Rick Steves & Gene Openshaw

CONTENTS

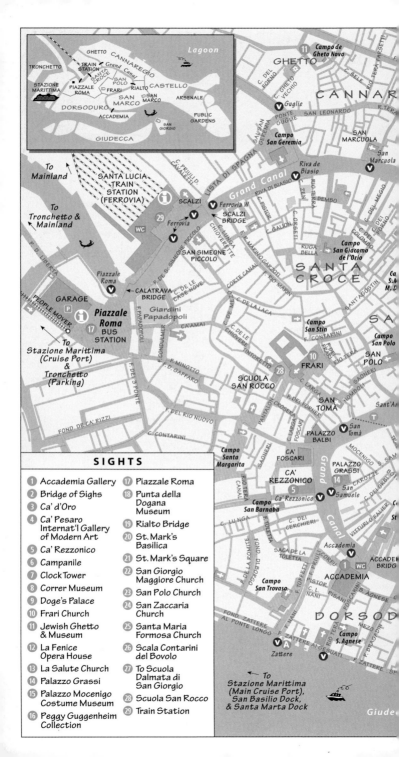

Venice

To San Michele, Murano, Burano & Torcello

SAN MICHELE (CEMETERY)

Lagoon

V Fondamente Nove
A

DORSODURO F. DE LA SENSA

F. DE L'ABAZIA

SINI F. D. MISERICORDIA

AL C. ZAN F. TRAPOLIN

ALENA

SANTA FOSCA

ALENA

GESUITI

STRADA NOVA

F. SAN FELICE

C. LARGA PRIULI

RUGA 2 POZZI

R. T. BARBA FRUTARIOL

C. DEL GORDION

C. DEL FUMO

C. DEI GORDINI

Stae

CA' PESARO

Ca' d'Oro **V** **T**

C. DELE VELE

S. VERDI

S. DEL PISTOR

C. DEL SQUERO

Campo Santi Apostoli

SAN CANZIAN

C. BANDI

C. WIDMANN

C. DEL MENDICANTI

FLO DEI

C. DEI BOTER

mpo ssiano

FISH MARKET

V Mercato Rialto

Campo de le Becarie

S. S. CANZIAN

S. GIOVANNI E PAOLO (SAN ZANIPOLO)

Campo S. Maria Nova

C. LARGA GALLINA

HOSPITAL

OLO

Campo San Aponal

SAN SILVESTRO

C. RAYANO

C. RASPI

RUGA RIALTO

C. DEL FERRO

RIALTO BRIDGE

RIVA DEL VIN

Rialto **A**

PRODUCE MARKET

ASEO

S. GRISOSTOMO

Campo San Bartolomeo

MIRACOLI

S. SCALETA MARCELLO

CA STELLO

C. CARMINATI

SALIZADA SAN LIO

Campo S. Maria Formosa

25

RUGA GIUFFA

F. S. SEVERO

San Silvestro **V**

ETA

C. DEL CARBON

G. LOREDAN

CAVALLI

R. DEL CARBON

BEMBO

C. TEATRO

PIGNOL

BAIOTO

Campo de la Fava

C. SAN ANTONIO

MONDO NOVO

C. DE LA GUERRA

QUERINI

27

MAG

C. DELLA MANDOLA

VERONA

Campo Manin

Campo San Luca

C. DEI FUSERI

LOCANDE

GOLDONI

C. DEI

FABBRI

POST

MERCERIE

DEI

FORSORO

S. MARCO

RUGA GIUFFA APOLLONIA

FOND. OS-MARIN

FOND. OS-MARIN

24 SAN ZACCARIA

26

C. FREZZARIA

P. FREZZARIA

CAFETIER

OCHER

Campo San Anzolo

LA FENICE 12

CORRER MUSEUM

8

7 ST. MARK'S BASILICA

20

21

6 DOGE'S PALACE 2

C. DEI ALBANESI

SAN MARCO

S. MARIA ZOBENIGO

WC

Piazza San Marco

9 RIVA

DEGLI SCHIAVONI

V **V** **A**

San Zaccaria **V**

To Public Gardens, Sant' Elena, Naval Museum & Arsenale

zio

22 MARZO

SAN MOISE

TRAGHETTO

VALLARESSO

SAN MOISE

WC

SAN MARCO & SAN THEODORE COLUMNS

G

OSTREGHE

S. Maria del Giglio

GGY **V** ENHEIM ECTION

zio

T

V Salute

13 18

PUNTA DELLA DOGANA MUSEUM

San Marco-Giardinetti

San Marco-Vallaresso **A**

St. Mark's Basin

C. BASTION

RIO TERA CATECUMENI

F. SALUTE

LA SALUTE

SECOLA

F. S. GORZAN FORNACE

ALSALONI

F. ZATTERE

nal

200 Meters
200 Yards

Zitelle **V** GIUDECCA

San Giorgio **V** 22

SAN GIORGIO MAGGIORE

SAN GIORGIO

LEGEND

- ■ Popular Shopping Area
- ■ Landmark or Point of Interest
- **V** Vaporetto Stop
- **T** Traghetto Crossing
- **G** Gondola Station
- **A** Alilaguna Stop to/from Airport
- Tourist Information

St. Mark's Square Area

Rialto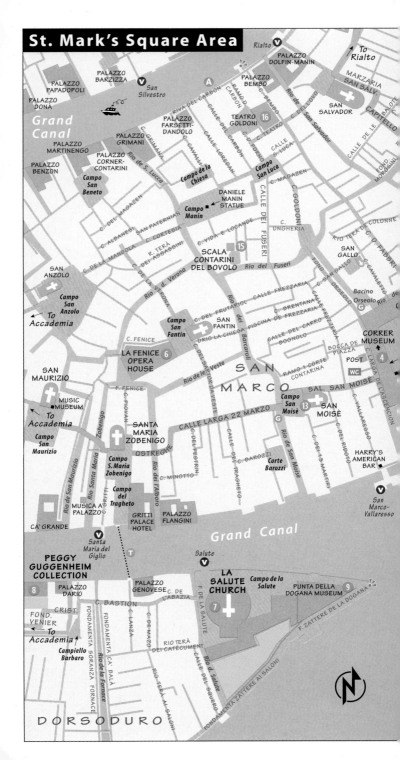

To Rialto

Grand Canal

PALAZZO PAPADOPOLI

PALAZZO BARZIZZA

PALAZZO DONA

San Silvestro

PALAZZO DOLFIN-MANIN

PALAZZO BEMBO

MARZARIA SAN SALV.

SAN SALVADOR

PALAZZO MARTINENGO

PALAZZO BENZON

PALAZZO GRIMANI

PALAZZO CORNER-CONTARINI

PALAZZO FARSETTI-DANDOLO

RIVA DEL CARBON

RAMO DEL CARBON

CALLE DEL CARBON

CALLE LOREDAN

C. CAVALLI

Rio di S. Lucca

Campo de la Chiesa

TEATRO GOLDONI 16

C. D. FORNO

C. TEATRO

CALLE S. LUCA

Campo San Luca

C. MAGAZEN

Rio DEL LOVO

Rio di San Salvador

CAPIELLO

CALLE DE LE

FOND. MOROSINI

CAPIELLO

Campo San Beneto

C. DEL MAGAZEN

SAN PATERNIAN

C. ALDANESI

C. CORTESIA

DANIELE MANIN STATUE

Campo Manin

CALLE DEI FUSERI

C. GOLDONI

C. UNGHERIA

RIO TERA C. D. COLONNE

C. DE LA MANDOLA

R. TERA DEI ASSASSINI

O. VIDA E LOCANDE

SCALA CONTARINI DEL BOVOLO 15

Rio del Fuseri

SAN GALLO

C. D. TRAGHI

C. CAVALETO

C. SAN GALLO

FOND. ORSEOLO

Bacino Orseolo

Rio de

RIO DE LA FORNASA

Rio di S. Verona

C. d. Verona

CALLE FREZZARIA

C. DEL FRUTARIOL

SAN FANTIN

CALLE FREZZARIA

BRENTANA

PISCINA DE FREZZARIA

CALLE FREZZARIA

CORRER MUSEUM

SAN ANZOLO

Campo San Anzolo

To Accademia

Campo San Fantin

C. FENICE

LA FENICE OPERA HOUSE 6

CALLE DEL CARRO

BOGNOLO

BOCCA DE PIAZZA

POST 4

LARGA DE L'ASCENSION

DRIO LA CHIESA

Rio de le Barcaroli

SAN MARCO

RAMO 1 CORTE CONTARINA

WC

SAN MAURIZIO

MUSIC MUSEUM

F. FENICE

C. PIOVAN

Rio de SANTO STEFANO

Rio de la Veste

CALLE LARGA 22 MARZO

Campo San Moisè 13

SAN MOISÈ

C. VALLARESSO

C. DEI RIDOTTO

To Accademia

Campo San Maurizio

Rio de San Maurizio

Rio Santa Maria

SANTA MARIA ZOBENIGO

OSTREGHE

Campo S.Maria Zobenigo

Rio de San Moisè

CALLE DEL PESTRIN

C. DEI 13 MARTIRI

HARRY'S AMERICAN BAR

C. DEL RIDOTTO

C. GRIFFITI

Campo del Traghetto

MUSICA A PALAZZO

C. BAROZZI

Corte Barozzi

San Marco-Vallaresso

CA' GRANDE

Santa Maria del Giglio

T

O. MINOTTO

Rio de l'Alboro

GRITTI PALACE HOTEL

PALAZZO FLANGINI

Grand Canal

Salute

PEGGY GUGGENHEIM COLLECTION 8

PALAZZO DARIO

PALAZZO GENOVESE

C. DE L'ABAZIA

LA SALUTE CHURCH 7

Campo de la Salute

PUNTA DELLA DOGANA MUSEUM 9

FOND. VENIER

CRIST.

C. BASTION

G. LANZA

C. DE MAZO

F. DE LA SALUTE

To Accademia

FONDAMENTA SORANZA

FONDAMENTA CA' BALA

Rio de la FORNACE

RIO TERA DEI CATECUMENI

Rio de SALUTE

CALLE DEL SQUERO

FONDAMENTA ZATTERE AI SALONI

F. ZATTERE DE LA DOGANA

Campiello Barbaro

RIO TERA AI SALONI

DORSODURO

N

SIGHTS

1. Bridge of Sighs
2. Campanile
3. Clock Tower
4. Correr Museum
5. Doge's Palace
6. La Fenice Opera House
7. La Salute Church
8. Peggy Guggenheim Collection
9. Punta della Dogana Museum
10. St. Mark's Basilica
11. St. Mark's Square
12. San Giorgio Maggiore Church
13. San Moisè Church
14. San Zaccaria Church
15. Scala Contarini del Bovolo
16. Teatro Goldoni

RESTAURANTS

17. Rist. Antica Sacrestia
18. Birreria Forst Café
19. Bar Verde
20. Ristorante alla Basilica
21. Rist. Cinese Capitol
22. Ristorante alla Conchiglia
23. Trattoria da Giorgio ai Greci
24. Gran Caffè Quadri (Bistro)
25. Gran Caffè Lavena (Gelato)
26. Todaro Gelato
27. Planet Restaurant
28. Co-op Supermarket

Rialto Area

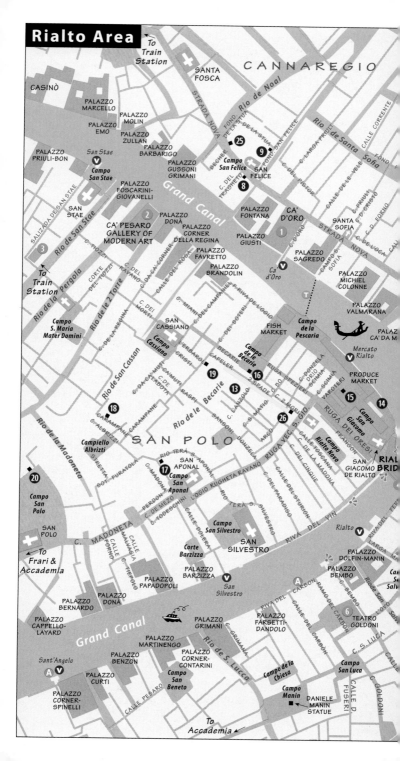

To Train Station

SANTA FOSCA

CANNAREGIO

CASINÒ

PALAZZO MARCELLO

PALAZZO EMO

PALAZZO MOLIN

PALAZZO ZULLAN

PALAZZO BARBARIGO

PALAZZO PRIULI-BON

San Stae

Campo San Stae

PALAZZO GUSSONI GRIMANI

STRADA NOVA

Rio de Noal

FOND. DE LA STUA

25

9

Campo San Felice

SAN FELICE

8

Rio de Santa Sofia

SAN STAE

SALIZADA DE SAN STAE

PALAZZO FOSCARINI-GIOVANELLI

Grand Canal

2

PALAZZO DONÀ

CA' PESARO GALLERY OF MODERN ART

PALAZZO CORNER DELLA REGINA

PALAZZO FAVRETTO

PALAZZO FONTANA

CA' D'ORO

1

PALAZZO GIUSTI

SANTA SOFIA

STRADA NOVA

Rio de la Pergola

3

To Train Station

PALAZZO BRANDOLIN

Ca' d'Oro

PALAZZO SAGREDO

PALAZZO MICHIEL COLONNE

PALAZZO VALMARANA

Campo S. Maria Mater Domini

Rio de la Regina

SAN CASSIANO

Campo Cassiano

RIVA DE L'OGIO

FISH MARKET

Campo de la Pescaria

T

PALAZ CA' DA M

Mercato Rialto

Rio de San Cassan

19

13

Campo de le Becarie

16

RUGA SPEZIERI

PRODUCE MARKET

15

14

Campo San Giacomo

RUGA DEI ORESI

18

Campiello Albrizti

Rio de le Becarie

26

SAN POLO

Campo Rialto Novo

SAN GIACOMO DE RIALTO

RIAL BRID

20

17

Campo San Polo

SAN APONAL

Campo San Aponal

RIO TERA S. APONAL

RUGA VEC. S. GIO

Rialto

V

SAN POLO

To Frari & Accademia

Campo San Silvestro

SAN SILVESTRO

RIVA DEL VIN

PALAZZO DOLFIN-MANIN

PALAZZO BEMBO

Corte Barzizza

PALAZZO PAPADOPOLI

PALAZZO BARZIZZA

V

San Silvestro

A

PALAZZO BERNARDO

PALAZZO DONÀ

Grand Canal

PALAZZO GRIMANI

PALAZZO FARSETTI-DANDOLO

6

TEATRO GOLDONI

PALAZZO CAPPELLO-LAYARD

PALAZZO MARTINENGO

Rio de S. Lucca

Campo San Luca

Sant'Angelo

A V

PALAZZO CURTI

PALAZZO BENZON

PALAZZO CORNER-CONTARINI

Campo San Beneto

Campo de la Chiesa

PALAZZO CORNER-SPINELLI

CALLE PESARO

Campo Manin

DANIELE MANIN STATUE

To Accademia

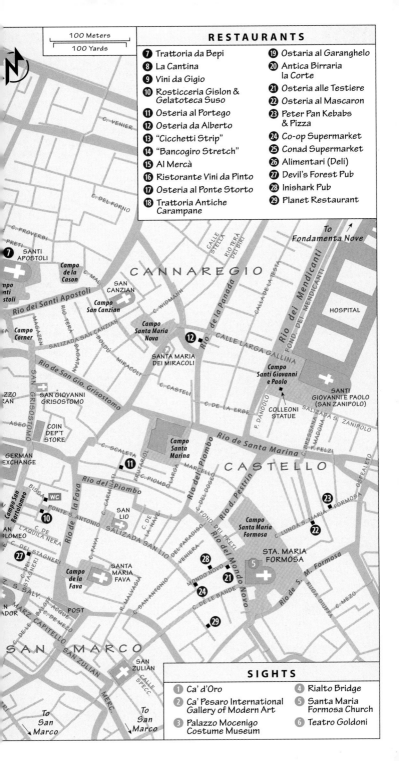

100 Meters
100 Yards

RESTAURANTS

7 Trattoria da Bepi
8 La Cantina
9 Vini da Gigio
10 Rosticceria Gislon & Gelatoteca Suso
11 Osteria al Portego
12 Osteria da Alberto
13 "Cicchetti Strip"
14 "Bancogiro Stretch"
15 Al Mercà
16 Ristorante Vini da Pinto
17 Osteria al Ponte Storto
18 Trattoria Antiche Carampane
19 Ostaria al Garanghelo
20 Antica Birraria la Corte
21 Osteria alle Testiere
22 Osteria al Mascaron
23 Peter Pan Kebabs & Pizza
24 Co-op Supermarket
25 Conad Supermarket
26 Alimentari (Deli)
27 Devil's Forest Pub
28 Inishark Pub
29 Planet Restaurant

SIGHTS

1 Ca' d'Oro
2 Ca' Pesaro International Gallery of Modern Art
3 Palazzo Mocenigo Costume Museum
4 Rialto Bridge
5 Santa Maria Formosa Church
6 Teatro Goldoni

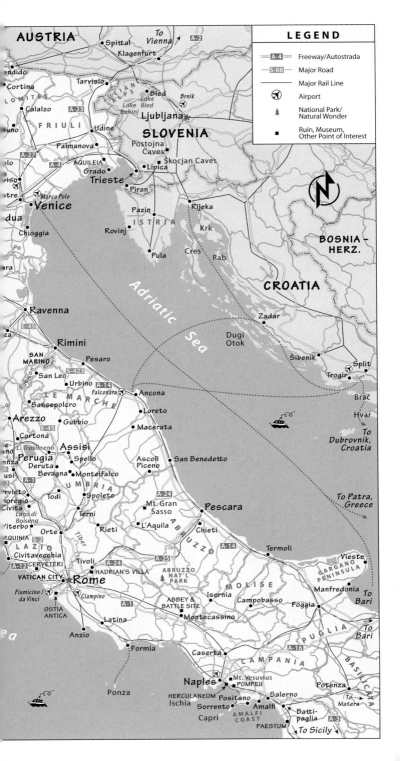

AUSTRIA

LEGEND

═A-4═ Freeway/Autostrada
═S-68═ Major Road
—— Major Rail Line
✈ Airport
🌲 National Park/Natural Wonder
■ Ruin, Museum, Other Point of Interest

Spittal
To Vienna A-2
Klagenfurt

ndido
Cortina
Tarvisio
JULIAN ALPS
Bled
Brnik ✈
Lake Bohinj
Lake Bled

LOMITES
Calalzo A-23

FRIULI
uno
Udine

A-27
Palmanova
Postojna Caves
Škocjan Caves

SLOVENIA
Ljubljana

A-4 AQUILEIA
Grado
Lipica
olo
Piran
viso
Marco Polo ✈
Trieste

stre
Venice
Pazin

dua
Rijeka

ISTRIA
Chioggia

BOSNIA-HERZ.

Po
Rovinj
Krk

ra
Pula
Cres
Rab

Adriatic Sea

CROATIA

Ravenna
E-45
za
Zadar

Rimini
Dugi Otok

SAN MARINO
Pesaro
S-423
San Leo
Urbino A-14
Šibenik

Sansepolcro
Falconara ✈ Ancona
Split
Trogir

Arezzo
Gubbio
Loreto
Brač

Cortona
E-45
Macerata
Hvar

eno
L. Trasimeno
Assisi
nza
To Dubrovnik, Croatia

Perugia
Spello
usi
Deruta
Ascoli Piceno
San Benedetto

Bevagna Montelfalco

UMBRIA
A-1
rvieto
Todi
Spoleto
To Patra, Greece

oregio
Civita
Lago di Bolsena
Terni
A-24
Mt. Gran Sasso
Pescara

iterbo
Orte
Rieti
L'Aquila
Chieti

RQUINIA S-2
Tiber
ABRUZZO

LAZIO
A-24
A-25
A-14
Termoli

Civitavecchia
Tivoli
Vieste

A-12 CERVETERI
HADRIAN'S VILLA
ABRUZZO NAT'L PARK
GARGANO PENINSULA

VATICAN CITY
MOLISE

Rome
Manfredonia
To Bari

Fiumicino / da Vinci ✈
Ciampino
ABBEY & BATTLE SITE
Isernia
Campobasso

OSTIA ANTICA
A-1
Montecassino
Foggia
To Bari

Latina
PUGLIA

Anzio
A-16

Formia
Caserta
To Bari

CAMPANIA
BASILICATA

Ponza
Naples ✈
Mt. Vesuvius
POMPEII
Potenza

HERCULANEUM Positano
Salerno
To Matera

a
Ischia Sorrento
Amalfi
Batti-paglia A-3

Capri
AMALFI COAST
PAESTUM
To Sicily

House of Juliet in Verona

Venetian masks

Gondoliers plying a Venetian canal

Rick Steves ®

VENICE

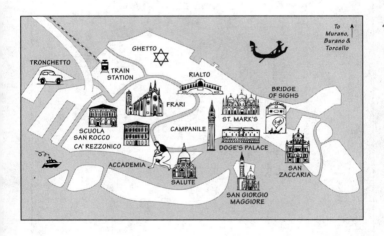

TRONCHETTO

TRAIN STATION

GHETTO

RIALTO

To Murano, Burano & Torcello

BRIDGE OF SIGHS

FRARI

SCUOLA SAN ROCCO

CA' REZZONICO

CAMPANILE

ST. MARK'S

ACCADEMIA

SALUTE

DOGE'S PALACE

SAN ZACCARIA

SAN GIORGIO MAGGIORE

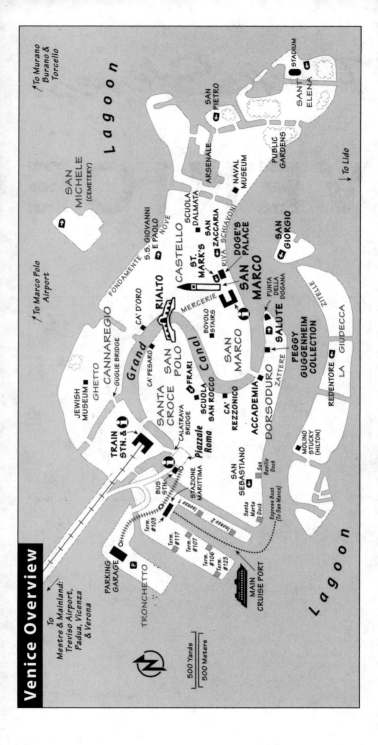

Venice Overview

To Murano, Burano & Torcello

To Marco Polo Airport

To Mestre & Mainland: Treviso Airport, Padua, Vicenza & Verona

Lagoon

Lagoon

SAN MICHELE (CEMETERY)

SANT' ELENA

STADIUM

SAN PIETRO

PUBLIC GARDENS

ARSENALE

NAVAL MUSEUM

To Lido

CANNAREGIO

S.S. GIOVANNI E PAOLO

FONDAMENTE NOVE

SCUOLA DALMATA

SAN ZACCARIA

CASTELLO

RIALTO

CA' D'ORO

GUGLIE BRIDGE

GHETTO

JEWISH MUSEUM

MERCERIE

ST. MARK'S

SAN MARCO

DOGE'S PALACE

RIVA SCHIAVONI

SAN GIORGIO

BOVOLO STAIRS

PUNTA DELLA DOGANA

SANTA CROCE

SAN POLO

FRARI

SCUOLA SAN ROCCO

CA' PESARO

Grand Canal

SAN MARCO

SALUTE

PEGGY GUGGENHEIM COLLECTION

ZATTERE

ZITELLE

TRAIN STN. &

CALATRAVA BRIDGE

CA' REZZONICO

ACCADEMIA

DORSODURO

Piazzale Roma

BUS STN.

STAZIONE MARITTIMA

SAN SEBASTIANO

San Basilio Dock

REDENTORE

LA GIUDECCA

MOLINO STUCKY (HILTON)

PARKING GARAGE

TRONCHETTO

Term. #105

Term. #117

Term. #107

Term. #106

Term. #123

MAIN CRUISE PORT

Santa Marta Dock

Express Boat (To San Marco)

Isonzo 1

Isonzo 2

500 Yards

500 Meters

N

INTRODUCTION

Engineers love Venice—a completely man-made environment rising from the sea, with no visible means of support. Romantics revel in its atmosphere of elegant decay, seeing the peeling plaster and seaweed-covered stairs as a metaphor for beauty in decline. And first-time visitors are often stirred deeply, awaking from their ordinary lives to a fantasy world unlike anything they've ever experienced before.

Those are strong reactions, considering that Venice today, frankly, can also be an overcrowded, prepackaged, tacky tourist trap. But Venice is unique. Built on a hundred islands with wealth from trade with the East, its exotic-looking palaces are laced together by sun-speckled canals. The car-free streets suddenly make walkers feel big, important, and liberated. It's basically one giant amusement park for grown-ups, centuries in the making. And yet, the longer you're here—and the more you explore its back streets—the clearer it becomes that this is also a real, living town, with its own personality and challenges.

By day, Venice is a city of museums and churches, packed with great art. Everything's within a half-hour walk. Cruise the canals on a vaporetto water bus. Climb towers for stunning seascape views. Shop for Venetian crafts (such as glass and lace), high fashions, or tacky souvenirs. Linger over lunch, trying to crack a crustacean with weird legs and antennae. Sip a *spritz* at a café on St. Mark's Square while the orchestra plays "New York, New York."

At night, when the hordes of day-trippers have gone, another Venice appears. Dance across a floodlit square. Glide in a gondola through quiet canals while music echoes across the water. Pretend it's Carnevale time, don a mask—or just a fresh shirt—and become someone else for a night.

INTRODUCTION

Map Legend

⚲ Viewpoint	✈ Airport	🍦 Gelato	
↑ Entrance	ⓣ Taxi Stand	▦ Pedestrian Zone	
❶ Tourist Info	Ⓑ Bus Stop	---- Railway	
🆆🅲 Restroom	🅿 Parking	·········· Ferry/Boat Route	
✡ Synagogue	)(Mtn. Pass		
🏠 Church	Park	+—Ⓣ—+ Tram	
Ⓥ Vaporetto Dock	▪ Statue/Point of Interest	▦ Stairs	
Ⓣ Traghetto (Venice)		· · · · · Walk/Tour Route	
Ⓖ Gondola Station			
Ⓐ Alilaguna Stop	🏰 Castle	- - - - - Trail	

Use this legend to help you navigate the maps in this book.

ABOUT THIS BOOK

Rick Steves Venice is a personal tour guide in your pocket. Better yet, it's actually two tour guides in your pocket: The co-author of this book is Gene Openshaw. Since our first "Europe through the gutter" trip together as high school buddies in the 1970s, Gene and I have been exploring the wonders of the Old World. An inquisitive historian and lover of European culture, Gene wrote most of this book's self-guided museum tours and neighborhood walks. Together, Gene and I keep this book current (though for simplicity, from this point "we" will shed our respective egos and become "I").

In this book, you'll find the following chapters:

Orientation to Venice includes specifics on public transportation, helpful hints, local tour options, easy-to-read maps, and tourist information. The "Planning Your Time" section suggests a schedule for how to best use your limited time.

Sights in Venice describes the top attractions and includes their cost and hours.

The **Self-Guided Walks** cover Venice's back streets. The walk from St. Mark's to Rialto follows a less touristy route between these two major landmarks, then loops back via Venice's high-end (and tourist-packed) shopping drag. The walk from Rialto to the Frari Church (with its exquisite art) takes you through bustling markets and by a mask-making shop. The walk from St. Mark's to San Zaccaria explores the area behind the basilica, featuring a historic church and a seldom-seen view of the famous Bridge of Sighs.

The **Self-Guided Tours** lead you through Venice's most fascinating museums and sights: the Grand Canal, St. Mark's Square, St. Mark's Basilica, Doge's Palace, Correr Museum, Accademia, Frari Church, Scuola San Rocco, Ca' Rezzonico (Museum of 18th-Century Venice), Peggy Guggenheim Collection, La Salute Church, San Giorgio Maggiore, and the islands in Venice's lagoon (including San Michele, Murano, Burano, and Torcello).

Key to This Book

Updates

This book is updated regularly—but once you pin down Italy, it wiggles. For the latest, visit www.ricksteves.com/update.

Abbreviations and Times

I use the following symbols and abbreviations in this book:
Sights are rated:

▲▲▲	Don't miss
▲▲	Try hard to see
▲	Worthwhile if you can make it
No rating	Worth knowing about

Tourist information offices are abbreviated as **TI**, and bathrooms are WCs. Accommodations are categorized with a **Sleep Code** (described on page 240); eateries are classified with a **Restaurant Price Code** (page 264). To indicate discounts for my readers, I include **RS%** in the listings.

Like Europe, this book uses the **24-hour clock.** It's the same through 12:00 noon, then keeps going: 13:00, 14:00, and so on. For anything over 12, subtract 12 and add p.m. (14:00 is 2:00 p.m.).

When giving **opening times,** I include both peak season and off-season hours if they differ. So, if a museum is listed as "May-Oct daily 9:00-16:00," it should be open from 9:00 a.m. until 4:00 p.m. from the first day of May until the last day of October (but expect exceptions).

A ◫ symbol in a sight listing means that the sight is described in greater detail elsewhere—either with its own self-guided tour, or as part of a self-guided walk. A ∩ symbol indicates that a free, downloadable self-guided Rick Steves audio tour is available.

For **transit** or **tour departures,** I first list the frequency, then the duration. So, a train connection listed as "2/hour, 1.5 hours" departs twice each hour and the journey lasts an hour and a half.

Sleeping in Venice describes my favorite hotels, from good-value deals to cushy splurges. I've focused on hotels conveniently located near St. Mark's Square, the Rialto Bridge, and the Accademia—all handy to the sights in this compact city. I also suggest hotels near the train station and on the mainland, in Mestre, and I cover alternatives such as dormitories and apartment rentals.

Eating in Venice serves up a range of options, from inexpensive cafés to fancy restaurants.

Venice with Children includes my top recommendations for keeping your kids (and you) happy.

Shopping in Venice gives you tips for shopping painlessly and enjoyably, without letting it overwhelm your vacation or ruin your budget.

Nightlife in Venice is your guide to after-dark Venice, including gondola rides, concerts, theaters, pubs, and clubs.

Venice Connections lays the groundwork for your smooth arrival and departure, covering transportation by train, bus, car, cruise ship, and plane. It provides detailed information on Venice's two airports (Marco Polo and Treviso), train station (Santa Lucia), and cruise port (Stazione Marittima).

Near Venice includes day trips to art-filled Padua and Ravenna, and romantic Verona.

Venetian History fills you in on the background of this fascinating city.

The **Practicalities** chapter near the end of this book is a traveler's tool kit, with my best travel tips and advice about money, sightseeing, sleeping, eating, staying connected, and transportation.

The **appendix** has the nuts-and-bolts: useful phone numbers and websites, a holiday and festival list, recommended books and films, a climate chart, a handy packing checklist, and Italian survival phrases.

Throughout this book, you'll find money- and time-saving tips for sightseeing, transportation, and more. Some businesses—especially hotels and walking tour companies—offer special discounts to my readers, indicated in their listings.

Browse through this book and select your favorite sights. Then have a great trip! Traveling like a temporary local, you'll get the absolute most out of every mile, minute, and dollar. As you visit places I know and love, I'm happy that you'll be meeting my favorite Venetians.

Planning

This section will help you get started planning your trip—with advice on trip costs, when to go, and what you should know before you take off.

TRAVEL SMART

Many people travel through Italy thinking it's a chaotic mess. They feel that any attempt at efficient travel is futile. This is dead wrong—and expensive. Italy, which seems as orderly as spilled spaghetti, actually functions well. Only those who understand this and travel smart can enjoy Italy on a budget.

This book can save you lots of time and money. But to have an "A" trip, you need to be an "A" student. Read it all before your trip, noting holidays, specific advice on sights, and days when sights are closed. If you save St. Mark's Basilica for Sunday morning (when it's closed), you've missed the gondola. You can sweat in line at the Doge's Palace, or you can buy your pass at the nearby Correr Museum and zip right through the palace turnstile. Day-tripping to Verona on Monday, when the major sights are closed, is bad news. A smart trip is a puzzle—a fun, doable, and worthwhile challenge.

Make your itinerary a mix of intense and relaxed stretches. Every trip—and every traveler—needs slack time (laundry, picnics, people-watching, and so on). Pace yourself. Assume you will return.

Even with the best-planned itinerary, you'll need to be flexible. Update your plans as you travel. Get online or call ahead to learn the latest on sights (special events, tour schedules, and so on), book tickets and tours, make reservations, reconfirm hotels, and research transportation connections.

Enjoy the friendliness of the Venetian people. Connect with the culture. Set up your own quest for the best little square, vaporetto ride, or gelato. Slow down and be open to unexpected experiences. Ask questions—most locals are eager to point you in their idea of the right direction. Keep a notepad in your pocket for confirming prices, noting directions, and organizing your thoughts. Wear your money belt, learn the currency, and figure out how to estimate prices in dollars. Those who expect to travel smart, do.

TRIP COSTS

Six components make up your trip costs: airfare to Europe, surface transportation in Europe, room and board, sightseeing/entertainment, shopping/miscellany, and gelato.

Airfare to Europe: A basic round-trip flight from the US to Venice (or even cheaper, Milan) can cost, on average, about $1,000-2,000 total, depending on where you fly from and when (cheaper in winter). If Venice is part of a longer trip, consider saving time and money in Europe by flying into one city and out of another; for instance, into Venice and out of Dubrovnik. Overall, Kayak.com is the best place to start searching for flights on a combination of mainstream and budget carriers.

Transportation in Europe: Venice's sights are within walking distance of each other, but vaporetto boat rides are fun and save time. Most visitors buy a vaporetto pass (figure about $22/day). For a one-way trip between Venice's airport and the city, allow about $10 by bus, $17 by Alilaguna water bus, or $120 by water taxi (can be shared by up to 4 people).

Round-trip, second-class train transportation to day-trip destinations is affordable as long as you avoid express trains (about $5 each way to Padua and $10 to Verona by local train). For more on public transportation and driving, see "Transportation" in Practicalities.

Venice Almanac

Population: While there are approximately 270,000 people in greater Venice, only 55,000 people live on the actual islands.

Currency: Euro

Nicknames: La Serenissima and The Queen of the Adriatic

City Layout: The city of Venice is built on more than 100 small islands in the Venetian Lagoon along the Adriatic Sea. The historic center is broken up into six districts (sestieri): Cannaregio, Castello, Dorsoduro, San Polo, Santa Croce, and San Marco.

Tallest Structure: The Campanile on St. Mark's Square reaches 325 feet and offers a beautiful view of the city. Good news: It has an elevator.

Tourist Tracks: Roughly 22 million tourists flock to Venice each year, with 30,000 roaming the streets each day of the Carnevale festival. St. Mark's Square is the most popular sight and the Rialto Bridge is the top photo spot.

Culture Count: Venice's population has long been almost entirely Italian—but that's changing. You'll notice lots of Asians working in shops and restaurants, as well as lots of Senegalese on the streets selling knockoff bags. While Italian is the official language of Italy, most of the Veneto region's 2 million people speak the Venetian dialect among themselves (you might notice how they don't roll their r's). The vast majority of native Venetians are Roman Catholics.

Fun Food Facts: Venice is known for its wine bars (bacari or enoteche) that serve small bite-sized snacks called cicchetti, which are similar to Spanish tapas.

Most Venerable Café: Caffè Florian, on the south side of St. Mark's Square, opened in 1720. Famous visitors have included Lord Byron and Charles Dickens.

Average Venetian: The average Venetian is 46 years old, has 1.4 children, and will live until the age of 82. Half of the Venetian population works in some sector of the tourism industry. Venetians are more likely to have a gondolier license than a driver's license. Many Venetians go weeks without seeing a car (unless they turn on a TV). Imagine the day a Venetian child realizes that what's normal in his or her world is actually not very normal at all.

Room and Board: You can manage comfortably in Venice on $135 a day per person for room and board. This allows $15 for lunch, $25 for dinner, and $90 for lodging (based on two people splitting the cost of a $180 double room that includes breakfast). That leaves you $5 for gelato. Students and tightwads can enjoy Venice for as little as $70 a day ($40 for a bed, $30 for meals and snacks).

Sightseeing and Entertainment: Figure about $15-25 per major sight (Accademia, Doge's Palace, Guggenheim), $8-12 for minor ones (climbing church towers), and $30-35 for splurge experiences (such as walking tours and concerts). A gondola ride starts at $90 (by day) or $110 (at night); split the cost by going with a pal. An overall average of $40 a day works for most people. Don't skimp here. After all, this category is the driving force behind your trip—you came to sightsee, enjoy, and experience Venice.

Shopping and Miscellany: Figure $3-4 per coffee, soft drink, or gelato. Shopping can vary in cost from nearly nothing to a small fortune. Good budget travelers find that this category has little to do with assembling a trip full of lifelong and wonderful memories.

WHEN TO GO

Venice's best travel months (also its busiest and most expensive) are April, May, June, September, and October.

Summer in Venice is more temperate (high 70s and 80s) than in Italy's scorching inland cities. Most Venetian hotels come with air-conditioning—important in the summer—but it's usually available only from May (at the earliest) through September. Spring and fall can be cool, and many hotels—thanks to a national interest in not wasting energy—are not allowed to turn on their heat until winter.

Between November and March you can usually expect mild winter weather (with lows in the 30s and 40s), occasional flooding, shorter lines, lower prices, and fewer tourists (except during the Carnevale festival, generally in February). While Carnevale comes with high hotel prices, it's a big party, with special concerts, lots of kids' events, fresh pastries, and costumed figures crowding through the city. March offers a good balance of low-season prices and reasonable weather. (For specifics, see the climate chart in the appendix.)

Venice has two main weather patterns: Wind from the southeast (the Balkans) brings cold and dry weather, while the sirocco wind from the south (north Africa) brings warm and wet weather, pushing more water into the lagoon and causing flooding *(acqua alta)*. This shouldn't greatly affect your sightseeing plans. *Tabacchi* (tobacco shops) and some souvenir shops sell boots to keep your feet dry. Elevated wooden walkways are sometimes set up in the busier, more flooded squares to keep you above the water. And it's worth a trip to St. Mark's Square to see waiters in fancy tuxes and rubber boots.

Off-Season Travel Tips: Off-season has none of the sweat and stress of the tourist season, but sights may have shorter hours, lunchtime breaks, and fewer activities. Here are several things to

INTRODUCTION

∩ **Rick Steves Audio Europe** ∩

My free **Rick Steves Audio Europe app** is a great tool for en-joying Europe. This app makes it easy to download my audio tours of top attractions, plus hours of travel interviews, all or-ganized into destination-specific playlists.

My self-guided **audio tours** of major sights and neighbor-hoods are free, user-friendly, fun, and informative. In this book, these audio tours include my Grand Canal Cruise, St. Mark's Square, St. Mark's Basilica, and Frari Church. Sights covered by my audio tours are marked with this symbol: ∩. These audio tours are hard to beat: Nobody will stand you up, your eyes are free to appreciate the sights, you can take the tour exactly when you like, and the price is right.

The Rick Steves Audio Europe app also offers a far-reach-ing library of insightful **travel interviews** from my public radio show with experts from around the globe—including many of the places in this book.

This app and all of its content are entirely free. (And new content is added about twice a year.) You can download Rick Steves Audio Europe via Apple's App Store, Google Play, or the Amazon Appstore. For more information, see www.ricksteves. com/audioeurope.

keep in mind if you visit Venice off-season, roughly November through March.

• Most sights close early, often at 17:00.

• The orchestras in St. Mark's Square may stop playing at 18:00 (and may not play at all in bad weather or during their an-nual vacations, usually in March).

• Vaporetto #2 (the Grand Canal fast boat) terminates at the Rialto stop before 9:00 and after 20:00, which means no stops at San Marco and Accademia early in the morning and late in the evening (you can take the slow boat, vaporetto #1, instead).

• Expect occasional flooding, particularly at St. Mark's Square and along Zattere (southern edge of Venice, opposite Giudecca Is-land).

• Room prices can be about 25-50 percent lower.

KNOW BEFORE YOU GO

Check this list of things to arrange while you're still at home.

You need a **passport**—but no visa or shots—to travel in Italy. You may be denied entry into certain European countries if your passport is due to expire within six months of your ticketed date of return. Get it renewed if you'll be cutting it close. It can take up to six weeks to get or renew a passport (for more on passports and

---

How Was Your Trip?

Were your travels fun, smooth, and meaningful? You can share tips, concerns, and discoveries at www.ricksteves.com/feedback. To check out readers' hotel and restaurant reviews—or leave one yourself—visit my travel forum at www.ricksteves.com/travel-forum. I value your feedback. Thanks in advance.

---

requirements for Italy, see www.travel.state.gov). Pack a photocopy of your passport in your luggage in case the original is lost or stolen.

Book rooms well in advance if you'll be traveling during peak season (June-Sept, plus Carnevale) or any major holidays (see page 470).

Call your **debit- and credit-card companies** to let them know the countries you'll be visiting, to ask about fees, to request your PIN if you don't already know it, and more. See page 416 for details.

Do your homework if you're considering **travel insurance.** Compare the cost of the insurance to the cost of your potential loss. Also check whether your existing insurance (health, homeowners, or renters) covers you and your possessions overseas. For more tips, see www.ricksteves.com/insurance.

If you're taking an **overnight train** and need a couchette *(cuccetta)* or sleeper—and you *must* leave on a certain day—consider booking it in advance through a US agent (such as www.ricksteves.com/rail), even though it may cost more than buying it in Italy. Other Italian trains, such as high-speed ES trains, require a seat reservation, but it's usually possible to make these arrangements in Italy just a few days ahead. (For more on train travel, see Practicalities.)

In Padua, **reservations** are mandatory to visit the Scrovegni Chapel, famous for its frescoes by Giotto, so book well in advance (easily done online; see page 330). Also consider reserving an entry slot for St. Mark's Basilica in Venice (see page 34).

If you plan to hire a **local guide,** reserve ahead by email. Popular guides can get booked up.

If you're bringing a **mobile device,** consider signing up for an international plan for cheaper calls, texts, and data (see page 448). Download any apps you might want to use on the road, such as translators, maps, and transit schedules, and **Rick Steves Audio Europe** (see page 8).

Check for recent **updates** to this book at www.ricksteves.com/update.

Traveling as a Temporary Local

We travel all the way to Italy to enjoy differences—to become temporary locals. You'll experience frustrations. Certain truths that we find "God-given" or "self-evident," such as cold beer, ice in drinks, bottomless cups of coffee, "the customer is king," and bigger being better, are suddenly not so true. One of the benefits of travel is the eye-opening realization that there are logical, civil, and even better alternatives. A willingness to go local ensures that you'll enjoy a full dose of Italian hospitality.

Europeans generally like Americans. But if there is a negative aspect to the Italians' image of Americans, it's that we are loud, wasteful, ethnocentric, too informal (which can seem disrespectful), and a bit naive.

Think about the rationale behind "crazy" Italian decisions. For instance, many hoteliers turn off the heat in spring and can't turn on air-conditioning until summer. The point is to conserve energy, and it's mandated by the Italian government. You could complain about being cold or hot...or bring a sweater in winter, and in summer, be prepared to sweat a little like everyone else.

While Italians, flabbergasted by our Yankee excesses, say in disbelief, *"Mi sono cadute le braccia!"* ("I throw my arms down!"), they nearly always afford us individual travelers all the warmth we deserve.

Judging from all the happy feedback I receive from travelers who have used this book, it's safe to assume you'll enjoy a great, affordable vacation—with the finesse of an independent, experienced traveler.

Thanks, and *buon viaggio!*

Back Door Travel Philosophy

From Rick Steves *Europe Through the Back Door*

Travel is intensified living—maximum thrills per minute and one of the last great sources of legal adventure. Travel is freedom. It's recess, and we need it.

Experiencing the real Europe requires catching it by surprise, going casual..."through the Back Door."

Affording travel is a matter of priorities. (Make do with the old car.) You can eat and sleep—simply, safely, and enjoyably—anywhere in Europe for $125 a day plus transportation costs. In many ways, spending more money only builds a thicker wall between you and what you traveled so far to see. Europe is a cultural carnival, and time after time, you'll find that its best acts are free and the best seats are the cheap ones.

A tight budget forces you to travel close to the ground, meeting and communicating with the people. Never sacrifice sleep, nutrition, safety, or cleanliness to save money. Simply enjoy the local-style alternatives to expensive hotels and restaurants.

Connecting with people carbonates your experience. Extroverts have more fun. If your trip is low on magic moments, kick yourself and make things happen. If you don't enjoy a place, maybe you don't know enough about it. Seek the truth. Recognize tourist traps. Give a culture the benefit of your open mind. See things as different, but not better or worse. Any culture has plenty to share. When an opportunity presents itself, make it a habit to say "yes."

Of course, travel, like the world, is a series of hills and valleys. Be fanatically positive and militantly optimistic. If something's not to your liking, change your liking.

Travel can make you a happier American, as well as a citizen of the world. Our Earth is home to seven billion equally precious people. It's humbling to travel and find that other people don't have the "American Dream"—they have their own dreams. Europeans like us, but with all due respect, they wouldn't trade passports.

Thoughtful travel engages us with the world. It reminds us what is truly important. By broadening perspectives, travel teaches new ways to measure quality of life.

Globetrotting destroys ethnocentricity, helping us understand and appreciate other cultures. Rather than fear the diversity on this planet, celebrate it. Among your most prized souvenirs will be the strands of different cultures you choose to knit into your own character. The world is a cultural yarn shop, and Back Door travelers are weaving the ultimate tapestry. Join in!

ORIENTATION TO VENICE

The island city of Venice is shaped like a fish. Its major thorough-fares are canals. The Grand Canal winds through the middle of the fish, starting at the mouth where all the people and food enter, passing under the Rialto Bridge, and ending at St. Mark's Square (Piazza San Marco). Park your 21st-century perspective at the mouth and let Venice swallow you whole.

VENICE: A VERBAL MAP

Venice is a car-less kaleidoscope of people, bridges, and odorless canals. It's made up of more than a hundred small islands—but for simplicity, I refer to the whole shebang as "the island."

Venice has six districts (*sestieri*, shown on map on next page): **San Marco** (from St. Mark's Square to the Accademia Bridge), **Castello** (the area east of St. Mark's Square), **Dorsoduro** (the "belly" of the fish, on the far side the Accademia Bridge), **Cannaregio** (between the train station and the Rialto Bridge), **San Polo** (west of the Rialto Bridge), and **Santa Croce** (the "eye" of the fish, across the canal from the train station).

The easiest way to navigate is by landmarks. Many street cor-ners have a sign pointing you to *(per)* the nearest major landmark, such as San Marco, Accademia, Rialto, and Ferrovia (train station). Obedient visitors stick to the main thoroughfares as directed by these signs...and miss the charm of back-street Venice.

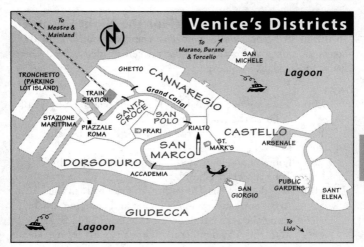

Beyond the city's core lie several other islands, including San Giorgio (with great views of Venice), Giudecca (more views), San Michele (old cemetery), Murano (famous for glass), Burano (lace-making), Torcello (old church), and the skinny Lido (with Venice's beach).

PLANNING YOUR TIME

Venice is small. You can walk across it, from head to tail, in about an hour. Nearly all of your sightseeing is within a 20-minute walk of the Rialto Bridge or St. Mark's Square. Remember that Venice itself is its greatest sight. Make time to wander, explore, shop, and simply be. When you cross a bridge, look both ways—you may be hit with a lovely view. Venice has what's considered one of the highest concentrations of art anywhere in the world. Art lovers need to be particularly well-organized to get the most out of their visit.

Key considerations: Ninety percent of tourists congregate in a very narrow zone in the center. But even the most touristy stretches of the city are almost ghostly peaceful early and late. Maximize your evening magic, and avoid the midday crowds around St. Mark's Basilica and the Doge's Palace. If you arrive in Venice late in the day, try taking my Grand Canal Cruise and St. Mark's Square Tour. These sights are more romantic and much less crowded after dark—and they provide a wonderful welcome to the city. (Also see "Crowd Control" tips in the "Daily Reminder" sidebar, later.)

Depending on when you visit, you may have to juggle the itineraries provided, as sights' visiting hours will vary by season and day of the week.

Venice in One Brutal Day (Plus the Night Before)

On the night before, walk or boat to the train station and then, aboard an empty vaporetto #1, take my self-guided Grand Canal Cruise to St. Mark's Square.

Day 1

9:00	Take my self-guided St. Mark's to Rialto Loop Walk as far as the Rialto Bridge.
10:00	Enjoy the action at the Rialto Bridge and Rialto Market.
11:00	Follow my self-guided Rialto to Frari Church Walk.
12:00	Tour the Frari Church.
13:00	Wander into the Dorsoduro district toward the Accademia museum, exploring and enjoying lunch along the way. Stroll across the Accademia Bridge (tour the Accademia only if you're an art lover—and really energetic) and back to St. Mark's Square.
15:30	Tour St. Mark's Basilica (closes at 17:00 in summer, at 16:00 in winter).
17:00	Visit the Doge's Palace (in summer closes at 19:00, last entry at 18:00; closes earlier in winter).
18:30	Take my self-guided St. Mark's Square Tour.
19:30	Dinner and a gondola ride (or vice versa, as a gondola ride at sunset is best).
22:00	Enjoy a drink with the orchestras on St. Mark's Square.

Venice in Two or More Days (Plus the Night Before)

On the night before, walk or boat to the train station and then, aboard an empty vaporetto #1, take my self-guided Grand Canal Cruise to St. Mark's Square.

Day 1

9:00	Ride to the top of the Campanile.
10:00	Take my self-guided St. Mark's Square Tour. Pop into a glass shop for a glass-blowing demo.
11:00	Take my self-guided St. Mark's to Rialto Loop Walk.
13:00	Lunch.
14:00	Tour Correr Museum (ticket purchased here includes Doge's Palace).
15:30	Tour St. Mark's Basilica (closes at 17:00 in summer, at 16:00 in winter).
17:00	Visit the Doge's Palace (in summer closes at 19:00, last entry at 18:00; closes earlier in winter).

| 19:00 | Dinner (if a nice one, make a reservation) and maybe a gondola ride (or vice versa, as a gondola ride at sunset is best). |
| 22:00 | Enjoy a drink with the orchestras on St. Mark's Square. |

Day 2

9:00	Enjoy the action at the Rialto Bridge and Rialto Market.
10:00	Follow my self-guided Rialto to Frari Church Walk.
11:00	Tour the Frari Church.
12:00	Wander into the Dorsoduro district toward Ca' Rezzonico, exploring and enjoying lunch along the way. (Visit Scuola San Rocco only if you're an art lover.)
14:00	Tour Ca' Rezzonico (Museum of 18th-Century Venice, closed Tue).
16:00	Tour the Accademia museum (only if you're an art lover), then stroll across the Accademia Bridge and back to St. Mark's Square.
18:00	Commence pub crawl for dinner (consider taking Alessandro's Classic Venice Bars Tour; see page 30).
20:00	Evening free for a concert or gondola ride.

Day 3—Lagoon Tour

10:00	Catch boat at Fondamente Nove to San Michele (old cemetery), then continue to Murano.
11:00	Tour Murano, and (on weekdays) see glassworks.
13:00	Boat to Burano for lunch and browsing.
15:00	Boat to Torcello, tour church, back to Burano.
18:00	Zip back to Fondamente Nove in 45 minutes, or—if you'd like to see more of the lagoon—take the long way back by boat via the mainland peninsula of Cavallino and the Lido (no need to stop there—just enjoy the cruise).
20:00	Dinner and/or concert in Venice.

Day 4 and Beyond

Shop and browse some of Venice's more characteristic areas (such as the zone between Campo Santa Margarita and Campo San Barnaba; the back lanes of Cannaregio, near the Jewish Ghetto; or the sleepy part of Dorsoduro behind the Accademia and Guggenheim).

Or consider these options: Take one of the many guided or theme tours available, visit the Church of San Giorgio Maggiore, or side-trip to Padua (30-50 minutes away by train).

Overview

TOURIST INFORMATION

With this book, a free city map from your hotel, and the events schedule on the TI's website, there's little need to make an in-person visit to a TI in Venice. That's fortunate, because though the city's TIs try to help, they are understaffed and don't have many free printed materials to hand out. If you need to check or confirm something, try phoning the TI information line at 041-2424 or visit www.turismovenezia.it; this website can be more helpful than the actual TI office. Other useful websites are www.veneziaunica. it (vaporetto and event schedules), www.venicexplorer.net (detailed maps), www.aguestinvenice.com (sights and events), www. veniceforvisitors.com (general travel advice), www.venicelink. com (public and private transportation tickets), and www. museicivicivineziani.it (city-run museums in Venice).

If you must visit a TI, you'll find four convenient branches: **St. Mark's Square** (in the far-left corner with your back to the basilica, open 9:00-19:00); **airport** (daily 9:00-20:00); **bus station** (inside the huge white Autorimessa Comunale parking garage, daily 8:30-14:00); and **train station** (white kiosk in front of the station near the vaporetto stop, daily 9:00-16:00).

Be wary of the travel agencies or special information services that masquerade as TIs but serve fancy hotels and tour companies. They're in the business of selling things you don't need.

Maps: Of all places, Venice demands a good map. Hotels give away freebies (similar in quality to the small color ones at the front of this book). TIs and vaporetto ticket booths sell decent €3 maps—but you can find a wider range at bookshops, newsstands, and postcard stands. The cheap maps are pretty bad, but if you spend €5, you'll get a map that shows all the tiny alleys. Investing in a good map can be the best €5 you'll spend in Venice.

Also consider a mapping **app** for your smartphone, which uses GPS to pinpoint your location—extremely useful if you get lost in twisty back streets. To avoid data-roaming charges, look for an offline map that can be downloaded in its entirety before your trip. The **City Maps 2Go** and **Google Maps** apps have good maps, including Venice, that are searchable even when you're not online—as long as you download them in advance.

ARRIVAL IN VENICE

For a rundown on Venice's train station, bus station, airport, and cruise terminal, and tips for drivers, see the Venice Connections chapter.

Daily Reminder

Sunday: While anyone is welcome to worship, most churches are closed to sightseers on Sunday morning. They reopen in the afternoon: St. Mark's Basilica (14:00-17:00, until 16:00 Nov-Easter), Frari Church (13:00-18:00), and the Church of San Zaccaria (16:00-18:00). The Church of San Polo is closed all day, and the Rialto open-air market consists mainly of souvenir stalls (fish and produce sections closed). It's a bad day for a pub crawl, as most pubs are closed.

Monday: All sights are open except the Rialto fish market, Ca' Pesaro, Palazzo Mocenigo Costume Museum, Lace Museum (on the island of Burano), and Torcello church museum (on the island of Torcello). The Accademia and Ca' d'Oro close at 14:00. Don't side-trip to Verona today, as most sights there are closed in the morning.

Tuesday: All sights are open except the Peggy Guggenheim Collection, Ca' Rezzonico (Museum of 18th-Century Venice), and Punta della Dogana.

Wednesday/Thursday/Friday: All sights are open.

Saturday: All sights are open except the Jewish Museum.

Notes: The Accademia is open earlier (daily at 8:15) and closes later (19:15 Tue-Sun) than most sights in Venice. Some sights close earlier off-season (such as the Correr Museum, Campanile bell tower, St. Mark's Basilica, and the Church of San Giorgio Maggiore). Modest dress is recommended at churches and required at St. Mark's Basilica—no bare shoulders, shorts, or short skirts.

Crowd Control: The city is inundated with cruise-ship passengers and tours from mainland hotels daily from 10:00 to about 16:00. Major sights are busiest in the late morning, so it's a delightful time to explore the back lanes. The sights that have crowd problems get even more packed when it rains.

To avoid the worst of the crowds at **St. Mark's Basilica,** go early or late, or reserve a time online. You can usually bypass the line if you have a large bag to check (see page 82).

At the **Doge's Palace,** purchase your ticket at the never-crowded Correr Museum across St. Mark's Square. You can also visit later in the day.

For the **Campanile,** ascend first thing in the morning or go late (it's open until 21:00 July-Sept), or skip it entirely if you're going to the similar San Giorgio Maggiore bell tower.

SIGHTSEEING PASSES FOR VENICE

Venice offers a dizzying array of combo-tickets and sightseeing passes. For most people, the best choice is the Museum Pass, which covers entry into the Doge's Palace, Correr Museum, and more. Note that seven of the most visit-worthy sights in town (the Accademia, Peggy Guggenheim Collection, Scuola San Rocco,

Campanile, and the three sights within St. Mark's Basilica that charge admission) are not covered by any pass.

All of the passes described below are sold at the TI (except for the combo-ticket), and most are also available at participating sights.

Combo-Ticket: A €19 combo-ticket covers both the Doge's Palace and the Correr Museum. To bypass the long line at the Doge's Palace, buy your combo-ticket at the never-crowded Correr Museum (or online). The two sights are also covered by the Museum Pass and Venice Card.

Museum Pass: Busy sightseers may prefer this more expensive pass, which covers these city-run museums: the Doge's Palace; Correr Museum; Ca' Rezzonico (Museum of 18th-Century Venice); Palazzo Mocenigo Costume Museum; Casa Goldoni (home of the Italian playwright); Ca' Pesaro (modern art); Museum of Natural History in the Santa Croce district; the Glass Museum on the island of Murano; and the Lace Museum on the island of Burano. At €24, this pass is the best value if you plan to see the Doge's Palace/Correr Museum and even just one of the other covered museums. You can buy it at any of the participating museums or via their websites.

Chorus Pass: This pass gives church lovers admission to 18 of Venice's churches and their art (generally €3 each) for €12 (www.chorusvenezia.org). The Frari church is included, but not St. Mark's. The typical tourist is unlikely to see more than two of these.

Venice Card: This pass (also called a "city pass") combines the 11 city-run museums and the 16 churches covered by the Chorus Pass, plus the Jewish Museum and a few minor discounts, for €40. A cheaper variation, San Marco Pack, is more selective: It covers the Correr Museum, Doge's Palace, and your choice of any three churches for €28. But it's hard to make either of these passes pay off (valid for 7 days, www.veneziaunica.com).

Rolling Venice: This youth pass offers discounts at dozens of sights and shops, but its best deal is for transit. If you're under 30 and want to buy a 72-hour transit pass, it'll cost you just €22—rather than €40—with the Rolling Venice pass (€6 pass for ages 14-29, sold at TIs, vaporetto ticket offices, and VèneziaUnica shops; for more info see www.veneziaunica.it and search for "Rolling Venice").

Transportation Passes: Venice sells transit-only passes that cover *vaporetti* and mainland buses. For a rundown on these, see "Getting Around Venice," later.

HELPFUL HINTS
Exchange Rate: €1 = about $1.10
Country Calling Code: 39 (see page 450 for dialing instructions)

Theft Alert: The dark, late-night streets of Venice are generally safe. Even so, pickpockets (often elegantly dressed) work the crowded main streets, docks, and *vaporetti*. Your biggest risk of pickpockets is inside St. Mark's Basilica, near the Accademia or Rialto bridges (especially if you're preoccupied with snapping photos), or on a tightly packed vaporetto.

A handy *polizia* station is on the right side of St. Mark's Square as you face the basilica (at #63, near Caffè Florian). To call the police, dial 113. The Venice TI handles complaints—which must be submitted in writing—about local crooks,

including gondoliers, restaurants, and hotel rip-offs (fax 041-523-0399, complaint.apt@ turismovenezia.it).

It's illegal for street vendors to sell knockoff handbags, and it's also illegal for you to buy them; both you and the vendor can get big fines.

Medical Help: Venice's Santi Giovanni e Paolo hospital (tel. 118) is a 10-minute walk from both the Rialto and San Marco neighborhoods, located behind the big church of the same name on Fondamenta dei Mendicanti (toward Fondamente Nove). You can take vaporetto #4.1 from San Zaccaria, or #5.2 from the train station or Piazzale Roma, to the Ospedale stop. Also, a first-aid station staffed by English-speaking doctors is on St. Mark's Square (at #63—same address as *polizia* station, daily 8:00-20:00), on the right-hand side as you face the basilica.

Be Prepared to Splurge: Venice is expensive for residents as well as tourists, as everything must be shipped in and hand-trucked to its final destination. I find that the best way to enjoy Venice is just to succumb to its charms, accept that prices are 20 percent higher than on the mainland, and blow through a little money. It's a unique place that's worth paying a premium to fully experience.

Picnics: Picnicking is illegal anywhere on St. Mark's Square, and offenders can be fined. The only place nearby for a legal picnic is in Giardinetti Reali, the small bench-filled park along the waterfront west of the Piazzetta near St. Mark's Square. Elsewhere in Venice, picnicking is no problem.

Dress Modestly: When visiting St. Mark's Basilica or other major churches, men, women, and even children must cover their shoulders and knees. Remove hats when entering a church.

Public Toilets: Handy public pay WCs are near major landmarks, including: St. Mark's Square (behind the Correr Museum and at the waterfront park, Giardinetti Reali), Rialto, and the Accademia Bridge. Use free toilets whenever you can—any museum you're visiting, or any café you're eating in. A cup of coffee at the counter of a nice bar and a trip to the WC is cheaper than the cost of using a pay WC.

Best Views: A slow vaporetto ride down the Grand Canal—ideally very early or just before sunset—is a shutterbug's delight (try to sit in the front seats, available on some older boats). On St. Mark's Square, enjoy views from the soaring Campanile or the balcony of St. Mark's Basilica (both require admission). The Rialto and Accademia bridges provide free, expansive views of the Grand Canal, along with a cooling breeze. Or get off the main island for a view of the Venetian skyline: Ascend San Giorgio Maggiore's bell tower, or venture to Giudecca Island to visit the swanky bar of the Molino Stucky Hilton Hotel (the free-to-"customers" shuttle boat leaves from near the San Zaccaria-B vaporetto dock).

Water: I carry a water bottle to refill at public fountains. Venetians pride themselves on having pure, safe, and tasty tap water piped in from the foothills of the Alps. You can actually see the mountains from Venice's bell towers on crisp, clear winter days.

Pigeon Poop: If your head is bombed by a pigeon, resist the initial response to wipe it off immediately—it'll just smear into your hair. Wait until it dries, and it should flake off cleanly. But if the poop splatters on your clothes, wipe it off immediately to avoid a stain.

SERVICES

Wi-Fi: Almost all hotels have Wi-Fi, many have a computer that guests can use, and most provide these services for free.

Useful App: ⌒ For free audio versions of my Grand Canal Cruise and tours of St. Mark's Square, St. Mark's Basilica, and Frari Church, get the **Rick Steves Audio Europe** app (see page 8).

Post Office: Use post offices only as a last resort, as simple transactions can take 45 minutes if you get in the wrong line. If mailing a letter or package, select "P" on the take-a-number machine. You can buy stamps from tobacco shops and mail postcards at any of the red postboxes in town.

The main post office is a little south of the Rialto Bridge on Marzaria San Salvador, part of the main shopping drag running toward San Marco (Mon-Fri 8:30-19:00, Sat 8:30-12:30, closed Sun, San Marco 5016). You'll find branch offices with shorter hours (generally mornings only) around town, including a handy one right behind St. Mark's Square (near the TI).

Bookstores: In keeping with its literary heritage, Venice has classy and inviting bookstores. The small **Libreria Studium,** a block behind St. Mark's Basilica, has a carefully chosen selection of new English books, including my guidebooks (daily 9:00-19:30, on Calle de la Canonica at #337—see map on page 71, tel. 041-522-2382). Used-

bookstore lovers shouldn't miss the funky **Acqua Alta** ("high water") bookstore, whose quirky owner Luigi has prepared for the next flood by displaying his wares in a selection of vessels, including bathtubs and a gondola. Look for the "book stairs" in his back garden (daily 9:00-20:00, large and classically disorganized selection includes prints of Venice, just beyond Campo Santa Maria Formosa on Lunga Santa Maria Formosa, Castello 5176, see map on page 249, tel. 041-296-0841). For a solid selection of used books in English, visit **Marco Polo,** on Calle del Teatro o de l'Opera, close to the St. Mark's side of the Rialto Bridge, just past the Coin department store and behind the church (daily 9:30-19:30, Cannaregio 5886a—see map on page 249, tel. 041-522-6343).

Baggage Storage: The train station has a pay **baggage check** (daily 6:00-23:00, no lockers; along track 1).

Laundry: Venice has two coin-operated launderettes. **Orange Self-Service Lavanderia** is across the Grand Canal from the train station (€15/load, daily 7:30-22:30, on Ramo de le Chioverete, Santa Croce 665b—see map on page 256, mobile 346-972-5446). The other, called **Effe Erre,** is off Campo Santa Maria Formosa (about €12/load, daily 6:30-23:00, on Ruga Giuffa, Castello 4826—see map on page 242, mobile 349-058-3881, Massimo).

To save time and spend about the same amount, take your laundry to the full-service **Lavanderia Gabriella,** a few streets north of St. Mark's Square (€15/load includes wash, dry, and fold; drop off Mon-Fri 8:00-12:30, closed Sat-Sun; pick up 2 hours later or next working day, on Rio Terà de le Colonne, San Marco 985—see map on page 242, tel. 041-522-1758, Elisabetta).

Travel Agencies: If you need to get train tickets, make seat reservations, or arrange a *cuccetta* (koo-CHET-tah—a berth on a night train), you can avoid a time-consuming trip to Venice's crowded train station by booking online or using a downtown travel agency. Most trains between Venice, Florence, and Rome require reservations, even for rail-pass holders. Booking online saves money. If using a travel agency, you'll be charged a booking fee (it should be no more than €7 per purchase—for example, four people buying round-trip Venice-Verona tickets together is considered one purchase, and therefore a total booking fee of €7; one person buying a €5 one-way ticket to Padua pays a €7 booking fee). Agencies won't tell you about special deals unless you ask (such as getting major savings if you buy non-changeable tickets). Tickets for simple, short train rides can be bought from a machine at the train station moments before you travel.

Oltrex Travel is handy (one bridge past the Bridge of Sighs, just across from the San Zaccaria vaporetto stop—see map on page 71, daily 9:00-13:00 & 14:00-17:30; tel. 041-476-1926, Luca and Beatrice).

Agenzie 365 is in the main lobby of the train station, where you can buy vaporetto and train tickets (about an 8 percent surcharge on train tickets, daily 8:00-19:30; tel. 041-275-9412).

English Church Services: San Zulian Church offers a Mass in English (generally May-Sept Mon-Fri at 9:30 and Sun at 11:30, Oct-April Sun at 10:30, 2 blocks toward Rialto off St. Mark's Square, tel. 041-523-5383). **St. George's Anglican Church** welcomes all to its English-language Eucharist (Sun at 10:30, located on Campo San Zio in Dorsoduro, midway between Accademia and Peggy Guggenheim Collection, www.stgeorgesvenice.com).

GETTING AROUND VENICE
On Foot

The city's "streets" are narrow pedestrian walkways connecting its docks, squares, bridges, and courtyards. To navigate, look for signs on street corners pointing you to *(per)* the nearest major landmark. The first landmarks you'll get to know are San Marco (St. Mark's Square), Rialto (the bridge), Accademia (another bridge), Ferrovia ("railroad," meaning the train station), and Piazzale Roma (the bus station). Determine whether your destination is in the direction of a major, signposted landmark, then follow the signs through the maze.

As you get more comfortable with the city, dare to disobey these signs, avoid the posted routes, and make your own discoveries. While 80 percent of Venice is, in fact, not touristy, 80 percent of the tourists never notice. Escape the crowds and explore on foot. Walk and walk to the far reaches of the town.

Don't worry about getting lost—in fact, get as lost as possible. Keep reminding yourself, "I'm on an island, and I can't get off." When it comes time to find your way, just follow the arrows on building corners or simply ask a local, *"Dov'è San Marco?"* ("Where is St. Mark's?") People in the tourist business (that's most Venetians) speak some English. If they don't, listen politely, watch where their hands point, say *"Grazie,"* and head off in that direction. If you're lost, refer to your map, your smartphone app, or pop into a hotel and ask for their business card—it probably comes with a map and a prominent "You are here."

Every building in Venice has a house number. The numbers relate to the district (each with about 6,000 address numbers), not the street. Therefore, if you need to find a specific address, it helps to know its district, street, house number, and nearby landmarks.

Some helpful street terminology: *Campo* means square, a *campiello* is a small square, *calle* (pronounced "KAH-lay" with an "L" sound) means "street," and a *ponte* is a bridge. A *fondamenta* is the embankment along a canal or the lagoon. A *rio terà* is a street that was once a canal and has been filled in. A *sotoportego* is a covered passageway. *Salizzada* literally means a paved area (usually a wide street). The abbreviations S. and S.S. mean "saint" and "saints" respectively. Don't get hung up on the exact spelling of street and square names, which may sometimes appear in Venetian dialect (which uses *de la, novo,* and *vechio*) and other times in standard Italian (which uses *della, nuovo,* and *vecchio*).

By Vaporetto

Venice's public transit system, run by a company called ACTV, is a fleet of motorized bus-boats called *vaporetti*. They work like city buses except that they never get a flat, the stops are docks, and if you jump off between stops, you might drown. For the same prices, you can purchase tickets and passes at docks and from ACTV affiliate VèneziaUnica (ACTV-tel. 041-2424, www.actv.it; VèneziaUnica—www.veneziaunica.it).

Tickets and Passes

Individual Vaporetto Tickets: A single ticket costs €7.50. Kids age 6 and up pay the same fare as an adult (kids under 6 travel free). Tickets are good for 75 minutes; you can hop on and off at stops and change boats during that time. Your ticket (a plastic card

ORIENTATION

Handy *Vaporetti* from San Zaccaria, near St. Mark's Square

Several *vaporetti* leave from the San Zaccaria docks, located 150 yards east of St. Mark's Square. There are four San Zaccaria docks spaced about 70 yards apart, with six different berths, lettered A to F. Check the big electronic board (next to the C/D dock), which indicates the departure time, line number, destination, and berth letter of upcoming *vaporetti*. Once you've figured out which boat you want, go to that letter berth and hop on.

Line #1: This vaporetto goes up the Grand Canal, making all the stops, including San Marco, Rialto, Ferrovia (train station), and Piazzale Roma (but it does not go as far as Tronchetto). In the other direction, it goes from San Zaccaria to Arsenale and Giardini before ending on the Lido.

Line #2: This vaporetto zips over to San Giorgio Maggiore, the island church across from St. Mark's Square (5 minutes, €5 ride). From there, it continues on to stops on the island of Giudecca, the parking lot at Tronchetto, and then down the Grand Canal. Note: You cannot ride the #2 up the Grand Canal (for example, to Rialto or the train station) directly from this stop—you'll need to walk five minutes along the waterfront, past St. Mark's Square, to the San Marco-Giardinetti dock and hop the #2 from there.

Line #4.1: This boat goes to San Michele and Murano (45 minutes).

Line #7: This is the summertime express boat to Murano (25 minutes).

Molino Stucky Shuttle Boat: This takes even non-guests to the Hilton Hotel, with its popular view bar (20-minute ride, 3/hour, from its own dock near the San Zaccaria-B dock).

Lines #5.1 and #5.2: These are the *circulare* (cheer-koo-LAH-ray), making a loop around the perimeter of the island, with a stop at

embedded with a chip) is refillable—don't toss it after the first use. You can put more money on it at the automated kiosks and avoid waiting in line at the ticket window. The fare is reduced to €5 for a few one-stop runs *(corsa semplice)* that are hard to do by foot, including from San Zaccaria to San Giorgio Maggiore. It's smart to keep your receipt (in case you're checked and your ticket is faulty).

Vaporetto Passes: You can buy a pass for unlimited use of *vaporetti*: €20/24 hours, €30/48 hours, €40/72 hours, €60/7-day pass. All passes must be validated each time you board by touching it to the small white machine on the dock. Because single tickets cost a hefty €7.50 a pop, these passes can pay for themselves in a hurry. Think through your Venice itinerary before you step up to the ticket booth to pay for your first vaporetto trip. The 48-hour pass pays for

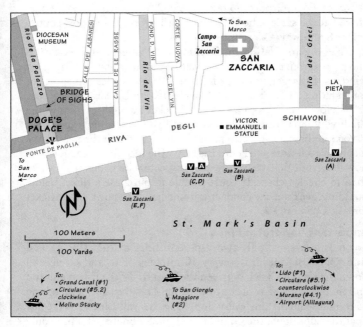

the Lido—perfect if you just like riding boats. Line #5.1 goes counterclockwise, and #5.2 goes clockwise. Both run less frequently in the evenings.

Alilaguna Shuttle Boat: This runs to and from the airport, stopping here as well.

itself with five rides (for example: to your hotel on your arrival, on a Grand Canal joyride, into the lagoon and back, and to the train station). Keep in mind that smaller and/or outlying stops, such as Sant'Elena and Biennale, are unstaffed—another good reason to buy a pass. It's fun to be able to hop on and off spontaneously, and avoid long ticket lines. On the other hand, many tourists just walk through Venice and rarely use a boat.

Travelers between ages 14-29 can get a 72-hour pass for €22 if they also buy a **Rolling Venice** discount card for €6 (see page 17). Those settling in for a much longer stay can ride like a local by buying the Vènezia Unica card (see www.veneziaunica.com for details).

Passes are also valid on some of ACTV's mainland buses,

including bus #2 to Mestre (but not the #5 to the airport nor the airport buses run by ATVO, a separate company). Pass holders get a discounted fare for all ACTV buses that originate or terminate at Marco Polo Airport (€6 one-way, €12 round-trip, must be purchased at the same time as the pass; otherwise, the airport shuttle costs €8 one-way, €15 round-trip).

Buying and Validating Tickets and Passes: Purchase tickets and passes from the automated machines at most stops, from ticket windows (at larger stops), or from the VèneziaUnica offices at the train station, bus station, and Tronchetto parking lot.

Before you board, validate your ticket by holding it up to the small white machine on the dock until you hear a pinging sound. If you purchase a vaporetto pass, you need to touch the pass to the machine each time you board the boat. The machine readout shows how long your ticket is valid—and inspectors do come by now and then to check tickets. If you're unable to purchase a ticket before boarding, seek out the conductor immediately to buy a single ticket (or risk a €50 fine).

Important Vaporetto Lines

For most travelers, only two vaporetto lines matter: **line #1** and **line #2.** These lines leave every 10 minutes or so and go up and down the Grand Canal, between the "mouth" of the fish at one end and St. Mark's Square at the other. Line #1 is the slow boat, taking 45 minutes and making every stop along the way. Line #2 is the fast boat that zips down the Grand Canal in 25 minutes, stopping only at Tronchetto (parking lot), Piazzale Roma (bus station), Ferrovia (train station), Rialto Bridge, San Tomà (Frari Church), San Samuele (opposite Ca' Rezzonico), Accademia Bridge, and San Marco (west end of St. Mark's Square, end of the line).

Sorting out the different directions of travel can be confusing. Some boats run on circular routes, in one direction only (for example, lines #5.1 and #5.2, plus the non-Murano sections of lines #4.1 and #4.2). Line #2 runs in both directions and is almost, but not quite, a full loop. The #2 boat leaving from the San Marco stop goes in one direction (up the Grand Canal), while from the San Zaccaria stop—just a five-minute walk away—it goes in the opposite direction (around the tail of the "fish"). Make sure you use the correct stop to avoid taking the long way around to your destination.

To clear up any confusion, ask a ticket-seller or conductor for help (sometimes they're stationed on the dock to help confused tourists). Get a copy of the most current ACTV map and timetable (in English and Italian, theoretically free at ticket booths but usually unavailable—can be downloaded from www.actv.it). System maps are posted at stops, but it's smart to print out your own copy of the map from the ACTV website before your trip.

Boarding and Riding

Many stops have two boarding platforms, and large stops—such as San Marco, San Zaccaria, Rialto, Ferrovia (train station), and

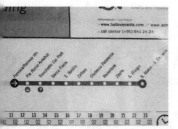

Piazzale Roma—have multiple platforms. At these larger stops, helpful electronic boards display which boats are coming next, and when, and from which platform they leave; each platform is assigned a letter (clearly marked above the gangway). At smaller stops without electronic displays, signs on each platform show the vaporetto lines that stop there and the direction they are headed. As you board, confirm your destination by looking for an electronic sign on the boat or just asking the conductor.

ORIENTATION

You may notice some *vaporetti* sporting a *corsa bis* sign, indicating that it's running a shortened or altered route, and that riders may have to hop off partway (at Rialto, for example) and wait for the next boat. If you see a *corsa bis* sign, before boarding ask the conductor whether the boat is going to your desired destination (e.g., simply ask "San Marco?").

Crowd-Beating Tips

For fun, take the Grand Canal Cruise (see that chapter). But be warned: Grand Canal *vaporetti* in particular can be absolutely jam-packed, especially during the tourist rush hour (during mornings heading in from Piazzale Roma, and in evenings heading out to Piazzale Roma). Riding at night, with nearly empty boats and chandelier-lit palace interiors viewable from the Grand Canal, can be a highlight of your Venetian experience.

By *Traghetto*

Only four bridges cross the Grand Canal, but *traghetti* (shuttle gondolas) ferry locals and in-the-know tourists across the Grand Canal at three additional locations (marked on the color map of Venice at the front of this book). Just step in, hand the gondolier €2, and enjoy the ride—standing or sitting. Some *traghetti* are seasonal, some stop running as early as

ORIENTATION

Is Venice Sinking?

Venice has battled rising water levels since the fifth century. But today, the water seems to be winning. Several factors, both natural and man-made, cause Venice to flood about 100 times a year—usually from October until late winter—a phenomenon called the *acqua alta*.

On my last trip I asked a Venetian how much the city is sinking. He said, "Less than the sea is rising." Venice sits atop sediments deposited at the ancient mouth of the Po River, which are still compacting and settling. Early industrial projects, such as offshore piers and the railroad bridge to the mainland, affected the sea floor and tidal cycles in ways that made the city more vulnerable to flooding. Twentieth-century industry worsened

things by pumping massive amounts of groundwater out of the aquifer beneath the lagoon for nearly 50 years before the government stopped the practice in the 1970s. In the last century, Venice has sunk by about nine inches.

Meanwhile, the waters around Venice are rising, a phenomenon that's especially apparent in winter. The highest so far was in November of 1966, when a huge storm (the same one that famously flooded Florence) raised Venice's water level to more than six feet above the norm. The notorious *acqua alta* happens when an unusually high tide combines with strong sirocco winds and a storm. Although tides are minuscule in the Mediterranean, the narrow, shallow Adriatic Sea has about a three-foot tidal range. When a storm—an area of low pressure—travels over a body of water, it pulls the surface of the water up into a dome. As strong sirocco winds from Africa blow storms north up the Adriatic, they push this high water ahead of the front, causing a surging storm tide. Add to that the worldwide sea-level rise that's resulted from recent climate change (melting ice caps, thermal expansion of the water, more frequent and more powerful storms) and it makes a high sea that much higher.

If the *acqua alta* appears during your visit, you'll see the first

12:30, and all stop by 18:00. *Traghetti* are not covered by any transit pass.

By Water Taxi

Venetian taxis, like speedboat limos, hang out at busy points along the Grand Canal. Prices are regulated: €15 for pickup, then €2 per minute; €5 per person for more than four passengers (boats can carry around 10 people); and €10 between 22:00 and 6:00. If

ORIENTATION

puddles in the center of paved squares, pooling around the limestone grates at the square's lowest point. These grates cover cis-terns that long held Venice's only source of drinking water. That's right: Surrounded by the lagoon and beset by constant flooding, this city had no natural source of fresh water. For centuries, residents carried water from the mainland with much effort and risk. In the ninth century, they devised a way to collect rainwater by using paved, cleverly sloped squares as catchment systems, with limestone filters covering underground clay tubs. Venice's population grew markedly once citizens were able to access fresh water by simply dropping buckets down into these "wells." Several thousand cisterns provided the city with drinking water up until 1884, when an aqueduct was built (paralleling the railroad bridge) to bring in water from nearby mountains. Now the wells are capped, the clay tubs are rotted out, and rain drains from squares into the lagoon—or up from it, as the case may be.

So, what is Venice doing about the flooding? After the 1966 flood, officials knew something had to be done, but it took about four decades to come up with a solution. In 2003, a consortium of engineering firms began construction on the MOSE Project. Named for the acronym of its Italian name, *Modulo Sperimentale Elettromeccanico*, it's also a nod to Moses and his (albeit temporary) mastery over the sea.

Underwater "mobile" gates are being installed on the floor of the sea at the three inlets where the open sea enters Venice's lagoon. When the seawater rises above a certain level, air will be pumped into the gates, causing them to rise and shut out the Adriatic. The first gates are already installed and on the verge of becoming operational. But, in good Italian fashion, greedy government officials were unable to resist the opportunity for personal enrichment and a corruption scandal has stranded the entire project for the foreseeable future.

you have more bags than passengers, the extra ones cost €3 apiece. (For information on taking the water taxi to/from the airport, see the Venice Connections chapter.) Despite regulation, prices can be soft; negotiate and settle on the price or rate before stepping in. For travelers with lots of luggage or small groups who can split the cost, taxi boat rides can be a worthwhile and time-saving convenience— and skipping across the lagoon in a classic wooden motorboat is a cool indulgence. For a little more than €100 an hour, you can have a private, unguided taxi-boat tour. You may find more competitive rates if you prebook through the Consorzio Motoscafi water taxi association tel. 041-522-2303, www.motoscafivenezia.it).

By Gondola

If you're interested in hiring a gondolier for your own private cruise, see the Nightlife in Venice chapter.

Tours in Venice

Local guides and tour companies offer plenty of walking tours that cater to a variety of interests.

𝄐 To sightsee on your own, download my **free audio tours** that illuminate some of Venice's top sights (see sidebar on page 8).

Avventure Bellissime Venice Tours

This company offers several English-only two-hour walks, including a basic St. Mark's Square introduction called the "Original Venice Walking Tour" (€25, includes church entry, most days at 11:00, Sun at 14:00; 45 minutes on the square, 15 minutes in the church, one hour along back streets), a 70-minute private boat tour of the Grand Canal (€48, daily at 16:00, 8 people maximum), a "Hidden Venice" tour (€25, in summer 3/week at 11:30), and mainland excursions (details at www.tours-italy.com, tel. 041-970-499, info@tours-italy.com). For a 10 percent Rick Steves discount, contact them ahead of time for a promo code.

Alessandro's Classic Venice Bars Backstreets Tours

Debonair Alessandro Schezzini is a connoisseur of Venetian *bacari*—classic old bars serving wine and traditional *cicchetti* snacks. He organizes two-hour Venetian bar tours (€35/person, most nights at 18:00) that include sampling *cicchetti* with wines at three *bacari*. (If you think of this tour as a light dinner with a local friend, it's a particularly good value.)

Alessandro is not a licensed guide, so he can't take you into sights. But his relaxed, 1.5-hour Backstreets Tour gets you beyond the clichés and into offbeat Venice (€20/person, most nights at 16:30).

Both tours depart almost daily in season when six or more sign up. They meet 50 yards north of the Rialto Bridge under the big clock on Campo San Giacomo. (Book via email, alessandro@schezzini.it, or by phone, mobile 335-530-9024; www.schezzini.it.)

Artviva Tours

This company offers several tours, including general intro-to-Venice tours, themed tours (Grand Canal, Venice Walk, Doge's Palace, Gondola Tour), or a private "Learn to Be a Gondolier" tour (for details, see www.italy.artviva.com). They offer a 10 percent Rick Steves discount (www.artviva.com/ricksteves, username "ricksteves" and password "reader").

Venicescapes

Michael Broderick's private, themed tours of Venice are intellectually demanding and beyond the attention span of most mortal tourists. But travelers with a keen interest and a desire to learn find him passionate and engaging. Your time with Michael is like a rolling, graduate-level lecture (see his website for various 4- to 6-hour itineraries, 2 people-$280-310 or the euro equivalent, $60/person after that, admissions and transport extra, tel. 041-850-5742, mobile 349-479-7406, www.venicescapes.org, info@venicescapes.org).

Local Guides

Plenty of licensed, trained guides are available. If you organize a small group from your hotel at breakfast to split the cost (figure on €75/hour with a 2-hour minimum), the fee becomes more reason-

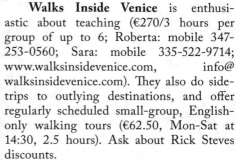

able. I've enjoyed working with the following guides:

Walks Inside Venice is enthusiastic about teaching (€270/3 hours per group of up to 6; Roberta: mobile 347-253-0560; Sara: mobile 335-522-9714; www.walksinsidevenice.com, info@walksinsidevenice.com). They also do side-trips to outlying destinations, and offer regularly scheduled small-group, English-only walking tours (€62.50, Mon-Sat at 14:30, 2.5 hours). Ask about Rick Steves discounts.

Corine Govi and **Elisabetta Morelli,** who run **2Guides4Venice,** are informative and reliable (Corine, mobile 347-966-8346, corine_g@libero.it; Elisabetta, tel. 041-526-7816, mobile 328-753-5220, bettamorelli@inwind.it, www.2guides4venice.com).

Venice with a Guide, a co-op of 10 good guides, offers a range of tours, (€150 for a 2-hour tour; for more, go to www.venicewithaguide.com).

Tour Leader Venice, a.k.a. **Treviso Car Service,** specializes in getting you outside of Venice by car or minivan—to countryside villas, wine-and-cheese tastings, and the Dolomites—but also offers guided walks in Venice (mobile 348-900-0700 or 333-411-2840; www.trevisocarservice.com, tvcarservice@gmail.com; for Venice tours also see www.tourleadervenice.com, info@tourleadervenice.com; Igor, Andrea, and Marta). They also provide

ORIENTATION

transfer services to Venice's airport and cruise terminal (see page 314).

Tour Packages for Students

Andy Steves (Rick's son) runs **Weekend Student Adventures** (WSA Europe), offering three-day and 10-day budget travel packages across Europe including accommodations, skip-the-line sightseeing, and unique local experiences. Locally guided and DIY unguided options are available for student and budget travelers in 12 of Europe's most popular cities, including Venice (guided trips from €199, see www.wsaeurope.com for details).

ORIENTATION

SIGHTS IN VENICE

Venice's greatest sight is the city itself. As well as seeing world-class museums and buildings, make time to wander narrow lanes, linger over a meal, or enjoy evening magic on St. Mark's Square. One of Venice's most delightful experiences—a gondola ride, worth ▲▲▲—is covered in the Nightlife in Venice chapter.

In this chapter, don't judge a listing by its length. Some of Venice's most important sights have the shortest listings and are marked with a 📖. These sights are covered in much greater detail in the individual tour chapters later in this book.

For information on sightseeing passes, see page 17. When you see a 🎧 in a listing, it means the sight is covered in a free audio tour (via my Rick Steves Audio Europe app—see page 8. Be sure to check www.ricksteves.com/update for any significant changes that may have occurred since this book was printed.

SAN MARCO DISTRICT
▲▲▲St. Mark's Square (Piazza San Marco)

This grand square is surrounded by splashy, historic buildings and sights: St. Mark's Basilica, the Doge's Palace, the Campanile bell tower, and the Correr Museum. The square is filled with music, lovers, pigeons, and tourists by day, and is your private rendezvous with the Venetian past late at night, when Europe's most magnificent dance floor is *the* romantic place to be.

For a slow and pricey evening thrill, invest €15 or so (including any cover charge for the music) for a drink at one of the elegant cafés with the dueling orchestras (see "Cafés on St. Mark's Square" on page 76). For an unmatched experience that offers the best people-watching, it's worth the splurge.

The **Clock Tower** (Torre dell'Orologio), built during the Renaissance in 1496, marks the entry to the main shopping drag, called

the Mercerie (or "Marzarie," in Venetian dialect), which connects St. Mark's Square with the Rialto Bridge. From the piazza, you can see the bronze men (Moors) swing their huge clappers at the top of each hour. In the 17th century, one of them knocked an unsuspecting worker off the top and to his death—probably the first-ever killing by a robot. Notice one of the world's first "digital" clocks on the tower facing the square (with dramatic flips every five minutes). You can go inside the Clock Tower with a prebooked guided tour that takes you close to the clock's innards and out to a terrace with good views over the square and city rooftops (€12 combo-ticket includes Correr Museum—where the tour starts—but not Doge's Palace; €7 for the tour if you already have a Museum Pass or Correr/Doge's Palace combo-ticket; tours in English Mon-Wed at 10:00 and 11:00, Thu-Sun at 14:00 and 15:00; no kids under age 6). While reservations are required for the Clock Tower tour, you have a decent chance of being able to "reserve" on the spot—try dropping by the Correr Museum for same-day (or day-before) tickets. To ensure a spot in advance, reserve by calling 848-082-000, or book online at http://torreorologio.visitmuve.it.

📖 See the St. Mark's Square Tour chapter or 🎧 download my free audio tour.

▲▲▲St. Mark's Basilica (Basilica di San Marco)

Built in the 11th century to replace an earlier church, this basilica's distinctly Eastern-style architecture underlines Venice's connec-

tion with Byzantium (which protected it from the ambition of Charlemagne and his Holy Roman Empire). It's decorated with booty from returning sea captains—a kind of architectural Venetian trophy chest. The interior glows mysteriously with gold mosaics and colored marble. Since about A.D. 830, the saint's bones have been housed on this site.

Cost and Hours: Basilica entry is free, except if you pay €2 for an online reservation that lets you skip the line. Three interior sights charge admission (see below). Church open Mon-Sat 9:45-17:00, Sun 14:00-17:00 (Sun until 16:00 Nov-Easter), interior brilliantly lit daily 11:30-12:30, museum open daily 9:45-16:45, including on Sunday mornings when the church itself is closed; if considering a Sunday visit, note that the museum has a balcony that provides a fine view down to the church's interior. The treasury and the Golden Altarpiece are both open Easter-Oct Mon-Sat 9:45-17:00, Sun 14:00-17:00; Nov-Easter Mon-Sat 9:45-16:00, Sun 14:00-16:00; St. Mark's Square, vaporetto: San Marco or San Zaccaria. The dress code is strictly enforced for everyone (no bare shoulders or bare knees). Lines can be long, and bag check is mandatory, free, and can save you time in line; for details, see the "Orientation" section in the St. Mark's Basilica Tour chapter. Tel. 041-270-8311, www.basilicasanmarco.it.

Three separate exhibits within the church charge admission: the **Treasury** (€3, includes audioguide), **Golden Altarpiece** (€2), and **San Marco Museum** (€5). The San Marco Museum has the original bronze horses (copies of these overlook the square), a balcony offering a remarkable view over St. Mark's Square, and various works related to the church.

📖 See the St. Mark's Basilica Tour chapter or 🎧 download my free audio tour.

▲▲▲Doge's Palace (Palazzo Ducale)

The seat of the Venetian government and home of its ruling duke, or doge, this was the most powerful half-acre in Europe for 400 years.

The Doge's Palace was built to show off the power and wealth of the Republic. The doge lived with his family on the first floor up, near the halls of power. From his once-lavish (now sparse) quarters, you'll follow the one-way tour through the public rooms of the top floor, finishing with the Bridge of Sighs and the prison. The place is wall-papered with masterpieces by Veronese and Tintoretto.

Cost and Hours: €19 combo-ticket includes Correr Museum, also covered by Museum Pass—see page 17, daily 8:30-19:00, Nov-March until 17:30, last entry one hour before closing, café, photos allowed without flash, next to St. Mark's Basilica, just off St. Mark's Square, vaporetto stops: San Marco or San Zaccaria, tel. 041-271-5911, http://palazzoducale.visitmuve.it.

Avoiding Lines: If the line is long at the Doge's Palace, buy your combo-ticket at the Correr Museum across the square; then you can go directly through the Doge's turnstile without waiting in line. Or, you can buy your ticket online—at least 48 hours in advance—on the museum website.

Tours: The audioguide costs €5, or €8 for two people. For a

SIGHTS

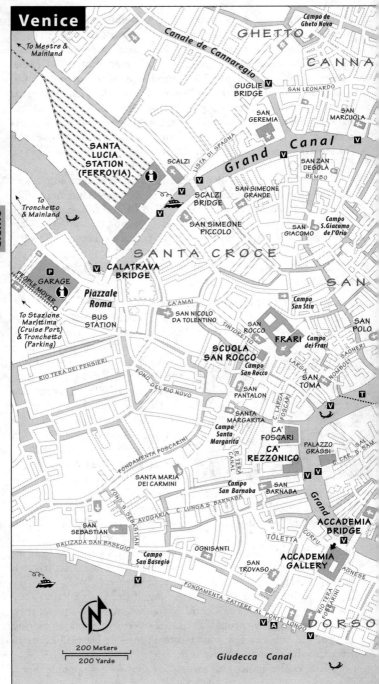

Venice

To Mestre & Mainland

Canale de Cannaregio

GHETTO

CANNA

Campo de Gheto Novo

SANTA LUCIA STATION (FERROVIA)

To Tronchetto & Mainland

SCALZI

GUGLIE BRIDGE

SAN LEONARDO

SAN GEREMIA

SAN MARCUOLA

LISTA DI SPAGNA

Grand Canal

SAN ZAN DEGOLA

BEMBO

SCALZI BRIDGE

SAN SIMEONE GRANDE

SAN SIMEONE PICCOLO

SAN GIACOMO

Campo S.Giacomo de l'Orio

SANTA CROCE

CALATRAVA BRIDGE

SAN

PEOPLE MOVER

GARAGE

Piazzale Roma

CA'AMAI

Campo San Stin

To Stazione Marittima (Cruise Port) & Tronchetto (Parking)

BUS STATION

SAN NICOLO DA TOLENTINO

TINTORETTO

SAN ROCCO

FRARI

Campo dei Frari

SAN POLO

SAONERI

RIO TERA DEI PENSIERI

FOND. DEL RIO NOVO

SCUOLA SAN ROCCO

Campo San Rocco

LARGA

SAN TOMA

NOMBOLI

T

SAN PANTALON

C. LARGA FOSCARI

SANTA MARGARITA

Campo Santa Margarita

CA' FOSCARI

CA' REZZONICO

PALAZZO GRASSI

FONDAMENTA FOSCARINI

SANTA MARIA DEI CARMINI

R. TERA CANAL

Campo San Barnaba

SAN BARNABA

C. CAR. S. SAM.

FOND. S. SEBASTIAN

C. LUNGA S. BARNABA

Grand

ACCADEMIA BRIDGE

SAN SEBASTIAN

SALIZADA SAN BASEGIO

AVOGARIA

OGNISANTI

TOLETTA

CORFU

ACCADEMIA GALLERY

AGNESE

Campo San Basegio

SAN TROVASO

FONDAMENTA ZATTERE AL PONTE LONGO

RIO TERA FOSCARINI

DORSO

N

200 Meters
200 Yards

Giudecca Canal

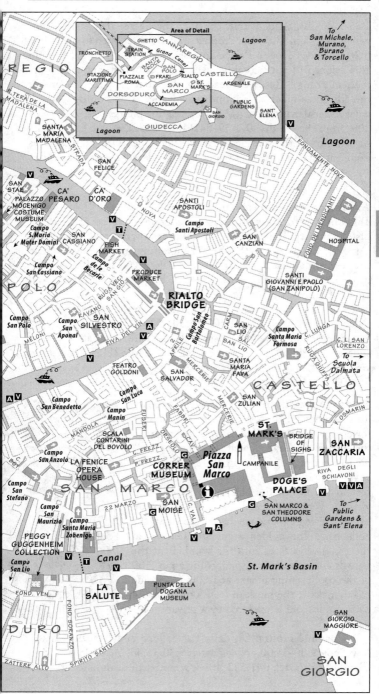

1.25-hour live guided tour, consider the Secret Itineraries Tour, which takes you into palace rooms otherwise not open to the public (€20, includes Doge's Palace admission but not Correr Museum admission; €14 with combo-ticket; three English-language tours each morning). Reserve ahead for this tour in peak season—it can fill up as much as a month in advance. Book online (http://palazzoducale.visitmuve.it), or reserve by phone (tel. 848-082-000, from the US dial 011-39-041-4273-0892), or you can try just showing up at the info desk. Avoid the Doge's Hidden Treasures Tour—it reveals little that would be considered a "treasure" and is a waste of €20.

📖 See the Doge's Palace Tour chapter.

▲▲Correr Museum (Museo Correr)

This uncrowded museum gives you a good overview of Venetian history and art. The doge memorabilia, armor, banners, statues (by Canova), and paintings (by the Bellini family and others) re-create the festive days of the Venetian Republic. And it's all accompanied—throughout the museum—by English descriptions and views of St. Mark's Square.

Cost and Hours: €19 combo-ticket also includes the Doge's Palace; daily April-Oct 10:00-19:00, Nov-March 10:00-17:00, last entry one hour before closing; elegant café, enter at far end of square directly opposite basilica, tel. 041-240-5211, http://correr.visitmuve.it.

📖 See the Correr Museum Tour chapter.

▲Campanile (Campanile di San Marco)

This dramatic bell tower replaced a shorter tower, part of the original fortress that guarded the entry of the Grand Canal. That tower crumbled into a pile of bricks in 1902, a thousand years after it was built. Ride the elevator 325 feet to the top of the bell tower for the best view in Venice (especially at sunset). For an ear-shattering experience, be on top when the bells ring. The golden archangel Gabriel at the top always faces into the wind. Beat the crowds and enjoy the crisp morning air at 9:00 or the cool evening breeze at 18:00. Go inside to buy tickets; the kiosk in front only rents €4 audioguides and is operated by a private company.

Cost and Hours: €8, daily Easter-June and Oct 9:00-19:00, July-Sept 9:00-21:00, Nov-Easter 9:30-15:45, may close during thunderstorms, tel. 041-522-4064, www.basilicasanmarco.it.

For more on the Campanile, see page 75 of the St. Mark's Square Tour chapter.

La Fenice Opera House (Gran Teatro alla Fenice)

During Venice's glorious decline in the 18th century, this was one of seven opera houses in the city, and one of the most famous in Europe. For 200 years, great operas and famous divas debuted here, applauded by ladies and gentlemen in their finery. Then in 1996, an arson fire completely gutted the theater. But La Fenice ("The Phoenix") rose from the ashes, thanks to an eight-year effort to rebuild the historic landmark according to photographic archives of the interior. To see the results at their most glorious, attend an evening **performance** (theater box office open daily 10:00-17:00, tel. 041-2424, www. teatrolafenice.it).

During the day, you can take an **audioguide tour** of the opera house. All you really see is the theater itself; there's no "backstage" tour of dressing rooms, or an opera museum, and the dry 45-minute guide mainly recounts two centuries of construction. But the auditorium, ringed with box seats, is impressive: pastel blue with sparkling gold filigree, muses depicted on the ceiling, and a starburst chandelier. It's also a bit saccharine and brings sadness to Venetians who remember the place before the fire. Other than a minor exhibit of opera scores and Maria Callas memorabilia, there's little to see from the world of opera. To save money and get just a peek at the place, walk into the entrance hall and browse the small bookshop.

For more on the opera house, see page 219 of the St. Mark's to Rialto Loop Walk chapter.

Cost and Hours: €10 audioguide tours, generally open daily 9:30-18:00, but can vary wildly, depending on the performance schedule—to confirm, call box office number (listed above) or check www.festfenice.com. La Fenice is on Campo San Fantin, between St. Mark's Square and the Accademia Bridge.

Palazzo Grassi

This former palace, gleaming proudly on the San Marco side of the Grand Canal, holds a branch of the Punta della Dogana contemporary art museum (for details, see "Punta della Dogana," later; www. palazzograssi.it).

Venice at a Glance

▲▲▲**St. Mark's Square** Venice's grand main square. **Hours:** Always open. See page 33.

▲▲▲**St. Mark's Basilica** Cathedral with mosaics, saint's bones, treasury, museum, and viewpoint of square. **Hours:** Mon-Sat 9:45-17:00, Sun 14:00-17:00 (until 16:00 Nov-Easter). See page 34.

▲▲▲**Doge's Palace** Art-splashed palace of former rulers, with prison accessible through Bridge of Sighs. **Hours:** Daily 8:30-19:00, Nov-March until 17:30. See page 35.

▲▲▲**Rialto Bridge** Distinctive bridge spanning the Grand Canal, with a market nearby. **Hours:** Bridge—always open; market—souvenir stalls open daily, produce market closed Sun, fish market closed Sun-Mon. See page 47.

▲▲**Correr Museum** Venetian history and art. **Hours:** Daily April-Oct 10:00-19:00, Nov-March 10:00-17:00. See page 38.

▲▲**Accademia** Venice's top art museum. **Hours:** Mon 8:15-14:00, Tue-Sun 8:15-19:15. See page 43.

▲▲**Peggy Guggenheim Collection** Popular display of 20th-century art. **Hours:** Wed-Mon 10:00-18:00, closed Tue. See page 44.

▲▲**Frari Church** Franciscan church featuring Renaissance masters. **Hours:** Mon-Sat 9:00-18:00, Sun 13:00-18:00. See page 47.

▲▲**Scuola San Rocco** "Tintoretto's Sistine Chapel." **Hours:** Daily 9:30-17:30. See page 48.

▲**Campanile** Dramatic bell tower on St. Mark's Square with elevator to the top. **Hours:** Daily Easter-June and Oct 9:00-19:00, July-Sept 9:00-21:00; Nov-Easter 9:30-15:45. See page 38.

▲**Bridge of Sighs** Famous enclosed bridge, part of Doge's Palace, near St. Mark's Square. **Hours:** Always viewable. See page 42.

▲**La Salute Church** Striking church dedicated to the Virgin Mary. **Hours:** Daily 9:00-12:00 & 15:00-17:30. See page 44.

SIGHTS

▲**Ca' Rezzonico** Posh Grand Canal palazzo with 18th-century Venetian art. **Hours:** Wed-Mon 10:00-18:00, Nov-March until 17:00, closed Tue year-round. See page 44.

▲**Punta della Dogana** Museum of contemporary art. **Hours:** Wed-Mon 10:00-19:00, closed Tue. See page 45.

▲**Ca' Pesaro International Gallery of Modern Art** Fine museum in a canalside palazzo. **Hours:** Tue-Sun 10:00-18:00, Nov-March until 17:00, closed Mon year-round. See page 45.

▲**Scuola Dalmata di San Giorgio** Exquisite Renaissance meeting house. **Hours:** Mon 13:30-17:30, Tue-Sat 9:30-17:30, Sun 9:30-13:30. See page 51.

Church of San Zaccaria Final resting place of St. Zechariah, plus a Bellini altarpiece and an eerie crypt. **Hours:** Mon-Sat 10:00-12:00 & 16:00-18:00, Sun 16:00-18:00. See page 42.

Church of San Polo Has works by Tintoretto, Veronese, and Tiepolo. **Hours:** Mon-Sat 10:00-17:00, closed Sun. See page 48.

Nearby Islands
▲**San Giorgio Maggiore** Island facing St. Mark's Square, featuring church with Palladio architecture, Tintoretto paintings, and fine views back on Venice. **Hours:** Daily 7:00-19:00, Nov-March closes at dusk. See page 42.

San Michele Cemetery island on the lagoon. **Hours:** Daily 7:30-18:00, Oct-March until 16:30. See page 54.

▲**Murano** Island famous for glass factories and glassmaking museum. **Hours:** Glass Museum open daily 10:00-18:00, Nov-March until 17:00. See page 54.

▲▲**Burano** Sleepy island known for lacemaking and lace museum. **Hours:** Museum open Tue-Sun 10:00-18:00, Nov-March until 17:00, closed Mon year-round. See page 54.

▲**Torcello** Near-deserted island with old church, bell tower, and museum. **Hours:** Church open daily March-Oct 10:30-18:00, Nov-Feb 10:00-17:00, museum closed Mon. See page 54.

▲**Lido** Family-friendly beach. See page 55.

SIGHTS

SIGHTS

BEHIND ST. MARK'S BASILICA
▲Bridge of Sighs
This much-photographed bridge connects the Doge's Palace with the prison. Travelers popularized this bridge in the Romantic 19th

century. Supposedly, a condemned man would be led over this bridge on his way to the prison, take one last look at the glory of Venice, and sigh. Though overhyped, the Bridge of Sighs is undeniably tingle-worthy—especially after dark, when the crowds have dispersed and it's just you and floodlit Venice. During the middle of the day, however, being immersed in the pandemonium of global tourism (and selfie sticks) can be a fascinating experience in itself.

Getting There: The Bridge of Sighs is around the corner from the Doge's Palace. Walk toward the waterfront, turn left along the water, and look up the first canal on your left. You can walk across the bridge (from the inside) by visiting the Doge's Palace.

📖 See the St. Mark's to San Zaccaria Walk chapter and the 📖 Doge's Palace Tour chapter.

Church of San Zaccaria
This historic church is home to a sometimes-waterlogged crypt, a Bellini altarpiece, a Tintoretto painting, and the final resting place of St. Zechariah, the father of John the Baptist.

Cost and Hours: Free, €1.50 to enter crypt, €0.50 coin to light up Bellini's altarpiece, Mon-Sat 10:00-12:00 & 16:00-18:00, Sun 16:00-18:00 only, two canals behind St. Mark's Basilica.

📖 See the St. Mark's to San Zaccaria Walk chapter.

ACROSS THE LAGOON FROM ST. MARK'S SQUARE
▲San Giorgio Maggiore
This is the dreamy church-topped island you can see from the waterfront by St. Mark's Square. The striking church, de-signed by Palladio, features art by Tintoretto, a bell tower, and good views of Venice.

Cost and Hours: Free entry to church; daily 7:00-19:00, Nov-March closes at dusk. The bell tower costs €6 and is accessible by elevator (runs until 15 minutes before the church closes but is not accessible Sun during services).

Venice Early and Late

Most sightseeing in Venice is restricted to the hours between 10:00 and 18:00. Here are some exceptions:

Sights Open Early

Accademia: Daily at 8:15.

Doge's Palace: Daily at 8:30.

Naval Museum (Ship Pavilion): Mon-Fri at 8:45.

Campanile: Daily Easter-Oct at 9:00, Nov-Easter at 9:30.

Frari Church: Mon-Sat at 9:00.

La Salute Church: Daily at 9:00.

San Giorgio Maggiore: Daily at 7:00.

Scuola Dalmata di San Giorgio: Tue-Sun at 9:30.

Scuola San Rocco: Daily at 9:30.

St. Mark's Basilica: Mon-Sat at 9:45.

San Marco Museum: Daily at 9:45.

Sights Open Late

Doge's Palace: Daily April-Oct until 19:00.

Correr Museum: Daily April-Oct until 19:00.

Punta della Dogana: Wed-Mon until 19:00.

Jewish Museum: June-Sept Sun-Fri until 19:00.

Campanile: Daily Easter-June and Oct until 19:00, July-Sept until 21:00.

Accademia: Tue-Sun until 19:15.

Ca' d'Oro: Tue-Sun until 19:15.

Always Open

St. Mark's Square and the Rialto Bridge are always open, un-crowded in the early morning, and magical at night.

Getting There: To reach the island from St. Mark's Square, take the one-stop, three-minute ride on vaporetto #2 from San Zac-caria (6/hour, €5 special vaporetto ticket, direction: Tronchetto).

📖 See the San Giorgio Maggiore Tour chapter.

DORSODURO DISTRICT
▲▲Accademia (Galleria dell'Accademia)

Venice's top art museum, packed with highlights of the Vene-tian Renaissance, features paintings by the Bellini family, Titian, Tintoretto, Veronese, Tiepolo, Giorgione, Canaletto, and Testos-terone. It's just over the wooden Accademia Bridge from the San Marco action.

Cost and Hours: €15, Mon 8:15-14:00, Tue-Sun 8:15-19:15, last entry one hour before closing, dull audioguide-€6, no flash

Billboards

As part of Venice's ongoing renovation, you will see scaffolding covering major monuments—and advertising covering the scaffolding. Cash-strapped Venice is seeking funding from corporations in exchange for advertising space. Might there be Coca-Cola ads covering St. Mark's Square? The mayor of Venice said of the possibility of more billboards: "It's not beautiful. It's not ugly. It's necessary."

photos allowed. At Accademia Bridge, vaporetto: Accademia, tel. 041-522-2247, www.gallerieaccademia.org.

☐ See the Accademia Tour chapter.

▲▲Peggy Guggenheim Collection

The popular museum of far-out art, housed in the American heiress' former retirement palazzo, offers one of Europe's best reviews of the art of the first half of the 20th century. Stroll through styles represented by artists whom Peggy knew personally—Cubism (Picasso, Braque), Surrealism (Dalí, Ernst), Futurism (Boccioni), American Abstract Expressionism (Pollock), and a sprinkling of Klee, Calder, and Chagall.

Cost and Hours: €15, usually includes temporary exhibits, Wed-Mon 10:00-18:00, closed Tue, audioguide-€7, pricey café, vaporetto: Accademia or Salute, tel. 041-240-5411, www.guggenheim-venice.it.

☐ See the Peggy Guggenheim Collection Tour chapter.

▲La Salute Church (Santa Maria della Salute)

This impressive church with a crown-shaped dome was built and dedicated to the Virgin Mary by grateful survivors of the 1630 plague.

Cost and Hours: Free entry to church, €3 to enter the Sacristy; daily 9:00-12:00 & 15:00-17:30. It's a 10-minute walk from the Accademia Bridge; the Salute vaporetto stop is at its doorstep, tel. 041-274-3928, www.seminariovenezia.it.

☐ See the La Salute Church Tour chapter.

▲Ca' Rezzonico (Museum of 18th-Century Venice)

This Grand Canal palazzo offers the most insightful look at the life of Venice's rich and famous in the 1700s. Wander under ceilings by Tiepolo, among furnishings from that most decadent century, enjoying views of the canal and paintings by Guardi, Canaletto, and Longhi.

Cost and Hours: €10, Wed-Mon 10:00-18:00, Nov-March until 17:00, closed Tue year-round; audioguide-€5 or €6/2 people; ticket office closes one hour before museum, no flash photography, café, at Ca' Rezzonico vaporetto stop, tel. 041-241-0100, http://carezzonico.visitmuve.it.

☐ See the Ca' Rezzonico Tour chapter.

▲Punta della Dogana

This museum of contemporary art, opened in 2009, makes the Dorsoduro a major destination for art lovers. Housed in the for-

mer Customs House at the end of the Grand Canal, it features cutting-edge 21st-century art in spacious rooms. This isn't Picasso and Matisse, or even Pollock and Warhol—those guys are ancient history. But if you're into the likes of Jeff Koons, Cy Twombly, Rachel Whiteread, and a host of newer artists, the museum is world class.

The displays change completely about every year, drawn from the museum's large collection—so large it also fills Palazzo Grassi, farther up the Grand Canal.

Cost and Hours: €15 for one locale, €20 for both; Wed-Mon 10:00-19:00, closed Tue, last entry one hour before closing; audioguide sometimes available, small café, tel. 199-112-112 within Italy, 041-200-1057 from abroad, www.palazzograssi.it.

Getting There: Punta della Dogana is near La Salute Church (or vaporetto: Salute). Palazzo Grassi is a bit upstream, on the east side of the Grand Canal (vaporetto #2: San Samuele).

SANTA CROCE DISTRICT
▲Ca' Pesaro International Gallery of Modern Art

This museum features 19th- and early 20th-century art in a 17th-century canalside palazzo. The collection is strongest on Italian (especially Venetian) artists, but also presents a broad array of other well-known artists. While the Peggy Guggenheim Collection is undisputedly Venice's best modern collection, Ca' Pesaro comes in a clear second—and features a handful of recognizable master-pieces (most notably Klimt's *Judith II*, Kandinsky's *White Zig Zags*, and Chagall's *Rabbi #2*).

Cost and Hours: €10; Tue-Sun 10:00-18:00, Nov-March until 17:00, closed Mon year-round, last entry one hour before

SIGHTS

A Dying City?

Venice's population (55,000 in the historic city) is half what it was just 30 years ago, and people are leaving at a rate of a thousand a year. Of those who stay, 25 percent are 65 or older.

Sad, yes, but imagine raising a family here: Apartments are small, high up, and expensive. Humidity and occasional flooding make basic maintenance a pain. Home-improvement projects require navigating miles of red tape, and you must follow regulations intended to preserve the historical ambience. Everything is expensive because it has to be shipped in from the mainland. You can easily get glass and tourist trinkets, but it's hard to find groceries or get your shoes fixed. Running basic errands involves lots of walking and stairs—imagine crossing over arched bridges while pushing a child in a stroller and carrying a day's worth of groceries.

With millions of visitors a year (150,000 a day at peak times), on any given day Venetians are likely outnumbered by tourists. Despite government efforts to subsidize rents and build cheap housing, the city is losing its residents. The economy itself is thriving, thanks to tourist dollars and rich foreigners buying second homes. But the culture is dying.

Greedy residents could sink Venice long before the sea swallows it up. Locals happily rent apartments to tourists a few times a month rather than affordably to local families, and shopkeepers sell trinkets to tourists before pots and pans to the local population. Even the most hopeful city planners worry that in a few decades Venice will not be a city at all, but a museum, a cultural theme park, a decaying Disneyland for adults.

closing, two-minute walk from San Stae vaporetto stop, tel. 041-721-127, http://capesaro.visitmuve.it.

Visiting the Museum: After buying your tickets, head upstairs and make your way through the rooms. You'll start with 19th-century sculpture (Rodin and Medardo Rossi, Room 1), then Romanticism (Room 2), and then in Rooms 3-4, Impressionism and turn-of-the-century art, including Klimt's beautiful/creepy *Judith II*, with her eagle-talon fingers. Room 5 has more sculpture (including by the Milanese sculptor Adolfo Wildt), as well as Chagall's surprisingly realistic portrait of his hometown rabbi, *Rabbi #2* (a.k.a. *The Rabbi of Vitebsk*). Room 6 shows off Venetian Impressionism. Rooms 7-9 are devoted to Modernist art from the

1920s and 1930s, including Bonnard's colorful *Nude in the Mirror*, which flattens the 3-D scene into a 2-D pattern of rectangles. Room 10 moves on to the 1930s and 1940s, while Room 11 has big international names including Klee, Kandinsky, Picasso, Calder, and Ernst. Abstract art is in Rooms 12-14, and finally, Dada and Pop Art in Room 15. Forgotten on the top floor is the skippable Museum of Oriental Art.

Palazzo Mocenigo Costume Museum (Museo di Palazzo Mocenigo)

The Museo di Palazzo Mocenigo offers a pleasant walk through a dozen rooms in a fine 17th-century mansion. Besides viewing period clothing and accessories, you can sniff an array of perfumes and spices and watch a video about the history of perfume in Venice (runs in a loop in three languages). The rooms provide a sense of aristocratic life during Venice's Golden Age, with furnishings, family portraits, ceilings painted (c. 1790) with family triumphs (the Mocenigos produced seven doges), and Murano glass chandeliers in situ. English-language cards in each room give sparse descriptions.

Cost and Hours: €8; Tue-Sun 10:00-17:00, Nov-March until 16:00, closed Mon year-round, a block in from San Stae vaporetto stop, tel. 041-721-798, http://mocenigo.visitmuve.it.

SAN POLO DISTRICT
▲▲▲Rialto Bridge

One of the world's most famous bridges, this distinctive and dramatic stone structure crosses the Grand Canal with a single con-

fident span. The arcades along the top of the bridge help reinforce the structure...and offer some enjoyable shopping diversions, as does the **market** surrounding the bridge (produce market closed Sun, fish market closed Sun-Mon).

For more on the Rialto Bridge, 📖 see the St. Mark's to Rialto Loop Walk chapter. For more on the markets, 📖 see the Rialto to Frari Church Walk chapter.

▲▲Frari Church (Basilica di Santa Maria Gloriosa dei Frari)

My favorite art experience in Venice is seeing art in the setting for which it was designed—as it is at the Frari Church. The Franciscan "Church of the Brothers" and the art that

SIGHTS

decorates it are warmed by the spirit of St. Francis. It features the work of three great Renaissance masters: Donatello, Giovanni Bellini, and Titian—each showing worshippers the glory of God in human terms.

Cost and Hours: €3, Mon-Sat 9:00-18:00, Sun 13:00-18:00, audioguide-€2, modest dress recommended, on Campo dei Frari, near San Tomà vaporetto and *traghetto* stops, tel. 041-272-8618, www.basilicadeifrari.it.

📖 See the Frari Church Tour chapter or 🎧 download my free audio tour.

▲▲Scuola San Rocco

Sometimes called "Tintoretto's Sistine Chapel," this lavish meeting hall (next to the Frari Church) has some 50 large, colorful Tintoretto paintings plastered to the walls and ceilings. The best paintings are upstairs, especially the *Crucifixion* in the smaller room. View the neck-breaking splendor with the mirrors available in the Grand Hall.

Cost and Hours: €10, daily 9:30-17:30, no flash photography, tel. 041-523-4864, www.scuolagrandesanrocco.it.

📖 See the Scuola San Rocco Tour chapter.

Church of San Polo

This nearby church, which pales in comparison to the two sights just listed, is only worth a visit for art lovers. One of Venice's oldest churches (from the ninth century), San Polo features works by Tintoretto, Veronese, and Tiepolo and son. For more information, see page 230 of the Rialto to Frari Church Walk chapter.

Cost and Hours: €3, Mon-Sat 10:00-17:00, closed Sun.

CANNAREGIO DISTRICT
Jewish Ghetto

Tucked away in the Cannaregio district is the ghetto where Venice's Jewish population once lived, segregated from their non-Jewish neighbors. While today's Jewish population is dwindling, the neighborhood still has centuries of history, not to mention Jewish-themed sights and eateries.

Getting There: From the train station, walk five minutes to the Ponte de Guglie bridge over the Cannaregio Canal. Cross the bridge and turn left. About 50 yards north of the bridge, a small covered alleyway (Calle del Gheto Vechio) leads be-

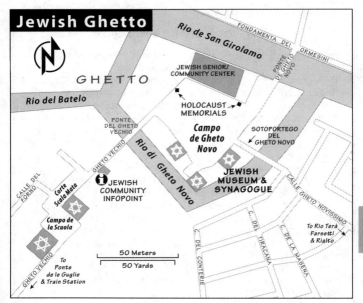

tween the *farmacia* and the Gam-Gam Kosher Restaurant, through a newer Jewish section, across a bridge, and into the historic core of the ghetto at Campo de Gheto Novo.

Visiting the Jewish Ghetto: Campo de Gheto Novo must have been quite a scene in the 17th century, ringed by 70 shops and with all of Venice's Jewish commerce compressed into this one spot. Today there are only about 500 Jews in all of Venice—and only a few dozen live in the actual ghetto. The square is still surrounded by the six-story "skyscrapers" that once made this a densely packed neighborhood.

Today the square, with its three cistern wells, is quiet. The Jewish people you may see here are likely tourists. Look for the large Jewish senior center/community center (Casa Israelitica di Riposo), flanked by two different Holocaust memorials by the Lithuanian artist Arbit Blatas. The barbed wire and bronze plaques remind us that it was on this spot that the Nazis rounded up 200 Jews for deportation (only 8 returned).

The **Jewish Museum** (Museo Ebraico), at #2902b, is small, but modern and well-presented—a worthwhile stop. Exhibits include silver menorahs, cloth covers for Torah scrolls, and a concise bilingual exhibit on the Venetian Jewish community (€4, Sun-Fri 10:00-19:00, Oct-May closes at 17:30, closed Jewish holidays and Sat year-round, modest dress required, bookstore, small café, Campo de Gheto Novo, tel. 041-715-359, www.museoebraico.it). You can see three of the ghetto's five **synagogues** with the 45-minute

Jews in Venice's Ghetto

In medieval times, Jews were grudgingly allowed to do business in Venice, but they weren't permitted to live here until 1385 (subject to strict laws and special taxes). Anti-Semitic forces tried to oust them from the city, but in 1516, the government compromised by restricting Jews to a special (undesirable) neighborhood. It was located on an easy-to-isolate island near the former foundry (geto). In time, the word "ghetto" caught on across Europe as a term for any segregated neighborhood.

The population swelled with immigrants from elsewhere in Europe, reaching 5,000 in the 1600s, the Golden Age of Venice's Jews. Restricted within their tiny neighborhood (the Gheto Novo—"New Ghetto"), they expanded upward, building six-story "skyscrapers" that still stand today. The community's five synagogues were built atop the high-rise tenements. (As space was very tight and you couldn't live above a house of worship, this was the most practical use of precious land.) Only two synagogues are still active. You can spot them (with their five windows) from the square, but to visit them you have to book a tour through the Jewish Museum.

Relations with the non-Jewish community were complex: While Jewish moneylenders were treated harshly, Jewish merchants were more valued and treated with more respect. The island's two bridges were locked at night, when only Jewish doctors—coming to the aid of Venetians—were allowed to come and go. Eventually the ghetto community was given more land and spread to adjacent blocks.

In 1797, Napoleon opened the ghetto gates and ended its isolation. Complete emancipation for Venice's Jews came with the founding of the Italian republic in the 1860s.

SIGHTS

English tour (€10, includes museum admission, tours run hourly on the half-hour Sun-Fri 10:30-17:30, Oct-May until 16:30, no tours Sat and Jewish holidays). Group sizes are limited (the 11:30 and 12:30 tours are the most popular), so show up 30 minutes early to be sure you get in—or reserve online or by phone (generally necessary only for groups of 15 or more).

Backtrack across the bridge that you came in on, and look on the left for the **information point** run by the Jewish community, at #1222, where Anat Shriki answers questions about ghetto history in fluent English (Mon-Fri 10:00-13:30, Wed until 17:00, closed Sat-Sun, on Calle del Gheto Vechio, tel. 041-523-7565, www. jvenice.org).

Return to the square and exit through Sotoportego del Gheto Novo for the best view of the "fortress ghetto," with tall tenement buildings rising from the canal and an easy-to-lock-up little bridge and gateway.

Calatrava Bridge (a.k.a. Ponte della Costituzione)

This controversial bridge, designed by Spanish architect Santiago Calatrava, is just upstream from the train station. Only the fourth

bridge to cross the Grand Canal, it carries foot traffic between the train station and bus terminal at Piazzale Roma.

The bridge draws snorts from Venetians. Its modern design is a sore point for a city with such rich medieval and Renaissance architecture. With an original price tag of €4 million, the cost rose to around €11 million by the time it finally opened, after lengthy delays, in 2008. Then someone noticed that people in wheelchairs couldn't cross, so the bridge was retrofitted with a special, orb-shaped carriage on a track. Today, this "egg cabin" is famously stuck, and those in wheelchairs still struggle. A bridge designed to look sleek and elegant, isn't. And, to add practical insult to aesthetic injury, critics say the heavy bridge is crushing the centuries-old foundations at either end, threatening nearby buildings.

Ca' d'Oro

This "House of Gold" palace, fronting the Grand Canal, is quintessential Venetian Gothic (Gothic seasoned with Byzantine and Islamic accents—see "Ca' d'Oro" on page 63). Inside, the permanent collection includes a few big names in Renaissance painting (Ghirlandaio, Signorelli, and Mantegna), a glimpse at a lush courtyard, and a grand view of the Grand Canal.

Cost and Hours: €6, daily 8:15-19:15, Mon until 14:00, dry audioguide-€4, vaporetto: Ca' d'Oro, tel. 041-520-0345, www.cadoro.org.

CASTELLO DISTRICT

▲Scuola Dalmata di San Giorgio

This little-visited *scuola* (which can mean either "school," or as in this case, "meeting place") features an exquisite wood-paneled chapel decorated with the world's best collection of paintings by Vittorio Carpaccio (1465-1526).

The Scuola, a reminder that cosmopolitan Venice was once Europe's trade hub, was one of more than a hundred such community centers for various ethnic, religious, and economic groups, supported by the government partly to keep an eye on foreigners. It was here that the Dalmatians (from a region of Croatia) worshipped in their own way, held neighborhood meetings, and preserved their culture.

Cost and Hours: €5, Mon 13:30-17:30, Tue-Sat 9:30-17:30, Sun 9:30-13:30, on Calle dei Furlani at Castello 3259a, tel. 041-522-8828.

Getting There: The Scuola is located midway between St. Mark's Square and the Arsenale. Go north from Campo San Provolo (by the Church of San Zaccaria), following the street as it changes names from L'Osmarin to St. George to Greci. At the second bridge, turn left on Fondamenta dei Furlani.

Visiting the Scuola: The chapel on the ground floor is one of the best-preserved Renaissance interiors in Venice. Ringing the room is the cycle of paintings that Carpaccio was hired to paint (1502-1507). For more information, you can buy an English booklet for €5.

The scenes run clockwise around the room, telling the story of St. George (Dalmatia's patron saint), who slew a dragon and metaphorically conquered paganism. Carpaccio cuts right to the climax. In the first panel on the far left, George meets the dragon on the barren plain, charges forward, and jams his lance through the dragon's skull, to the relief of the damsel in distress (in red). George gets there a bit too late—notice half a damsel on the ground. This painting is one of Carpaccio's masterpieces. He places George and the dragon directly facing each other. Meanwhile, the center of the composition—where George meets dragon—is also the "vanishing point" that draws your eye to the distant horizon. Very clever.

The story of St. George continues in the next panel, as George leads the bedraggled dragon (lance still in its head) before the thankful, wealthy pagan king and queen. Next, they kneel before George (now with a red sash, far right) as he holds a pan of water, baptizing them.

The rest of the panels (about St. Jerome and St. Tryphone) are also by Carpaccio. In the last panel on the right, St. Augustine pauses while writing. He hears something. The dog hears it, too. It's the encouraging voice of St. Jerome, echoing mysteriously through the spacious room. Carpaccio sweated small details like the scattered books and the shadow cast by the statue of Christ.

In the adjoining room, see the cross and censers (incense burners) used by the community in religious processions. Upstairs is another paneled room with more depictions of St. George (but not by Carpaccio).

Naval Museum, Arsenale, and Ship Pavilion

The mighty Republic of Venice was home to the first great military-industrial complex: a state-of-the-art shipyard that could build a powerful warship of standardized parts in an assembly line (and did so to intimidate visiting heads of state).

The Naval Museum (Museo Storico Navale), which may be closed for restoration, is old-school and military-run, but anyone into maritime history or sailing will find its several floors of exhibits interesting. When it reopens you'll see the evolution of warships, displays on old fishing boats, and gondolas (all described in English).

The Arsenale is still a military base and is therefore closed to the public, but its massive and evocative gate, the Porta Magna, is worth a look (to see the gate, turn left at the Naval Museum and follow the canal).

The Ship Pavilion (Padiglione delle Navi), open during the museum restoration, is across the Arsenale Bridge and has military vessels and ancient ceremonial gondolas.

Cost and Hours: €5, Ship Pavilion—Mon-Thu 8:45-13:00, Fri 8:45-17:00, Sat-Sun 10:00-17:00; off Riva San Biasio, Castello 2148, tel. 041-244-1399, www.visitmuve.it/en/museums.

Getting There: From the Doge's Palace, hike six bridges east along the waterfront to the Naval Museum.

Sant'Elena

For a pleasant peek into a completely nontouristy, residential side of Venice, walk or catch vaporetto #1 from St. Mark's Square to the neighborhood of Sant'Elena (at the fish's tail, get off at S. Elena stop). This 100-year-old suburb lives as if there were no tourism. You'll find a kid-friendly park, a few lazy restaurants, and beautiful sunsets over San Marco.

La Biennale

From roughly June through November, Venice hosts an annual world's fair—contemporary art in odd years, modern architecture in even years—in buildings and pavilions scattered throughout Giardini park and the Arsenale. The festival is an excuse for temporary art exhibitions, concerts, and other cultural events around the city (for more information, see page 471; www.labiennale.org).

VENICE'S LAGOON

With more time, venture to some nearby islands in Venice's lagoon. While still somewhat touristy, they offer an escape from the crowds, a chance to get out on a boat, and some enjoyable diversions for fans of glassmaking, lace, and sunbathing.

The first four islands are listed in order of proximity to Venice, from nearest to farthest. For more information, 📖 see the Venice's Lagoon Tour chapter. The fifth island has the beach.

San Michele (a.k.a. Cimitero)

This island is the final resting place of Venetians and a few foreign VIPs, from poet Ezra Pound to composer Igor Stravinsky (cemetery open daily 7:30-18:00, Oct-March until 16:30).

▲Murano

Famous for its glassmaking, this island is home to several glass factories and the **Glass Museum** (Museo Vetrario), which traces the history of this delicate art (€10, daily 10:00-18:00, Nov-March until 17:00, tel. 041-739-586, http://museovetro.visitmuve.it).

▲▲Burano

This island's claim to fame is lacemaking, and (along with countless lace shops) it offers a delightful pastel village alternative to big, bustling Venice. Its **Lace Museum** (Museo del Merletto di Burano) shows the island's lace heritage (€5, Tue-Sun 10:00-18:00, Nov-March until 17:00, closed Mon year-round, tel. 041-730-034, http://museomerletto.visitmuve.it).

▲Torcello

This sparsely populated island features Venice's oldest church—Santa Maria Assunta—with impressive mosaics, a climbable bell tower, and a modest museum of Roman sculpture and medieval sculpture and manuscripts (€12 combo-ticket covers museum, church, and bell tower; €9 combo-ticket covers church and bell tower; both combo-tickets include audioguide; museum only—€3; church and bell tower—€5 each; church open daily March-Oct 10:30-18:00, Nov-Feb 10:00-17:00, museum and campanile close 30 minutes earlier, museum closed Mon year-round; museum tel. 041-730-761, church/bell tower tel. 041-730-119).

▲Lido Beach

Venice's nearest beach is the Lido, across the lagoon on an island connected to the mainland (which means car traffic). The sandy beach is pleasant, family-friendly, and good for swimming. You can rent an umbrella, buy beach gear at the shop, get food at the self-service café, or have a drink at the bar. Everything is affordable and in the same building (vaporetto: Lido S.M.E., walk 10 minutes on Gran Viale S. Maria Elisabetta to beach entry).

GRAND CANAL CRUISE

Canal Grande

Take a joyride and introduce yourself to Venice by boat. Cruise the Canal Grande all the way to St. Mark's Square, starting at the train station (Ferrovia) or the bus station (Piazzale Roma).

If it's your first trip down the Grand Canal, you might want to stow this book and just take it all in—Venice is a barrage on the senses that hardly needs narration. But these notes give the cruise a little meaning and help orient you to this great city.

This tour is designed to be done on the slow boat #1. The express boat #2 travels the same route, but it skips many stops, making hop-on/hop-off sightseeing difficult.

To help you enjoy the visual parade of canal wonders, the tour is keyed to each boat stop. I'll point out both what you can see from the current stop, and what to look forward to as you cruise to the next stop. Because it's hard to see everything in one go, you may want to do this tour twice (perhaps once in either direction).

🎧 If you download my free audio tour, you won't even have to look at the book.

Orientation

Length of This Tour: Allow 45 minutes. With limited time, take the 25-minute express vaporetto #2. Or do only half the trip—choose either Ferrovia-to-Rialto or Rialto-to-San Marco. Early and late in the day, the vaporetto #2 terminates at Rialto; you'll have to get off and switch to #1 to do the whole tour.

Cost: €7.50 for a 75-minute vaporetto ticket, or covered by a pass—best choice if you want to hop on and off (see page 23).

When to Go: Boats run every 10 minutes or so. Enjoy the best light and the fewest crowds by riding #1 late in the day. Avoid the morning rush hour (8:00-10:00), when local workers and tourists commute into town from Ferrovia to San Marco. In the evening, the crowds head the opposite way, and boats to San Marco are less crowded. Sunset bathes the buildings in gold (particularly on the left side, the San Marco side). After dark, boats are nearly empty as chandeliers light up building interiors. (Slow boat #1 goes 3/hour through the night, and is labeled "N.")

Seating Strategies: As the *vaporetti* can be jammed, strategize about where to sit—then, when the boat pulls up, make a bee-line for your preference. You're more likely to find an empty seat if you catch the vaporetto at Piazzale Roma—the stop *before* Ferrovia.

Some *vaporetti* have seats in the bow (in front of the captain's bridge), the perfect vantage point for spotting sights left, right, and forward. Otherwise, your options include sitting inside (and viewing the passing sights through windows); standing in the open middle deck (where you can move from side to side when the boat's not crowded—especially easy after dark); or sitting outside in the back (where you'll miss the wonderful forward views). For views, the left side has a slight edge, with more sights and the best light late in the day.

Getting There: This tour starts at the Ferrovia vaporetto stop (at Santa Lucia train station). If you want to board upstream at the less-crowded Piazzale Roma, it's a five-minute walk over the Calatrava Bridge from the Ferrovia stop. At Piazzale Roma, check the electronic boards to see which dock the next #1 or #2 is leaving from, hop on board to get your pick of seats, and start reading the tour when your vaporetto reaches Ferrovia.

Stops to Consider: You can break up the tour by hopping on and off at various sights—but remember, a single-fare vaporetto ticket is good for just 75 minutes (passes let you hop on and off all day). These stops are all worth considering: San Marcuola (Jewish Ghetto), Rialto Mercato (fish market and famous bridge), Ca' Rezzonico (Museum of 18th-Century Venice), Accademia (art museum and the nearby Peggy Guggenheim Collection), and Salute (huge and interesting church and nearby Punta della Dogana contemporary art museum).

Tours: ∩ Download my free Grand Canal Cruise audio tour.

Starring: Palaces, markets, boats, bridges—Venice.

BACKGROUND

The Grand Canal is Venice's "Main Street." At more than two miles long, nearly 150 feet wide, and nearly 15 feet deep, it's the city's largest canal, lined with its most impressive palaces. It's the remnant of a river that once spilled from the mainland into the

GRAND CANAL

Grand Canal

Vaporetto Stops

1. Ferrovia
2. Riva de Biasio
3. San Marcuola
4. San Stae
5. Ca' d'Oro
6. Rialto Mercato
7. Rialto
8. San Silvestro
9. Sant'Angelo
10. San Tomà
11. Ca' Rezzonico
12. Accademia
13. Santa Maria del Giglio
14. Salute
15. San Marco – Giardinetti
16. San Marco – San Zaccaria

GRAND CANAL

Lagoon

FONDAMENTE NOVE

PALAZZO MARCELLO

PALAZZO MOLIN

PALAZZO ZULLAN

❹

SAN STAE

PALAZZO BARBARIGO

PALAZZO FONTANA

PALAZZO GIUSTI

CA' PESARO

PALAZZO DONÀ

PALAZZO FAVRETTO

CA' D'ORO

STRADA NOVA

PALAZZO SAGREDO

PALAZZO MICHIEL COLONNE

CANNAREGIO

PALAZZO CORNER DELLA REGINA

PALAZZO BRANDOLIN

❺

T

PALAZZO VALMARANA

FISH MARKET

❻

PALAZZO CA' DA MOSTO

PRODUCE MARKET

PALAZZO CIVRAN

P O L O

GERMAN EXCHANGE (FORMER POST)

RIALTO BRIDGE

A

SAL. S. LIO

S. MARIA FORMOSA

PALAZZO PAPADOPOLI

PALAZZO BARZIZZA

❼

PALAZZO DOLFIN-MANIN

❽

PALAZZO DONÀ

PALAZZO CORNER-CONTARINI

PALAZZO BEMBO

MERCERIE

PALAZZO BERNARDO

PALAZZO FARSETTI-DANDOLO

C A S T E L L O

PALAZZO BENZON

PALAZZO MARTINENGO

PALAZZO GRIMANI

PALAZZO CORNER-SPINELLI

FABBRI

MERCERIE

ST. MARK'S BASILICA

CAMPANILE

BRIDGE OF SIGHS

S A N   M A R C O

SAN MARCO

DOGE'S PALACE

❶❻

CALLE LARGA XXII MARZO

HARRY'S AMERICAN BAR

SAN MARCO & SAN THEODORE COLUMNS

To Lido

CA' GRANDE

GRITTI PALACE HOTEL

PALAZZO FLANGINI

❶❺

A

❶❸

T

Canal

❶❹

LA SALUTE CHURCH

St. Mark's Basin

Grand

PALAZZO DARIO

PALAZZO GENOVESE

PEGGY GUGGENHEIM COLLECTION

PUNTA DELLA DOGANA MUSEUM

To San Giorgio Maggiore & Giudecca

N

200 Meters

200 Yards

Adriatic. The sediment it carried formed barrier islands that cut Venice off from the sea, forming a lagoon.

Venice was built on the marshy islands of the former delta, sitting on wood pilings driven nearly 15 feet into the clay (alder was the preferred wood). About 25 miles of canals drain the city, dumping like streams into the Grand Canal. Technically, Venice has only three canals: Grand, Giudecca, and Cannaregio. The 45 small waterways that dump into the Grand Canal are referred to as rivers (e.g., Rio Novo).

Venice is a city of palaces, dating from the days when the city was the world's richest. The most lavish palaces formed a grand architectural cancan along the Grand Canal. Once frescoed in reds and blues, with black-and-white borders and gold-leaf trim, they made Venice a city of dazzling color. This cruise is the only way to truly appreciate the palaces, approaching them at water level, where their main entrances were located. Today, strict laws pro-hibit any changes in these buildings, so while landowners gnash their teeth, we can enjoy Europe's best-preserved medieval/Renaissance city—slowly rotting. Many of the grand buildings are now vacant. Others harbor chandeliered elegance above mossy, empty (often flooded) ground floors.

The Tour Begins

❶ Ferrovia

This site has been the gateway into Venice since 1860, when the first train station was built. The **Santa Lucia station,** one of the few modern buildings in town, was built in 1954. The "F.S." logo above the entry stands for "Ferrovie dello Stato," the Italian state railway system. Consider that before the causeway was built in the mid-1800s, Venice was an island with no road or train access and no water system. With the causeway the city got a train line, an aqueduct, and a highway.

More than 20,000 people a day commute in from the mainland, making this the busiest part of Venice during rush hour. The **Calatrava Bridge,** spanning the Grand Canal between the train station and Piazzale Roma upstream, was built in 2008 to alleviate some of the congestion (for more about the bridge, see page 51).

Opposite the train station, atop the green dome of **San Simeon Piccolo** church, St. Simeon waves *ciao* to whoever enters or leaves the "old" city. The pink church with the white Carrara-marble facade, just beyond the station, is the **Church of the Scalzi** (Church of the Barefoot, named after the shoeless Carmelite monks), where the last doge (Venetian ruler) rests. It looks relatively new because it was partially rebuilt after being bombed in 1915 by Austrians aiming (poorly) at the train station. The stately Scalzi Bridge was rebuilt simply and elegantly under Mussolini.

❷ Riva de Biasio

Venice's main thoroughfare is busy with all kinds of **boats:** taxis, police boats, garbage boats, ambulances, construction cranes, and even brown-and-white UPS boats. Somehow they all manage to share the canal in relative peace.

About 25 yards past the Riva de Biasio stop, look left down the broad Cannaregio Canal to see what was the Jewish Ghetto (described on page 48). The twin, pale-pink, six-story "skyscrapers"—the tallest buildings you'll see at this end of the canal—are reminders of how densely populated the world's original ghetto was. Set aside as the local Jewish quarter in 1516, this area became extremely crowded. This urban island developed into one of the most closely knit business and cultural quarters of all the Jewish communities in Italy, and gave us our word "ghetto" (from *geto,* the copper foundry located here).

❸ San Marcuola

At this stop, facing a tiny square just ahead, stands the unfinished Church of San Marcuola, one of only five churches fronting the Grand Canal. Centuries ago, this canal was a commercial drag of expensive real estate in high demand by wealthy merchants. About 20 yards ahead on the right (across the Grand Canal) stands the stately gray **Turkish Exchange** (Fondaco dei Turchi), one of the oldest houses in Venice. Its horseshoe arches and roofline of triangles and dingle balls are reminders of its Byzantine heritage. Turkish traders in turbans docked here, unloaded their goods into the warehouse on the bottom story, then went upstairs for a home-style meal and a place to sleep. Venice in the 1500s was very cosmopolitan, welcoming every religion and ethnicity, so long as they carried cash. (Today the building contains the city's Museum of Natural History—and Venice's only dinosaur skeleton.)

Just 100 yards ahead on the left (the tallest building with the red canopy), Venice's **Casinò** is housed in the palace where German composer Richard *(The Ring)* Wagner died in 1883. See his distinct, strong-jawed profile in the white plaque on the brick wall. In the 1700s, Venice was Europe's Vegas, with casinos and prostitutes everywhere. *Casinòs* ("little houses" in Venetian dialect) have long provided Italians with a handy escape from daily life. Today they're run by the state to keep Mafia influence at bay. Notice the fancy front porch, rolling out the red carpet for high rollers arriving by taxi or hotel boat. Across the canal, the plain brick 15th-century building was a granary. Now it's a grade school.

❹ San Stae

The San Stae Church sports a delightful Baroque facade. Opposite the San Stae stop is a little canal opening—on the second building to the right of that opening, look for the peeling plaster that once made up **frescoes** (you can barely distinguish the scant remains of little angels on the lower floors). Imagine the facades of the Grand Canal at their finest. Most of them would have been covered in frescoes by the best artists of the day. As colorful as the city is today, it's still only a faded, sepia-toned remnant of a long-gone era, a time of lavishly decorated, brilliantly colored palaces.

Just ahead (on the right, with blue posts) is the ornate white facade of **Ca' Pesaro** (which houses the International Gallery of Modern Art—see page 45). "*Ca'*" is short for *casa* (house). Because only the house of the doge (Venetian ruler) could be called a palace *(palazzo)*, all other Venetian palaces are technically "*Ca'.*"

In this city of masks, notice how the rich marble facades along the Grand Canal mask what are generally just simple, no-nonsense brick buildings. Most merchants enjoyed showing off. However, being smart businessmen, they only decorated the sides of the buildings that would be seen and appreciated. But look back as you pass Ca' Pesaro. It's the only building you'll see with a fine side facade. Ahead (about 100 yards on the left) is Ca' d'Oro, with its glorious triple-decker medieval arcade (just before the next stop).

❺ Ca' d'Oro

The lacy **Ca' d'Oro** (House of Gold) is the best example of Venetian Gothic architecture on the canal. Although a simple brick con-

struction, its facade is one of the city's finest. Its three stories offer different variations on balcony design, topped with a spiny white roofline. Venetian Gothic mixes traditional Gothic (pointed arches and round medallions stamped with a four-leaf clover) with Byzantine styles (tall, narrow arches atop thin columns), filled in with Islamic frills. Like all the palaces, this was originally painted and gilded to make it even more glorious than it is now. Today the Ca' d'Oro is an art gallery (described on page 51).

Look at the Venetian chorus line of palaces in front of the boat. On the right is the arcade of the covered **fish market,** with the open-air **produce market** just beyond. It bustles in the morning but is quiet the rest of the day. This is a great scene to wander through—even though European Union hygiene standards have made it cleaner but less colorful than it once was.

Find the *traghetto* gondola ferrying shoppers—standing like Washington crossing the Delaware—back and forth. While once

much more numerable, today only three *traghetto* crossings survive along the Grand Canal, each one marked by a classy low-key green-and-black sign. Piloting a *traghetto* isn't the normal day job of these gondoliers. As a public service, all gondoliers are obliged to row a *traghetto* a few days a month. Make a point to use them. At €2 a ride, *traghetti* offer the cheapest gondola ride in Venice (but at this price, don't expect them to sing to you).

➏ Rialto Mercato

This stop serves the busy market. The long, official-looking building at the stop is the Venice courthouse. Directly ahead (on the left), is the former German Exchange (Fondaco dei Tedeschi, a trading center for German merchants in the 16th century). It was the central post office and is slated to be a modern shopping center. Rising above it is the tip of the Campanile (bell tower), crowned by its golden-angel weathervane at St. Mark's Square, where this tour will end.

You'll cruise by some trendy and beautifully situated wine bars on the right, but look ahead as you round the corner and see the impressive Rialto Bridge come into view.

A major landmark of Venice, the **Rialto Bridge** is lined with shops and tourists. Constructed in 1588, it's the third bridge built

on this spot. Until the 1850s, this was the only bridge crossing the Grand Canal. With a span of 160 feet and foundations stretching 650 feet on either side, the Rialto was an impressive engineering feat in its day. Earlier bridges here could open to let big ships in, but not this one. By the time it was completed in the 16th century, Venetian trading power was ebbing. After that, much of the Grand Canal was closed to shipping and became a canal of palaces.

When gondoliers pass under the fat arch of the Rialto Bridge, they take full advantage of its acoustics: *"Volare, oh, oh..."*

➐ Rialto

Rialto, a separate town in the early days of Venice, has always been the commercial district, while San Marco was the religious and governmental center. Today, a winding street called the Mercerie connects the two, providing travelers with human traffic jams and a mesmerizing gauntlet of shopping temptations. This is one of the only stretches of the historic Grand Canal with landings upon which you can walk. Boats unloaded the city's basic necessities here: oil, wine, charcoal, iron. Today, the quay is lined with tourist-trap restaurants.

Venice's sleek, black, graceful **gondolas** are a symbol of the city (for more on gondolas, see page 301). With about 500 gondoliers joyriding amid the churning *vaporetti*, there's a lot of congestion on the Grand Canal. Pay attention—this is where most of the gondola and vaporetto accidents take place. While the Rialto is the highlight of many gondola rides, gondoliers understandably prefer the quieter small canals. Watch your vaporetto driver curse the better-paid gondoliers.

Ahead 100 yards on the left, two gray-colored **palaces** stand side by side (City Hall and the mayor's office). Their horseshoe-shaped, arched windows are similar and their stories are the same height, lining up to create the effect of one long balcony.

❽ San Silvestro

We now enter a long stretch of important **merchants' palaces,** each with proud and different facades. Because ships couldn't navigate beyond the Rialto Bridge, the biggest palaces—with the major shipping needs—line this last stretch of the navigable Grand Canal.

Palaces like these were multifunctional: ground floor for the warehouse, offices and showrooms upstairs, and living quarters above, on the "noble floors" (with big windows to allow in maximum light). Servants lived and worked on the very top floors (with the smallest windows). For fire-safety reasons, kitchens were also located on the top floors. Peek into the noble floors to catch a glimpse of their still-glorious chandeliers of Murano glass.

The **Palazzo Grimani** (across from the San Silvestro dock) sports a heavy white Roman-style facade—a reminder that the Grimani family included a cardinal and had strong Roman connections.

The **Palazzo Papadopoli,** with the two obelisks on its roof (50 yards beyond the San Silvestro stop on the right, with the blue posts), is the very fancy Aman Hotel where George Clooney was married in 2014.

❾ Sant'Angelo

Notice how many buildings have a foundation of waterproof white stone *(pietra d'Istria)* upon which the bricks sit high and dry. Many canal-level floors are abandoned as the rising water level takes its toll.

The **posts**—historically painted gaily with the equivalent of family coats of arms—don't rot underwater. But the wood at the waterline, where it's exposed to oxygen, does. On the smallest canals, little "no motorboats" signs indicate that these canals are for gondolas only (no motorized craft, 5 kph speed limit, no wake).

⑩ San Tomà

Fifty yards ahead, on the right side (with twin obelisks on the rooftop) stands **Palazzo Balbi,** the palace of an early-17th-century captain general of the sea. These Venetian equivalents of five-star admirals were honored with twin obelisks decorating their palaces. This palace, like so many in the city, flies three flags: Italy (green-white-red), the European Union (blue with ring of stars), and Venice (a lion on a field of red and gold). Today it houses the administrative headquarters of the regional government.

Just past the admiral's palace, look immediately to the right, down a side canal. On the right side of that canal, before the bridge, see the traffic light and the **fire station** (the 1930s Mussolini-era building with four arches hiding fireboats parked and ready to go).

The impressive **Ca' Foscari,** with a classic Venetian facade (on the corner, across from the fire station), dominates the bend in the canal. This is the main building of the University of Venice, which has about 25,000 students. Notice the elegant lamp on the corner—needed in the old days to light this intersection.

The grand, heavy, white **Ca' Rezzonico,** just before the stop of the same name, houses the Museum of 18th-Century Venice (☐ described in the Ca' Rezzonico Tour chapter). Across the canal is the cleaner and leaner **Palazzo Grassi,** the last major palace built on the canal, erected in the late 1700s. It was purchased by a French tycoon and now displays part of Punta della Dogana's contemporary art collection.

⓫ Ca' Rezzonico

Up ahead, the Accademia Bridge leads over the Grand Canal to the **Accademia Gallery** (right side), filled with the best Venetian paintings (𝕞 described in the Accademia Tour chapter). There was no bridge here until 1854, when a cast-iron one was built. It was replaced with this wooden bridge

in 1933. While meant to be temporary, it still stands today, nearly a century later.

⓬ Accademia

From here, look through the graceful bridge and way ahead to enjoy a classic view of **La Salute Church,** topped by a crown-shaped

dome supported by scrolls (𝕞 described in the La Salute Church Tour chapter). This Church of St. Mary of Good Health was built to ask God to deliver Venetians from the devastating plague of 1630 (which had killed about a third of the city's population).

The low, white building among greenery (100 yards ahead, on the right, between the Accademia Bridge and the church) is the **Peggy Guggenheim Collection.** The American heiress "retired" here, sprucing up a palace that had been abandoned in mid-construction. Peggy willed the city her fine collection of modern art (𝕞 described in the Peggy Guggenheim Collection Tour chapter).

As you approach the next stop, notice on the right how the fine line of higgledy-piggledy palaces evokes old-time Venice. Two

doors past the Guggenheim, Palazzo Dario has a great set of characteristic **funnel-shaped chimneys.** These forced embers through a loop-the-loop channel until they were dead— required in the days when stone palaces were surrounded by humble, wooden buildings,

and a live spark could make a merchant's workforce homeless. Notice this early Renaissance building's flat-feeling facade with "pasted-on" Renaissance motifs. Three doors later is the **Salviati building,** which once served as a glassworks. Its fine Art Nouveau mosaic, done in the early 20th century, features Venice as a queen being appreciated by the big shots of society.

⑬ Santa Maria del Giglio

Back on the left stands the fancy Gritti Palace hotel. Hemingway and Woody Allen both stayed here (but not together).

Take a deep whiff of Venice. What's all this nonsense about stinky canals? All I smell is my shirt. By the way, how's your captain? Smooth dockings?

⑭ Salute

The huge La Salute Church towers overhead as if squirted from a can of Catholic Reddi-wip. Like Venice itself, the church rests

upon pilings. To build the foundation for the city, more than a million trees were piled together, reaching beneath the mud to the solid clay. Much of the surrounding countryside was deforested by Venice. Trees were imported and consumed locally—to fuel the furnaces of Venice's booming glass industry, to build Europe's biggest merchant marine, to form light and flexible beams for nearly all the buildings in town, and to prop up this city in the mud.

As the Grand Canal opens up into the lagoon, the last building on the right with the golden ball is the 17th-century **Customs House,** which now houses the Punta della Dogana contemporary art museum (see page 45). Its two bronze Atlases hold a statue of Fortune riding the ball. Arriving ships stopped here to pay their tolls.

⑮ San Marco

Up ahead on the left, the green pointed tip of the Campanile marks **St. Mark's Square,** the political and religious center of Venice...and the final destination of this tour. You could get off at the San Marco stop and go straight to St. Mark's Square (and you'll have to if you're on vaporetto #2, which terminates here). But I'm staying

on the #1 boat for one more stop, just past St. Mark's Square (it's a quick walk back).

Survey the lagoon. Opposite St. Mark's Square, across the water, the ghostly white church with the pointy bell tower is San Giorgio Maggiore, with great views of Venice (□ see the San Giorgio Maggiore Tour chapter). Next to it is the residential island Giudecca, stretching from close to San Giorgio Maggiore past the Venice youth hostel (with a nice view, directly across) to the Hilton Hotel (good nighttime view, far right end of island).

Still on board? If you are, as we leave the San Marco stop look left and prepare for a drive-by view of St. Mark's Square. First comes the bold white facade of the old mint (in front of the bell tower) marked by a tiny cupola yet as sturdy as Fort Knox, where Venice's golden ducat, the "dollar" of the Venetian Republic, was made. Next door is the library, its facade just three windows wide. Then comes the city's ceremonial front door: twin columns topped by St. Theodore and the winged lion of St. Mark, who've welcomed visitors since the 15th century. Between the columns, catch a glimpse of two giant figures atop the **Clock Tower**—they've been whacking their clappers every hour since 1499. The domes of **St. Mark's Basilica** are soon eclipsed by the lacy facade of the **Doge's Palace.** Next you'll see many gondolas with their green breakwater buoys, the **Bridge of Sighs** (leading from the palace to the prison— check out the maximum-security bars), and finally the grand harborside promenade—the **Riva.**

Follow the Riva with your eye, past elegant hotels to the green area in the distance. This is the largest of Venice's few **parks,** which hosts the annual Biennale festival (see page 471). Much farther in the distance is the **Lido,** the island with Venice's beach. Its sand and casinos are tempting, though given its car traffic, it lacks the medieval charm of Venice.

⑯ San Zaccaria

OK, you're at your last stop. Quick—muscle your way off this boat! (If you don't, you'll eventually end up at the Lido.)

At San Zaccaria, you're right in the thick of the action. A number of other *vaporetti* depart from here (see page 24). Otherwise, it's a short walk back along the Riva to St. Mark's Square. Ahoy!

ST. MARK'S SQUARE TOUR

Piazza San Marco

Venice was once Europe's richest city, and Piazza San Marco was its center. As middleman in the trade between Asia and Europe, wealthy Venice profited from both sides. In 1450, at its peak, Venice had 150,000 citizens (many more than London) and a gross "national" product that exceeded that of entire countries.

The rich Venetians taught the rest of Europe about the good life—silks, spices, and jewels from the East, crafts from northern Europe, good food and wine, fine architecture, music, theater, and laughter. Venice was a vibrant city full of painted palaces, glittering canals, and impressed visitors. Five centuries after its power began to decline, Venice still has all of these things, with the added charm of romantic decay. In this tour, we'll spend an hour in the heart of this Old World superpower.

Orientation

Getting There: Signs all over town point to *San Marco*—meaning both the square and the basilica—located where the Grand Canal spills out into the lagoon. Vaporetto stops: San Marco or San Zaccaria.

Campanile: If you ascend the bell tower, it'll cost you €8 (daily Easter-June and Oct 9:00-19:00, July-Sept 9:00-21:00; Nov-Easter 9:30-15:45).

Clock Tower: To see the interior, you need to book a spot on a tour through the Correr Museum (see page 33 for specifics).

Information: There a TI in the square's southwest corner.

Tours: ∩ Download my free St. Mark's Square audio tour.

Services: Handy pay WCs are behind the Correr Museum and also at the waterfront park, Giardinetti Reali (near San Marco-Vallaresso vaporetto dock).

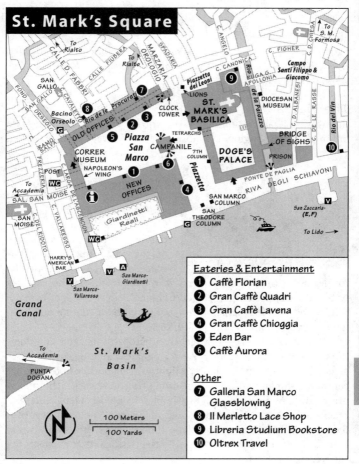

St. Mark's Square

Eateries & Entertainment
1 Caffè Florian
2 Gran Caffè Quadri
3 Gran Caffè Lavena
4 Gran Caffè Chioggia
5 Eden Bar
6 Caffè Aurora

Other
7 Galleria San Marco Glassblowing
8 Il Merletto Lace Shop
9 Libreria Studium Bookstore
10 Oltrex Travel

Eating: Cafés with live music provide an engaging soundtrack for St. Mark's Square (see "Cafés on St. Mark's Square" sidebar, later in this chapter). The Correr Museum (at the end of the square opposite the basilica) has a quiet upstairs coffee shop overlooking the crowded square. For a list of restaurants in the area, see page 269.

Necessary Eyesores: Expect scaffolding and advertising billboards to cover parts of the square and its monuments when you visit.

Cardinal Points: The square is aligned (roughly) east-west. So, facing the basilica, north is to your left.

Starring: Byzantine domes, Gothic arches, Renaissance arches... and the wonderful, musical space they enclose.

The Tour Begins

• *For an overview of this grand square and the buildings that surround it, view it from the west end of the square (away from St. Mark's Basilica).*

The Piazza

St. Mark's Basilica dominates the square with its Eastern-style onion domes and glowing mosaics. Mark Twain said it looked

like "a vast warty bug taking a meditative walk." (I say it looks like tiara-wearing ladybugs copulating.) To the right of the basilica is its 325-foot-tall Campanile. Behind the Campanile, you can catch a glimpse of the pale pink Doge's Palace. Lining the square are the former government offices *(procuratie)* that managed the treasury of St. Mark's, back when the church and state were one, and administered the Venetian empire's vast network of trading outposts, which stretched all the way to Turkey.

The square is big, but it feels intimate with its cafés and dueling orchestras. By day, it's great for people-watching and pigeon-chasing. By night, under lantern light, it transports you to another century, complete with its own romantic soundtrack. The piazza draws Indians in saris, English nobles in blue blazers, and Nebraskans in shorts. Napoleon called the piazza "the most beautiful living room in Europe." Napoleon himself added to the intimacy by building the final wing, opposite the basilica, that encloses the square.

For architecture buffs, here are three centuries of styles, bam, side by side, *uno-due-tre,* for easy comparison:

1. On the left (as you face the basilica) are the "old" offices, built about 1500 in solid, column-and-arch Renaissance style.

2. The "new" offices (on the right), in a High Renaissance style from a century later (c. 1600), are a little heavier and more ornate. This wing mixes arches and the three orders of columns in layers from bottom to top—Doric, Ionic, and Corinthian.

3. Napoleon's wing, at the end opposite from the basilica, is later and designed to fit in. The dozen Roman emperors decorating the

parapet were once joined by Napoleon in the middle, but today the French emperor is gone.

The arcade ringing the square, formerly lined with dozens of fine cafés, still provides an elegant promenade—complete with drapery that is dropped when necessary to provide relief from the sun.

Imagine this square full of water. That happens every so often at very high tides *(acqua alta)*, a reminder that Venice and the sea are intertwined. (Now that one is sinking and the other is rising, they are more intertwined than ever.)

Venice became Europe's richest city from its trade with northern Europeans, Ottoman Muslims, and Byzantine Christians. Here in St. Mark's Square, the exact center of this East-West axis, we see both the luxury and the mix of Eastern and Western influences.

Watch out for pigeon speckle. Venetians don't like pigeons, but they do like seagulls—because they eat pigeons. In 2008, Venice outlawed the feeding of pigeons. But tourists—eager for a pigeon-clad photo op—haven't gotten that message. Vermin are also a problem on this small island, where it's said that each Venetian has two pigeons and four rats. (The rats stay hidden, except when high tides flood their homes.)

• *Now approach the basilica. If it's hot and you're tired, grab a shady spot at the foot of the Campanile.*

St. Mark's Basilica

The facade is a wild mix of East and West, with round, Roman-style arches over the doorways, golden Byzantine mosaics, a roof-line ringed with pointed Gothic pinnacles, and Muslim-shaped onion domes (wood, covered with lead) on the roof. The brick-structure building is blanketed in marble that came from Constantinople (in 1204), which had itself looted it from throughout

the eastern Mediterranean: columns from Alexandria, capitals from Sicily, and carvings from Anatolia. The columns flanking the doorways show the facade's variety—purple, green, gray, white, yellow, some speckled, some striped horizontally, some vertically, some fluted—all topped with a variety of different capitals.

What's amazing isn't so much the variety as the fact that the whole thing comes together in a bizarre sort of harmony. St. Mark's is simply the most interesting church in Europe, a church that (to paraphrase Goethe) "can only be compared with itself."

For more on the basilica, inside and out, □ see the St. Mark's Basilica Tour chapter.

• *Facing the basilica, turn 90 degrees to the left to see the...*

Clock Tower (Torre dell'Orologio)

Any proper Renaissance city wanted to have a fine, formal entry and a clock tower. In Venice's case, its entry was visible from the sea and led from the big religious and governmental center to the rest of the city. The Clock Tower retains some of its original blue and gold pigments, a reminder that, in centuries past, this city glowed with bright color.

Two bronze "Moors" stand atop the Clock Tower (built originally in 1499 to be Caucasian giants, they only switched their ethnicity when their metal darkened over the centuries). At the top of each hour they swing their giant clappers. The clock dial shows the 24 hours, the signs of the zodiac, and in the blue center, the phases of the moon—practical information, as a maritime city with a shallow lagoon needs to know the tides. Above the dial is the world's first digital clock (added in 1858), which changes every five minutes.

An alert winged lion, the symbol of St. Mark and the city, looks down on the crowded square. He opens a book that reads *"Pax Tibi Marce,"* or "Peace to you, Mark." As legend goes, these were the comforting words that an angel spoke to the stressed evangelist, assuring him he would find serenity during a stormy night that the saint spent here on the island. Eventually, St. Mark's body found its final resting place inside the basilica, and now his winged-lion symbol is everywhere. (Find four in 20 seconds. Go.)

Venice's many lions express the city's various mood swings

through history—triumphant after a naval victory, sad when a favorite son has died, hollow-eyed after a plague, and smiling when the soccer team wins. Every Venetian child born since the dawn of cameras has probably been photographed riding one of the pair of lions squatting between the Clock Tower and the basilica.

Campanile

The original Campanile (bell tower) was an observation tower and a marvel of medieval and Renaissance architecture until 1902, when it toppled into the center of the piazza. It had groaned ominously the night before, sending people scurrying from the cafés. The next morning... crash! The golden angel on top landed right at the basilica's front door, standing up.

The Campanile was rebuilt 10 years later complete with its golden archangel Gabriel, who always faces the breeze. You can ride a lift to the top for the best view of Venice. It's crowded at peak times, but well worth it.

Because St. Mark's Square is the first place in town to start flooding, there are tide gauges at the outside base of the Campanile (near the exit, facing the square) that show the current sea level *(livello marea)*. Find the stone plaque (near the exit door) that commemorates the high-water 77-inch level from the disastrous floods of 1966. In December 2008, Venice suffered another terrible high tide, cresting at 61 inches.

If the tide is mild (around 20 inches), the water merely seeps up through the drains. But when there's a strong tide (around 40 inches), it looks like someone's turned on a faucet down below. The water bubbles upward and flows like a river to the lowest points in the square, which can be covered with a few inches of water in an hour or so. When the water level rises one meter above mean sea level, a warning siren sounds, and it repeats if a serious flood is imminent.

Many doorways have three-foot-high wooden or metal barriers to block the high water *(acqua alta)*, but the seawater still seeps in through floors and drains, rendering the barriers nearly useless. (For background on what causes the flooding, see the sidebar on page 28.)

You might see stacked wooden benches in the square; during floods, the benches are placed end-to-end to create elevated sidewalks. If you think the square is crowded now, when it's flooded it turns into total gridlock, as all the people normally sharing the whole square jostle for space on the narrow, raised wooden walkways.

In 2006, the pavement around St. Mark's Square was taken up, and the entire height of the square was raised by adding a layer of sand and then replacing the stones. If the columns along the ground floor of the Doge's Palace look stubby, it's because this process has

Cafés on St. Mark's Square

In Venice's heyday, it was said that the freedoms a gentleman could experience here went far beyond what any true gentleman would actually care to indulge in. But one extravagance all could enjoy was the ritual of publicly consuming coffee: showing off with an affordable luxury, doing something trendy, while sharing the ideas of the Enlightenment.

Exotic coffee was made to order for the fancy café scene. Traders introduced coffee, called the "wine of Islam," from the Middle East (the plant is native to Ethiopia). The first coffeehouses opened in the 17th century, and by 1750 there were dozens of cafés lining Piazza San Marco and 200 operating in Venice.

Today, several fine old cafés survive and still line the square. Those with live music feature similar food, prices, and a three- to five-piece combo playing a selection of classical and pop hits, from Brahms to "Bésame Mucho."

You can wander around the square listening to the different orchestras, or take a seat at a café and settle in. At any café with live music, it's perfectly acceptable to nurse a cappuccino for an hour—you're paying for the music with the cover charge. And remember, you can sip your coffee at the bar at a nearly normal price—even with the orchestra playing just outside.

Caffè Florian (on the right as you face the church) is the most famous Venetian café and was one of the first places in Europe to serve coffee (daily 9:00-24:00, shorter hours in winter,

been carried out many times over the centuries, buying a little more time as the sea slowly swallows the city.

• *The small square between the basilica and the water is the...*

Piazzetta

This "Little Square" is framed by the Doge's Palace on the left, the library on the right, and the waterfront of the lagoon. In former days, the Piazzetta was closed to the public for a few hours a day so that government officials and bigwigs could gather in the sun to strike shady deals.

The pale pink **Doge's Palace** is the epitome of the style known as Venetian Gothic. Columns support tra-

www.caffeflorian.com). It was originally named "Triumphant Venice" (Venezia Triomfante). But under French occupation, in the early 19th century, that politically incorrect name was changed. If you sit outside and get just an espresso—your cheapest option—expect to pay €12.50: €6.50 for the coffee and a €6 cover charge when the orchestra is playing (which is most of the day).

The Florian has been a popular spot for a discreet rendezvous in Venice since 1720. Each room has a historic or artistic theme. For example the "Room of the Illustrious Men" features portraits of great Venetians from Marco Polo to Titian. The outside tables are the main action, but do walk inside through the richly decorated, old-time rooms where Casanova, Lord Byron, Charles Dickens, and Woody Allen have all paid too much for a drink. The café's orchestra—the most serious on the square—plays daily from 10:00 to 24:00. Each hour comes with a musical theme (operetta, Latin, Romantic, jazz, Venetian, and so on—you can ask for the program).

Gran Caffè Quadri, opposite the Florian and established in 1780, has another illustrious roster of famous clientele.

Gran Caffè Lavena, near the Clock Tower, is less storied—although it dates from 1750 and counts composer Richard Wagner as a former regular. Drop in to check out its dazzling but politically incorrect chandelier.

Gran Caffè Chioggia, on the Piazzetta facing the Doge's Palace, charges no cover and has one or two musicians playing—usually a pianist (€7 cocktails, music from 10:30 to 23:00—jazz after 21:00).

Eden Bar and **Caffè Aurora** are less expensive and don't have live music.

ditional, pointed Gothic arches, but with a Venetian flair—they're curved to a point, ornamented with a trefoil (three-leaf clover), and topped with a round medallion of a quatrefoil (four-leaf clover). The pattern is found on buildings all over Venice and on the formerly Venetian-controlled Croatian coast, but nowhere else in the world (except Las Vegas).

The two large 12th-century **columns** near the water were (like so much else) looted from Constantinople. Mark's winged lion sits on top of one. The lion's body (nearly 15 feet long) predates the wings and is more than 2,000 years old. The other column holds St. Theodore (battling a crocodile),

Venetian Gothic

$$\bigwedge + \bigcap + \bigwedge + \clubsuit = $$

the former patron saint who was replaced by Mark. I guess stabbing crocs in the back isn't classy enough for an upwardly mobile world power. After public ridicule, criminals were executed by being hung from these columns in the hope that the public could learn its lessons vicariously.

Venice was the "Bride of the Sea" because she depended on sea trading for her livelihood. This "marriage" was celebrated annually by the people on Ascension Day. The doge, in full regalia, boarded a ritual boat (his Air Force One equivalent) here at the edge of the Piazzetta and sailed out into the lagoon. There a vow was made, and he dropped a jeweled ring into the water to seal the marriage.

In the distance, on an island across the lagoon, is one of the grandest views in the city, of the Church of San Giorgio Maggiore. With its four tall columns as the entryway, the church, designed by the late-Renaissance architect Andrea Palladio, influenced the appearance of future government and bank buildings around the world.

Palladio's sober classical lines are pure and intellectual, but with their love of extravagance, Venetians wanted something more exuberant. More to local taste was the High Renaissance style of Jacopo Sansovino, who (around 1530) designed the library (here on the Piazzetta) and the delicate Loggetta at the base of the Campanile (destroyed by the collapse of the tower in 1902 and then pieced back together).

Tetrarchs and the Doge's Palace's Seventh Column

Where the basilica meets the Doge's Palace is the traditional entrance to the palace, decorated with four small Roman statues—the **Tetrarchs**, which date from the fourth century A.D. No one knows for sure who they are, but I like the legend that says they're the scared leaders of a divided Rome during its fall, holding their swords and each other as all hell breaks loose around them. Some believe that they are the leaders of the Eastern and West-

> # Escape from St. Mark's Square
>
> Crowds getting to you? Here are some relatively quiet areas on or near St. Mark's Square.
>
> **Correr Museum:** Sip a cappuccino in the café of this uncrowded history museum that overlooks St. Mark's Square (entrance at far end of the piazza, no museum ticket necessary). ☐ See the Correr Museum Tour chapter.
>
> **Giardinetti Reali:** This small park along the waterfront is the only place near the square for a legal picnic (it's west of the Piazzetta—facing the water, turn right).
>
> **Il Merletto:** This lace shop is in a small, decommissioned chapel near the northwest corner of St. Mark's Square (daily 10:00-17:00, go through Sotoportego del Cavalletto and across the little bridge on the right; for more details, see page 298).
>
> **La Salute Church:** This cool church in a quiet neighborhood is a short hop on vaporetto #1 from the San Marco-Vallaresso stop. ☐ See the La Salute Church Tour chapter.
>
> **Caffè Florian:** The plush interior of this luxurious 18th-century café on St. Mark's Square is generally quiet and nearly empty. A coffee here can be a wonderful break (see "Cafés on St. Mark's Square," earlier).

ern empires (the bearded ones) with their chosen successors (the clean-shaven, younger ones). Whatever the legend, these statues—made of precious purple porphyry stone—are symbols of power. They were looted, likely from Constantinople (1204), and then placed here proudly as spoils of war.

About two-thirds of the way down the Doge's Palace, look for a **column** that's slightly shorter and fatter than the rest (it's the

seventh from the water). Its carved capital tells a story of love, romance, and tragedy: 1) In the first scene (the carving facing the Piazzetta), a woman on a balcony is wooed by her lover, who says, "Babe, I want *you!*" 2) She responds, "Why, little ol' *me?*" 3) They get married. 4) Kiss. 5) Hit the sack—pretty racy for 14th-century art. 6) Nine months later, guess what? 7) The baby takes its first steps. 8) And as was all too common in the 1300s...the child dies.

• *Continue down the Piazzetta to the waterfront. Turn left and walk (east) along the water. At the top of the first bridge, look inland at the...*

Bridge of Sighs

In the Doge's Palace (on your left), the government doled out justice. On your right are the prisons. (Don't let the palatial facade fool you—see the bars on the windows?) Prisoners sentenced in the palace crossed to the prisons by way of the covered bridge in front of you. This was called the Prisons' Bridge until the Romantic poet Lord Byron renamed it in the 19th century. From this bridge, the convicted got their final view of sunny, joyous Venice before entering the black and dank prisons. According to the Romantic legend, they sighed.

Venice has been a major tourist center for four centuries. Anyone who's ever come here has stood on this very spot, looking at the Bridge of Sighs. Lean on the railing leaned on by everyone from Casanova to Byron to Hemingway.

> *I stood in Venice, on the Bridge of Sighs;*
> *A palace and a prison on each hand:*
> *I saw from out the wave, her structures rise*
> *As from the stroke of the enchanter's wand:*
> *A thousand years their cloudy wings expand*
> *Around me, and a dying glory smiles*
> *O'er the far times when many a subject land*
> *Looked to the winged Lion's marble piles,*
> *Where Venice sat in state, throned on her hundred isles!*
> —Lord Byron, *Childe Harold's Pilgrimage,* Canto 4

ST. MARK'S SQUARE

ST. MARK'S BASILICA TOUR

Basilica di San Marco

Among Europe's churches, St. Mark's is peerless. From the outside, it's a riot of domes, columns, and statues, completely unlike the towering Gothic churches of northern Europe or the heavy Baroque of much of the rest of Italy. Inside is a decor of mosaics, colored marbles, and Byzantine treasures that's rarely seen elsewhere. The Christian symbolism is unfamiliar to Western eyes, done in the style of Byzantine icons and even Islamic designs. Older than most of Europe's churches, it feels like a remnant of a lost world.

This is your best chance in Italy (outside of Ravenna) to glimpse a forgotten and somewhat mysterious part of the human story—Byzantium.

Orientation

Cost: Entering the church is free, though you can pay €2 for a reservation that lets you skip the line. Three separate, optional sights inside require paid admission: the Treasury (€3, includes audioguide), Golden Altarpiece (€2), and San Marco Museum—the sight most worth its entry fee (€5, enter museum up stairs from atrium either before or after you tour the church).

Hours: The **church** is open Mon-Sat 9:45-17:00, Sun 14:00-17:00 (Sun until 16:00 Nov-Easter). The interior is brilliantly lit daily from 11:30 to 12:30; although this is an especially busy time, the additional lighting brings the otherwise dim gold-leaf domes and mosaics to glowing life.

The **museum** is open daily 9:45-16:45, including on Sunday mornings when the church itself is closed. If considering a Sunday visit, note that the museum has a balcony that allows you to view some, but not all, of the church's interior. The

Treasury and the Golden Altarpiece are both open Easter-Oct Mon-Sat 9:45-17:00, Sun 14:00-17:00; Nov-Easter Mon-Sat 9:45-16:00, Sun 14:00-16:00.

Lines: There's almost always a long line to get into St. Mark's, and there are several ways to avoid it: You can try going early or late. Or, if you have a large, bulky day bag, you can check it at a church around the corner: Your claim tag usually allows you to skip to the front of the line (see "Bag Check," below). Or you can reserve a time slot online (also described below). If you wind up in a long line, don't fret; it gives you time to enjoy one of Europe's finest squares as you read ahead in this chapter—and besides, the line moves pretty fast. Once inside, it can be packed, and you just have to shuffle through on a one-way system (another good reason to read this chapter before you enter).

Online Reservations: You can book an entry time, even for the same day, for €2 at www.venetoinside.com (April-Oct only). You get a 17-digit confirmation number that you need to show to the guards—either printed out, on a smartphone, or simply noted on a piece of paper.

Dress Code: Modest dress (no bare knees or bare shoulders) is strictly enforced for men, women, and even kids. Shorts are OK if they cover the knees.

Theft Alert: St. Mark's Basilica is the most notorious place in Venice for pickpocketing—inside, it's always a crowded jostle.

Getting There: Signs throughout Venice point to *San Marco*, meaning both the square and the church (vaporetto: San Marco or San Zaccaria).

Information: Tel. 041-270-8311, www.basilicasanmarco.it.

Church Services: Experience the church in its uncrowded glory at any Mass outside of visiting hours (e.g., daily at 8:00 or 18:45; see www.basilicasanmarco.it for full schedule). Enter through the "worship only" door around the left side of the basilica.

Tours: Free, hour-long English **tours** (heavy on the mosaics' religious symbolism) are offered many days at 11:30 (meet in atrium, schedule varies, see schedule board just inside entrance).

🎧 Download my free St. Mark's Basilica **audio tour**.

Length of This Tour: Allow one hour. If you have less time, forgo one (or all) of the basilica's three museums. The most skippable is the Golden Altarpiece (elaborate gold altarpiece near Mark's burial place), followed by the Treasury (fascinating but obscure old objects).

Bag Check (and Skipping the Line): Small purses and shoulder bags are usually allowed inside, but larger bags and backpacks are not. Check them for free for up to one hour at the nearby church called Ateneo San Basso, 30 yards to the left of the basilica, down narrow Calle San Basso (see map page 85; daily 9:30-17:00). Note that you generally can't check small bags that would be allowed inside.

Those with a bag to check usually get to skip the line, as do their companions (meaning about one or two others—keep it within reason; this is at the guard's discretion). Leave your bag at Ateneo San Basso and pick up your claim tag. Take your tag to the basilica's tourist entrance. Keep to the left of the railing where the line forms and show your tag to the gate-keeper. He'll generally let you in, ahead of the line.

Services: A free WC is inside the San Marco Museum. For restaurant suggestions nearby, see page 269.

Photography: Although officially forbidden inside the church, it is allowed on the balcony of the San Marco Museum, which has great views overlooking the square.

Starring: St. Mark, Byzantium, mosaics, and ancient bronze horses.

The Tour Begins

EXTERIOR
• *Start outside in the square, far enough back to take in the whole facade. Then zero in on the details.*

❶ Mosaic of Mark's Relics
St. Mark's Basilica is a treasure chest of booty that was looted during Venice's glory days. That's most appropriate for a church built on the stolen bones of a saint.

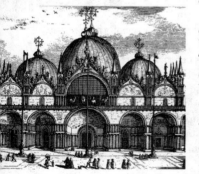

The **mosaic over the far left door** shows the theft that put Venice on the pilgrimage map. Two men (in the center, with crooked staffs) enter the church bearing a coffin with the body of St. Mark, who looks pretty grumpy from the long voyage.

St. Mark was the author of one of the Gospels, the four Bible books (Matthew, Mark, Luke, and John) telling the story of Jesus' life. Eight centuries after Mark's death, his holy body was in Muslim-occupied Alexandria, Egypt. In A.D. 829, two visiting Venetian merchants "rescued" the body from the "infidels" and spirited it away to Venice.

The merchants presented the body—not to a pope or bishop—but to the doge (with white ermine collar, on the right) and his

St. Mark's...Cathedral, Church, or Basilica?

All three are correct. The church is also a cathedral, because it's the home church of the local bishop. It's a basilica, because the Roman Catholic Church gives that special designation to certain churches of religious importance. Coincidentally, it's also a basilica in the architectural sense. Its floor plan (if you ignore the transepts) has a central nave with flanking side aisles, a layout patterned after the ancient Roman public buildings called "basilicas." The transepts turn the basilica plan into a cross—in this case, a Greek cross, as it has four equal arms.

wife, the dogaressa (with entourage, on the left), giving instant status to Venice's budding secular state. They built a church here over Mark's bones and made him the patron saint of the city. You'll see his symbol, the winged lion, all over Venice.

The original church burned down in A.D. 976. Today's structure was begun in 1063. The mosaic, from 1260, shows that the church hasn't changed much since then—you can see the onion domes and famous bronze horses on the balcony.

The St. Mark's you see today, mostly from the 11th century, was modeled after a great fourth-century church in Constantinople (Istanbul), the Church of the Holy Apostles (now long gone). Venice needed roots. By building a retro church, the city could imply that it had been around for longer than it actually had been. (Throughout European history, upstarts loved to fake deep roots this way. Germany embraced mystic, medieval lore as it emerged as a modern nation in the 19th century, England cooked up the King Arthur legend, and so on.)

In subsequent centuries, the church was encrusted with materials looted from buildings throughout the Venetian empire (see sidebar on page 92). Their prize booty was the four bronze horses that adorn the balcony, stolen from Constantinople during the Fourth Crusade (these are copies; the originals are inside the church museum); the atrium you're about to enter was added on to the church as their pedestal. Later, it was decorated with a mish-

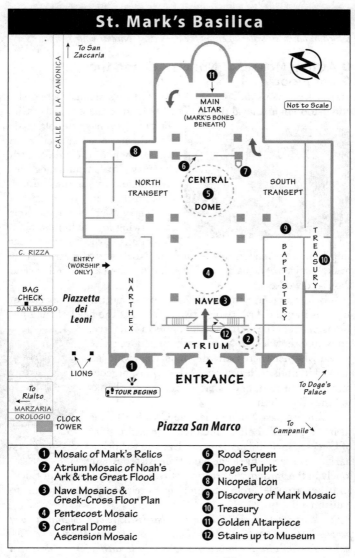

St. Mark's Basilica

To San
Zaccaria

CALLE DE LA CANONICA

11

MAIN
ALTAR
(MARK'S BONES
BENEATH)

Not to Scale

8

6

NORTH
TRANSEPT

CENTRAL
5
DOME

7

SOUTH
TRANSEPT

9

C. RIZZA

ENTRY
(WORSHIP
ONLY)

NARTHEX

4

NAVE **3**

BAPTISTERY

TREASURY

10

BAG
CHECK
SAN BASSO

Piazzetta
dei
Leoni

12

2

ATRIUM

To
Rialto

MARZARIA
OROLOGIO

LIONS

1

ENTRANCE

TOUR BEGINS

CLOCK
TOWER

Piazza San Marco

To Doge's
Palace

To
Campanile

❶ Mosaic of Mark's Relics
❷ Atrium Mosaic of Noah's
Ark & the Great Flood
❸ Nave Mosaics &
Greek-Cross Floor Plan
❹ Pentecost Mosaic
❺ Central Dome
Ascension Mosaic

❻ Rood Screen
❼ Doge's Pulpit
❽ Nicopeia Icon
❾ Discovery of Mark Mosaic
❿ Treasury
⓫ Golden Altarpiece
⓬ Stairs up to Museum

mash of plundered columns. The architectural style of St. Mark's has been called "Early Ransack."

INTERIOR

• *Enter the atrium of the basilica through a sixth-century, bronze-paneled Byzantine door—which likely once swung in Constantinople's Hagia Sophia church. Immediately after being admitted by the dress-code guard, look up and to the right into an archway decorated with fine mosaics. Don't be bullied by the crowd. Step aside and find an eddy from which to pause in order to enjoy the amazing space at your tempo.*

❷ Atrium Mosaic of Noah's Ark and the Great Flood

St. Mark's famous mosaics, with their picture symbols, were easily understood in medieval times, even by illiterate masses. Today's lit-

erate masses have trouble reading them, so let's practice on these, some of the oldest (13th century), finest, and most accessible mosaics in the church.

In the scene to the right of the entry door, Noah and sons are sawing logs to build a boat. Venetians—who were great ship builders—related to the story of Noah and the Ark. At its peak, Venice's Arsenale warship-building plant employed several thousand workers.

Below that are three scenes of Noah putting all species of animals into the Ark, two by two. (Who's at the head of the line? Lions.) Across the arch, the Flood hits in full force, drowning the wicked. Noah sends out a dove twice to see whether there's any dry land where he can dock. He finds it, leaves the Ark with a gorgeous rainbow overhead, and offers a sacrifice of thanks to God. Easy, huh?

Venture past Noah under the Creation Dome (if it's not blocked off), which tells the entire story of Genesis, including Adam and Eve and the original sin. In a scene-by-scene narration, we see Adam lonely in the garden, the creation of Eve, the happy couple in Eden, and then trouble: from succumbing to temptation, to fig leaf, to banishment.

• *Now that our medieval literacy rate has risen, rejoin the slow flow of people. Notice the entrance to the San Marco Museum (Loggia dei Cavalli). You can visit the museum now or save it until after you've toured the main part of the church. Survey the lay of the (holy) land and consider the flow of the masses.*

Assuming you're following the tour as written, climb seven steps, pass through the doorway, and enter the nave. Just inside the door, step to the far left, stop, let your eyes adjust, and survey the church.

❸ Nave Mosaics and Greek-Cross Floor Plan

The initial effect is dark and unimpressive (unless they've got the floodlights on). But as your pupils slowly unclench, notice that

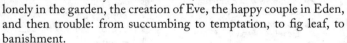

ST. MARK'S BASILICA

Christ as Pantocrator

Most Eastern Orthodox churches have at least one mosaic or painting of Christ in a standard pose—as "Pantocrator," a Greek word meaning "Ruler of All." St. Mark's features several images of Christ as Pantocrator (for example, over the altar, in the central dome, and over the entrance door). The image, so familiar to Orthodox Christians, may be a bit foreign to Protestants, Catholics, and secularists.

As King of the Universe, Christ sits (usually on a throne) facing directly out, with penetrating eyes. He wears a halo divided with a cross. In his left hand is a Bible, while his right hand blesses, with the fingers forming the Greek letters *chi* and *rho*, the first two letters of "Christos." The thumb touches the fingers, symbolizing how Christ unites both his divinity and his humanity. On either side of Christ's head are the Greek letters "IC XC," short for "IesuC XristoC."

the entire upper part is decorated in mosaic—nearly 5,000 square yards (imagine paving a football field with contact lenses). These golden mosaics are in the Byzantine style, though many were designed by artists from the Italian Renaissance and later. The often-overlooked lower walls are covered with green-, yellow-, purple-, and rose-colored marble slabs, cut to expose the grain, and laid out in geometric patterns. Even the floor is mosaic, with mostly geometrical designs. It rolls like the sea. Venice is sinking and shifting, creating these cresting waves of stone.

The church is laid out with four equal arms, topped with domes, radiating out from the center to form a Greek cross (+). Those familiar with Eastern Orthodox churches will find familiar elements in St. Mark's: a central floor plan, domes, mosaics, and iconic images of Mary and Christ as Pantocrator—ruler of all things. As your eyes adjust, the mosaics start to give off a mystical, golden luminosity, the atmosphere of the Byzantine heaven. The air itself seems almost visible, like a cloud of incense. It's a subtle effect, one that grows as the filtered light changes. There are more

ST. MARK'S BASILICA

beautiful, bigger, more overwhelming, and even holier churches, but none is as stately.

• *Find the chandelier near the entrance doorway (in the shape of a Greek cross cathedral space station), and run your eyes up the support chain to the dome above.*

❹ Pentecost Mosaic

In a golden heaven, the dove of the Holy Spirit shoots out a pinwheel of spiritual lasers, igniting tongues of fire on the heads of the 12 apostles below, giving them the ability to speak other languages without a Rick Steves phrase book. You'd think they'd be amazed, but their expressions are as solemn as... icons. One of the oldest mosaics in the church (c. 1125), it has distinct "Byzantine" features: a gold background and apostles with halos, solemn faces, almond eyes, delicate blessing hands, and rumpled robes, all facing forward.

This is art from a society still touchy about the Bible's commandment against making "graven images" of holy things. Byzantium had recently emerged from two centuries of iconoclasm, in which statues and paintings were broken and burned as sinful "false gods." The Byzantine style emphasizes otherworldliness rather than literal human detail.

• *Shuffle along with the crowds up to the central dome.*

❺ Central Dome Ascension Mosaic

Gape upward to the very heart of the church. Christ—having lived his miraculous life and having been crucified for man's sins—ascends into the starry sky on a rainbow. He raises his right hand and blesses the universe. This isn't the dead, crucified, mortal Jesus featured in most churches, but a powerful, resurrected God, the ruler of all.

Christ's blessing radiates, rippling down to the ring of white-robed apostles below. They stand amid the trees of the Mount of Olives, waving goodbye as Christ ascends. Mary is with them, wearing blue with golden Greek crosses on each shoulder and looking ready to play patty-cake. From these saints, goodness descends, creating the Virtues and Beatitudes that ring the base of the dome between the windows. In Byzantine churches, the window-lit dome represented heaven, while the dark church below represented earth—a microcosm of the hierarchical universe.

Beneath the dome at the four corners, the four Gospel writers

Mosaics

St. Mark's mosaics are designs or pictures made by pressing small tiles of colored stone or glass (called *tesserae*) into wet plaster. Ancient Romans paved floors, walls, and ceilings with them. When Rome "fell," the art form died out in the West but was carried on by Byzantine craftsmen. They perfected the gold background effect by sandwiching pieces of gold leaf between glass. The surfaces of the tiles are purposely cut unevenly to capture light and give off a shimmering effect. The reflecting gold mosaics helped to light thick-walled, small-windowed, lantern-lit Byzantine churches, creating a golden glow that symbolized the divine light of heaven.

St. Mark's mosaics tell the entire Christian history from end to beginning. Entering the church, you're greeted with scenes from the end of the world (Apocalypse) and the Pentecost. As you approach the altar, you walk backward in time to the source, experiencing Jesus' Passion and Crucifixion, his miraculous life, and continuing back to his birth and Old Testament predecessors. Over the altar at the far end of the church (and over the entrance door at the near end) are images of Christ—the beginning and the end, the Alpha and Omega of the Christian universe.

("Matev," "Marc," "Luca," and "Ioh") thoughtfully scribble down the heavenly events. This wisdom flows down as water pouring from jugs, symbolizing the four great rivers below them, spreading through the church's four equal arms (the "four corners" of the world), and baptizing the congregation with God's love. The church building is a series of perfect circles within perfect squares—the cosmic order—with Christ in the center solemnly blessing us. God's in his heaven, saints are on earth, and all's right with the world.

The Church as Theater

Look around at the church's furniture and imagine a service here. The ❻ **rood screen,** (like the iconostasis in a Greek church) topped with 14 saints, separates the congregation from the high altar, heightening the "mystery" of the Mass. The ❼ **pulpit** on the right was reserved for the doge, who led prayers and made important announcements.

The Venetian church service is a theatrical multimedia spectacle, combining words (prayers, biblical passages, Latin and Greek phrases), music (chants, choir, organ, horns, strings), images (mosaics telling Bible stories), costumes and props (priests' robes, golden reliquaries, candles, incense), set design (mosaics, rood screen, Golden Altarpiece), and even stage direction (processionals through the crowd, priests' motions, standing, sitting, kneeling, crossing yourself). The symmetrical church is itself part of the set design. The Greek-cross floor plan symbolizes perfection, rather than the more common Latin cross of the Crucifixion (emphasizing man's sinfulness). Coincidentally or not, the first modern opera—also a multimedia theatrical experience—was written by St. Mark's *maestro di cappella,* Claudio Monteverdi (1567-1643).

North Transept

In the north transept (left of the altar), today's Venetians pray to a painted wooden icon of Mary and Baby Jesus known as ❽ **Nicopeia,** or Our Lady of Victory (it's a small painting crusted over with a big stone canopy). In its day, this was the ultimate trophy—the actual icon, used to protect the Byzantine army in war, looted by the Crusaders. Supposedly painted by the evangelist Luke, it was once enameled with bright paint and precious stones, and Mary was adorned with a crown and necklace of gold and jewels (now on display in the Treasury). Now the protector of Venetians, this Madonna has helped the city persevere through plagues, wars, and crucial soccer games.

• *In the south transept (right of main altar), find the dim mosaic high up on the three-windowed wall above the entrance to the treasury.*

❾ Discovery of Mark Mosaic

This mosaic isn't a biblical scene; it depicts the miraculous event that capped the construction of the present church. (It's high up and hard to read.)

It's 1094, the church is nearly complete (see the domes shown in cutaway fashion), and it's time to reinter Mark's bones under the new altar. There's just one problem: During the decades of construction, locals forgot where they'd stored his body!

So (on the left), all of Venice gathers inside the church to bow down and pray for help finding the bones. The doge (from the Latin *dux,* meaning leader) leads them. Soon after (on the right), the patriarch (far right) is inspired to look inside a hollow column where he finds the relics. Everyone turns and applauds, including the womenfolk, who stream in from the upper-floor galleries. The relics were soon placed under the altar in a ceremony that inaugurated the current structure.

At the far end of the transept, the door under the rose window, with the green curtain, leads directly from the Doge's Palace. On important occasions, the doge entered the church through here, ascended the steps of his pulpit, and addressed the people.

ST. MARK'S THREE MUSEUMS

Inside the church are three sights, each requiring a separate admission. These provide an easy way to experience the richness of Byzantium. The San Marco Museum also gives you access to great views over the inside of the church, as well as to St. Mark's Square outside.

⓾ Treasury (Tesoro)

• *The two-room Treasury is in the south transept.*

If you're not into metalworking or religious objects, you may find the Treasury's cramped collection somewhat underwhelming, but the objects become more interesting when you consider their illustrious past. These rooms hold an amazing collection of precious items most of them stolen from Constantinople: Byzantine chalices, silver reliquaries, monstrous monstrances (for displaying the Communion wafer), and icons done in gold, silver, enamels, gems, and semiprecious stones. These pieces, highlighting finely worked and translucent material, are the ones that show up in art textbooks as the finest surviving Byzantine treasures (assuaging any Venetian guilt). As Venice thought of itself as the granddaughter of Rome and the daughter of Byzantium, Venetians consider these treasures not stolen, but inherited—rock crystal, jasper, alabaster, and marble that was rightfully theirs. Less sophisticated thieves would have smelted these pieces, but the Venetians safely stored them here for posterity.

Some of the items represent the fruits of labor by different civilizations over a thousand-year period. For example, an ancient rock-crystal chalice made by the Romans might have been decorated centuries later with Byzantine enamels and then finished still later with gold filigree by Venetian goldsmiths. This is marvelous handiwork, but all the more marvelous for having been done when Western Europe was still mired in Dark Age mud.

• *Enter the main room, to the right. Start with the large glass case in the center of the room.*

Main Room: This display case holds the most precious Byzantine objects (mostly war booty brought here during the Fourth

ST. MARK'S BASILICA

Byzantium, the Fourth Crusade, and Venice

The Byzantine Empire was the eastern half of the ancient Roman Empire that *didn't* "fall" in A.D. 476. It remained Christian, Greek-speaking, and enlightened for another thousand years.

In A.D. 330, Constantine, the first Christian emperor, moved the Roman Empire's capital to the newly expanded city of Byzantium, which he humbly renamed Constantinople. With him went Rome's best and brightest. When the city of Rome decayed and fell, plunging Western Europe into its "Dark Ages," Constantinople lived on as the greatest city in Europe.

From its earliest days, Venice had strong ties with Byzantium. In the sixth century, Byzantine Emperor Justinian invaded northern Italy, briefly reuniting East and West, and making Ravenna his regional capital. In 810, Venetians asked the emperor in Constantinople to protect them from Charlemagne's marauding Franks.

Soon Venetian merchants were granted trading rights to Byzantine ports in the Adriatic and eastern Mediterranean. They traded raw materials from Western Europe for luxury goods from the East. By the 10th century, about 10,000 Venetian merchants lived and worked in Constantinople. Meanwhile, relations between Byzantine Christians and Roman Catholics were souring across Europe over religious grounds—and because Constanti-

nople's local merchants felt crowded out by the powerful Venetians, the corporate titans of the day. In 1171, the Byzantine emperor expelled the Venetian merchants from Constantinople; after another decade of conflict, the entire Roman Catholic population—about 60,000 people—was either slaughtered or expelled from the city.

Powerful, rich Venice wasn't about to stand for it—the Venetians had virtually no economy without trade. Two decades later, they saw their chance: The pope was organizing the Fourth Crusade to "save" the Holy Land from Muslim influence. Venice offered her ships to transport more than 30,000 Crusaders. They set out bound for Jerusalem—but the ships, led by the Venetian doge, diverted to Constantinople. The Crusaders sacked the Byzantine capital and occupied it from 1204 to 1261, turning the city

into a quarry—one wide open for plunder. During that period, any ship traveling from Constantinople to Venice was required to bring with it a souvenir for the Venetian Republic. Eventually the riches of Constantinople ended up in Venice—much of it here, in St. Mark's Basilica.

You can still see much of what the Venetians carried home: the bronze horses, bronze doors of Hagia Sophia, Golden Altarpiece enamels, the Treasury's treasures, the Nicopeia icon, and much of the marble that now covers the (brick) church. A good portion of the artistic riches adorning the church and filling its treasury was 700 years old when it was brought here...800 years ago.

The Venetians were clearly thieves, albeit thieves with good taste. While you could argue that much of the treasure belongs in Turkey today, a good Venetian would argue that had they not "rescued" it, much of it (especially anything made from precious metal) never would have survived the centuries.

After the Fourth Crusade, Venice rose while the Byzantine Empire faded. Then both civilizations nose-dived when Constantinople finally fell to the Ottomans in 1453, severely damaging Venice's trading empire and ending Byzantium entirely. Constantinople, however, soon began to thrive again—once a bustling Christian city of a thousand churches, it flourished again as the newly Islamic city of Istanbul.

ST. MARK'S BASILICA

Crusade in 1204). The hanging lamp with the protruding fish features fourth-century Roman rock crystal framed in 11th-century Byzantine metalwork.

Just behind the lamp, a black bucket, carved in the fourth century with scenes of satyrs chasing nymphs, epitomizes the pagan world that was fading as Christianity triumphed. Also in the case are blue-and-gold lapis lazuli icons of the Crucifixion and (opposite side) of the Archangel Michael—standing like an action hero, ready to conquer evil in the name of Christ. This features a Byzantine specialty: enamel work (more on that craft at the Golden Altarpiece). See various chalices (cups used for the bread and wine during Mass) made of onyx, agate, and rock crystal, and an incense burner shaped like a domed church.

• *Along the walls, find the following displays (working counterclockwise around the room).*

The first three glass cases have bowls and urns made of glass or rock crystal, gold and silver, and precious stones, and laced with elaborate filigree (twisted wires of precious metal). The styles blend elements from the three medieval cultures that cross-pollinated in the Eastern Mediterranean: Venetian, Byzantine, and Islamic.

Next, on a wooden pedestal, comes the Urn of Artaxerxes I (next to window in right wall), an Egyptian-made object that once held the ashes of the great Persian king who ruled 2,500 years ago (r. 465-425 B.C.).

The next cases hold religious paraphernalia used for High Mass—chalices, reliquaries, candlesticks, bishops' robes, and a 600-year-old ceremonial crosier (reminiscent of a shepherd's staff) still used today by the chief priest on holy days.

Next is the Ciborio di Anastasia (far left corner), a small marble canopy that once arched over the blessed communion wafer during Mass. The object may be a gift from "Anastasia," the name carved on it in Greek. She was a lady-in-waiting in the court of the emperor Justinian (483-565). Christian legend has it that she was so beautiful that Justinian (a married man) pursued her amorously, so she had to dress like a monk and flee to a desert monastery.

Moving to the next wall, you'll see two large golden panels that once fronted an altar. The bottom one shows 14 scenes from the life of St. Mark. Flanking the panels are two golden candlesticks. Study the one on the left. What detail! The smiling angels at the top, the literary lion, the man with the weight on his shoulders, the row of queens flanking the Crucifixion...all the way down to the roots. Continuing counterclockwise, see a photo of a Madonna adorned with jewels, gold, and enamel.

Next to the Madonna, notice the granite column that extends below current floor level—you can see how the floor has risen as the basilica has settled in the last 1,000 years.

Relics/Sanctuary Room: This room is filled with relics so precious they were stored in this treasury. Straight ahead, the glass case over the glowing alabaster altar contains elaborate gold-and-glass reliquaries holding relics of Jesus' Passion—his torture and execution. The reliquary showing Christ being whipped (from 1125) holds a stone from the column he was tied to. You may scoff, but of Europe's many "Pieces of the True Cross" and "Crown of Thorns" relics, these have at least some claim of authenticity. Legend has it that Christ's possessions were gathered up in the fourth century by Constantine's mother and taken to Constantinople. During the Crusade heist of 1204, Venetians brought them here. They've been paraded through the city every Good Friday for 800 years.

Back by the room's entrance is a glass reliquary with the bones of Doge Orseolo (r. 976-978), who built the church that preceded the current structure. Another contains the bones of St. George, legendary dragon slayer.

• *Return to the nave and follow the crowds through the turnstile and behind the main altar to the …*

⓫ Golden Altarpiece (Pala d'Oro)

Under the green marble canopy, supported by four intricately carved 7th-century alabaster columns (plundered from far away), sits the **high altar.** Inside the altar is an urn (not visible) with the mortal remains of Mark, the Gospel writer. (Look through the grate of the altar to read *Corpus Divi Marci Evangelistae,* or "Body of the Evangelist Mark.") He rests in peace, as an angel had promised him. Shh.

As you shuffle along, notice the marble canopy's **support columns** carved with New Testament scenes.

The **Golden Altarpiece** itself is a stunning golden wall made of 250 blue-backed enamels with religious scenes, all set in a gold

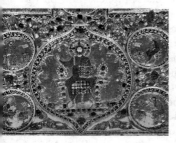

frame and studded with 15 hefty rubies, 300 emeralds, 1,500 pearls, and assorted sapphires, amethysts, and topaz. The Byzantine-made enamels were part of the Venetians' plunder of 1204, subsequently pieced together by Byzantine craftsmen specifically for St. Mark's high altar. It's a bit much to take in all at once, but get up close and find several details you might recognize:

In the center, Jesus as Ruler of the Cosmos sits on a golden throne, with a halo of pearls and jewels. Like a good Byzantine Pantocrator, he dutifully faces forward and gives his blessing while stealing a glance offstage at Mark ("Marcus") and the other saints.

The Legend (Mixed with a Little Truth) of Mark and Venice

Mark (died c. A.D. 68) was a Jewish-born Christian, and he might have actually met Jesus. He traveled with fellow convert Paul, eventually settling in Alexandria as the city's first Christian bishop. On a trip to Rome, Peter—Jesus' right-hand man—asked him to write down the events of Jesus' life. This became the Gospel of Mark.

During his travels, Mark stopped in the lagoon (in Aquileia on the north coast of the Adriatic), where he dreamed of a Latin-speaking angel who said, *"Pax tibi Marce, evangelista meus"* ("Peace to you, Mark, my evangelist"), promising him rest after death. Back in Alexandria, Mark was attacked by an anti-Christian mob. They tied him with ropes and dragged his body through the streets until he died.

Eight centuries later, his body lay in an Alexandrian church that was about to be vandalized by Muslim fanatics. Two Venetian traders on a business trip saved the relics from desecration by hiding them in a basket of pork—a meat considered unclean by Muslims—and quickly setting sail. The doge received the body, and in 832 they built the first church of St. Mark's to house it. After construction of the current church started in 1063, Mark's relics were temporarily lost, and it took another miracle to find them, hidden inside a column. Today, Venetians celebrate Mark on the traditional date of his martyrdom, April 25.

Along the bottom row, Old Testament prophets show off the books of the Bible they've written. With halos, solemn faces, and elaborately creased robes, they epitomize the Byzantine icon style.

Follow Mark's story in the vertical series of panels on each side (up on the left and then down on the right). In the bottom left panel, Mark meets Peter (seated) at the gates of Rome. It was Peter (legend has it) who gave Mark the eyewitness account of Jesus' life that Mark wrote down in his Gospel. Mark's story ends in the bottom right panel with the two Venetian merchants returning by ship, carrying his coffin here in 829 to be laid to rest.

Byzantium excelled in the art of cloisonné enameling. A piece of gold leaf is stamped with a design, then filled in with pools of enamel paste, and then fired. Look at a single saint to see the detail work: The gold background around the saint is the gold-leaf medallion that gets stamped. The golden folds in the robe are the raised edges of the impression; in the recessed areas, each different color of the robe was baked on in a separate firing. Some saints even have pearl crowns or jewel collars pinned on. This kind of craftsmanship—and the social infrastructure that could afford it—made Byzantium seem like an enchanted world during Europe's dim Middle Ages.

After you've looked at some individual scenes, back up as far as this small room will let you and let yourself be dazzled by the whole picture—this "mosaic" of Byzantine greatness—and marvel at the fact that it's still here. While the altarpiece contains 30 pounds of gold, Napoleon's men thought it was just gold leaf, so they didn't bother melting it down. And during World War II, the altarpiece almost certainly would have been snatched by the Nazis, had it not been hidden away in an Umbrian villa.

This magnificent altarpiece sits on a swivel (notice the mechanism at its base) and is swung around on festival Sundays so the entire congregation can enjoy it, as Venetians have for so many centuries.

⓬ San Marco Museum (Museo di San Marco)

• *The steep staircase up to the museum is in the atrium near the main entrance. The sign says* Loggia dei Cavalli, Museo. *In the first room, you'll see several models of the church at various stages of its history. Notice how the original domes, once squat, were made taller in the 13th century, leaving today's church with a dome-within-a-dome structure. Notice also the historic drawings here.*

Next are the museum's three highlights: view of the interior (right), view of the square (out the door to the left), and bronze horses (directly ahead). Belly up to the stone balustrade (on the right) to survey the interior.

View of Church Interior

Scan the church, with its thousands of square meters of mosaics, then take a closer look at the Pentecost Mosaic (first dome above you). The unique design at the very top signifies the Trinity: throne (God), Gospels (Christ), and dove (Holy Spirit). The couples below the ring of apostles are the people of the world (I can find Judaea, Cappadocia, and Asia), who, despite their different languages, still understood the Spirit's message.

If you were a woman in medieval Venice, you'd enjoy this same close-up view, because in the Middle Ages, women climbed the same stairs you just did and found a spot along the balconies at your feet. The balcony was for women, the nave for men, and the altar for the priests. Back then the rood screen (the fence with the 14 figures on it) separated the priest from the public. The doge was also allowed to address his public from the pulpit, thereby amplifying the power of his political speeches with the force of God.

Looking down at the nave, appreciate the patterns of the mosaic floor—one of the finest in Italy—that unfurl like a Persian carpet.

• *From here, the museum loops you along the left gallery to the far (altar) end of the church, then back to the bronze horses. Along the way, you'll see…*

Mosaic Fragments

These mosaics once hung in the church, but when they became damaged or aesthetically old-fashioned, they were replaced by new and more fashionable mosaics. These few fragments avoided the garbage can. You'll see mosaics from the church's earliest days (and most "Byzantine" style, c. 1070) to more recent times (1700s, more realistic and detailed). Many are accompanied by small photos that show where the fragment used to fit into a larger scene.

The mosaics—made from small tiles of stone or colored glass pressed into wet clay—were assembled on the ground, then cemented onto the walls. Artists drew the pattern on paper, laid it on the wet clay, and slowly cut the paper away as they replaced it with tiles. The first mosaic on your left as you enter shows a reproduction of a paper "cast" of a mosaic.

Continuing on, down a set of stairs, you'll see other artwork and catch glimpses of the interior of the church from the north transept. Here you get a close-up view of the **Tree of Jesse mosaic,** showing Jesus' distant ancestor at the root and his mom at the top. This mosaic is from 1540, during the High Renaissance—it's much more modern than those decorating the domes, which date mostly from the 1200s.

• *Take this opportunity to compare the styles, then continue on to the Sala dei Banchetti (WCs near the room's entrance).*

Sala dei Banchetti

This large, ornate room—once the doge's banquet hall—is filled with religious objects, tapestries, and carpets that once adorned the church, Burano-made lace vestments, illuminated music manuscripts, a doge's throne, and much more.

Try reading some music. The manuscripts date from the 16th century—before the age of treble and bass clefs. You'll see a C clef along the left margin of each staff (which could slide along the staff to locate middle C). From this, you could chant notes in proper relationship to each other, following the rhythm indicated.

In the center of the hall stands the most prestigious artwork here, the *Pala Feriale,* by Paolo Veneziano (1345). On ordinary days, these 14 scenes painted on wood formed a cover for the basilica's Golden Altarpiece. The top row shows seven saints, including crucified Christ. Below are seven episodes in Mark's life. In the first panel, Mark kneels before a red-robed Saint Peter and receives his calling. Next, he arrives in Alexandria and makes his first convert. Then Jesus appears to Mark. Mark is beaten to death and dragged through the streets. The panel of the sailboat recounts the Venetian merchants' trip home with Mark's relics. A storm at sea billows their sails, ripples the flag, churns the waves, and scares the crew as the ship heads toward the rocks. But then Mark himself appears miraculously at the stern and calms the storm, bringing the ship (and his own body) safely to Venice. Paolo proudly signed his name (along the bottom) and the names of his two assistants, his sons Luca and Giovanni. In the next panel, Mark's long-lost body is rediscovered hidden in a column. Finally, worshippers gather at Mark's tomb by the altar of the basilica.

• *Now double back toward the museum entrance, through displays of stone fragments from the church, finally arriving at...*

The Bronze Horses (La Quadriga)

Stepping lively in pairs and with smiles on their faces, the horses exude energy and exuberance. Art historians don't know how old

they are—they could be from ancient Greece (fifth century B.C.) or from ancient Rome, during its fall (fourth century A.D.). Professor Carbon Fourteen says they're from around 175 B.C. Originally, the horses pulled a chariot driven by an emperor, *Ben-Hur* style. These bronze statues were not hammered and bent into shape by metalsmiths, but were cast from clay molds using what is called the lost-wax technique. The heads are detachable and adjustable—even swappable. The bronze is high quality, with 97 percent copper. Originally gilded, they still have some streaks of gold. Long gone are the ruby pupils that gave the horses the original case of "red eye." While four-horse statues were once relatively common, this is the only intact group of four horses to survive from ancient times. That they survived at all is amazing, as bronze work like this almost always ends up being smelted down by conquerors.

Megalomaniacs through the ages have coveted these horses not only for their artistic value, but because they symbolize Apollo, the Greco-Roman god of the sun...and of secular power. Legend says they were made in the time of Alexander the Great, then taken by Nero to Rome. Constantine took them to his new capital in Constantinople to adorn the chariot racecourse. The Venetians then stole them from their fellow Christians when they sacked the city in 1204 and erected them on the exterior of St. Mark's in about 1255. The doge spoke to his people while standing between the horses when they graced the balcony atop the church's facade (where the copies—which you'll see next—stand today).

What goes around comes around, and Napoleon came around and took the horses when he conquered Venice in 1797. They stood atop a triumphal arch in Paris until Napoleon's empire was "blown-aparte" and they were returned to their "rightful" home. Their expressive faces seem to say, "Oh boy, Wilbur, have we done some travelin'."

The horses were again removed from their spot when they were attacked by their most dangerous enemy yet—modern man. The threat of oxidation from pollution sent them galloping for cover inside the church in the 1970s.

• *The visit ends outside on the balcony overlooking St. Mark's Square.*

The Loggia and View of St. Mark's Square

You'll be drawn repeatedly to the viewpoint of the square, but remember to look at the facade to see how cleverly all the looted architectural elements blend together. Ramble among the statues of water-bearing slaves that serve as drain spouts. The horses are modern copies (note the 1978 date on the hoof of the horse to the right).

Be a doge, and stand aside the bronze horses overlooking St. Mark's Square. Under the gilded lion of St. Mark, in front of the four great evangelists (who once stood atop the columns), and flanked—like Apollo—by the four glorious horses, he inspired the Venetians in the square below to great things.

Admire the mesmerizing, commanding view of the center of this city, which so long ago was Europe's only superpower, and today is just a small town with a big history—one that's filled with tourists.

DOGE'S PALACE TOUR

Palazzo Ducale

Venice is a city of beautiful facades—palaces, churches, carnival masks—that cover darker interiors of intrigue and decay. The Doge's Palace, with its frilly pink exterior, hides the fact that the "Most Serene Republic" (as Venice called itself—"serene" meaning stable) was far from serene in its heyday.

The Doge's Palace housed the fascinating government of this rich and powerful empire. It also served as the home for the Venetian ruler known as the doge (pronounced "dohzh"), or duke. For four centuries (about 1150 to 1550), this was the most powerful half-acre in Europe. The rest of Europe marveled at the way Venice could govern itself without a dominant king, bishop, or tyrant. The doges wanted their palace to reflect the wealth and secular values of the Republic, impressing visitors and serving as a reminder that the Venetians were Number One in Europe.

Orientation

Cost: €19 combo-ticket includes the Correr Museum. The palace is free and crowded the first Sun of the month.

Hours: Daily April-Oct 8:30-19:00, Nov-March until 17:30, last entry one hour before closing.

Crowd Control: To avoid the long peak-season line, you have several options (the first is best):

• Buy your combo-ticket at the Correr Museum. Or if you're purchasing a Museum Pass (which covers the Doge's Palace—see page 17), get it at one of the less-crowded museums covered by the pass. Then go straight to the Doge's Palace turnstile, skirting along to the right of the long ticket-buying line and entering at the "prepaid tickets" entrance.

• Pay €0.50 extra to buy your ticket online—at least 48 hours

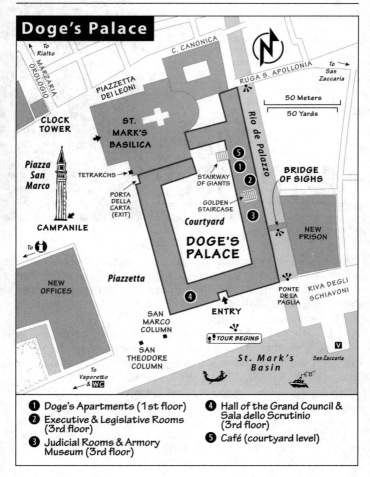

Doge's Palace

To Rialto

MARZARIA OROLOGIO

C. CANONICA

RUGA S. APOLLONIA

To San Zaccaria

PIAZZETTA DEI LEONI

50 Meters

50 Yards

CLOCK TOWER

ST. MARK'S BASILICA

Rio de Palazzo

Piazza San Marco

TETRARCHS

STAIRWAY OF GIANTS

5
1
2

BRIDGE OF SIGHS

CAMPANILE

PORTA DELLA CARTA (EXIT)

GOLDEN STAIRCASE

3

NEW PRISON

To ℹ

Courtyard

DOGE'S PALACE

NEW OFFICES

Piazzetta

PONTE DE LA PAGLIA

RIVA DEGLI SCHIAVONI

4

ENTRY

SAN MARCO COLUMN

🚩 TOUR BEGINS

SAN THEODORE COLUMN

St. Mark's Basin

San Zaccaria

To Vaporetto & WC

1 Doge's Apartments (1st floor)	**4** Hall of the Grand Council & Sala dello Scrutinio (3rd floor)
2 Executive & Legislative Rooms (3rd floor)	**5** Café (courtyard level)
3 Judicial Rooms & Armory Museum (3rd floor)	

in advance—on the museum website (http://palazzoducale. visitmuve.it).

• In peak season, visit the palace after about 16:00, when the line diminishes.

• Book a guided Secret Itineraries Tour (see "Tours," below).

Getting There: The palace is next to St. Mark's Basilica, on the lagoon waterfront, and just off St. Mark's Square. Vaporetto stops: San Marco or San Zaccaria.

Information: Guidebooks are on sale in the bookshop. Tel. 041-271-5911, http://palazzoducale.visitmuve.it.

Tours: The fine **Secret Itineraries Tour** follows the doge's footsteps through rooms not included in the general admission price. Though the tour skips the palace's main hall, you're welcome to visit the hall afterward on your own. Three 1.25-hour

English-language tours run each morning. Reserve ahead, as tours fill up—although you can try just showing up at the information desk (€20, includes Doge's Palace admission but not Correr Museum—don't confuse this with the Doge's Hidden Treasures Tour, which isn't worth its fee; to reserve from the US dial 011-39-041-4273-0892, within Italy call 848-082-000, or reserve online for €0.50 extra at http://palazzoducale.visitmuve.it).

The **audioguide** tour is dry but informative (€5 or €8/2 people, 1.5 hours, need ID for deposit). Pick it up after you pass through the turnstile after the ticket counter.

Length of This Tour: Allow 1.5 hours. If you need to shave some time off your visit, head straight to the third floor (the Square Room) and follow the tour from there to the Hall of the Grand Council. Skip the prisons.

Services: Some WCs are in the courtyard; more are halfway up the stairs to the balcony level. An elevator (off the courtyard) is available for those who have difficulty climbing stairs. Any bag bigger than a large purse must be checked (free) in the courtyard.

Photography: Photos are allowed without flash.

Cuisine Art: A café is off the palace courtyard (it's tucked in the gallery behind the Stairway of Giants, and the tour route also deposits you there). I'd head instead for the good sandwich bars on Calle de le Rasse (two blocks behind the palace—see page 269).

Starring: Big rooms bare of furnishings but crammed with history, Tintoretto masterpieces, and the doges.

The Tour Begins

Exterior

"The Wedding Cake," "The Tablecloth," or "The Pink House" is also sometimes known as the Doge's Palace. The style is called Vene-

tian Gothic—a fusion of Italian Gothic with a delicate Islamic flair. The columns originally had bases on the bottoms, but these were covered over as the columns sank, and the square was built up over the centuries. If you compare this lacy, top-heavy structure with the massive fortress-palaces of Florence, you realize the wisdom of building a city in the middle of the sea—you have no natural enemies except gravity. This unfortified palace in a city with no city wall was the doge's way of saying, "I am an elected and loved ruler. I do not fear my own people."

The palace was originally built in the 800s, but most of what we see came after 1300, as it was expanded to meet the needs of the empire. Each doge wanted to leave his mark on history with a new wing, but so much of the city's money was spent on the palace that finally a law was passed levying an enormous fine on anyone who even mentioned any new building. That worked for a while, until one brave (and wealthy) doge proposed a new wing, paid his fine... and started building again.

• *Enter the Doge's Palace from along the waterfront. After you pass through the turnstile, ignore the signs and cross the courtyard, noticing the two fine wellheads (the courtyard once functioned as a cistern), and stand at the foot of the grand staircase topped by two statues.*

Stairway of Giants (Scala dei Giganti)

Imagine yourself as a foreign dignitary on business to meet the doge. In the courtyard, you look up a grand staircase topped with

two nearly nude statues of, I think, Moses and Paul Newman (more likely, Neptune and Mars, representing Venice's prowess at sea and at war). The doge and his aides would be waiting for you at the top, between the two statues and beneath the winged lion. No matter who you were—king, pope, or emperor—you'd have to hoof it up. The powerful doge would descend the stairs for no one.

Many doges were crowned here, between the two statues. The doge was something like an elected king—which makes sense only in the dictatorial republic that was Venice. Technically, he was just a noble selected by other nobles to carry out their laws and decisions. Many doges tried to extend their powers and rule more as divine-right kings. Many others just put on their funny hats and accepted their role as figureheads and ceremonial ribbon-cutters. Because doges served a lifelong term, most were geezers, elected in their 70s and committed to preserving Venetian traditions.

The palace is attached to the basilica, symbolically welding church and state. Both buildings have ugly brick behind a painted-lady veneer of marble. In this tour, we'll see the similarly harsh inner workings of an outwardly serene, polished republic.

The courtyard is a hodgepodge of architectural styles, as the palace was refurbished over the centuries. There are classical statues in Renaissance niches, shaded by Baroque awnings, topped by

Flamboyant Gothic spires, and crusted with the Byzantine onion domes of St. Mark's Basilica.

• *Cross back to near the entrance and follow the signs up the tourists' staircase to the first-floor balcony (loggia), where you can look back down on the courtyard. From this point on, it's hard to get lost. It's a one-way system, so just follow the arrows.*

Midway along the balcony, you'll find a face in the wall, the...

Mouth of Truth

This fierce-looking androgyne opens his/her mouth, ready to swallow a piece of paper, hungry for gossip. Letterboxes like this (some

with lions' heads) were scattered throughout the palace. Originally, anyone who had a complaint or suspicion about anyone else could accuse him anonymously *(denontie secrete)* by simply dropping a slip of paper in the mouth. This set the blades of justice turning inside the palace.

• *A few steps toward Paul Newman is the entrance to the...*

Golden Staircase (Scala d'Oro)

The palace was architectural propaganda, designed to impress visitors. This staircase with a 24-karat gilded ceiling was something for them to write home about. As you ascend the stairs, look back at the floor below and marvel at its 3-D pattern.

• *Start up the first few steps of the Golden Staircase. Midway up, at the first landing, turn right, which loops you through a dozen rooms (often closed). You then return to the Golden Staircase and climb up to the...*

Doge's Apartments
(Appartamento del Doge)

The dozen or so rooms on the first floor are where the doge actually lived. The blue-and-gold-hued Sala dei Scarlatti (Room 5) is typical of the palace's interior decoration: gold-coffered ceiling, big stone fireplace, silky walls with paintings, and a speckled floor. There's very little original furniture, as doges were expected to bring their own. Despite his high office, the doge had to obey several rules that bound him to the city. He couldn't leave the palace unescorted, he couldn't open official mail in private, and he and his family had to leave their own home and live in the Doge's Palace.

DOGE'S PALACE

Paintings by Titian, Veronese, and Tintoretto

Only the top Venetian painters decorated the Doge's Palace. It was once rich in Titians, but fires in the late 1500s destroyed nearly all the work by the greatest Venetian master. As the palace was hastily reconstructed, the empty spaces left by the Titians were quickly patched in with works by Veronese and Tintoretto.

Veronese used the best pigments available—made from minerals and precious stones —and his colors have survived vividly. These Veronese paintings are by the artist's hand and are fine examples of his genius. Tintoretto, on the other hand, didn't really have his heart in these commissions, and the pieces here were done by his workshop.

The paintings of the Doge's Palace are a study of long-ago Venice, with fine views of the old city and its inhabitants. The extravagant women's gowns in the paintings by Veronese show off a major local industry—textiles. While the paintings are not generally of masterpiece quality, they're historically interesting. They prove that in the old days, Venice had no pigeons.

The large Room 6, the Sala dello Scudo (Shield Hall), is full of maps and globes. The main map illustrates the reach of Venice's maritime realm, which stretched across most of the eastern Mediterranean. The Venetian Republic was a mighty trading empire, built not on vast land holdings but upon a network of ports and a mastery of the sea. With the maps in this room you can trace the eye-opening trip across Asia—from Italy to Greece to Palestine, Arabia, and "Irac"—of local boy Marco Polo (c. 1254-1325). Finally, he arrived at the other side of the world. This last map (at the far end of the room) is shown "upside-down," with south on top, giving a glimpse of the Venetian worldview circa 1550. It depicts China, Taiwan (Formosa), and Japan (Giapan), while America is a nearby island made up of California and lots of Terre Incognite with *antropofagi* (cannibals).

In Room 7, the Sala Grimani, are several paintings of the lion of St. Mark, including the famous one by Vittore Carpaccio of a smiling lion (on the long wall). The lion holds open a book with these words, *"Pax*

Tibi Marce..." ("Peace to you, Mark"), which, according to legend, were spoken by an angel welcoming St. Mark to Venice. In the background are the Doge's Palace and the Campanile.

Find Room 10, the Sala dei Filosofi (Philosophers' Hall), look for the first doorway on the right, pop up the humble stairway, and look back at a Titian quickie, painted in just three days. This fresco of St. Christopher carrying the Christ Child across the lagoon was made for a doge who believed that if you looked at St. Christopher, you wouldn't die that day.

• *Finish browsing the dozen or so rooms of the Doge's Apartments, and continue up the Golden Staircase to the third floor, which was the "public" part of the palace. The room right at the top of the stairs is the...*

Square Room (Atrio Quadrato)

The ceiling painting, *Justice Presenting the Sword and Scales to Doge Girolamo Priuli*, is by Jacopo Tintoretto. (Stand at the top of the painting for the full 3-D effect.) It's a late-Renaissance masterpiece. So what? As you'll soon see, this palace is wall-papered with Titians, Tintorettos, and Veroneses. Many have the same theme you see here: a doge, in his ermine cape, gold-brocaded robe, and funny one-horned hat with earflaps, kneeling in the presence of saints, gods, or mythological figures.

• *Enter the next room.*

Room of the Four Doors (Sala delle Quattro Porte)

This was the central clearinghouse for all the goings-on in the palace. Visitors presented themselves here and were directed to their destination—the courts, councils, or the doge himself.

The room was designed by Andrea Palladio, the architect who did the impressive Church of San Giorgio Maggiore, across the Grand Canal from St. Mark's Square. On the intricate stucco ceiling, notice the feet of the women dangling down below the edge (above the windows), extending the illusion.

On the wall to the right of the door you entered from is a painting by (ho-hum) Titian, showing a **doge kneeling** with great piety before a woman embodying Faith holding the Cross of Jesus. Notice old Venice in the misty distance under the cross. This is one of many paintings you'll see of doges in uncharacteristically humble poses—paid for, of course, by the doges themselves.

G. B. Tiepolo's well-known *Venice Receiving Neptune* is now

Executive & Legislative Rooms

ROOM 11 — COLLEGIO HALL
ROOM 12 — SENATE HALL

Courtyard

6
9
7
8
5 4
ROOM OF THE 4 DOORS
2   3

Not to Scale

SQUARE ROOM
1

GOLDEN STAIRCASE
HALL OF THE COUNCIL OF 10

1 TINTORETTO – Justice Presenting the Sword and Scales
2 TITIAN – Doge Kneeling
3 TIEPOLO – Venice Receiving Neptune
4 VERONESE – The Rape of Europa
5 TINTORETTO – Bacchus and Ariadne
6 VERONESE – Discussion
7 VERONESE – Mars and Neptune with Campanile and Lion
8 TINTORETTO – Triumph of Venice
9 Clocks

displayed on an easel, but it was originally hung on the wall above the windows where they've put a copy (you'll get a closer look at the painting when you loop back through this room in a few minutes). The painting shows Venice as a woman—Venice is always a woman to artists—reclining in luxury, dressed in the ermine cape and pearl necklace of a doge's wife (dogaressa). Crude Neptune, enthralled by the First Lady's beauty, arrives bearing a seashell bulging with gold ducats. A bored Venice points and says, "Put it over there with the other stuff."

• *Enter the small room with the big fireplace and several paintings.*

Ante-Collegio Hall (Sala dell'Anticollegio)

If accepted for a visit, you would wait here before you entered, combing your hair, adjusting your robe, popping a breath mint, and

preparing the gifts you'd brought. While you cooled your heels and warmed your hands at the elaborate fireplace, you might look at some of the paintings—among the finest in the palace, worthy of any museum in the world.

The Rape of Europa (on the wall opposite the fireplace), by Paolo Veronese, most likely shocked many small-town visitors with its risqué subject matter. Here

Zeus, the king of the Greek gods, appears in the form of a bull with a foot fetish, seducing a beautiful earthling, while cupids spin playfully overhead. The Venetian Renaissance looked back to pagan Greek and Roman art, a big change from the saints and crucifixions of the Middle Ages. This painting doesn't portray the abduction in a medieval condemnation of sex and violence, but rather as a celebration in cheery pastel colors of the earthy, optimistic spirit of the Renaissance.

Tintoretto's **Bacchus and Ariadne** (to the right of the fireplace) is another colorful display of Venice's sensual tastes. The God of Wine seeks a threesome, offering a ring to the mortal Ariadne, who's being crowned with stars by Venus, who turns slowly in zero gravity. The ring is the center of a spinning wheel of flesh, with the three arms like spokes.

But wait, the doge is ready for us. Let's go in.

• *Enter the next room and approach your imaginary doge.*

Collegio Hall (Sala del Collegio)

Flanked by his cabinet of six advisers—one for each Venetian neighborhood—the doge would sit on the wood-paneled platform at the far end to receive ambassadors, who laid their gifts at his feet and pleaded their countries' cases. All official ceremonies, such as the ratification of treaties, were held here.

At other times, it was the "Oval Office" where the doge and his cabinet (the executive branch) met privately to discuss proposals to give to the legislature, pull files from the cabinets (along the right wall) regarding business with Byzantium, or rehearse a meeting with the pope. The wooden benches around the sides (where they sat) are original. The clock on the wall is a backward-running 24-hour clock with Roman numerals and a sword for its single hand.

The **ceiling** is gilded, with paintings by Veronese. These are not frescoes (painting on wet plaster), like those in the Sistine Chapel, but actual canvases painted in Veronese's studio and then placed on the ceiling.

The T-shaped painting of the woman with the spider web (on the ceiling, opposite the big window) represents the Venetian symbol of *Discussion.* You can imagine the webs of truth and lies woven in this room by the doge's scheming advisers.

In *Mars and Neptune with Campanile and Lion* (the ceiling painting near the entrance), Veronese presents four symbols of the

Republic's strength—military, sea trade, city, and government (plus a cherub about to be circumcised by the Campanile).

You'll note that nearly every painting features a different doge, each identified by his oval family crest.

• *Enter the large Senate Hall.*

Senate Hall (Sala del Senato)

While the doge presided from the stage, senators mounted the podium (middle of the wall with windows) to address their 120 colleagues. The legislators, chaired by the doge, debated and passed laws in this room.

Venice prided itself on its self-rule (independent of popes, kings, and tyrants), with most power placed in the hands of these annually elected noble men. Which branch of government really ruled? All of them. It was an elaborate system of checks and balances to make sure no one rocked the gondola, no one got too powerful, and the ship of state sailed smoothly ahead.

Tintoretto's large *Triumph of Venice* on the ceiling (central painting, best viewed from the top) is an allegory of the city in all her glory. Lady Venice is up in heaven with the Greek gods, while barbaric lesser nations swirl up to give her gifts and tribute. Do you get the feeling the Venetian aristocracy was proud of its city?

On the wall are two large clocks, one of which has the signs of the zodiac and phases of the moon. And there's one final oddity in this room, in case you hadn't noticed it yet. In one of the wall paintings (above the entry door), there's actually a doge... not kneeling.

• *Exiting the Senate Hall, pass again through the Room of the Four Doors, then around the corner into a hall with a semicircular platform.*

Hall of the Council of Ten (Sala del Consiglio dei Dieci)

By the 1400s, Venice had a worldwide reputation for swift, harsh, and secret justice. The dreaded Council of Ten—10 judges, plus the doge and his six advisers—met here to dole out punishment to traitors, murderers, and "morals" violators.

Slowly, they developed into a CIA-type unit with their own force of police officers, guards, spies, informers, and even assassins. They had their own budget and were in practice accountable to no

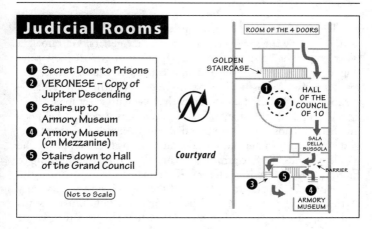

one, soon making them the de facto ruling body of the "Republic." It seemed no one was safe from the spying eye of the "Terrible Ten." You could be accused of certain crimes anonymously (by a letter dropped into a Mouth of Truth), swept off the streets, tried, judged, and thrown into the dark dungeons in the palace for the rest of your life without so much as a Miranda warning.

It was in this room that the Council decided who lived or died, and who was decapitated, tortured, or merely thrown in jail. The small, hard-to-find **door** leading off the platform (the fifth panel to the right of center) leads through secret passages to the prisons and torture chambers.

The large, central, oval ceiling painting by Veronese (a copy of the original stolen by Napoleon and still in the Louvre) shows *Jupiter Descending from Heaven to Strike Down the Vices*, redundantly informing the accused that justice in Venice was swift and harsh. To the left of that, Veronese painted Juno showering Lady Venice with coins, crowns, and peace.

Though the dreaded Council of Ten was eventually disbanded, today their descendants enforce the dress code at St. Mark's Basilica.
• *Pass through the next room, turn right, and head up the stairs to the Armory Museum.*

Armory Museum (L'Armeria)

The aesthetic of killing is beyond me, but I must admit I've never seen a better collection of halberds, falchions, ranseurs, targes, morions, and brigandines in my life. The weapons in these three rooms make you realize the important role the military played in keeping the East-West trade lines open.

DOGE'S PALACE

Room 1: In the glass case on the right, you'll see the suit of armor worn by the great Venetian mercenary general Gattamelata (far right, on horseback), as well as "baby's first armor" (how soon they grow up!). A full suit of armor could weigh 66 pounds. Before gunpowder, crossbows (look up) were made still more lethal by turning a crank on the end to draw the bow with extra force.

Room 2: In the thick of battle, even horses needed helmets. The hefty broadswords were brandished two-handed by the strongest and bravest soldiers who waded into enemy lines. Opposite the window stands the fine armor of Henry IV, a 16th-century king of France. Behind him is a cell for VIP prisoners.

Room 3: At the far (left) end of the room is a very, very early (17th-century) attempt at a 20-barrel machine gun. On the walls and weapons, the "C-X" insignia means that this was the private stash of the "Council of Ten."

Room 4: In this room, rifles and pistols enter the picture. Don't miss the glass case in the corner, with a tiny crossbow, some torture devices (including an effective-looking thumbscrew), the wooden "devil's box" (a clever item that could fire in four directions at once), and a nasty, two-holed chastity belt. These disheartening "iron breeches" were worn by the devoted wife of the Lord of Padua. Out the windows are fine views of San Giorgio Maggiore. And the window around the corner, to the left, comes with fine views of the Riva.

• *Exit the Armory Museum (after enjoying a closer look at that early machine gun). Go downstairs, turn left, and traverse the long hall that's lined with wood-carved benches and has a wood-beam ceiling (you'll pass interesting exhibits branching off this hall). Now turn right and open your eyes as wide as you can to see the...*

Hall of the Grand Council (Sala del Maggiore Consiglio)

It took a room this size to contain the grandeur of the Most Serene Republic. This huge room (175 by 80 feet) could accommodate up to 2,600 people at one time. The engineering is remarkable. The ceiling is like the deck of a ship—its hull is the rooftop, creating a huge attic above that.

The doge presided from the raised **dais,** while the nobles—the backbone of the empire—filled the center and lined the long walls. Nobles were generally wealthy men over 25, but the title had less to do with money than with long bloodlines. In theory, the doge, the Senate, and the Council of Ten were all subordinate to the Grand Council of nobles who met here to elect them.

On the wall over the doge's throne is Tintoretto's monsterpiece, ***Paradise,*** the largest oil painting in the world. At 570 square

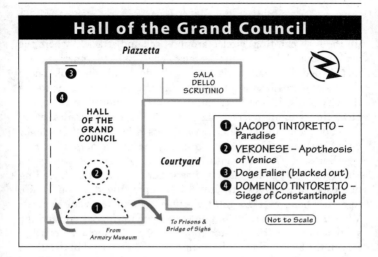

Hall of the Grand Council

Piazzetta

SALA DELLO SCRUTINIO

HALL OF THE GRAND COUNCIL

Courtyard

① JACOPO TINTORETTO – Paradise

② VERONESE – Apotheosis of Venice

③ Doge Falier (blacked out)

④ DOMENICO TINTORETTO – Siege of Constantinople

Not to Scale

To Prisons & Bridge of Sighs

From Armory Museum

feet, it could be sliced up to wallpaper an apartment with enough left over for placemats.

Christ and Mary are at the top of heaven, surrounded by 500

people. It's rush hour in heaven, and all the good Venetians made it. The painting leaves you feeling that you get to heaven not by being a good Christian, but by being a good Venetian. Tintoretto worked on this in the last years of his long life. On the day it was finished, his daughter died. He got his brush out again and painted her as saint number 501. She's dead center with the blue skirt, hands clasped, getting sucked up to heaven. (At least, that's what an Italian tour guide told me.)

Veronese's *Apotheosis of Venice* (on the ceiling at the Tintoretto end—view it from the top) is a typically unsubtle work showing Lady Venice being crowned a goddess by an angel.

Ringing the top of the hall are portraits, in chronological order, of the first 76 doges. The one at the far end that's blacked out (in the left corner) is the notorious **Doge Marin Falier,** who opposed the will of the Grand Council in 1355. He was tried for treason, beheaded, and airbrushed from history.

Along the entire wall to the right of *Paradise,* the *Siege of Constantinople* (by Tintoretto's son, Domenico) shows Venice's greatest military (if not moral) victory, the conquest of the fellow-Christian city of Constantinople during the Fourth Crusade (1204, see sidebar on page 92). The mighty walls of Constantinople repelled every attack for nearly a thousand years. But the sneaky Venetians (in the fifth painting) circled around back and attacked where the walls rose straight up from the water's edge. Skillful Venetian oarsmen cozied their galleys right up to the dock, allowing soldiers to scoot along crossbeams attached to the masts and on to the top of the city walls. In the foreground, an archer cranks up his crossbow. The gates are opened, the Byzantine emperor parades out to surrender, and tiny Doge Dandolo (dressed in gold with his fancy doge's hat) says, "Let's go in and steal some bronze horses."

But soon Venice would begin its long slide into historical oblivion. One by one, the Ottomans gobbled up Venice's trading outposts. In the West, the rest of Europe ganged up on Venice to reduce her power. By 1500, Portugal had broken Venice's East-West trade monopoly by finding a sea route to the East around the southern tip of Africa. To top it off, despite winning a famous victory in the bloody Battle of Lepanto in 1571 (depicted in paintings in the adjoining Sala dello Scrutinio), Venice's reputation as a naval power began to suffer; their ships could not compete with Spain's more modern, more effective armada. Over the centuries, Venice remained a glorious city, but not the world power she once was. Finally, in 1797, the French general Napoleon marched into town shouting, *"Liberté, égalité, fraternité."* The Most Serene Republic was finally conquered, and the last doge abdicated in the name of modern democracy.

Out the windows (if they're open) is a fine view of the domes of the basilica, the palace courtyard below, and Paul Newman.

The adjoining **Sala dello Scrutinio** features paintings bursting with action. This room overlooks the Piazzetta; from its balcony, a newly elected doge was presented to the people of Venice. A noble would announce, "Here is your doge, if it pleases you." That was fine, until one time when the people weren't pleased. From then on they just said, "Here is your doge."

• *Consider reading about the prisons here in the Grand Council Hall, where there are more benches and fewer rats.*

To reach the prisons, exit the Grand Hall by squeezing through the door to the left of Tintoretto's monsterpiece. Follow signs for Prigioni/ Ponte dei Sospiri, *passing through several rooms. In a room adjoining Room 31, you'll find a narrow staircase going down, following signs to the prisons. (Don't miss it, or you'll miss the prisons altogether and end up at the bookshop near the exit.) Then cross the covered Bridge of Sighs over the canal to the prisons. Start your visit in the cells to your left.*

Prisons

The palace had its own dungeons. In the privacy of his own home, a doge could oversee the sentencing, torturing, and jailing of politi-

cal opponents. The most notorious cells were "the wells" in the basement, so-called because they were deep, wet, and cramped.

By the 1500s, the wells were full of po-litical prisoners. New prisons were built across the canal (to the east of the palace) and con-nected with a covered bridge.

Medieval justice was harsh. The cells con-sisted of cold stone with heavily barred win-dows, a wooden plank for a bed, a shelf, and

a bucket. (My question: What did they put on the shelf?) You can feel the cold and damp.

Circle the cells. Notice the carvings made by prisoners—from olden days up until 1930—on some of the stone windowsills of the cells, especially in the far corner of the building.

While a small taste of the prisons is enough for most visitors, if you have more time and interest, explore the cellblocks one and two floors down (following signs for *Complete Tour*). Or stay on this floor, where there's a room displaying ceramic shards found in archaeological digs. Adjoining that are more cells, including one (the farthest) where you can see the bored prisoners' compelling and sometimes artistic graffiti. The singing gondoliers outside are a reminder of how tantalizingly close these pitiful prisoners were to one of the world's finest cities.

• *Wherever you roam, you'll end up where you entered. Now recross the...*

Bridge of Sighs

According to romantic leg-end, criminals were tried and sentenced in the palace, then marched across the canal here to the dark prisons. On this bridge, they got one last look at Venice. They gazed out at the sky, the water, and the beautiful build-ings.

• *As you cross the Bridge of Sighs, pause to look through the marble-trellised windows at all the tourists* and the heavenly Church of San Giorgio Maggiore. Heave one last sigh and leave the palace.

CORRER
MUSEUM TOUR

Museo Correr

A doge's hat, an empress's bathroom, gleaming statues by Canova, and paintings by the illustrious Bellini family—for some people, that's a major museum; for others, it's a musty bore. But the Correr Museum has one more thing to offer, and that's a quiet refuge—an elegant Neoclassical space—in which to rise above St. Mark's Square when the piazza is too hot, too rainy, or too overrun with tourists. Besides, the museum is included if you've bought a ticket to the Doge's Palace...whether you want it or not. Those who enter are rewarded with an easy-to-manage overview of Venice's art and history.

Orientation

Cost: €19 combo-ticket also includes the Doge's Palace, free and crowded on the first Sun of the month.

Tickets to tour the Clock Tower (€12, requires reservation, see page 33) include admission to the Correr but not the Doge's Palace.

Hours: Daily April-Oct 10:00-19:00, Nov-March until 17:00, last entry one hour before closing.

Getting There: The entrance is on St. Mark's Square in Napoleon's wing—the building at the far end of the square, opposite the basilica. Climb the staircase to the first-floor ticket office and bookstore.

Information: English descriptions are provided throughout. Tel. 041-240-5211, http://correr.visitmuve.it.

Renovation: Like many museums in Venice, the Correr is often under renovation, occasionally causing room numbers and locations of pieces to change.

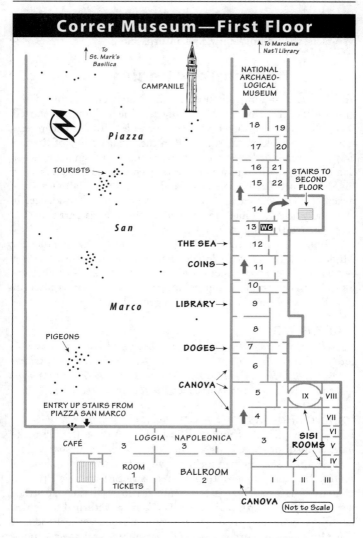

Correr Museum—First Floor

To St. Mark's Basilica

To Marciana Nat'l Library

CAMPANILE

NATIONAL ARCHAEO-LOGICAL MUSEUM

Piazza

TOURISTS →

18 | 19

17 | 20

16 | 21

15 | 22

STAIRS TO SECOND FLOOR

14

San

13 **WC**

THE SEA → 12

COINS → 11

10

Marco

LIBRARY → 9

8

DOGES → 7

6

PIGEONS

CANOVA 5

IX | VIII

VII

VI

4

3

SISI ROOMS

V

IV

ENTRY UP STAIRS FROM PIAZZA SAN MARCO

CAFÉ

LOGGIA 3

NAPOLEONICA 3

3

ROOM 1

TICKETS

BALLROOM 2

I | II | III

CANOVA (Not to Scale)

Length of This Tour: Allow one hour. With less time, stick to the first floor and skip the second-floor paintings.

Baggage Check: Free and mandatory for bags bigger than a large purse.

Photography: Photos are allowed without flash.

Cuisine Art: The classy museum café offers a peaceful retreat. It has good sandwiches, pastas, and salads, and a few tables have outstanding views of St. Mark's Square (same hours as museum, no museum entry required).

Starring: Canova statues, a royal suite, Venetian historical artifacts, the Bellini family, and a Carpaccio.

The Tour Begins

The Correr Museum is housed in the Napoleonic Wing of the grand edifice that rings St. Mark's Square. The building was started in 1809 by Napoleon, who wanted a private ballroom and reception hall overlooking the square. (On the facade, a line of Roman emperors reminded everyone of his authority.) Napoleon never danced in the ballroom, which was only completed five years after his Waterloo. After Napoleon fell and the Austrian Habsburgs annexed Venice, this palatial wing was their imperial residence. It eventually became a museum, named for the Venetian art collector who donated the collection to the city.

This tour covers the two long, skinny floors that parallel St. Mark's Square: The first floor contains imperial rooms, Canova statues, and Venetian history; the second floor displays a chronological overview of Venetian paintings. The collection is often in flux. Be flexible and enjoy things in a general way.

FIRST FLOOR

• *You'll enter the museum either through the grand ballroom (Room 2, used for gala events) or the skinny Loggia Napoleonica (Room 3, with a view over St. Mark's Square). Whichever entrance you're sent through, make your way to a group of nine rooms in the corner, the...*

Imperial Rooms for Empress Sisi

In 1856, 18-year-old Empress Elizabeth of Austria (fondly nicknamed "Sisi," or "Sissi") arrived in Venice with her husband Emperor Franz Josef. The two spent a few weeks in these chandeliered rooms. The famously beautiful-yet-reclusive Sisi was the Princess Diana of the age. Though the Venetians loathed their Austrian overlords, Sisi's charm won many over, and she returned to Venice later for a longer stay. Years later, estranged from her husband and court life, she was murdered by an Italian anarchist while vacationing in Switzerland.

The nine opulent rooms reflect styles from several periods. The dining room (Room I)—with its squiggly-lined "grotesque" walls and ceiling, and motifs of Winged Victories and tritons—traces its roots to the Neoclassical style Napoleon originally had in mind. The red-walled throne room (II) is where the Habsburg Emperor Ferdinand arrived in 1838 to consolidate his Italian holdings.

Next come rooms decorated especially for Sisi: where she received visitors (Room III, with color-coordinated walls, drapes, and furniture), her bathroom (IV), and study (V, with a Murano chandelier). In her dressing room (Room VI), admire the special touches the Venetians added to make Sisi feel at home. On the cornice, eagles bear the Austrian coat of arms. Her favorite flower, the lily, was woven into the various decorations on the walls and ceiling. And in the center of the ceiling, the painting of the Goddess of Art is actually Sisi.

In Sisi's bedroom (VII), the fine "marble" on the lower walls is actually a distinctive Venetian specialty—cheap plaster made to simulate precious marble, called marmorino. The room's 1810 ceiling (geometric panels and classical frescoes of Venus, Cupid, and Jupiter) would have reminded Sisi of the man who married her husband's aunt—Napoleon. The bed (not Sisi's) belonged to Napoleon's stepson, who, when Napoleon conquered Italy, was declared "Prince of Venice." Finally, pass through Sisi's private passageway (VIII, with a view across the Giardinetti Reali), to the Oval Room (IX), where Sisi and close friends enjoyed their private meals together.

Canova Rooms

Rooms 2-6 are dedicated to the famed Neoclassical sculptor Antonio Canova (1757-1822). Son of a Venetian stonemason, Canova grew up with a chisel in his hand in a studio along the Grand Canal, precociously mastering the sentimental, elegant Rococo style of the late 1700s. At 23, he went to Rome and beyond, studying ancient statues at the recently discovered ruins of Pompeii. These archaeological finds inspired a revival of classical style. Canova's pure, understated "neo"-classical style soon became the rage all over Europe.

Called to Paris, Canova became Napoleon's court sculptor and carved perhaps his best-known work: Napoleon's sister as a semi-nude Venus, reclining on a couch (now in the Borghese Gallery in Rome). Canova combined Rococo sentiment with the cool, minimal lines of classicism.

Among a scattering of his white statues are reliefs on walls, artifacts in cases, and his death mask. Look for these Canova works:

Canova, *Daedalus and Icarus (Dedalo e Icaro)*, 1778-1779

Serious Daedalus straps wax-and-feather wings, which he's just crafted, onto his son's shoulders. The boy is thrilled with the new toy, not knowing what we know—that the wax in the wings will soon melt in the sun and plunge him to his death. Daedalus' middle-aged, slightly saggy skin contrasts with Icarus' supple form. Canova displays the tools of his family's stonemason trade on the base.

Canova was only 20 when Venice's procurator commissioned this work from the hometown prodigy. It was so realistic that it caused a stir—skeptics accused Canova of not really sculpting it, but making it from plaster casts of live humans.

Canova, *Paris (Paride)*, 1807

The guy with black measles is not a marble statue of Paris; it's a plaster of Paris, a life-size model that Canova used in carving the real one in stone. The dots are sculptor's "points," which tell the sculptor how far into the block he should chisel to establish the figure's rough outline.

Canova, *Orpheus and Eurydice (Orfeo e Euridice)*, 1776

Orpheus is leading his beloved back from hell when she is tugged from behind by the cloudy darkness. She calls for help. Orpheus looks back and smacks his forehead in horror...but he can do noth-

ing to help, and he has to hurry on.

In this youthful work, Canova already shows elements of his later style: high-polished, slender, beautiful figures; an ensemble arrangement, with more than one figure; open space between the figures that's almost as compelling as the figures themselves; and a statue group that's interesting from many angles.

Carved by a teenage Canova, this piece captures the Rococo spirit of Venice in the late 1700s—it's beautiful, but tinged with bittersweet loss. Even Canova's later works—which were more sober, minimalist, and emotionally restrained—retained the grace and romantic sentiment of the last days of the Venetian Republic.

Other Canovas

The other large statues in the Canova rooms are either lesser works or more plaster studies for works later executed in marble. You'll also see small clay models in which Canova worked out ideas before chiseling into an expensive block of marble.

• *Now, enter the world of Venice's doges. The displays in Rooms 7-10 can change often. Browse the exhibits, but also appreciate the fact that these rooms were once government offices.*

Rooms 7-10: Government Offices

Some of the rich furnishings in these rooms are reminders that this wing once housed the administrative offices of a wealthy, so-phisticated, trade-oriented republic. You'll see pictures of doge processions (often in Room 7); rare books in walnut bookcases and a Murano chandelier under a wood-beamed ceiling (Room 8); and portraits of political bigwigs.

Ducal Processions in St. Mark's Square (a woodcut by Matteo Pagan, and a painting by Cesare Vecellio)

The woodcut shows the doge and his court parading around St. Mark's Square in the kind of traditional festivities that Venetians enjoy even today. At the head of the parade (to the right) come the flag bearers and the trumpet players sounding the fanfare. Next are the bigwigs, the archbishop, the bearer of the doge cap, the doge's chair, and finally *Il Serenissimo* himself, under an umbrella. The ladies look on from the windows above.

Some doges were imposing dictators, but in general their power was severely restricted by the Venetian constitution and

powerful senators. Many doges were simply ceremonial figure-heads, expected to show up in their funny hats for ribbon-cut-ting ceremonies and state funer-als. Doges even needed permis-sion to leave the city.

In the painting, locate the very same windows of the room you're standing in (at far right of the painting). The square looks much like it does today.

• *Move to Room 11 to view Venetian coins. The collection runs chrono-logically, clockwise around the room.*

Room 11: Coins and the Treasury

The Venetian ducat weighed only a bit more than a US penny, but was mostly gold (by decree, 99 percent pure gold, weighing 3.5 grams). First minted around 1280 (find Giovanni Dandolo's *zec-chino*, or "sequin," in the first glass case to the right of the door that leads into the next room), it became the strongest currency in all Europe for nearly 700 years, eventually replacing the Florentine florin. In Renaissance times, 100 ducats would be an excellent sal-ary for a year, with a single ducat worth about $1,000. The most common design shows Christ on the "heads" side, standing in an oval of stars. "Tails" features the current doge kneeling before St. Mark and the inscription "sacred money of Venice" *(SM Veneti)*.

Hanging above the newest coins, find **Tintoretto's painting** of three red-robed treasury officials who handled ducats in these offices (*St. Justina and the Treasurers*, 1580). The richness of their fur-lined robes suggests the almost religious devotion that officials were expected to have as caretakers of the "sacred money" of Venice.

Room 12: Venice and the Sea

Venice's wealth came from its sea trade. Raw materials from Europe were exchanged for luxury goods from eastern lands controlled by Muslim Ottomans and Byzantine Christians.

Models of Galleys *(Modello di Galera)*

These fast oar- and wind-powered warships rode shotgun for Venice's commercial fleets plying the Mediterranean. With up to 150 men (four per oar, some prisoners, most proud professionals) and three horizontal sails, they could cruise from Venice to Constantinople in about a month. In battle, they specialized in turning on a dime to aim cannons, or in quickly building up speed to ram other ships with their formidable prows. Also displayed are large lanterns from a galley's stern.

• *Find two similar paintings depicting...*

The Battle of Lepanto
(Battaglia di Lepanto), c. 1571

The two paintings (flanking the door behind the galleys, by unknown Venetian artists) capture the confusion of a famous battle fought off the coast of Greece in 1571 between Muslim Ottomans and a coalition of Christians. This battle ended Ottoman dominance at sea. Sort it out by their flags. The turbaned Ottomans fought under the crescent moon. On the Christian side, Venetians had the winged lion, the pope's troops flew the cross, and Spain was marked with the Habsburg eagle.

The fighting was fierce and hand-to-hand as the combatants boarded each other's ships and cannons blasted away point-blank. Miguel de Cervantes fought in this battle; he lost his hand and had to pen *Don Quixote* one-handed.

The Christians won, sinking 113 enemy ships and killing up to 30,000. It was a major psychological victory, as it was a turning point in the Ottoman threat to Europe.

But for Venice, it marked the end of an era. The city lost 4,000 men and many ships, and never fully recovered its trading empire in Ottoman lands. Moreover, Spain's cannon-laden sailing ships proved to be masters of the waves, making Spain the next true naval power. Venice's shallow-hulled galleys, so swift in the placid Mediterranean, were no match on the high seas.

Room 13: The Arsenale

The Arsenale shipbuilding center, located near the tail of Venice, was a rectangular, artificial harbor surrounded by workshops

 where ships could be mass-produced as though on a modern assembly line (but it was the workers who moved). If needed, they could crank out a galley a day. Look for various sketches and paintings of the Arsenale, including a 17th-century pen-and-ink plan *(Pianta dell'Arsenale)* by Antonio di Natale showing a bird's-eye view. The Arsenale's entrance (lower left of Natale's painting) is still guarded today by the two lions.

• *From here wander through rooms (14 through 18) designed for showing off. They lead to two sections technically considered separate museums but included as if part of the Correr.*

National Archaeological Museum and Marciana National Library

I'd walk straight through the archaeological museum, passing through six rooms of ancient statues (mostly copies that aren't that ancient) before reaching the sumptuous library hall. This is a ceremonial space (imagine this as a reading room); the books are in another part of the building. In Renaissance times, Venice was a major center of printing and secular knowledge, and you'll see and manuscripts on display.

On the ceiling are tondi (round) paintings of virtues and allegories of the liberal arts, such as mathematics, geometry, and music. The three tondi immediately above where you enter are by Paolo Veronese. The walls are richly decorated with portraits of renowned scholars and ancient philosophers who twist and turn in their niches in classical Baroque style.

The smaller room beyond the large hall was a high school for Venice's noble children. It features Roman copies of Greek statuary and a trompe l'oeil ceiling that tries to make the wood-beam ceiling appear even higher. The painting in the center of the ceiling by Titian shows Lady Wisdom seated in the clouds reading a book and a scroll. Check out the antique globes and a huge, preColumbian map of the world.

• *That's it for the first floor. To get to the upper floor, backtrack to Room 14 (WCs nearby) and climb the stairs, following signs to* La Quadreria—Picture Gallery. *Enter Room 25.*

SECOND FLOOR
Rooms 25-26: Venetian Painting

The painting highlights (the Bellinis) are located at the far end of this wing, and you have permission to hurry there. But along the way, trace the development of Venetian painting from golden Byzantine icons to Florentine-inspired 3-D to the natural beauty of Bellini and Carpaccio.

Correr Museum— Second Floor

Paolo Veneziano, *Six Saints (Sei Santi)*, 1340s

Gold-backed saints combine traits from Venice's two stylistic sources:

Byzantine (serene, elongated, somber, and iconic, with gold background, like the mosaics in St. Mark's) and the Gothic of mainland Europe (curvy, expressive bodies posed at a three-quarter angle, colorful robes, and individualized faces).

Lorenzo Veneziano, *Figures and Episodes of Saints (Figure e Storie di Santi)*, second half of 14th century

Influence from the mainland puts icons in motion, adding drama

to the telling of the lives of the saints (here, in the small scenes above the three saints). St. Nicholas grabs the executioner's sword and lifts him right off the ground before he even knows what's happening.

CORRER

Room 27: Flamboyant Gothic

Architectural fragments of Gothic buildings remind us that Venice's distinctive architecture is Italian Gothic, filtered through Eastern exoticism. You'll see examples, in both paint and stone, of pointed arches decorated with the flame-like curlicues that gave the Flamboyant Gothic style its name.

Room 29: International Gothic
Master of the Jarves Cassoni, *Story of Alatiel (Storie di Alatiel)*, first half of 15th century

As humanism spread, so did art that was not exclusively religious. Find the two wide panels at the far end of the room. These scenes, painted on the panels of a chest, depict a story from Boccaccio's bawdy *Decameron*. Done in the elegant, detailed naturalism of the International Gothic style, the painting emphasizes decorative curves—curvy filigree patterns in clothes, curvy boats, curvy sails, curvy waves, curvy horses' rumps—all enjoyed as a pleasing pattern.

Room 31: Ferrarese Painters
Baldassare Estense, *Portrait of a Young Man (Ritratto di Gentiluomo)*, c. 1475

The young man in red is not a saint, king, or pope, but an ordinary citizen painted, literally, wart and all. On the window ledge is a strongly foreshortened book. And behind the young man, the curtain opens to reveal a new world—a spacious 3-D vista courtesy of the Tuscan Renaissance.

Room 33: Flemish Artists
Pieter Brueghel II, *Adoration of the Magi (Adorazione dei Magi)*, 1617-1633

The detailed, everyday landscapes of Northern masters strongly influenced Venetian artists. Lost in this snowy scene of the secular working world is Baby Jesus in a stable (lower left), worshipped by the Magi. Venetians learned that landscape creates its own mood, and humans don't have to be the center of every painting.

Room 34
Antonello da Messina, Pietà (La Pietà), c. 1475

The Sicilian painter Messina wowed Venice with this work when he visited in 1475, bringing a Renaissance style and Flemish painting techniques. After a thousand years of standing rigidly on medieval crucifixes, the body of Christ finally softens into a natural human posture. The scene is set in a realistic, distant landscape. Remember this work, as I'll refer to it later.

Room 36: The Bellini Family (I Bellini)
One family single-handedly brought Venetian painting into the Renaissance—the Bellinis.

Jacopo Bellini, Crucifixion (La Crocifissione), c. 1450

Father Jacopo (c. 1400-1470) had studied in Florence when Donatello and Brunelleschi were pioneering 3-D naturalism.

Daughter Nicolosia (not a painter) married the painter Mantegna, whose precise lines and statuesque figures influenced his brothers-in-law.

Gentile Bellini, Portrait of Doge Mocenigo (Ritratto del Doge Mocenigo), c. 1478-1485

Elder son Gentile (c. 1429-1507) took over the family business and established a reputation for documenting Venice's rulers and official ceremonies. His straightforward style and attention to detail capture the ordinary essence of this doge.

Giovanni Bellini, Crucifixion (La Crocifissione), c. 1453-1455

Younger son Giovanni (c. 1430-1516) became the most famous Bellini, the man who pioneered new techniques and subject matter,

trained Titian and Giorgione, and almost single-handedly invented the Venetian High Renaissance.

Compare this early *Crucifixion* (young Giovanni's earliest doc-
umented work) with his father's version. Young Giovanni weeds
out all the crowded, medieval mourners, leaving only Mary and
John. Behind, he paints a spacious (Mantegnesque) landscape,
with a lake and mountains in the distance. Our eyes follow the
winding road from Christ to the airy horizon, ascending like a soul
to heaven.

Giovanni Bellini, *The Dead Christ Supported by Two Angels (Cristo Morto Sorretto da Due Angeli)*, 1453-1455

In another early work, Giovanni explores human
anatomy, with exaggerated veins, a heaving dia-
phragm, and even a hint of pubic hair. Mentally
compare this stiff, static work with Antonello
da Messina's far more natural *Pietà*, done 20
years later, to see how far Giovanni still had to
go. In fact, Giovanni was greatly influenced by
Messina, appreciating the full potential of the
new invention of oil-based paint. Armed with
this more transparent paint, he could add subtler shades of color and rely less on the sharply
outlined forms we see here.

Room 38
Vittore Carpaccio, *Two Venetian Gentlewomen (Due Dame Veneziane)*, c. 1490

Two well-dressed Venetians look totally bored, despite being surrounded by a wealth of exotic pets and amusements. One lady

absentmindedly plays with a dog, while
the other stares into space. Romantics
imagined them to be kept ladies awaiting lovers, but the recent discovery of the
once-missing companion painting tells
us they're waiting for their menfolk to
return from hunting. If you like Carpaccio, the Scuola Dalmata di San Giorgio
(between St. Mark's Square and Arsenale) has the world's best collection; see
page 51.

The colorful details and love of lux-
ury are elements that would dominate the Venetian High Renaissance. Fascinating stuff, but my eyes—like theirs—are starting to
glaze...

ACCADEMIA TOUR

Galleria dell'Accademia

The Accademia (ack-ah-DAY-mee-ah) is the greatest museum anywhere for Venetian Renaissance art and a good overview of painters whose works you'll see all over town. Venetian art is underrated and, I think, misunderstood. It's nowhere near as famous today as the work of the florescent Florentines, but—with historical slices of Venice, ravishing nudes, and very human Madonnas—it's livelier, more colorful, and simply more fun.

Orientation

Cost: €15, sometimes more during special exhibitions; free and crowded the first Sun of the month; passes that cover Venice's city-run museums are not valid here.

Hours: Mon 8:15-14:00, Tue-Sun 8:15-19:15, last entry one hour before closing.

Avoiding Lines: Just 360 people are allowed into the gallery at one time, so you may have to wait. It's most crowded on Tue mornings and whenever it rains; it's least crowded Wed, Thu, and Sun mornings (before 10:00) and late afternoons (after 17:00). While it's possible to book tickets in advance (€1.50/ticket surcharge; either book online at www.gallerieaccademia.org or call 041-520-0345), it's generally not necessary if you avoid the busiest times.

Getting There: The museum faces the Grand Canal, just over the Accademia Bridge (vaporetto stop: Accademia). It's a 15-minute walk from St. Mark's Square—just follow the signs to *Accademia*.

Information: Some of the Accademia's rooms have information in English. The dull audioguide costs €6, and the book-

shop sells guidebooks for €14. Tel. 041-522-2247, www.
gallerieaccademia.org.

Renovation: This museum seems to be in a constant state of disarray. A major expansion and renovation has been dragging on for years. Paintings come and go, and the actual locations of the pieces are hard to pin down. Still, the museum contains sumptuous art—the best in Venice. Be flexible: You'll probably just end up wandering around and matching descriptions to blockbuster paintings when you find them. If you don't find a particular piece, check Room 23, which seems to be their catchall holding pen for displaced art.

Length of This Tour: Allow one hour.

Baggage Check: You must use a pay locker for large bags.

Photography: Allowed without flash.

Cuisine Art: For forgettable food at inflated prices but priceless Grand Canal views, **Bar Foscarini** is right next door (at the base of the Accademia Bridge); for a less expensive, far more characteristic Venetian experience, walk less than five minutes to the delightful **Enoteca Cantine del Vino Già Schiavi** *cicchetti* bar (both described on page 273, along with other options nearby). A cheap café is at the opposite end of the embankment from Bar Foscarini, and a handful of cafés line Calle Nuova Sant'Agnese, which connects this area to the Peggy Guggenheim Collection.

Nearby: While you're in the Accademia neighborhood, consider visiting the Ca' Rezzonico, Peggy Guggenheim Collection, historic La Salute Church, and Punta della Dogana contemporary art museum (see page 45).

Starring: Titian, Veronese, Giorgione, Bellini, and Tintoretto.

The Tour Begins

VENICE—SWIMMING IN LUXURY

The Venetian love of luxury shines through in Venetian painting. We'll see grand canvases of colorful, spacious settings peopled with happy locals in extravagant clothes having a great time. The museum proceeds chronologically from the Middle Ages to the 1700s. But before we start at the medieval beginning, let's sneak a peek at a work by the greatest Venetian Renaissance master, Titian.

• *Buy your ticket, check your bag, and head upstairs to a large hall filled with gold-leaf altarpieces. At the top of the stairs, turn left and enter the small Room 24.*

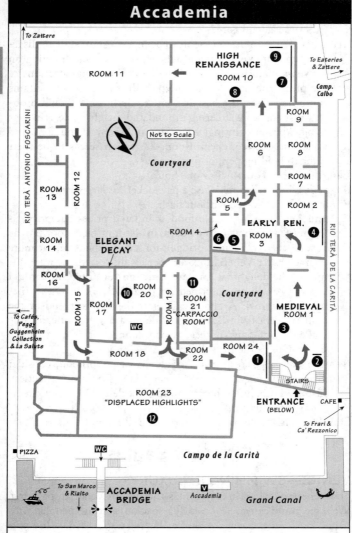

Accademia

To Zattere

HIGH RENAISSANCE

ROOM 11

ROOM 10

To Eateries & Zattere

Camp. Calbo

❾
❼
❽

ROOM 9

ROOM 12

ROOM 13

Courtyard

Not to Scale

RIO TERÀ ANTONIO FOSCARINI

ROOM 6

ROOM 8

ROOM 7

ROOM 5

ROOM 2

ROOM 14

ELEGANT DECAY

ROOM 4

EARLY REN.

ROOM 3

❻
❺
❹

RIO TERÀ DE LA CARITÀ

ROOM 16

ROOM 15

To Cafés, Peggy Guggenheim Collection & La Salute

❿

ROOM 20

ROOM 19

⓫

ROOM 21 "CARPACCIO ROOM"

Courtyard

MEDIEVAL
ROOM 1

ROOM 17

WC

❸

ROOM 18

ROOM 22

ROOM 24

❷

❶

STAIRS

ROOM 23 "DISPLAYED HIGHLIGHTS"

⓬

ENTRANCE (BELOW)

CAFE

To Frari & Ca' Rezzonico

PIZZA

WC

Campo de la Carità

To San Marco & Rialto

ACCADEMIA BRIDGE

Accademia

Grand Canal

❶ TITIAN – Presentation of the Virgin

❷ VENEZIANO – Madonna and Child with Two Donors

❸ JACOBELLO – Coronation of the Virgin in Paradise

❹ GIOVANNI BELLINI – Enthroned Madonna with Child

❺ MANTEGNA – St. George

❻ GIO. BELLINI – Madonna and Child between St. Catherine and Mary Magdalene

❼ VERONESE – Feast in the House of Levi

❽ TITIAN – Pietà

❾ TINTORETTO – The Removal of St. Mark's Body

❿ GENTILE BELLINI – Procession in St. Mark's Square

⓫ CARPACCIO – The Legend of Saint Ursula

⓬ GIORGIONE – The Tempest

Titian, *Presentation of the Virgin (Presentazione della Vergine)*, 1534-1538

A colorful crowd gathers at the foot of a stone staircase. A dog eats a bagel, a mother handles a squirming baby, an old lady sells eggs, and onlookers lean out the windows. Suddenly the crowd turns and points at something. Your eye follows up the stairs to a larger-than-life high priest in a jeweled robe.

But wait! What's that along the way? In a pale blue dress that sets her apart from all the other colored robes, dwarfed by the enormous staircase and columns, the tiny, shiny figure of the child Mary almost floats up to the astonished priest. She's unnaturally small, easily overlooked at first glance. When we finally notice her, we realize all the more how delicate she is amid the bustling crowd, hard stone, and epic grandeur. Venetians love this painting and call it, appropriately enough, the "Little Mary."

The painting is a parade of colors. Titian leads your eyes from the massive buildings to the deep blue sky and mountains in the background to the bright red robe of the man in the crowd to glowing Little Mary. Titian painted the work especially for this room, fitting it neatly around the door on the right. The door on the left was added later, cutting into Titian's masterpiece.

This work is typical of Venetian Renaissance art. Here and throughout this museum, you will find: 1) bright, rich color; 2) big canvases; 3) Renaissance architectural backgrounds; 4) slice-of-life scenes of Venice; and 5) 3-D realism. It's a religious scene, yes, but it's really just an excuse to display secular splendor—Renaissance architecture, colorful robes, and human details.

Now that we've gotten a taste of Renaissance Venice at its peak, let's backtrack and see art by some of Titian's predecessors.

• *Return to Room 1, stopping at a painting (near the stairs) of Mary and Baby Jesus.*

ACCADEMIA

MEDIEVAL ART
Paolo Veneziano, *Madonna and Child with Two Donors (Madonna col Bambino e Due Committenti)*, c. 1325

Mary sits in heaven. The child Jesus is a baby in a bubble, a symbol of his "aura" of holiness.

Notice how two-dimensional and unrealistic this painting is. The sizes of the figures reflect their religious importance—Mary is huge, being the mother of Christ as well as the "Holy Mother Church." Jesus is next in size, then the two angels who crown Mary. Finally, in the corner, are two mere mortals kneeling in devotion. The golden halos let us know who's holy and who's not. Medieval Venetian artists, with their close ties to the East, borrowed techniques such as gold-leafing, frontal poses, and "iconic" faces from the religious icons of Constantinople (modern-day Istanbul).

Most of the paintings in Room 1 are altarpieces, intended to sit in the center of a church for the faithful to meditate on during services. Many feature the Virgin Mary being crowned in triumph. Very impressive. But it took Renaissance artists to remove Mary from her golden never-never land, clothe her in human flesh, and bring her down to the real world we inhabit.

• *On the left side of the room, you'll find...*

Jacobello del Fiore, *Coronation of the Virgin in Paradise (Incoronazione della Vergine in Paradiso)*, 1438

This swarming beehive of saints and angels is an attempt to cram as much religious information as possible into one space. The architectural setting is a clumsy try at three-dimensionality (the railings of the wedding-cake structure are literally glued on). The color-coordinated saints are simply stacked one on top of the other, rather than receding into the distance as they would in real life.

• *Enter Room 2 at the far end of this hall.*

EARLY RENAISSANCE (1450-1500)
Only a few decades later, artists rediscovered the natural world and ways to capture it on canvas. With this Renaissance, or "rebirth," of the arts and attitudes of ancient Greece and Rome, painters took a

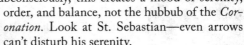

giant leap forward. They weeded out the jumble of symbols, fleshed out cardboard characters into real people, and placed them in spacious 3-D settings.

Giovanni Bellini, *Enthroned Madonna with Child,* a.k.a. *San Giobbe Altarpiece (Madonna in Trono col Bambino),* c. 1480

Mary and the Baby Jesus meet with saints beneath an arched half-dome, engaging in a sacred conversation *(sacra conversazione)*. A trio of musician angels jams at her feet. In its original church setting, the painting's pillars and arches matched the real ones around it, as though Bellini had blown a hole in the wall and built another chapel, allowing us mortals to mingle with the saints.

Giovanni Bellini (bell-EE-nee) takes only a few figures, places them in this spacious architectural setting, and balances them, half on one side of Mary and half on the other. Left to right, you'll find St. Francis (medieval founder of an order of friars), John the Baptist, Job, St. Dominic (founder of another order of monks), St. Sebastian, and St. Louis.

The painting has a series of descending arches. At the top is a Roman arch. Hanging below that is a triangular canopy. Then comes a pyramid-shaped "arch" formed by the figures themselves, with Mary's head at the peak, echoed below by the pose of the three musicians. Subconsciously, this creates a mood of serenity,

order, and balance, not the hubbub of the *Coronation.* Look at St. Sebastian—even arrows can't disturb his serenity.

In Bellini's long career, he painted many altarpieces in the *Sacra Conversazione* formula: The Virgin and Child surrounded by saints "conversing" informally about holy matters while listening to some tunes. The formula, developed in the 1430s and 1440s by Fra Angelico (1400-1455) and other Florentine artists, became a common Renaissance theme. Compare this painting with other *sacras* by Bellini in the Frari Church (see page 144) and the Church of San Zaccaria (see page 235).

• *Climb the small staircase and pass through Room 3 into the small Room 4.*

Andrea Mantegna, *St. George (San Giorgio),* c. 1460

This Christian dragon slayer is essentially a Greek nude sculpture with armor painted on. He rests his weight on one leg in the same asymmetrical pose *(contrapposto)* as a classical sculpture, Michelangelo's *David,* or an Italian guy on the street corner. The doorway he stands in resembles a niche designed for a classical statue.

Mantegna (mahn-TAYN-yah) was trained in the Tuscan tradition, in which painters were like sculptors, "carving" out figures (like this) with sharp outlines, filling them in with color, and setting them in distant backdrops like the winding road behind George. When Mantegna married Giovanni Bellini's sister, he brought Florentine realism and draftsmanship to his in-laws.

St. George radiates Renaissance optimism—he's alert but relaxed, at rest but ready to spring into action, humble but confident. With the broken lance in his hand and the dragon at his feet, George is the strong Renaissance Man slaying the medieval dragon of superstition and oppression.

• *Find three women and a baby on a black background.*

Giovanni Bellini, *Madonna and Child between St. Catherine and Mary Magdalene (Madonna col Bambino tra Sta. Caterina e Maria Maddalena),* c. 1490

In contrast to Mantegna's sharp-focus 3-D, this painting features three female heads on a flat plane with a black-velvet backdrop.

Their features are soft, hazy, and atmospheric, glowing out of the darkness as though lit by soft candlelight. It's not the sculptural line that's important here, but color—warm, golden, glowing flesh tones. The faces emerge from the canvas like cameos.

Bellini painted dozens of Madonna and Childs in his day. (Others are nearby.) This Virgin Mary is pretty, but she's upstaged by the sheer idealized beauty of Mary Magdalene (on the right). Mary Magdalene's hair is down, like the prostitute that legend says she was, yet she has a childlike face, thoughtful and repentant. This is the perfect image of the innocent woman who sinned by loving too much.

Bellini was the teacher of two more Venetian greats, Titian and Giorgione, schooling them in the new medium of oil painting. Mantegna painted *St. George* using tempera paint (pigments dissolved in egg yolk), while Bellini pioneered oils (pigments in vegetable oil)—a more versatile medium. Applying layer upon transparent layer, Bellini painted creamy complexions with soft outlines, bathed in an even light. His gift to the Venetian Renaissance was the "haze" he put over his scenes, giving them an idealized, glowing, serene, and much-copied atmosphere. (You can see more of Bellini's work at the Correr Museum, Frari Church, and the Church of San Zaccaria.)

• *Browse through several rooms, eventually climbing five steps into the large Room 10 to see three epic Venetian Renaissance canvases.*

VENETIAN HIGH RENAISSANCE (1500-1600)
Paolo Veronese, *Feast in the House of Levi* *(Convito in Casa di Levi),* 1573

Parrrrty!! Stand about 10 yards away from this enormous canvas, to where it just fills your field of vision...and hey, you're invited. Venice loves the good life, and the celebration is in full swing. You're in a huge room with a great view of Venice. Everyone's dressed to kill in colorful silk and velvet robes. Conversation roars, and the servants bring on the food and drink.

This captures the Venetian attitude (more love, less attitude) as well as the style of Venetian Renaissance painting. Remember: 1) bright colors, 2) big canvases, 3) Renaissance architectural settings, 4) scenes of Venetian life, and 5) 3-D realism. Painters had mastered realism and now gloried in it.

The *Feast in the House of Levi* is, believe it or not, a religious work painted for a convent. The original title was *The Last Supper*. In the center of all the wild goings-on, there's Jesus, flanked by his disciples, sharing a final meal before his Crucifixion.

This festive feast captures the optimistic spirit of Renaissance Venice. Life was a good thing and beauty was to be enjoyed. Renaissance men and women saw the divine in the beauties of Nature and glorified God by glorifying man.

Uh-uh, said the Church. In its eyes, the new humanism was the same as the old hedonism. The false spring of the Renaissance froze quickly after the Reformation, when half of Europe left the Catholic Church and became Protestant, and the Catholic Church countered with the Counter-Reformation.

Veronese (vayr-oh-NAY-zay) was hauled before the Inquisition, the Church tribunal that punished heretics. What did he mean by painting such a bawdy Last Supper? With dwarf jesters? And apostles picking their teeth (between the columns, left of center)? And dogs and cats? And a black man, God forbid? And worst of all, some German soldiers—maybe even Protestants!—at the far right?

Veronese argued that it was just artistic license, so they asked to see his—it had expired. But the solution was simple. Rather than change the painting, just fine-tune the title. *Sì, no problema.* Veronese got out his brush, and *The Last Supper* became the *Feast in the House of Levi*, written in Latin on the railing to the left: *"FECIT D. COVI. MAGNV. LEVI".*

Titian, *Pietà*, c. 1573

Jesus has just been executed, and his followers grieve over his body before burying it. Titian painted this to hang over his own tomb.

Titian was the most famous painter of his day—perhaps even more famous than Michelangelo. He excelled in every subject: portraits of dukes, kings, and popes; racy nudes for their bedrooms; solemn altarpieces for churches; and pagan scenes from Greek mythology. He was cultured and witty, a fine musician and businessman—an all-around Renaissance kind of guy.

Titian was old when he painted this. He had seen the rise and decline of the Renaissance and had experienced much sadness in his own life. Unlike Titian's colorful and exuberant "Little Mary," done at the height of the Renaissance, this canvas is dark, the mood more somber.

The dead Christ is framed by a Renaissance arch like the one in Bellini's *Enthroned Madonna,* but here the massive stones overpower the figures, making them look puny and helpless. The lion statues are downright scary. Instead of the clear realism of Renaissance paintings, Titian uses rough, messy brushstrokes, a technique that would be picked up by the Impressionists three centuries later. Titian adds a dramatic compositional element—starting with the lion at lower right, a line of motion sweeps up diagonally along the figures, culminating in the grief-stricken Mary Magdalene, who turns away, flinging her arm and howling out loud.

The kneeling figure of an old, bald man is a self-portrait of the aging Titian, tending to the corpse of Jesus, who symbolizes the once powerful, now dead Renaissance Man. In the lower right, a painting-within-the-painting shows Titian and his son kneeling, asking the Virgin to spare them from the plague of 1576. Unfortunately, Titian's son eventually died of the plague.

Tintoretto, *The Removal of St. Mark's Body (Trafugamento del Corpo di San Marco)*, 1562-1566

The event that put Venice on the map is frozen at its most dramatic moment. Muslim fundamentalists in Alexandria are about to burn

St. Mark's body (there's the smoke from the fire in the center), when suddenly a hurricane appears miraculously, sending them running for cover. (See the wisps of baby-angel faces in the storm, blowing on the infidels? Look hard, on the left-hand side.) Meanwhile, Venetian merchants whisk away the body.

Tintoretto makes us part of the action. The square tiles in the courtyard run straight away from us, an extension of our reality, as though we could step right into the scene—or the merchants could carry Mark into ours.

Tintoretto would have made a great black-velvet painter. His colors burn with a metallic sheen, and he does everything possible to make his subject popular with common people.

In fact, Tintoretto was a common man himself, self-taught, who apprenticed only briefly with Titian before striking out on his own. He sold paintings in the marketplace in his youth and insisted on living in the poor part of town, even after he became famous.

Tintorettos abound here, in the next room, and throughout Venice. Look for these characteristics, some of which became standard features of the Mannerist and Baroque art that followed the Renaissance: 1) heightened drama, violent scenes, strong emotions; 2) elongated bodies in twisting poses; 3) strong contrasts between dark and light; 4) bright colors; and 5) diagonal compositions.

(Tintoretto fans will want to see his "Sistine Chapel"; 📖 see the Scuola San Rocco Tour chapter.)

• *Spend some time in this room, the peak of the Venetian Renaissance and the climax of the museum. From here on, there are three must-visit spots: Room 20 (Gentile Bellini), Room 21 (Vittore Carpaccio), and Room 23 ("displaced highlights"). Find each room with the help of your map. Start in Room 20, with...*

Gentile Bellini, *Procession in St. Mark's Square (Processione in Piazza San Marco)*, 1496

Here's a chance to look back at Venice in its heyday. Painted by Giovanni's big brother, this wide-angle view—more than any human eye could take in at once—reminds us how little Venice has changed over the centuries. There is St. Mark's:

ACCADEMIA

gleaming gold with mosaics, the four bronze horses, the three flag-poles out front, the old Campanile on the right, and the Doge's Palace. There's the guy selling 10 postcards for a euro. (But there's no Clock Tower with the two bronze Moors yet, the pavement's different, the church is covered with gold, and there are no café orchestras playing "New York, New York.") Every detail is in perfect focus, regardless of its distance from us, and presented for our inspection.

Take some time to linger over this and the other views of old Venice in this room. Opposite the big procession is a painting by Carpaccio showing a slice of Venetian life circa 1500: the old wooden drawbridge version of the Rialto, nobles in private gondolas with their fancy-pants gondoliers, elegant faces of city folk, pent-up promiscuity awaiting carnival. Notice it's a man's world. (According to an old Venetian rhyme, "A woman is to be silent, good looking, and stay at home with children.")

• From here, walk left through Room 19 and into Room 21.

Vittore Carpaccio, *The Legend of Saint Ursula,* c. 1490

This ensemble of nine paintings tells the story of Ursula, patron saint of girls needing to get married (and needing a dowry). Working clockwise around the room you follow her odyssey.

The first scene sets things up: She wants to escape marriage to a non-Christian. Her father, the king, sends her and her suitor from Brittany to Rome to see the pope in hopes that the young man will convert. (Notice how the artist had no idea what Brittany looked like.) Then the story ramps up: Somehow she meets Attila and his Huns, she and her 11,000 ladies in waiting are massacred, and it all ends with her funeral and ascension. While the scenes are hard to follow, they nicely show off Venice's architecture, ships, and textiles. Carpaccio gives us a trip back in time—a fantasy chance to visit Venice 500 years ago.

• Finally, visit the largest room in the museum, Room 23.

Displaced Highlights

This giant hall is the upper half of an old Gothic church. The nave was divided under Napoleon's rule, and this became the fine arts academy—the Accademia. It's where art displaced by the gallery's ongoing renovation often ends up. If you missed any of the works described up until now, use this book's photos to see if you can track them down here. The room's inner court generally holds the finest works—including masterpieces by Giovanni Bellini (such as his *Madonna degli Alberetti*) and Giorgione (such as *The Tempest*).

Giorgione, *The Tempest (La Tempesta),* c. 1505

It's the calm before the storm. The atmosphere is heavy—luminous but ominous. There's a sense of mystery. Why is the woman nursing her baby in the middle of the countryside? And the soldier—is he

ogling her or protecting her? Will lightning strike? Do they know that the serenity of this beautiful landscape is about to be shattered by an approaching storm?

The mystery is heightened by contrasting elements. The armed soldier contrasts with the naked mother and her baby. The austere, ruined columns contrast with the lusciousness of Nature. And, most important, the stillness of the foreground scene is in direct opposition to the threatening storm in the background. The landscape itself is the main subject, creating a mood, regardless of what the painting is "about."

Giorgione (jor-JONE-ay) was as mysterious as his few paintings, yet he left a lasting impression. A student of Bellini, he learned to use haziness to create a melancholy mood of beauty. But nothing beautiful lasts—flowers fade, Mary Magdalenes grow old, and Giorgione died at 33. In *The Tempest*, the fleeting stillness is about to be shattered by the slash of lightning, the true center of the composition.

• *You've seen the highlights of the Accademia, which means you've seen the highlights of the Venetian Renaissance. Now you're free to get back out into the amazing city that inspired all this beauty.*

FRARI CHURCH TOUR

Basilica di Santa Maria Gloriosa dei Frari

For me, this church offers the best art-appreciation experience in Venice, because so much of its great art is in situ—right where it was designed to be seen, rather than hanging in museums. Because Venice's spongy ground could never support a real stone Gothic church (such as those you'd find in France), the Frari is made of light and flexible brick. As with Venetian architecture in general, the white limestone foundation insulates the building from the wet soil.

The church was built by the Franciscan order, which arrived in Venice around 1230 (the present building was consecrated in 1492). Franciscan men and women were inspired by St. Francis of Assisi (c. 1182-1226), who dedicated himself to a nonmaterialistic lifestyle—part of a reform movement that spread across Europe in the early 1200s. The Roman Church felt distant and corrupt, and there was a hunger for religious teaching that connected with everyday people. While some of these movements were dubbed heretical (like that of the Cathars in southern France), the Franciscans (and Dominicans) eventually earned the Church's blessing.

The spirit of St. Francis of Assisi warms both the church of his "brothers" *(frari)* and the art that decorates it. The Franciscan love of all of creation—Nature and Man—later inspired Renaissance painters to capture the beauty of the physical world and human emotions, showing worshippers the glory of God in human terms.

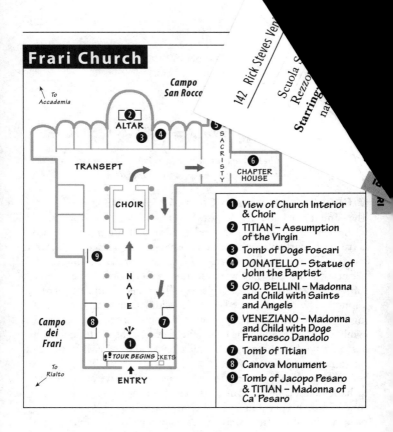

Frari Church

Campo San Rocco

To Accademia

ALTAR ❷

❸ ❹

❺ SACRISTY

CHAPTER HOUSE ❻

TRANSEPT

CHOIR

❾

N A V E

Campo dei Frari

❽ ❼

To Rialto

❶ TOUR BEGINS | TICKETS

ENTRY

❶ View of Church Interior & Choir
❷ TITIAN – Assumption of the Virgin
❸ Tomb of Doge Foscari
❹ DONATELLO – Statue of John the Baptist
❺ GIO. BELLINI – Madonna and Child with Saints and Angels
❻ VENEZIANO – Madonna and Child with Doge Francesco Dandolo
❼ Tomb of Titian
❽ Canova Monument
❾ Tomb of Jacopo Pesaro & TITIAN – Madonna of Ca' Pesaro

Orientation

Cost: €3.

Hours: Mon-Sat 9:00-18:00, Sun 13:00-18:00.

Dress Code: Modest dress is recommended.

Getting There: It's on Campo dei Frari, near the San Tomà vaporetto and *traghetto* stops. From the dock, follow signs to *Scuola Grande di San Rocco*. For a pleasant stroll from the Rialto Bridge, 🕮 take the Rialto to Frari Church Walk.

Information: Tel. 041-272-8611, www.basilicadeifrari.it.

Tours: You can rent an audioguide for €2.

🎧 Download my free Frari Church **audio tour**.

Length of This Tour: Allow one hour. Don't miss Titian's *Assumption*, Donatello's statue, or Bellini's altarpiece.

Photography: Allowed without flash.

Eating: The church square is ringed with small, simple, reasonably priced cafés. The Bottega del Caffè Dersut (around to the left, facing the side of the church, inside seating only) serves salads and fresh sandwiches.

Nearby: For efficient sightseeing, combine your visit with the

an Rocco, located behind the Frari Church. The Ca'
nico is a seven-minute walk away.

Titian, Giovanni Bellini, Paolo Veneziano, and Do-
ello.

The Tour Begins

*Enter the church, let your eyes adjust, and stand just inside the door
with a good view down the long nave toward the altar.*

❶ Church Interior and Choir, 1250-1443

The simple, spacious (110-yard-long), well-lit Gothic church—
with rough wood crossbeams and a red-and-white color scheme—
is truly a remarkable sight in a city otherwise crammed with exotic
froufrou. Traditionally, churches in Venice were cross-shaped, but
because the Franciscans were an international order, they weren't
limited to Venetian tastes. This new T-shaped footprint featured
a long, lofty nave—flooded with light and suited to large gather-
ings—where common people heard sermons. The T, or tau, is the
symbol of the Franciscan order. St. Francis chose the tau as his
personal symbol, wearing it on his clothes and using it in place of
his signature.

The wooden choir area in the center of the nave allowed friars
to hold smaller, more intimate services. From the early 16th century, as worshippers entered the church and looked down the long
nave to the altar, they were greeted by Titian's glorious painted
altarpiece—then, as now, framed by the arch of the choir entrance.
(The architecture predates the painting by nearly 200 years. Titian
must have enjoyed this perspective.)

Walk prayerfully toward the Titian, stopping in the gorgeously carved 1480s choir. Notice the fine inlay above the chairs,
showing the Renaissance enthusiasm for Florentine-style depth
and perspective. Surviving choirs such as this
are rare. (In response to Luther's challenge,
Counter-Reformation churches discarded the
idea of the choirs and altar screens in order to
get priests closer to their flocks.)
• *Approach Titian's heavenly vision.*

❷ Titian, *Assumption of the Virgin*, 1516-1518

Glowing red and gold like a stained-glass window, this altarpiece sets the tone of exuberant
beauty found in this church. At the end of her
life (though looking 17 here), Mary was miraculously "assumed" into heaven. As cherubs

lift her up to meet a Jupiter-like God, the stunned apostles on earth reach up to touch the floating bubble of light.

Look around. The church is littered with chapels and tombs "made possible by the generous financial support" of rich people who donated to the Franciscans for the good of their souls (and usually for tomb-topping statues of themselves, as well). But the Franciscans didn't sell their main altar; instead they hired the new whiz artist, Titian, to create a dramatic altar painting.

Unveiled in 1518, the work scandalized a Venice accustomed to simpler, more contemplative church art. The rich colors, twisting poses, and mix of saccharine angels with blue-collar apostles were unheard of. Most striking, this Virgin is fully human—a real woman in the golden glow of heaven, not a stiff icon on a throne. The Franciscans thought this woman aroused excitement rather than spirituality. They agreed to pay Titian only after the Holy Roman Emperor offered to buy the altar if they refused.

In a burst of youthful innovation, Titian (c. 1490-1576) had rewritten the formula for church art, hinting at changes to come with the Mannerist and Baroque styles. He energized the scene with a complex composition, overlapping a circle (Mary's bubble) and a triangle (draw a line from the apostle reaching up to Mary's face and down the other side) on three horizontal levels (God in heaven, Man on earth, Mary in between). Together, these elements draw our eyes from the swirl of arms and legs to the painting's focus—the radiant face of a triumphant Mary, "assumed body and soul into heaven."

• *Flanking the painting are marble tombs lining the walls. On the wall to the right of the altar is the...*

❸ Tomb of Doge Foscari, 15th century

This heavy, ornate tomb marks the peak of Venice's worldly power. Doge Francesco Foscari (1373-1457) assumed control of the city's powerful seafaring empire and then tried to expand it onto the mainland, battling Milan in a 31-year war of attrition that swept through northern Italy. Meanwhile, on the unprotected eastern front, the Ottomans took Constantinople (1453) and scuttled Venice's trade. Venice's long slide into historical oblivion had begun. Financially drained city fathers forced Foscari to resign, turn in his funny hat, and hand over the keys to the Doge's Palace.

• *In the first chapel to the right of the altar, you'll find...*

FRARI

❹ Donatello, *Statue of John the Baptist,* 1438

In the center of the altarpiece, the cockeyed prophet of the desert—emaciated from his breakfast of bugs 'n' honey and dressed in animal skins—freezes mid-rant when he spies something in the distance. His jaw goes slack, he twists his face and raises his hand to announce the coming of...the Renaissance.

The Renaissance began in the Florence of the 1400s, where Donatello (1386-1466) created realistic statues with a full range of human emotions. This warts-and-all John the Baptist contrasts greatly with, say, Titian's sweet Mary. Florentine art (including painting) was sculptural, strongly outlined, and harshly realistic, with muted colors. Venetian art was painterly, soft focus, and beautiful, with bright colors.

Florentine expatriates living in Venice commissioned Donatello to make this wooden statue for their local chapel. Notice how the statues flanking John (sculpted at about the same time but by lesser artists) are clearly behind Donatello's work in realism.
• *Enter the sacristy through the door at the far end of the right transept. You'll bump into an elaborate altar crammed with reliquaries. Opposite that (near the entrance door) is a clock, intricately carved from a single piece of wood. At the far end of the room, you'll find Bellini's glowing altarpiece.*

❺ Giovanni Bellini, *Madonna and Child with Saints and Angels,* 1488

The Pesaro family, who negotiated an acceptable price and place for their family tomb, funded this delightful chapel dominated by a Bellini masterpiece.

Mary sits on a throne under a half-dome, propping up Baby Jesus (who's just learning to stand), flanked by saints and serenaded by musician angels. Giovanni Bellini (c. 1430-1516), the father of the Venetian Renaissance, painted fake columns and a dome to match the real ones in the gold frame, making the painting seem to be an extension of the room. He completes the illusion with glimpses of open sky in the background. Next, he fills the artificial niches with symmetrically posed, thoughtful saints—left to right, find Saints Nicholas, Peter, Mark, and Sean Connery (Benedict).

Bellini combined the meditative poses of the Venetian Byzantine tradition with Renaissance improvements in modern art. He made the transition from painting with medieval tempera (egg yolk-based) to painting in oil (pigments dissolved in vegetable oil). Oils allowed a subtler treatment of colors because artists could apply them in successive layers. And because darker colors aren't so muddy when painted in oil, they "pop"—effectively giving the artist a brighter palette.

Bellini virtually invented the formula (later to be broken by his precocious pupil, Titian) for Venetian altarpieces. This type of holy conversation *(Sacra Conversazione)* between saints and Mary can also be seen in Venice's Accademia and Church of San Zaccaria.

Renaissance humanism demanded Madonnas and saints that were accessible and human. Bellini delivers, but places them in a physical setting so beautiful that it creates its own mood of serene holiness. The scene is lit from the left, but nothing casts a harsh shadow—Mary and the babe are enveloped in a glowing aura of reflected light from the golden dome. The beauty is in the details— the writing in the dome, the red brocade backdrop, the swirls in the marble steps, and the angels' dimpled legs.

• *In the adjoining room, facing a grand cloister with the most extravagant wellhead in Venice, find a painting in the shape of a Gothic arch.*

❻ Paolo Veneziano, *Madonna and Child with Doge Francesco Dandolo,* c. 1339

Bellini's Byzantine roots can be traced to Paolo Veneziano (literally, "Paul the Venetian"), the first "name" artist in Venice, who helped

shape the distinctive painting style of his city. In turn, Veneziano was inspired by Byzantine artists who had come to Venice in search of greater freedom of expression. They had chafed under strict societies (Byzantine and, in some locales, Islamic) that frowned on painting figurative images. In Venice, these expats found an eager community of rich patrons who indulged their love of deeper color, sentiment, movement, and decoration. (Venice clung to this style for so long that its art eventually lagged behind the rest of Western Europe.)

In this altarpiece, Veneziano paints Byzantine icons and sets them in motion. Baby Jesus turns to greet a kneeling Doge Dandolo, while Mary turns to acknowledge the doge's wife. None other than St. Francis presents "Francis" (Francesco) Dandolo to the Madonna. Both he and St. Elizabeth (on the right) bend at the waist and gesture as naturally as 14th-century icons can.

Notice the color. Venetians were enthusiastic about color. All these paintings have the city's colors—blue, gold, and red—in common. And with the thriving colored glass industry, Venetian painters had access to more and better pigments than did rival painters from other towns.

• *Return to the nave and head left, toward the door you entered through. Turn around and face the altar. The Tomb of Titian is in the second bay on your right.*

❼ Tomb of Titian, 1852

The enormous carved marble monument is labeled "Titiano Ferdinandus MDCCCLII." The tomb celebrates both the man (the

center statue shows Titian with a beard and crown of laurels) and his famous paintings (depicted in the background reliefs).

Titian was the greatest Venetian painter, excelling equally in inspirational altarpieces, realistic portraits, joyous mythological scenes, and erotic female nudes.

He moved to Venice as a child, studying first as a mosaic-maker and then under Giovanni Bellini and Giorgione before establishing his own bold style, which featured teenage Madonnas (see a relief of *The Assumption of the Virgin* behind Titian). He became wealthy and famous, traveling Europe to paint stately portraits of kings and nobles, and colorful, sexy works for their bedrooms. Titian resisted the temptation of big money that drew so many of his contemporary Venetian artists to Rome. Instead he always returned to his beloved Venice (see winged lion on top)...and favorite Frari Church.

In his old age, Titian painted dark, tragic masterpieces, including the *Pietà* (see relief in upper left) that was intended for his tomb but ended up in the Accademia (see page 136). Nearing 90, he labored to finish the *Pietà* as the plague enveloped Venice. Over a quarter of the population died, including Titian's son and assistant, Orazio. Heartbroken, Titian died soon afterward. His tomb was built three centuries later to remember and honor this great

Venetian. The inscription reads: "To Titian from Ferdinand I, the Habsburg Emperor who paid for this."
• *On the opposite side of the nave is the pyramid-shaped...*

❽ Canova Monument, 1827

Antonio Canova (1757-1822, see his portrait above the door) was Venice's greatest sculptor. He created gleaming white, highly pol-

ished statues of beautiful Greek gods and goddesses in the Neo-classical style. (See several of his works at the Correr Museum.)

The pyramid shape is time-less, suggesting pharaohs' tombs and the Christian Trinity. Mourn-ers, bent over with grief, shuffle up to pay homage to the master artist.

Even the winged lion is choked up.

Follow me here. Canova himself designed this pyramid-shaped tomb, not for his own use but as the tomb of an artist he greatly admired: Titian. But the Frari picked another design for Titian's tomb, so Canova used the pyramid for an Austrian prin-cess...in Vienna. After his death, Canova's pupils copied the design here to honor their master. In fact, Canova isn't buried here. But inside the tomb's open door, you can (barely) see an urn, which contains his heart.

Next to the Canova Monument is the massive tomb of the only member of the Pesaro family to become a doge. It's supported by hardworking Ottoman sailors (represented by black figures of African prisoners). From the 1600s, it's very Baroque—wildly emotional and quite a contrast to the calm Neoclassical Canova Monument adjacent.

• *Head back toward the altar. Halfway up, on the left, is the private altar of the Pesaro family and the tomb of Jacopo Pesaro. Calling your attention to this tomb is a grandiose painting on the wall...*

❾ Titian, *Madonna of Ca' Pesaro*, 1519-1526

Titian's second altarpiece for the Frari Church displays all his many skills. Fol-lowing his teacher Bellini, he puts Mary (seated) and baby (standing) on a throne, surrounded by saints having a holy con-versation. And, like Bellini, he paints fake columns that echo the church's real ones.

But wait. Mary is off-center, Titian's

idealized saints mingle with Venetians sporting five o'clock shadows, and the stairs run diagonally away from us. Mary sits not on a throne but on a pedestal. Baby Jesus is restless. The precious keys of St. Peter seem to dangle unnoticed. These things upset traditional Renaissance symmetry, but they turn a group of figures into a true scene. St. Peter (center, in blue and gold, with book) looks down at Jacopo Pesaro, who kneels to thank the Virgin for his recent naval victory over the Ottomans (1502). A flag-carrying lieutenant drags in a turbaned captive. Meanwhile, St. Francis talks to Baby Jesus while gesturing down to more members of the Pesaro family. The little guy looking out at us (lower right) is the Pesaro descendant who administered the trust fund to keep prayers coming for his dead uncle.

FRARI

Titian combines opposites: a soft-focus Madonna with photo-realistic portraits, chubby winged angels with a Muslim prisoner, and a Christian cross with a battle flag. In keeping with the spirit of St. Francis' humanism, Titian lets mere mortals mingle with saints. And we're right there with them.

• *While this church is a great example of art* in situ, *in a sense, all of Venice is art* in situ. *At the Frari, you're away from the touristy center. Before returning to the mobs, why not explore some back lanes and lonely canals from here and enjoy a softer, more meditative side of town?*

SCUOLA SAN ROCCO TOUR

Scuola Grande di San Rocco

The 50-plus paintings in the Scuola Grande di San Rocco—often called "Tintoretto's Sistine Chapel"—present one man's very personal vision of Christian history. Tintoretto spent the last 20 years of his life working practically for free, driven by the spirit of charity that the Scuola, a Christian organization, promoted. For Tintoretto fans, this is the ultimate. Even for the art-weary, his large, dramatic canvases, framed in gold on the walls and ceilings of a grand upper hall, are an impressive sight.

Orientation

Cost: €10.

Hours: Daily 9:30-17:30.

Getting There: It's next to the Frari Church (vaporetto: San Tomà). For an easy route on foot from the Rialto Bridge, 📖 take the Rialto to Frari Church Walk, following signs to *Scuola Grande di San Rocco*.

Information: Tel. 041-523-4864, www.scuolagrandesanrocco.org.

Audioguide: The €5 audioguide provides only sketchy descriptions.

Mirrors: Use the mirrors scattered about the museum's Great Upper Hall, because much of this art is on the ceiling and, therefore, a pain in the neck.

Length of This Tour: Allow one hour. If you have less time, skip the Ground Floor Hall and focus on the Great Upper Hall and Albergo Hall.

Photography: OK without flash.

Services: WCs are on the ground floor (through the bookstore).

Nearby: Right next door is the Church of San Rocco, featuring still more Tintorettos (free, same hours as the Scuola).

Starring: Tintoretto, Tintoretto, and Tintoretto.

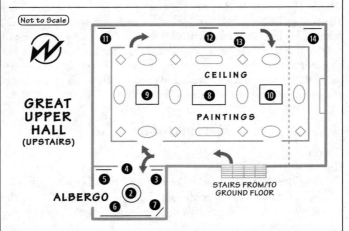

Scuola San Rocco

To Frari

To Accademia

Campo San Rocco

① TOUR BEGINS

⑮

TICKETS & AUDIOGUIDE KIOSK

ENTRY →

GROUND FLOOR

To San Rocco Church

STAIRS UP TO GREAT HALL

⑯

SHOP

WC

SCUOLA SAN ROCCO

Not to Scale

⑪ ⑫ ⑬ ⑭

CEILING

⑨ ⑧ ⑩

PAINTINGS

GREAT UPPER HALL (UPSTAIRS)

⑤ ④ ③

②

⑥ ⑦

ALBERGO

STAIRS FROM/TO GROUND FLOOR

① The Annunciation
② St. Roch in Glory
③ Christ Before Pilate
④ Christ Crowned with Thorns
⑤ The Way to Calvary
⑥ The Crucifixion
⑦ Three Apples
⑧ The Miracle of the Bronze Serpent

⑨ Moses Strikes Water from the Rocks
⑩ The Fall of Manna in the Desert
⑪ The Adoration of the Shepherds
⑫ The Resurrection
⑬ Tintoretto's Carved Face
⑭ The Last Supper
⑮ The Flight into Egypt
⑯ The Circumcision

The Tour Begins

The art of the Scuola is contained in three rooms—the Ground Floor Hall (where you enter) and two rooms upstairs, including the Great Upper Hall, with the biggest canvases. Your ticket also admits you to the Scuola's small and skippable treasury (one more flight up).

• *Enter on the ground floor, which is lined with big, colorful Tintoretto canvases. Begin with the first canvas on the left.*

Ground Floor Hall
❶ *The Annunciation*

An angel swoops through the doorway, dragging a trail of naked baby angels with him, to tell a startled Mary that she'll give birth to Jesus. This canvas has many of Tintoretto's typical characteristics:

• **The miraculous and the everyday mingle side by side.** Glorious angels are in a broken-down house with stacks of lumber and a frayed chair.

• **Bright light and dark shadows.** A bright light strikes the brick column, highlighting Mary's face and the angel's shoulder, but casting dark shadows across the room.

• **Strong 3-D sucks you into the scene.** Tintoretto literally tears down Mary's wall to let us in. The floor tiles recede sharply into the distance, making Mary's room an extension of our real space.

• **Colors that are bright, almost harsh,** with a metallic "black-velvet" sheen, especially when contrasted with the soft-focus haze of Bellini, Giorgione, Veronese, and (sometimes) Titian.

• **Twisting, muscular poses.** The angel turns one way, Mary turns the other, and the baby angels turn every which way.

• **Diagonal composition.** Shadows run diagonally on the floor as Mary leans back diagonally.

• **Rough brushwork.** The sketchy pattern on Mary's ceiling contrasts with the precise photo-realism of the brick column.

And finally, *The Annunciation* exemplifies the general theme of the San Rocco paintings—God intervenes miraculously in our everyday lives in order to save us.

• *We'll return to the ground floor later, but let's get right to the highlights. Climb the staircase (taking time to admire the plague scenes that are not by Tintoretto) and enter the impressive Great Upper Hall.*

Jacopo Tintoretto (1518-1594)

The son of a silk dyer ("Tintoretto" is a nickname meaning "little dyer"), Tintoretto applied a blue-collar work ethic to painting, becoming one of the most prolific artists ever. He trained briefly under Titian, but their egos clashed. He was influenced more by Michelangelo's recently completed *Last Judgment*, with its muscular, twisting, hovering nudes and epic scale.

By age 30, Tintoretto was famous, astounding Venice with the innovative *St. Mark Freeing the Slave* (now in the Accademia). He married, had eight children (three of whom became his assistants), and dedicated himself to work and family, shunning publicity and living his whole life in his old Venice neighborhood.

Twenty years of his life were spent decorating the Scuola di San Rocco. It was a labor of love, showing his religious faith, his compassion for the poor, and his artistic passion.

Wow! Before we tackle the big canvases in this huge room, let's start where Tintoretto did, in the Albergo Hall—the small room in the left corner of the Great Upper Hall. On the ceiling of the Albergo Hall is an oval painting of St. Roch, best viewed from the doorway.

Albergo Hall (Sala d'Albergo)—Christ's Passion
❼ St. Roch in Glory, 1564
Start at the feet of St. Roch (San Rocco), a French medical student in the 1300s who dedicated his short life to treating plague victims.

The Scuola di San Rocco was a kind of Venetian "Elks Club" whose favorite charity was poor plague victims.

This is the first of Tintoretto's 50-plus paintings in the Scuola. It's also the one that got him the job, beating entries by Veronese and others.

Tintoretto amazed the judges by showing the saint from beneath, as though he hovered above in a circle of glory. This Venetian taste for dramatic angles and illusion would later become standard in Baroque ceilings. Tintoretto trained by dangling wax models from the ceiling and lighting them from odd angles.

• On the walls are scenes of Christ's trial, torture, and execution. Work *counterclockwise around the room. Start with the one to the right of the door (as you face it).*

❸ Christ Before Pilate (Ecce Homo)

Jesus has been arrested and brought before the Roman authorities in a cavernous hall. Although he says nothing in his own defense, he stands head and shoulders above the crowd, literally "rising above" the slanders. Tintoretto shines a bright light on his white robe, making Christ radiate innocence.

At Christ's feet, an old, bearded man in white stoops over to record the events on paper—it's Tintoretto himself.

❹ Christ Crowned with Thorns

Jesus was beaten, whipped, then mocked by the soldiers, who dressed him as a king "crowned" with thorns. Seeing the bloodstains on the cloth must have touched the hearts of Scuola members, generating compassion for those who suffer.

❺ The Way to Calvary

Silhouetted against a stormy sky, Jesus and two other prisoners trudge up a steep hill, carrying their own crosses to the execution site. The cycle culminates with...

❻ The Crucifixion

The crucified Christ is the calm center of this huge and chaotic scene that fills the wall. Workers struggle to hoist crosses, mourners swoon, riffraff gamble for Christ's clothes, and soldiers mill about aimlessly. Scarcely anyone pays any attention to the Son of God...except us, because Tintoretto directs our eye there.

All the lines of sight point to Christ at the center: the ladder on the ground, the cross being raised, the cross still on the ground, the horses on the right, and the hillsides that slope in. In a trick of multiple perspectives, the cross being raised seems to suck us in toward the center, while the cross still on the ground seems to cause the figures to be sucked toward us.

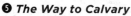

SCUOLA SAN ROCCO

Above the chaos stands Christ, high above the horizon, higher than everyone, glowing against the dark sky. Tintoretto lets us appreciate the quiet irony lost on the frenetic participants—that this minor criminal suffering such apparent degradation is, in fact, triumphant.

• *Displayed on an easel to the left of and beneath* The Crucifixion *is a small fragment of...*

❼ Three Apples

This fragment, from the frieze around the upper reaches of the Albergo Hall, was discovered folded under the frieze in 1905. Because it was never exposed to light, it still retains Tintoretto's original bright colors. All of his paintings are darker today, despite cleaning, due to the irreversible chemical alteration of the pigments. Imagine the original brightness of these rooms.

• *Now step back out into the Great Upper Hall.*

Great Upper Hall—Understanding What You're Standing Under

Thirty-four enormous oil canvases, set into gold frames on the ceiling and along the walls of this impressive room, tell biblical history from Adam and Eve to the Ascension of Christ. Tintoretto's storytelling style is straightforward, and anyone with knowledge of the Bible can quickly get the gist. Tintoretto's success in the Albergo Hall won him the job of the enormous Great Upper Hall.

The ceiling displays Old Testament scenes; the walls show events from the New Testament. Beyond that, the layout is not chronological but symbolic, linked by common themes. Tintoretto shows how God leads mankind to salvation. Evil enters the world with the Original Sin of *Adam and Eve* (at the Albergo end of room, on the ceiling). From there, man must go through many trials, as the ceiling shows—the struggles of Moses and the Israelites, Jonah, and Abraham. But God is always there to help. In the three largest paintings on the ceiling, God saves man from thirst *(Moses Strikes Water from the Rocks)*, illness *(The Miracle of the Bronze Serpent)*, and hunger *(The Fall of Manna in the Desert)*. Christ's story (along the walls) parallels the struggles of men (on the ceiling). But while the first humans *(Adam and Eve)* succumb to Satan's temptation, Christ does not (see *Christ Tempted by Satan,* on the wall nearby). And ultimately—at the altar—mankind is saved by Christ's sacrifice *(The Passover* overhead on the ceiling and *The Last Supper* on the wall to the left). The art captures the charitable spirit of the school—just as God helps those who suffer, so should we.

• *Let's look at a few pieces in depth. Start with the largest painting, in the center of the ceiling. View it from the top (the Albergo end), not directly underneath.*

❽ The Miracle of the Bronze Serpent

The tangle of half-naked bodies (at the bottom of the painting) represents the children of Israel, wrestling with poisonous snakes

and writhing in pain. At the top of the pile, a young woman gestures toward Moses (in pink), who points to a pole carrying a bronze serpent. Those who looked at the statue were miraculously healed. His work all done, God (above in the clouds) high-fives an angel.

This was the first of the Great Hall panels Tintoretto painted in response to a terrible plague that hit Venice in 1575. About one in three died. Four hundred a day were buried. Like today's Red Cross, the Scuola sprang into action, raising funds, sending doctors, and giving beds to the sick—and aid to their families. Tintoretto saw the dead and dying firsthand. While capturing their suffering, he gave a ray of hope that help was on the way: Turn to the cross, and be saved by your faith.

There are dozens of figures in the painting, shown from every conceivable angle. Tintoretto was well aware of where it would hang and how it would be viewed. Walk around beneath it and see the different angles come alive. The painting becomes a movie, and the children of Israel writhe like snakes.

• *The rectangular panel at the Albergo end of the hall is...*

❾ Moses Strikes Water from the Rocks

Moses (in pink, in the center) hits a rock in the desert with his staff, and it miraculously spouts water, which the thirsty Israelites catch in jars. The water spurts like a ray

of light. Moses is a strong, calm center to a spinning wheel of activity.

Tintoretto worked fast, and, if nothing else, his art is exuberant. He trained in fresco painting, which must be finished before the plaster dries. With these paintings, he sketched an outline right onto the canvas, then improvised details as he went.

The sheer magnitude of the San Rocco project is staggering. This canvas alone is 300 square feet—like painting a bathroom with an artist's tiny brush. The whole project, counting the Albergo Hall, Great Upper Hall, and the Ground Floor Hall together, totals some 8,500 square feet—more than enough to cover a typical house, inside and out. (The Sistine Chapel ceiling, by comparison, is 5,700 square feet.)

• *The rectangular panel at the altar end of the hall is...*

➓ The Fall of Manna in the Desert

It's snowing bread, as God feeds the hungry Israelites with a miraculous storm. They stretch a blanket to catch it and gather it up in baskets. Up in the center of the dark cloud is a radiant, almost transparent God, painted with sketchy brushstrokes to suggest he's an unseen presence.

Tintoretto tells these Bible stories with a literalness that was very popular with the poor, uneducated sick people who sought help from the Scuola. He was the Spielberg of his day, with the technical know-how to bring imagination to life, to make the miraculous tangible.

• *You could grow old studying all the art here, so we'll select just a couple of the New Testament paintings on the walls. Start at the Albergo end, on the right, with...*

⓫ The Adoration of the Shepherds

Christ's glorious life begins in a straw-filled stable with cows, chickens, and peasants who pass plates of food up to the new parents. It's night, with just a few details lit by moonlight: the kneeling shepherd's forehead and leggings, the serving girl's shoulders, the faces of Mary and Joseph...and little Baby Jesus, a smudge of light.

Notice the different points of view. Tintoretto clearly has placed us on the lower floor, about eye level with the cow, looking up through the roof beams at the night sky. But we also see Mary and Joseph in the loft above as though they were at eye level. By using multiple perspectives (and ignoring the laws of physics), Tintoretto could portray every

detail at its perfect angle and create an otherworldly atmosphere.

• *In the middle of the long wall, on the same side, find...*

⓬ The Resurrection

Angels lift the sepulchre lid, and Jesus springs forth in a blaze of light. The contrast between dark and light is extreme, with great dramatic effect.

• *Head for* The Last Supper, *in the corner to the left of the altar. On the way there, look on the wall for a* ⓭ **woodcarving of Tintoretto** *(third statue from altar, directly opposite entry staircase). The artist holds the tools of his trade. His craggy, wrinkled face peers out from under a black cap and behind a scraggly beard.*

⓮ *The Last Supper*

A dog, a beggar, and a serving girl dominate the foreground of Christ's final Passover meal with his followers. More servants work

in the background. The disciples themselves are dining in the dark, some with their backs to us, with only a few stray highlights to show us what's going on. Tintoretto emphasizes the human, everyday element of that gathering, in contrast to, say, Leonardo da Vinci's more stately version. And he sets the scene at a diagonal for dramatic effect. The angle connects this holy scene with Mass as it's being performed.

The table stretches across a tiled floor, a commonly used device to create 3-D space. But Tintoretto makes the more distant tiles unnaturally small to exaggerate the distance. Similarly, the table and the people get proportionally smaller and lower until, at the far end of the table, tiny Jesus (with glowing head) is only half the size of the disciple at the near end.

Theatrically, Tintoretto leaves it to us to piece together the familiar narrative. The disciples are asking each other, "Is it I who will betray the Lord?" Jesus, meanwhile, unconcerned, hands out Communion bread.

• *Before leaving this hall, enjoy the amazing wooden carvings by Francesco Pianta (done about 40 years after Tintoretto's death) that ring the room.*

After you've gotten your fill of the Great Upper Hall, head back downstairs for Tintoretto's last works. The first one is directly across from the foot of the stairs.

Ground Floor Hall—The Life of Mary

⓯ *The Flight into Egypt*

There's Mary, Joseph, and the baby, but they're dwarfed by palm trees. Tintoretto, in his old age, returned to composing a Venetian specialty—landscapes—after years as champion of the Michelangelesque style of painting beefy, twisting nudes. The leafy greenery, the still water, the supernatural sunset, and the hut whose inhabitants go about their work tell us better than any human action could that the holy family has found a safe haven.

• *Over your right shoulder, above the door, is...*

⓰ *The Circumcision*

This painting, featuring the circumcision of the Baby Jesus, is one of the last canvases that Tintoretto did for the Scuola. He collaborated on this work with his son Domenico, who carried on the family business.

In his long and prolific career, Tintoretto saw fame and many well-paying jobs. But at the Scuola, he asked for almost no money. It stands as one man's very personal contribution to the poor, to the Christian faith, and to art.

SCUOLA SAN ROCCO

CA' REZZONICO TOUR

*Museum of 18th-Century Venice
(Museo del Settecento Veneziano)*

Endowed by nature with a pleasing physical appearance, a confirmed gambler, a great talker, far from modest, always running after pretty women...I was certain to be disliked. But, as I was always willing to take responsibility for my actions, I decided I had a right to do anything I pleased.

—The Memoirs of Giacomo Casanova

Venice in the 1700s was the playground for Europe's aristocrats, including the wealthy Rezzonico (ret-ZON-ee-koh) family, who owned this palace. Today, the Ca' Rezzonico (a.k.a. the Museo del Settecento Veneziano) contains furniture, decoration, and artwork from the period. This grand home on the Grand Canal is the best place in town to experience the luxurious, decadent spirit of Venice in the Settecento (the 1700s).

Orientation

Cost: €10. Free and crowded on first Sun of month.

Hours: Wed-Mon 10:00-18:00, Nov-March until 17:00, closed Tue year-round, ticket office closes one hour before museum.

Getting There: The museum is located in Dorsoduro, on the west bank of the Grand Canal at the Ca' Rezzonico vaporetto stop. It's a 10- or 20-minute walk from the Accademia and Rialto bridges, respectively.

Information: Tel. 041-241-0100, http://carezzonico.visitmuve.it.

Audioguide: The audioguide costs €5 (€6/2 people) and lasts 1.5 hours.

Length of This Tour: Allow one hour, or more if you want to explore the third floor on your own. If you have less than an hour, focus on Rooms 1-7 on the first floor, with their Tiepolo ceilings and ambience.

Baggage Check: Free and required for large items.

Services: The Ca' Rezzonico has a bookstore and WCs.

Photography: Allowed without flash.

Cuisine Art: The museum's café has simple fare (€5-6 *panini,* no museum entry required). The delightful Campo San Barnaba is just a three-minute walk away; for eateries on and near that square, see page 276.

Starring: A beautiful palace with 18th-century furnishings and paintings by G. B. Tiepolo, Canaletto, and Guardi.

OVERVIEW

Our Ca' Rezzonico tour covers two floors. The first floor has rooms decorated with period furniture and ceiling frescoes by G. B. Tiepolo. The second floor displays paintings by Canaletto, Guardi, G. D. Tiepolo, Longhi, and others. (The third-floor painting gallery—which is skippable—shows lots of flesh in lots of rooms.)

The Tour Begins

• *If you're arriving by vaporetto, admire Ca' Rezzonico's heavy stone facade facing the Grand Canal. The dock was, of course, the main entrance back in the 1700s. Then, as you enter the palazzo courtyard, admire the 1700s-era gondola on display. Picture this arriving at the Ca's dock for a party during Carnevale. A char-coal heater inside kept the masked and caped passengers warm, as they sipped Prosecco and chatted in French, enjoying their winter holiday away from home...*

FIRST FLOOR

• *Buy tickets on the ground floor, then ascend the grand staircase to the first floor (where you show your ticket), entering the ballroom. From here, simply follow the one-way route through the numbered rooms.*

Room 1: Ballroom

This would be a great place for a wedding reception. At 5,600 square feet, it could be the biggest private venue in the city. Stand in the center, and the room gets even bigger, with a ceiling painting that opens up to the heavens and trompe l'oeil (optical illusion) columns and arches that open onto fake alcoves.

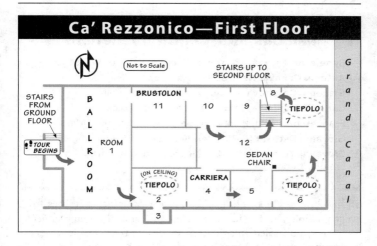

Ca' Rezzonico—First Floor

Not to Scale

STAIRS UP TO
SECOND FLOOR

STAIRS FROM GROUND FLOOR

TOUR BEGINS

BALLROOM

ROOM 1

BRUSTOLON

11   10   9   8

TIEPOLO 7

12

SEDAN CHAIR

(ON CEILING) TIEPOLO

2

3

CARRIERA

4   5

TIEPOLO 6

Grand Canal

Imagine dancing under candlelit chandeliers to Vivaldi's *Four Seasons*. Servants glide by with drinks and finger foods. The gentlemen wear powdered wigs, linen shirts with lacy sleeves, tight velvet coats and breeches, striped stockings, and shoes with big buckles. They carry snuffboxes with dirty pictures inside the lids. The ladies powder their hair, pile it high, and weave in stuff—pictures of their children or locks of a lover's hair. And everyone carries a mask on a stick to change identity in a second.

The chandeliers of gold-covered wood are original. But while most of the furniture we'll see is from the 1700s, it's not from the Rezzonico family collection.

• *Promenade across the floor, bearing right into the next room.*

Room 2: Nuptial Allegory Salon

In fact, there *was* a wedding here—see the happy couple on the ceiling, arriving in a chariot pulled by four white horses and serenaded by angels, cupids, and Virtues. In 1758, Ludovico Rezzonico exchanged vows with Faustina Savorgnan in this room, under the bellies of the horses painted for the occasion by Giovanni Battista ("John the Baptist") Tiepolo. G. B. Tiepolo (1696-1770), the best-known decorator of Europe's palaces, was at the height of his fame and technique. He knocked this

Famous 18th-Century Venetians

Canaletto (Giovanni Antonio Canal): Painter of Venice views

Antonio Canova: Neoclassical sculptor

Giacomo Casanova: Gambler, womanizer, revolutionary

Carlo Goldoni: Playwright of realistic comedies

Francesco Guardi: Painter of romantic Enlightened ideas

Giovanni Battista (G. B.) Tiepolo: Painter of Rococo ceilings

Giovanni Domenico (G. D.) Tiepolo: Painter son of the more famous Tiepolo

off in 12 days. His bright colors, mastery of painting figures from every possible angle, wide knowledge of classical literary subjects, and sheer, unbridled imagination made his frescoes blend seamlessly with ornate Baroque and Rococo furniture.

The Rezzonico were a family of *nouveaux riches* who bought their way into the exclusive club of Venetian patrician families. The state, which needed money for its military adventures, actually sold noble status to parvenu families like the Rezzonico. These upwardly mobile families then followed a strategy to be accepted by the old nobility. Over the course of several generations, the Rezzonico bought and decorated this fancy palace, married into high society, managed to secure a prestigious Venetian office, and even put one of their relatives on the papal throne. In early times, art was about scoring religious points to gain entry to heaven. In the 18th century, wealthy people commissioned art like the works in this palace simply to gain respect.

The *Portrait of Clement XIII,* pink-cheeked and well-fed, shows the most famous Rezzonico. As pope (elected in 1758), Clement spent his reign defending the Jesuit society from anti-Catholic European nobles. A **prayer kneeler** (in the tiny adjoining chapel, Room 3) looks heavily used, dating from the sin-and-repent era of Settecento Venice.

Room 4: Pastel Room

Europe's most celebrated painter of portraits in pastels was a Venetian, Rosalba Carriera (1673-1757). Wealthy French and English tourists on holiday wanted a souvenir of Venice, and Carriera obliged, with miniature portraits on ivory rather than the traditional vellum (soft animal skin). These were products of narcissism—the Facebook photos of the 18th century that proclaimed, "Look how charming/interesting I am."

She progressed to portraits in pastel, a medium that caught the luminous, pale-skin, white-haired, heavy-makeup look that was considered so desirable. Still, her *Portrait (Ritratto) of Sister Maria Caterina* has a warts-and-all realism that doesn't hide the nun's heavy eyebrows, long nose, and forehead vein, which only intensifies the spirituality she radiates.

At age 47, Carriera was invited by tourists whom she'd befriended to visit them in Paris. There she became the toast of the town. Returning triumphantly to Venice, she settled into her home on the Grand Canal and painted until her eyesight failed.

Also in the room is a **portrait of Cecilia Guardi Tiepolo:** wife of famous painter Giovanni Battista Tiepolo, sister of famous painter Francesco Guardi, and mother of not-very-famous painter Lorenzo Tiepolo, who painted this when he was 21.

Room 5: Tapestry Room

Tapestries, furniture, a mirror, and a door with Asian themes that shows an opium smoker on his own little island paradise (lower panel) give a sense of the Rococo luxury of the wealthy. In a century dominated by the French court at Versailles, Venice was one of the few cities that could hold its own. The furniture ensemble of gilded wood chairs, tables, and chests hints at the Louis XIV (claw-foot) style, but the pieces were made in a Venetian workshop.

Despite Venice's mask of gaiety, in the 1700s it was a poor, politically bankrupt, dirty city. Garbage floated in the canals, the streets were either unpaved or slippery with slime, and tourists could hardly stand visiting St. Mark's Basilica or the Doge's Palace because of the stench of mildew. But its reputation for decay and sleaze was actually romanticized into a metaphor for adventures into shady morality. With licensed casinos and thousands of courtesans (prostitutes), it was a fun city for foreigners freed from hometown blinders.

Room 6: Throne Room

"Nowhere in Europe are there so many and such splendid fêtes, ceremonies, and public entertainments of all kinds as there are in Venice," wrote a visitor from France. As you check out the view of the Grand Canal, imagine once again that you're attending a party here. You could watch the *Forze d'Ercole* (Force of Hercules) acrobats, who stood in boats and kept building a human pyramid—of up to 50 bodies—until they tumbled, laughing, into the Grand Canal. At midnight the hosts would dim the mirrored candleholders on the walls, so you could look out on a fireworks display over the water.

Carnevale, Venice's prime party time, stretched from the day after Christmas to Lent. Everyone wore masks. Frenchmen, dressed as turbaned Ottoman Turks, mingled with Turkish traders dressed as harlequins. Fake Barbary pirates fought playfully with skin-blackened "Moors." And long-nosed Pulcinella clowns were everywhere, reveling in the time when all social classes partied as one because "the mask levels all distinctions."

The **ceiling fresco,** again by Giovanni Battista Tiepolo, certainly trompes my oeil. (It's best viewed from the center.) Tiepolo opens the room's sunroof, allowing angels to descend to earth to pick up the Rezzonico clan's patriarch. The old, bald, bearded fellow is crowned with laurels and begins to rise on a cloud up to the translucent temple of glory. The angels hold Venice's Golden Book, where the names of the city's nobles were listed. In 1687, the Rezzonico family bought their way into the exclusive club. Tiepolo captures the moment just as the gang is exiting through the "hole" in the ceiling. The leg of the lady in blue hangs over the "edge" of the fake oval. Tiepolo creates a zero-gravity universe that must have astounded visitors. Walk in circles under the fresco, and watch the bugling angel spin.

• *Pass through the large next room and into...*

Room 7: Tiepolo

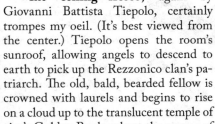

The ceiling painting by G. B. Tiepolo depicts Nobility and Virtue as a kind of bare-breasted, Thelma-and-Louise duo defeating Treachery, who tumbles down. The painting—which is on canvas, not a fresco like the others—was moved here from another palazzo.

Portraits around the room are by Tiepolo and his sons, Lorenzo and Giovanni Domenico. The paintings are sober and down-to-earth, demonstrating the artistic range of this exceptional family. G. B. was known for his flamboyance, but he passed to his sons his penchant for painting wrinkled, wizened old men in the Rembrandt style. In later years, G. B. had the pleasure of traveling with his sons to distant capitals, meeting royalty, and working on palace ceilings. Giovanni Domenico (G. D.) contributed some of the minor figures in the Ca' Rezzonico ceilings and went on to a successful artistic career of his own. (We'll see his work upstairs.)

This was the game room, and you can see a card table in the center. The big walnut cabinet along the wall is one of the few original pieces of furniture from the Rezzonico collection.

Room 9: Library

Ca' Rezzonico was the home of the English poet Robert Browning (1812-1889) in his later years. Imagine him here in this study, in a melancholy mood after a long winter, reading a book and thinking of words from a poem of his: "Oh to be in England, now that April's there...."

Room 10: Lazzarini

The big, colorful paintings are by Gregorio Lazzarini (1655-1730), Tiepolo's teacher. Tiepolo took Lazzarini's color, motion, and twisted poses and suspended them overhead.

Room 11: Brustolon

Andrea Brustolon (1662-1732) carved Baroque fantasies into the custom-made tables, chairs, and vase stands that he crafted in his Venice workshop. In black ebony, reddish boxwood, and brown walnut, they overwhelm with the sheer number of figures, yet each carving is a gem worth admiring. The big vase stand is a harmony of different colors: a white vase supported by ebony slaves in chains and a brown boxwood Hercules. The slaves' chains are carved from a single piece of wood—a racist motif, but an impressive artistic feat.

The room's flowery Murano glass chandelier—of pastel pinks, blues, and turquoise—is original.

• *Backtrack to Room 10, then turn right into the large, sparsely decorated reception space called the...*

Room 12: Portico *(Portego)*

That funny little cabin in the room is a **sedan chair,** a servant-powered taxi for Venice's nobles. Four strong-shouldered men ran

Giacomo Casanova (1725-1798)

I began to lead a life of complete freedom, caring for nothing except what pleased me.
   —The Memoirs of Giacomo Casanova

Casanova, a real person who wrote an exaggerated autobiography, typifies the Venice that so entranced the rest of Europe. In his life, he adopted many personae, worked in a number of professions, and always took the adventurous path.

Casanova was born just across the Grand Canal from the Ca' Rezzonico. The son of an actor, Casanova trained to be a priest, but was expelled for seducing nuns. To Venetians he was first known as a fiery violinist at fancy parties in palaces such as the Ca' Rezzonico. He would later serve time in the Doge's Palace prison, accused of being a magician.

As a professional gambler and charmer, he roamed Europe's capitals seducing noblewomen, dueling with fellow men of honor, and impressing nobles with his knowledge of Greek literature, religion, politics, and the female sex. His memoirs, published after his death, cemented his reputation as a genial but cunning rake, rogue, and rapscallion.

poles through the iron brackets on either side, then carried it on their shoulders, while the rich rode in red-velvet luxury above the slimy streets.

• *The staircase to the second floor is here in Room 12, in the middle of the long wall. On the second floor, you emerge into Room 13 and find the two Canaletto paintings on the opposite wall.*

SECOND FLOOR
The first floor showed the rooms and furniture of the 1700s. The second-floor paintings depict the people who sat in those chairs.

Room 13: Painting
Portego—Canaletto

Rich tourists wanting to remember their stay in Venice sought out Canaletto (1697-1768) for a "postcard" view. The **Grand Canal from Palazzo Balbi to Rialto** (by Giovanni Antonio Canal, called Il Canaletto) captures the view you'd see from the palazzo two doors down. With photographic clarity, Canaletto depicts buildings, boats, and

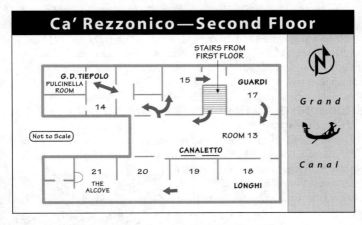

shadows on the water, leading the eye to the tiny, half-hidden Rialto Bridge on the distant horizon.

The ***View of Rio dei Mendicante*** chronicles every chimney, every open shutter, every pair of underwear hanging out to dry.

Canaletto was a young theater-set painter working on Scarlatti operas in Rome when he decided his true calling was painting reality, not Baroque fantasy. He moved home to Venice, set up his

easel outside, and painted scenes like these two, directly from nature. It was considered a very odd thing to do in his day.

Despite the seeming photo-realism and crystal clarity, these wide-angle views are more than any human eye could take in without turning side to side. Canaletto, who meticulously studied the mathematics of perspective, was not above tweaking those rules to compress more of Venice into the frame.

In the *Grand Canal from Palazzo Balbi to Rialto,* notice there are shadows along both sides of the canal—physically impossible, but more picturesque. His paintings still have a theater-set look to them, but here, the Venice backdrop is the star.

To meet the demand for postcard scenes of Venice, Canaletto resorted in later years to painting from engravings or following formulas. But these two early works reflect his pure vision to accurately paint the city he loved.

Grand Tour visitors routinely reported that Venice pleased the eye but not the heart or mind. Just as they experienced the city without feeling any real passion, these paintings let you see it, marvel, and move on.

• From here, we'll move roughly clockwise around the second floor. Head for the door behind your right shoulder. Room 14 is actually a maze of several rooms.

Room 14: G. D. Tiepolo's Frescoes from the Villa Zianigo

The son of G. B. Tiepolo decorated the family villa with frescoes for his own enjoyment. They're far more down-to-earth than G. B.'s high-flying fantasies. *New World* features butts, as ordinary folk crowd around a building with a peep-show window. The only faces we see are the two men in profile—Giovanni Domenico Tiepolo (far right, with eyeglass) and his father, G. B. (arms folded)—and baby brother Lorenzo (center). The **Pul-**

cinella Room (far right corner) has several scenes (including one overhead) of the hook-nosed, white-clothed, hunchbacked clown who, at Carnevale time, represented the lovable country bumpkin. But here, he and his similarly dressed companions seem tired, lecherous, and stupid. The decadent gaiety of Settecento Venice was at odds with the *Liberté, Egalité,* and *Fraternité* erupting in France.

The 18th century was a time of great change. The fresh ideas and innovations of the Enlightenment swept more adaptable societies upward into a thriving new modern age. Meanwhile, a Venice in denial declined.

Venetians bought into their own propaganda. The modern ideas coming out of France threatened the very foundation of what La Serenissima was all about. Over time Venetians stopped trading, stopped traveling, and became stuck in the mud. Like Marie Antoinette retreating into her little hamlet at Versailles, the aristocracy of Venice withdrew into their palaces. Insisting their city remained exceptional, Venetian society chose to dance rather than to adapt. As Venice fell, its appetite for decadence grew. Through the 18th century, the Venetians partied and partied, as if drunk on the wealth accumulated through earlier centuries as a trading power.

• Backtrack through the maze of Room 14, winding your way into a room with a harpsichord, or spinet, cleverly named the...

Room 15: Spinet Room

The 1700s saw the development of new keyboard instruments that would culminate by century's end in the modern piano. This particular specimen has strings that are not hammered (like a piano) but plucked. At this point, a pluck was just a pluck—always the same volume. When hammers were introduced shortly after this, the novelty of being able to play both soft and loud sounds prompted Italians to name the instrument the *pianoforte* (the soft-loud).

Room 17: Parlor

Francesco Guardi (1712-1793), like Canaletto, supplied foreigners with scenes of Venice. But Guardi uses rougher brushwork that casts a romantic haze over the decaying city.

The Parlor (Il Parlatorio delle Monache di S. Zaccaria) is an interior landscape featuring visiting day at a convent school. The girls,

secluded with their servant girls behind grills, chat and have tea with family members, friends, ladies with their pets, and potential suitors. Convents were like finishing schools for aristocratic girls, where they got an education and learned manners before re-entering the world. Note the puppet show (starring spouse-abusing Pulcinella).

Guardi's *Il Ridotto di Palazzo Dandolo* shows partygoers in masks at a Venetian palace licensed for gambling. Casanova and others claimed that these casino houses had back rooms for the private use of patrons and courtesans. The men wear the traditional *bautta*—a three-piece outfit consisting of a face mask, three-cornered hat, and cowl. This getup was actually required by law in certain seedy establishments to ensure that every sinner was equally anonymous. The women wear Lone Ranger masks, and parade a hint of cleavage to potential customers.

• *Continuing along, you'll pass back through the Painting Portico and into...*

Room 18: Longhi

There is no better look at 1700s Venice than these genre scenes by Pietro Longhi (1701-1785), depicting everyday life among the upper classes. See ladies and gentlemen going to the hairdresser or to the dentist, dressed in the finery that was standard in every public situation.

These small easel works provide a psychoana-lytic insight into society. They come with an overwhelming sense of boredom. There's no dynamism. There aren't even any windows. It's a society closed to the world, without initiative, and—it seems—with no shortage of leisure time.

Contrast these straightforward scenes with G. B. Tiepolo's sumptuous ceiling painting of nude gods and goddesses. The Rococo fantasy world of aristocrats was slipping increasingly into the more prosaic era of the bourgeoisie.

• *Pass through several rooms to the far corner.*

Room 21: Alcove
Casanova daydreamed of fancy boudoirs like this one, complete with a large bed (topped with a Madonna by Rosalba Carriera), a walnut dresser, Neoclassical wallpaper, and silver toiletries. Even the presence of the baby cradle would not have dimmed his ardor.

THE TOP FLOOR
The final and most skippable part of the museum is a large collection of Venetian paintings amassed by a local scholar named Egidio Martini. Most are by lesser-known artists from the 1600s and 1700s, but there's one room of 19th- and early 20th-century works, including a few Impressionists.

CA' REZZONICO

PEGGY GUGGENHEIM COLLECTION TOUR

Peggy Guggenheim (1898-1979)—an American-born heiress to the Guggenheim mining fortune and niece of Solomon Guggenheim (who built New York's modern-art museum of the same name)—made her mark as a friend, lover, and patron of modern artists.

As a gallery owner, she introduced Europe's avant-garde to a skeptical America. As a collector, she gave instant status to modern art that was too radical for serious museums. As a patron, she fed starving artists such as Jackson Pollock. And as a person, she lived larger than life, unconventional and original, with a succession of lovers that enhanced her reputation as a female Casanova.

In 1948, Peggy "retired" to Venice, renovating a small, unfinished palazzo on the Grand Canal. Today it's a fun museum, decorated much as it was during her lifetime, with one of the best collections anywhere of 20th-century art. It's the only museum I can think of where the owner is buried in the garden.

Orientation

Cost: €15, usually includes any temporary exhibits.

Hours: Wed-Mon 10:00-18:00, closed Tue.

Avoiding Lines: To dodge crowds, don't come on rainy days. It tends to be a bit less busy at lunchtime. While it's possible to prebook tickets online, it's generally unnecessary.

Getting There: The museum overlooks the Grand Canal, a five-minute walk from the Accademia Bridge (vaporetto: Accademia) or from La Salute Church (vaporetto: Salute). A cool way to cross the Grand Canal is via the S.M. del Giglio *traghetto* (runs 9:00-18:00, €2), see map on page 58).

Information: The ticket desk and museum shop sell an excellent

€5 miniguidebook. Tel. 041-240-5411, www.guggenheim-venice.it.

Tours: Audioguides cost €7. You can book a 1- to 1.5-hour **guided tour** (€85) by calling the museum. Art interns guarding the works are happy to tell you about particular pieces if you ask.

Length of This Tour: Allow one hour.

Baggage Check: Free and required for anything bigger than a small purse.

Services: The WCs inside the main building (between the Kitchen and Living Room) are crowded; less crowded ones are across the garden (at the left end of the café/shop building as you face it; enter from side courtyard).

Photography: Permitted without flash.

Cuisine Art: I'd skip the pricey café on site (€6-14 sandwiches, €13-14 pastas, big €16-17 salads). Instead, see page 272 in the Eating in Venice chapter for recommendations in the Dorsoduro neighborhood. Also consider the options noted for the Accademia Tour, as that museum is just a five-minute walk away, along a street lined with many eateries.

Nearby: If you like contemporary art, this is your neighborhood. Browse the art galleries, and visit the Punta della Dogana museum (next to La Salute, see page 45).

Starring: Picasso, Kandinsky, Mondrian, Dalí, Pollock...and Peggy herself.

The Tour Begins

You'll enter a garden courtyard sprinkled with statues. There's a wing to the left (with the café) and a wing to the right (with the main collection, where you start), plus a modern annex. The collection is (very) roughly chronological, starting to the left with Cubism and ending to the right with post-World War II artists.

The collection's strength is its Abstract, Surrealist, and Abstract-Surrealist art. The placement of the paintings may change, so use this chapter as an overview, not a painting-by-painting tour. What makes this collection unique is that it hangs here in Peggy's home, much as it did in her lifetime. Another plus is that it's staffed by fresh young art students, not the tired civil servants that you meet at Venice's publicly run museums.

• *You'll walk through Peggy's collection and her life. From the sculpture garden, head right, up the stairs and through the black iron-grille doors, into the...*

ENTRANCE HALL: MEET PEGGY GUGGENHEIM

Picture Peggy Guggenheim greeting guests here—standing before the **trembling-leaf mobile by Alexander Calder,** flanked by two

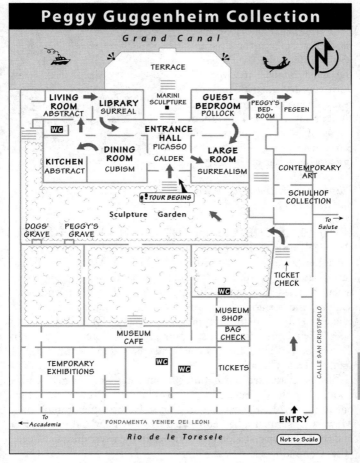

Picasso paintings, surrounded by her yapping dogs and meowing cats, and wearing her Calder-designed earrings, Mondrian-print dress, and "Catwoman" sunglasses.

During the 1950s and 1960s, this old palazzo on the Grand Canal was a mecca for "Moderns," from composer Igor Stravinsky to actor Marlon Brando, from painter Mark Rothko to writer Truman Capote, from choreographer George Balanchine to Beatle John Lennon and performance artist Yoko Ono. They came to sip cocktails, tour the great art, talk about ideas, and meet the woman who had become a living legend.

Pablo Picasso, *On the Beach,* 1937

Curious, balloon-animal women play with a sailboat while their friend across the water looks on. Of all of Peggy's many paintings, this was her favorite.

By the time Peggy Guggen-
heim first became serious about
modern art (about the time this
was painted), Pablo Picasso—
the most famous and versatile
20th-century artist—had already been through his Blue,
Rose, Fauve, Cubist, Synthetic
Cubist, Classical, Abstract, and
Surrealist phases, finally arriving at a synthesis of these styles.
Peggy had some catching up to do.

• *Enter the first room to the left, and you'll see a skinny dining-room table in the center.*

1900-1920: CUBISTS IN THE DINING ROOM

Peggy's **dining-room table** reminds us that this museum was, indeed, her home for the last 30 years of her life. Most of the furniture is now gone, but the walls are decorated much as they were
when she lived here, with paintings and statues by her friends, colleagues, and mentors. Here, she entertained countless artists and
celebrities (more name-dropping), from actor Paul Newman to
poet Allen Ginsberg, from sculptor Henry Moore to playwright
Tennessee Williams, from James Bond creator Ian Fleming to glass
sculptor Dale Chihuly.

Most of the art in the dining room dates from Peggy's child-
hood, when she was raised in the lap of luxury in New York, oblivious to the artistic upheavals going on in Europe. Her grandfather,
Meyer Guggenheim, had emigrated from Switzerland to America
and then had the good fortune to invest in the silver mines at Lead-
ville, Colorado.

In 1912, the *Titanic* went down, taking Peggy's playboy tycoon father with it...and leaving his 14-year-old daughter with a
small but comfortable trust fund and a man-sized hole in her life.

Approaching adulthood, Peggy rejected her traditional American upbringing. She started hanging out at a radical bookstore, got
a nose job (a botched operation, leaving her with a rather bulbous
schnozz)...and began planning a trip to Europe.

In 1920, 21-year-old Peggy arrived in Paris, where a revolution
in art was taking place.

• *Find the following early 20th-century art (or similar pieces) in the Dining Room. (These and other items sometimes move around—if you don't see them where I mention them, keep looking.)*

Pablo Picasso, *The Poet,* 1911

Picasso, a Spaniard living in Paris, shattered the Old World into brown shards ("cubes") and reassembled it in Cubist style. It's a vaguely recognizable portrait of a man from the waist up—tapering to a head at the top, smoking a pipe (?), and cradling the traditional lyre of a poet. While the newfangled motion-picture camera could capture a moving image, Picasso suggests motion with a collage of stills.

Marcel Duchamp, *Nude (Study)—Sad Young Man on a Train,* 1911-1912

In a self-portrait, Duchamp poses gracefully with a cane, but the moving train jiggles the image into a blur of brown. Duchamp is best known not for paintings like this, but for his outrageous conceptual pieces: his urinal-as-statue *(Fountain)* and his moustache on the *Mona Lisa* (titled *L.H.O.O.Q.,* which—when spoken aloud in French—is a pun that translates loosely as "she has a hot ass"). In a 2004 poll of

British artists, Duchamp's urinal was named the most influential modern artwork of all time.

Constantin Brancusi, *Maiastra,* c. 1912

For the generation born before air travel, flying was magical. This high-polished bird is the first of many by Brancusi, who dreamed of flight. But this bronze bird just sits there. For centuries, a good sculptor was one who could capture movement in stone. Brancusi reverts to the essential forms of "primitive" African art, in which even the simplest statues radiate mojo.

• *Head next door, into the Kitchen.*

Marc Chagall, *Rain,* 1911

The rain clouds gather over a farmhouse, the wind blows the trees and people, and everyone prepares for the storm. Quick, put the horse

GUGGENHEIM COLLECTION

in the barn, grab an umbrella, take a leak, and round up the goats in the clouds.

Marc Chagall, a Russian living in France, reinvented scenes from his homeland with a romantic, weightless, childlike joy in topsy-turvy Paris.

1920s: ABSTRACTION AND VARIOUS "-ISMS"

In the Roaring Twenties, Peggy spent *her* twenties right in the center of avant-garde craziness: Paris. For the rest of her life, Europe—not America—would be her permanent address.

In Paris, trust-funded Peggy lived the bohemian life. Post-WWI Paris was cheap and, after the bitter war years, ready to party. Days were spent drinking coffee in cafés, talking ideas with the likes of activist Emma Goldman, writer Djuna *(Nightwood)* Barnes, and photographer Man Ray. Nights were spent abusing the drug forbidden in America (alcohol), dancing to jazz music into the wee hours, and talking about Freud and s-e-x.

One night, at the top of the Eiffel Tower, a dashing artist and intellectual nicknamed "The King of Bohemia" popped the question. Peggy and Laurence Vail soon married and had two children, but the partying only slowed somewhat. This thoroughly modern couple dug the wild life and the wild art it produced.

Vassily Kandinsky, *White Cross,* 1922

I see white, I see crosses, but where's the white cross? Oh, there it is on the right, camouflaged among black squares.

Like a jazz musician improvising from a set scale, Kandinsky plays with new patterns of related colors and lines, creating something that's simply beautiful, even if it doesn't "mean" anything. As Kandinsky himself would say, his art was like "visual music—just open your eyes and look."

• *Continue across the hall, into the Living Room.*

Piet Mondrian, *Composition with Red,* 1938-1939

Like a blueprint for Modernism, Mondrian's T-square style boils painting down to its basic building blocks—black lines, white canvas, and the three primary colors (red, yellow, and blue) arranged in orderly patterns. This stripped-down canvas even omits yellow and blue.

Mondrian started out painting realistic landscapes of the orderly fields in his native Holland. Increasingly, he simplified things into horizontal and vertical grids, creating rectangles of different

proportions. This one has horizontal lines to the left, vertical ones to the right. The horizontals appear to dominate, until we see that they're balanced by the tiny patch of red.

For Mondrian, who was heavily into Eastern mysticism, up vs. down and left vs. right were metaphors for life's ever-shifting dualities: good vs. evil, man vs. woman, fascism vs. communism. The canvas is a bird's-eye view of Mondrian's personal landscape.

• *Head next door, into the Library.*

1930s: ABSTRACT SURREALISTS

In 1928, Peggy's marriage to Laurence Vail ended, and she entered into a series of romantic attachments. Though not stunningly attractive, she was easy to be with, and she truly admired artistic men.

In 1937, she began an on-again, off-again sexual relationship with playwright Samuel *(Waiting for Godot)* Beckett. Beckett steered her toward Modern painting and sculpture—things she'd never paid much attention to.

She started hanging out with the French Surrealists, from artist Marcel Duchamp to writer André Breton to filmmaker/artist Jean *(Beauty and the Beast)* Cocteau. Duchamp, in particular, mentored her in modern art, encouraging her to use her money to collect and promote it. Nearing 40, she moved to London and launched a new career.

Yves Tanguy, *The Sun in Its Jewel Case,* 1937

In May of 1938, this painting was featured at Guggenheim Jeune, the art gallery Peggy opened in London. Tanguy's painting sums up the turbulent art that shocked a sleepy London during that first season.

Weird, phallic, tissue-and-bone protuberances cast long shadows across a moody, dreamlike landscape—the landscape of the mind. (Peggy said the picture "frightened" her, but added, "I got over my fear...and now I own it.") The figures are Abstract (unrecognizable), and the mood is Surreal, producing the style cleverly dubbed Abstract Surrealism.

Peggy was drawn to Yves Tanguy and had a short but intense affair with the married man. Tanguy, like his art, was wacky and

Abstract Art

Abstract art simplifies. A man becomes a stick figure. A squiggle is a wave. A streak of red expresses anger. Arches make you want a cheeseburger. These are universal symbols that everyone from a caveman to a banker understands. Abstract artists capture the essence of reality in a few lines and colors, even things a camera can't—emotions, theoretical concepts, musical rhythms, and spiritual states of mind.

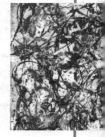

Most 20th- and 21st-century paintings are a mix of the real world ("representation") and the colorful patterns of "abstract" art. An abstract artist purposely "abstracts" only some elements of camera-eye reality to make the resulting canvas more provocative, expressive, or challenging.

spontaneous, occasionally shocking friends by suddenly catching and gobbling up a spider and washing it down with white wine. The Surrealists saw themselves as spokesmen for Freud's "id," the untamed part of the personality that thinks dirty thoughts when the "ego" goes to sleep.

The Guggenheim Jeune gallery exhibited many of the artists we see in this museum, including Kandinsky, Mondrian, and Calder. Guggenheim Jeune closed as a financial flop after just two years, but its shocking paintings certainly created a buzz in the art world, and as the years passed the gallery's failure gained a rosy glow of success.

Salvador Dalí, *The Birth of Liquid Desires,* 1931-1932

Salvador Dalí could draw exceptionally well. He painted "unreal" scenes with photographic realism, making us believe they could truly happen. This air of mystery—the feeling that anything is possible—is both exciting and unsettling. His men explore the caves of the dream world and morph into something else before our eyes.

Personally, Peggy didn't like Dalí or his work, but she dutifully bought this canvas (through his wife, Gala) to complete her collection.

1939-1940: PEGGY'S SHOPPING SPREE IN PARIS

Peggy moved back to Paris and rented an apartment on the Ile St. Louis. In September, Nazi Germany invaded Poland, sparking World War II. All of France waited...and waited...and waited for the inevitable Nazi attack on Paris.

Meanwhile, Peggy spent her days shopping for masterpieces. Using a list compiled by Duchamp and others, she personally visited artists in their studios—from Brancusi to Dalí to Giacometti—often negotiating directly with them. (Picasso initially turned Peggy down, thinking of her as a gauche, bargain-hunting housewife. When she entered his studio he said, "Madame, you'll find the lingerie department on the second floor.") In a few short months, she bought 37 of the paintings now in the collection, perhaps saving them from a Nazi regime that labeled such art "decadent."

In 1941, with the Nazis occupying Paris and most of Europe, Peggy fled her adopted homeland. With her stash of paintings and a new companion—painter Max Ernst—she sailed from Lisbon to safety in New York.

• *Pass back through the Entrance Hall—where Peggy welcomed celebrity guests, from writer Somerset Maugham to actor Rex Harrison to painter Marc Chagall—and into the east wing. The right entryway leads to a room filled with Surrealist canvases.*

1941-1945: SURREALISTS INVADE NEW YORK

Trees become women, women become horses, and day becomes night. Balls dangle, caves melt, and things cast long shadows across film-noir landscapes—Surrealism. The world was moving fast, and Surrealists caught the jumble of images. They scattered seemingly unrelated things on the canvas, leaving us to trace the connections in a kind of connect-the-dots game without numbers.

Peggy spent the war years in America. She married Max Ernst, and their house in New York City became a gathering place for exiled French Surrealists and young American artists.

In 1942, she opened a gallery/museum in New York called Art of This Century that featured, well, essentially the collection we see here in Venice. But patriotic, gung-ho America was not quite ready for the nonconformist, intellectual art of Europe.

Max Ernst, *The Antipope*, c. 1942

The horse-headed nude in red is a portrait of Peggy—at least, that's what she thought when she saw it. She loved the painting and insisted that Max give it to her as a wedding present, renamed *The Mystic Marriage*.

Others read more into it. Is the horse-headed warrior (at right) Ernst himself? Is he being wooed by one of his art students? Is that Peggy's daughter, Pegeen (center), watching the scene, sadly, from a distance? And is Peggy turning toward her beloved Max, subconsciously suspicious of the young student...who would (in fact) soon steal Max from her? Ernst uses his considerable painting skill to bring to light a tangle of secret urges, desires, and fears—hidden like the grotesque animal faces in the reef they stand on.

Paul Delvaux, *The Break of Day,* **1937**
Full-breasted ladies with roots cast long shadows and awaken to a mysterious dawn. If you're counting boobs, don't forget the one reflected in the nightstand mirror.

René Magritte, *Empire of Light,* **1953-1954**
Magritte found that, even under a sunny blue sky, suburbia has its dark side. The improbable combination of daylight sky and nighttime street in one scene is the kind of bizarre paradox that Surrealists loved.

• *Across the hall is the Guest Bedroom, with a fireplace and works by Pollock.*

1945-1948: THE POSTWAR YEARS: POLLOCK IN THE GUEST BEDROOM

Certain young American painters—from Mark Rothko to Robert Motherwell to Robert De Niro Sr. (the actor's father)—were strongly influenced by Peggy's collection. Adopting the Abstract style of Kandinsky, they practiced Surrealist spontaneity to "express" themselves in the physical act of putting paint on canvas. The resulting style (duh): Abstract Expressionism.

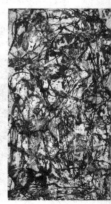

Jackson Pollock, *Enchanted Forest,* **1947**
"Jack the Dripper" attacked America's postwar conformity with a can of paint, dripping and splashing a dense web onto the canvas. Picture Pollock in his studio, jiving to the hi-fi, bouncing off the walls, throwing paint in a moment of alcohol-fueled enlightenment.

Peggy helped make Pollock a celebrity. She bought his earliest works (which show Abstract-Surrealist roots), exhibited his work at her gallery, and even paid him a monthly stipend to keep experimenting.

By the way, if you haven't yet tried the Venetian specialty *spaghetti al nero di seppia* (spaghetti with squid in its own ink), it looks something like this.

In 1946, Peggy published her memoirs, titled *Out of This Century: The Informal Memoirs of Peggy Guggenheim*. The front cover was designed by Max Ernst, the back by Pollock. Peggy herself was now a celebrity.

• *The room on the other side of the fireplace was Peggy's Bedroom.*

1950s: PEGGY IN THE BEDROOM

As America's postwar factories turned swords into kitchen appliances, Peggy longed to return "home" to Europe. The one place that kept calling to her was Venice, ever since she visited here with Laurence Vail in the 1920s. "I decided Venice would be my future home," she wrote. "I felt I would be happy alone there."

In 1947, after a grand finale exhibition by Pollock, she closed the Art of This Century gallery, crated up her collection, and moved to Venice. In 1948, she bought this palazzo and moved in.

This was Peggy's bedroom. She painted it turquoise. She commissioned the **silver headboard by Alexander Calder** for her

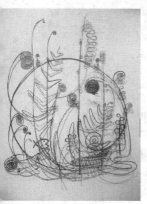

canopy bed, using its silver frame to hang her collection of earrings, handmade by the likes of Calder and Tanguy. Venetian mirrors hung on the walls, along with a sentimental portrait of herself and her sister as children. Ex-husband Laurence Vail's collage-decorated bottles sat on the nightstand.

The same year she moved in, Peggy showed her collection in its own pavilion at the Biennale, Venice's world's fair of art, and it was the hit of the show. Europeans were astounded and a bit dumbfounded, finally seeing the kind of "degenerate" art forbidden during the fascist years, plus the radical new stuff coming out of New York City.

In 1951, Peggy met the last great love of her life, an easygoing, blue-collar Italian with absolutely no interest in art. She was 53, Raoul was 30. When Raoul died in 1954 in a car accident, Peggy comforted herself with her pets.

• *The tiny corner room adjoining the bedroom displays paintings by Pegeen.*

PEGEEN

Peggy's daughter, Pegeen, inherited some of Laurence Vail's artistic talent, painting childlike scenes of Venice, populated by skinny Barbie dolls with antennae. She married twice, had four children, suffered badly from depression, and died of a barbiturate overdose in 1967.

The guest bedroom (where the Pollocks are) was a busy place. Pegeen and her brother, Sinbad, visited their mother in Venice, as did Peggy's ex-husbands and their new loves. Other overnight guests ranged from sculptor Alberto Giacometti (who honeymooned here), to author and cultural explorer Paul Bowles, to artist Jean Arp.

• *Return to the Entrance Hall, then go out onto the Terrace, overlooking the Grand Canal.*

EXHIBITIONISTS ON THE TERRACE

You fall in love with the city itself. There is nothing left over in your heart for anyone else.

—Peggy Guggenheim

The obviously exuberant figure in Marino Marini's equestrian statue, *The Angel of the City* (1948), faces the Grand Canal, spreads his arms wide, and tosses his head back in sheer joy, with an eternal hard-on for the city of Venice. Every morning, Peggy must have felt a similar exhilaration as she sipped coffee while taking in this unbelievable view.

Marini originally designed his bronze rider with a screw-off penis (which sounds dirtier than it is) that could be removed for prudish guests or by curious ones. Someone stole it for some unknown purpose, so the current organ is permanently welded on.

The palazzo—formally Palazzo Venier dei Leoni—looks modern but is old. Construction began in 1748, but only the ground floor was completed. Legend has it that members of a rival family across the canal squelched plans for the upper stories so their home wouldn't be upstaged. The palazzo remained unfinished until Peggy bought it in 1948 and spruced it up. She added the annex in 1958. The **lions** *(leoni)* of the original palace still guard the waterfront entrance.

Peggy's outlandish and rather foreign presence in Venice—drinking, dressing up outrageously, and sunbathing on her rooftop for all to see—was not immediately embraced by the Venetians. But for artists in the 1950s and 1960s, Peggy's palazzo was *the* place to be, especially when the Biennale brought the jet set. Everyone from actor Alec Guinness, to political satirist Art Buchwald, to gossip columnist Hedda Hopper signed her guest book. Picture Peggy and guests, decked out in evening clothes, hopping into her custom-built gondola (nicknamed *La Barchessa,* after the doge's

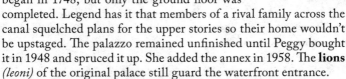

private boat) to ride slowly down the canal for a martini and a Bellini at Harry's Bar.

THE REST OF THE MUSEUM

• *We've seen the core of Peggy's collection (and home). But the museum complex also houses two other collections donated by Peggy's fellow art lovers, as well as a fine garden.*

Schulhof and Mattioli Collections

The recently acquired **Schulhof Collection** brings the museum into the late 20th century. It's exhibited in the small wing perpendicular to the main house (which you can enter from near Peggy's bedroom).

In the 1950s and '60s, the trend was toward bigger canvases, abstract designs, and experimentation with new materials and techniques. Enjoy the simple lines and colors of big, empty canvases by Americans such as Ellsworth Kelly, Barnett Newman, and Mark Rothko. They were following in the footsteps of Abstract artists such as Mondrian and Kandinsky (whose work they must have considered busy). Calder's mobile is like a hanging Kandinsky, brought to life by a gust of wind. The geometrical forms here reflect the same search for order, but these artists painted to the 5/4 asymmetry of Dave Brubeck's jazz classic, "Take Five."

Other painters explored a new dimension: texture. Some works (such as those by de Kooning) have very thick paint piled on. Some (by Dubuffet or Tapies) applied material such as real dirt and organic waste to the canvas. Fontana punctured the canvas so that the fabric itself (and the hole) becomes the subject. The canvas is a tray, serving up a delightful array of substances with interesting colors, patterns, shapes, and textures.

In the psychedelic '60s, Pop Art (Warhol) raised pop-ular cultural icons to the level of high art, and Op Art (Riley) featured optical illusions that mess with your mind when you stare at them. Cy Twombly added crayon-scribbled doodles to the canvas, suggesting handwritten messages with mysterious meanings. Also in the collection are a number of sculptures by Chillida, Calder, Hepworth, and Arp. By the way, many of the Schulhof artists—Calder, Fontana, Chillida, Riley, and Twombly—were first introduced to the world at the Venice Biennale.

The **Mattioli Collection,** normally housed in the café/shop building across the garden from the main palazzo, features paintings and sculptures by well-known Italians, as well as the less-famous postwar generation of young Italians who were strongly influenced by Peggy's collection.

You'll see a lone canvas by Modigliani, pieces by the Futurists, and some fine sculptural works by the father of Futurism, **Umberto**

Boccioni. His *Dynamism of a Speeding Horse + Houses* (1915), as-sembled from wood, cardboard, and metal, captures the blurred motion of a modern world—accelerated by technology, then shat-tered by World War I, which would leave nine million Europeans dead and everyone's moral compass spinning. (In fact, this statue was shattered by the destructive force of Boccioni's own kids, who scattered the cardboard "houses" while using it as a rocking horse.)

Boccioni's *Unique Forms of Continuity in Space* (1913, one of a dozen authorized bronze casts in the world's museums) seems inspired by the flowing works by Picasso and Duchamp we saw earlier. The energetic cyborg speeds forward, rippled by the winds of history, as it strides purposefully into the future. This work may look familiar—check your pocket for one of Italy's €0.20 coins and compare.

Peggy sponsored young artists, including **Tancredi**—just one name, back when that was odd—who was given a studio in the palazzo's basement. Tancredi had a relationship with daughter Pe-geen, with her mother's blessing.

Sculpture Garden

Peggy opened her impressive collection of sculpture to the Vene-tian public for free. It features first-rate works by all the greats, from Brancusi to Giacometti. After so much art already, you might find the trees—so rare in urban Venice—more interesting.

If, after your visit here, you still don't like modern art, think of what Peggy used to tell puzzled visitors: "Come back again in 50 years."

Café/Shop and More Exhibitions

The long building facing the main palazzo from across the garden houses the overpriced **café, shop, WCs,** and (in the back) halls for the **Mattioli Collection** (described earlier) and **temporary exhib-its.** Step into the café just to peruse the fascinating black-and-white photos of Peggy standing alongside her art, taken in the very same rooms in which the paintings now hang.

• *Finally, in the southwest corner of the garden (along the brick wall), find...*

Peggy's Grave and Her Dogs' Graves

"Here Lie My Beloved Babies" marks the grave of Peggy's many dogs, her steady companions as she grew old. Note the names of some of these small, long-haired Lhasa Apsos. Along with "Cappuccino" and

"Baby," you'll see "Pegeen," after her dau[ghter] [and] for Herbert Read, the art critic who helped [build the col]lection.

Peggy's ashes are buried alongside, marked wi[th a] plaque: "Here Rests Peggy Guggenheim 1898-1979."

Over your right shoulder, the flourishing olive tree is a g[ift] from one of Peggy's old traveling buddies—Yoko Ono.

In the nonconformist 1960s, Peggy's once shocking art and unconventional lifestyle became more acceptable, even commonplace. By the 1970s, she was universally recognized as a major force in early modern art and was finally even honored by the Venetians with the nickname, *L'Ultima Dogaressa*— The Last Dogaressa.

LA SALUTE CHURCH TOUR

Santa Maria della Salute

Where the Grand Canal opens up into the lagoon stands one of Venice's most distinctive landmarks, the church dedicated to Santa Maria della Salute (Our Lady of Health). The architect, Baldassare Longhena—who also did St. Mark's Square's "new" wing and the Ca' Rezzonico—remade Venice in the Baroque style. Crown-shaped La Salute was his crowning achievement, and the last grand Venetian structure built before Venice's decline began.

Orientation

Cost: Free entry to church; €3 to visit the Sacristy.

Hours: Daily 9:00-12:00 & 15:00-17:30, tel. 041-274-3928, http://www.seminariovenezia.it.

Getting There: The church is on the Grand Canal, near the point where the canal spills into the lagoon. It's a 10-minute walk from the Accademia Bridge (past the Peggy Guggenheim Collection). By boat, vaporetto #1 delivers you to its doorstep (€5 from San Marco, 5 minutes). The *traghetto* from San Marco to Salute no longer runs, but you can still take one from S.M. del Giglio.

Musical Services: Vespers service with organ music Mon-Thu at 15:30, followed by Mass at 16:00. Mass also on Sun at 11:00, followed by organ music at 11:45.

Length of This Tour: Allow 30 minutes.

Photography: OK without flash.

Starring: Baldassare Longhena's church, minor works by Titian and Giordano, and the Sacristy, with major works by Tintoretto and Titian.

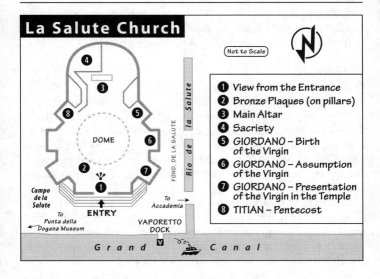

The Tour Begins

EXTERIOR

The white stone church has a steep dome that rises above the octagonal structure. It's encrusted with Baroque scrolls, leafy Corinthian columns, and 125 statues, including the lovely ladies lounging over the central doorway. The architect conceived of the church in the shape of a crown.

During the bitter plague of 1630, the Virgin Mary took pity on the city of Venice, miraculously allowing only one in three Venetians (46,000 souls) to die. During this terrible time, Venetians built this church in honor of Our Lady of Health. Her statue tops the lantern, and she's dressed as an admiral, hand on a rudder, welcoming ships to the Grand Canal.

Even today, Mary's intercession is celebrated every November 21, when a floating bridge is erected across the Grand Canal so Venetians can walk from San Marco across the water and right up the seaweed-covered steps to the front door.

At age 32, architect Baldassare Longhena (1598-1682) supported the city's heaviest dome by sinking countless pilings (locals claim over a million) into the sandy soil to provide an adequate

LA SALUTE CHURCH

foundation. The 12 Baroque scrolls at the dome's base function as buttresses to help support the mammoth structure.

INTERIOR
❶ View from the Entrance
The church has a bright, healthy glow, with white stone (turned gray because of a fungus) illuminated by light filtering through the dome's windows. The nave is circular, surrounded by chapels. In contrast to the ornate Baroque exterior, the inside is simple, with only Corinthian columns and two useless balcony railings up in the dome. The red, white, and yellow marble of the floor adds a cheerful note.

Longhena focuses our immediate attention on the main altar. Every other view is blocked by heavy pillars. A master of "theatrical architecture," Longhena reveals the side chapels only one by one, as we walk around and explore. Viewed from the center of the church, the altar and side chapels are framed by arches.

Some of the "marble" is actually brick covered with marble dust. The windows, with clear glass in a honeycomb pattern, bring in maximum light.

• Look at the pillars near the entrance, opposite the altar, to find the...

❷ Bronze Plaques
The church is dedicated not just to physical health but to spiritual health as well. The plaques relate that on September 16, 1972, Albino Luciani, the future Pope John Paul I, visited here and paid homage to the Virgin of Health (six years later, he fell sick and died after only 30 days in office).

❸ Main Altar
The marble statues on the top of the main altar tell the church's story: The Virgin and Child (center) are approached for help by a kneeling, humble Lady Venice (left). Mary shows compassion and sends an angel baby (right) to drive away Old Lady Plague.

The icon of a black, sad-eyed Madonna with a black baby (12th-century Byzantine) is not meant to be ethnically accurate. Here, a "black" Madonna means an otherworldly one.

• Find the entrance to the Sacristy, if it's open (entry location varies). It costs €3 to get in, but cheapskates can get a glimpse of the paintings for free by standing outside the entry.

❹ Sacristy
Along the right wall is Tintoretto's big and colorful *Marriage at*

Cana (1551). The receding dinner table leads the eye to Jesus, who is surrounded by the bustle of the wedding feast. On the right, the host (in gray) orders the servant to bring more wine. The apostles at the table portray leading Venetian artists of the day.

On the ceiling are three ultra-dramatic paintings by Titian, with gruesome subjects: *Cain Clubbing Abel, Abraham Sacrificing His Son,* and *David Slaying Goliath* (c. 1543-1544). The panels—featuring stormy clouds, windblown hair, flat tones, and overwrought poses—date from Titian's "Mannerist crisis." After visiting Rome and seeing the work of Michelangelo in the Sistine Chapel, Titian abandoned his standard, sweet, and tested style to paint epic, statuesque, and dramatic works in the Mannerist style. To appreciate his range of styles, contrast the ceiling panels with the painting over the altar, Titian's stately *St. Mark Enthroned with Saints* (c. 1511).

• *Back in the circular nave, there are six side chapels—three to the left, three to the right. Start near the main altar, on the right side (to your right as you face the altar).*

Side Chapel Paintings

Luca Giordano (1632-1705) celebrates the Virgin in three paintings with similar compositions—heaven and angels above, dark earth below.

Giordano, a prolific artist from Naples, was known as "Luca fa presto" (Fast Luke) for the speed (some would say sloppiness) with which he dashed off his paintings.

• *In the chapel to the right of the altar is...*

❺ Giordano, *Birth of the Virgin,* 1674

Little baby Mary in her mom's arms seems like nothing special. But God the Father looks down from above and sends the dove of the Holy Spirit.

• *In the middle chapel (on the right side), look for...*

❻ Giordano, *Assumption of the Virgin,* 1667

Mary, at the end of her life, is being taken gloriously, by winged babies, up from the dark earth to the golden light of heaven. The apostles cringe in amazement. A later artist thought his statue was better and planted it right in our way.

• *In the chapel closest to the entrance, see...*

❼ Giordano, *Presentation of the Virgin in the Temple,* early 1670s

Notice how the painting fits the surrounding architecture. It's great to enjoy art in situ. The child Mary (in blue, with wispy halo) ascends a staircase that goes diagonally "into" the canvas. Giordano places us viewers at the foot of the stairs. The lady in the lower left asks her kids, "Why can't you be more like her?!"

• *From here, look directly across to the other side of the nave at Titian's* Pentecost, *in the chapel closest to the main altar. The painting looks its best from this distance and angle.*

❽ Titian, *Pentecost,* 1546

The dove of the Holy Spirit sends spiritual rays that fan out to the apostles below, giving them tongues of fire above their heads. They gyrate in amazement, each one in a different direction. Using floor tiles and ceiling panels, Titian has created the 3-D illusion of a barrel-arched chapel, with the dove coming right into the church through a fake window. But the painting was not designed for this location and, up close, the whole fake niche looks...fake.

SAN GIORGIO MAGGIORE TOUR

If you stand at the southern end of St. Mark's Square, you can't miss the classical facade, dome, and tower of San Giorgio Maggiore just across the water. This iconic church is only a five-minute vaporetto ride away. Even if you're not interested in Palladio's influential architecture, Tintoretto's famous *Last Supper,* or the stunning bell-tower views of Venice and the lagoon, it's worth a trip just to escape from tourist-mobbed St. Mark's Square.

Orientation

Cost: Admission to the church is free. It costs €6 to go up the bell tower. Bring €0.50 coins to light the artwork.

Hours: Church open daily April-Oct 7:00-19:00, Nov-March 7:00-dusk. Tower opens at 9:00; the last ascent in the tower elevator is 15 minutes before closing time. The elevator is closed during Sunday Mass. Tel. 041-522-7827.

Avoiding Crowds: The church is never crowded, but the bell tower and elevator can be. Come early or late to have it to yourself.

Getting There: Getting to San Giorgio Maggiore (alone on its own island) requires a vaporetto  ride so, unless you have a pass, it's pricey. The one-hop, three-minute ride on #2 from the San Zaccaria docks (pier is just past the Bridge of Sighs, direction: Tronchetto) is discounted at €5. Also, remember that the normal €7.50 ticket gives you 75 minutes—which could cover your return trip if you do a quick visit. To get back to St. Mark's Square, take the #2 headed the opposite way (direction: San Zaccaria).

Mass: Mass is held on Sundays and holidays at 11:00 and on other days at 8:00; the church remains open during Mass to welcome worshippers, not sightseers. In the winter, when it's too cold inside the church, Mass is held in the adjacent chapel (enter to the right of the high altar). Benedictine monks who live at San Giorgio perform Gregorian chants during each Mass and at evening vespers (daily at 19:00, stay after closing).

Length of This Tour: Allow one hour.

Visitor Services: A WC is at the base of the elevator. A fine little harborside café, rarely used by tourists, is about 150 yards around the left of the church. Its terrace is peaceful—except at lunchtime, when it's mobbed by librarians (€4 *panini*, €8.50 pastas and salads, €10 *secondi*, daily 10:00-20:00, off-season 11:00-15:00).

Photography: Permitted without flash.

The Rest of the Island: You can walk along the left side of the church to the café and view the pleasure boats in the marina. Inside the pink building just beyond the café is **Le Stanze del Vetro,** a super-modern space with rotating exhibits relating to glass. Typically their spring exhibition features contemporary glass art, while their fall show highlights a historic Venetian maestro (free entry, Thu-Tue 10:00-19:00, closed Wed, tel. 041-522-9138, www.lestanzedelvetro.org).

Starring: Palladio, Tintoretto, and views of Venice.

The Tour Begins

EXTERIOR

The facade looks like a Greek temple, a style well-known today because of its architect, Andrea Palladio (1508-1580). Palladio's

SAN GIORGIO MAGGIORE

hugely influential treatise on architecture inspired centuries of architects in England and America with its expert application of Greco-Roman styles. Countless villas, palaces, and churches look like this. They are "Palladian."

Palladio's ingenious facade overlaps two temple fronts. Four tall columns, topped by a triangular pediment resembling a Greek porch, mark the entryway to the tall, central nave. This is superimposed over the facade of the lower side aisles. Behind the facade rises a dome topped with a statue of St. George (the Christian slayer of medieval dragons) holding a flag. The whole complex is

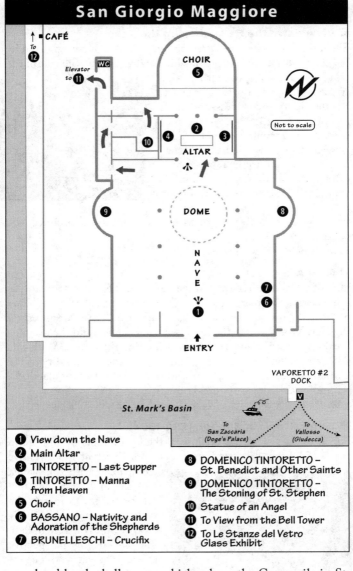

San Giorgio Maggiore

CAFÉ
To **12**

Elevator to **11**

WC

CHOIR
5

Not to scale

4 **2** **3**
10
ALTAR

DOME

9 N A V E **8**

7
6
1

ENTRY

VAPORETTO #2
DOCK

St. Mark's Basin

To
San Zaccaria
(Doge's Palace)

To
Vallosso
(Giudecca)

1 View down the Nave
2 Main Altar
3 TINTORETTO – Last Supper
4 TINTORETTO – Manna from Heaven
5 Choir
6 BASSANO – Nativity and Adoration of the Shepherds
7 BRUNELLESCHI – Crucifix
8 DOMENICO TINTORETTO – St. Benedict and Other Saints
9 DOMENICO TINTORETTO – The Stoning of St. Stephen
10 Statue of an Angel
11 To View from the Bell Tower
12 To Le Stanze del Vetro Glass Exhibit

SAN GIORGIO MAGGIORE

completed by the bell tower, which echoes the Campanile in St. Mark's Square across the water.

This church feels so striking because it just doesn't fit with old-school Venice. Palladio makes no concession to the Byzantine legacy of Venice that you see across the water at the Doge's Palace.
• *Walk into the interior of the church.*

INTERIOR
❶ View down the Nave, then up the Nave

The interior matches the outer facade, with a high nave flanked by lower side aisles. The walls are white (Palladio's favorite color); the windows have clear, rather than stained, glass; and the well-lit church has the clarity, orderliness, and mathematical perfection of the classical world. In keeping with Palladio's classical sensitivity, all decor is in harmony (compared to the relative chaos of, say, the Frari Church). Oh, the stout, stony symmetry and mathematical purity—with light spilling in from the canal—it's enough to give a Renaissance architect a... never mind.

• *Head down the nave to the...*

❷ Main Altar

The altar, made after the voyages of Columbus and company, is topped with a bronze globe of the world. When this place was being built, Church doctrine was being challenged by the discovery of the New World, the founding of secular societies, and the groundbreaking scientific advancements of the Enlightenment. With this altar, the globe is embraced as if to declare the universality of the Christian message. God, overhead, is wearing a triangular halo, reminding us he's part of the Trinity.

• *On the wall to the right of the altar is...*

❸ Tintoretto, *Last Supper*, 1592-1594

This is the last of several versions of the Last Supper by Tintoretto (1518-1594) that decorate Venice, each one different and inventive

(compare it with the Scuola San Rocco version, pictured on page 157). Here, the table stretches diagonally away from us on a tiled floor. The convincing perspective effect is theatrical, engaging the viewer. The scene is crowded—servants and cats mingle with wispy angels. A blazing lamp, radiating supernatural light, illuminates the otherwise dark interior. At the far left, a beggar is fed, illustrating Christ's concern for the poor. The devilish guy on the right rejects a basket of communion wafers while eyeing a more hedonistic banquet. Your eyes go straight to a well-lit Christ, serving his faithful with both hands—wholeheartedly.

San Giorgio was the church for a Benedictine monastery, an order that stressed a simple lifestyle and concern for the poor. They hired Tintoretto (a common-man's painter) and worked closely with him to hone the message that all are welcome—saints, servants, beggars, sinners—into the Christian faith. The monks appreciated Tintoretto's jumble of the spiritual with the mundane, proclaiming that God works miraculously with us on an everyday level.

This canvas works together theologically with the other canvas flanking the altar.

• *On the wall to the left of the altar is...*

❹ Tintoretto, *Manna from Heaven*, 1591-1592

This painting illustrates the Benedictine motto: Work and pray.

Here we see the sunny morning after the storm, when God rained bread down on the hungry Israelites. Some work, others relax prayerfully, and others gather the heavenly meal in baskets, basking in the glow of the miracle. The message: Work and pray, and God will take care of you.

• *Behind the altar is the...*

❺ Choir

This beautiful space features 82 stalls elaborately carved in walnut. Here, monks stood and sang, carrying on the prayers, chants, and traditions of the Benedictine order, whose relationship with the island stretched back to A.D. 982 (the monastery closed in 1807, but was revived on a smaller scale in the 20th century). The choir was designed with acoustics in mind, and the barrel-vault ceiling

is backed up with a woofer-shaped apse—ideal for amplifying Gregorian chant. (Suddenly I feel a cough coming on...my, the echoes.)

MORE ART INSIDE THE CHURCH

As long as you're here, check out a few more works. They're minor pieces in art-drenched Venice, but they'd be stars in any American museum.

Back near the entrance, in the first chapel on the right as you face the altar, is Jacopo Bassano's ❻ *Nativity and Adoration of the Shepherds,* where a radiant Baby Jesus lights the dim canvas. In the next chapel is a carved ❼ **Crucifix** by Florentine dome-builder Filippo Brunelleschi.

In the transepts are two works by Jacopo Tintoretto's son, Domenico. In the right transept, the static ❽ *St. Benedict and Other Saints* shows the early monk (to left, in black, bald and bearded) along with Pope Gregory (who wrote about him) having a heavenly vision. ❾ *The Stoning of St. Stephen* (left transept) shows that Domenico had his father's raw talent, but not his flair for dramatic compositions that recede into the distance.

On your way to the bell tower, you'll pass the original ❿ **statue of an angel** that once stood atop the tower (a copy stands there today). Made in the 18th century of laminated wood covered in lead, it was destroyed by lightning in 1993. Restorers have pieced it back together.

• *You'll find the elevator to the top of the bell tower in the far left corner.*

THE BELL TOWER
⓫ View from the Bell Tower

The bell tower here is less crowded than the Campanile at St. Mark's and has an unobstructed view in all directions (St. Mark's has a lattice grill to keep suicidal people from jumping).

Start by looking at the city (to the north), and go clockwise:

Facing North (toward the city): This is the famous view of Venice's skyline, dominated by St. Mark's Campanile. The big,

long, brick church farther inland is Santi Giovanni e Paolo. Farther to the right (east) is the barely visible basin of the Arsenale, the former shipyard, which in its medieval heyday bragged that it was capable of producing a ship a day. Farther still is the green parkland where the Venice Biennale international exhibition is held annually (alternating each year between art and architecture). North of Venice, in the hazy distance (just to the right of Santi Giovanni e Paolo), you can glimpse several islands. Tiny San Michele (with cypress trees) is the city's cemetery—from here, the island looks connected to Venice. Murano, the next closest, appears to be an extension of the forested cemetery. Burano is to the distant

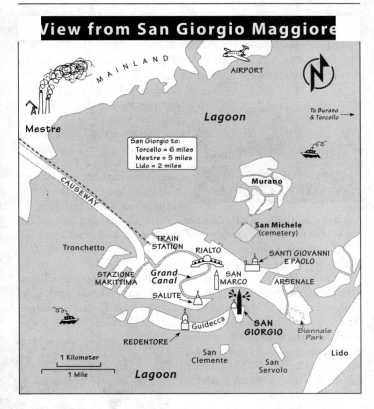

View from San Giorgio Maggiore

MAINLAND

AIRPORT

Mestre

Lagoon

To Burano
& Torcello →

CAUSEWAY

San Giorgio to:
Torcello = 6 miles
Mestre = 5 miles
Lido = 2 miles

Murano

San Michele
(cemetery)

Tronchetto

TRAIN
STATION

RIALTO

SANTI GIOVANNI
E PAOLO

STAZIONE
MARITTIMA

*Grand
Canal*

SAN
MARCO

ARSENALE

SALUTE

Guidecca

**SAN
GIORGIO**

Biennale
Park

REDENTORE

San
Clemente

San
Servolo

Lido

1 Kilometer

1 Mile

Lagoon

right, with its leaning bell tower. And Torcello (trust me) is just beyond Burano.

Facing East and South: Look out at the lagoon, which leads to the open Adriatic. This tower was once used to spot approaching enemy boats. The lagoon is too shallow for serious shipping; posts mark the channels dredged to let boats pass through. There's a strict speed limit: 5 knots per hour (kph) on the small canals, 7 kph on the Grand Canal, and 11 kph around the perimeter of the island city.

The long, narrow sandbar island of Lido in the distance is six miles long and only a half-mile wide (with cars and ferry service to the mainland). The green dome on the island marks the Lido's town center, home to modern hotels and beaches. The Lido serves as a natural breakwater against the wind and waves of the Adriatic Sea, helping create the placid waters of the Venetian lagoon. At the right end of the Lido (visible from here, but not obvious) is the narrow opening to the Adriatic, where the long-delayed underwater flood barriers are being built. Designed to block the *acqua alta* flooding, the multibillion-dollar project involves the construction of a series of hinged barriers that will rise up to block high tides threatening the lagoon.

Once a year, the mayor of Venice sails to the opening of the Adriatic to celebrate the ritual marriage of Venice and the sea—the

same ritual performed centuries ago by the doges in their gold-leaf boat.

Between the Lido and San Giorgio are several smaller islands, which have been home over the centuries to monasteries and hospitals. The plain, rectangular white building on San Servolo, the little island just before the Lido, was a hospital for the insane in the 18th century and now houses a university.

At your feet are the green gardens and the cloisters of the former abbey of San Giorgio.

Facing West: Below is the church, with its dome topped by a green St. George carrying a flag (or is his arm still missing?). You can see the back sides of the white statues atop Palladio's facade. Arcing gracefully to the left is the island of Giudecca, which is oh-

so-close to the island you're on, but must be reached by a short swim or vaporetto #2. The Giudecca, which has always been isolated from the rest of the city, was a popular place to build villas in Venice's heyday. The island's separation also made it a perfect place for exiles such as Michelangelo, who found refuge and peace here between com-

missions. Today, except for a few churches, a youth hostel, and a couple of luxury hotels, the Giudecca is home to locals going about their quiet lives, oblivious to the tourism that dominates the rest of Venice. You can see the swimming pool of the jet-setty Ciprani Hotel, the domes of other Palladian churches (the only sights on this otherwise residential island), and, at the far end, the Molino Stucky, an old, industrial flour mill that reopened in 2007 as the Hilton Hotel.

Directly across from you is the grand dome of La Salute Church. At the head of the Grand Canal stands the golden globe of the old Customs House, now the Punta della Dogana contemporary art museum. Looming beyond La Salute's dome, and a bit to the right, is Venice's cruise port. How many megaships are in town today? And in the far distance, through the smog, are the burning smokestacks and cranes of lovely Mestre, on the mainland.

Looking Up: The bells chime the hours and half-hours, and ring especially loudly at noon. Try being here then, and when people ask you, "How did you enjoy San Giorgio Maggiore?" you can say, "What?"

VENICE'S LAGOON TOUR

San Michele • Murano • Burano • Torcello

Fascinating islands hide out in Venice's lagoon, a calm section of the Adriatic protected from wind and waves by the natural break-water of the Lido. The brackish marsh—a mix of fresh water and silt from the mainland's rivers, plus the tide-driven saltwater of the Adriatic—is set among a maze of sandbars. The lagoon is big (212 square miles) and so shallow that you could walk across most of it without getting your hair wet. Centuries ago, the shallow water and treacherous sandbars made the isle of Venice safe from attack by land or sea. Venice is the only great medieval city that never needed a wall.

Cradled by the lagoon, north of the city, are four islands easily laced together in a pleasant day trip, a nice escape from the hubbub of Venice. Though they're all basically satellites of Venice, each one has its own personality and claims to fame: Murano is known for glass; Burano for lace and photogenic, exuberantly colorful houses; and tranquil Torcello for its antique church's fine mosaics. San Michele is the cemetery island, the last stop for its residents, but the first stop for the vaporetto from Venice. The lagoon is home to many more islands, but these four are the most worthwhile for visitors.

We'll sail first from Venice to Murano (stopping at San Michele on the way), and then to Burano, from where we'll make a side-trip to Torcello before returning to Venice.

Orientation

Getting There: We'll travel by vaporetto, but there are other options (see sidebar in this chapter). Since single vaporetto tickets (€7.50) are only valid for 75 minutes, getting a vaporetto pass for this lagoon excursion makes

Venice's Lagoon

more sense (such as a 24-hour pass for €20; see page 23 for more on vaporetto tickets). You can recheck vaporetto times by downloading the latest schedule in PDF form from www.actv.it.

When to Go: If you want to visit all of the lagoon sights, keep in mind that Burano's good Lace Museum and Torcello's dull church museum are closed Mondays.

Avoiding Crowds: You aren't the only tourist in Venice spending your day seeing these sights, in this same order. *Vaporetti* can be very crowded; if you want a seat for the longer rides, consider showing up at the boat dock a bit early to get in line.

Planning Your Time: Since it takes a minimum of three hours round-trip from St. Mark's to Torcello, allow at least six hours to blitz all four islands. Eight hours (or more) lets you slow down, browse, and enjoy. For an hour-by-hour itinerary, see page 15. If you only have a few hours to spare, stick to visiting either Murano or Burano/Torcello. Murano is much quicker to reach and a must for glass enthusiasts, but Burano and Torcello have more compelling sights overall.

Cemetery (San Michele): Daily 7:30-18:00, Oct-March until

LAGOON

16:30; reception to the left as you enter, free WC to the right, no picnicking.

Glass Museum (Murano): €10, daily 10:00-18:00, Nov-March until 17:00, Fondamenta Giustinian 8, tel. 041-739-586, www.museovetro.visitmuve.it.

Lace Museum (Burano): €5, Tue-Sun 10:00-18:00, Nov-March until 17:00, closed Mon year-round, some English descriptions, tel. 041-730-034, www.museomerletto.visitmuve.it.

Santa Maria Assunta Church (Torcello): €5, €12 combo-ticket covers museum, church, and bell tower; daily March-Oct 10:30-18:00, Nov-Feb 10:00-17:00; museum and bell tower close 30 minutes earlier, museum closed Mon year-round; museum tel. 041-730-761, church/bell tower tel. 041-730-119.

Information: Pick up a free map of the lagoon and its islands from any TI. Two words you'll see all day: *vetri* (glass, Murano's specialty) and *merletti* (lace, Burano's specialty).

Starring: World-famous Venetian glass and lace, the mosaics of the oldest Venetian church, outrageously colorful fishermen's villages, and the quieter side of Venice.

WHERE TO START

You can start from St. Mark's Square, from the train or bus station, or from the Fondamente Nove vaporetto stop (15 minutes' walk from Rialto or San Marco). Wherever you start, your first goal is to locate a vaporetto heading to the Colonna stop on the island of Murano (listed on signs and schedules as Murano-Colonna).

From Fondamente Nove: The Fondamente Nove vaporetto stop is on the north shore of Venice (the "back" of the fish, an enjoyable 15-minute walk from the Rialto or San Marco area—see directions below). Lines #4.1 and #4.2 converge here before heading out to Murano. Catch either one (about every 10 minutes). From Fondamente Nove the boats cross to San Michele (whose stop is called Cimitero) in six minutes, then continue another three minutes to Murano-Colonna.

Walking to Fondamente Nove is easy and scenic, passing through two of Venice's most pleasant squares: First head for Campo Santa Maria Formosa (north of St. Mark's), then navigate north to Campo San Zanipolo/Santi Giovanni e Paolo (with its hulking church). Behind the church is Venice's gigantic, brick hospital *(ospedale);* walk between that building and the canal (on Fondamenta dei Mendicanti) until you reach the lagoon; turn left and walk a few more minutes to the vaporetto stops.

From St. Mark's Square: From the San Zaccaria stop, catch vaporetto #4.1, which leaves every 20 minutes (check the reader-board to find the right dock). It travels around the "tail" of fish-shaped Venice, making several stops before reaching Murano-

LAGOON

Colonna after 45 minutes. (During the summer—roughly June through early September—you can also take the express #7 vaporetto directly to Murano in 25 minutes, but you'll miss the cemetery.)

From the Train Station or Bus Station: Catch vaporetto #4.2, which leaves every 20 minutes and takes 40 minutes to reach Murano-Colonna. (You can also take the express #3 vaporetto, which goes directly to Murano-Colonna twice an hour, but skips the cemetery.)

THE ROUTE

Here's the plan: On the way from Fondamente Nove to Murano, get off at the Cimitero stop on the island of San Michele if you want to see the cemetery. On Murano, you'll arrive at the Colonna stop, but leave from a different stop, Murano-Faro, where you'll board vaporetto #12 for the 30-40-minute trip to Burano. From Burano, you can side-trip to Torcello (on the #12, 5-minute trip each way). To return to Venice from Burano, take vaporetto #12 back in the other direction (45 minutes to Fondamente Nove). For a longer, more scenic return past even more lagoon islands, see page 212.

The Tour Begins

• *After leaving Fondamente Nove, the next stop of the #4.1 and #4.2 vaporetto lines is Cimitero. On the way you may see a sculpture in the water of two people in a boat heading toward the cemetery. It's* The Barque of Dante, *ferrying Dante and Virgil to the afterlife. At the dock, hop off for a short visit to...*

SAN MICHELE

The cemetery island's location—directly across the water from the emergency room of Venice's Santi Giovanni e Paolo hospital—is

just a coincidence. The stopover is easy, since boats come every 10 minutes. If you even half-enjoy wandering through old cemeteries, you'll dig this one—it's full of flowers, trees, scurrying lizards, and birdsong, and has an intriguing chapel.

The island, which is dedicated to St. Michael and holds a Renaissance church, became Venice's cemetery in 1806 when Napoleon decreed that it was unhygienic to bury bodies within a city. As a result, Venice's coffins were shipped out to San Michele, and

LAGOON

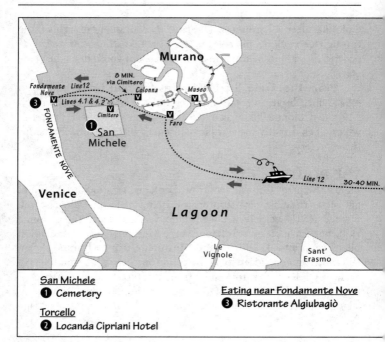

San Michele
❶ Cemetery

Torcello
❷ Locanda Cipriani Hotel

Eating near Fondamente Nove
❸ Ristorante Algiubagiò

since then, Venetians have been buried here. You'll find the dearly departed (many with their photos) sorted into sections *(campi)* of priests *(preti)*, nuns *(suore)*, monks *(frati)*, children *(bambini)*, civilian victims of war, soldiers, military sailors *(marinai)*, and so on. The cemetery is divided into numbered zones called *recinti*.

Foreign Romantics and artists who made Venice their adopted hometown have also chosen this spot as their final resting place. Because many came from other cultures and weren't Catholic, you'll find them in the Evangelico (Protestant) section, Recinto XV; and the Greco (Orthodox) section, Recinto XIV. To find these sections—with the graves of the most famous foreigners—go basically straight ahead from the entrance to the far end, following the maps and signs.

In Recinto XV lies Idaho-born poet **Ezra Pound.** While his works are less familiar than his contemporaries', he was a huge influence on his fellow Modernists, most notably James Joyce and T. S. Eliot. A fan of Mussolini, he made anti-American broadcasts during World War II. Instead of being tried for treason after the war, he spent 12 years in a hospital for the "criminally insane." Eliot, Robert Frost, Ernest Hemingway, and others eventually lobbied for his re-

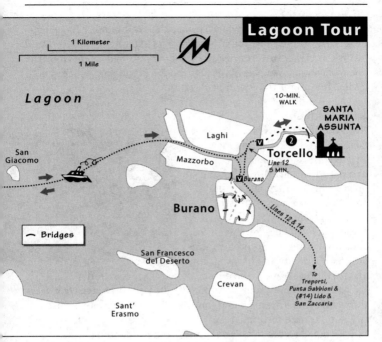

Lagoon Tour

1 Kilometer

1 Mile

Lagoon

Laghi

10-MIN. WALK

SANTA MARIA ASSUNTA

San Giacomo

Mazzorbo

Torcello ②
Line 12
5 MIN.

Burano

Burano

~ Bridges

San Francesco del Deserto

Lines 12 & 14

Crevan

Sant' Erasmo

To Treporti, Punta Sabbioni & (#14) Lido & San Zaccaria

lease, which came in 1958. From the Evangelico gate, he's in the near-left quarter of the section—look for a small stone in a large plot, with three large bushes.

Nearby is the grave of Nobel Laureate and onetime US Poet Laureate **Joseph Brodsky** (1940-1996), who was expelled from Soviet Russia, lived the rest of his life in America, and asked to be buried here in Venice. It's in the far-left quarter, facing the gravel path and Ezra Pound.

Recinto XIV (the "Greco" section) is nearby: Exit the Evangelico gate and turn left, following the wall until you reach the gate marked *Rec. Greco*. Inside, find Russian-born Modernist composer **Igor Stravinsky** (far right corner, alongside his wife) and the Russian dancer/choreographer **Diaghilev** (the canopied tomb along the far wall, piled with ballet slippers left in homage by his admirers).

• *Return to the dock and catch any #4.1 or #4.2 vaporetto heading toward the right (boats leave every 10 minutes). While you're waiting, look for the blue funeral boat with a rack on wheels for the coffin. It's usually moored next to the vaporetto.*

It's just a three-minute crossing to the Murano-Colonna stop.

(If the vaporetto's too crowded, you could just swim it.) As you approach the island of Murano, you'll see its ghostly lighthouse *(faro)* off to the right. In centuries past, the *faro* guided boats from the open sea into town. Near the lighthouse is the stop where you'll leave Murano for the island of Burano.

▲MURANO

Murano is famous for its glass factories. A 1292 Venetian law restricted glass production (and its dangerous furnaces) to Murano to prevent fires on the main island... and to protect the secrets of Venetian glassmaking. Originally, glassmakers made mosaic tiles, later branching out to produce the ornate vases, beaded necklaces, glass sculptures, and wine decanters you'll see here today.

Murano may seem dominated by glassworks and the glass shops that line its main canal, but there's much more to the island. If you take time to wander, you'll find impressive churches, scenically situated restaurants, and untouristed residential areas.

From the Colonna vaporetto stop, skip the glass shops in front of you, walk to the right, and wander up the street along the canal, **Fondamenta dei Vetrai** (Glassmakers' Embankment). The Faro district of Murano, on the other side of the canal, is packed with factories *(fabriche)* and their furnaces *(fornaci)*. The brick buildings give Murano a 19th-century, Industrial Age look and feel. At #14 is the entry to the island's small indoor **shopping mall,** with a Despar supermarket on the upper floor (Mon-Sat 8:00-19:30, closed Sun).

You'll pass dozens more **glass shops** along the canal. Window-shopping here can be as much fun as buying—the personality, style, and prices of wares vary wildly from place to place. Early along this promenade, at #47, is the venerable **Venini** shop, with glass that's a cut above much of what else is on offer here, and with an interior showing off the ultimate in modern Venetian glass design (Mon-Sat 9:30-18:00, closed Sun). The storefronts along here display everything from knickknacks (glass menageries) to vases to decorative items to, well, glasses. If a window display grabs your attention, step inside; you may even see a glass maestro working on small-

Murano

① Fondamenta dei Vetrai
② Church of San Pietro Martire
③ Residential Murano: Ram o da Mula

④ Glass Museum
⑤ Santa Maria e San Donato Church

scale works in one corner of a showroom. Note that the really cheap places likely aren't selling authentic Murano glass; if that matters to you, ask before you buy. (Several shops sport signs pointedly reminding potential customers that their glass may be a bit more expensive...because it's not made in China.) If your browsing starts turning to buying, be sure to read my tips on page 293.

Continue up Fondamenta dei Vetrai until you see a tower on your right and a church on your left. The **tower** was built as a fire lookout in this city of furnaces. The **Church of San Pietro Martire**

(free but donations appreciated, open erratic hours with demand, possibly closed 12:00-15:00 when it's not busy, www.sandonatomurano.it) features Giovanni Bellini's solid-color *Virgin Enthroned with Mark and a Kneeling Doge* (right wall of the nave in the center). This votive painting—showing a doge being introduced to

LAGOON

the Virgin Mary by St. Mark—was the doge's way of asking for divine protection and favor during his reign. The doge wears a luxurious ermine cloak (a symbol of royalty) and a ducal crown hat. The sacristy/museum has ornately carved caryatids (human pillars, c. 1660) with expressive faces and arms posed every which way (€1.50 admission). The carved panels between the caryatids depict scenes from the life of John the Baptist, culminating in his beheading in the far corner. In the next rooms, see ceremonial religious objects and statues, then check out the photos (at the landing midway up the steps) of these objects being used in modern-day Venetian parades. Upstairs are piles of relics in glass cases.

For a slice of **residential Murano,** continue past the church along the canal, bending left and passing the big, green metal bridge. Keep going as the promenade bears left and feeds you down the street called Ramo da Mula, and wander this very tidy "subdivision." In this old shell there's a new vibrancy, as tourist-swamped Venice's high rents and real-estate prices have driven locals to the outlying islands. Behind the glass shops, Murano is a workaday community of 6,000 residents. It has real neighborhoods, with moms shopping at markets, schools filled with noisy children, bikes in the front yards, and benches warmed by Venetian old-timers.

Backtrack to the embankment, and use the green bridge to cross the Grand Canal of Murano. Once across, turn right. Just after the first real side street, you'll pass another unique shop, **La Murina,** with elegant and modern home-decor items (such as striking chandeliers; Wed-Mon 10:30-13:00 & 14:00-17:00, Sat-Sun until 17:30, closed Tue, Riva Longa 17, tel. 041-527-4605).

Continue past the shop, then pass a smaller Co-op supermarket and the Murano-Museo vaporetto stop. Where the canal bends left, look for Murano's **Glass Museum** *(Museo Vetrario)* in a large white building, where recent renovations give visitors a much improved look at the history of glassmaking. The museum emphasizes ancient glass and glassmaking techniques in order to illustrate how Venice has carried on making the same colors and using the same techniques from its earlier days. Also on display, of course, are the very best examples of 500 years of Venetian glassmaking.

One hundred yards farther along the canal is **Santa Maria e San Donato Church,** the architectural highlight of Murano (free, erratic opening hours, www. sandonatomurano.it). Before entering, note the fine Byzantine Romanesque exterior—especially the stonework of its apse, facing the canal. At the base of the towering campanile is an elaborate memorial to residents

Guided Tours to Murano

I recommend the self-guided tour in this chapter. But if you'd like to test your ability to resist a smooth-talking Italian glass salesman, or if you'd like to join a group for your trip out to Murano, consider these two other ways to get there.

By Speedboat Tour: The easiest—and priciest—way to see Murano, Burano, and Torcello is to pay €20 for a rushed and touristy four-hour speedboat tour, run by Alilaguna (the same outfit that runs the airport boats; this trip is called the "green line"). They leave three times a day in summer from the San Marco-Giardinetti dock; look and listen for guides calling out for potential passengers (April-Oct usually at 9:30, 11:00, and 14:30, fewer cruises Nov-March, tel. 041-240-1711, www.alilaguna.it). The tours are speedy indeed—live guides race through the commentary in up to five languages—and boats stop for roughly 40 minutes at each island. The stops are for glassblowing and lacemaking demonstrations followed by sales spiels, leaving no time to explore on your own.

A Free Ride with a Sales Pitch: You can also get to Murano for free on a speedboat. Tourists are practically kidnapped from St. Mark's Square by the aggressive sales reps who then ferry them out to the island (35-minute ride). Your only obligation is to sit through a fairly interesting 20-minute glassmaking demonstration and sales pitch. After that, you're on your own. (In fact, they don't promise you a trip back to Venice.)

During the demonstration, the glassblower typically sticks a rod with raw glass on the end into a furnace, melts the glass, and expands it by blowing through the hollow rod. Then he shapes it with tongs into a vase, a glass, or a piece of art. This is followed by an almost comically high-pressure sales pitch in the showroom. (The spiel is brief, and there really is no obligation to buy anything.) If you do buy something, see page 293 for tips on having a purchase shipped home.

If you just want to see a glassblower in action, you don't need to go out to Murano—visit Galleria San Marco, just off St. Mark's Square (at 181a Calle del Cappello Nero; see Shopping in Venice chapter). But if you do visit Murano, you'll likely be approached by a local salesman trying to lure you into his shop for a free demo. If you'd rather see a similar demo in a lower-pressure environment, drop into the Ai Dogi shop near the Murano-Faro vaporetto stop, at the end of my Murano tour (see page 210).

of the Veneto (the region surrounding Venice) who have been lost fighting in all wars. Now head inside the church. The interior takes you back to the 12th century. Built when St. Mark's Basilica was under construction, the highlights are its inlaid stone floor and the gorgeous mosaic above the altar. It features Mary as God's mother,

LAGOON

gliding in from heaven on her carpet, blessing the faithful with two open hands.

When you're ready to leave Murano, find your way back to the green bridge and cross back toward San Pietro Martire. Near the church, cross the narrow canal and turn right onto Fondamenta Daniele Manin. Before the next bridge, turn left on the street called Bressagio, which takes you toward the white-stone light-house *(faro)* and its Murano-Faro vaporetto dock.

To your right are some of Murano's actual glass factories and their showrooms. At #25, the **Ai Dogi** factory's showroom has an open kiln area where you can watch a glassblower at work. While most such demos on Murano come with a pushy sales pitch, Ai Dogi just lets you watch a maestro work his magic (Mon-Fri roughly 9:30-15:30—often with a lunch break, no activity on Sat-Sun or on particularly hot days).

• *To continue our tour, walk over to the Murano-Faro vaporetto stop and catch the #12 vaporetto to* **Burano** *(2-3/hour, 30-40 minutes, boat destination may say* Treporti *or* Punta Sabbioni*). If you'd prefer to head straight back to Venice, take either the #3 vaporetto (for the train station and bus station), the #4.2, #12, or #13 (for Fondamente Nove), or the #7 (for St. Mark's Square). The #4.1 is a much slower way back, as it loops around Murano before heading back to Fondamente Nove.*

▲▲BURANO

Famous for its lace and outlandishly colorful houses, Burano is a sleepy island with a sleepy community (pop. 2,700)—village Venice without the glitz. Its vibrantly painted homes look like Venice before the plaster peeled off. Each adjoining townhouse is painted its own color. When Venice was a showy city of merchants, Burano was a humble town of fishermen. Though tourists clog the island's main drag by day, at night it's quiet. Laundry hangs over alleyways, and sunshades (typical of the area) cover the doors of residents' homes. The church's

bell tower leans at a five-degree angle...the same as Pisa's. Beyond the touristy core, Burano holds many back lanes and Technicolor-tranquil canals.

This town's history is ancient, dating back to when the island was, like Torcello, a haven for mainlanders fleeing from barbarian invasions. "Burano" likely comes from "Porta Boreana"—the city gate from the settlers' hometown that faced the bracing Bora wind. It's that same wind that meant survival on the lagoon. It kept away the malaria-carrying mosquitoes that made other places (like Tor-

LAGOON

1 Merletti d'Arte dalla
   Lidia Lace Shop

2 Lace Museum

3 Bell Tower

4 Trattoria al Gatto
   Nero da Ruggero

cello) less habitable, and whisked sailing fishermen away from the stagnant waters nearby. (Nevertheless, Burano is often engulfed in the fog that's so common on the lagoon—the island's vividly painted facades helped those fishermen find their way home in the mist.)

Burano can be covered in a 15-minute stroll. From the vaporetto dock, follow the crowds into the center. The tight **main drag** is packed with tourists and lined with shops, some of which sell Burano's locally produced white wine. Soon you'll hit the first

of many picture-perfect Burano canals; turn left and follow it straight ahead to a bridge, which deposits you on the main square, **Piazza Galuppi**—jammed with lace shops, restaurants, and happy shutterbugs.

Most tourists visit Burano for its lace, and they're not disappointed. Lace is cheaper in Burano than in Venice, and serious shoppers should comparison-shop in Venice before visiting Burano. Of the many lace shops, I like **Merletti d'Arte dalla Lidia** for its fine private museum (in the rear of the shop and upstairs). Paola, who speaks English, gives visitors a warm welcome as she shows off masterpieces of lace from all over Europe. Use a magnifying glass to marvel at the intricate knots, and be sure to go upstairs (daily 9:30-18:00, until 17:00 in winter, just off the big square opposite the leaning tower at Via Baldassarre Galuppi 215, tel. 041-730-052, www.dallalidia.com).

Lace fans enjoy the **Lace Museum** (Museo del Merletto di Burano), with a small but modern and well-presented exhibit about Burano's favorite product. The visit begins on the ground floor, with a 20-minute film telling the history of Burano and the significance of lace during Venice's golden age. You'll learn how the intricate patterns of lace were inspired by the ornate Gothic facades of Venice, the city where they claim the craft was invented, or at least perfected. Then you'll head upstairs to see lots of actual antique lace (slide the drawers to see more samples) as well as some actual, antique lacemakers, squinting at the windows while they work.

Back outside, gaze at Burano's famous leaning church **bell tower.** Enter the church (of San Martino Vescovo) from the corner of the square. It has a fine, restored Tiepolo painting of the Crucifixion (along the left wall of the nave, near the back; free entry but donations appreciated, typically closed 12:00-15:00).

Now circle around the back of the church to appreciate the tower's angle of repose (from the main street, it actually looks straight). Here at the far end of the island, the mood shifts. A grassy area, with benches and a waterside promenade, makes for a pretty picnic spot. Continuing all the way around the church brings you into a peaceful yet intensely colorful, small-town world and, eventually, back to the main street or the vaporetto dock. The park next to the dock is also good for a picnic.

Eating on Burano: You'll find plenty of touristy eateries on Burano, all enthusiastic about their fish. While you have plenty of options for a quick bite, if you want to dine, consider family-run **$$$ Trattoria al Gatto Nero da Ruggero.** For three generations, they've been serving pricey, good, traditional dishes outside overlooking the peaceful canal or in the dressy interior (Tue-Sat 12:30-15:00 & 18:00-21:00, Sun 12:30-15:00, closed Mon, crisp service, 5-minute walk from the ferry dock and from the thriving main tourist drag at Fondamenta de la Giudecca 88, tel. 041-730-120, www.gattonero.com).

• *To reach our tour's next stop,* **Torcello,** *reboard vaporetto #12, making sure it's stopping at Torcello (likely at :00, :12, and :32 past each hour; five-minute trip).*

If you want to skip Torcello and head right back to Venice, #12 boats

Boating in Venice

Italian law stipulates that a luxury tax is levied on all boats—except in Venice, where they're considered a necessity. Venetians go everywhere by boat. Calling a taxi? A boat comes. Going to the hospital to have a baby? Just hop on the vaporetto. Garbage day? You put your bag on the canal edge, and a garbage boat mashes it and takes it away.

Many residents own a boat, though it's not always practical for everyday activities. If you want to cruise to the grocery store, you first have to check the tide table to make sure your boat can fit beneath certain bridges. And parking is always a huge problem everywhere—either you know a friend nearby with a grandfathered parking space, or your partner has to "circle the block" while you shop.

Locals rely more on the public *vaporetti* and *traghetti*. While tourists pay plenty for these boats, Venetians ride cheap and easy. An all-year pass costs less than €1 a day.

Gondolas are strictly for tourists these days, but in earlier times, these flat-bottomed boats were the only way to negotiate the tricky, shallow lagoon. The oarsman had to stand up in the back of the boat to see oncoming sandbars. Today, boats ply confidently between the shifting sandbanks of the lagoon, thanks to thoroughfares defined by modern pilings.

While many Venetians own a car for driving on the isle of Lido or the mainland, they admit they're "not very much beloved on the road."

generally depart at :00, :24, and :44 (45 minutes to Fondamente Nove, runs less frequently in the evening). If your ultimate destination is near St. Mark's Square or if you'd just like to cruise more of the lagoon, consider the #14 vaporetto, which leaves Burano once an hour (from 9:26-18:26) on a 70-minute trip, running first to Treporti and Punta Sabbioni on the mainland peninsula of Cavallino, then the Lido, and finally the San Zaccaria dock near St. Mark's Square. You can also get to St. Mark's via the #12 to Fondamente Nove, and from there to San Zaccaria on the #4.2 (an additional 30 minutes).

▲TORCELLO

This is the birthplace of Venice, where some of the first mainland refugees settled, escaping the barbarian hordes. Yet today, it's the least-developed island (pop. 20) in the most natural state, marshy and shrub-covered. There's little for tourists to see except the church, the oldest in Venice, which still sports some impressive

LAGOON

mosaics. It's a 10-minute walk, with full sun, from the vaporetto dock to the church.

As you stroll from the dock through a salty canalside land-scape, think of the original inhabitants. Romanized farmers came

here, escaping the Germanic barbar-ians who started streaming through the mainland in the fifth century. By the 11th century, the teeny island had 11 churches. But one look around makes it easy to understand why this place was inhospitable—the farming was poor, there was no fresh water, and mosquitoes and malaria were big problems. Even though residents diverted the flow of mainland rivers, the lagoon silted up around them anyway, and the island was slowly abandoned.

Approaching the church, you'll pass by the remote yet fancy **Locanda Cipriani Hotel** next door. With just five rooms, it's hosted Thomas Mann, Queen Elizabeth II, and Princess Diana. Its res-taurant is the most expensive of the five or so that vie to feed the lunch crowd on Torcello. Of these, the best pick is probably the **$$$ Villa 600,** with its shaded garden terrace (closed Wed, tel. 041-527-2254, www.villa600.it).

The **Santa Maria Assunta Church** complex consists of four sights: the church itself, the bell tower (behind the church, climb

a ramped stairway for great lagoon views), a small museum (facing the church, in two separate buildings, but with little to see—mainly just sparsely described old artifacts, including a few sixth-century mosaic fragments), and the smaller, free church of Santa Fosca (by the Sacrum sign). The main church is the only one of these really worth paying to visit (€5), but vari-ous combo-tickets, which include an audioguide, let you get into the other sights as you like. There's a pay WC in a corner behind the museum.

The circular ruins in front of the church are what's left of a baptistery from the ninth century; in those days, you couldn't enter a church until you were baptized.

Inside the church, the brick walls and wood beams of the ceil-ing are classically Venetian building materials—that is, flexible, to accommodate the ever-shifting sands underneath.

The **altar** has the relics of St. Heliodorus (d. 390), a local-born bishop who was the travel partner of the famed St. Jerome on a trip to the Holy Land. The columns of the rood screen (separating the altar area from the congregation) were obviously scavenged from elsewhere—note the variety of capitals.

The **apse mosaic** (over the altar) shows Mary and Baby Jesus above and the 12 apostles below. Her three stars symbolize her virginity: before, during, and after giving birth to Jesus.

In the **right apse,** with its sumptuous vault, find Christ Pantocrator, ruler of all, flanked by archangels Michael and Gabriel. On the ceiling, Christ is represented by the sacrificial lamb.

The mosaic on the **back wall** is justifiably famous and worth examining. Six horizontal bands depict the Last Judgment (and other scenes). From top to bottom, see:

1. The Crucifixion.

2. A striding Christ pulling an elderly, bearded Adam (with Eve behind him) out from Limbo while stepping on a devil.

3. Christ, in an almond-shaped bubble, as the Creator, flanked by John the Baptist, Mary, and other holy souls in Paradise. From the bottom of the bubble pours a river of fire, which runs down the wall to hell.

4. Angels preparing the Throne of Judgment—empty except for a book (whose seven seals, it was predicted, will be broken during Judgment Day). Note Adam and Eve kneeling below.

5 and 6. Archangel Michael (over the door) weighing souls on a scale, while mischievous devils try to tip the scales in their favor.

On the right are the fires of hell, where sinners—many of them turbaned Muslims—are tormented by black-skinned demons. A

crude display of the seven deadly sins appears at the lower right: pride (crowned heads in flames), lust (bodies in flames), gluttony (guys eating even their fingers), envy (skulls with worms eating out their coveting eyes), anger (men waist-deep in cold water to cool down), greed (fancy earrings), and laziness (useless hands and cut-off feet).

• *Avoid the eighth deadly sin—missing your vaporetto—by allowing at least 10 minutes to get from the church back to the boat dock. The #12 vaporetto generally departs at :05, :17, :32, and :51 (5 minutes). The :05 goes straight back to Venice's Fondamente Nove (40 minutes); the :17 and :32 head first to Burano, where you may have to switch boats to continue to Fondamente Nove (55 minutes). Unless you just want to get back to Burano, skip the :51 departure, which heads via Burano to Treporti and Punta Sabbioni, ports on a northern arm of the mainland. For a longer cruise back to Venice that ends near St. Mark's Square, change at Burano to the #14 (mentioned earlier).*

LAGOON

ST. MARK'S TO RIALTO LOOP WALK

Two rights and a left (simple!) can get you from St. Mark's Square to the Rialto Bridge via a completely different route from the one most tourists take. Along the way, take in some lesser sights in the area west of St. Mark's Square. Then we'll return to St. Mark's along the tourists' main drag, the Mercerie.

Orientation

Length of This Walk: Allow one hour for a leisurely walk.
San Moisè Church: Free, Mon-Sat 9:30-12:30 & 15:30-18:30, tel. 041-296-0630.
La Fenice Opera House: €10 for dry 45-minute audioguide tour, generally open daily 9:30-18:00, theater box office open daily 10:00-17:00, box office tel. 041-2424, www.teatrolafenice.it.
Rialto Market: The souvenir stalls are open daily; the produce market is closed on Sunday; and the fish market is closed on Sunday and Monday. The market is lively only in the morning.

The Walk Begins

St. Mark's Square
• *From the square, walk to the waterfront and stop between the two columns. You're walking on recently raised Venice—in 2006, the stones were taken up and six inches of extra sand put down to minimize flooding.*

You're at the front porch of Venice. Survey this grand scene with your back to the water. It reflects the Renaissance ideal of an urban layout: A proper city needs a formal entry. These pillars say "welcome to an aristocratic republic." The library (on your left) represents wisdom. The palace (right), with Lady Justice (never

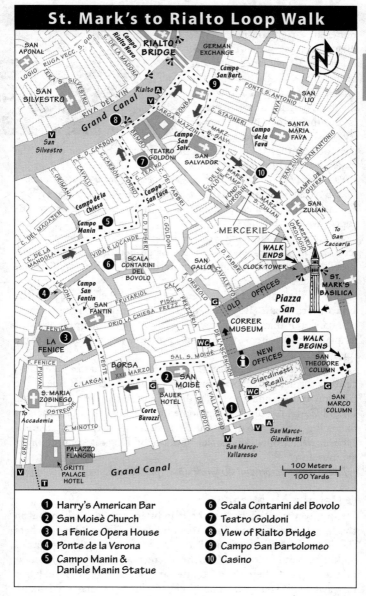

St. Mark's to Rialto Loop Walk

1. Harry's American Bar
2. San Moisè Church
3. La Fenice Opera House
4. Ponte de la Verona
5. Campo Manin & Daniele Manin Statue
6. Scala Contarini del Bovolo
7. Teatro Goldoni
8. View of Rialto Bridge
9. Campo San Bartolomeo
10. Casino

blindfolded in Venice) on top, represents righteousness. Medieval towns were cluttered. A grand Renaissance city has grand vistas. At the far end, the Clock Tower lets all know how much daylight is left (sunset is on top). This monumentality wasn't always here. Before  the 16th century there was no library. That's where you'd find the baker, butcher, and cheese shops.

• *Now, turn left to walk past the library, heading for a white pavilion.*

Beyond the library stands the old mint—looking pretty Fort Knox-y. In the 16th century the Venetian ducat—the dollar of Europe—was minted here.

Along the waterfront, you'll see the various boats that ply Venice's waters. Classic wooden motorboats operating as water taxis. Hotel shuttle boats bringing guests here from distant, $700-a-night hotels.

Run the gauntlet of souvenir stands to the entrance to the **Giardinetti Reali** (Royal Gardens, once the site of a huge grain-storage depot that was destroyed by Napoleon). The grounds (with ample benches) offer some precious greenery in a city built of stone on mud.

After the park entrance, the walkway takes you to a cute 18th-century former coffeehouse pavilion. Go around the left side of the pavilion and—from atop the bridge—look across the mouth of the Grand Canal to view the big dome of La Salute Church. The guy balancing a bronze ball on one foot is on top of the old Customs House, which now houses the Punta della Dogana contemporary art museum.

• *Twelve steps down and 20 yards ahead on the right is...*

❶ Harry's American Bar

Hemingway put this bar on the map by making it his hangout in the late 1940s. If Brad and Angelina are in town, this is where they'll be. If they're not, you'll see plenty of dressed-up Americans looking around for celebrities. The discreet (and overpriced) restaurant upstairs is where the glitterati hang out. The street-level bar is for gawkers. If you wear something a bit fancy (or artsy bohemian), you can pull up a stool at the tiny bar by the entrance and pay too much for a Bellini (Prosecco and peach puree), which was invented right here.

• *Head inland down Calle Vallaresso, one of Venice's most exclusive streets, past fancy boutiques such as Tiffany, Brunello Cucinelli, and Roberto Cavalli. At the T intersection, turn left and head west on Sal-*

izada San Moisè (which becomes Calle Larga XXII Marzo)—the Fifth Avenue of Venice with Gucci, Prada, Versace, and company. Continue to the first bridge and a square dominated by the fancy facade of a church. Climb the bridge and, against a soundtrack of tourists negotiating with hustling gondoliers, look back at the ornate...

❷ San Moisè Church

This is the parish church for St Mark's; because of tourist crowds at the basilica, this is where the community used to worship, but it no longer offers Mass. While it's one of Venice's oldest churches, dating from the 10th century (note the old tower on the right), its busy facade is 17th-century Baroque. This was an age when big shots who funded such projects expected to see their faces featured (see the bust of Mr. Fini in the center—flanked by tombs of his brother and nephew all actually buried into the facade). Moses (Moisè) caps the facade.

Inside, the altarpiece depicts Mount Sinai, with Moses (kneeling) receiving the two tablets with the Ten Commandments. The alcove to the left of the altar has Tintoretto's 16th-century *Christ Washing the Disciples' Feet.*

The modern building on the right is the ritzy five-star **Bauer Hotel,** originally an 18th-century palace. While it was closed throughout the 1940s, the owners added this Fascist-deco wing, defying Italian historical-preservation codes. Its facade still gives locals the Mussolini-creeps. Now it's one of the few modern buildings in town. You can take a few minutes to wander through the hotel for a James Bond-meets-Mussolini architectural experience.

• Continue over the bridge, down Calle Larga XXII Marzo, a big street that seems too wide and large for Venice. It was created during the 19th century by filling in a canal. You can make out the outline of the sidewalks that once flanked the now-gone canal. Pass by the Vivaldi look-alikes selling concert tickets and (mostly Senegalese) immigrants illegally selling knockoffs of Prada bags.

Halfway down the street, after passing the grand Borsa (the former stock exchange), turn right on tiny Calle del Sartor da Veste. Go straight, crossing a bridge. At the next square, you'll find...

❸ La Fenice Opera House
(Gran Teatro alla Fenice)

Venice's famed opera house, completed in 1792 (read the MDC-CXCII on the facade), was started as a business venture by a group of nobles who recognized that Venice was short on entertainment

opportunities for the well-heeled set. (In the 18th century, aristocrats strolled around several months out of the year with little to do.)

La Fenice was reduced to a hollowed-out shell by a disastrous fire in 1996. After a vigorous restoration campaign, "The Phoenix"—true to its name—has risen again from the ashes. La Fenice resumed opera productions in 2004, opening with *La Traviata*. The theater is usually open daily to the public (for information, see page 39).

Venice is one of the cradles of the art form known as opera. An opera is a sung play and a multimedia event, blending music, words, story, costume, and set design. Some of the great operas were first performed here in this luxurious setting. Verdi's *Rigoletto* (1851) and *La Traviata* (1853) were actually commissioned by La Fenice. The man who put words to some of Mozart's opera tunes was a Venetian, Lorenzo da Ponte, who drew inspiration from the city's libertine ways and joie de vivre. In recent years, La Fenice's musical standing was overshadowed by its reputation as a place for the wealthy to parade in furs and jewels.

• *Passing La Fenice, continue north along the same street (though its name is now Calle de la Verona), to a small bridge over a quiet canal.*

❹ Ponte de la Verona

Pause atop this bridge, where reflections can make you wonder which end is up. Looking above you, see bridges of stone propping up leaning buildings, and there's a view of the "Leaning Tower" of San Stefano.

People actually live in Venice. Notice their rooftop gardens, their laundry, their plumbing, the electricity lines snaking into their apartments, and the rusted iron bars and bolts that hold their crumbling homes together. On one building, find centuries-old relief carvings—a bearded face and a panel of an eagle with its prey. Below you is an old water gate indicating that this was once a merchant's house.

While many Venetians own (and love) their own boats, parking watercraft is a huge problem. Getting a spot is tough, and when you finally find one, it's very expensive and rarely near your apartment. (For more on boating in Venice, see page 213.)

People once swam freely in the canals. Find the sign that reads *Divieto di Nuoto* ("swimming not allowed").

• *Continue north. At the T intersection, turn right on Calle de la Mandola. You'll cross over a bridge into a spacious square dominated by a statue and an out-of-place modern building.*

❺ Campo Manin

The centerpiece of the square is **a statue of Daniele Manin** (1804-1857), one of a group of patriotic visionaries who foresaw the unification of Italy (the Risorgimento) 20 years before it happened. The statue faces the red house Manin lived in. Chafing under Austrian rule, the Venetians rose up in 1848. The Austrians laid siege to the city (1849) and bombarded it into surrender. The fiery leader Manin was banished and spent his final years in Paris, still proudly drumming up support for modern Italy. In a rare honor, he's buried at St. Mark's Basilica.

• *Scala Contarini del Bovolo is a block south of here, with yellow signs pointing the way. Facing the Manin statue, turn right and exit the square down an alley. Turn left with the street, then immediately follow yellow signs to the right, into a courtyard with one of Venice's hidden treasures...*

❻ Scala Contarini del Bovolo

The Scala is a cylindrical brick tower with five floors of spiral staircases faced with white limestone banisters.

Built in 1499, it was the external staircase of a palace (external stairs saved interior space for rooms). Architecture buffs admire the successful blend of a Gothic building with a Renaissance staircase. The garden is a graveyard of old cistern wellheads.

If the tower is open, you can pay €5 to wind your way up the "snail shell" (*bovolo* in the local dialect). It's 113 steps to the top, where you're rewarded with views of the Venetian skyline.

• *Unwind and return to the Manin statue. Continue east, circling around the right side of the big Cassa di Risparmio bank, marveling at its Modernist ugliness. At Campo San Luca, walk halfway through the square, then turn left (north) on Calle del Forno. Note the 24-hour pharmacy vending machine (on the right) that dispenses shower gel, Band-Aids, bug repellent, toothbrushes, toothpaste, condoms, and other after-hours necessities.*

Heading north, glance 20 yards down the street to the right at the flag-bedecked...

❼ Teatro Goldoni

Though this theater dates from the 1930s, there's been a theater here since the 1500s, when Venice was at the forefront of secular entertainment. Many of Carlo Goldoni's (1707-1793) groundbreaking comedies were first performed here. Before Goldoni's time, most Italian theater was formulaic and somewhat contrived, but Goldoni portrayed real-life situations of the new middle class—and with a refreshing sense of humor and honesty. Thanks in part to his ample use of the Venetian dialect, he remains especially popular in his native city, and the theater was renamed in his honor. Today, Teatro Goldoni is still a working theater of mainly Italian productions.

• *Continue north on Calle del Forno. You're very close to the Grand Canal. Keep going north. At the small square, jog left and then right onto a lane that leads past a big modern Co-op supermarket to the Grand Canal. Walk right out to the end of the small wooden pier for a grand view. On your right is the Rialto Bridge. The two palaces a few steps behind you are Venice's City Hall—blue posts with golden lions mark city government buildings. Notice the speedboats with shiny varnish parked and awaiting their VIPs. Now look down the Grand Canal (opposite the Rialto Bridge). Obelisks atop the palace across the canal mark the former home of a five-star admiral—a rank only bestowed in wartime—and the family gets obelisk bragging rights for centuries. (Today those twin obelisks mark the ritzy hotel where George Clooney got hitched.)*

❽ Rialto Bridge

Of Venice's more than 400 bridges, only four cross the Grand Canal. Rialto was the first among these four.

The original Rialto Bridge, dating from 1180, was a platform supported by boats tied together. It linked the political side (Palazzo Ducale) of Venice with the economic center (Rialto). Rialto, which takes its name from *riva alto* (high bank), was one of the earliest Venetian settlements. When Venice was Europe's economic superpower, this was where bankers, brokers, and merchants conducted their daily business.

Rialto Bridge II was a 13th-century wooden drawbridge. It was replaced in 1588 by the current structure, with its bold single arch (spanning 160 feet) and arcades on top designed to strengthen the stone span. Its immense foundations stretch 650 feet on either side. Heavy buildings were then built atop the foundations to hold everything in place. The Rialto remained the only bridge crossing the Grand Canal until 1854.

Marking the geographical center of Venice (midway down the Grand Canal), the Rialto is the most sensible location for retail shops. The government built it with the (accurate) expectation that it'd soon pay for itself with rent from the shops built into it. Like the (older) Ponte Vecchio in Florence, the Rialto was originally lined with luxury gold and jewelry shops. The bridge is cleverly designed to generate maximum rent: three lanes, two rows of 12 shops each, with a warehouse area above each shop under the lead-and-timber roof.

Reliefs of the Venetian Republic's main mascots, St. Mark and St. Theodore, crown the arch. Barges and *vaporetti* run the busy waterways below, and merchants vie for tourists' attention on top.

The Rialto has long been a symbol of Venice. Aristocratic inhabitants built magnificent palaces just to be near it. The poetic Lord Byron swam to it all the way from Lido Island. And thousands of marriage proposals have been sealed right here, with a kiss, as the moon floated over La Serenissima.

• *From here, you can continue this walk and return to St. Mark's Square or pick up my Rialto to Frari Church Walk (next chapter). Either way, you might want to take a break to check out the fish and produce market that lies just over the bridge. To continue this walk, follow me along the Mercerie, the most direct (and tourist-clogged) route back to St. Mark's. From the base of the Rialto Bridge (on the San Marco side), go 100 yards directly to...*

❾ Campo San Bartolomeo

This square is one of the city's main crossroads. Locals routinely meet at the statue of Carlo Goldoni, the beloved and innovative 18th-century playwright for whom Teatro Goldoni, which we saw earlier, was named. The pharmacy on this square (marked by a green cross) keeps an electronic counter in its window, ticking down the population of Venice as it shrinks (55,415 on my last visit).

• *Head to the right 100 yards, down Via 2 Aprile, setting your sights on the green and red umbrellas on the corner. They mark a stretch of town once famous for selling umbrellas and handbags. From there, turn left and follow the crowds 100 yards more along Marzaria San Salvador, a.k.a. the...*

Mercerie

You're in the city's high-rent district. The Mercerie (or "Marzarie," in Venetian dialect) is a string of connecting streets lined mostly with tacky tourist shops. Much of the glass displayed here is Chinese, not Venetian. (If you're shopping for glass that's actually made in Venice, look for the Murano seal.)

• *When you get to the yellow two-way arrow "directing" you to San Marco, head right and then follow the flow left another 100 yards until you reach a bridge that makes for a fun gondola-viewing perch. At the top of the bridge, belly up to the railing on the left. Above the arcade on your left is the little iron balcony of the city's best-preserved...*

⑩ Casino

While humble from the outside, the interior is a great example of a classic Venetian space. If the windows are open, spy the lacy pastel and stucco ceilings inside. Though only a few of Venice's casinos still exist, the city once had over a hundred of these "little houses"—city-center retreats for the palazzo-dwelling set. For many patricians, they served as 18th-century man caves, used for entertaining, gambling, and/or intimate encounters. For well-to-do women, casinos provided a different kind of escape: Inspired by Madame de Pompadour (Louis XV's mistress), ladies would hold court with writers, artists, and avant-garde types.

• *Cross the bridge and continue straight for 100 yards along Marzaria San Zulian. On the way, notice the metal, two-foot-high flood barrier braces at shop doors—and how merchandise is elevated in anticipation of high water (local insurance doesn't cover floods).*

When you hit the next schizophrenic Per S. Marco *arrow (in front of the church), go right a few steps, then left onto Marzaria dell'Orologio, a street named for where you're heading: the Clock Tower. You're approaching St. Mark's Square (back where you started this walk) and the city's front door.*

RIALTO TO FRARI CHURCH WALK

Cross the Rialto Bridge, and dive headlong into Venice's thriving market area. The area west of the Grand Canal feels less touristy—a place where more "real" Venetians live. This 20-minute walk is the most direct route from the Rialto Bridge to the Frari Church and Scuola San Rocco. This chapter is less a collection of sights than it is a tour of the Rialto market area, followed by a convenient, easy-to-follow route through the San Polo area. After exploring the lively produce and stinky fish markets, you'll see pubs and squares that are at least a bit off the tourist path.

Orientation

Length of This Walk: Allow a leisurely hour.

When to Go: The markets are lively only in the morning. The produce market is closed on Sunday, and the fish market is closed on Sunday and Monday.

Ancient Musical Instruments Collection (in the Church of San Giacomo de Rialto): Free, Mon-Sat 9:00-17:00, closed Sun.

Church of San Polo: €3, Mon-Sat 10:00-17:00, closed Sun.

Tragicomica Mask Shop: Daily 10:00-19:00, on Calle dei Nomboli at #2800, tel. 041-721-102, www.tragicomica.it. The owners are generally happy to show their workshop on weekdays to customers who buy a mask, though it's best to make a reservation.

Eateries: Many pubs and restaurants in the Rialto area are recommended in the Eating in Venice chapter.

The Walk Begins

• From the top of the Rialto Bridge, walk down the bridge (heading away from the St. Mark's side) and about 50 yards onward until you see an old square on your right. Go to its fountain.

❶ Campo San Giacomo

This square, named for the church that faces it, looks today much like it did in the 16th century. The buildings lining the square are High

Renaissance, mostly built after a 1514 fire devastated this area. Find the MDXX date on the arcade: It was built in 1520. Only the church predates that fire. The square is designed to collect rainwater and store it in a cistern that once fed this fountain (for more on this system, see page 28).

Back when the Rialto Bridge was a drawbridge (until the 1590s), big ships would dock alongside this historic market. Imagine the commotion as ships tied up to load and unload their spices, oil, wine, and jewels. The line of buildings between Campo San Giacomo and the canal was once a strip of banks. It's still called Bancogiro, which means the place where merchants banked. In the days when carrying cash meant carrying gold and silver—heavy and dangerous—paper transfers between bank accounts were a godsend. Today you'll find a line of popular eateries here (described on page 268). Behind the trashy jewelry stands are real jewelry shops. In fact, the street across from the market has been called "Street of Jewelers" for more than 500 years.

Opposite the church, a granite hunchback supports steps leading to a column. Until the 1550s, when a financial crisis knocked it for an economic loop, Venice was Europe's trading capital. You could call this neighborhood the "Wall Street" of medieval Europe. In those days, this column was the closest thing they had to a *Wall Street Journal*. Someone climbed the stair each noon and stood on the column to read aloud the daily news from the doge: which ships had docked, which foreign ambassadors were in town, the price of pepper, and so on. Behind the hunchback is Calle de la Sicurtà, named for the maritime insurance companies that once did business here.

The church facade is one of the oldest in town. Back before

clocks had minute hands, its porch was
a shelter for the poor. The spirit of St.
James the Minor, for whom the church is
named, watched over the business community, encouraging honesty in a time
when banking regulations were nonexistent. Today the church's tranquil interior
hosts an exhibition of historical musical
instruments.

Walk along the canal side of the
church. The large white building behind the church was and still is
the city's fiscal administration building. Walk out to the canal, and
look back at the structure. Notice how it tilts out (probably because
the bridge's huge foundation is compressing the mud beneath it).

Now walk toward the Rialto Bridge along the canal to a little
canalside dead-end. Take in the great view of the bridge. The former post office (directly across from you) was originally the German merchants' hall (see the seal). It's about to be reincarnated as a
Benetton-owned shopping center.

You're standing under a former prison. Study the iron grills
over the windows. Notice the interlocking pipes with alternating
joints—you couldn't cut just one and escape.

• *From the prison, walk back along the canal, proceed through the triple
archway, cross the square, and enter the square named Casaria (for the
historic cheese market). Today, this is Venice's...*

❷ Produce Market *(Erberia)*

Colorful stalls offer fresh fruit and vegetables, some quite exotic.
Nothing is grown on the island of Venice, so everything is shipped
in daily from the main-
land or distant points on
the lagoon. The Mercato
Rialto vaporetto stop is a
convenient place for boats
to unload their wares, here
in the heart of fish-shaped
Venice. At #203-204 (halfway down the first set of
stalls, on the left), the shop
called Macelleria Equina

sells horse *(cavallo)* and donkey *(asino)* meat. Continue along the
canal, exploring all the produce stalls.

• *Follow your nose straight ahead (passing six alleyways on your left)
until you see* Mercato del Pesce *on the brick wall of the open–air arcade
that houses the...*

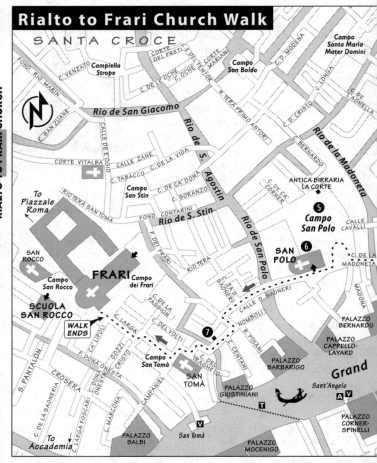

Rialto to Frari Church Walk

➌ Fish Market *(Pescaria)*

This market is especially vibrant and colorful in the morning. The open-air stalls have the catch of the day—Venice's culinary spe-

cialty. Find eels, scallops, crustaceans with five-inch antennae, and squid destined for tonight's risotto soaking in their own ink. This is the Venice that has existed for centuries: Workers toss boxes of fish from delivery boats while shoppers step from the *traghetto* (gondola shuttle) into the action. It's a good peek at workaday Venice. Shoppers are exacting and expect to know if

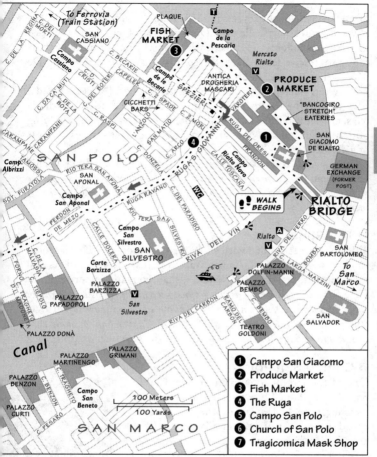

RIALTO TO FRARI CHURCH

1 Campo San Giacomo
2 Produce Market
3 Fish Market
4 The Ruga
5 Campo San Polo
6 Church of San Polo
7 Tragicomica Mask Shop

the fish is fresh or frozen, farmed or wild, Atlantic or Mediterranean (look for labels at some stands). Local fish are small and considered particularly tasty because of the high concentration of salt at this end of the Adriatic. Any salmon you see are farmed, mostly from northern Europe. It's not unusual to pay €30 per kilo (about 2.2 pounds) for the best fish.

In the courtyard between market buildings, locate a square, white Istrian stone on the wall between two arches. It lists the minimum length a fish must be for it to be sold. Sardines must be seven centimeters; *peocio* (mussels) must be three centimeters. (Below that, someone has added a penis joke.)

Now walk away from the water to the end of the fish market. You're on **Campo de la Becarie** ("Butchers Square"). If the market has you ready for a fishy nibble, you'll find many good options near here (listed on page 268 of the Eating in Venice chapter). Several of my favorite local bars serving the Venetian version of tapas, *cicchetti*, line up along Calle de le Do Spade (we'll pass it in just a moment). If it's lunchtime, consider dropping by one or more of these for a progressive feast: Bar all'Arco, Osteria ai Storti, Cantina Do Mori, and Cantina Do Spade.

When you're ready, follow Ruga dei Spezieri ("Spicers Road") back toward the Rialto. Along the way, pop into Antica Drogheria Mascari (on the right at #380), which hides a vast *enoteca* holding 600 different Italian wines arranged by region, plus spices and lots of gifty edibles.

• *At the end of Ruga dei Spezieri, you'll see a sign for* Ruga Vechia San Giovanni. *Turn right along it. (The second street you pass on the right, Sotoportego dei Do Mori, leads in just a block to the* cicchetti *bars mentioned later.)*

❹ The Ruga

This busy street is lined with shops that get progressively less touristy and more practical. As you walk, you'll see fewer trinkets and more clothes, bread, shoes, watches, shampoo, and underwear.

• *The Ruga changes names as you go. Just keep heading basically straight (little jogs are OK). When in doubt, follow signs pointing to* Ferrovia *(train station). You'll pass straight through Campo San Aponal, then cross a wide bridge, and later a narrow bridge, soon after arriving at...*

❺ Campo San Polo

One of the largest squares in Venice, Campo San Polo is shaped like an amphitheater, with its church tucked away in the corner (just ahead of you). Antica Birraria la Corte, a fine and family-friendly pizzeria/*ristorante,* is located at the far side (see listing under "Other Good Eateries near the Rialto Market," page 268). The square's amphitheater shape was determined by a curved canal at the base of the buildings on the right. Today, the former canal is now a *rio terà*—a street made of landfill. A few rare trees grace the square, as do rare benches occupied by grateful locals. In the summer, bleachers and a screen are erected for open-air movies.

• *On the square is the...*

❻ Church of San Polo (S. Paolo Apostolo)

This church, one of the oldest in Venice, dates from the ninth century (English description at ticket desk). The wooden, boat-shaped ceiling recalls the earliest basilicas built after Rome's fall. While the church is skippable for many, art enthusiasts visit to see

Tintoretto's *Last Supper,* Giovanni Battista Tiepolo's *Virgin Appearing to St. John of Nepomuk* and his son Domenico's *Stations of the Cross,* and Veronese's *Betrothal of the Virgin with Angels.*

• *From the Church of San Polo, continue about 200 yards (following* Ferrovia *signs). You'll cross a bridge, jog left when you have to, then right, onto Calle dei Nomboli. On the right at #2800, directly across the alley from the Casa Goldoni museum, you'll see the...*

❼ Tragicomica Mask Shop

One of Venice's best mask stores, Tragicomica is also a workshop that offers a glimpse into the process of mask making. Venice's

masks have always been a central feature of the celebration of Carnevale—the local pre-Lent, Mardi Gras-like blowout. (The translation of Carnevale is "goodbye to meat," referring to the lean days of Lent.) You'll see Walter, Alessandra, and Giuliana hard at work.

Many masks are patterned after standard characters of the theater style known as commedia dell'arte: the famous trickster Harlequin, the beautiful and cunning Columbina, the country bumpkin Pulcinella (who later evolved into the wife-beating Punch of marionette shows), and the solemn, long-nosed Doctor *(dottore).* For more on masks, see page 297.

• *Continuing along, cross the bridge and veer right, passing San Tomà Church and its square. You'll soon see purple signs directing you to* Scuola Grande di San Rocco. *Follow these until you bump into the back end of the Frari Church, with Scuola San Rocco next door.*

ST. MARK'S TO SAN ZACCARIA WALK

San Zaccaria, one of the oldest churches in Venice, is just a few minutes on foot from St. Mark's Square. The church features a Bellini altarpiece and a submerged crypt that might be the oldest place in Venice. This short walk gets you away from the bustle of St. Mark's, includes a stroll along the waterfront, and brings you right back to where you started.

Orientation

Length of This Walk: Allow about an hour for a leisurely walk (though the actual distance is short).

Church of San Zaccaria: Free, €1.50 to enter crypt, €0.50 coin to illuminate Bellini's altarpiece, Mon-Sat 10:00-12:00 & 16:00-18:00, Sun 16:00-18:00 only. Mass is held daily at 18:30 and Sun also at 10:00 and 12:00.

The Walk Begins

❶ St. Mark's—Piazzetta dei Leoni

Facing St. Mark's Basilica, start in the small square to the left of the church (Piazzetta dei Leoni), with the 18th-century stone lions that kids love to play on. See those drains in the pavement? You're standing on a cistern, fed by four drains.

Notice the nicely restored north side of the basilica, with fine 14th-century reliefs. Notice also the prayer entrance below the exquisite Porta dei Fiori. To the left, behind a black metal fence, is the tomb of Daniele Manin, the great 19th-century Italian and Venetian patriot.

The white Neoclassical building at the far east end of the square (built in 1834, when Venice was under Austrian rule) houses

St. Mark's to San Zaccaria Walk

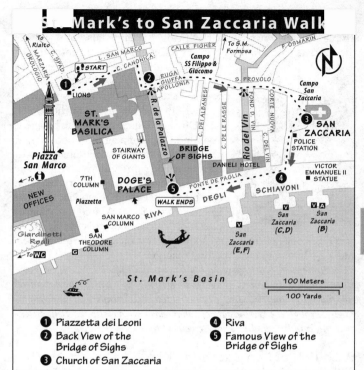

① Piazzetta dei Leoni
② Back View of the Bridge of Sighs
③ Church of San Zaccaria
④ Riva
⑤ Famous View of the Bridge of Sighs

the offices of Venice's "patriarch," the special title given to the local bishop. In the 1950s, this is where the future Pope John XXIII

presided as Venice's patriarch and cardinal. The popular, warmhearted cardinal went on to become the "Sixties Pope," who oversaw major reforms in the Catholic Church (Vatican II). Locals still refer to him as "Il Papa Buono" (the good pope). You'll see a plaque dedicated to "Papa Giovanni XXIII" on this building. (Historically, the Venetian bishop was given the position of cardinal automatically, but Pope Francis hasn't done so because he is working to make the College of Cardinals more representative of global Catholicism...which is no longer so Italian.)

• *Head east along Calle de la Canonica, past a fine English-language bookstore, then turn right and circle behind the basilica. Passing some of the sexiest gondoliers in town, you'll reach a bridge (Ponte Selfie Stick) with a...*

❷ View of the Bridge of Sighs

This lesser-known view of the Bridge of Sighs also lets you see the tourists who are ogling it, with cameras cocked. You can just

see the Lady Justice relief (centered above the windows), with her sword and scales—a reminder that the courts were to the right and the prison to the left.

On the basilica side of the bridge is a common sight in neighborhood Venice: a streetside altarpiece and donation box. As the street signs tell you, the bridge you're on marks the boundary between two traditional neighborhoods, the *sestiere* (district) of San Marco and that of Castello. Throughout this walk, you'll pass relics of a fast-fading era: newspaper stands, public telephones, and a 24-hour cigarette vending machine.

• *Continue east, passing through a lively, small square. You'll cross another bridge with a view of a "Modern Bridge of Sighs," which connects two wings of the exclusive Danieli Hotel. Continue east another 50 yards, through the Gothic gate of what was once a cloistered Benedictine convent, and into a square where you see the...*

❸ Church of San Zaccaria

Back in the ninth century—when Venice was just a collection of wooden houses and before there was a St. Mark's Basilica—a stone

church and monastery stood here. Today's structure dates mostly from the 15th century.

The tall facade by Mauro Codussi (who also did the Clock Tower in St. Mark's Square) and others is early Renaissance. The "vertical" effect produced by the four support pillars that rise up to an arched crown is tempered by the horizontal, many-layered stories and curved shoulders.

In the northwest corner of Campo San Zaccaria (near where you entered) is a plaque from 1620 listing all the things that were prohibited "in this square" *(in questo campo),* including games, obscenities, dishonesty, and robbery, all "under grave penalty" *(sotto gravis pene).*

• *Enter the church. The second chapel on the right holds the...*

Body of Zechariah (S. Zaccaria)

Of the two bodies in the chapel, the lower one in the glass case is the reputed body of Zechariah, the father of John the Baptist. Back when mortal remains were venerated and thought to bring miracles to the faithful, Venice was proud to own the bones of St. Zechariah ("San Zaccaria," also known as Zacharias).

• *The church is blessed with fine art. On the opposite side of the nave (second chapel on the left), you'll find...*

Giovanni Bellini, *Madonna and Child with Saints,* 1505

Mary and the baby, under a pavilion, are surrounded by various saints interacting in a so-called *sacra conversazione* (holy conversation), which in this painting is more like a quiet meditation. The saints' mood is melancholy, portrayed with lidded eyes and down-turned faces. A violinist angel plays a sad solo at Mary's feet.

This is one of the last of Bellini's paintings in the *sacra conversazione* formula, the newer type of altarpiece that liberated the

Virgin, Child, and saints from the separate cells of the older triptych style. Compare this to his other variations on this theme in the Accademia (see Accademia Tour chapter) and Frari Church (see Frari Church Tour chapter). The life-size saints stand in an imaginary extension of the church—the pavilion's painted columns match those of the real church. We see a glimpse of trees and a cloudy sky beyond. Bellini establishes a 3-D effect using floor tiles. The four saints pose symmetrically, and there's a harmony in the big blocks of richly colored robes—blue, green, red, white, and yellow. A cool white light envelops the whole scene, creating a holy ambience. (To add even more light, drop a €0.50 coin in the box in front of the altar.)

The ever-innovative Bellini was productive until the end of his long life—he painted this masterpiece at age 75. The German artist Albrecht Dürer said of him: "He is very old, and still he is the best painter of them all."

• *On the right-hand side of the nave is the entrance (€1.50 entry fee) to the...*

Crypt

Before you descend into the crypt, the first room (Chapel of Sant'Atanasio) contains **Tintoretto's *Birth of John the Baptist*** (c. 1560s, on the altar), which tells the back story of Zechariah. In the background, old Zechariah's wife, Elizabeth, props herself up in bed while nurses hold and coo over her newborn son, little John the Baptist. The birth was a miracle, as she was past childbearing age. On the far right, Zechariah—the star of this church—witnesses the heavens opening up, bringing this miracle to earth.

The five **gold thrones** (displayed in this room or one of the next rooms) were once seats for doges. Every Easter, the current doge would walk from St. Mark's Square to this religious center and thank the nuns of San Zaccaria for giving the land for the square.

The small next room contains religious objects as well as an engraving of the doge parading into Campo San Zaccaria.

Next comes the **Chapel of San Tarasio,** dominated by an impressive 15th-century prickly gold altarpiece by Antonio Vivarini. The predella (seven small scenes beneath the altarpiece) may be by Paolo Veneziano, the 14th-century grandfather of Venetian painting. Look down through glass in the floor to see the 12th-century mosaic floor from the original church. In fact, these rooms were parts of the earlier churches.

Finally, go downstairs to the **crypt**—the foundation of a church built in the 10th century. The crypt is low and the water

table high, so the room is often flooded, submerging the bases of the columns. It's a weird experience, calling up echoes of the Dark Ages.

• *Emerge from the Church of San Zaccaria back into the small campo. Before leaving the campo, check out the small art gallery on the left (free), the thirst-quenching water fountain, and the pink Carabinieri police station (a former monastery), marked by the Italian flag. Then exit the square at the far end, and head south until you pop out at the waterfront, right on the...*

❹ Riva

The waterfront promenade known as the "Riva" was built not for tourists but as part of the port of San Marco. Until recently, big ships tied up here. Today it's home to some of the town's finest and most famous hotels—and provides a great view of the Church of San Giorgio Maggiore (one stop away on vaporetto #2).

The big equestrian monument depicts **Victor Emmanuel II,** who helped lead Italy to unification and became the country's first king in 1861. Beyond that (over the bridge) is the four-columned **La Pietà Church,** where Antonio Vivaldi once directed the music. Five bridges farther along (not visible from here) are the Arsenale and Naval Museum (described on page 53).

For a peek at the *most* famous and luxurious hotel, turn right, cross over one bridge, and nip into the **Danieli Hotel.** Tuck in your shirt, stand tall and aristocratic, and (with all the confidence of a paying guest) be swept by the revolving door into the sumptuous interior of what was once the Gothic Palazzo Dandolo. As you check out the Danieli's restaurant menu (that's why you're there, isn't it?), admire the lobby, the old-style chandeliers, the water-taxi drive-up entrance, and the occasional celebrity. Since 1820, the Neo-Gothic Danieli has been Venice's most exclusive hotel. Exquisite as all this is, it still gets flooded routinely in the winter.

• *Facing the water, turn right and head west toward St. Mark's Square. The commotion atop a little bridge marks the...*

❺ Famous View of the Bridge of Sighs

The Bridge of Sighs connects the Doge's Palace (left) with the doge's prison (right). The bridge let justice be very swift indeed,

as convicted criminals could, upon sentencing, be escorted directly from the palace's secretive court-room to prison without being seen in public.

Notice the beefy bars on the prison. There were no windows, so throughout the year it would alternate between very hot and very cold. The top floor, below the lead roof, was nicknamed "The Oven." While designed for 300 people, the prison routinely held 500.

From this historic bridge (according to romantic legend), prisoners took one last look at Venice before entering the dark and unpleasant prison. And sighed. Lord Byron picked up on the legend in the early 1800s and gave the bridge its famous nickname, making this sad little span a big stop on the Grand Tour. Look high up on your left—although that rogue Casanova wrote of the bridge in his memoirs, he was actually imprisoned here in the Doge's Palace. Check out the carved relief on the palace corner, to your left, showing the biblical scene of drunken Noah spilling his wine but still being thoughtfully cared for by his sons. The message: Even if your superiors don't deserve respect because of their actions, cut them some slack and treat them well.

Nowadays, while the bridge is a human traffic jam of gawking tourists during the day, it remains breathtakingly romantic in the lonely late-night hours.

• *Your tour's over. (By the way, if you need some quick cash, this is a great place to pick a pocket. There's lots of bumping, and everyone's distracted...)*

Flexible Floors

All over town, from palaces to cheap, old hotels, you'll find speckled floors *(pavimento alla Veneziana)*. While they might look like cheap linoleum, these are historic—protected by the government and a pain for Venetian landlords to maintain. As Venice was built, it needed flexible flooring to absorb the inevitable settling of the buildings. Through an expensive and laborious process, several layers of material were built up and finished with a broken marble top that was shaved and polished to what you see today. While patterns were sometimes designed into the flooring, it's often just a speckled hodgepodge. Keep an eye open for this. Once a year, the floor is rubbed with natural oil to maintain its flexibility, and craftspeople still give landlords fits when repairs are needed.

using your ride to follow my tour of the Grand Canal (see Grand Canal Cruise chapter); to make sure you arrive via the Grand Canal, confirm that your boat goes *"via Rialto."*

Nearby Laundries: Lavanderia Gabriella offers full service a few streets north of St. Mark's Square; **Effe Erre** is a modern self-service *lavanderia* near the recommended Hotel al Piave. For details see page 21.

East of St. Mark's Square

Located near the Bridge of Sighs, just off the Riva degli Schiavoni waterfront promenade, these places rub drainpipes with Venice's most palatial five-star hotels.

$$$$ Hotel Campiello, lacy and bright, was once part of a 19th-century convent. Ideally located 50 yards off the waterfront on a tiny square, its 16 rooms offer a tranquil, friendly refuge for travelers who appreciate comfort and professional service (RS%, air-con, elevator, just steps from the San Zaccaria vaporetto stop, Castello 4647; tel. 041-520-5764, www.hcampiello.it, campiello@ hcampiello.it; family-run for four generations, currently by Thomas, Nicoletta, and Monica). They also rent three modern family apartments, under rustic timbers just steps away.

$$$$ Hotel Fontana, two bridges behind St. Mark's Square, is a pleasant family-run place with 15 sparse but classic-feeling rooms overlooking a lively square (two rooms with terraces, family

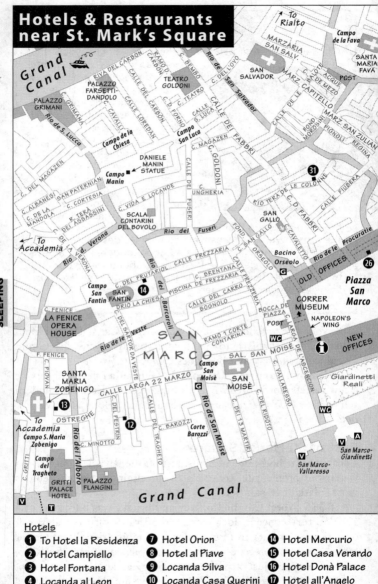

Hotels & Restaurants near St. Mark's Square

Hotels

1. To Hotel la Residenza
2. Hotel Campiello
3. Hotel Fontana
4. Locanda al Leon
5. Albergo Doni
6. Casa per Ferie Santa Maria della Pietà
7. Hotel Orion
8. Hotel al Piave
9. Locanda Silva
10. Locanda Casa Querini
11. Corte Campana B&B
12. Hotel Flora
13. Hotel Bel Sito
14. Hotel Mercurio
15. Hotel Casa Verardo
16. Hotel Donà Palace
17. Hotel all'Angelo
18. Hotel al Ponte dei Sospiri
19. Hotel Ca' Dei Conti

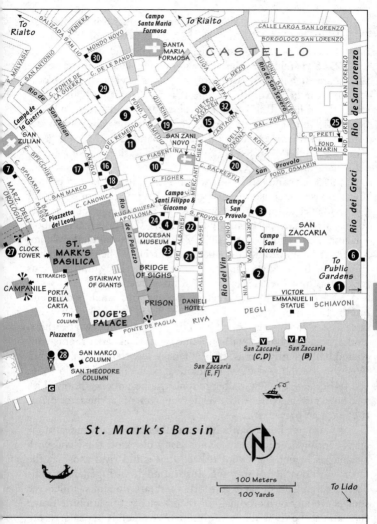

Eateries & Other

- ⑳ Ristorante Antica Sacrestia
- ㉑ Birreria Forst Café
- ㉒ Bar Verde
- ㉓ Ristorante alla Basilica
- ㉔ Ristorante Cinese Capitol
- ㉕ Ponte dei Greci Canalside Eateries
- ㉖ Gran Caffè Quadri (Bistro)
- ㉗ Gran Caffè Lavena (Gelato)
- ㉘ Todaro Gelato
- ㉙ Planet Restaurant
- ㉚ Co-op Supermarket
- ㉛ Lavanderia Gabriella
- ㉜ Lavanderia Effe Erre

rooms, air-con, elevator, Wi-Fi in common areas, on Campo San Provolo at Castello 4701, tel. 041-522-0533, www.hotelfontana.it, info@hotelfontana.it, cousins Diego and Gabriele).

$$$$ Hotel la Residenza is a grand old palace facing a peaceful square. It has 16 small rooms on three levels (with no elevator) and a huge, luxurious lounge that comes with a piano and a stingy breakfast. This is a good value for romantics—you'll feel like you're in the Doge's Palace after hours (some view rooms, air-con, Wi-Fi in most rooms, on Campo Bandiera e Moro at Castello 3608, tel. 041-528-5315, www.venicelaresidenza.com, info@venicelaresidenza.com, Giovanni).

$$$$ Locanda al Leon, which feels a little like a medieval tower house, is conscientiously run and rents 12 rooms just off Campo Santi Filippo e Giacomo (RS%, some view rooms, family rooms, air-con, 2 apartments with kitchens, Campo Santi Filippo e Giacomo, Castello 4270, tel. 041-277-0393, www.hotelalleon.com, leon@hotelalleon.com, Giuliano and Marcella). Their annex down the street, **B&B Marcella,** has three newer, classy, and spacious rooms for the same rates (check in at main hotel).

$$$ Albergo Doni, situated along a quiet canal, is dark and quiet. This time-warp—with creaky floors and 13 well-worn, once-classy rooms—is run by friendly Tessa and her two brothers, Barnaba and an Italian stallion named Nikos (cheaper rooms with shared bath, family rooms, ceiling fans, a few rooms have air-con, Wi-Fi in common areas, on Fondamenta del Vin at Castello 4656, tel. 041-522-4267, www.albergodoni.it, albergodoni@hotmail.it). The hotel also has three nice overflow apartments at the same prices (but without breakfast).

¢ Casa per Ferie Santa Maria della Pietà is a wonderful facility renting 53 beds in 15 rooms just a block off the Riva, with a fabulous lagoon-view roof terrace that could rival those at the most luxurious hotels in town. Institutional, with generous public spaces and dorm-style comfort, there are no sinks, toilets, or showers in any of its rooms, but there's plenty of plumbing down the hall (cash only, 2-night minimum on weekends in peak season, only twin beds, private rooms available, air-con, 100 yards from San Zaccaria-Pietà vaporetto dock, down Calle de la Pietà from La Pietà Church at Castello 3701, take elevator to third floor, tel. 041-244-3639, www.bedandvenice.it, info@bedandvenice.it).

North of St. Mark's Square
$$$ Hotel Orion rents 21 simple, welcoming rooms in the center of the action. Steep stairs (there's no elevator) take you from the touristy street into a peaceful world high above (RS%—use code RSTEVES, air-con, 2 minutes inland from St. Mark's Square, 10

steps toward St. Mark's from San Zulian Church at Calle Spadaria 700a, tel. 041-522-3053, www.hotelorion.it, info@hotelorion.it).

$$$ Hotel al Piave, with 28 rooms above a bright, tight lobby and breakfast room, is comfortable and cheery, and you'll enjoy the neighborhood (RS%, family rooms, lots of narrow stairs, air-con, on Ruga Giuffa at Castello 4838, tel. 041-528-5174, www.hotelalpiave.com, info@hotelalpiave.com; Mirella, Paolo, Ilaria, and Federico).

$$$ Locanda Silva is a big, scruffy, but beautifully located hotel with a functional 1960s feel and a peaceful terrace. It rents 23 decent, old-school rooms that are particularly worth considering if you're willing to share a bathroom to save some money (RS%, closed Dec-Jan, family rooms, air-con, lots of stairs, on Fondamenta del Remedio at Castello 4423, tel. 041-522-7643, www.locandasilva.it, info@locandasilva.it; Sandra, Katia, and Massimo).

$$$ Locanda Casa Querini rents six bright, high-ceilinged rooms on a quiet square tucked away behind St. Mark's. You can enjoy your breakfast or a sunny happy-hour picnic sitting at their tables right on the sleepy little square (RS%, family rooms, in-room fridges, air-con, halfway between San Zaccaria vaporetto stop and Campo Santa Maria Formosa at Castello 4388 on Campo San Zaninovo/Giovanni Novo, tel. 041-241-1294, www.locandaquerini.com, info@locandaquerini.com; Patrizia and Caterina).

$$ Corte Campana B&B, run by enthusiastic and helpful Riccardo and his Californian wife Grace, rents three quiet, spacious, characteristic rooms in a homey flat just behind St. Mark's Square. For one room, the private bath is down the hall (cash only, 2-night minimum, family rooms, air-con, slow elevator, on Calle del Remedio at Castello 4410, tel. 041-523-3603, mobile 389-272-6500, www.cortecampana.com, info@cortecampana.com).

Near Campo Santa Maria Formosa

A bit farther north of the options listed above, these are in the quiet, somewhat less touristy Castello area, beyond the inviting Campo Santa Maria Formosa.

$$$ Locanda la Corte is perfumed with elegance without being snooty. Its 14 attractive, high-ceilinged, wood-beamed rooms—Venetian-style, done in earthy pastels—circle a small, sun-drenched courtyard and a ground-level restaurant (RS%, family rooms, air-con, on Calle Bressana at Castello 6317, tel. 041-241-1300, www.locandalacorte.it, info@locandalacorte.it, Marco and Oscar the dog).

$$ Alloggi Barbaria, a good budget choice, rents eight simple, characterless rooms on one floor around a bright but institutional-feeling common area. Beyond Campo San Zanipolo/Santi Giovanni e Paolo, it's a fair walk from the action, but in a pleasant residential neighborhood. The Ospedale vaporetto stop is two minutes away on foot, with no steps (RS%, limited breakfast of bread and jam, air-con in summer, Wi-Fi in common areas, on Calle de le Capucine at Castello 6573, tel. 041-522-2750, www. alloggibarbaria.it, info@alloggibarbaria.it, well-traveled Fausto). You can reach the Ospedale stop on vaporetto #5.2 from the train or bus stations, or (on request) via the Alilaguna blue line from the airport.

West of St. Mark's Square
These more expensive hotels are solid choices in a more elegant neighborhood.

$$$$ Hotel Flora sits buried in a sea of fancy designer boutiques and elegant hotels almost on the Grand Canal. It's formal, with uniformed staff and grand public spaces, yet the 40 rooms have a homey warmth and the garden oasis is a sanctuary for well-heeled, foot-weary guests (RS%, air-con, elevator, family apartment, on Calle Bergamaschi at San Marco 2283a, tel. 041-520-5844, www.hotelflora.it, info@hotelflora.it).

$$$$ Hotel Bel Sito offers pleasing Old World character, 34 smallish rooms, generous public spaces, a peaceful courtyard, and a picturesque location—facing a church on a small square between St. Mark's Square and the Accademia (some view rooms, air-con, elevator; near Santa Maria del Giglio vaporetto stop—line #1, on Campo Santa Maria Zobenigo/del Giglio at San Marco 2517, tel. 041-522-3365, www.hotelbelsitovenezia.it, info@hotelbelsitovenezia.it, graceful Rossella).

$$$$ Hotel Mercurio, a lesser value a block in front of La Fenice Opera House, offers 29 peaceful, comfortable rooms (some view rooms, family rooms, air-con, lots of stairs, on Calle del Fruttariol at San Marco 1848, tel. 041-522-0947, www.hotelmercurio.com, info@hotelmercurio.com; Monica, Vittorio, Marco, Pierangelo, and Giacomo).

NEAR THE RIALTO BRIDGE
These places are on opposite sides of the Grand Canal, within a short walk of the Rialto Bridge. Express vaporetto #2 brings you to the Rialto quickly from the train station, the Piazzale Roma bus station, and the parking-lot island of Tronchetto, but you'll need to take the "local" vaporetto #1 to reach the minor stops closer to the last two listings. To locate the following hotels, see the map on page 249.

$$$$ Hotel al Ponte Antico is exquisite, professional, and small. With nine plush rooms, a velvety royal living/breakfast room, and its own dock for water taxi arrivals, it's perfect for a romantic anniversary. Because its wonderful terrace overlooks the

Grand Canal, Rialto Bridge, and market action, its rooms without a canal view may be a better value (air-con, 100 yards from Rialto Bridge at Cannaregio 5768, use Rialto vaporetto stop, tel. 041-241-1944, www.alponteantico.com, info@alponteantico.com, Matteo makes you feel like royalty).

$$$ Pensione Guerrato, right above the colorful Rialto produce market and just two minutes from the Rialto Bridge, is run by friendly, creative, and hardworking Roberto and Piero. Their 800-year-old building—with 22 spacious, charming rooms—is simple, airy, and wonderfully characteristic (RS%, cheaper rooms with shared bath, family rooms, air-con, on Calle drio la Scimia at San Polo 240a, take vaporetto #1 to Rialto Mercato stop to save walk over bridge, tel. 041-528-5927, www.hotelguerrato.com, info@hotelguerrato.com, Monica and Rosanna). My tour groups book this place for 60 nights each year. Sorry. The Guerrato also rents family apartments in the old center (great for groups of 4-8) for around €60 per person.

$$$ Hotel al Ponte Mocenigo is off the beaten path—a 10-minute walk northwest of the Rialto Bridge—but it's a great value. This 16th-century Venetian palazzo has a garden terrace and 10 comfy, beautifully appointed, and tranquil rooms (air-con, Santa Croce 2063, tel. 041-524-4797, www.alpontemocenigo.com, info@alpontemocenigo.com, Sandro and Valter). Take vaporetto #1 to the San Stae stop, head inland along the right side of the church, and take the first left down tiny Calle della Campanile.

NEAR THE ACCADEMIA BRIDGE

As you step over the Accademia Bridge, the commotion of touristy Venice is replaced by a sleepy village laced with canals. This quiet area, next to the best painting gallery in town, is a 15-minute walk from the Rialto or St. Mark's Square. The fast vaporetto #2 to the Accademia stop is the typical way to get here from the train station, Piazzale Roma bus station, Tronchetto parking lot, or St. Mark's Square (early and late, #2 terminates at the Rialto stop, where you change to #1). For hotels near the Zattere stop, vaporetto #5.1 (or the Alilaguna speedboat from the airport) are good options.

To locate the following hotels, see the map on page 253.

South of the Accademia Bridge, in Dorsoduro

$$$$ Pensione Accademia fills the 17th-century Villa Maravege like a Bellini painting. Its 27 comfortable, elegant rooms gild the lily. You'll feel aristocratic gliding through its grand public spaces and lounging in its wistful, breezy gardens (family rooms, must pay first night in advance, air-con, no elevator but most rooms on ground floor or one floor up, on Fondamenta Bollani at

SLEEPING

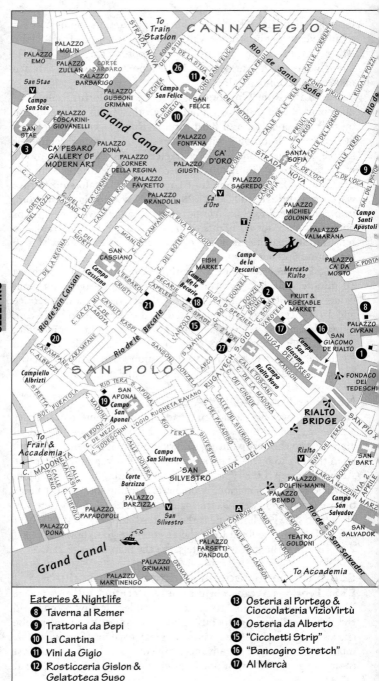

Eateries & Nightlife

- 8 Taverna al Remer
- 9 Trattoria da Bepi
- 10 La Cantina
- 11 Vini da Gigio
- 12 Rosticceria Gislon & Gelatoteca Suso
- 13 Osteria al Portego & Cioccolateria VizioVirtù
- 14 Osteria da Alberto
- 15 "Cicchetti Strip"
- 16 "Bancogiro Stretch"
- 17 Al Mercà

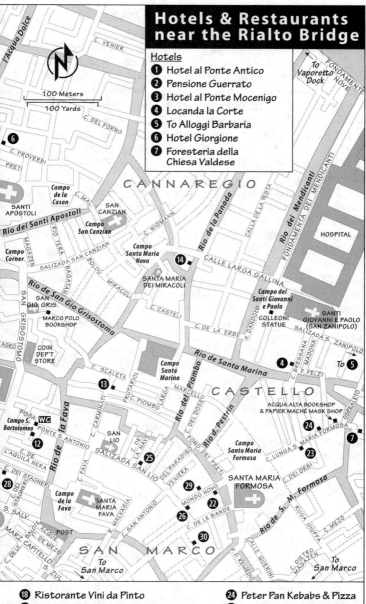

Hotels & Restaurants near the Rialto Bridge

Hotels
1. Hotel al Ponte Antico
2. Pensione Guerrato
3. Hotel al Ponte Mocenigo
4. Locanda la Corte
5. To Alloggi Barbaria
6. Hotel Giorgione
7. Foresteria della Chiesa Valdese

18. Ristorante Vini da Pinto
19. Osteria al Ponte Storto
20. Trattoria Antiche Carampane
21. Ostaria al Garanghelo
22. Osteria alle Testiere
23. Osteria al Mascaron
24. Peter Pan Kebabs & Pizza
25. La Boutique del Gelato
26. Supermarkets (2)
27. Alimentari (Deli)
28. Devil's Forest Pub
29. Inishark Pub
30. Planet Restaurant

SLEEPING

Dorsoduro 1058, tel. 041-521-0188, www.pensioneaccademia.it, info@pensioneaccademia.it).

$$$$ Hotel la Calcina, the home of English writer John Ruskin in 1876, maintains a 19th-century formality. It comes with three-star comforts in a professional yet intimate package. Its 26 nautical-feeling rooms are squeaky clean, with nice wood furniture, hardwood floors, and a peaceful waterside setting facing Giudecca Island (some view rooms, air-con, no elevator and lots of stairs, rooftop terrace, buffet breakfast outdoors in good weather on platform over lagoon, near Zattere vaporetto stop at south end of Rio de San Vio at Dorsoduro 780, tel. 041-520-6466, www.lacalcina.com, info@lacalcina.com).

$$$$ Hotel Belle Arti, with a stiff, serious staff, lacks personality but has a grand entry, an inviting garden terrace, and 67 heavily decorated rooms (air-con, elevator, 100 yards behind Accademia art museum on Rio Terà A. Foscarini at Dorsoduro 912a, tel. 041-522-6230, www.hotelbellearti.com, info@hotelbellearti.com).

$$$$ Casa Rezzonico, a tranquil getaway far from the crowds, rents seven inviting, nicely appointed rooms with a grassy private garden terrace. All the rooms overlook either the canal or the garden (RS%, family rooms, air-con, near Ca' Rezzonico vaporetto stop—line #1, a few blocks past Campo San Barnaba on Fondamenta Gherardini at Dorsoduro 2813, tel. 041-277-0653, www.casarezzonico.it, info@casarezzonico.it, brothers Matteo and Mattia).

$$$$ Hotel Galleria has nine tight, old-fashioned, velvety rooms, most with views of the Grand Canal. Some rooms are quite narrow. It's run with a family feel by Luciano and Stefano (cheaper rooms with detached private bath, breakfast in room, ceiling fans, free minibar, 30 yards from Accademia art museum, next to recommended Foscarini pizzeria at Dorsoduro 878a, tel. 041-523-2489, www.hotelgalleria.it, info@hotelgalleria.it).

$$$ Don Orione Religious Guest House is a big cultural center dedicated to the work of a local man who became a saint in modern times. With 80 rooms filling an old monastery, it feels cookie-cutter-institutional (like a modern retreat center), but is also classy, clean, peaceful, and strictly run. It's beautifully located, comfortable, and a good value supporting a fine cause: Profits go to mission work in the developing world (family rooms, groups welcome, air-con, elevator, on Rio Terà A. Foscarini, Dorsoduro 909a, tel. 041-522-4077, www.donorione-venezia.it, info@donorione-venezia.it). From the Zattere vaporetto stop, turn right, then turn left. It's just after the church at #909a.

$$$ Ca' San Trovaso rents six newly renovated rooms in a little three-floor, formerly residential building. The location is peaceful, on a small, out-of-the-way canal (RS%, some view rooms, breakfast in your room, tiny roof terrace, apartments available with 3-night minimum, near Zattere vaporetto stop, off Fondamenta de le Romite at Dorsoduro 1350, tel. 041-241-2215, mobile 349-125-3890, www.casantrovaso.com, info@casantrovaso.com, Anna and Alessandra).

$$$ Casa di Sara, a colorfully decorated B&B, is hidden in a leafy courtyard in a humble back-street area overlooking a canal. Their four quiet rooms and tiny roof terrace offer the maximum in privacy (air-con, along Fondamenta de le Romite at Dorsoduro 1330, mobile 342-596-3563, www.casadisara.com, info@casadisara.com, Aniello).

North of the Accademia Bridge

These places are between the Accademia Bridge and St. Mark's Square.

$$$$ Novecento Hotel rents nine plush rooms on three floors, complemented by a big, welcoming lounge, an elegant living room, and a small breakfast garden. This boutique hotel is nicely located and has a tasteful sense of style, mingling Art Deco with North African and Turkish decor (air-con, lots of stairs, on Calle del Dose, off Campo San Maurizio at San Marco 2683, tel. 041-241-3765, www.novecento.biz, info@novecento.biz).

$$$$ Foresteria Levi, run by a foundation that promotes research on Venetian music, offers 32 quiet, institutional yet comfortable and spacious rooms—some are loft quads, a good deal for families (RS%, air-con, elevator, on Calle Giustinian at San Marco 2893, tel. 041-277-0542, www.foresterialevi.it, info@foresterialevi.it).

$$$ Istituto Ciliota is a big, efficient, and sparkling-clean place—well-run, well-located, church-owned, and plainly furnished—with 30 dorm-like rooms and a peaceful courtyard. If you want industrial-strength comfort with no stress and little character, this is a fine value. During the school year, half the rooms are used by students (air-con, in-room fridges, elevator, on Calle de le Muneghe just off Campo San Stefano, San Marco 2976, tel. 041-520-4888, www.ciliota.it, info@ciliota.it).

$$$ Hotel San Samuele rents 10 rooms in an old *palazzo* near Campo San Stefano. It's in a great locale, and the rooms with shared bath can be a good deal (no breakfast, fans, some stairs, on Salizada San Samuele at San Marco 3358, tel. 041-520-5165, www.hotelsansamuele.com, info@hotelsansamuele.com, Judith).

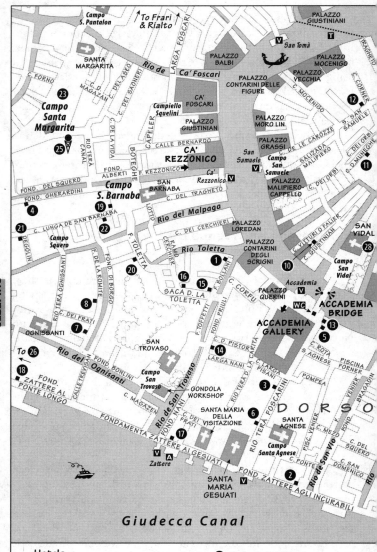

Hotels

1 Pensione Accademia
2 Hotel la Calcina
3 Hotel Belle Arti
4 Casa Rezzonico
5 Hotel Galleria
6 Don Orione Religious Guest House
7 Ca' San Trovaso
8 Casa di Sara
9 Novecento Hotel
10 Foresteria Levi
11 Istituto Ciliota
12 Hotel San Samuele

Eateries & Nightlife

13 Bar Foscarini
14 Enoteca Cantine del Vino Già Schiavi

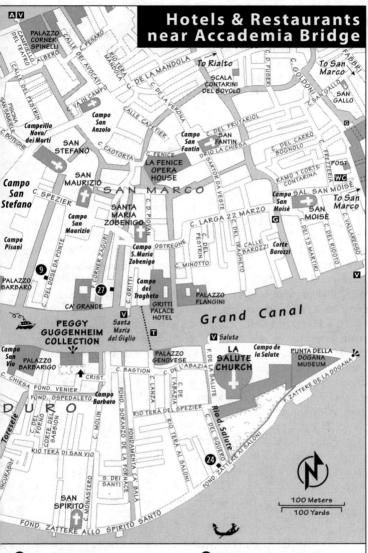

Hotels & Restaurants near Accademia Bridge

SLEEPING

- **15** Bar al Maraveje
- **16** Al Vecio Marangon
- **17** Terrazza del Casin dei Nobili
- **18** Oke Pizzeria
- **19** Ristoteca Oniga
- **20** Osteria Enoteca Ai Artisti
- **21** Pizzeria al Profeta
- **22** Enoteca e Trattoria la Bitta
- **23** Campo Santa Margarita Eateries & Nightlife
- **24** Ristorante Lineadombra
- **25** Il Doge Gelateria
- **26** Supermarket
- **27** Venice Jazz Club
- **28** El Chioschetto alle Zattere
- **29** Musica a Palazzo
- **30** Interpreti Veneziani Concerts
- **31** Music Museum

NEAR THE TRAIN STATION

I don't recommend the train station area. It's crawling with noisy, disoriented tourists with too much baggage and people whose life's calling is to scam visitors out of their money. It's so easy just to hop on a vaporetto upon arrival and sleep in the Venice of your dreams. Still, some like to park their bags near the station, and if so, these places stand out. The farther you get from the station, the more pleasant the surroundings.

Nearby Laundry: The nearest self-service launderette is across the Grand Canal from the station (see page 21).

Close to the Station

These hotels are very close to the station, but each is down a side street, away from the throngs along the main drag.

$$$$ Hotel Abbazia fills a former abbey with both history and class. The refectory makes a grand living room for guests, a garden fills the old courtyard, and the halls leading to 50 rooms are monkishly wide (RS%, air-con, no elevator but plenty of stairs, fun-loving staff, 2 blocks from the station on the very quiet Calle Priuli dei Cavaletti, Cannaregio 68, tel. 041-717-333, www.abbaziahotel.com, info@abbaziahotel.com).

$$ Hotel S. Lucia, 150 yards from the train station, is oddly modern and sterile, with bright and spacious rooms and tight showers. Its 13 rooms are simple and clean. Guests enjoy their sunny garden area out front (cheaper rooms with shared bath, air-con, closed Nov-Feb, on Calle de la Misericordia at Cannaregio 358, tel. 041-715-180, www.hotelslucia.com, info@hotelslucia.com, Gianni, Alessandra, and their son, Lorenzo).

$ Hotel Rossi, sitting quietly at the end of a dead-end street off the main Lista di Spagna, rents 17 tired, well-worn rooms that are cheap in every sense—the budget-minded will find it tolerable for a night or two, but consider yourself forewarned (cheaper rooms with shared bath, air-con, lots of stairs, on Calle de le Procuratie, Cannaregio 262, tel. 041-715-164, www.hotelrossi.ve.it, info@hotelrossi.ve.it).

Across the Bridge from the Train Station

These two places are in a quieter area on the other side of the Grand Canal from the train station—you'll have to haul your bags across a big bridge. Both are also convenient to the bus station at Piazzale Roma.

$$$ Albergo Marin is loosely run, with 20 nice but sloppily kept rooms. It's close enough to the station to be convenient, but far enough to be quiet, sane, and residential (cheaper rooms with shared bath, air-con, on Ramo de le Chioverete at Santa Croce

670b, tel. 041-718-022, www.albergomarin.it, info@albergomarin. it, brothers Giacomo and Filippo).

$$ Hotel Ai Tolentini is a pleasant couple-hundred yards from the Piazzale Roma bus station—just far enough to make you feel like you're actually in Venice. The seven rooms are on two floors, up narrow stairs above a restaurant that can be noisy (no breakfast, air-con, on Calle Amai at Santa Croce 197g, tel. 041-275-9140, www.albergoaitolentini.it, info@albergoaitolentini.it).

Farther from the Station, Toward the Jewish Ghetto and Rialto

While still walkable from the station, these listings are just outside the chaotic station neighborhood, in a far more pleasant residential zone close to the former Jewish Ghetto. The nearest Grand Canal vaporetto stop is San Marcuola.

$$$ Locanda Ca' San Marcuola is a peaceful, characteristic, good-value oldie-but-goodie renting 14 fine rooms a few steps from the Grand Canal (some view rooms, family rooms, air-con, elevator, next to San Marcuola vaporetto stop on Campo San Marcuola, Cannaregio 1763, tel. 041-716-048, www.casanmarcuola.com, info@casanmarcuola.com).

$$$ Locanda Herion, tucked down a sleepy lane just off a busy shopping street, rents 13 beige-tiled, homey rooms (RS%— use code STEVES, a few shared terraces, one room is wheelchair accessible, air-con, pay Wi-Fi, on Campiello Augusto Picutti, Cannaregio 1697a, tel. 041-275-9426, www.locandaherion.com, info@locandaherion.com).

$$ Hotel Henry, a small family-owned hotel, rents 15 simple, flowery, nicely maintained rooms with few public spaces. It's in a sleepy residential neighborhood near the Jewish Ghetto, a 10-minute walk from the train station (RS%, family rooms, no breakfast but bars nearby, apartments available, air-con, on Calle Ormesini at Campiello Briani, Cannaregio 1506e, tel. 041-523-6675, www. hotelhenry.it, info@hotelhenry.it, Manola and Henry).

OTHER ACCOMMODATIONS IN VENICE
More Venice Hotels

Big, Fancy Hotels that Discount Shamelessly: Several big, plush, **$$$$** places with greedy, sky-high rack rates frequently have steep discounts if you book through their websites. All the ones I've listed here are on the map on page 242, except Hotel Giorgione. If you want sliding-glass-door, uniformed-receptionist kind of comfort and formality in the old center, these are worth considering: **Hotel Giorgione** (big, garish, shiny, near Rialto Bridge—see map on page 249; www.hotelgiorgione.com); **Hotel Casa Verardo** (elegant and quietly parked on a canal behind St. Mark's, more

Hotels & Restaurants near the Train Station

Hotels
1. Hotel Abbazia
2. Hotel S. Lucia
3. Hotel Rossi
4. Albergo Marin & Launderette
5. Hotel Ai Tolentini
6. Locanda Ca' San Marcuola
7. Locanda Herion
8. Hotel Henry

Eateries
9. To Osteria L'Orto dei Mori
10. To Osteria Ai 40 Ladroni
11. Osteria Enoteca Timon
12. Trattoria Al Mariner
13. Gam Gam Kosher
14. Pizzeria Vesuvio
15. Osteria di Bentigodi
16. Enoteca Cicchetteria Do Colonne
17. Antica Birraria la Corte
18. Brek Cafeteria
19. Il Doge Gelateria

SLEEPING

Road to Mestre & Mainland

To Road to Mestre & Mainland

To Tronchetto

SANTA LUCIA TRAIN STATION (FERROVIA)

Ferrovia W

Ferrovia Scalzi

SCALZI BRIDGE

Ferrovia

SAN SIMEONE PICCOLO

CAMP DE LE CHIOVERETE

WC

To Stazione Marittima & Tronchetto

Canale de Santa Chiara

PONTE DELLA LIBERTA

PEOPLE MOVER

RIO TERA SAN ANDREA

PUBLIC PARKING GARAGE

CO-OP SUPERMARKET

Piazzale Roma

CALATRAVA BRIDGE

Giardino Papadopoli

CASE NOVE

CAMPO D. LA

SAN MARCO GARAGE

Piazzale Roma

BUS STATION

Novo

Campiello de Lana

C. DE CA'AMAI

SAN NICOLO DA TOLENTINO

PHARMACY

SANTA   CROCE

Canale de Santa Maria Maggiore

Rio de la Cazziola

F. MINOTTO

F.D. GAFFARO

C. D. BRIACA. GALLO

C. BASEGO

F. DEL RIO NUOVO

100 Meters
100 Yards

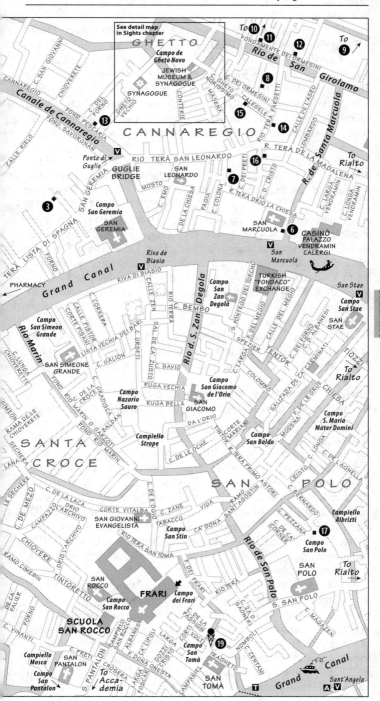

SLEEPING

stately, 22 rooms, www.casaverardo.it); **Hotel Donà Palace, Hotel all'Angelo,** and **Hotel al Ponte dei Sospiri** (three sister hotels sitting Las Vegas-like in the touristy zone a few blocks behind St. Mark's Basilica, with formal service and 100 overpriced rooms that are getting a bit long in the tooth, all on Calle Larga San Marco, www.carrainhotelsgroup.com); and **Hotel Ca' Dei Conti** (5 minutes northeast of St. Mark's Square, palatial and perfectly located but its high-priced rooms are worth it only when deeply discounted, www.cadeiconti.com).

Other Options: If all my other listings are full, try one of the following **$$$** hotels. Rates for these places vary widely with the season and demand: **Hotel Violino d'Oro** is a beautiful boutique hotel (Via XXII Marzo, San Marco 2091, tel. 041-277-0841, www.violinodoro.com). Its sister hotel, **Hotel Anastasia,** is more modest, with limited reception staff (San Marco 2141, tel. 041-277-0776, www.hotelanastasia.com). **Hotel American Dinesen** offers 30 plush rooms with all the comforts (near Peggy Guggenheim Collection at Fondamenta Bragadin, Dorsoduro 628, tel. 041-520-4733, www.hotelamerican.com). **Hotel La Fenice et des Artistes** has 68 classy but unpretentious rooms on a sleepy square (near opera house at Campiello della Fenice, San Marco 1936, tel. 041-523-2333, www.fenicehotels.com). **Hotel dei Dragomanni** is modern, stylish, and pricey (facing Grand Canal at San Marco 2711, tel. 041-277-1300, www.hoteldragomanni.com).

Cheap Dormitory Accommodations

$$ Foresteria della Chiesa Valdese is ramshackle, chilly, run-down, yet charming. It rents 75 beds—mostly in tight (6- to 10-bed) dorms, but with nine fine doubles and some larger private rooms sleeping up to six. It comes with generous public spaces and classic paintings on the walls and ceilings. Its profits support the charity work of the Waldesian and Methodist Church. Reservations for the dorms are accepted only four days in advance (some view rooms; must check in and out when office is open—8:30-20:00; free concerts on site Wed and Sat, no air-con, elevator, near Campo Santa Maria Formosa on Fondamenta Cavagnis at Castello 5170, see map on page 249, tel. 041-528-6797, www.foresteriavenezia.it, info@foresteriavenezia.it).

¢ **Venice's youth hostel,** on Giudecca Island, with 243 beds and grand views across the Bay of San Marco, is a godsend for backpackers shell-shocked by Venetian prices. Though the facility was recently renovated, at heart it's still a classic hostel—big rooms stacked with bunk beds (rates vary wildly, private and family rooms available, office open 24 hours, Fondamenta Zitelle 86, tel. 041-877-8288, www.hostelvenice.org, info@ostellovenezia.it). From the bus or train stations, take vaporetto #4.1 (faster) or #2 (more frequent) to the Zitelle stop, then walk right along the embankment to #86. (From the Tronchetto parking lot, take vaporetto #2.)

Apartments

Consider this option if you're traveling as a family, in a group, or staying five days or longer. Websites such as Airbnb and VRBO let you correspond directly with property owners or managers. Alternatively, the following recommended hotels also rent apartments (with small kitchens) on the side; see their earlier listings for contact information. For more information on renting apartments in Italy, see page 427 in the Practicalities chapter.

Hotel Campiello, east of St. Mark's Square, has three modern, upscale, and quiet family apartments for up to six people, just steps away from their hotel. Nearby, **Locanda al Leon** has a pair of two-bedroom, two-bathroom apartments with kitchens. **Hotel Flora,** west of St. Mark's Square, has a great family-size apartment. **Pensione Guerrato,** west of the Rialto Bridge, has apartments for four to eight people. East of the Rialto Bridge, **Locanda la Corte** has two quads for up to eight (in hotel, no kitchen), and **Albergo Doni** has three basic apartments. So does **Hotel Henry**, near the train station.

STAYING ON THE MAINLAND, IN MESTRE

Drivers wanting to do a one-day blitz of Venice can sleep in Mestre for two nights and park right at their hotel. Mestre (MEH-streh) is a gloomy, industrial, concrete burg where Venice's causeway meets the mainland. The streets surrounding the Mestre station are a stark contrast to Venice: big, dingy buildings, rough corners, and modern roads buzzing with traffic. These places are cheaper than hotels of a similar standard in Venice proper, but unless you have a car, it's hard to justify sleeping here when the magic of Venice is so close. Bunking here does have a few other advantages, though: Your money buys more comfort and amenities; it's extra handy for side-tripping by rail to other towns (such as Padua, Vicenza, and Verona); and it's more likely to have affordable rooms when Venice proper is chockablock with festivals.

It's easy to get between Mestre and Venice. From the big Mestre station, trains depart about every 10 minutes, zipping to Venezia Santa Lucia Station (right on the Grand Canal) in about 10 minutes for €1.25 (buy tickets at machines; validate before boarding). Alternatively, you can catch bus #2, right in front of Mestre's train station, and ride it to Venice's Piazzale Roma (also right on the Grand Canal, across from the train station) in 15 minutes (€1.30, covered by Venice's transit passes).

These hotels all charge around €100-150 for a double in peak season, but rates are extremely soft. In slow times, you can get a

SLEEPING

much better deal. All of these are quite modern when compared to the typically musty, Old World options in Venice. My Mestre recommendations all have parking—mostly pay on-site or discounted at the big Parcheggio Stazione garage across from the station (figure €10-16/day; request when you reserve), but a few offer free parking.

Right in Front of the Station

$$$ Hotel Tritone, a high-rise business hotel with 60 rooms and a borderline-gaudy lobby, has the most convenient location, facing Mestre's train station (cheaper if you pay in advance, air-con, elevator, pay parking; leaving the station, cross the street, turn right, and walk to the end of the block to find Viale Stazione 16, tel. 041-538-3125, www.hoteltritonevenice.com, info@hoteltritonevenice.com).

$$ Hotel Paris is a few doors down from the station and worth considering if you can get a deal. It has 18 small, modern, modestly stylish rooms (air-con, on-site parking, Via Venezia 11, tel. 041-926-037, www.hotelparis.it, info@hotelparis.it). It's hiding in a drab sea of apartment blocks: Leaving the station, cross the street, turn left along Viale Stazione, and turn right after one block up Via Venezia.

A Bit Farther, but Still Walkable

While slightly less handy to the station (about a 10-minute walk), these options are a better value and have more of a neighborhood feel. To reach them from the station, cross the street and go up Via Piave. After about four blocks, turn left for Hotel Villa Costanza or Hotel Cris, or (soon after) right for Hotel Aaron. For these hotels, the bus (which stops along Via Piave) can be a faster and easier way to reach Venice than the train (and lets you skip the station-area chaos).

$$ Hotel Villa Costanza is the nicest place I could find in Mestre. This stylish, professional-feeling boutique hotel fills an old villa on a sleepy residential street with 26 classy rooms, an inviting modern lounge, and a covered terrace (RS%, air-con, minibar, elevator, on-site pay parking, Via Monte Nero 25, tel. 041-932-624, www.hotelvillacostanza.com, info@hotelvillacostanza.com, Monica).

$$ Hotel Cris, a simpler option with a quiet courtyard up the street from Hotel Villa Costanza, has 18 nondescript rooms (air-con, free on-site parking, Via Monte Nero 3a, tel. 041-926-773, www.hotelcris.it, info@hotelcris.it).

$$ Hotel Aaron oozes modern artistic style, with 20 sleek, good-value rooms on a pleasant street just off Viale Piave (air-con, elevator, on-site pay parking, Via Felisati 187, tel. 041-538-5868, www.hotelaaron.com, info@hotelaaron.com).

Behind Mestre Station, in Marghera

If you leave the station through its back door (follow the underground tunnel connecting platforms to the end beyond tracks 12/13), you'll pop out into Marghera, a much more pleasant, residential-feeling area, with freestanding homes, gardens, and trees. Exiting the station, turn left down the first street, then right onto Via Rizzardi. This main drag is lined with lots of big tour hotels (where cut-rate tour companies shoehorn their groups at Venice's doorstep), as well as this smaller, charming option.

$$ Casa Villa Gardenia, just before the roundabout on the right (about a 10-minute walk from the station's tracks), is sweetly run by Lorenza, who rents six rooms in a pleasant old villa (family rooms, air-con, free on-site parking, Via Rizzardi 36c, Marghera, tel. 041-930-207, info@casavillagardenia.com, www.casavillagardenia.it).

Beyond Mestre

This place, beyond the urban core of Mestre, combines fine prices with easy bus links into Venice.

$ Villa Mocenigo Agriturismo, about 10 miles from Marco Polo Airport, is a working, family-run farm with 10 simple rooms in a peaceful rural location between Venice and Padua (dinner about €20/person, air-con, free parking, Via Viasana 59 in Mirano-Venezia, tel. 041-433-246, mobile 335-547-4728, www.villamocenigo.com, info@villamocenigo.com). Email for directions. Buses to Venice stop a 10-minute walk away (3/hour, 45 minutes).

EATING IN VENICE

Looking for an "untouristy restaurant" in Venice is like looking for the same thing at Disneyland. A restaurateur once confided in me that no restaurant in Venice can be truly untouristy: They all want and need the tourist euro. Simply put, Venice's restaurants exist to feed tourists. But while some cater to groups and sloppy big spenders, others respect their clientele—both locals and travelers. My recommended places, even though they're touristy, are popular with actual Venetians, who still eat out and have their favorites.

EATING TIPS

For even more advice on eating in Italy, including details on ordering, dining, and tipping in restaurants, where to find budget meals, picnicking help, and Italian cuisine and beverages (including wine), see page 430.

Restaurant Hours: Most restaurants close their kitchens between lunch and dinner, typically reopening around 19:00 or later. Even if a restaurant is fully booked for later that evening, it may accommodate walk-in diners who are willing to eat early and quickly.

Eating Well: While touristy restaurants are the norm in Venice, you can still make the most of your meal by dining at one of my recommended listings and following these tips. First trick: Walk away from triple-language menus. Second trick: For freshness, eat fish. Many seafood dishes are the catch-of-the-day. Third trick: Eat later. A place may feel really touristy at 19:00, but if you come back at 21:00, it can be filled with locals. Tourists eat barbarically early, which is fine with the restaurants because they fill tables that would otherwise be used only once in an evening.

Budget Eating: The keys to eating affordably in Venice are pizza, bars/cafés (see next), self-service cafeterias, and picnics. For a colorful picnic experience, gather your ingredients in the morning at a produce market (most fun at and around the big Rialto Market). See page 438 for more picnicking tips.

Bars/Cafés: Venetians often eat a snack—*cicchetti* or *panini*—while standing at a bar. (You'll usually pay more if you sit; see page 436). You can get a filling plate of typically Venetian appetizers at nearly any bar.

I like small, fun, stand-up mini meals at *cicchetti* **bars** best. Unique to Venice, *cicchetti* bars specialize in finger foods and appetizers that combine to make a speedy and tasty meal. *Cicchetti* (the Venetian version of tapas) was designed as a quick meal for working people. The selection and ambience are best on workdays—Monday through Saturday for lunch or early dinner (see "The Stand-Up Progressive Venetian Pub-Crawl Dinner," on page 270). An *ombra* ("shadow") is a small glass of wine often offered with *cicchetti*. I list a couple of stretches in Venice where you can go from bar to bar sampling *cicchetti* (see page 267).

Sandwiches are sold fast and cheaply at bars everywhere and can stave off midmorning hunger (order a *panini, piadini,* or *tramezzini;* described on page 274). A great "sandwich row" of cheap cafés is near St. Mark's Square (see page 270). You can eat your sandwich at the bar or take it with you.

Aperitivo: One of my favorite Italian traditions is the *aperitivo* (predinner drink). The dominant *aperitivo* among Venetians is the *spritz*. This refreshing cocktail mixes white wine, soda, and ice with a liquor of your choice and is garnished with an olive or skewer of fruit. When you order, you'll be asked if you'd like your *spritz con Campari* (bitter—traditionally the man's choice) or *con Aperol* (sweeter, a supposedly feminine choice). Between 18:00 and 20:00, this happy pink drink dominates Venice's watering holes.

NEAR THE RIALTO BRIDGE
For locations, see the map on page 249.

EATING

Restaurant Price Code

I've assigned each eatery a price category, based on the average cost of a typical main course (pasta or *secondi*). Drinks, desserts, and splurge items (steak and seafood) can raise the price considerably.

$$$$	**Splurge:**	Most main courses over €20
$$$	**Pricier:**	€15-20
$$	**Moderate:**	€10-15
$	**Budget:**	Under €10

In Italy, pizza by the slice and other takeaway food is $; a basic trattoria or sit-down pizzeria is $$; a casual but more upscale restaurant is $$$; and a swanky splurge is $$$$.

North of the Bridge

These restaurants and wine bars are located near or beyond Campo Santi Apostoli, on or near the Strada Nova, the main drag going from Rialto toward the train station.

$$$ Taverna al Remer is a creative place with its own private square overlooking the Grand Canal (across from the Rialto Market). Its restaurant seating is deep in an old, candlelit warehouse, and its happy-hour "yard" offers a chance to sit on their private pier and enjoy the Grand Canal and Rialto Bridge action (free buffet accompanying drinks, Thu-Tue 17:30-19:00). They also offer a good lunch buffet (€20 plus drink, Mon-Tue & Thu-Fri 12:00-15:00) and have live jazz after 21:00 (closed Wed, Cannaregio 5701, tel. 041-522-8789). From Campo San Bartolomeo, head north (behind the statue) and cross one bridge. Then, just past the pink church (San Giovanni Crisostomo), about 10 yards before the next bridge, venture down the tiny dark lane on the left.

$$$ Trattoria da Bepi, bright and alpine-paneled, feels like a classic, where Loris carries on his mother's passion for good, traditional Venetian cuisine. Ask for the seasonal specialties: The seafood appetizer plate and crab dishes are excellent. There's good seating inside and out. If you trust Loris, you'll walk away with a wonderful dining memory (Fri-Wed 12:00-14:30 & 19:00-22:00, closed Thu, reservations recommended, half a block off Campo Santi Apostoli on Salizada Pistor, Cannaregio 4550, tel. 041-528-5031, www.anticatrattoriadabepi.it).

$$$ La Cantina is an elegant *enoteca*, both rustic and sophisticated—you won't find a menu here. Rather than cook (there's no kitchen), they serve wonderful gourmet cold plates of meat, cheese, and fish. Though short on smiles and expensive (meat-and-cheese plates-€18/person, seafood plates-€35/person), you'll enjoy the best ingredients paired with fine wines. You can sit inside and watch the preparation scene or enjoy the parade of passersby from great seats right on the Strada Nova (Mon-Sat 11:00-22:00, closed Sun, facing Campo San Felice on Strada Nova near Ca' d'Oro, Cannaregio 3689, tel. 041-522-8258).

$$$$ Vini da Gigio, a more expensive option, has a traditional Venetian menu and a classy but unsnooty setting that's a pleasant mix of traditional and contemporary (Wed-Sun 12:00-14:30 & 19:00-22:30, closed Mon-Tue, 4 blocks from Ca' d'Oro vaporetto stop on Fondamenta San Felice, behind the church on Campo San Felice, Cannaregio 3628a, tel. 041-528-5140, www.vinidagigio.com).

East of the Rialto Bridge

The next few places hide away in the twisty lanes between the Rialto Bridge and Campo Santa Maria Formosa. Osteria da Alberto is a tad farther north of the others, in Cannaregio.

$ Rosticceria Gislon is a cheap—if confusing—self-service diner. This throwback budget eatery—kind of an Italian Mel's Diner—has a surly staff: Don't take it personally. Notice that the different counters serve up different types of food—pastas, *secondi*, fried goodies, and so on. You can get it to go, grab one of the few tiny tables, or munch at the bar—but I'd skip their upper-floor restaurant option (great fried *mozzarella al prosciutto*, fruit salad, cheap glasses of wine, prices listed on wall behind counter, no cover and no service charge, daily 9:00-21:30, San Marco 5424, tel. 041-522-3569). To find it, imagine the statue on Campo San Bartolomeo walks backward 20 yards, turns left, and goes under a passageway. Follow him.

$$ Osteria al Portego is a small and popular neighborhood eatery near Campo San Lio. Carlo serves good meals, bargain-priced house wine, and excellent €1-3 *cicchetti*—best enjoyed early, around 18:00. The *cicchetti* here can make a great meal, but consider sitting down for a dinner from their menu. From 12:00-14:30 & 17:30-21:30, their six tables are reserved for those ordering from the menu; the *cicchetti* are picked over by 21:00. Reserve ahead if you want a table (daily 11:30-15:00 & 17:30-22:00, on Calle de la Malvasia, Castello 6015, tel. 041-522-9038, www.osteriaalportego.it, Federica). From Rosticceria Gislon (listed above), continue over a bridge to Campo San Lio, turn left, and follow Calle Carminati straight 50 yards over another bridge.

$$ Osteria da Alberto, up near Campo Santa Maria Novo, is one of my standbys. They offer up excellent daily specials: seafood dishes, pastas, and a good house wine in a woody and characteristic interior (although it's set along a canal, you can't see it from the dining area). It's smart to reserve at night—I'd request a table in front (daily 12:00-15:00 & 18:30-22:30; on Calle Larga Giacinto Gallina, midway between Campo Santi Apostoli and Campo San Zanipolo/Santi Giovanni e Paolo, and next to Ponte

Pizza in Venice

For a killer canalside setting without a killer price, stick to pizza. While not the home of pizza, Venice is enthusiastic about it. For tourists, a great way to enjoy a delightful Venetian setting at a painless price is to have a €9-10 pizza with a beer or carafe of house wine at a canalside restaurant. Even at an expensive eatery, ordering a pizza won't break the bank, and you can enjoy a great setting and classy service. If you're in the mood for pizza, consider one of these places (all described in more detail later in this chapter):

Several fun-loving, youthful pizzerias feature inexpensive and good pizzas, big pizza parlor-type interiors, and relaxing outdoor seating, such as **Pizzeria al Profeta** (with a leafy garden, near Campo San Barnaba), **Oke Pizzeria** (with casual tables overlooking the Giudecca Canal), **Antica Birraria la Corte** (on a big, breezy neighborhood square), and **Pizzeria Vesuvio** (with streetside tables, near the Jewish Ghetto).

For basic pizza with one of the city's most picturesque settings—on the Grand Canal under the Accademia Bridge—check out **Bar Foscarini.**

For top-shelf pizza served in a more formal restaurant setting, consider **Terrazza del Casin dei Nobili** (with elegant seating overlooking the Giudecca Canal) and **Ristorante Antica Sacrestia** (a classy restaurant near St. Mark's Square).

Takeout pizza is one of the least expensive ways to eat in Venice. Hole-in-the-wall shops in every neighborhood bake huge, round, family-size pizzas (about 20 inches across) for €8-15, or "normal" ones (12 inches) for €4-8. Some sell *pizza al taglio* (by the slice, usually reheated) as well as kebabs. Takeout prices increase dramatically as you near the Rialto and St. Mark's Square. At the base of the Rialto Bridge, family-size pizzas are cut into eight slices that sell for €4.50 each, but around Campo Santa Maria Formosa or Campo San Barnaba, they're cut into six larger slices and cost €2 each. (For tips on ordering takeout pizza, see page 436; for a list of common types of pizza, see page 439.)

Away from the crowds, you'll get more for your money—whether you get takeout or eat in restaurants.

de la Panada bridge, Cannaregio 5401; tel. 041-523-8153, www.osteriadaalberto.it, run by Graziano and Giovanni).

Rialto Market Area

The north end of the Rialto Bridge is a great area for menu browsing, bar-hopping, drinks, and snacks; it also has fine sit-down restaurants. As with market neighborhoods anywhere, you'll find lots of hard-working holes-in-the-wall with a line on the freshest of ingredients and catering to local shoppers needing a quick, affordable, and tasty bite. This area is very crowded by day, nearly empty early in the evening, and packed with young Venetian clubbers later.

My listings below include a stretch of dark and rustic pubs serving *cicchetti* (Venetian tapas), a strip of trendy places fronting the Grand Canal, a few little places on the market, and a couple of "normal" restaurants serving solid pasta, pizza, and *secondi*. All but the last two eateries are within 200 yards of the market and each other.

The *Cicchetti* Strip: Four Venetian Tapas Bars

The 100-yard-long stretch starting two blocks inland from the Rialto Market (along Sotoportego dei Do Mori and Calle de le Do Spade) is beloved among Venetian *cicchetti* enthusiasts for its delightful bar munchies, good wine by the glass, and fun stand-up conviviality. These four **$** places serve food all day, but the spread is best at around noon (generally open daily 12:00-15:00 & 18:00-20:00 or 21:00; two of the places I list are closed Sun). Each place offers a fine bar-and-stools scene, and a couple can be treated like a restaurant—order from their rustic menu and grab a table. Scout these places in advance (listed in the order you'll reach them, if coming from the Rialto Bridge) to help decide which ambience is right for the experience you have in mind. Then pick one, dig in, and drink up.

At each place, look for the list of snacks and wine by the glass at the bar or on the wall. When you're ready for dessert, try dipping a Burano biscuit in a glass of strawberry-flavored *fragolino* or another sweet dessert wine. Most bars are closed 15:00-18:00 and offer glasses of house wine for under €1, better wine for around €2.50, and *cicchetti* for €1.50-2.

Bar all'Arco, a bustling one-room joint, is particularly enjoyable for its tiny open-face sandwiches (closed Sun, San Polo 436; Francesco, Anna, Matteo).

Cantina Do Mori has been famous with locals (since 1462) and savvy travelers (since 1982) as a convivial place for fine wine. They serve a forest of little edibles on toothpicks and *francobolli* (a spicy selection of 20 tiny, mayo-soaked sandwiches nicknamed "stamps"). Go here to be abused in a fine atmosphere—the frowns are part of the shtick (closed Sun, can be shoulder-to-shoulder, San Polo 430).

Osteria ai Storti, with a cool photo of the market in 1909, is more of a sit-down place (tables inside and on street). It's run by Alessandro, who speaks English and enjoys helping educate travelers, and his sister Baby—pronounced "Bobby" (daily, around corner from Cantina Do Mori on Calle San Matio—follow signs, San Polo 819).

Cantina Do Spade is expertly run by Francesco, who clearly lists the *cicchetti* and wines of the day (also good for sit-down meals, 30 yards down Calle de le Do Spade from Osteria ai Storti at San Polo 860, tel. 041-521-0583).

The "Bancogiro Stretch": Five Places Overlooking the Grand Canal

Just past the Rialto Bridge, between Campo San Giacomo and the Grand Canal, this strip of five popular places in a recently reno-vated old building has some of the best canalside seating in Venice. I call this the "Bancogiro Stretch" (the restaurants front a former banking building called Bancogiro).

Each place has a unique character and formula. Unless other-wise noted, all are open daily and serve drinks, *cicchetti,* and inven-tive, somewhat pricey sit-down meals. While you can get a drink anytime, dinner is typically served only after 19:00 or 19:30. Dur-ing meals, they charge more and limit table seating to those order-ing full lunches or dinners; but between mealtimes you can enjoy a drink or a snack at fine prices. After dinner hours, the Bancogiro Stretch—especially in the surrounding alleys that house low-rent bars—becomes a youthful and trendy nightspot. Before or after dinner, this strip is one of the best places in town for a *spritz.*

Here's the rundown (in the order you'll reach them from the Rialto Bridge): **$$$ Bar Naranzaria** serves Italian dishes with a few Japanese options. **$$ Caffè Vergnano** is your cheapest op-tion—especially during mealtimes (vegan dishes and a busy mi-crowave oven). **$$$ Osteria al Pescador** has a friendly staff and serves local specialties. **$$$ Bar Ristorante Bancogiro** has the best reputation for dinner, a passion for the best cheese, and good *cicchetti* options at the bar (nice €17 cheese plate, closed Mon, tel. 041-523-2061, www.osteriabancogiro.it). The more modern **$$ Bar Ancòra** seems to be most popular with the local bar crowd, with a live piano player crooning lounge music during busy times (*cicchetti* at the bar).

Other Good Eateries near the Rialto Market

$ Al Mercà ("At the Market"), a few steps away and off the canal, is a lively little nook with a happy crowd, where law-office workers have lunch and young locals gather in the evening for drinks and little snacks. The price list is clear, and the youthful crowd seems to enjoy connecting with curious tourists (stand at bar or in square—there are no tables and no interior, Mon-Sat 10:00-14:30 & 18:00-21:00, closed Sun, on Campo Cesare Battisti, San Polo 213).

$$ Ristorante Vini da Pinto is a tourist-friendly eatery facing the fish market, with a large menu and relaxing outdoor seating. Owner George visits the market each morning to select the day's best catch. Enjoy the fixed-price, three-course seafood meal for €17, including a pasta, seafood sampler plate, veggies, and dessert. Grander versions cost €20-25. Rick Steves readers receive a welcoming prosecco and a farewell *limoncello* and homemade cookie (daily 11:00-23:00, Campo de le Becarie, San Polo 367a, tel. 041-522-4599).

$$ Osteria al Ponte Storto, a little family-run place on a quiet canalside corner a block off the main drag, is worth seeking out for its good-value main dishes, daily specials, and peaceful location (Tue-Sun 12:00-15:00 & 19:00-21:45, closed Mon, down Calle Bianca from San Aponal church, San Polo 1278, tel. 041-528-2144).

Between the Rialto Bridge and Frari Church

$$$$ Trattoria Antiche Carampane is a dressy, family-run place with an open kitchen and a local following. They have a passion for fish (and make a point: no pizza) and serve traditional Venetian dishes with a fresh twist that change with the season. It's small—there are just 30 seats with six tables on the street (closed Sun-Mon, reservations necessary, Rio Tera delle Carampane, San Polo 1911, tel. 041-524-0165, www.antichecarampane.com, Francesco).

$$ Ostaria al Garanghelo is a happy little eatery with an inviting menu, a love for fresh fish, and an old but shiny ambience. They have a few seats on the street—good for people-watching—and offer a seafood tasting platter and vegetarian dishes (daily, Calle dei Boteri, San Polo 1570, tel. 041-721-721).

$$ Antica Birraria la Corte is an everyday eatery on the delightful Campo San Polo. Popular for its pizza, calzones, and wonderful selection of hearty salads, it fills the far side of this cozy, family-filled square. Although the interior is sprawling and modern, it's a joy to eat on the square, where metal tables teeter on the cobbles, the wind plays with the paper mats, and children run free (daily 12:00-15:00 & 18:00-23:30, on Campo San Polo at #2168—see map on page 256, tel. 041-275-0570).

NEAR ST. MARK'S SQUARE

While my first listing is a serious restaurant, the other places listed here are cheap-and-cheery options convenient to your sightseeing. For locations, see the map on page 242.

$$$$ Ristorante Antica Sacrestia is a classic restaurant where the owner, Pino, takes a hands-on approach to greeting guests. His staff serves creative fixed-price meals (€35, €55, or €80), a humdrum *menù del giorno,* and wonderful pizzas. (Be warned: These meals seem designed to overwhelm you with too much food.

EATING

The Stand-Up Progressive Venetian Pub-Crawl Dinner

My favorite Venetian dinner is a pub crawl *(giro d'ombra)* — a tradition unique to Venice, where no cars means easy crawling. *(Giro* means stroll, and *ombra* —slang for a glass of wine—means shade, from the old days when a portable wine bar scooted with the shadow of the Campanile bell tower across St. Mark's Square.)

Venice's residential back streets hide plenty of characteristic bars *(bacari)*, with countless trays of interesting toothpick munchies *(cicchetti)* and blackboards listing the wines that are uncorked and served by the glass. This is a great way to mingle and have fun with the Venetians. Bars don't stay open very late, and the *cicchetti* selection is best early, so start your evening by 18:00. Most bars are closed on Sunday. For a stress-free pub crawl, consider taking a tour with the charming Alessandro Schezzini (see page 30).

***Cicchetti* bars** have a social stand-up zone and a cozy gaggle of tables where you can generally sit down with your *cicchetti* or order from a simple menu. In some of the more popular places, the crowds happily spill out into the street. Food generally costs the same price whether you stand or sit.

There's no wine by the glass. Order carefully. Pizza is your only budget escape.) You can also order à la carte; their €22 antipasto spread looks like a lagoon aquarium spread out on a plate. My readers are welcome to a free *sgroppino* (lemon vodka after-dinner drink) upon request (Tue-Sun 11:30-15:00 & 18:00-23:00, closed Mon, behind San Zaninovo/Giovanni Novo Church on Calle Corona, Castello 4463, tel. 041-523-0749, www.anticasacrestia.it).

"Sandwich Row": On Calle de le Rasse, just steps away from the tourist intensity at St. Mark's Square, is a handy strip I call "Sandwich Row." Lined with sandwich bars, it's the closest place to St. Mark's to get a decent sandwich at an affordable price with a place to sit down (most places open daily 7:00-24:00, €1 extra to sit; from the Bridge of Sighs, head down the Riva and take the second lane on the left). I particularly like **$ Birreria Forst,** a pleasantly unpretentious café that serves busy local workers a selection of meaty €3 sandwiches with tasty sauce on wheat bread, or made-

I've listed plenty of pubs in walking order for a quick or extended crawl. If you've crawled enough, most of these bars make a fine one-stop, sit-down dinner.

While you can order a plate, Venetians prefer going one-by-one...sipping their wine and trying this...then give me one of those...and so on. Try deep-fried mozzarella cheese, gorgonzola, calamari, artichoke hearts, and anything ugly on a toothpick. *Crostini* (small toasted bread with a topping) are popular, as are marinated seafood, olives, and prosciutto with melon. Meat and fish (*pesce*; PESH-ay) munchies can be expensive; veggies (*verdure*) are cheap, at about €3 for a meal-sized plate. In many places, there's a set price per food item (e.g., €1.50). To get a plate of assorted appetizers for €8 (or more, depending on how hungry you are), ask for "*Un piatto classico di cicchetti misti da €8*" (oon pee-AH-toh KLAH-see-koh dee cheh-KET-tee MEE-stee dah OH-toh eh-OO-roh). Bread sticks (*grissini*) are free for the asking.

Bar-hopping Venetians enjoy an *aperitivo*, a before-dinner drink. Boldly order a Bellini, a *spritz con Aperol*, or a prosecco, and draw approving looks from the natives.

Drink the house wines. A small glass of house red or white wine (*ombra rosso* or *ombra bianco*) or a small beer (*birrino*) costs about €1. The house keg wine is cheap—€1 per glass, about €4 per liter. *Vin bon*, Venetian for fine wine, may run you from €2 to €6 per little glass. There are usually several fine wines uncorked and available by the glass. A good last drink is *fragolino*, the local sweet wine—*bianco* or *rosso*. It often comes with a little cookie (*biscotto*) for dipping.

to-order sandwiches (daily 9:30-23:00, air-con, rustic wood tables, Castello 4540, tel. 041-523-0557, Romina), and **$ Bar Verde,** a more modern sandwich bar with clear and good pricing plus fun people-watching views from its corner tables (also splittable salads, fresh pastries, at the end of Calle de le Rasse facing Campo Santi Filippo e Giacomo, Castello 4526).

$$ Ristorante alla Basilica, just one street behind St. Mark's Basilica, is a church-run, indoor, institutional-feeling place that serves a solid €16 fixed-price lunch, often amid noisy school groups. It's not self-serve—you'll be seated and can choose a pasta, a *secondi,* and a vegetable side dish off the menu. Don't expect high cuisine or ingratiating service—but it's efficient and filling (Wed-Mon 12:00-15:00, closed Tue, air-con, Calle dei Albanesi, Castello 4255, tel. 041-522-0524).

$ Ristorante Cinese Capitol, around the corner from the listings above, provides a break from Italian. It serves inexpensive but tasty Chinese standards to eat in or take out (daily 11:00-15:30 & 17:30-23:00, on Campo S.S. Filippo e Giacomo, Castello 4294, tel. 041-522-5331).

Picnicking: Though you can't picnic on St. Mark's Square, you can legally take your snacks to the nearby Giardinetti Reali, the small park along the waterfront west of the Piazzetta.

NORTH OF ST. MARK'S SQUARE, NEAR CAMPO SANTA MARIA FORMOSA

For a (marginally) less touristy scene, walk a few blocks north to the inviting Campo Santa Maria Formosa. For locations, see the map on page 249.

$$$$ Osteria alle Testiere is my top dining splurge in Venice. Hugely respected, Luca and his staff are dedicated to quality, serving up creative, artfully presented market-fresh seafood (there's no meat on the menu), homemade pastas, and fine wine in what the chef calls a "Venetian Nouvelle" style. With only 22 seats, it's tight and homey, with the focus on food and service. They have daily specials, 10 wines by the glass, and one agenda: a great dining experience. This is a good spot to let loose and trust your host. They're open for lunch (12:00-15:00), and reservations are a must well in advance for their two dinner seatings: 19:00 and 21:30 (plan on spending €50 for dinner, closed Sun-Mon, on Calle del Mondo Novo, just off Campo Santa Maria Formosa, Castello 5801, tel. 041-522-7220, www.osterialletestiere.it).

$$$ Osteria al Mascaron is a rustic little bar-turned-restaurant where I've gone for years to watch Gigi, Momi, and their food-loving band of ruffians dish up rustic-yet-sumptuous pastas with steamy seafood to salivating foodies. The €16 *antipasto misto* plate—have fun pointing—and two glasses of wine make a terrific light meal (Mon-Sat 11:00-15:00 & 17:30-23:00, closed Sun, reservations smart Fri-Sat, Wi-Fi; on Calle Lunga Santa Maria Formosa, a block past Campo Santa Maria Formosa, Castello 5225; tel. 041-522-5995, www.osteriamascaron.it). While they advertise pastas only for two, you are welcome to have a half-order for half-price—still plenty big.

Fast and Cheap Eats: The veggie stand on Campo Santa Maria Formosa is a fixture. For *döner kebabs* and pizza to go, head down Calle Lunga Santa Maria Formosa to **$ Peter Pan** at #6249 (daily 12:00-23:00, Castello).

DORSODURO

All of these recommendations are within a 10-minute walk of the Accademia Bridge (for locations, see the map on page 253). Dorsoduro is great for restaurants and well worth the walk from the more touristy Rialto and San Marco areas. The first listings, near the Accademia, are best for lunch. The places in Zattere overlook the Giudecca Canal. Best for dinner are the four restaurants near Campo San Barnaba. Last are a handful of pizzerias and *cicchetti* bars on Campo Santa Margarita. My top Dorsoduro listing, **Ristorante Lineadombra,** is described later in "Splurging on a Water (or Otherwise Great) View."

Near the Accademia Bridge
$$ Bar Foscarini, next to the Accademia Bridge and Galleria, offers decent pizzas and *panini* in a memorable Grand Canal-view setting. The food is forgettable and drinks are pricey. But you're paying a premium for this premium location. On each visit to Venice, I grab a pizza lunch here while I ponder the Grand Canal bustle. They also serve breakfast (daily 8:00-23:00, until 20:30 Nov-April, on Rio Terà A. Foscarini, Dorsoduro 878c, tel. 041-522-7281, Paolo and Simone).

$ Enoteca Cantine del Vino Già Schiavi, with a wonderfully characteristic *cicchetti*-bar ambience, is much loved for its €1.20 *cic-*

chetti, €4 sandwiches (order from list on board), and €1-2 glasses of wine. You're welcome to enjoy your wine and finger food at the bar or out on the sidewalk. This is primarily a wine shop with great prices for bottles to go—and plastic glasses for picnickers (Mon-Sat 8:30-20:30, closed Sun, 100 yards from Accademia art museum on San Trovaso canal; facing the Accademia, take a right and then a forced left at the canal to the second bridge—it's at Dorsoduro 992, tel. 041-523-0034).

$ Bar al Maraveje is handy for a sandwich, with quiet, comfy tables just minutes from the Accademia. They serve a range of fresh sandwiches, from less expensive *topolini* (four-bite sandwiches) and *tramezzini* (crustless sandwich triangles) to heartier ciabatta sandwiches (daily, 100 yards west of the Accademia, just over a bridge on Calle de la Toletta, Dorsoduro 1185, tel. 041-523-5768).

$ Al Vecio Marangon glows like a dream come true on its corner tucked away from the frenzy of Venice, about 100 yards west of the Accademia. This stylishly rustic bar serves *cicchetti*-style dishes and pastas within its tight and picturesque interior or at a line of outdoor tables. Consider their splittable *piatto di cicchetti misti,* a sampler of sardines, octopus, codfish, and seafood salad. As they take no reservations, arrive early or be prepared to wait (daily 12:00-23:00, on Calle de la Toletta, Dorsoduro 1210, tel. 041-525-5768).

Venetian Cuisine

Even more so than the rest of Italy, Venetian cuisine relies heavily on fish, shellfish, risotto, and polenta. Along with the usual pizza-and-pasta fare, here are some typical foods you'll encounter. For more on Italian food, including *salumi*, and cheeses, see page 439.

Sandwiches

Panini: Sandwiches made with rustic bread, filled with meat, vegetables, and cheese, served cold or toasted *(riscaldato)*.

Piadini: Flatbread or wrap-like sandwiches.

Tramezzini: Sandwiches served cold and stuffed with fillings (like egg, tuna, or shrimp) mixed with mayonnaise.

Antipasti (Appetizers)

Venetians start a meal with a light *antipasti* or some *cicchetti*—finger-food appetizers sold in many bars.

Antipasto di mare: Marinated mix of chilled fish and shellfish.

Asiago cheese: A regional specialty, this cow's-milk cheese is either *mezzano* (young, creamy) or *stravecchio* (aged, pungent).

Sarde in saor: Sardines marinated with onions.

Risi (Rice), Pasta, and Polenta

Bigoli in salsa: Long, fat, whole-wheat noodle in anchovy sauce.

Pasta alla buzzara: Pasta in a rich seafood-tomato sauce, generally with shrimp.

Pasta al pomodoro: Pasta in a simple tomato sauce.

Pasta al vongole: Pasta with clams.

Pasta e fagioli: Bean-and-pasta soup.

Polenta: Thick cornmeal porridge served soft or cut into firm slabs and grilled.

Risi e bisi: Rice and peas.

Risotto: Short-grain rice simmered in broth and flavored with seafood, meat, or veggies. *Risotto nero* is made with squid and its ink.

Frutti di Mare (Seafood)

Venetian fish are generally smaller than American salmon and trout (think sardines and anchovies). The weirder the seafood (eel, octopus, frogfish), the more local it is.

Baccalà: Atlantic salt cod that's rehydrated and served with polenta; or chopped up and mixed with mayonnaise as a topping for *cicchetti* (appetizers), called *baccalà mantecato*.

Branzino: Sea bass, grilled and served whole.

Calamari: Squid, often cut into rings and deep-fried or marinated.

Cozze: Mussels, often steamed in an herb broth with tomato.

Gamberi: Shrimp—*gamberetti* are small, and *gamberoni* are large.

Moleche col pien: Fried soft-shell crabs.

Orata: Sea bream (usually farmed).

Pesce fritto misto: Deep-fried seafood (often calamari and prawns).

Pesce spada: Swordfish.

Rombo: Turbot, a flatfish similar to flounder.

Rospo: Frogfish, a small marine fish.

Salmone: Salmon (typically farm-raised).

Seppia: Cuttlefish, a squid-like creature. *Seppia al nero* is the squid served in its own ink, often over spaghetti.

Sogliola: Sole, served poached or oven-roasted.

Vitello di mare: "Sea veal," like swordfish—firm, mild, and grilled.

Vongole: Clams, often steamed with fresh herbs and wine, or served as *spaghetti alle vongole.*

Zuppa di pesce: Seafood stew.

Dolci (Desserts)

Rather than order dessert in a restaurant, I like to stroll with a cup or cone of gelato from one of Venice's popular *gelaterie.* Cookies are also popular. The numerous varieties are due perhaps to Venice's position in trade (spices) and love of celebrations.

Bisse: Seahorse-shaped cookies.

Bussola: Ring-shaped cookies made for Easter.

Croccante: Toasted almond confection, similar to peanut brittle.

Fritole: Tiny doughnuts associated with Carnevale (Mardi Gras).

Pinza: Rustic cornmeal and wheat-flour cake filled with dried fruit; made for Epiphany, January 6.

Tiramisù: Spongy ladyfingers soaked in coffee and Marsala, layered with mascarpone cheese and bitter chocolate.

Cocktails and Local Wines

Amarone: Rich and intense red, made from dried Valpolicella grapes that yield a wine high in alcohol—often around 15 percent.

Bardolino: Beaujolais-like wine made from Valpolicella grapes.

Bellini: Cocktail of Prosecco and white-peach puree (invented at the pricey Harry's American Bar near St. Mark's Square).

Fragolino: A sweet, slightly fizzy dessert wine made from a strawberry-flavored grape.

Prosecco: Sparkling white wine. Connoisseurs say the best hails from Valdobbiadene.

Recioto: Dessert wine made with dried, aged Valpolicella grapes.

Sgroppino: Traditional after-dinner drink of squeezed lemon juice, lemon gelato, and vodka.

Soave: Crisp, dry white wine, great with seafood.

Spritz: White wine, soda, and ice mixed with Campari (bitter) or Aperol (sweeter).

Tiziano: Grape juice and Prosecco.

Valpolicella: Light, dry, fruity red wine, often served as the *vino della casa* (house wine).

EATING

Zattere

$$$ Terrazza del Casin dei Nobili takes full advantage of the warm, romantic evening sun. They serve regional specialties at tolerable prices. The breezy and beautiful seaside seating comes with the rumble of *vaporetti* from the nearby stop. The interior is bright and hip (daily 12:00-24:00; from Zattere vaporetto stop, turn left to Dorsoduro 924; tel. 041-520-6895).

$ Oke Pizzeria is playful, with casual tables on the embankment and a sprawling pizza-parlor interior. It's a hit with young Venetians for its fun atmosphere (daily 11:30-15:30 & 18:30-23:00, a couple of hundred yards from the Zattere vaporetto stop, Dorsoduro 1414, tel. 041-520-6601).

On or near Campo San Barnaba

This small square is a delight—especially in the evening. As these places are within a few steps of each other—and the energy and atmosphere can vary—I like to survey the options before choosing (although reservations may be necessary to dine later in the evening).

$$$ Ristoteca Oniga is all about fresh fish and other sea creatures, with a chic-and-shipshape interior, great tables on the square, and the enthusiastic direction of Raffaele. The menu is accessible and always includes a good vegetarian dish (daily 12:00-14:30 & 19:00-22:30, except closed Tue in winter, reservations smart, Campo San Barnaba, Dorsoduro 2852, tel. 041-522-4410, www.oniga.it).

$$$ Osteria Enoteca Ai Artisti serves well-presented quality dishes, with seating within its tight little wine-snob interior or at a few petite, romantic canalside tables. They serve good wines by the glass. When reserving, make sure they know your preference—a table on the canal or inside (Mon-Sat 12:30-15:00 & 19:00-21:00, closed Sun, Fondamenta de la Toletta, Dorsoduro 1169a, tel. 041-523-8944, www.enotecaartisti.com, Vicenzo).

$$ Pizzeria al Profeta is a casual place popular for great pizza and steak. Its sprawling interior seems to stoke conviviality, as does its leafy garden out back (Wed-Mon 12:00-14:30 & 19:00-23:30, closed Tue; from Campo San Barnaba, a long walk down Calle Lunga San Barnaba to #2671, tel. 041-523-7466).

$$$ Enoteca e Trattoria la Bitta is dark and woody, with a soft-jazz bistro feel, tight seating, and a small, forgettable back patio. They serve beautifully presented, traditional Venetian food with—proudly—no fish. Their helpful wait staff and small, handwritten daily menu are focused on local ingredients (including rabbit) and a "slow food" ethic. As it has an avid following, they do two dinner seatings (19:00 and 21:00) and require reservations (dinner only, Mon-Sat 18:30-23:00, closed Sun, cash only, just off Campo

San Barnaba on Calle Lunga San Barnaba, Dorsoduro 2753a, tel. 041-523-0531, Debora and Marcellino).

On Campo Santa Margarita

For a fresh, youthful, and neighborhood vibe away from the tourist crowds and cutesy Venice, hike out to Campo Santa Margarita, where you'll find a multigenerational slice-of-life scene by day and a trendy college-bar scene after dark. The square is ringed by bakeries, pubs, pizzerias, and fruit stands offering options for everything from picnics to finer dining. If slumming, a picnic or takeout pizza on this square (with fine benches and trees) is great. The area gets a little sketchy late at night.

$$ Osteria Do Torri, is a family affair delightfully situated with tables overlooking the square. Loretta and Paolo offer wines, little Venetian plates, love, and passion (closed Mon, tel. 041-522-0686).

$$ Osteria alla Bifora is a former butcher shop, serving lots of polenta and classic dishes in their candlelit woody interior and tables on the square. For rustic *cicchetti* plates ranging from sardines, anchovies, and cod to platters of fine salamis and cheeses, this is a good choice (daily, tel. 041-523-6119, Franco and Mirella).

$$ Pier Dickens Ristorante-Pizzeria, with good tables on the square, serves a huge selection of pizzas as well as three-course fixed-price meals (daily, tel. 041-241-1979).

Various **hole-in-the-wall** *cicchetti* **bars** (on the square and just off it) serve drinks and tapas plates to local eaters with a contagious love of life.

CANNAREGIO

Cannaregio, along the fish's "back," offers the classic chance in Venice to get off the beaten path. I've listed restaurants both near the Jewish Ghetto and near a main thoroughfare (see map on page 256; these zones are about a 10-minute walk apart). Also listed are a few convenient, last-resort options next to the train station.

Near the Jewish Ghetto

This sleepy neighborhood—more residential than touristic—features a grid layout with straight and spacious canalside walks (part of an expansion from the 1400s). Although it lacks the higgledy-piggledy feel of the older part of town, it's worth the long walk for a look. Instead of coming here just for a meal, I'd make time to explore and then grab a bite while in the neighborhood. Cannaregio is most peaceful at sunset.

$$$ Osteria L'Orto dei Mori is a chic place serving nicely presented, creative Venetian cuisine. You can eat in the elegant, modern interior or on a great neighborhood square with 10 tables

Romantic Canalside Settings

Of course, if you want a meal with a canal view, it generally comes with lower quality and/or a higher price. But if you're determined to take home a canalside memory, these places (many described elsewhere in this chapter) can be great.

Near the Rialto Bridge: The five places I call the "Bancogiro

Stretch" offer wonderful canal-side dining and a great place to enjoy a drink and/or a snack between meals or after dinner (see page 268).

Rialto Bridge Tourist Traps: Venetians are embarrassed by the lousy food and aggressive "service" at the string of joints dominating the best romantic, Grand Canal-fringing real estate in town. Still, if you want to lin-

ger over dinner with a view of the most famous bridge and the songs of gondoliers oaring by (and don't mind eating with other tourists), this can be enjoyable. Don't trust the waiter's recommendations for special meals. The budget ideal would be to get a simple pizza or pasta and a drink for €15, and savor the ambience without getting ripped off. But few restaurants will allow you to get off that easy. To avoid a dispute over the bill, ask if there's a minimum charge before you sit down (most places have one).

Near the Accademia: Bar Foscarini, next to the Accademia Bridge, offers decent pizzas overlooking the canal with no cover or service charge (see page 273).

Ponte dei Greci, East of St. Mark's Square: Two delightful canals meet at the Ponte dei Greci. Restaurants have gobbled up every inch of canalside real estate to feed tourists forgettable food—and great memories. Three cheap pizzerias are busy along Canal San Provolo. For nicer fare, two pricier restaurants on Fon-

surrounded by a classic scene of wellhead, bridges, and canal (smart to reserve for dinner, Wed-Mon 12:30-15:30 & 19:00-24:00, closed Tue, on Campo dei Mori, facing a bridge on Fondamenta dei Mori, Cannaregio 3386; tel. 041-524-3677, www.osteriaortodeimori.com).

$$ Osteria Ai 40 Ladroni ("The 40 Thieves") is a characteristic, unpretentious old standby with a few tables on the canal, a rustic interior, and a convivial garden out back. The action is near the bar (they're proud of their mixed seafood *antipasti,* Tue-Sun 12:00-14:30 & 19:00-22:15, closed Mon, on Fondamenta de la Sensa near the corner of Calle del Capitello, Cannaregio 3253, tel. 041-715-736).

damenta San Lorenzo (**Ristorante alla Conchiglia** and **Trattoria da Giorgio ai Greci**) are lit up like Christmas trees after dark. With gondolas gliding by, you can't argue with the setting.

Overlooking the Giudecca Canal: **Terrazza del Casin dei Nobili** is located in Zattere—on the Venice side of the wide Giudecca Canal—and is particularly nice just before sunset (vaporetto: Zattere, and for a cheaper perch on the same canal, consider **Oke Pizzeria,** (both described on page 276). **I Figli delle Stelle Ristorante,** on the island of

Giudecca, is a classy restaurant offering romantic canalside seating and a wonderful experience (vaporetto: Zitelle, see page 281). **Ristorante Lineadombra,** with a terrace on the Giudecca Canal, serves gourmet dishes to a dressy crowd (see page 280).

In Cannaregio, near the Jewish Ghetto: **Gam Gam Kosher** offers memorable canalside kosher dining. And nearby, just north of the ghetto, a number of rustic eateries with rickety tables are set up along a peaceful canal, including **Osteria Enoteca Timon** and **Trattoria Al Mariner** (see page 277).

On Fondamente Nove with a View of the Open Lagoon: **Ristorante Algiubagiò** offers a good opportunity to eat well while overlooking the north lagoon (see page 281).

On Burano: **Trattoria al Gatto Nero da Ruggero** sits on a tranquil canal under a tilting bell tower in the pastel townscape of Burano. If you're touring the lagoon and want to enjoy Burano without the crowds, go late and consider a dinner here (see page 212).

EATING

$$ Osteria Enoteca Timon, while nothing earthshaking, has a relaxing canalside setting with a hipster vibe, nice wines, and *cicchetti* (a block past the Jewish Ghetto on Fondamenta Ormesini near the corner of Calle de la Malvasia, Cannaregio 2754, tel. 041-524-6066).

$$ Trattoria Al Mariner, just one bridge east of Osteria Timon, is another fun eatery, with a rustic interior and romantic canalside tables serving delightful local dishes (Mon-Sat 7:00-24:00, closed Sun, Cannaregio 2679, tel. 041-720-036).

$$ Gam Gam Kosher is your best bet for all-kosher Venetian dishes with canalside seating near the Ghetto. While the interior seating is forgettable, the canalside tables will make the meal memorable (great vegetarian options; Sun-Thu 12:00-22:00, Fri 12:00-two hours before Shabbat, Sat one hour after Shabbat-23:00, a few steps past the bridge where Lista di Spagna crosses the canal called Fondamenta di Cannaregio at #1122, tel. 366-250-4505).

Along the Main Drag

Closer to the Grand Canal than the options listed above, the following places are a few steps from the main drag that connects the train station to the Rialto/San Marco area. All are near the San Marcuola vaporetto stop.

$$ Pizzeria Vesuvio, a neighborhood favorite, has classy indoor seating and pleasant tables outside (daily 11:00-23:00 except closed Wed Oct-April, on Rio Terà Farsetti, Cannaregio 1837, tel. 041-795-688).

$$$ Osteria di Bentigodi serves traditional Italian dishes with a creative flair and a passion for what's in season. Chef Domenico overcomes his hidden location and simple ambience with a fun personality, great food, and live music—nightly from 19:00. Reservations are smart for dinner (daily 12:00-14:30 & 19:00-23:00, down a dead-end directly across from recommended Pizzeria Vesuvio at Calesele-Cannaregio 1423, tel. 041-822-3714, www.bentigodi.com).

$$ Enoteca Cicchetteria Do Colonne is a local dive with a loyal following and a good spread of *cicchetti* and sandwiches (no hot food). It's handy for a drink and a snack. While the food is mediocre, the scene—both at the bar and at the tables outside—feels real and is fun (daily 10:00-21:30, on Rio Terà del Cristo, Cannaregio 1814, tel. 041-524-0453).

Near the Train Station

There are piles of eateries near the station. The buffet in the station itself is not bad, with big sandwiches and slices of pizza for €3. A block away is a small branch of the efficient and economical **$ Brek,** a self-service cafeteria chain (cheap pastas and *secondi*, daily 11:30-22:00, head left as you leave the station and walk about 50 yards past the bridge along Rio Terà Lista di Spagna, Cannaregio 124).

SPLURGING ON A WATER (OR OTHERWISE GREAT) VIEW

Overlooking the Giudecca Canal: **$$$$ Ristorante Lineadombra**, immediately behind La Salute Church, is peacefully situated on the Giudecca Canal, with commanding lagoon views from their big floating terrace and a spacious, modern, and dressy interior. This is a gourmet treat, with gorgeously presented dishes that are local and modern at the same time. Each dish is a memory, and even though plates are pricey (€20 appetizers and pastas, €30 *secondi*), you are welcome to share. The appetizers especially are big and are happily served on two smaller plates. Reserve ahead and choose seating inside or on their terrace. Service is friendly yet professional (daily 12:00-15:00 & 19:00-22:00, closed Tue off-season, a short walk behind La Salute Church, directly across the island from the Salute vaporetto stop, Dorsoduro 19, tel. 041-241-1881, www. ristorantelineadombra.com).

On Fondamente Nove, with a Lagoon View: **$$$$ Ristorante Algiubagiò** is a good place to eat as you look over the northern lagoon. You could combine a meal here with a trip to Murano or Burano. The name joins the names of the four owners—Alberto, Giulio, Barbara, and Giovanna—who strive to impress visitors with quality, creative Venetian cuisine made with the best ingredients. Reserve a waterside table or sit in their classy cantina dining room (daily 12:00-15:00 & 19:00-22:30, between the two sets of vaporetto docks on Fondamente Nove, Cannaregio 5039—see map on page 205, tel. 041-523-6084, www.algiubagio.net).

On Giudecca Island, with a View of St. Mark's Square: **$$$ I Figli delle Stelle Ristorante** offers a delightful dining experience with an excuse to ride the boat from St. Mark's Square across to the island of Giudecca. Simone and his staff artfully serve Venetian classics with a dash of Rome and Puglia and a passion for fish and lamb. While they have inside seating, the reason to venture here is to sit canalside with fine views of Venice across the broad Giudecca Canal and all the water traffic. Reserve ahead to specify "first line" seating along the water, "second line" seating a few steps away, or a table inside (Wed-Mon 12:30-14:30 & 19:00-23:00, closed Tue, 50 yards from Zitelle vaporetto dock—from San Marco, ride line #4.2 or #2, Giudecca 70/71, tel. 041-523-0004, www.ifiglidellestelle.it).

On St. Mark's Square: **$$$$ Gran Caffè Quadri** is the place to go if you want to eat fancy on Piazza San Marco. Upstairs is their Michelin star restaurant, but this bistro, also dressy and a bit pretentious, shares the same kitchen, with a more traditional and accessible menu, and prices that won't ruin your appetite. While its 15 tables are all inside, the orchestra is just out the window (daily for lunch and dinner, reservations smart, San Marco 121, tel. 041-522-2105).

PICNICS AND SWEETS
Picnicking

You're legally forbidden from picnicking anywhere on or near St. Mark's Square except for Giardinetti Reali, the waterfront park near the San Marco vaporetto docks. Though it's legal to eat outdoors elsewhere around town, you may be besieged by pigeons who are, in turn, besieged by aggressive seagulls.

EATING

Venice has one main produce market and several convenient supermarkets:

Outdoor Market near the Rialto Bridge: The **fruit and vegetable market** that sprawls for a few blocks to the north of the Rialto Bridge is a fun place to assemble a picnic (best Mon-Sat 8:00-13:00, liveliest in the morning, closed Sun). The adjacent **fish market** is wonderfully slimy (closed Sun-Mon). Side lanes in this area are speckled with fine hole-in-the-wall munchie bars, bakeries, and cheese shops. The Rialto Mercato vaporetto stop is convenient to both.

Neighborhood Deli near the Rialto Market: This tiny *alimentari* just down the street from the market sells a flavorful concoction of cheese, Kalamata olives, sun-dried tomatoes, olive oil, and hot peppers that they call *intruglio*. It goes great with a fresh roll. It's at Sotoportego dei do Mori, at the end of my favorite strip of *cicchetti* bars (Mon-Sat 9:00-20:00, Sun 11:00-19:00, San Polo 414; see map on page 249).

Produce Stands: Many larger squares have a produce stand. To find the one nearest St. Mark's Square, face St. Mark's Basilica, then walk along its left side, heading east down Calle de la Canonica. Cross the bridge and turn left at Campo Santi Filippo e Giacomo. There are also stands on Campo Santa Maria Formosa and Campo Santa Margarita.

Supermarket near St. Mark's Square: A handy **Co-op** supermarket is between St. Mark's and Campo Santa Maria Formosa, on the corner of Salizada San Lio and Calle del Mondo Novo at Castello 5817. It has a deli counter and a great selection of picnic supplies, including packaged salads for €3 and fresh sandwiches (daily 8:30-20:30).

Other Supermarkets: The largest supermarket in town is the **Co-op** at Piazzale Roma, next to the vaporetto stop at Santa Croce 504 (daily 8:30-20:00). It's an easy walk from the train station, as is the **Conad** supermarket on Campo San Felice (daily 8:00-23:30, along the Strada Nova between the train station and Rialto area, Cannaregio 3660). Another **Conad** supermarket is convenient for those staying in Dorsoduro: It's at #1492, as far west as possible on the Zattere embankment, by the San Basilio vaporetto stop and the cruise-ship docks (daily 8:00-23:00). And just beyond the Rialto vaporetto stop is another handy **Co-op** (facing the Grand Canal on Riva del Carbon).

Good Gelato and Chocolate Spots

You'll find good *gelaterie* in every Venetian neighborhood, typically offering one-scoop cones for about €1.50 (plus €1 per extra scoop). Look for the words *artigianale* or *produzione propria,* which indicates that a shop makes its own gelato. All of these are open long hours daily. Here are a few to consider:

St. Mark's Side of the Rialto Bridge: An expensive gourmet gelato shop, **Gelatoteca Suso,** serves delectable flavors in bowls you can eat (next to recommended Rosticceria Gislon on Calle de la Bissa, San Marco 5453).

St. Mark's Square: Several of the cafés have gelato counters in summer. Try **Gran Caffè Lavena** at #134, or **Todaro** (on the corner of the Piazzetta at #5, near the water and just under the column topped by St. Theodore slaying a crocodile).

On Campo Santa Margarita and Campiello San Tomà: Il Doge has Sicilian-style *granita*—slushy ice flavored with fresh fruit—as well as regular flavors.

Near Campo Santa Maria Formosa: On Salizada San Lio is the popular **La Boutique del Gelato** (next to Hotel Bruno). And nearby is a hit with chocolate lovers: **Cioccolateria Vizio Virtù** (Vice and Virtue). Across from the recommended Osteria al Portego, it's a modern lab of deliciousness with fine gelato as a bonus (10:00-19:30, closed Mon, Castello 5988, tel. 041-275-0149).

EATING

VENICE WITH CHILDREN

Some of the best fun I've had with my kids has been in Venice. The city doesn't need an amusement park...it is one big fantasy world. It's safe, friendly, and like nothing else your kids have ever seen. Though there's lots of pavement and few parks or playgrounds, just being there—and free to wander—can be delightful.

However, while Venice is great for older children and teens, it presents challenges if you're traveling with toddlers or infants. You'll need to keep small children safely in hand, as there are rarely any fences or walls between the sidewalk and the water. (Campo Santa Maria Formosa is a rare place with railings, because a preschool uses it as their playground.) Holding hands also makes it easy to keep track of your child in narrow, crowded passageways.

With hundreds of stepped bridges, Venice is a frustrating obstacle course for strollers. But considering the dangers, bringing a stroller—the smallest, lightest umbrella stroller possible—is still a good tactic for navigating Venice with a wily preschooler. Parents of infants might find a baby carrier less hassle.

Trip Tips

EATING

Venetian fare can be different from the "Italian food" you have at home. While there's plenty of pasta, it's often prepared with seafood rather than tomatoes or meat. Picky eaters will want to avoid local seafood dishes such as eel *(anguilla)* and cuttlefish *(seppia)*. Here are more tips to keep your kids content and well-fed.

- Start the day with a good breakfast (at hotels, kids sometimes eat free).
- For lunch or a snack, it's fun to buy pizza by the slice, fold it in half, and eat it as you stroll...or find a perch on a nearby square.

Favorite pizza choices for kids include *margherita* (tomato sauce, cheese, and basil) and spicy *diavola* or *salame piccante,* which are the closest things on the menu to sliced pepperoni sausage (if you ask for *peperoni,* you'll get bell peppers).

- For ready-made sandwiches and other portable food, drop by an *alimentari* (deli) or a supermarket. Be aware that you can't picnic on St. Mark's Square (but you can at Giardinetti Reali, the nearby waterfront park; see page 79).

- Choose easy eateries. For good old American food, check out one of the American hamburger joints between the Rialto Bridge and St. Mark's Square. A good, safe (though not exotic) bet is the Brek self-serve restaurant near the train station (see page 280). Having snacks on hand can avoid meltdowns. Stock your day bag with trail mix or crackers, and plan to buy plenty of gelato.

- Eat dinner early (19:00 at restaurants), and skip the romantic places. If you eat early you'll find that children are comfortable and welcome in better restaurants. Eating *al fresco* is great with kids. Try places on squares where kids can run free while you dine. You can nearly always get some kind of plain noodles.

SIGHTSEEING

The key to a successful Venetian family vacation is to slow down. Tackle one or two key sights each day, mix in a healthy dose of pure fun in a square or on a boat, and take extended breaks when needed. A vaporetto ride is a great way to start your visit. Consider these other tips:

- Incorporate your child's interests into each day's plans. Let your kids make some decisions: choosing lunch spots or deciding when to take a gondola ride. Let them lead you through the maze of Venice's back streets. Get lost together. If your children are old enough, they can be the tour guides and read this book's self-guided tours. (Standard tip for good guides: a two-scoop gelato.)

- Give your child a money belt and an expanded allowance; you are on vacation, after all. Let your children budget their funds and compare and contrast the dollar and euro. Allowing your children the freedom to buy whatever they want will teach them responsibility, and it will be fun for them.

- Buy your child a trip journal, and encourage them to write down their observations, thoughts, and favorite memories. This journal could end up being their favorite souvenir.

- While Venice is short on parks, its many small squares have served as playgrounds for local children for centuries. Let your kids run around while you take a seat at a café or bench.

- It's good to have a "what if" procedure in place in case something goes wrong, such as getting separated in a crowd. Give your kids a business card from your hotel, your own contact information (if you brought a mobile phone), and a few euros to cover the cost of a phone call if they don't have their own mobile phones.

- If you allow kids to explore a museum or neighborhood on their own, be sure to establish a clear meeting time and place.

- If your kids love playing in the sand, consider staying in an apartment near the Lido. Easy beach access offers a convenient daily activity.

- Apartments, typically with multiple bedrooms and kitchen facilities, can save money over hotel rooms and eliminate the stress that can accompany restaurant dining with small children. See page 427 for some options.

- Give your kid a cheap camera. Venice turns anyone into a photographer.

- Follow this book's crowd-beating tips. Kids dislike long lines even more than you do.

- Seek out museums with kid appeal, such as the Peggy Guggenheim Collection—though be aware that art may feature nudes or erotic themes. If you're visiting art museums with younger children, hit the gift shop first so you can buy postcards; then hold a scavenger hunt to find the pictured artwork.

- Italy's national museums generally offer free admission to children under age 18—always ask before buying tickets for your kids.

- Look for family and child discounts. If buying the Doge's Palace/Correr Museum combo-ticket or a Museum Pass, ask for the family discount. A family ticket is also available for the Chorus Pass, which covers church visits.

The **Rolling Venice** youth discount pass gives discounts on many sights and transportation for young travelers (€6 pass for ages 14-29; with the pass, kids pay just €22 for a 72-hour transit pass; see page 17).

CHILDREN

Top Sights and Activities

KID-CENTRIC ATTRACTIONS

Boat Rides

Ride lots of boats (vaporetto, gondola, *traghetto*, or speedboat tours of the lagoon). If you can, try to sit in the front seat of a vaporetto for my Grand Canal Cruise (see page 56). See how many kinds of service boats you can spot while on the canal (UPS, police, fire, garbage, and so on). Venice feels safe; if you have responsible teenagers, you could turn them loose with your hotel card, some euros for lunch, and a vaporetto pass (see Rolling Venice pass, earlier). Note that *vaporetti* are free for kids under age 6, but everyone else pays full fare, and there is no discount-pass option for those between 6 and 13.

St. Mark's Square

This grand square is surrounded by splashy historic buildings and sights: St. Mark's Basilica, the Doge's Palace, the Campanile bell tower, and the Correr Museum. The square is filled with music, romantics, pigeons, and tourists by day. By night, the historical buildings are lit up, small orchestras put on free concerts, and good gelato is only a walk away. Anyone of any age will enjoy the magic of St. Mark's Square day or night.

The **pigeons** on the square offer a new breed of bird-watching. (Though feeding them is now against the law, most tourists don't realize that—and enjoy trying to lure as many birds to drape over their kids as possible.) If you yell, the birds will just ignore you, but tossing a sweater into the air will cause a flocking flurry in a hurry.

Elevator Ride

Ride the elevator to the top of the Campanile bell tower to enjoy the grand view, and be there as the huge bells whip into ear-shattering action at the top of each hour (see St. Mark's Square Tour, page 70). Some prefer the better view from the bell tower on the island of San Giorgio Maggiore (see page 289).

Glassblowing Demonstration

For a quick and entertaining demo of Venice's favorite craft, stop by the Galleria San Marco (in an alley on the north side of St. Mark's Square; see page 293).

Rialto Bridge and Fish Market

The Rialto fish market is as fishy as they get (closed Sun-Mon, on the canal two blocks west of Rialto Bridge). Get there early in the

Venetian Adventures

To help your kids realize the magic of Venice, stoke their imagination with some of these recommended books:

This Is Venice (Miroslav Slasek) Classic 1960s picture book captures Venice's charm with witty illustrations.

Kids Go Europe: *Treasure Hunt Venice* Tiny, spiral-bound book takes kids on a scavenger hunt through Venice.

Stravaganza: *City of Masks* (Mary Hoffman) First in the time-traveling series set in 16th-century "Talia," an alternate-universe Italy.

The Dragon's Pearl (Devin Jordan) Fictional early adventures of 16-year-old Venetian Marco Polo.

Daughter of Venice (Donna Jo Napoli) A young girl disguises herself as a beggar boy to avoid entering a convent in 16th-century Venice.

Stones in Water and its sequel, *Fire in the Hills* (Donna Jo Napoli) Fictional account of a young Venetian boy sent to a Nazi labor camp, and his struggles to return to his beloved Venice.

Venice for Kids (Elisabetta Pasqualin) Great guidebook for tweens and up, available at many museum bookshops.

VivaVenice: *A Guide to Exploring*, *Learning*, *and Having Fun* (Paola Zoffoli) Full of interesting facts, and sold at many bookstores in the city.

day to watch people unload the boats at the market. You can leave by *traghetto* and cross the Grand Canal (*traghetto* dock at market).

MUSEUMS AND EXHIBITS

Be choosy when taking kids to museums. The venerable and fascinating (to adults) Accademia will probably bore children. But don't skip art entirely. Kids like holding mirrors to see the ceiling paintings at the Scuola San Rocco. The Peggy Guggenheim Collection has colorful modern art by Picasso and others.

Doge's Palace

The building is more impressive than the art inside. If your children aren't wowed by the architecture, they may enjoy the tour of the dark, dank prison. The dungeon held the notorious lover Giacomo Casanova, sentenced to prison for being a magician. In his memoirs, he describes how he used an iron rod and the help of a fellow prisoner to make his escape. Young swashbucklers may like the swords and crossbows in the Armory (🕮 see the Doge's Palace Tour chapter).

Cost and Hours: €12 combo-ticket for kids ages 6-14 and students ages 15-25 includes Correr Museum, €19 for adults; families with two adults and at least one child get reduced rates; daily April-

Oct 8:30-19:00, Nov-March 8:30-17:30, last entry one hour before closing, tel. 041-271-5911, http://palazzoducale.visitmuve.it.

Scuola San Rocco

This museum houses some of the best paintings by Tintoretto, which cover not only the walls, but the ceilings. Your kids may get a kick out of using the provided mirrors to look at the paintings on the ceiling without straining their necks (□ see the Scuola San Rocco Tour chapter).

Cost and Hours: Free for those under age 18 with a paying parent, €10 for adults; €5 audioguide, daily 9:30-17:30, tel. 041-523-4864, www.scuolagrandesanrocco.it.

The Peggy Guggenheim Collection

This museum shows major works from the first half of the 20th century, including pieces by Picasso, Pollock, Chagall, Magritte, and Dalí. Your children may not understand Surrealism, Futurism, or Abstract Expressionism, but there's enough variety here that they'll find something "cool." For younger kids, the outdoor sculpture garden is a rare green space in Venice where they can burn off some energy. Free workshops every Sunday from 15:00 to 16:30 give kids ages 4-10 a chance to experiment with techniques; though usually in Italian, the activity is sometimes offered in English (□ see the Peggy Guggenheim Collection Tour chapter).

Cost and Hours: €9 for ages 10-18 and students under age 26, free for kids under age 10, €15 for adults, Wed-Mon 10:00-18:00, closed Tue, pricey café, vaporetto: Accademia or Salute, tel. 041-240 5411, www.guggenheim-venice.it.

San Giorgio Maggiore

Located on an island a short boat ride away, this is a great church to visit after battling the hordes of St. Mark's Square. Enjoy a lagoon ride to the island, then take an elevator to the top of the bell tower (□ see the San Giorgio Maggiore Tour chapter).

Cost and Hours: Free entry to church; €0.50 to light the artwork, elevator to bell tower-€6; April-Oct daily 7:00-19:00; Nov-March daily 7:00-dusk. The last ascent in the tower elevator is 15 minutes before closing time.

PARKS
Giardino Papadopoli

This tiny park, next to Venice's bus station, has one of the city's rare playgrounds. The nearest vaporetto stop is Piazzale Roma. Coming from the train station, take the Calatrava Bridge across the Grand Canal, turn left, and take the next bridge over a side canal to the park.

CHILDREN

Giardini Pubblici (Public Gardens)

An ideal spot for children who want an American park experience, the Public Gardens have swings, slides, a play area, and big trees (unusual in Venice). It's about a 20-minute walk along the water from St. Mark's Square, past the Arsenale, going toward the tail of the fish (vaporetto: Giardini).

Parco Delle Rimembranze (Memorial Park)

Farther out on the tail, in the Sant'Elena neighborhood, this park contains a soccer field, along with basketball and tennis courts. It's one of the largest open spaces in Venice (vaporetto: S. Elena).

BEACHES AND OTHER EXPERIENCES

Lido

The Lido has a fun, free, clean, sandy beach that's good for swimming, with an affordable self-service café, a bar, rentable umbrellas, and a well-priced beach-gear shop. Even the ride across the lagoon is enjoyable (vaporetto: Lido S.M.E., walk 10 minutes on Gran Viale S. Maria Elisabetta to beach entry).

Soccer

Consider attending a soccer game at the stadium located in the Sant'Elena neighborhood. Venice's team, Venezia FC, is currently in the Lega Pro league (not so good), so the crowds aren't as enthusiastic as they might be, but games are fun nonetheless—and the owner is a lawyer from New York who is promising major upgrades. Matches take place on Sundays from September to May (ask at the TI). Buy a scarf with the team colors—black, orange, and green—and join the fun.

Signor Blum

This shop, on Campo San Barnaba—about a 10-minute walk northwest of the Accademia—has an array of colorfully painted wooden decorations. It's a good place to shop for kid-friendly souvenirs (for details, see page 300 in the Shopping in Venice chapter).

CHILDREN

SHOPPING IN VENICE

The merchants of Venice are abundant, making this a fun city for window-shoppers. Long a city of aristocrats, luxury goods, and trade, Venice was built to entice. While no one claims it's great for bargains, it has a shopping charm that makes paying too much strangely enjoyable. Carnevale masks, lace, glass, antique paper products, designer clothing, one-of-a-kind jewelry, custom-made shoes, fancy accessories, hand-painted or printed velvet and silk tapestries, and paintings are all popular with tourists visiting Venice.

Around the train station and the Rialto Bridge, Venice feels like one big open-air shopping mall. Trinket stands tuck themselves between internationally famous designer stores and hole-in-the-wall artisan workshops. While there are plenty of temptations, remember: Anything not made locally is brought in by boat—and therefore generally more expensive than elsewhere in Italy. And, given Venice's tourist cachet, even items made here are priced at a premium. The shops near St. Mark's Square charge the most.

In touristy areas, shops are typically open from 9:00 to 19:30 (sometimes with a break from about 13:00 until 15:00 or 16:00), and more stores are open on Sunday here than in the rest of the country. If you're buying a substantial amount from nearly any shop, bargain—it's accepted and almost expected. Offer less and offer to pay cash; merchants are very conscious of the bite taken by credit-card companies.

While you'll see many tourists in these shops, you'll also encounter locals. Italians shop for quality; they tend to spend less on entertainment and more on looking good. With their limited budgets, they'd rather buy three top-quality shirts rather than ten mediocre ones. They don't impulse buy: Italian shoppers are on a strategic mission. For example, "I need this belt to match this out-fit." Watch them in action and appreciate the difference.

The first part of this chapter briefly introduces you to Venice's shopping neighborhoods; the second half recommends specific shops for different items you might be interested in (such as Carnevale masks, glass, jewelry, and lace).

For information on VAT refunds and customs regulations, see page 419.

For a private tour focusing on shopping and crafts, contact Walks Inside Venice, which offers several different itineraries (www.walksinsidevenice.com; for details, see page 31).

Shopping Neighborhoods

The streets closest to **St. Mark's Square,** and those along the Mercerie (the route between St. Mark's and the Rialto Bridge, also called "Marzaria"), are the most-trafficked, the highest-rent, and the highest-priced in town. This is where you'll see all of the big international names; it seems you can't be a fashion-world staple until you have a branch in San Marco. The neighborhood to the west of St. Mark's, going toward the Accademia Bridge, is more elegant and exclusive, with high-fashion shops along Calle Vallaresso (southwest of St. Mark's). As you get closer to the Accademia Bridge, you'll find more cutting-edge, slightly more characteristic and affordable stores, such as the Bevilacqua and Venetia Studium textile shops (both described later), and art boutiques and galleries around Campo San Stefano and Salizzada San Samuele.

Dorsoduro, across the Accademia Bridge, is a fine shopping neighborhood. The area immediately around and between the Accademia and Peggy Guggenheim Collections is touristy and can feel tacky, but does have some worthwhile places selling glass and/or jewelry with an artistic bent. In the opposite direction, a 10-minute walk past the Accademia, is the somewhat lower-rent area around Campo San Barnaba that attracts more innovative, less established artisans; this is a great place to window-shop.

The **Rialto Bridge**—Venice's historic market area—is still a cancan of shopping opportunities. Many of the products here are edible, but there are lots of hole-in-the-wall jewelry and trinket stores on the bridge, under the arcades to the north, and on the Ruga (the street running from the Rialto toward Campo San Polo and the Frari Church).

The route from the east side of the **Rialto Bridge** to the **train station** is where you're most likely to find two-euro stores, discount joints with jeans in the basement for €10, cheap plastic goods, and—at holiday times—shops selling Easter or Christmas decorations. You'll see peddlers who lay out knockoff handbags on sheets that can be gathered up quickly if the police happen by (see the sidebar on page 298). Near the Rialto end of this stretch is Venice's department store, Coin, which has predictable clothing and house-wares sections.

What to Buy

Popular souvenirs and gifts include Murano glass, Burano lace (fun lace umbrellas for little girls), Carnevale masks (fine shops and

artisans all over town), art re-productions (posters, postcards, and books), prints of Venetian scenes, traditional stationery (pens and marbled paper prod-ucts of all kinds), calendars with Venetian scenes (and sexy gon-doliers), silk ties, scarves, and plenty of goofy knickknacks (Titian mouse pads, gondolier T-shirts, and little plastic gon-dola condom holders).

But beyond the typical souvenirs, Venice has a wealth of unique and locally made items, such as artisan jewelry, handcrafted fabrics, and made-to-order shoes. Note that many shops selling ar-tisan goods can be quite expensive. But they are still atmospheric, engaging places to window-shop and daydream. If you're curious about the product, dip into a shop and ask a few questions. The vendor never knows when browsing might turn to buying...and nei-ther do you.

VENETIAN GLASS

Popular Venetian glass is available in many forms: vases, tea sets, decanters, glasses, jewelry, lamps, mod sculptures (such as solid-glass aquariums), and on and on. Shops will ship it home for you, but you're likely to pay as much or more for the shipping as you are for the item(s), and you may have to pay duty on larger purchases. Make sure the shop insures their merchandise *(assicurazione)*, or you're out of luck if it breaks. If your item arrives bro-ken and it has been insured, take a photo of the pieces, send it to the shop, and they'll replace it for free.

Some visitors feel that because they're in Venice, they ought

Shopping in Venice

Masks
1. Ca' del Sol
2. Atelier Marega (3)
3. Papier Mâché Mask Shop
4. Tragicomica Mask Shop
5. Ca' Macana

Glass & Jewelry
6. Galleria San Marco
7. Attombri
8. Marina e Susanna Sent (3)
9. Caron

Lace & Textiles
10. Il Merletto
11. Annelie
12. Venetia Studium
13. Bevilacqua (2)

Stationery
14. Il Pavone (2)
15. Il Prato
16. Il Papiro

Shoes
17. Daniela Ghezzo
18. Giovanna Zanella
19. Dittura

Bookstores
20. Libreria Studium
21. Acqua Alta
22. Marco Polo

Gondola Workshops
23. Le Fórcole di Saverio Pastor
24. Paolo Brandolisio

SHOPPING

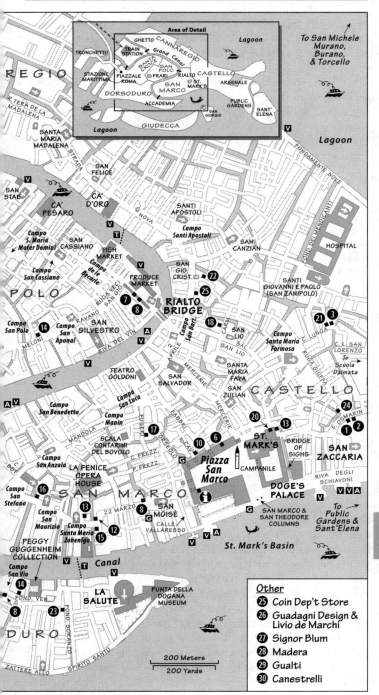

Other

25 Coin Dep't Store

26 Guadagni Design & Livio de Marchi

27 Signor Blum

28 Madera

29 Gualti

30 Canestrelli

SHOPPING

to grab the opportunity to buy glass. Remember that you can buy fine glass back home, too (Venice stopped forbidding its glassblowers from leaving the republic a few centuries ago)—and under less time pressure.

Also be aware that much of the cheap glass you'll see in Venice is imported (a sore point for local vendors dealing in the more expensive, locally produced stuff). Venetian glass producers, up in arms about the influx of Chinese glass, claim that a big percentage of the glass that tourists buy is actually not Venetian. Genuine Venetian glass comes with the Murano seal.

If you'd like to watch a quick glassblowing demonstration, try **Galleria San Marco,** a tour-group staple just off St. Mark's Square, which offers great demos every few minutes. They typically let individual travelers flashing this book sneak in with tour groups until 16:00 to see the show (and sales pitch). If you buy anything, show this book and they'll take 20 percent off the listed price. The gallery is in an alley that runs behind the north side of the square; walk through the passageway between #140 and #141, then look for #181a on your left and go up to the second floor (daily 8:30-18:00, on Calle del Cappello Nero, San Marco 181a, tel. 041-271-8671, info@galleriasanmarco.it, manager Aldo Dinon).

If you're serious about glass, visit the island of **Murano,** its glass museum, and ·many shops (see page 54). You'll find greater variety on Murano, but prices are usually the same as in Venice.

JEWELRY

Jewelers abound in Venice. Not surprisingly, glass jewelry and beadwork are particularly popular—you'll see references to *perle de Venezia* or *perle veneziane,* colorfully speckled glass beads. In addition to buying premade pieces, at many shops you can select the beads you like to create your own masterpiece. As with other glass, you can assume that cheap beads are imported, not local.

Because jewelry is such a subjective taste, I recommend that you browse around to find the styles and prices that suit you. But if you need help, here are some places to start: Several jewelers can be found under the arcades (behind the chintzy souvenir stands) on the west (market) side of the Rialto Bridge, including **Attombri,** selling pieces with a classic, filigree-plus-beads look (Sotoportego dei Orefici, San Polo 65, www.attombri.com). **Marina e Susanna Sent** sells contemporary designs in three upscale-feeling showrooms (near St. Mark's next to Campo San Moisè at San Marco 2090, near the Accademia on Campo San Vio at Dorsoduro 681, and across Rialto Bridge at Sotoportego dei Oresi San Polo 70, www.marinaesusannasent.com). **Caron** sells handmade glass jewelry, west of the Accademia along Calle de la Toleta (daily, Dorsoduro 1195).

Mask Making

In the 1700s, when Venice was Europe's party town, masks were popular—sometimes even mandatory—to preserve the anonymity of visiting nobles doing things forbidden back home. At Carnevale (the weeks-long Mardi Gras leading up to Lent), everyone wore masks. The most popular were based on characters from the lowbrow comedic theater called commedia dell'arte. We all know Harlequin (simple, Lone Ranger-type masks), but there were also long-nosed masks for the hypocritical plague doctor, pretty Columbina masks, and so on.

Masks are made with the simple technique of papier-mâché. You make a mold of clay, smear it with Vaseline (to make it easy to remove the finished mask), then create the mask by draping layers of paper and glue atop the clay mold.

You'll see mask shops all over town. Just behind St. Mark's Square, on a quiet canal just inland from the Church of San Zaccaria (on Fondamenta de l'Osmarin), is a corner with two fascinating mask and costume shops: **Ca' del Sol** at #4964 (with two showrooms to either side of a little bridge, www.cadelsolmaschere.com) and **Atelier Marega** at #4968 and #4976a (www.marega.it; also has two shops near the Frari Church).

Just a bit north, a block off Campo Santa Maria Formosa (next to the Acqua Alta bookstore) is the **Papier Mâché Mask Shop,** where Stefano Gottardo proudly sells only masks made in his store. The masks are both traditional and modern, and you're welcome to watch the artisans at work (daily 9:00-19:30, at the end of Calle Lunga Santa Maria Formosa, Castello 5174b, tel. 041-522-9995, www.papiermache.it).

Out near the Frari Church, the **Tragicomica Mask Shop** is highly respected and likely to have artisans at work (workshop usually open on weekdays to customers who've bought a mask, though it's best to make a reservation). You'll pass this shop if you take my 📖 Rialto to Frari Church Walk (daily 10:00-19:00, 200 yards past Church of San Polo on Calle dei Nomboli at #2800, tel. 041-721-102, www.tragicomica.it). Another good option is **Ca' Macana**, near Campo San Barnaba, a shop that designed masks for Stanley Kubrick's film *Eyes Wide Shut* (they also offer mask-painting classes—arrange in advance; open daily, Dorsoduro 3172, tel. 041-520-3229, www.camacana.com).

Beware of Cheap Knockoff Bags

Along Venice's many shopping streets, you'll notice fly-by-night street vendors selling knockoffs of famous designer handbags (Louis Vuitton, Gucci, etc.). These vendors are willing to bargain. Beware: If you're caught purchasing fakes, you could get hit with a fine. Legitimate manufacturers are raising a stink about these street merchants, and the government is trying to rid the city of them. Caught up in a city-wide game of cat and mouse (with the police playing the  role of cat), the vendors spend as much time lurking in alleys waiting for the coast to clear as they do selling. Authorities, frustrated in their attempts to actually arrest the merchants, have made it illegal to buy counterfeit items. Their hope: The threat of a huge fine will scare potential customers away—so unlicensed merchants will be driven out of business and off the streets.

LACE

Lace, made from cotton or silk thread, is another Venetian specialty. Prior to the Industrial Revolution, the city was a major trading point for luxury fabrics like lace, silk, and satin. Venice was a European fashion hot spot, and Venetian Burano lace adorned the clothing of royalty. Venice is particularly known for "needle lace," with intricate flowers, leaves, and curling stems, which was used for cuffs, gowns, and frilly collars.

In recent decades the lace industry has been on life support as cheap imitations flood the market. But lately Venetians are attempting to revive the art. Today, popular lace goods include tablecloths, doilies, clothing, and even lace pictures suitable for framing.

But buyer beware. Note that much of the lace sold in Venice (and on the island of Burano) is cheap, machine-made, and imported—so stick to reputable shops to ensure that you are buying an authentic product.

The **Il Merletto** shop just off St. Mark's Square is the most convenient, and perhaps most authentic place to start—the store sells pieces crafted by students of the Scuola dei Merletti, the local lace-making school in Burano (exit the square near the northwest corner through Sotoportego del Cavaletto, then across the little bridge to the right, daily

10:00-17:00, San Marco 95, tel. 041-520-8406). **Annelie,** in the Dorsoduro district, is another well-respected shop (on Calle Lunga San Barnaba, Dorsoduro 2748). Lace lovers will find the journey out to Burano worthwhile. Here you'll find many shops such as **Merletti d'Arte dalla Lidia** and the **Lace Museum** (both described under the "Burano" section, page 210).

TEXTILES

Venetia Studium carries on the Venetian tradition for hand-painted and woodblock-printed fabrics. In addition to velvet cushions and runners, they specialize in hanging lamps decorated with delicate hand-painted silk shades (daily 10:00-19:30, just east of Campo Santa Maria Zobenigo, San Marco 2425, tel. 041-523-6953, www. venetiastudium.com).

Bevilacqua is a big and well-established producer of velvet cushions, tapestries, and so on. Mario and Paola have a few high-profile shops around Venice, as well as an 18th-century, hand-operated loom that they still use. For the budget-conscious, they also sell equally fine machine-made products (both open daily 10:00-19:00; easiest to find at the Canonica Bridge behind St. Mark's Basilica at San Marco 337b, another location just to the right as you look at the Church of Santa Maria Zobenigo at San Marco 2520; tel. 041-528-7581, www.bevilacquatessuti.com).

STATIONERY

A number of shops around town sell handmade paper, colorfully bound books, and fine prints. **Il Pavone** is known for its marbleized paper and custom stamps (locations at Campiello dei Meloni, San Polo 1478, between Rialto Bridge and Campo San Polo, sign says *Zaga;* and at Fondamenta Venier, Dorsoduro 721, near the Guggenheim; www.ilpavonevenezia.it). **Il Prato,** on a side corner of Campo Santa Maria Zobenigo west of St. Mark's Square, specializes in vividly bound books, trays, and other items, as well as glass (daily, on Calle de le Ostreghe, San Marco 2456, www. ilpratovenezia.com). A couple of blocks away is a branch of the Italy-wide chain **Il Papiro** (daily, Calle del Piovan, San Marco 2764, www.ilpapirofirenze.it).

HANDMADE SHOES

Fashion-conscious travelers may find it worth the splurge to indulge in custom-made shoes from a trained Venetian cobbler. Some of the well-regarded options include **Daniela Ghezzo** (tucked in an adorably cluttered hole-in-the-wall on Calle dei Fuseri near St. Mark's Square, San Marco 4365, www.danielaghezzo.it) and **Giovanna Zanella** (closed Sun, Castello 5641, www.giovannazanella.it). For something distinctly Venetian, check out **Dittura,** which makes and sells velvet gondolier's slippers (on the main drag between the Accademia and Guggenheim, Dorsoduro 871).

ART GALLERIES AND BOUTIQUES
You'll find a fascinating smattering of mostly cutting-edge art boutiques in the zone north and west of Campo San Stefano (on the St. Mark's side of the Accademia Bridge). From that square, head west on Calle Botteghe, which becomes Crosera before it runs into the skinny square called Salizzada San Samuele. Fronting this square are a half-dozen low-profile galleries worth a browse. At the bottom of the square, peek into the shop of **Livio de Marchi,** who specializes in outlandish and/or remarkably detailed wood carvings—from handbags and ballet shoes to gloves and teddy bears to a bizarre phallus-medusa head (at #3157a, www.liviodemarchi. com).

OTHER GOODS
Department Store: The only one is **Coin,** just north of the Rialto Bridge (daily 10:00-20:00, Cannaregio 5787).

Housewares: **Guadagni Design** sells sleek and unique housewares, halfway down Salizzada San Samuele (San Marco 3336, www.guadagnidesign.it).

Toys: **Signor Blum** makes and sells delightfully colorful wood-carved letters, symbols, mobiles, and scenes of Venice—fun for kids and grown-ups. It's located at the bottom corner of Campo San Barnaba, overlooking the canal (daily, at #2840, www. signorblum.com).

Accessories: **Madera** is an attractive boutique with smart, modern, high-quality accessories, on Campo San Barnaba next to the Grom *gelateria* (closed Sun-Mon, Dorsoduro 2762, www. maderavenezia.it). To see more, check out their bigger showroom, just a few short blocks down Calle Lunga San Barnaba. Or follow Rio Terà Canal one block toward Campo Santa Margarita; you'll pass the **Gualti** boutique on the left, worth a peek for its contemporary accessories and shoes (closed Sun, Dorsoduro 3111, www. gualti.it).

Mirrors: At **Canestrelli,** soft-spoken Stefano Coluccio makes unique convex mirrors in circular frames, like the ones in old paintings. It's along Calle de la Toleta, between the Accademia Bridge and Campo San Barnaba (Dorsoduro 1173, www.venicemirrors. com).

Books: See "Services" on page 20.

SHOPPING

NIGHTLIFE IN VENICE

You must experience Venice after dark. The city is quiet at night, as tour groups stay in the cheaper hotels of Mestre on the mainland, and the masses of day-trippers return to their beach resorts and cruise ships.

Do what you must to reserve energy for the evening: Take a nap, or skip a few sights during the day. When the sun goes down, a cool breeze blows in from the lagoon, the lanterns come on, the peeling plaster glows in the moonlight, and Venice resumes its position as Europe's most romantic city.

Though Venice comes alive after dark, it does not party into the wee hours. By 22:00, restaurants are winding down; by 23:00, many bars are closing; and by midnight, the city is shut tight. Evenings are made for wandering—even Venice's dark and distant back lanes are considered safe after nightfall. Enjoy the orchestras on St. Mark's Square. Experience Vivaldi's *Four Seasons* in a candlelit 17th-century church. Pop into small bars for an appetizer and a drink. Lick gelato. As during the day, it's the city itself that is the star. But Venice under a cloak of darkness has an extra dose of magic and mystery—the ambience that has attracted visitors since the days of Casanova.

GONDOLA RIDES

Riding a gondola is simple, expensive, and one of the great experiences in Europe. Gondoliers hanging out all over town are eager to have you hop in for a ride. While this is a rip-off for some, it's a traditional must for romantics.

The price for a gondola starts at €80 for a 40-minute ride during the day. You can divide the cost—and the romance—among up to six people per boat, but only two get the love seat. Prices jump to €100 after 19:00—when it's most romantic and relaxing. Adding a singer and an accordionist will cost an additional €120. If you value budget over romance, you can save money by recruiting fellow travelers to split a gondola. Prices are standard and listed on the gondoliers' association website (go to www.gondolavenezia.it, click on "Using the Gondola," and look under "charterage").

Dozens of gondola stations *(servizio gondole)* are set up along canals all over town. Because your gondolier might offer narration or conversation during your ride, talk with several and choose one you like. You're welcome to review the map and discuss the route. Doing so is also a good way to see if you enjoy the gondolier's personality and language skills. Establish the price, route, and duration of the trip before boarding, enjoy your ride, and pay only when you're finished. While prices are pretty firm, you might find them softer during the day. Most gondoliers honor the official prices, but a few might try to scam you out of some extra euros, particularly by insisting on a tip. (While not required or even expected, if your gondolier does the full 40 minutes and entertains you en route, a 5-10 percent tip is appreciated; if he's surly or rushes through the trip, skip it.)

If you've hired musicians and want to hear a Venetian song *(un canto Veneziano),* try requesting *"Venezia La Luna e Tu."* Asking to hear *"O Sole Mio"* (which comes from Naples) is like asking a Chicago lounge singer to sing "Swanee River."

Glide through nighttime Venice with your head on someone's shoulder. Follow the moon as it sails past otherwise unseen buildings. Silhouettes gaze down from bridges while window glitter spills onto the black water. You're anonymous in the city of masks, as the rhythmic thrust of your striped-shirted gondolier turns old crows into songbirds. This is extremely relaxing (and, I think, worth the extra cost to experience at night). Suggestion: Put the camera down

and make it a point for you and your partner to enjoy a threesome with Venice. Women, beware...while gondoliers can be extremely charming, locals say that anyone who falls for one of these Venetian Romeos "has slices of ham over her eyes."

For cheap gondola thrills during the day, stick to the €2 one-minute ferry ride on a Grand Canal *traghetto.* At night, *vaporetti* are nearly empty, and it's a great time to cruise the Grand Canal on the slow boat #1. Or hang out on a bridge along the gondola route and wave at romantics.

ST. MARK'S SQUARE

For tourists, St. Mark's Square is the highlight, with lantern light and live music echoing from the cafés. Just being here after dark is a thrill, as **dueling café orchestras** entertain. The ultimate Venetian music scene is at the venerable Caffè Florian. But Gran Caffè Chioggia (facing the Doge's Palace) doesn't charge extra for music and has good jazz nightly (see sidebar on page 76). Every night, enthusiastic musicians play the same songs, creating the same irresistible magic. Hang out for free behind the tables (allowing you to move easily on to the next orchestra when the musicians take a break), or spring for a seat and enjoy a fun and gorgeously set concert. If you sit a while, it can be about €13-22 well spent (for a drink and the cover charge for music). Dancing on the square is free—and encouraged.

Several venerable cafés and bars on the square serve expensive drinks outside but cheap drinks inside at the bar. The scene

in a bar like **Gran Caffè Lavena** (in spite of its politically incorrect chandelier) can be great. The touristy **Bar Americano** is lively until late (under the Clock Tower). You'll hear people talking about the famous **Harry's American Bar,** which sells overpriced food and American cocktails to dressy tourists near the San Marco-Vallaresso vaporetto stop. But it's a rip-off...and the last place Hemingway would drink today. It's far cheaper to get a drink at any of the hole-in-the-wall bars just off St. Mark's Square; you can get a bottle of beer or even prosecco-to-go in a plastic cup.

Wherever you end up, streetlamp halos, live music, floodlit history, and a ceiling of stars make St. Mark's magic at midnight. You're not a tourist, you're a living part of a soft Venetian night...an alley cat with money. In the misty light, the moon has a golden hue. Shine with the old lanterns on the gondola piers, where the sloppy lagoon splashes at the Doge's Palace...reminiscing.

ENTERTAINMENT

Venice has a busy schedule of events, church concerts, festivals, and entertainment. Check at the TI or the TI's website (www.turismovenezia.it) for listings. The free monthly *Un Ospite di Venezia* lists all the latest happenings in English (free at fancy hotels, or check www.aguestinvenice.com).

Gondolas

Two hundred years ago, there were 10,000 gondolas in Venice. Although the aristocracy preferred horses to boats through the early Middle Ages, beginning in the 14th century, when horses were outlawed from the streets of Venice, the noble class embraced gondolas as a respectable form of transportation.

The boats became *the* way to get around the lagoon's islands. To navigate over the countless shifting sandbars, the boats were flat (no keel or rudder) and the captains stood up to see. During the Age of Decadence, wannabe Casanovas would enjoy trysts in gondolas. Part of the gondolier's professional code was to never reveal what happened under the canopy of his little love boat.

Today, there are about 400 gondolas in service, used only for tourists. The boats are prettier now, but they work the same way they always have. Single oars are used both to propel and to steer the boats, which are built curved a bit on one side so that an oar thrusting from that side sends the gondola in a straight line.

These sleek yet ornate boats typically are about 35 feet long and five feet wide, and weigh about 1,100 pounds. They travel about three miles an hour (same as walking) and take the same energy to row as it does to walk. They're always painted black (six coats)—the result of a 17th-century law a doge enacted to eliminate competition between nobles for the fanciest rig. But each has unique upholstery, trim, and detailing, such as the squiggly shaped, carved-wood oarlock *(fórcola)* and metal "hood ornament" *(ferro)*. All in all, it takes about two months to build a gondola.

The boats run about €35,000-50,000, depending on your options (air-con, cup holders, etc.). Every so often, the boat's hull must be treated with a new coat of varnish to protect against a lagoon-dwelling creature that eats into wood. A gondola lasts

Baroque Concerts

Venice is a city of the powdered-wig Baroque era. For about €25, you can take your pick of traditional Vivaldi concerts in churches throughout town. Homegrown Vivaldi is as ubiquitous here as Strauss is in Vienna and Mozart is in Salzburg. In fact, you'll find frilly young Viv-

about 15 years, after which it can be refinished (once) to last another 10 years.

You can see Venice's most picturesque gondola workshop (from the outside; it's not open to the public) in the Accademia neighborhood. (Walk down the Accademia side of the canal  called Rio San Trovaso; as you approach Giudecca Canal, you'll glimpse the beached gondolas on your right across the canal.) The workmen, traditionally from Italy's mountainous Dolomite region (because they need to be good with wood), maintain this refreshingly alpine-feeling little corner of Venice.

Carving the uniquely curvy oarlock is an art form. To see the work in action, visit the woodcarving shop of **Paolo Brandolisio.** His shop is just behind St. Mark's Square, inland from the Church of San Zaccaria on Fondamenta de l'Osmarin—look for it down an alley from the Ca' del Sol mask shop. You can pop in to watch Paolo carving both *fórcole* and traditional oars (workshop open Mon-Fri 9:30-13:00 & 15:30-19:00, closed Sat-Sun, on Calle Corte Rota at #4725, tel. 041-522-4155, www.paolobrandolisio.altervista.org). Search for *"fórcole e remi"* on YouTube to watch Paolo at work.

In the Dorsoduro district, you can visit the workshop of **Saverio Pastor,** another *fórcola* maker, who has scale models for sale (workshop open Mon-Fri 8:00-18:00, closed Sat-Sun, one canal east of the Peggy Guggenheim Collection, detour south along Fondamenta Soranzo de la Fornace to #341, www.forcole.com).

There are about 400 licensed gondoliers. When one dies, the license passes to his widow. And do the gondoliers sing, as the popular image has it? My mom asked our gondolier that very question, and he replied, "Madame, there are the lovers and there are the singers. I do not sing."

aldis hawking concert tickets on many corners. Most shows start at 20:30 and generally last 1.5 hours. You'll see posters in hotels all over town (hotels sell tickets at face-value).

Tickets for Baroque concerts in Venice can usually be bought the same day as the concert, so don't bother with websites that sell tickets with a surcharge. The general rule of thumb: Musicians in wigs and tights offer better spectacle; musicians in black-and-white suits are better performers.

The **Interpreti Veneziani orchestra,** considered the best group in town, generally performs 1.5-hour concerts nightly at

21:00 inside the sumptuous San Vidal Church (€28, church ticket booth open daily 9:30-21:00, north end of Accademia Bridge, tel. 041-277-0561, www.interpretiveneziani.com).

If you just want a quick, free Vivaldi moment, stop by the **Music Museum** inside the San Maurizio Church, which Interpreti Veneziani has turned into a bilingual exhibition on the music and instruments of Vivaldi's time (free, daily 9:30-19:00, between St. Mark's Square and the Accademia on Campo San Maurizio, tel. 041-241-1840, www.museodellamusica.com).

Other Performances

Venice's most famous theaters are **La Fenice** (grand old opera house, box office tel. 041-2424, see page 39), **Teatro Goldoni** (mostly Italian live theater), and **Teatro Fondamenta Nuove** (theater, music, and dance).

Musica a Palazzo is a unique evening of opera at a Venetian palace on the Grand Canal. You'll spend about 45 delightful minutes in each of three sumptuous rooms (about 2.25 hours total) as eight musicians (generally four instruments and four singers) perform. They generally present three different operas on successive nights—enthusiasts can experience more than one. With these kinds of surroundings, and under Tiepolo frescoes, you'll be glad you dressed up. As there are only 70 seats, you must book by phone or online in advance (€75, nightly at 20:30, Palazzo Barbarigo Minotto, Fondamenta Duodo o Barbarigo, vaporetto: Santa Maria del Giglio, San Marco 2504, mobile 340-971-7272, www.musicapalazzo.com).

Venezia is advertised as "the show that tells the great stories of Venice" and "simply the best show in town." I found the performance to be slow-moving and a bit cheesy, and the venue disappointing (€39, nightly March-Oct at 20:00, Nov-Feb at 19:00; 80 minutes, just off St. Mark's Square on Campo San Gallo, San Marco 1097, tel. 041-241-2002, www.teatrosangallo.net).

Movies

Venetian cinema is rarely in the original language; expect to hear it in Italian. Every September, Venice's **film festival** (with some English-language films, www.labiennale.org) doubles the viewing choices and brings the stars out to Venice's Lido, a 10-minute vaporetto ride from St. Mark's Square.

PUBS, CLUBS, AND LATE-NIGHT SPOTS

Unlike other Italian cities, Venice doesn't have a good dance scene. The close proximity of apartments means loud music isn't tolerated late at night. The few *discoteche* are overpriced and exclusive (not tourist-friendly), with expensive drinks and little actual dancing.

But there are plenty of zones where people gather to enjoy the late hours. The scene in front of St. Mark's Basilica is seductive (described earlier), but also consider the following options.

Near the Rialto Market
Each night, but especially on weekends, young Venetians and local night owls congregate in bars near the Rialto Market and along a nearby section of the Grand Canal. A strip of canalside restaurants I've dubbed the "Bancogiro Stretch" is a great place to enjoy a drink and the scene late at night (see page 268).

Between the Rialto and St. Mark's Square
Perhaps the best place to drink beer with an Italian is in an Irish pub—and Venice has several near the Rialto Bridge, including **Devil's Forest Pub** (daily 11:00-late, a block off Campo San Bartolomeo on Calle dei Stagneri at San Marco 5185, tel. 041-520-0623, www.devilsforestpub.com) and **Inishark Pub** (closed Mon, free Wi-Fi, on Calle del Mondo Novo, just west of Campo Santa Maria Formosa off Salizada San Lio, at Castello 5787, tel. 041-523-5300, www.inisharkpub.com). For locations, see the map on page 249.

   Planet Restaurant shows sports coverage on TV while serving up pizzas, expensive pastas, and drinks until very late (no cover, between Campo Santa Maria Formosa and St. Mark's Square on Calle Cas[sellerie at Castello 5281—see map on page 249, tel. 041-522-0808, www.planetpubve.com).

Zattere
At the south end of Dorsoduro, a canalfront strip called Zattere (near the Zattere vaporetto stop) has a youthful vibe, with fun-loving pizzerias, *gelaterie,* and bars open late in season. **El Chioschetto alle Zattere** is a simple outdoor bar right on the promenade (8:00-21:00, just west of Zattere vaporetto dock—see map on page 253; mobile 348-396-8466). The popular **Gelateria Nico** has a floating terrace for views with your dessert.

Campo Santa Margarita
For location, see #23 the map on page 252.

   The university student zone of Campo Santa Margarita, near the Accademia Bridge, is popular with young Venetians. It has a good restaurant, café, and bar scene—especially from May through September. **Caffè Rosso** is a favorite (unsigned at #2963—with a tiny interior and tons of outdoor seating, tel. 041-528-7998). A few doors down (at #2944), **Pizza al Volo** sells cheap, hearty slices to go until 2:00 in the morning. Across the square, find the excellent

Il Doge *gelateria* (see page 256). For more suggestions, see page 277.

A block away, facing the canal (across Campo San Barnaba), the **Venice Jazz Club** has live music from 21:00 to 23:00 (nightly except Thu and Sun). Doors open at 19:00 and light meals are served before the music starts (€20 includes first drink, no smoking, near Ponte dei Pugni, Dorsoduro # 3102, tel. 041-523-2056, mobile 340-150-4985, www.venicejazzclub.com, Federico).

Cannaregio

Il Paradiso Perduto ("Paradise Lost"), in the back streets of Cannaregio, is notorious for being noisy late at night. When locals complain, night owls say there's got to be someplace in Venice that stays open late. The restaurant and bar has a huge following for its good casual food and ambience; there are often live concerts on Monday nights (closed Tue-Wed, on Fondamenta della Misericordia, Cannaregio 2540, vaporetto: San Marcuola, tel. 041-720-581).

VENICE CONNECTIONS

This chapter addresses your arrival and departure from Venice—by train, plane, car, bus, and cruise ship.

A two-mile-long causeway (with highway and train lines) connects Venice to the mainland. Mestre, the sprawling mainland section of Venice, has fewer crowds, cheaper hotels, and plenty of inexpensive parking lots, but zero charm. Don't stop in Mestre unless you're changing trains, parking your car, or sleeping there.

By Train

SANTA LUCIA TRAIN STATION

All trains to "Venice" stop at Venezia Mestre (on the mainland). Most continue on to Santa Lucia Station (a.k.a. Venezia S.L.) on the island of Venice itself. If your train happens to terminate at Mestre, you'll need to buy a €1.25 Mestre-Santa Lucia ticket and validate it before hopping any nonexpress, regional train (with an R or RV prefix) for the ride across the causeway to Venice (6/hour, 10 minutes).

Santa Lucia train station plops you right into the old town on the Grand Canal, an easy vaporetto ride or fascinating 45-minute walk to St. Mark's Square. You'll find the **TI** in a white kiosk out front, next to the vaporetto dock. If the station TI is crowded when you arrive, visit the TI at St. Mark's Square instead.

The station has a **baggage check** (€6/5 hours, €17/24 hours, daily 6:00-23:00, no lockers; along track 1). Pay **WCs** are at track 1 and in the back of the big bar/cafeteria area inside the station.

Before heading into town, confirm your departure plan (use the ticket machines or study the *partenze*/departures posters on walls). The banks of user-friendly ticket machines are handy (but cover Italian destinations only). They take euros and credit cards,

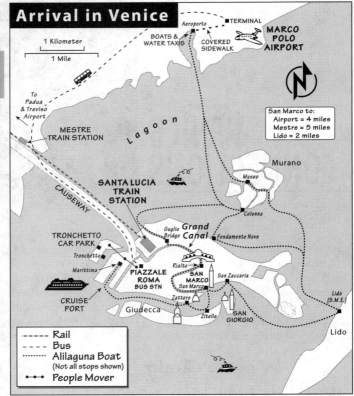

Arrival in Venice

1 Kilometer
1 Mile

TERMINAL

Aeroporto

BOATS &
WATER TAXIS

COVERED
SIDEWALK

**MARCO
POLO
AIRPORT**

To
Padua
& Treviso
Airport

MESTRE
TRAIN STATION

Lagoon

San Marco to:
Airport = 4 miles
Mestre = 5 miles
Lido = 2 miles

Murano

Museo

SANTA LUCIA
TRAIN
STATION

CAUSEWAY

Colonna

TRONCHETTO
CAR PARK

Guglie Grand
Bridge Canal

Fondamente Nove

Tronchetto

Marittima

Rialto

PIAZZALE
ROMA
BUS STN

SAN
MARCO
San Marco

San Zaccaria

CRUISE
PORT

Zattere

Giudecca

Zitelle

SAN
GIORGIO

Lido
(S.M.E.)

Lido

---- Rail
---- Bus
.... Alilaguna Boat
(Not all stops shown)
•–•–• People Mover

display schedules, and issue tickets. The green-and-white machines are for Trenitalia trains (toll tel. 892-021, www.trenitalia.it); the red machines are for the high-speed Italo service (tel. 06-0708, www.italotreno.it).

If you need international tickets or live help, head to the ticket windows in the corner, near track 14 (Trenitalia open 6:00-21:00; Italo open 8:15-20:10). Or you could take care of these tasks online or at a downtown travel agency (ticket fee, see page 21). For more on train travel in Italy—including your ticket-buying options—see page 454.

Getting from the Train Station to Central Venice

It's best by **vaporetto**. Walk straight out of the station to the canal, where you'll see five vaporetto docks, each serving different boats. Electronic signboards show which boats are leaving when and from which dock. From left to right, it's dock A, bridge, and docks B, C, D, and E: Dock A (circular-route boats #4.1 and #5.1), Dock B (circular-route boats #4.2

and #5.2), Dock C (fast boat #2, wrong direction), Dock D (fast boat #2 to Rialto and San Marco), and Dock E (slow boat #1, making every stop down the Grand Canal all the way to San Marco). Buy a €7.50 ticket before you board, and even though you're an expert now, confirm that your boat is going to your stop as you hop on. For details on vaporetto tickets and passes, see page 23.

A **water taxi** from the train station to central Venice costs about €60-70 (the taxi dock is straight ahead).

From Venice by Train to Other Destinations

When taking the train to nearby cities such as Padua and Verona, prices and journey times vary greatly depending on whether you take an express or regional train.

Destinations in Italy: Padua (2/hour, 25-50 minutes), **Vicenza** (2/hour, 45-75 minutes), **Verona** (2/hour, 1.5-2.5 hours), **Ravenna** (roughly hourly, 3 hours, transfer in Ferrara or Bologna), **Florence** (hourly, 2 hours, often crowded so make reservations), **Bolzano/Dolomites** (to Bolzano about hourly, 3 hours, transfer in Verona; catch bus from Bolzano into mountains), **Milan** (2/hour, most direct on high-speed ES trains, 2.5 hours), **Cinque Terre/ Monterosso** (5/day, 6 hours, change in Milan), **Rome** (roughly hourly, 3.5 hours, overnight possible), **Naples** (almost hourly, 5.5 hours, some change in Bologna or Rome), **Brindisi** (5/day, 9 hours, change in Rome or Bologna). These departures are operated by Trenitalia; Italo offers additional high-speed connections to major Italian cities including **Bologna, Florence,** and **Rome** (see page 454).

International Destinations: Interlaken (4/day, 6-6.5 hours with 2 changes), **Munich** (1/day direct, 6.5 hours, more with change in Verona; reservable only at ticket windows or via www. bahn.com), **Innsbruck** (1/day direct, 5 hours, more with change in Verona; reservable only at ticket windows or via www.bahn.com), **Salzburg** (4/day, 6-7 hours with change in Villach), **Paris** (2/day direct, 11 hours; 1 direct night train, 14.5 hours, reserve up to 4 months in advance, no rail passes accepted, www.thello.com), **Geneva** (1/day direct, 7 hours). Travelers to **Ljubljana** and **Vienna** can take an Austrian Railways bus (1-2/day in the morning) to Villach in Austria, and continue from there by direct train (bus leaves from Tronchetto and Mestre railway station; buy tickets from windows in train station). To **Ljubljana,** there's also a direct DRD bus from Mestre (1/day, 3.25 hours, www.drd.si) and a private shuttle service (www.goopti.com). To **Vienna,** you can also take a direct evening train (1/day, 8 hours) or night train (1/day, 11 hours).

By Plane

MARCO POLO AIRPORT

Venice's small, modern airport is on the mainland shore of the lagoon, six miles north of the city (airport code: VCE). There's one sleek terminal, with a TI (daily 9:00-20:00), car-rental agencies, ATMs, a bank, and a few shops and eateries. For flight information, call 041-260-9260, visit www.veniceairport.com, or ask your hotel.

Getting Between the Airport and Venice

You can get between the airport and central Venice in any of four ways: by Alilaguna boat, water taxi, airport bus, or land taxi.

Type	Speed	Cost	Notes
Alilaguna boat	Slow	Moderate	No transfer
Water taxi	Fast	Expensive	No transfer
Airport bus to Piazzale Roma	Medium	Cheap	Transfer to vaporetto
Land taxi to Piazzale Roma	Medium	Moderate	Transfer to vaporetto

The Alilaguna boats reach most of this book's recommended hotels very simply, with no changes. Hotels near the train station, however, are better served by the bus to Piazzale Roma.

Both Alilaguna boats and water taxis leave from the airport's boat dock, an eight-minute walk from the terminal. Exit the arrivals hall and turn left, following signs along a covered sidewalk.

When flying out of Venice, allow yourself plenty of time to get to the airport. Water transport can be slow—just getting there can take up to two hours. Alilaguna boats are small and can fill up. In an emergency, you can always hop in a water taxi and get to the airport in 30 minutes.

Alilaguna Airport Boats

These boats make the scenic journey across the lagoon, shuttling passengers between the airport and the island of Venice (€15, €27 round-trip, €1 surcharge if bought on boat, discount if bought online, includes 1 suitcase and 1 piece of hand luggage, additional bags-€3 each, roughly 2/hour, 1-1.5-hour trip depending on destination). Alilaguna boats are not covered by city transit passes, but they do use the same docks and ticket windows as the regular *vaporetti*. You can buy Alilaguna tickets online at www.alilaguna.it or www.venicelink.com.

There are three key Alilaguna lines for reaching St. Mark's Square. From the airport, the **blue line** *(linea blu)* heads first to Fondamente Nove (40 minutes), then loops around to San Zaccaria and San Marco (about 1.5 hours) before continuing on to Zattere and the cruise terminal (almost 2 hours). The **orange line** *(linea arancio)* runs down the Grand Canal, reaching Guglie (handy for Cannaregio hotels, 45 minutes), Rialto (1 hour), and San Marco (1.25 hours). In high season, the **red line** *(linea rossa)* runs to St. Mark's in just over an hour. It circumnavigates Murano and then runs parallel to the blue line, ending at Giudecca Zitelle. For a full schedule, visit the TI, see the website (www.alilaguna.it), call 041-240-1701, ask your hotelier, or scan the schedules posted at the docks.

From the Airport to Venice: You can buy Alilaguna tickets at the airport's TI, the ticket desk in the terminal, and at the ticket booth at the dock. Any ticket seller can tell you which line to catch to get to your destination. Blue- and orange-line boats from the airport run roughly twice an hour; red goes once an hour (blue line from 6:15, orange line from 7:45, red line from 9:40; blue and orange lines run until about midnight, red line makes its last run at 18:40).

From Venice to the Airport: Ask your hotelier which dock and which line is best. Blue-line boats start leaving Venice as early as 3:50 in the morning. Scope out the dock and buy your ticket in advance to avoid last-minute stress.

Water Taxis

Luxury taxi speedboats zip directly between the airport and the closest dock to your hotel, getting you within steps of your final destination in about 30 minutes. The official price is €110 for up to four people; add €10 for every extra person (10-passenger limit). You may get a higher quote—politely talk it down. A taxi can be a smart investment for small groups and those with an early departure.

From the airport, arrange your ride at the water-taxi desk or with the boat captains at the dock. From Venice, book your taxi trip the day before your departure, either through your hotel or directly with the Consorzio Motoscafi water taxi association (tel. 041-522-2303, www.motoscafivenezia.it).

Airport Shuttle Buses

Buses between the airport and Venice are fast, frequent, and cheap. They drop you at Venice's bus station, at the square called Piazzale Roma. From there, you can catch a vaporetto down the Grand Canal—convenient for hotels near the Rialto Bridge and St. Mark's Square. If you're staying near the train station, you can walk from Piazzale Roma to your hotel.

Two bus companies serve this route: ACTV and ATVO. ATVO buses take 20 minutes and go nonstop. ACTV buses make a few stops en route and take slightly longer (30 minutes), but you get a discount if you buy a Venice vaporetto pass at the same time (see page 23). The service is equally good (either bus: €8 one-way, €15 round-trip, runs about 5:00-24:00, 2/hour, drops to 1/hour early and late, check schedules at www.atvo.it or www.actv.it).

From the Airport to Venice: Buses leave from just outside the arrivals terminal. Buy tickets from the TI, the ticket desk in the terminal, the kiosk near baggage claim, or ticket machines. ATVO tickets are not valid on ACTV buses and vice versa. Double-check the destination; you want Piazzale Roma. If taking ACTV, you want bus #5.

From Venice to the Airport: At Piazzale Roma, buy your ticket from the ACTV windows (in the building by the bridge) or the ATVO office (at #497g) before heading out to the platforms. The newsstand in the center of the lot also sells tickets.

Land Taxi or Private Minivan

It takes about 20 minutes to drive from the airport to Piazzale Roma or the cruise port. A **land taxi** can do the trip for about €50. To reserve a private minivan, contact **Treviso Car Service** (minivan-€55, seats up to 8; car-€50, seats up to 3; mobile 338-204-4390 or 333-411-2840, www.trevisocarservice.com).

TREVISO AIRPORT

Several budget airlines, such as Ryanair and Wizz Air, use Treviso Airport, 12 miles northwest of Venice (airport code: TSF, tel. 042-231-5111, www.trevisoairport.it). The fastest option into Venice (Tronchetto parking lot) is on the **Barzi express bus,** which does the trip in just 40 minutes (€12, buy tickets on board, every 1-2 hours, www.barziservice.com). From Tronchetto, hop on a vaporetto, or take the People Mover monorail to Piazzale Roma for €1.50. **ATVO buses** are a bit more frequent and drop you right at Piazzale Roma (saving you the People Mover ride), but take nearly twice as long (€12 one-way, €22 round-trip, about 2/hour, 70 minutes, www.atvo.it; buy tickets at the ATVO desk in the airport and stamp them on the bus). **Treviso Car Service** offers minivan service to Piazzale Roma (minivan-€75, seats up to 8; car-€65, seats up to 3; for contact info, see listing above).

By Bus

PIAZZALE ROMA BUS STATION

Venice's "bus station" is actually an open-air parking lot called Piazzale Roma. The square itself is a jumble of different operators, platforms, and crosswalks over busy lanes of traffic. But bus stops are well-signed. The ticket windows for ACTV (including #5 to

Marco Polo Airport) are in a building between the bridge and va-poretto stop. The ATVO ticket office (express buses to Marco Polo and Treviso airports and to Padua) is at #497g in the big, white building, on the right side of the square as you face away from the canal (office open daily 7:30-22:30).

Piazzale Roma also has two big parking garages and the Peo-ple Mover monorail (€1.50, links to the cruise port and then the parking-lot island of Tronchetto). A baggage-storage office is next to the monorail at #497m (€7/24 hours, daily 6:00-21:00).

If you arrive here, find the vaporetto docks (just left of the modern bridge) and take #1 or the faster #2 down the Grand Canal to reach the Rialto, Accademia, or San Marco (St. Mark's Square) stops. Electronic boards direct you to the dock you want. Before buying a single-ride vaporetto ticket, consider getting a transit pass (see page 23). If your hotel is near here or near the train station, you can get there on foot.

By Car

PARKING IN VENICE

The freeway (monitored by speed cameras) dead-ends after cross-ing the causeway to Venice. At the end of the road you have two parking-garage choices: Tronchetto or Piazzale Roma. As you drive into the city, signboards with green and red lights indicate which lots are full. (You can also park in Mestre, on the mainland, but this is less convenient.)

Parking at Tronchetto: This big garage is a bit farther out, but it's a little cheaper and well-connected by vaporetto (€3-5/hour, €21/24 hours, tel. 041-520-7555, www.veniceparking.it).

From the garage, cross the street to the brick building and go right to the vaporetto dock (not well-signed, look for *ACTV*). At the dock, catch vaporetto #2 in one of two directions: via the Grand Canal (more scenic, stops at Rialto, 40 minutes to San Marco), or via Giudecca (around the city, faster, no Rialto stop, 30 minutes to San Marco).

Don't be waylaid by aggressive water-taxi boatmen. They charge €100 to take you where the vaporetto will for far less. Also avoid the travel agencies masquerading as TIs; deal only with the ticket booth at the vaporetto dock or the VèneziaUnica public transport office. If you're going to buy a local transport pass, do it now.

If you're staying near the bus or train station, you can take the €1.50 **People Mover** monorail, which brings you from Tronchetto to the bus station at Piazzale Roma. From there, it's a five-minute walk across the Calatrava Bridge to the train station (buy tickets with cash or credit card from machine, 3-minute trip).

Parking at Piazzale Roma: The two garages here are more convenient but a bit more expensive and likelier to be full. Both garages face the busy Piazzale Roma, where the road ends. The big white building on your right is the **Autorimessa Comunale** city garage (€26/24 hours, TI office in payment lobby open daily 8:30-14:00, tel. 041-272-7211, www.avmspa.it). In a back corner of the square is the private **Garage San Marco** (€30/24 hours, tel. 041-523-2213, www.garagesanmarco.it). At either of these, you'll have to give up your keys. Near the Garage San Marco, avoid the Parcheggio Sant'Andrea, which charges obscene rates.

Parking in Mestre: The **Parcheggio Stazione** garage across from the train station in Mestre (on the mainland) makes sense only if you have light bags and are staying within walking distance of Santa Lucia Station (€2.50/hour, €14/day, www.sabait.it).

By Cruise Ship

Most cruise ships dock at Venice's Stazione Marittima, at the west end of town. From the cruise port, the most direct way to reach St. Mark's Square is to take the Alilaguna **express boat** (2/hour in each direction, 30 minutes, www.alilaguna.it).

Another option is to take the **People Mover** monorail from the port to Piazzale Roma, then hop on a **vaporetto**. It's about a five-minute walk to the People Mover, then a three-minute ride to Piazzale Roma, where you'll find a stop for *vaporetti* to St. Mark's Square (45 minutes on boat #1, 25 minutes on boat #2).

Other options for getting to the center from the cruise port include **walking** (about an hour to St. Mark's Square) or an expensive **water taxi** ride (at least €70-80).

For more details, see my *Rick Steves Mediterranean Cruise Ports* guidebook.

NEAR VENICE

Venice is just one of many towns in the Italian region of Veneto (VEN-eh-toh), but few visitors venture off the lagoon. That's a shame, as there's much to see within a very short hop of Venice: the important and worthwhile towns of **Padua, Verona, Vicenza,** and **Ravenna.**

If you can't make it to all four, pick the one that interests you. Art lovers will want to head to **Padua** to see Giotto's celebrated Scrovegni Chapel or to **Ravenna** for its sumptuous Byzantine mosaics. History buffs should see **Verona's** impressive Roman ruins. Verona is also the pick for star-crossed lovers retracing Romeo and Juliet's steps. Architecture fans could consider a quick stop in Palladio-designed **Vicenza,** located about halfway between Padua and Verona.

If you're Padua-bound, remember that you need to reserve ahead to see the Scrovegni Chapel. Don't bother visiting Vicenza

on a Monday, when many of the top sights are closed; in Verona, several sights don't open until 13:30 on Mondays.

Spending a day at one of these towns as a side-trip from Venice is exciting and efficient. Padua, Verona, and Vicenza are on the same train line. Connected by at least two trains per hour, they're easy to visit. Only Ravenna is not on the main Venice-Milan train line. To reach Ravenna, you'll need to make at least one change, either in Bologna or Ferrara.

Train travelers find that the "fast regional" trains (marked with an RV prefix on schedules and ticket machines) offer the best mixture of speed, convenience, and savings. Frecce express trains cost three to four times as much—and though rail-pass holders don't have to pay the fare, they do have to commit to a time and pay to reserve a seat. Regional trains don't require (or even accept) seat reservations. The regular regional trains (R prefix) offer the same savings as the RV ones but are much slower, especially on the longer journey to Verona or Ravenna.

Type of Train	Venice-Padua	Venice-Verona	Venice-Ravenna
R (Regional)	€4, 50 minutes	€9, 2.5 hours	none
RV (Fast Regional)	€4, 25 minutes	€9, 1.5 hours	€14-18, 3-3.5 hours (includes regional train)
Frecce (Express)	€17, 25 minutes	€26, 70 minutes	€25-30, 2.5-3 hours (includes regional train)

PADUA

Padova

This inexpensive, easily appreciated city is a fine destination on its own and a convenient base for day trips all around the region. Nicknamed "The brain of Veneto," Padua (*Padova* in Italian) is home to the prestigious university (founded in 1222) that hosted Galileo, Copernicus, Dante, and Petrarch. Pilgrims know Padua as the home of the Basilica of St. Anthony, where the reverent assemble to touch his tomb and ogle his remarkably intact lower jaw and tongue. And lovers of early-Renaissance art come here

to make a pilgrimage of their own: to gaze at the remarkable frescoes by Giotto in the Scrovegni Chapel. But despite the fact that Padua's museums and churches hold their own in Italy's artistic big league, its hotels are reasonably priced, and the city doesn't feel touristy. Padua's old town center is elegantly arcaded, filled with students, and sprinkled with surprises, including some of Italy's most inviting squares for lingering over an *aperitivo* as the sun slowly dips low in the sky.

From Padua, architecture fans can ride by train (15-25 minutes) to Vicenza and its celebrated Palladian buildings (see page 350).

PLANNING YOUR TIME: PADUA IN SIX HOURS

Day-trippers can do a quick but enjoyable blitz of Padua—including a visit to the Scrovegni Chapel—in six hours. Trains from Venice are cheap, take 25-50 minutes, and run frequently. Once in Padua, everything is a 10-minute walk or a quick tram ride apart.

To see Giotto's Scrovegni Chapel, you need to make a reservation; your entry time will dictate the order of your sightseeing (see

"Reservations" on page 332). When planning your day, also consider these factors: The station has a reliable baggage-check desk; the open-air markets are vibrant in the morning; student life is best at the university late in the day; and the Basilica of St. Anthony is open all day, but the reliquary chapel closes midday, from 12:45 to 14:30.

Ideally, I'd do it this way: 9:00—market action and sightseeing in town center, 11:00—Basilica of St. Anthony, 13:00—lunch, 15:00—Scrovegni Chapel tour.

Orientation to Padua

Padua's main tourist sights lie on a north-south axis through the heart of the city, from the train station to Scrovegni Chapel to the market squares (the center of town) to the Basilica of St. Anthony. It's roughly a 10-minute walk between each of these sights, or about 30 minutes from end to end. I've designed this chapter around Padua's wonderful, single tram line, which makes lacing things together quick and easy (see "Getting Around Padua," later).

TOURIST INFORMATION

Padua has two TIs: in the **center** (in the alley behind Caffè Pedrocchi at Vicolo Cappellato Pedrocchi 9, Mon-Sat 9:00-19:00, closed Sun) and at the **train station** (Mon-Sat 9:00-19:00, Sun 10:00-16:00, tel. 049-201-0080, www.turismopadova.it).

At either TI, pick up the seasonal *Padova Today* entertainment listing (with a list of sights in the back). The TI's free I-PADova audio tour is creative and works well; you can download it to your smartphone or tablet from their website and follow any of the five routes in town (www.discoverpadova.com, search for "audio guide"; smart to print out audio-tour map ahead of time).

The **Padova Card** includes entry to all the recommended sights in this chapter—except the university's Anatomy Theater and the Oratory of St. George—plus unlimited tram rides and free parking near Prato della Valle (€16/48 hours, €21/72 hours, buy at either TI, the Scrovegni Chapel, or online at www.padovacard. it). The card will likely pay off if you're doing at least two of these three things: seeing the Scrovegni Chapel, parking a car, or staying overnight (giving you time to sightsee the next day).

While the Padova Card covers the Scrovegni Chapel, you still need to make a reservation in advance to enter the chapel (€1 extra reservation fee). If you go through the chapel website (www.cappelladegliscrovegni.it), you can buy the card and make a chapel reservation at the same time. Collect your prepurchased cards from either TI or at the chapel.

ARRIVAL IN PADUA

By Train: The efficient station is a user-friendly shopping mall with whatever you may need (Despar supermarket open Mon-Sat 7:00-21:00, Sun 10:00-21:00). Along track 1 are pay WCs and baggage storage (daily 6:30-18:00, bring photo ID).

For a travel agency, go to **Leonardi Viaggi-Turismo,** which is only a block from the station and offers ticketing services for trains, planes, and boats for a small fee (Mon-Fri 9:00-19:00, Sat 9:00-13:00, closed Sun, up the main drag, Corso del Popolo 14, tel. 049-650-455, www.leonardiviaggi.com).

To get downtown, simply hop on Padua's handy **tram** (see "Getting Around Padua," below). Purchase your ticket (€1.30, or €3.80 day pass) from shops inside the station or in the low brown rectangular booth in front of the station, which has both machines and a staffed window. Leaving the station, the tram stop is 100 yards to the right at the foot of the bridge. A **taxi** into town (a good option after dark) costs about €8-10.

By Bus: The bus station is 100 yards east of the train station. Buses arrive here from Venice's Piazzale Roma and Marco Polo Airport.

HELPFUL HINTS

Exchange Rate: €1 = about $1.10

Country Calling Code: 39 (see page 450 for dialing instructions)

Pronunciation: You say Padua (PAD-joo-wah), they say Padova (PAH-doh-vah). The city's top sight, Scrovegni Chapel, is pronounced skroh-VEHN-yee.

Wi-Fi: There's public Wi-Fi at both TIs and on the square in front of Café Pedrocchi (network name: Padova WiFi). The central TI has a guest computer (free for 15 minutes).

Bookstore: Feltrinelli, with books in English, is one block from the main university building (Mon-Sat 9:00-19:45, Sun 10:00-13:00 & 15:30-20:00, Via San Francesco 7, tel. 199-151-173).

Launderette: Lavami is central, tiny, and modern. Two of the three washers are supersized and cost more (€5-8/wash, €1.50/12 minutes to dry, daily 7:00-21:30, Via Marsala 22 near intersection with Via dell'Arco, tel. 049-876-4532).

Local Guide: Charming and helpful **Cristina Pernechele** is a great teacher (€110/half-day, mobile 338-495-5453, cristina@pernechele.eu).

GETTING AROUND PADUA

Ignore the city buses; pretend there is only the **tram** and rely on it. There's just one line, which efficiently and without stress connects everything you care about. Buy tickets from tobacco shops, newsstands, or the booth on the square in front of the train station

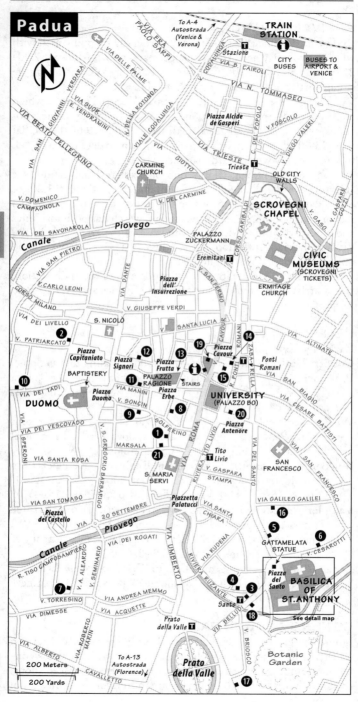

Padua

To A-4 Autostrada (Venice & Verona)

TRAIN STATION

Stazione

CITY BUSES

BUSES TO AIRPORT & VENICE

VIA FRA PAOLO SARPI

VIA DELLE PALME

VIA VERDARA

VIA SUOR E. VENDRAMIN

VIA GIOVANNI

VIA BEATO PELLEGRINO

VIA SAN PIETRO

VIA DELLA ROTONDA

VIALE CODALUNGA

VIA B. CAIROLI

VIA N. TOMMASEO

V. FOSCOLO

V. DIEGO VALERI

C. DEL POPOLO

Piazza Alcide de Gasperi

VIA TRIESTE

GIOTTO

VIA DANTE

Trieste

OLD CITY WALLS

V. GASPARE GOZZI

V. GASO

V. ALTINATE

CARMINE CHURCH

V. DEL CARMINE

SCROVEGNI CHAPEL

CIVIC MUSEUMS (SCROVEGNI TICKETS)

Piovego

Canale

V. DOMENICO CAMPAGNOLA

VIA DEI SAVONAROLA

PALAZZO ZUCKERMANN

Eremitani

CORSO GARIBALDI

ERMITAGE CHURCH

V. SAN PIETRO

V. CARLO LEONI

CORSO MILANO

VIA DEI LIVELLO

V. PATRIARCATO

S. NICOLÒ

Piazza dell'Insurrezione

V. GIUSEPPE VERDI

V. SANTA LUCIA

V. SAN FERMO

Piazza Cavour

CAVOUR

Ponti Romani

ROMANI

V. PONTI

VIA SAN BIAGIO

VIA CESARE BATTISTI

②

Piazza Capitaniato

BAPTISTERY

Piazza Signori

⑫

Piazza Frutta

⑬

⑲

⑭

⑮

ZABARELLA

⑩

Piazza Duomo

DUOMO

VIA DEI TADI

Piazza Erbe

⑪ PALAZZO RAGIONE

VIA MANIN

Stairs

UNIVERSITY (PALAZZO BO)

⑳

VIA DEI VESCOVADO

V. SONCIN

⑨

⑧

V. S. GREGORIO BARBARIGO

SOLFERINO

VIA SPERONI

VIA SANTA ROSA

①

Piazza Antenore

VIA DEL SANTO

VIA SAN FRANCESCO

MARSALA

�21

VIA ROMA

RIVIERA TITO LIVIO

Tito Livio

V. GASPARA STAMPA

SAN FRANCESCO

VIA SAN TOMASO

S. MARIA SERVI

Piazza del Castello

VIA 20 SETTEMBRE

Piovego

Piazzetta Palatucci

VIA SANTA CHIARA

VIA GALILEO GALILEI

⑯

⑤

VIA GALILEO GALILEI

Canale

R. TISO CAMPOFAMPIERO

VIA DEI ROGATI

RIVIERA RUZANTE

GATTAMELATA STATUE

⑥

V. CESAROTTI

⑦

V. A. ALEARDO

V. SEMINARIO

V. TORRESINO

VIA ANDREA MEMMO

VIA ACQUETTE

RIVIERA RUZANTE

④

③

Santo

⑱

Piazza del Santo

BASILICA OF ST. ANTHONY

See detail map

VIA DIMESSE

VIA ROBERTO MARIN

VIA ALBERTO

Prato della Valle

VIA BELLUDI

V. BRIOSCO

Botanic Garden

200 Meters

200 Yards

To A-13 Autostrada (Florence)

CAVALLETTO

Prato della Valle

⑰

Padua Key

❶ Hotel Majestic Toscanelli
❷ Albergo Verdi
❸ Hotel Belludi 37
❹ Hotel Al Fagiano
❺ Hotel Al Santo & Antica Trattoria dei Paccagnella
❻ Hotel/Rist. Casa del Pellegrino
❼ Ostello Città di Padova
❽ Osteria dei Fabbri
❾ Osteria L'Anfora
❿ Enoteca dei Tadi

⓫ Rist. Dante alle Piazze
⓬ La Lanterna Ristorante
⓭ Bar dei Osei
⓮ Brek Cafeteria
⓯ PAM Supermarket & Brek
⓰ Pizzeria Pago Pago
⓱ Zairo Rist./Pizzeria
⓲ Pollodoro la Gastronomica
⓳ Caffè Pedrocchi
⓴ Feltrinelli Bookstore
㉑ Launderette

PADUA

and validate them on board; there are also ticket machines at some stops, but they sell only single tickets and don't give change (€1.30 single ticket good for 1.25 hours, €3.80 *biglietto giornaliero* good for one calendar day; departs every 8 minutes during the day Mon-Sat, every 20 minutes evenings and Sun). The rubber-wheeled trams run on a single rail.

Before boarding, note the tram direction on posted schedules and above the front window (Pontevigodarzere is northbound, Capolinea Sud is southbound). Stops that matter to tourists include Stazione FS (train and bus stations), Eremitani (Scrovegni Chapel), Ponti Romani (old town center, market squares, university), Tito Livio (ghetto, old town center, Hotel Majestic Toscanelli), Santo (Basilica of St. Anthony and neighborhood hotels), and Prato della Valle (hostel).

Padua's **hop-on, hop-off tour buses** are not worth the time or money.

Sights in Padua

IN THE CENTER

Padua's two main sights (Basilica of St. Anthony and Scrovegni Chapel) are, respectively, at the southern and northern reaches of downtown. But its atmospheric, cobbled core—with bustling markets, vibrant student life, and inviting sun-and-café-speckled piazzas—is its own ▲▲▲ attraction. You could simply stroll the area aimlessly or seek out some of the following spots.

▲▲Market Squares

The stately Palazzo della Ragione (described later) provides a dramatic backdrop for Padua's almost exotic-feeling produce market, which fills the surrounding squares—**Piazza delle Erbe** and **Piazza della Frutta**—each morning and all day Saturday (Mon-Fri roughly 8:00-13:00, Sat 8:00-19:00 but a bit quieter in the afternoon, closed Sun). Second only to the produce market in Italy's gastronomic capital of Bologna, this market has been renowned for centuries as having the freshest and greatest selection of herbs, fruits,

and vegetables. The presentation is an art in itself. As you wander, appreciate the local passion for good food: Residents can tell the month by the seasonal selections, and merchants share recipe tips with shoppers. You'll notice quite a few Sri Lankans working here (Italy took in many refugees from Sri Lanka's civil war).

PADUA

Don't miss the **indoor market** zone on the ground floor of the Palazzo della Ragione. Wandering through this H-shaped arcade—where you'll find various butchers, *salumerie* (delicatessens), cheese shops, bakeries, and fishmongers at work—is a sensuous experience. For centuries, this was a market for luxury items (furs, fine fabrics, silver, and gold—notice the imposing iron gates used to lock it up each evening). Then, the devastating loss to the French in 1797 marked the end of good times, and with no market for luxury items, the arcade was used to sell perishables—meat and cheese—out of the sun.

Students gather in the squares after the markets have closed, spilling out of colorful bars and cafés, drinks in hand (see sidebar). Pizza by the slice is dirt-cheap. For pointers on a recommended local sandwich stand, **Bar dei Osei,** and a neighboring seafood-snack stand, see page 348. Just a few steps away from these is a classic old pharmacy that dates to 1841: The licorice-perfumed **Ai Due Cantini d'Oro,** which stocks retail items like it did before World War II, sells odd foods and specialty items for every dietary need (Tue 16:00-19:30, Wed-Sun 9:00-13:00 & 16:00-19:30, closed Mon, Piazza della Frutta 46, tel. 049-875-0623).

Piazza dei Signori, just a block away, is a busy clothing mar-

ket in the morning and the most popular gathering place in the evening for students out for a drink (see sidebar). The circa-1400 clock decorates the former palace of the ruling family. The aggressive lion with unfurled wings on the column was a reminder of the Venetian determination to assert its control. Today that lion can be seen as representing the Veneto region's independence from Rome: Italy's North

Drinking a *Spritz* with the Student Crowd

Each early evening, before dinner, students enliven Padua by enjoying a convivial drink in their favorite places. Piazza dei Signori is trendier, with people of all ages, while the scene on Piazza della Erbe is more bohemian and alternative. Or you could sit in front of the university, nurse your drink, and watch the graduates get roasted with their crazy gangs of friends.

The drink of choice is a *spritz*, an aperitif generally made with Campari (a red liqueur infused with bitter herbs), white wine, and sparkling water, and garnished with a blood-orange wedge. Traditionally, men opt for the heavier and bitterer Campari *spritz*, while women prefer a sweeter and lighter *spritz* made with Aperol (an orange-flavored liqueur with less alcohol content).

Grab a table and be part of the scene. This is a classic opportunity to enjoy a real discussion with smart, English-speaking students who see tourists not as pests, but as interesting people from far away. For an instant conversation starter, ask about the current political situation in Italy, the right-wing party's policy on immigrants, or the cultural differences between Italy's North and South.

(Veneto and Lombardy) is tired of subsidizing the South. Grumbling about this issue continues to stir talk of splitting the country.

Palazzo della Ragione

Looming over Padua's two big central market squares (Piazza delle Erbe and Piazza della Frutta), this grand 13th-century palazzo—

commonly called *il Salone* (the great hall)—once held the medieval law courts. Its first floor consists of a huge hall—265 feet by 90 feet—that was at one time adorned with frescoes by Giotto. A fire in 1412 destroyed those paintings, and the palazzo was redecorated with the 15th-century art you see today: a series of 333 frescoes depicting the signs of the zodiac, labors of the month, symbols representing characteristics of people born under each sign, and, finally, figures of saints to legitimize the power of the courts in the eyes of the Church.

The hall is topped with a hull-shaped roof, which helps to support the structure without the use of columns—quite an architectural feat in its day, considering the building's dimensions. The biggest thing in the hall is the giant, very anatomically correct horse. Its prominent placement represents the pride locals feel for the Veneto's own highly respected breed of horse. (After the bronze ones in St. Mark's Basilica, these are the favorite horses in the region.) The curious black stone in the corner opposite the big wooden horse is the "Stone of Shame," which was the seat of debtors being punished during the Middle Ages. It was introduced as a compassionate alternative to prison by St. Anthony in 1230. Instead of being executed or doing prison time, debtors sat upon this stone, surrendered their possessions, and denounced themselves publicly before being exiled from the city. The computer kiosks provide excellent information with entertaining videos.

Cost and Hours: €4, more during special exhibitions; Tue-Sun 9:00-19:00, Nov-Jan until 18:00, closed Mon year-round; enter through the east end of Piazza delle Erbe and go up the long staircase, Ponti Romani tram stop, tel. 049-820-5006. The WCs are through the glass doors at the opposite end of the hall from the wooden horse.

Caffè Pedrocchi

The white-columned, Neoclassical Pedrocchi building is much more than just a café on the ground floor. A complex of meeting rooms and entertainment venues, it stirs the Italian soul (or the patriotic Italian soul, at least). Built in 1831 during the period of Austrian rule, Caffè Pedrocchi was inaugurated for the fourth Italian Congress of Scientists, which convened during the mid-19th century to stir up nationalistic fervor as Italy struggled to become a united nation. As a symbol of patriotic hope, it was the target (no surprise) of a student uprising plot in 1848.

Each of the café's three dining rooms is decorated and furnished in a different color (denoted by the hue of velvet on the chairs): red, white, or green—representing the colors of the Italian flag. In the outer, unheated Sala Verde (Green Room), people are welcome to sit and relax without ordering anything or having to pay. This is where Italian gentlemen read their newspapers and gather with friends to chat about the old days. In the Sala Rossa (Red Room), the clock over the bar is flanked by marble reliefs of morning and night, signal-

ing that it was once open 24 hours a day (in the 19th century). In the rooms on either side, the maps of the hemispheres with south up top reflect the anti-conventional spirit of the place. In the Sala Bianca (White Room), where one of the revolutionaries in that ill-fated 1848 uprising was killed, you can still see a bullet hole in the wall (framed in tarnished silver).

The menu offers teahouse fare, including sandwiches and ice-cream sundaes, a variety of breakfast combos, and the writer Stendhal's beloved *zabaglione,* a creamy custard made with *marsala* wine. A shiny new bar in the center of the building has a praline and ice-cream counter and serves sandwiches at outdoor tables. Remember that in Italy, you can order a basic coffee standing up at the bar of any place, no matter how fancy, and pay the same low, government-regulated price.

Cost and Hours: Café interior free, daily 8:00-23:00, two entrances across from Via VIII Febbraio 14 and 20 near Ponti Romani tram stop, tel. 049-878-1231, www.caffepedrocchi.it.

Visiting the Café's Piano Nobile: To see the café's even more elaborate upstairs, you can pay to enter this "noble floor" of the Pedrocchi building (€4, Tue-Sun 9:30-12:30 & 15:30-18:00, closed Mon; to find entrance, head outside to Piazza Cavour, face café, and go through the door on the right; tel. 049-878-1231). The rooms are all in different styles, such as Greek, Etruscan, or Egyptian. These rooms were intended to evoke memories of the glory of past epochs, which a united Italy had hopes of reliving.

The Piano Nobile also hosts the small **Museum of the Risorgimento,** which traces Padua's role in Italian history, from the downfall of the Venetian Republic (1797) to the founding of the Republic of Italy (1948). Exhibits include uniforms, medals, weaponry, old artillery, fascist propaganda posters, and a 30-minute propagandistic video (in Italian, but mostly fascinating footage without narration). The video, played on demand, is a "Luce" production (meaning a Mussolini production) and features great scenes of the town in the 1930s, including clips of Il Duce's visit and later WWII bombardments. The war and propaganda posters in the last room are haunting. An old woman pleads to those who question the fascist-driven war effort: "Don't betray my son." Another declares, "The Germans are truly our friends." And another asks, "And you...what are *you* doing?"

University of Padua

The main building of this prestigious university, known as Palazzo Bò, is adjacent to Caffè Pedrocchi. Founded in 1222, it's one of the first, greatest, and most progressive universities in Europe. Back when the Church controlled university curricula, a group of professors and students broke free from the University of Bologna to create this liberal school, which would be independent of Catholic constraints and accessible to people of other faiths.

A haven for free thought, the university attracted intellectuals from all over Europe, including the great astronomer Copernicus, who realized here that the universe didn't revolve around him. And Galileo—notorious for disagreeing with the Church's views on science—called his 18 years on the faculty here the best of his life.

Access to Palazzo Bò is via a mostly underwhelming 45-minute guided tour, but the gawking public can get a peek at a few of its exterior courtyards (see below). The most exciting part of the tour is Europe's first great **Anatomy Theater** (from 1594). Despite the Church's strict ban on autopsies, more than 300 students would pack this theater to watch professors dissect human cadavers (the bodies of criminals from another town). This had to be done in a "don't ask, don't tell" kind of way, because the Roman Catholic Church only started allowing the teaching of anatomy through dissection in the late 1800s.

Cost and Hours: Grounds—free; Palazzo Bò tour—€5, March-Oct Mon-Sat generally three tours a day, no tours on Sun, reduced schedule Nov-Feb; Ponti Romani tram stop, 049-827-3047, www.unipd.it/en/guidedtours.

Confirm tour times and availability on website or by calling or stopping by the ticket desk (opens 15 minutes before each tour, through a door off the fascist-era courtyard, described next). School groups often book the entire visit. Tours are in Italian and another language (depending on the composition of the group). The tiny bar by the ticket desk is fun for a cheap drink and to see photos of university life.

Visiting the University Courtyards on Your Own: On weekdays and Saturday mornings, you can poke into two of the university's **courtyards** (when closed, just peer through the gate). Find the entrance at Via VIII Febbraio 7, under the "Gymnasium" inscription (30 yards from Caffè Pedrocchi, facing City Hall). You'll pop into a 16th-century courtyard, the school's historic core. It's littered with the coats of arms of important faculty and leaders of the university over the ages. Classrooms, which open onto the square, are still used.

Graduation Antics in Padua

With 60,000 students, Padua's university always seems to be hosting graduation ceremonies. There's a constant trickle of happy grads and their friends and families celebrating the big event.

During the school year, every 20 minutes or so, a student steps into a formal room (upstairs, above the university courtyard) to officially meet with the leading professors of his or her faculty. When they're finished, the students are given a green laurel wreath. They pose for ceremonial group photos and family snapshots. It's a sweet scene. Then, craziness takes over.

The new graduates replace their somber clothing with raunchy outfits, as gangs of friends gather around them on Via VIII Febbraio, the street in front of the university. The roast begins. The gang rolls out a giant butcher-paper poster with a generally obscene caricature of the student and a litany of *This Is Your Life* photos and stories. The new grad, subject to various embarrassing pranks, reads the funny statements out loud. The poster is then taped to the university wall for all to see. (Find the plastic panels to the right of the main entry, facing Via VIII Febbraio. Graduation posters are allowed to stay there for 24 hours. The panels are emptied each morning, but by nighttime a new set of posters is affixed to the plastic shields.)

During the roast, the friends sing the catchy but obscene local university anthem, reminding their newly esteemed friend not to get too huffy: *Dottore, dottore, dottore del buso del cul. Vaffancul, vaffancul* (loosely translated: "Doctor, doctor. You're just a doctor of the a-hole...go f-off, go f-off"). After you've heard this song (with its fanfare and oom-pah-pah catchiness) and have seen all the good-natured fun, you can't stop singing it.

The crazy show is usually staged late in the afternoon. Outdoor café tables afford great seats to enjoy the spectacle.

Today, students gather here, surrounded by memories of illustrious alumni, including the first woman in the world to receive a university degree (in 1678).

A passageway leads from here to an adjacent second courtyard, dating from the fascist era (c. 1938). The relief celebrates heroic students in World War I. Off this courtyard, notice the richly decorated stairway, frescoed fascist-style in the 1930s with themes celebrating art, science, and the pursuit of knowledge.

▲Baptistery

Located next to Padua's skippable Duomo, this richly frescoed little building was once the private chapel of Padua's ruling family, the Carraresi. In the 1370s, they hired a local artist, Giusto de' Menabuoi, to do a little interior redecoration. Later, in 1405, Venice conquered Padua and deposed the Carraresi; the building was turned into a baptistery, but the decorations survived.

Cost and Hours: €3, daily 10:00-18:00, on Piazza Duomo.

Visiting the Baptistery: The Baptistery's frescoes, like those in St. Mark's Basilica in Venice, show Byzantine influence. Almighty Christ, the Pantocrator, is in majesty on top, while approachable Mary and the multitude of saints provide the devout with access to God. Find the world as it was known in the 14th century (the disk below Mary's feet). It kicks off a cycle of scenes illustrating Creation (clockwise from the creation of Adam). The four evangelists (Matthew, Mark, Luke, and John) with their books and symbols fill the corners. A vivid Crucifixion scene faces a gorgeous Annunciation. And the altar niche features a dim, blue-toned, literal Apocalypse from the book of Revelation.

While the Baptistery was created 70 years after Giotto, it feels older. Because de' Menabuoi was working for a private family, he needed to be politically correct and not threaten or offend the family's allies—especially the Church. While still mind-blowing, the Baptistery's art seems relatively conservative compared to Giotto's Scrovegni Chapel. Giotto, supported by the powerful Scrovegni family and the Franciscans, could get away with being more progressive and bold.

▲▲▲SCROVEGNI CHAPEL AND CIVIC MUSEUMS

Wallpapered with Giotto's beautifully preserved cycle of nearly 40 frescoes, the glorious, renovated Scrovegni Chapel holds scenes depicting the lives of Jesus and Mary. You must make reservations in advance to see the chapel. Scrovegni Chapel tickets also cover the Civic Museums, featuring the worthwhile Pinacoteca and Multimedia Room, as well as the skippable Archaeological Museum and the little-visited Palazzo Zuckermann.

Cost: The €13 ticket covers the Scrovegni Chapel and Civic Museums. It's €10 for just the museums.

Hours: The **chapel** is open daily 9:00-19:00; tel. 049-201-0020, www.cappelladegliscrovegni.it. The **Multimedia Room** has the same hours, as do the **Pinacoteca** and **Archaeological Museum**, except they are closed Mon;

Giotto di Bondone (c. 1267-1337)

Although details of his life are extremely sketchy, we know that the 12-year-old shepherd Giotto was discovered painting pictures of his father's sheep on rock slabs. He grew to become the wealthiest and most famous painter of his day. His achievement is especially remarkable because painters at that time weren't considered anything more than craftsmen—and weren't expected to be innovators.

After making a name for himself by painting frescoes of the life of St. Francis in Assisi, the Florentine tackled the Scrovegni Chapel (c. 1303-1305). At age 35, he was at the height of his powers. His scenes were more realistic and human than anything that had been done for a thousand years. Giotto didn't learn technique by dissecting corpses or studying the mathematics of 3-D perspective; he had innate talent. And his personality shines through in the humanity of his art.

The Scrovegni frescoes break ground by introducing nature—rocks, trees, animals—as a backdrop for religious scenes. Giotto's people, with their voluminous, deeply creased robes, are as sturdy and massive as Greek statues, throwbacks to the Byzantine icon art of the Middle Ages. But these figures exude stage presence. Their gestures are simple but expressive: A head tilted down says dejection, an arm flung out indicates grief, clasped hands indicate hope. Giotto created his figures not just by drawing outlines and filling them in with single colors; he filled the outlines in with subtle patchworks of lighter and darker shades, and in doing so pioneered modern modeling techniques. Giotto's storytelling style is straightforward, and anyone with knowledge of the episodes of Jesus' life can read the chapel like a comic book.

The Scrovegni represents a turning point in European art and culture—away from scenes of heaven and toward a more down-to-earth, human-centered view.

Palazzo Zuckermann is open Tue-Sun 10:00-19:00, closed Mon; museums tel. 049-820-4551, palazzo tel. 049-820-5664.

Chapel Entry Times: To protect the paintings from excess humidity, only 25 people are allowed in the chapel at a time. Every 15 minutes (on the quarter-hour), a new group is admitted for a 15-minute video presentation in an anteroom, followed by 15 minutes in the chapel itself. In the evening, visitors can pay €12 (plus

€1 reservation fee) to stay inside for a double period (40 minutes)—reservation must be made by phone.

Reservations: Prepaid reservations are required. It's wise to reserve at least two days in advance and easiest to do online at www.cappelladegliscrovegni.it. (If you'll be staying overnight in Padua or parking a car, consider paying the €3 extra for a Padova Card—described on page 320.) You can also reserve by phone (tel. 049-201-0020).

Without a reservation, it's sometimes possible to buy a same-day ticket (especially for single visitors), but don't count on it. Drop by the ticket office and see if anything is available (you might see a Post-it note stuck to the desk indicating the next available entry time). Tickets for daytime visits are generally released at 9:00; showing up early will increase your chances of getting a slot (likely for later in the day). You can't book next-day reservations in person—only online or by phone. You might also see local tour guides, who have to book blocks of tickets, trying to unload unneeded tickets.

Helpful Hint: If you packed binoculars, bring them along for a better—and more comfortable—view of the uppermost frescoes. No photos are allowed.

Getting There: From the train station, it's a 10- to 15-minute walk, or a quick, two-stop tram ride to the Eremitani stop.

Getting In: To reach the chapel, enter through the Eremitani building, where you'll find the museums, ticket office, and a free but mandatory bag check. Though you're instructed to pick up your tickets at the ticket office at least one hour before your visit, in practice, I've found that 30 minutes is enough to weather any commotion at the desk. Present your confirmation number at the ticket desk, verify your time, pick up your ticket, and check any bags or purses.

While waiting for your reserved time, blitz the Pinacoteca and Multimedia Room (described later). Read the chapel description before you enter, since you'll only have a short time in the chapel itself.

The chapel is well-signed: From the ticket office, go outside and walk 100 yards down the path, passing some ruins of Roman Padua (described later). Be at the chapel doors at least five minutes before your scheduled visit. The doors are automatic, and if you're even a minute late, you'll forfeit your visit and have to rebook and repay to enter.

At your appointed time, you first enter an anteroom to watch

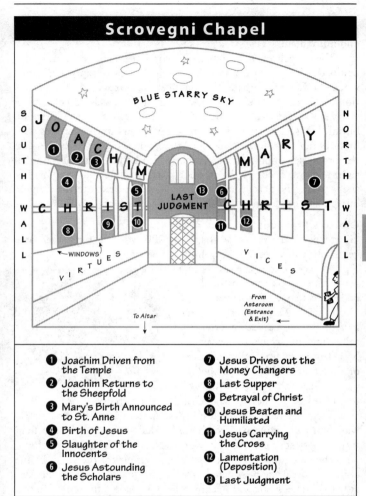

Scrovegni Chapel

BLUE STARRY SKY

SOUTH WALL

NORTH WALL

JOACHIM
MARY
CHRIST
CHRIST

LAST JUDGMENT

WINDOWS

VIRTUES

VICES

To Altar

From Anteroom (Entrance & Exit)

PADUA

1 Joachim Driven from the Temple
2 Joachim Returns to the Sheepfold
3 Mary's Birth Announced to St. Anne
4 Birth of Jesus
5 Slaughter of the Innocents
6 Jesus Astounding the Scholars

7 Jesus Drives out the Money Changers
8 Last Supper
9 Betrayal of Christ
10 Jesus Beaten and Humiliated
11 Jesus Carrying the Cross
12 Lamentation (Deposition)
13 Last Judgment

a very instructive 15-minute video (with English subtitles) and to establish humidity levels before continuing into the chapel. Although you have only a short visit inside the chapel, it is divine. You're inside a Giotto time capsule, looking back at an artist ahead of his time.

Scrovegni Chapel (Cappella degli Scrovegni)

Painted by Giotto and his assistants from 1303 to 1305 and considered by many to be the first piece of modern art, this work makes it clear: Europe was breaking out of the Middle Ages. A sign of the Renaissance to come, Giotto placed real people in real scenes, expressing real human emotions. These frescoes were radical for their 3-D nature, lively colors, light sources, emotion, and humanism.

The chapel was built out of guilt for white-collar crimes. Reginaldo degli Scrovegni charged sky-high interest rates at a time when the Church forbade the practice. He even caught the attention of Dante, who placed him in one of the levels of hell in his *Inferno.* When Reginaldo died, the Church denied him a Christian burial. His son Enrico tried to buy forgiveness for his father's sins by building this superb chapel. After seeing Giotto's frescoes for the Franciscan monks of St. Anthony, Enrico knew he'd found the right artist to decorate the interior (and, he hoped, to save his father's soul). The Scrovegni residence once stood next to the chapel, but it was torn down in 1824.

Giotto's Frescoes

Giotto painted the entire chapel in 200 working days over two years, but you'll get only 15 minutes to see it.

As you enter the long, narrow chapel, look straight to the far end—the rear wall is covered with Giotto's big *Last Judgment.* Christ in a bubble is flanked by crowds of saints and by scenes of heaven and hell. This is the final, climactic scene of the story told in the chapel's 38 panels—the three-generation history of Jesus, his mother Mary, and Mary's parents.

The story begins with Jesus' grandparents, on the long south wall (with the windows) in the upper-left corner. ❶ In the first frame, a priest scolds the man who will be Mary's father (Joachim, with the halo) and kicks him out of the temple for the sin of being childless. ❷ In the next panel to the right, Joachim returns dejectedly to his sheep farm. ❸ Meanwhile (next panel), his wife is in the bedroom, hearing the miraculous news that their prayers have been answered—she'll give birth to Mary, the mother of Jesus.

From this humble start, the story of Mary and Jesus spirals clockwise around the chapel, from top to bottom. The top row (both south and north walls) covers Mary's birth and life.

Jesus enters the picture in the middle row of the south (windowed) wall. ❹ The first frame shows his birth in a shedlike manger. In the next frame, the Magi arrive and kneel to kiss his little toes. Then the child is presented in the tiny temple. Fearing danger, the family gets on a horse and flees to Egypt. ❺ Meanwhile, back home, all the baby boys are slaughtered in an attempt to prevent the coming of the Messiah *(Slaughter of the Innocents)*.

Spinning clockwise to the opposite (north) wall, you see (in a badly damaged fresco) ❻ the child Jesus astounding scholars with his wisdom. Next, Jesus is baptized by John the Baptist. His first miracle, at a wedding, is turning jars of water into wine. Next, he raises a mummy-like Lazarus from the dead. Riding a donkey, he enters Jerusalem triumphantly. ❼ In the temple, he drives out the wicked money changers.

Turning again to the south wall (bottom row), we see scenes from Jesus' final days. ❽ In the first frame, he and his followers gather at a table for a Last Supper. Next, Jesus kneels humbly to wash their feet. ❾ He is betrayed with a kiss and arrested. Jesus is tried. ❿ Then he is beaten and humiliated.

PADUA

⓫ Finally (north wall, bottom row), he is forced to carry his own cross, crucified, and prepared for burial, while his followers mourn (⓬ *Lamentation*). Then he is resurrected and ascends to heaven, leaving his disciples to carry on.

⓭ The whole story concludes on the rear wall, where Jesus reigns at the Last Judgment. The long south wall (ground level) features the Virtues that lead to heaven, while the north wall has the (always more interesting) Vices. And all this unfolds beneath the blue, starry sky overhead on the ceiling.

Some panels deserve a closer look:

Joachim Returns to the Sheepfold (south wall, upper left, second panel): Though difficult to appreciate from ground level, this oft-reproduced scene is groundbreaking. Giotto—a former shepherd himself—uses nature as a stage, setting the scene in front of a backdrop of real-life mountains and adding down-home details like Joachim's jumping dog, frozen in midair.

Betrayal of Christ, a.k.a. *Il Bacio*, "The Kiss" (south wall, bottom row, center panel): Amid the crowded chaos of Jesus' arrest, Giotto skillfully creates a focus upon the central action, where Judas ensnares Jesus in his yellow robe (the color symbolizing envy), establishes meaningful eye contact, and kisses him.

Lamentation, a.k.a. *Deposition* (north wall, bottom row, middle): Jesus has been crucified, and his followers weep and wail over the lifeless body. John the Evangelist spreads his arms wide and shrieks, his cries echoed by anguished angels above. Each face is a study in grief. Giotto emphasizes these saints' human vulnerability.

Last Judgment (big west wall): Christ in the center is a glorious vision, but the real action is in hell (lower right). Satan is a Minotaur-headed ogre munching on sinners. Around him, demons give sinners their just desserts in a scene right out of Dante... who was Giotto's friend and fellow Florentine. Front and center is Enrico Scrovegni, in a violet robe (the color symbolizing penitence), donating the chapel to the Church in exchange for forgiveness of his father's sins.

Before the guard scoots you out, take a look at the actual altar. Though Enrico's father's tomb is lost, Enrico Scrovegni himself is in the tomb at the altar. The three statues are by Giovanni Pisano—Mary (in the center) supports Baby Jesus on her hip with a perfectly natural, maternal, S-shape. She's flanked by anonymous deacons.

Nearby: Between the museum and the chapel are the scant remains of **Roman Padua.** The remnants are from the wall of an arena and also include nicely fitting pipes that once channeled water so that the arena could be flooded for special spectacles.

Civic Museums (Musei Civici agli Eremitani)

The Eremitani, the building next to the Scrovegni Chapel, was once an Augustinian hermit's monastery and now houses several museums. While you can skip the ground-floor Archaeological Museum (with Roman and Etruscan artifacts and no English descriptions), the Pinacoteca and the Multimedia Room are worth visiting. Another part of the museum, Palazzo Zuckermann, is across the street.

Pinacoteca

The museum's highlight is upstairs, in the Pinacoteca (picture gallery). The collection has 13th- to 18th-century paintings by Titian, Tintoretto, Giorgione, Tiepolo, Veronese, Bellini, Canova, Guariento, and other Veneto artists. But I'd make a beeline for the room with the Giotto crucifix (upstairs and to the right, through the upper gallery). Ask for *"La Croce di Giotto?"* (lah KROH-cheh dee JOH-toh?)

The remarkable crucifix, painted by Giotto on wood, originally hung in the Scrovegni Chapel between the Scrovegni family's private zone and the public's worshiping zone. If you actually sit on the floor and look up, the body really pops. The adjacent "God as Jesus" piece *(L'Eterno)* was the only painting in the otherwise frescoed chapel. (The original hangs here for conservation purposes; its copy is the only nonoriginal art in the chapel.) Studying these two masterpieces affirms Giotto's greatness.

Behind the crucifix room is a collection of 14th- and 15th-century art. While the works here are exquisite—and came well after Giotto—they're clearly not as modern.

Multimedia Room

Dedicated to taking a closer look at the Scrovegni Chapel, this small but interesting exhibit is downstairs. To head straight from the museum entrance to the Multimedia Room, use the entrance to the right of the main entry, step into the courtyard, make a sharp right, go through the glass doors at the end of the corridor, and head down the stairs.

Rows of computer screens offer a virtual Scrovegni Chapel visit and provide cultural insights into daily life in the Middle Ages. There are explanations of the individual panels, Giotto's fresco technique, close-ups of the art, and a description of the restoration. You'll also see a life-size re-creation of the house of Mary's mother, St. Anne, as depicted in Giotto's fresco. A 12-minute video (English headphones available) tells the history of the chapel and is similar—but not identical—to the one that precedes your chapel visit. For me, it's worth just taking some time to enjoy a second video that features a mesmerizing, slow montage of close-ups of the Giotto frescoes.

Palazzo Zuckermann

This overlooked wing of the Civic Museum is just across a busy street. Its first two floors offer a commotion of applied and decorative arts—clothes, furniture, and ceramics—from the Venetian Republic (1600s-1700s). On the top floor, the Bottacin collection takes you to the 19th century with coins and delightful (but no-name) pre-Impressionist paintings.

▲▲▲BASILICA OF ST. ANTHONY

Friar Anthony of Padua, "Christ's perfect follower and a tireless preacher of the Gospel," is buried here. Construction of this impressive Romanesque/ Gothic church (with its Byzantine-style domes) started immediately after St. Anthony's death in 1231. As a mark of his universal appeal and importance in the medieval Church, he was sainted within a year of his death. Speedy.

St. Anthony of Padua (1195-1231)

One of Christendom's most popular saints, Anthony is known as a powerful speaker, a miracle worker, and the finder of lost articles.

Born in Lisbon to a rich, well-educated family, his life changed at 25, when he saw the mutilated bodies of some Franciscan martyrs. Their sacrifice inspired him to join the poor Franciscans and dedicate his life to Christ. He moved to Italy and lived in a cave, studying, meditating, and barely speaking to anyone.

One day, he joined his fellow monks for a service. The appointed speaker failed to show up, so Anthony was asked to say a few off-the-cuff words to the crowd. He started slowly, but, filled with the Spirit, he became more confident and amazed the audience with his eloquence. Up in Assisi, St. Francis heard about Anthony and sent him on a whirlwind speaking tour.

Anthony had a strong voice, knew several languages, had an encyclopedic knowledge of theology, and could speak spontaneously as the Spirit moved him. It's said that he even stood on the shores of the Adriatic Sea in Rimini and enticed a school of fish to listen. Anthony also was known as a prolific miracle worker.

In 1230, Anthony retired to Padua, where he founded a monastery and initiated reforms for the poor. An illness cut his life short at 36. Anthony said, "Happy is the man whose words issue from the Spirit and not from himself!"

And for nearly 800 years, his remains and this glorious church have attracted pilgrims to Padua.

Cost and Hours: The **basilica** is free and open daily 6:20-19:45 (Nov-March Mon-Fri closes at 18:45). The various sights within the basilica have slightly different hours: The important **Chapel of the Reliquaries** (free) keeps the basilica's hours but closes for lunch (12:45-14:30). Other, less important sights include a **museum** (€2.50, Tue-Fri 9:00-13:00, Sat-Sun 9:00-13:00 & 14:00-18:00, closed Mon), a **multimedia exhibit** (free, daily 9:00-12:30 & 14:00-17:30), and the **Oratory of St. George** and **Scuola del Santo** (€3 apiece or €5 together, 9:00-12:30 & 14:30-18:00, Nov-March closes at 17:00). The nearest tram stop is Santo.

Dress Code: A modest dress code is enforced.

Information: Look for the information desk at the southern entrance to the cloisters (near the basilica entry), where you can pick up a free pamphlet on the saint's life and the basilica; make a donation in the Chapel of the Reliquaries to get a more detailed booklet. Tel. 049-822-5652, www.basilicadelsanto.org.

Church Services: The church hosts six separate Masses each

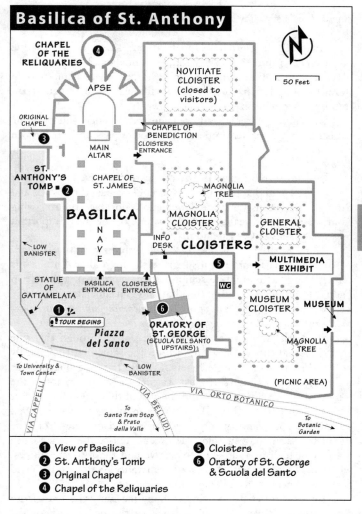

Basilica of St. Anthony

CHAPEL OF THE RELIQUARIES
4
APSE

NOVITIATE CLOISTER
(closed to visitors)

50 Feet

ORIGINAL CHAPEL
3

CHAPEL OF BENEDICTION
CLOISTERS ENTRANCE

MAIN ALTAR

ST. ANTHONY'S TOMB
2

CHAPEL OF ST. JAMES

MAGNOLIA TREE

MAGNOLIA CLOISTER

GENERAL CLOISTER

BASILICA

N A V E

LOW BANISTER

INFO DESK

CLOISTERS

MULTIMEDIA EXHIBIT

5

STATUE OF GATTAMELATA

BASILICA ENTRANCE

CLOISTERS ENTRANCE

WC

MUSEUM CLOISTER

MUSEUM

1
TOUR BEGINS

6

Piazza del Santo

ORATORY OF ST. GEORGE
(SCUOLA DEL SANTO UPSTAIRS)

MAGNOLIA TREE

To University & Town Center

LOW BANISTER

(PICNIC AREA)

VIA CAPPELLI

VIA BELLUDI

VIA ORTO BOTANICO

To Santo Tram Stop & Prato della Valle

To Botanic Garden

PADUA

1 View of Basilica
2 St. Anthony's Tomb
3 Original Chapel
4 Chapel of the Reliquaries

5 Cloisters
6 Oratory of St. George & Scuola del Santo

---

morning (the last at 11:00), as well as at 17:00 and 18:00 in summer and on Sunday year-round, plus additional Sunday services at 12:15, 16:00, and 19:00.

Services: WCs and a picnic area are inside the cloisters.

○ Self-Guided Tour: Before heading inside, take a look at the basilica's red-brick facade. St. Anthony looks down and blesses all. He holds a book, a symbol of all the knowledge he had accumulated as a quiet monk before starting his preaching career.

A golden angel—the weathervane atop the spire—points her trumpet into the wind. (While you can never really be sure with angels, locals say they know it's a woman because she always tells the truth.)

Guarding the church is Donatello's life-size equestrian statue of the Venetian mercenary general, Gattamelata. Though it looks like a thousand other man-on-a-horse statues, it was a landmark in Italy's budding Renaissance—the first life-size, secular, equestrian statue cast from bronze in a thousand years.

The church is technically outside Italy. When you pass the banisters that mark its property line, you're passing into Vatican territory.

• *Enter the basilica.*

Interior: Grab a pew in the center of the nave and let your eyes adjust. Sit and appreciate the space. Gaze past the crowds and through the incense haze to Donatello's glorious crucifix rising from the altar, and realize that this is one of the most important pilgrimage sites in Christendom.

Along with the crucifix, Donatello's bronze statues—Mary with Padua's six favorite saints—grace the high altar. Late in his career, the great Florentine sculptor spent more than a decade in Padua (1444-1455), creating the altar and Gattamelata.

• *Head to the left side of the nave to find the gleaming marble masterpiece that is the focus of the visiting pilgrims—the tomb of St. Anthony.*

St. Anthony's Tomb: Pilgrims file slowly through this side chapel around the tomb, so focused on the saint that they hardly notice the nine fine marble reliefs. (While the long queue looks intimidating, these folks are just waiting their turn to touch the tomb; you can easily skirt around the side of this group for a closer look at each panel.) These Renaissance masterpieces were carved during the 16th century and show scenes and miracles from the life of the saint. As you enjoy each scene, notice the Renaissance mastery of realism and 3-D perspective and the intricate frames, which celebrate life with a burst of exuberance. Note also the vivid faces with their powerful emotions.

The **first relief** depicts St. Anthony receiving the Franciscan tunic. The architectural setting (such as the perspective of the arches on the left and the open door) illustrates the new ability to show depth by using mathematics. The cityscape above is Padua in about 1500.

In the **second relief,** a jealous husband has angrily stabbed his wife. Notice the musculature, the emotion, and the determination in the faces of loved ones. Above, Anthony intercedes with God to bring the woman back to life.

The **third panel** shows Anthony bringing a young man back to life. Above is the Palazzo della Ragione looking as it still does today.

The **fourth scene,** by the famous Florentine sculptor Jacopo

Sansovino, shows three generations: a dead girl, her distraught mom, and a grandmother who's seen it all. A boy on the right realistically leans on his stick. Of course, Anthony will eventually change the mood, but right now it's pretty dire. Above is a relief of this basilica.

In the **fifth relief,** a fisherman holds a net, sadly having retrieved a drowned boy. The mother looks at Anthony, who blesses and revives the boy. Across from here is the saint's actual tomb. Under thoughtful lighting, it reads *Corpus S. Antonii.* Prayer letters are dropped behind the iron grill.

The **sixth relief** shows "the miracle of the miser's heart." Anthony's helper dips his hand into a moneylender's side to demonstrate the absence of his heart. At his foot, the square tray with coins and a heart illustrates the scriptural verse "for where your treasure is, there your heart will be also."

For the **seventh relief,** Anthony holds the foot of a young man who confessed to kicking his mother. Taking a lesson from the saint about respecting your mother a little too literally, the man had cut off his own foot. The hysterical mother implores Anthony's help, and the saint's prayers to God enabled him to reattach the foot.

Stand in the corner for a moment, observing the passionate devotion that pilgrims and Paduans alike have for Anthony. Touching his tomb or kneeling in prayer, the faithful believe Anthony is their protector—a confidant and intercessor for the poor. And they believe he works miracles. Believers leave offerings, votives, and written prayers to ask for help or to give thanks for miracles they believe Anthony has performed. By putting their hands on his tomb while saying silent prayers, pilgrims show devotion to Anthony and feel the saint's presence.

Popular Anthony is the patron saint of dozens of things: travelers, amputees, donkeys, pregnant women, infertile women, and flight attendants. Most pilgrims ask for his help in his role as the "finder of things"—from lost car keys to a life companion. You'll see dozens of photos posted on his tomb in prayer or as thanks, including many of fervently wished-for newborns.

The **eighth scene** makes the point that—unlike St. Francis, who was a rowdy youth—Anthony was holy even as a toddler. He tosses the glass (representing his faith), which, rather than shattering, breaks the marble floor.

In the **ninth relief,** a jealous husband (the bearded man behind Anthony) accuses his wife of cheating. The wife asks Anthony to identify her baby's father. Anthony asks the child, who speaks and says that the husband is his real dad and his mother was not messing around. Everyone is relieved—whew!

PADUA

Before leaving, pause to appreciate how the entire chapel is an integrated artistic wonder.

• *Leave the chapel (between scenes eight and nine) and step into the oldest part of the church. This is the...*

Original Chapel: This is where Anthony was first buried in 1231. To the left of the altar, note the fine (and impressively realistic for the 14th century) view of medieval Padua, with this church outside the wall (finished by 1300 and looking like it does today). Below the cityscape, in a circa-1380 fresco, Anthony on his cloud promises he'll watch over Padua.

As you exit this chapel, you'll notice many tombs nearby. People wanted to be buried near a saint. If you could afford it, this was about the best piece of real estate a dead person could want. (The practice was ended with Napoleonic reforms in 1806.)

• *Continue your circuit of the church by going behind the altar into the apse, to the Chapel of the Reliquaries. (At busy times, you may have to line up and trudge slowly up the stairs past the reliquaries.)*

Chapel of the Reliquaries

The most prized relic is in the glass case at center stage—Anthony's tongue. When Anthony's remains were exhumed 32 years after his death (in 1263), his body had decayed to dust, but his tongue was found miraculously unspoiled and red in color. How appropriate for the great preacher who, full of the Spirit, couldn't stop talking about God.

Entering the chapel, join the parade of pilgrims working their way clockwise around the chapel and up the stairs. First, on the left, look for the red, triangular vestment in which Anthony's body was wrapped. Next is his rough-hewn wood coffin. Then, up the stairs, is his pillow—a comfy rock (chest level in first glass case). The center display case contains (top to bottom) the saint's lower jaw with all his teeth impressively intact *(il mento,* located about 8 feet high), his uncorrupted tongue *(lingua,* at about eye level), and, finally, his vocal chords *(apparato vocale,* at about waist level) discovered intact when his remains were examined in 1981. In the last display case, a fragment of the True Cross *(la croce)* is held in a precious cross-shaped reliquary. Finally, descend the stairs and pass St. Anthony's holy, and holey, tunic *(tonaca).*

Above the relics, decorating the cornice, is the *Glorification of St. Anthony.* In this Baroque fantasy—made in 1691 of carved marble and stucco—a cloud of angels and giddy putti tumble to the left and right in jubilation as they play their Baroque-era musical instruments to celebrate Anthony's arrival in heaven.

• *Leaving this relic chapel, continue circling the apse. You'll come to the* **Chapel of Benediction.** *Here, under a powerful modern fresco of the*

Crucifixion (by Pietro Annigoni, who died in 1982), a priest is waiting to bless anyone who cares to be blessed.

Next, past the sacristy (where you can peek in at priests preparing for Mass), is a door leading to the cloisters. But before heading out, walk just beyond this passage to the...

Chapel of St. James

Exactly opposite the tomb of St. Anthony, this chapel features an exquisite 14th-century fresco by Altichiero da Zevio. Study the vivid commotion around the Crucifixion, clearly inspired by Giotto (this was created 70 years after the Scrovegni Chapel). The faces are real—right off the streets of 14th-century Padua.

• *Next, head out into the cloisters. From the right side of the nave as you face the altar, follow signs to* chiostro; *from outside, find signs on the right side of the church.*

Cloisters

The main cloister is dominated by an exceptionally bushy magnolia tree, planted in 1810 (the magnolia tree was exotic for Europe

when it was imported from America in 1760). Also in the cloister are the graves of the most illustrious Paduans, such as Gabriel Fallopius, the scientist who gave his name to his discovery, the Fallopian tube. When Napoleon decreed that graves should be moved out of cities, this once grave-covered courtyard was cleared of tombstones. But the bodies were left in the ground, perhaps contributing to the magnolia tree's fecundity. Today the tree remains an explosion of life.

Of the four cloisters here, you can wander in three. In one, picnic tables invite pilgrims and tourists to enjoy meals (it's covered and suitable even when rainy, also has WCs).

The **multimedia exhibit** on the life of St. Anthony is kitschy, as pilgrimage multimedia exhibits tend to be (30 minutes, free, you move three times as you use headphones to listen to the story of each tableau).

At the far end, a fascinating little **museum** is filled with votives and folk art recounting miracles attributed to Anthony. The abbreviation *PGR* that you'll see on many votives stands for *per grazia ricevuta*—for answered prayers.

Oratory of St. George and Scuola del Santo

The small but sumptuous **Oratory of St. George** faces the little square in front of the basilica. The oratory ("ora" means prayer) is not actually a church, though it's certainly a fine place to pray—it's

PADUA

344 Rick Steves Venice

filled with vivid, circa-1370 frescoes showing scenes not of Anthony but from the life of St. Catherine. Because many lovers credit St. Anthony with finding them their partners—and this is the closest place to St. Anthony where you can be married—it's popular for weddings. While you can see it all from the door, paying the entry fee lets you sit and enjoy this peaceful spot.

Next door and upstairs (buy ticket and get info sheet in the oratory) is the skippable **Scuola del Santo** (a.k.a. La Scoletta), the former meeting hall of the Confraternity of Anthony, with frescoes and paintings by various artists—including some by Titian.

NEAR THE BASILICA
Prato della Valle

The square is 150 yards southwest of the basilica (down Via Luca Belludi). Once a Roman theater and later Anthony's preaching grounds, this square claims to be the largest in Italy. It's a pleasant, 400-yard-long, oval-shaped piazza with fountains, walkways, dozens of statues of Padua's eminent citizens, and grass. It's also a lively **market** scene (though smaller than those previously listed): fruit and vegetables (Mon-Fri 8:00-13:00), clothing, shoes, and household goods (Sat 8:00-19:00), and antiques (third Sun 8:00-19:00). This place is often busy with special events and festivals. Ask at the TI or your hotel if anything's going on at Prato della Valle.

Botanic Garden (Orto Botanico)

Green thumbs appreciate this nearly five-acre botanical garden, which contains the university's vast collection of rare plants. Founded in 1545 to cultivate medicinal plants, it's the world's oldest academic botanical garden still in its original location. A visitors center—in a little cottage to the right of the garden's entrance—houses models of the garden's layout and computer terminals that describe the history and composition of the garden.

Cost and Hours: €10; daily 9:00-19:00, closes earlier off-season; last entry one hour before closing; entrance 150 yards south of Basilica of St. Anthony—with your back to the facade, take a hard left; Santo tram stop, tel. 049-201-0222, www.ortobotanicopd.it.

Sleeping in Padua

Rooms in Padua's hotels are more spacious and a better value than those in Venice. I've listed two hotels in the center and a group of accommodations near the basilica. All are reachable from the station by tram; only Albergo Verdi is more than a five-minute walk from the nearest tram stop.

IN THE CENTER

$$ Hotel Majestic Toscanelli, an old-fashioned, borderline-gaudy, family-run, 34-room hotel, owns a perfectly convenient location right in the town center—buried in the characteristic ghetto with wonderful cobbled ambience. At night, this area is popular with noisy students; request a quiet room on the back side (RS%, spacious attic "loft" rooms with kitchenettes and low beams, air-con, elevator, pay parking, Via dell'Arco 2, Tito Livio tram stop, tel. 049-663-244, www.toscanelli.com, majestic@toscanelli.com, Mario Morosi and family). From the tram stop, follow the passageway next to #26, then jog left down Via Marsala and turn right on Via dell'Arco.

$$ Albergo Verdi, an Ikea-mod little place, is crammed into an old building on a small back street beyond Piazza dei Signori. While public spaces are tight, the 14 rooms are comfortable (air-con, tiny elevator, Via Dondi dall'Orologio 7, Ponti Romani tram stop, tel. 049-836-4163, www.albergoverdipadova.it, info@albergoverdipadova.it). From Piazza dei Signori, walk through the arch under the clock tower and go to the far end of Piazza del Capitaniato; the hotel is on the side street to your right.

NEAR THE BASILICA OF ST. ANTHONY

Santo is the nearest tram stop for the following hotels. Use the Prato della Valle tram stop for the hostel.

$$$ Hotel Belludi 37 is a slick, stylish, almost pretentious place renting 16 modern rooms shoehorned into an old building. The decor is dark, woody, and fresh (RS%, some rooms with basilica view, air-con, lots of stairs with no elevator, apartments available nearby, a block from the Santo tram stop at Via Beato Luca Belludi 37, tel. 049-665-633, www.belludi37.it, info@belludi37.it).

$$ Hotel Al Fagiano feels like an art gallery with crazy, sexy, modern art everywhere. The hotel is all about the union of a man and a woman (quite romantic). They rent 37 bright and cheery rooms, each uniquely decorated with Rossella Fagiano's canvases (RS%, air-con, elevator, pay parking, 50 yards from the Santo tram stop at Via Locatelli 45, tel. 049-875-0073, www.alfagiano.com, info@alfagiano.com; Anita, artist Rossella, and husband Amato).

$ Hotel Al Santo, run with charm by Valentina and Antonio,

Sleep Code

Hotels are classified based on the average price of a standard double room with breakfast in high season.

$$$$	**Splurge:**	Most rooms over €170
$$$	**Pricier:**	€130-170
$$	**Moderate:**	€90-130
$	**Budget:**	€50-90
¢	**Backpacker:**	Under €50
RS%	**Rick Steves discount**	

Unless otherwise noted, credit cards are accepted, hotel staff speak basic English, and free Wi-Fi is available. Comparison-shop by checking prices at several hotels (on each hotel's own website, on a booking site, or by email). For the best deal, *book direct with the hotel.* Ask for a discount if paying in cash; if the listing includes **RS%**, request a Rick Steves discount.

offers 15 spacious rooms with all the comforts on two floors above their restaurant, a few steps from the basilica. Given the warm welcome and pleasant location, it's a fine value (family rooms, double-paned windows, quieter rooms off street, some rooms with basilica views, air-con, elevator, pay parking, Via del Santo 147, tel. 049-875-2131, www.alsanto.it, alsanto@alsanto.it).

$ Hotel Casa del Pellegrino, with 148 spotless, cheap, bare rooms and straight pricing, is owned by the friars of St. Anthony. It's home to the pilgrims who come to pay homage to the saint in the basilica next door. Any visitor to Padua is welcome, making it popular with professors and students. Some rooms with basilica views also come with more noise—both from the street and, starting at 6:00 in the morning, the church bells—while others are in *dipendenza,* the hotel's modern wing (cheaper rooms with shared bath, family rooms, ask for a room off the street, breakfast extra, air-con, elevator, pay parking, Via Melchiorre Cesarotti 21, tel. 049-823-9711, www.casadelpellegrino.com, info@casadelpellegrino.com).

Hostel: **¢ Ostello Città di Padova,** near Prato della Valle, is well-run and has 90 beds (private rooms available, includes breakfast, reception open 7:30-9:30 & 15:30-23:00, 23:30 curfew unless you get a key, Via Aleardo Aleardi 30, Prato de Valle tram stop, tel. 049-875-2219, www.ostellopadova.it, ostellopadova@gmail.com). From the tram stop, exit the square ahead of you to the right and make an immediate left down Via Memmo; after the church, continue straight one block on Via Torresini and turn right on Via Aleardi.

Eating in Padua

The university population means cheap, good food abounds. My recommended restaurants are all centrally located in the historic core. You'd think there would be fine dining on the charming market squares, but on the piazzas it's a takeout-pizza and casual-bar scene (dominated by students after dark). La Lanterna, at the neighboring Piazza dei Signori, is the best on-square option—but they only offer functional Italian classics. The dreamily atmospheric ghetto neighborhood (just two blocks off the market squares) thrives after dark with trendy bars and a lively student *spritz* scene.

DINING NEAR THE CENTER

$$ Osteria dei Fabbri, with shared rustic tables, offers a good mix of class and accessibility, quality, and price. The dining room is spacious, and the dishes are traditional Venetian and Paduan. Ask to peek into their back courtyard, where you can see the door of an old synagogue (daily 12:30-14:30 & 19:00-22:30, but closed Sun for dinner, Via dei Fabbri 13, on a side street on south side of Piazza Erbe, tel. 049-650-336).

$$ Osteria L'Anfora is a classic place serving classic dishes in an informal, fun-loving space. Don't be put off by the woody, ruffian decor, the squat toilet, and the fact that it's a popular hangout for a premeal drink. They take food seriously and serve it at good prices, and the energy and commotion add to a great dining experience (meals served Mon-Sat 12:30-15:00 & 19:30-22:30, bar open 9:00-24:00, closed Sun, reservations smart for dinner, Via dei Soncin 13, tel. 049-656-629).

$ Enoteca dei Tadi is a small, quirky place with seven tables filling a cozy back room behind a convivial little bar (avoid their basement). Roberto and Anna serve traditional Paduan dishes and have earned a local following for their small but tasty menu. The selection is driven by what's fresh and in season, and they offer good wines by the glass (Tue-Sun 18:30-24:00, closed Mon, Via dei Tadi 16, tel. 049-836-4099, mobile 338-408-3434).

$$$ Ristorante Dante alle Piazze is a respected fixture in town for its dressy white-tablecloth dining. They are passionate about their meat and fish dishes. Reservations are smart at night (Wed-Sat and Mon 12:00-14:30 & 18:15-22:00, Sun 12:00-14:30, closed Tue, Via Daniele Manin 8, tel. 049-836-0973, www. dadanteallepiazze.com).

CHEAP EATS NEAR THE CENTER

Affordable Meals on Piazza dei Signori: **$$ La Lanterna** has a forgettable interior and a predictable menu of pizzas, pastas, and *secondi.* But its prime location on Piazza dei Signori provides a rare-

Restaurant Price Code

I've assigned each eatery a price category, based on the average cost of a typical main course (pasta or *secondi*). Drinks, desserts, and splurge items (steak and seafood) can raise the price considerably.

$$$$	**Splurge:** Most main courses over €20
$$$	**Pricier:** €15-20
$$	**Moderate:** €10-15
$	**Budget:** Under €10

In Italy, pizza by the slice and other takeout food is **$**; a basic trattoria or sit-down pizzeria is **$$**; a casual but more upscale restaurant is **$$$**; and a swanky splurge is **$$$$**.

in-Padua chance to sit in a grand square under the stars, surrounded by great architecture (reservations recommended). Its pizzas are a local favorite—takeaway available (Fri-Wed 12:00-15:00 & 18:00-24:00, closed Thu, Piazza dei Signori 39, tel. 049-660-770, www.lalanternapadova.it).

Light Meals on Piazza della Frutta: **$ Bar dei Osei,** on Piazza della Frutta, is a very simple sandwich bar with some of the best outdoor seats in town. While Paduans love their delicate *tramezzini*—white-bread sandwiches with crusts cut off, I'd choose their *porchetta*—savory roasted pork sandwiches. You'll find a two-footlong mother lode waiting on the counter for you; tell friendly Marco how big a slice you'd like. Wines are listed on the board (Mon-Sat 7:00-21:00, closed Sun, Piazza della Frutta 1, tel. 049-875-9606). In the evenings, just a few feet away, a **snack stand** selling all kinds of fresh, hot, and ready-to-eat seafood appetizers sets up between 17:00 and 20:30 (daily except Sun). Belly up to the bar with your drink and try whatever Massimiliano's serving.

Fast Food: **$ Brek,** with one entrance next to the Ponti Romani tram stop and another tucked into a corner of Piazza Cavour at #20, is an easy self-service chain *ristorante* with healthy and affordable choices. It's big, bright, practical, and family-friendly (daily 11:30-15:00 & 18:30-22:00, tel. 049-875-3788). **$ Brek Foccacceria** (part of the same chain), across from Caffè Pedrocchi and next door to the PAM supermarket, is a café selling big sandwiches and slices of pizza that you can eat at outdoor tables. During happy hour (18:30-21:00), you can buy a drink and pay €1.50 more to fill a plate at their *antipasti* buffet, which can easily turn into a light dinner (open daily 9:00-21:00, Piazzetta della Garzeria 6, tel. 049-876-1651).

Groceries: Stock up on picnic items at the outdoor markets, or visit the **PAM supermarket,** in the tiny *piazzetta* east of Caffè

Pedrocchi (Mon-Sat 8:00-21:00, Sun 9:00-20:00, Piazzetta Garzeria 3).

NEAR THE BASILICA OF ST. ANTHONY

$$ Antica Trattoria dei Paccagnella, the most serious restaurant near the basilica, serves up nicely presented, seasonal local dishes with modern flair and an impressive attention to ingredients. The place has friendly service, modern art on the walls, and no pretense. It's thoughtfully run by two brothers, Raffaele and Cesare, who happily explain why they are so excited about local hens (Mon 19:00-22:00, Tue-Sun 12:00-14:00 & 19:00-22:00 except closed Sun in summer, Via del Santo 113, tel. 049-875-0549).

$ Pizzeria Pago Pago dishes up wood-fired Neapolitan pizzas (a local favorite) and daily specials depending on what's in season. Get there early for dinner or wait (Wed-Mon 12:00-14:00 & 19:00-24:00, closed Tue; 2 blocks from Basilica of St. Anthony, up Via del Santo and right onto Via Galileo Galilei to #59; tel. 049-665-558, Gaetano and Modesto).

$ Casa del Pellegrino Ristorante caters to St. Anthony pilgrims with simple, basic, and hearty meals, served in a cheery dining room just north of the basilica (good €15 fixed-price meal, kid-friendly, Tue-Sun 12:00-14:00 & 19:00-21:00, closed Mon, Via Cesarotti 21, tel. 049-876-0715).

$ Zairo is a huge indoor/outdoor *ristorante*/pizzeria with reasonable prices, delicious homemade pastas, Veneto specialties, snappy service, and a local clientele. As it's next to the vast and inviting Prato della Valle square/park, consider combining dinner here with a relaxing stroll through the park (Tue-Sun 11:30-15:30 & 18:30-late, closed Mon, east side of Prato della Valle at #51, tel. 049-663-803).

$ Pollodoro la Gastronomica, my pick of the takeout delis near the basilica, sells roast chicken, pastas, pizza, and veggies. They'll also make sandwiches (Wed-Sat and Mon 9:00-14:00 & 17:00-20:00, Sun 8:30-14:00, closed Tue, 100 yards from basilica at Via Belludi 34, tel. 049-663-718). You can picnic at the nearby cloisters of the basilica.

Padua Connections

From Padua by Train on Trenitalia to: Venice (2/hour, 25-50 minutes), **Vicenza** (at least 2/hour, fewer on weekends, 15-25 minutes), **Milan** (1-2/hour, 2-3 hours), **Verona** (2/hour, 40-80 minutes), **Ravenna** (roughly hourly, change in Bologna or Ferrara, 2.5-3.5 hours). When taking the train to Venice, Vicenza, Verona, or Ravenna, buy a ticket on a regional train (R or RV). The Trenitalia Frecce or Italo express trains cost much more and get you there only marginally faster (especially when compared to a Trenitalia RV train).

By Bus to: Venice's Marco Polo Airport (65 minutes, €8.50 from ticket windows, €10 on board, hourly at :25 past the hour from 6:25 to 21:25, leaves from platform 11 at Padua's bus station, next to the train station; recheck times at www.fsbusitalia.it). If flying into the airport, take this bus to get directly to Padua (buy tickets at windows in arrivals hall or at airport TI). It's also possible—but not recommended—to connect the airport and Padua **by bus and train**—from the airport ride ACTV bus #15 (2/hour, 30 minutes, www.actv.it) to Venice's Mestre train station and take a train from there (4-5/hour, 15 minutes).

By Minibus to Airports: An Air Service minibus runs from Padua to **Marco Polo Airport** (€32/person) or **Treviso Airport** (€41/person, reservations required, tel. 049-870-4425, www. airservicepadova.it).

Near Padua: Vicenza

To many architects, Vicenza (vih-CHEHN-zah) is a pilgrimage site. Entire streets look like the back of a nickel. This is the city of Andrea Palladio (1508-1580), the 16th-century Renaissance architect who defined the Palladian style that is now so influential in countless British country homes. But as grandiose as Vicenza's Palladian facades may feel, there is little marble here because the city lacked the wealth to build with much more than painted wood and plaster.

If you're an architecture buff, Vicenza merits a quick day trip on any day but Monday, when major sights are closed. If you're packing light, it's an easy stop, located on the same train line as Padua, Verona, and Venice. However, because you can't store bags at the train station, it's not worth stopping here if you have lots of luggage (though in a pinch, the TI may be willing to store bags for you while you walk around town).

Tourist Information: The TI is next to the Olympic Theater at Piazza Matteotti 12 (daily 9:00-13:30 & 14:00-17:30, tel. 0444-320-854, www.visitvicenza.org). Ask for the free brochure on Palladio's buildings. Architecture fans appreciate the booklet titled *Vicenza and the Villas of Andrea Palladio*.

Arrival in Vicenza: From the **train station,** I'd head straight for the most distant sight, the Olympic Theater (with a TI next door) and then see other sights on the way back. Go straight out the train station's front door, and use the crosswalk on the right side of the roundabout. From here, it's a five-minute walk straight ahead up wide Viale Roma to the PAM supermarket at the bottom of Corso Palladio; turn right through the gate, and then it's a good

Vicenza

ARCHAEOLOGICAL &
NATURAL HISTORY MUSEUM
OLYMPIC
THEATER
To A-4 &
Padua
PALAZZO
LEONI MONTANARI
SANTA
CORONA
PEDEMURO SAN BIAGIO
C. CANOVE
SANTA CORONA
River Bacchiglione
GIACOMO ZANELLA
C. PORTI
S. STEFANO
Piazza
Matteotti
SAN
LORENZO
STALLI
SAN
STEFANO
PINACOTECA
C. RIALE
FOGAZZARO
PALLADIO
Piazza
San Lorenzo
VIA B. SAN LORENZO
MOTTON
CORDENONS
SAN MARCELLO
ORATORIO
S. FAUSTINO
S. FAUSTINO
GIURIOLO
CONTRA DELLE BARCHE
CARPAGNA
CORSO BATTISTI
LOGGIA
MONTE
CAVOUR
DO RODE
MORETTE
COLUMNS
Piazza
Biade
Piazza
Signori
BASILICA
PALLADIANA
ORATORIO SERVI
PIANCOLI
Giardino
Salvi
To A-4 &
Verona
Piazzale
del Castello
DUOMO
Piazza
Erbe
SAN PAOLO
River Retrone
Piazzale
de Gasperi
Piazza
Duomo
POST
PROTI
PASINI
SUPER-
MKT
VIALE ROMA
VIA GORIZIA
CARPAGNON
C. DELLA FASCINA
To
Villa Valmarana
ai Nani
& Villa Rotonda
200 Meters
200 Yards
200 yards to
train station

PADUA

10 minutes more down the Corso to the Olympic Theater (a taxi costs €8). **Drivers** can park in one of the cheap parking lots (Parcheggio Bassano and Parcheggio Cricoli) and catch a free shuttle bus to the center.

Sights in Vicenza

Helpful bilingual signs in front of Palladio's buildings explain their history. Arrows around town point you to his major works.

All the sights mentioned (except the villas outside town) are covered by the **Museum Card** combo-ticket (€15, €18 family pass, good for 3 days, sold at Olympic Theater and Palazzo Leoni Montanari Galleries).

▲▲Olympic Theater (Teatro Olimpico)

Palladio's last work, one of his greatest, shouldn't be missed. This

indoor theater is a wood-and-stucco festival of classical columns, statues, and an oh-wow stage bursting with perspective tricks. When you step back outside, take another look at the town's main drag—named after Palladio. It's the same main street you saw on the stage of his theater.

Cost and Hours: €12.50, also

covered by Museum Card; Tue-Sun 9:00-17:00, closed Mon, very occasionally closed when theater is in use, audioguide available, entrance to left of TI at Piazza Matteotti 11, info tel. 0444-222-800, tickets tel. 044-496-4380, www.teatrolimpicovicenza.it.

▲Church of Santa Corona (Chiesa di Santa Corona)

A block away from the Olympic Theater, this "Church of the Holy Crown" was built in the 13th century to house a thorn from the Crown of Thorns, given to the Bishop of Vicenza by the French King Louis IX. The church has two artistic highlights: Paolo Veronese's *Adoration of the Magi* (1573) and Giovanni Bellini's fine *Baptism of Christ* (c. 1502).

Cost and Hours: Free, Tue-Sun 9:00-12:00 & 15:00-18:00, closed Mon, Contrà Santa Corona 2, tel. 0444-323-644.

Archaeological and Natural History Museum (Museo Naturalistico Archeologico)

Located next door to the Church of Santa Corona, this museum's ground floor features Roman antiquities (mosaics, statues, and artifacts excavated from Rome's Baths of Caracalla, plus swords) and a barbarian warrior skeleton complete with sword and helmet. Prehistoric scraps are upstairs. Look for English description sheets near exhibit entryways throughout.

Cost and Hours: €3.50, covered by Museum Card, Tue-Sun 9:00-17:00, closed Mon, Contrà Santa Corona 4, tel. 0444-222-815, www.museicivicivicenza.it.

Palazzo Leoni Montanari Galleries (Gallerie di Palazzo Leoni Montanari)

Across the street from the Church of Santa Corona, this small museum is a palatial riot of Baroque, with cherub-cluttered ceilings jumbled like a preschool in heaven. A quick stroll shows off Venetian paintings and a floor of Russian icons.

Cost and Hours: €8.50, Tue-Sun 10:00-18:00, closed Mon, Contrà Santa Corona 25, tel. 800-578-875, www.palazzomontanari.com.

Piazza dei Signori

Vicenza's main square has been the center of town ever since it was the site of the ancient Roman forum. The commanding **Basilica Palladiana,** with its 270-foot-tall, 13th-century tower, dominates the square. This was once the meeting place for local big shots. It was young Palladio's proposal—to redo Vicenza's dilapidated Gothic palace of justice in the Neo-Greek style—that established him as the city's favorite architect. The rest of Palladio's

PADUA

career was a one-man construction boom. The basilica hosts special exhibitions that sometimes involve a fee, but you can often pop in for a free look.

Villas on the Outskirts of Vicenza

Vicenza is surrounded by dreamy Venetian villas. Venice's commercial empire receded in the 1500s when trade began to pick up along the Atlantic seaboard and dwindle in the Mediterranean. Venice redirected its economic agenda to agribusiness, which led to the construction of lavish country villas, such as **Villa la Rotonda,** the inspiration for Thomas Jefferson's Monticello (www.villalarotonda. it), and **Villa Valmarana ai Nani** (www.villavalmarana.com). Located southeast of the town center, both houses are furnished with period pieces (closed Mon). Pick up the free brochure on Palladio's villas from the TI if you plan to visit.

Vicenza Connections

From Vicenza by Train to: Venice (2/hour, 45-75 minutes), **Padua** (at least 2/hour, fewer on weekends, 15-25 minutes), **Verona** (2/hour, 30-60 minutes), **Milan** (1-2/hour, 2 hours). You'll save money by taking the slow R or the faster RV trains to Vicenza instead of the speedy Freccia or ES trains.

PADUA

VERONA

Romeo and Juliet made Verona a household word. Alas, a visit here has nothing to do with those two star-crossed lovers. You can pay to visit the house that falsely claims to be Juliet's (with an almost believable balcony and a courtyard swarming with tour groups), join in the tradition of rubbing the breast of Juliet's statue to help find a lover (or to pick up the sweat of someone who can't), and even make a pilgrimage to what isn't "La Tomba di Giulietta."

Fiction aside, Verona has been an important crossroads for 2,000 years and is, therefore, packed with genuine history. R&J fans will take some solace in the fact that two real feuding families, the Montecchi and the Cappellos, were the models for Shakespeare's Montagues and Capulets. And, if R&J had existed and were alive today, they would still recognize much of their "hometown."

Verona's main attractions are its wealth of Roman ruins; the remnants of its 13th- and 14th-century political and cultural boom brought about by its leading family, the Scaligeri; its 21st-century, pedestrian-only ambience; and its world-class opera festival, held each summer. After Venice's festival of tourism, the Veneto region's second city is a cool and welcome sip of pure Italy, where dumpsters are painted by schoolchildren as class projects and public spaces are primarily the domain of locals, not tourists. If you like Italy but don't need blockbuster sights, this town is a joy.

Orientation to Verona

Verona's old town fills an easy-to-defend bend in the River Adige. The vibrant and enjoyable core of Verona lies along Via Mazzini between Piazza Brà (pronounced "bra") and Piazza Erbe, Verona's market square since Roman times. Each evening the two main streets from Piazza Brà to Piazza Erbe, Via Mazzini and Corso Porta Borsari, are enlivened by a wonderful *passeggiata*...bustling with a slow and elegant parade of strollers. For a good day trip to Verona, take my self-guided walk, beginning with a visit to the Roman Arena.

TOURIST INFORMATION

Verona's helpful TI is just off **Piazza Brà**—from the square, head to the big yellow building with columns and cross the street to Via degli Alpini 9 (Mon-Sat 10:00-13:00 & 14:00-18:00, Sun 10:00-15:00, shorter hours and closed Sun off-season, tel. 045-806-8680, www.tourism.verona.it). If you're staying the night, ask the TI about concerts. The monthly entertainment guide, *Carnet Verona,* sold at newsstands, is in Italian only (€2).

Sightseeing Passes: The **Verona Card** covers city transportation and entry to all recommended Verona sights except the Arena-MuseOpera (though you can get a discount there with the card). The card can save day-trippers intent on blitzing the city almost a third off their sightseeing costs (€18/24 hours, €22/48 hours, sold at TI and at participating sights, www.tourism.verona.it).

The €6 **Church Card,** sold at four churches that require admission (San Zeno, Duomo, Sant'Anastasia, and San Fermo, normally €2.50 each), pays off if you visit three (www.chieseverona.it).

Walking Tours: The TI organizes 75-minute tours in English (March-Oct Sat-Sun at 11:30, €10/person). Tours meet inside the Piazza Brà TI and stroll all the way through the old town (confirm schedule, no reservation necessary).

ARRIVAL IN VERONA

By Train: Verona's main train station is called Verona Porta Nuova. In the main hall, you'll find pay WCs and a baggage-check office (daily 8:00-20:00). Buses and taxis are immediately outside.

Avoid the boring 15-minute walk from the station to Piazza Brà. Buses are cheap, easy, and leave every few minutes. Buy a ticket from the tobacco shop inside the station (€1.30/90 minutes, €4 day pass valid until midnight), or buy one on board using coin-op machines for €0.70 more. Leaving the station, angle right across the street to the bus stalls, find platform A, and hop on a bus: #11, #12, and #13 run Monday-Saturday before 20:00; #90, #92, #93, and #98 run after 20:00 and all day Sunday; and #51 and #52 run daily, even after 20:00. If in doubt, confirm that your bus is headed to the city center by asking, *"Per il centro?"* (pehr eel CHEN-troh). Validate your ticket by stamping it in the machine on the bus.

Drivers don't announce stops, but you'll know Piazza Brà because of the mass exodus and the can't-miss-it Roman Arena (bus stops in front of big, yellow, Neoclassical building). The TI is just a few steps beyond the bus stop, against the medieval wall. You can catch return buses to the station (same numbers) from the stop on the piazza side of the street, or from another bus stop on Piazza Brà, near the WCs.

Taxis pick up only at taxi stands (at Piazza Brà, Piazza Erbe, and the train station) and cost about €8-10 for the quick ride between the train station and the center of town (€2 more on Sundays and after 22:00, €1/big bag).

If you're in downtown Verona and need train tickets or reservations, drop by Welcome Travel (see "Helpful Hints," later).

By Car: The old town center (where nearly all my recommended hotels are located) is closed to traffic. Your hotel can get you permission to drive in—ask when you book. Otherwise your license plate will be photographed, and a €100 ticket might be waiting in the mail when you get home.

Drivers will find reasonably priced parking in well-marked lots and garages just outside the center. The underground **Cittadella garage,** at Piazza Cittadella (a block off Piazza Brà, behind the TI), is huge, convenient, and easy to find (€2/hour, €16/24 hours). The **Città di Nimes/Parking Stazione** lot is near the wall, a five-minute walk from the train station (€1.50/hour, €7/day). **Street parking** is limited to two hours and costs €1/hour (spaces marked with blue lines, buy ticket at a tobacco shop or ticket machine, place ticket on dashboard; some hotels can give you a free street-parking permit—ask).

By Plane: Efficient buses connect Verona's airport (known as Catullo or Verona-Villafranca, 12 miles southwest of the city, airport code: VRN, tel. 045-809-5666, www.aeroportoverona.it) with its train station (€6, buy tickets on board or at tobacco shop, daily about 5:15-23:00, 3/hour, 15 minutes, bus stop is by front door of train station, to the right).

HELPFUL HINTS

Exchange Rate: €1 = about $1.10

Country Calling Code: 39 (see page 450 for dialing instructions)

Sightseeing Schedules: Most sights (except churches) are closed on Monday mornings and typically open at 13:30.

Opera: From mid-June through early September, Verona's opera festival brings the city to life, with 15,000 music fans filling the Roman Arena for almost nightly performances. The city is packed and festive—restaurants have prescheduled seatings for dinner, and hotels jack up their prices (cheap upper-level seats-€29, day-of-show tickets often available). You can book tickets at the TI (extra charge if paying by credit card) or through the official box office (buy online at www.arena.it or call 045-800-5151; box office open Mon-Fri 9:00-12:00 &

15:15-17:45, Sat 9:00-12:00, closed Sun; during opera season, open daily 10:00-17:45, or until 21:00 on performance days; Via Dietro Anfiteatro 6B). If you're not here for the festival, you can still explore the arena and/or visit Verona's opera-focused ArenaMuseOpera museum.

Travel Agency: If you need train tickets or reservations, stop by **Welcome Travel** (small fee added to tickets but saves a trip to the station, Mon-Fri 9:00-19:00, Sat 9:30-12:30 & 15:00-18:00, closed Sun, Corso Porta Nuova 11, tel. 049-806-0111).

Private Guides: Three excellent and enthusiastic Verona guides enjoy giving private tours of the town and region tailored to your interests—villas, wine tasting, and so on (€120-125/2 hours, €260/5 hours). They are **Marina Menegoi** (mobile 328-958-1108, www.marinamenegoi.com, mmenegoi@gmail.com), **Valeria Biasi** (€32 for small-group tour, €130 for 2.5-hour private tour, mobile 348-903-4238, www.aguideinverona.com or www.veronatours.com, valeria@aguideinverona.com), and **Franklin Baumgarten** (mobile 347-566-6765, franklin_baumgarten@web.de).

Verona Walk

This walk covers the essential sights in the town core, starting at Piazza Brà and ending at the cathedral. Allow two hours (including the tower climb and some dawdling).

❶ Piazza Brà

If you're wondering about the name, it comes from the local dialect and means "big open space." A generation ago this piazza was noisy with cars. Now it's open and people friendly—it's become the community family room and natural festival grounds.

Grab a bench near the central **fountain** called "The Alps." This was a gift from Verona's sister city Munich, which is just over

the mountains to the north. You'll see in the middle of the fountain the symbols of the two cities separated by the Alps, carved out of pink marble from this region. In general, Verona has a bit of an alpine feel; historically it was the place where people rested and prepared before crossing the mountains, and to this day it's the place where the main west-east, Milan-Venice train line meets the north-south line up to Bolzano, the Dolomites, and Austria.

The ancient **arena** looming over the piazza is a reminder that

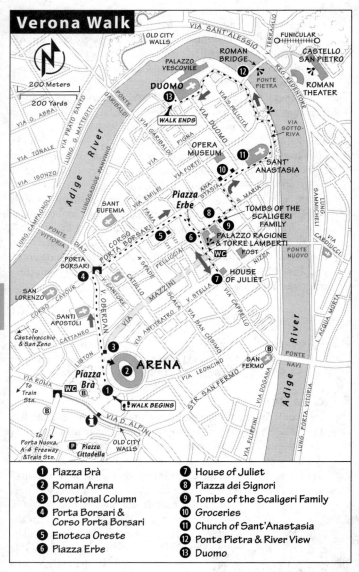

Verona Walk

VIA SANT'ALESSIO

OLD CITY WALLS

PALAZZO VESCOVILE

ROMAN BRIDGE

FUNICULAR

CASTELLO SAN PIETRO

ROMAN THEATER

200 Meters

200 Yards

DUOMO 🔟

PONTE PIETRA

VIA DUOMO

WALK ENDS

VIA G. ABBA.

VIA PRATO SANTO

LUNG. G. MATTEOTTI

PONTE GARIBALDI

VIA GARIBALDI

PIGNA

VIA SOTTO-RIVA

VIA TONALE

VIA ISONZO

Adige River

LUNGADIGE PANVINIO

VIA

VIA EMILEI

OPERA MUSEUM

⓫

🔟

SANT' ANASTASIA

VIA CAMPAGNOLA

LUNG. VITTORIA

PONTE VITTORIA

SANT EUFEMIA

VIA FAMA

Piazza Erbe

ANA STASIA

LUNG. DIAZ

CORSO PORTA BORSARI

8️⃣

9️⃣

TOMBS OF THE SCALIGERI FAMILY

PORTA BORSARI

4️⃣

5️⃣

6️⃣

PALAZZO RAGIONE & TORRE LAMBERTI

WC

POST

NIZZA

PONTE NUOVO

SAN LORENZO

CORSO CAVOUR

SANTI APOSTOLI

V. GANFORE

V. OBERDAN

VIA CATTANEO

CASTELLO

PELLICCIAI

V. SPADE

VIA AMFITEATRO

MAZZINI

VIA SCALA

7️⃣

HOUSE OF JULIET

V. STELLA

VIA BAN COSIMO

VIA CAPPELLO

LUNG. SAMMICHELI

VIA CARDUCCI

L. ACQUA MORTA

To Castelvecchio & San Zeno

LISTON

3️⃣

2️⃣ ARENA

VIA LEONCINO

SAN FERMO

Adige River

PONTE NAVI

Piazza Brà

1️⃣

WC

B

STR. SAN FERMO

B

VIA D. ALPINI

WALK BEGINS

1️⃣

VIA ROMA

To Train Stn.

B

To Porta Nuova, A-4 Freeway & Train Stn.

P Piazza Cittadella

OLD CITY WALLS

VIA FILIPPINI

VIA DOGANA

LUNG. PORTA VITTORIA

1️⃣ Piazza Brà	7️⃣ House of Juliet
2️⃣ Roman Arena	8️⃣ Piazza dei Signori
3️⃣ Devotional Column	9️⃣ Tombs of the Scaligeri Family
4️⃣ Porta Borsari & Corso Porta Borsari	🔟 Groceries
5️⃣ Enoteca Oreste	⓫ Church of Sant'Anastasia
6️⃣ Piazza Erbe	⓬ Ponte Pietra & River View
	⓭ Duomo

VERONA

the city's history goes back to Roman times. On this walk, we'll meander across what was the ancient city, from the arena on this side to the theater across the river.

With the fall of Rome in the fifth century, Verona became a favored capital of barbarian kings. In the Middle Ages, noble families had to choose sides in the civil struggles between emperors (Ghibellines) and popes (Guelphs). During this time (1200s),

the town bristled with several hundred San Gimignano-type towers, built by different families to symbolize their power. When the
Scaligeri family rose to power here in the 14th century, they established stability on their terms and made the other noble families
lop off their proud towers—only the Scaligeri were allowed to keep
theirs. To add insult to injury, the Scaligeri paved the city's roads
with bricks from the other families' toppled towers. But interfam-
ily feuds made it impossible for the Scaligeri to maintain a stable
government, and in 1405 the town essentially gave itself to Venice,
which ruled Verona until Napoleon stopped by in 1796. During
the 19th century, a tug-of-war between France and Austria actually divided the city for a time, with the river marking the border
of each country's domain. Eventually Verona, like Venice, fell into
Austrian hands. Reminders of Austrian rule remain: The huge, yellow, Neoclassical **city hall** facing Piazza Brà (look for the flags)
was built by the Austrians to serve as their 19th-century military
headquarters. Their former arsenal stands just across the river, and
an Austrian fortress caps the hill looking over the city. But the
big **equestrian statue** is of Italy's first king, Victor Emmanuel II,
celebrating Italian independence and unity, which was won in the
1860s. The **statue of a modern soldier** striking a *David* pose, with
a machine gun instead of a sling over his shoulder, honors Verona's
war dead.

VERONA

Apart from all its history, Piazza Brà is about strolling—the
evening *passeggiata* is a national sport in Italy. The broad, shiny
sidewalk (named "Liston" after a Venetian promenade; note the
fine, Venetian-style marble pavement slabs) was built by 17th-cen-
tury Venetians, who made it big and wide so that promenading
socialites could see and be seen in all their finery.

❷ Roman Arena
The Romans built this stadium outside their town walls, just as
modern stadiums are usually located outside downtown districts.

With 72 aisles, this elliptical, 466-by-400-
foot amphitheater is the third largest in Italy
(and it was originally 50 percent taller). Most
of the stone you see is original. Dating from
the first century A.D., it looks great in its pink
marble. Over the centuries, crowds of up to
25,000 spectators have cheered Roman glad-
iator battles, medieval executions, rock concerts, and modern plays, all taking advantage of the arena's famous acoustics. This is
also where the popular opera festival is held
every summer. Started in 1913, the festival
has run continuously ever since, except for

brief breaks during both World Wars, when the arena was used as a bomb shelter. While there's little to see inside except the impressive stonework, it's memorable to visit a Roman arena that is still a thriving concert venue. If you climb to the top, you'll enjoy great city views.

The gladiators posing with tourists out front are mostly from Albania and part of a local gang; they're notorious for overcharging for photos. While they're a nuisance, the police say it's better that they're scamming a living here than finding even more disreputable ways to get by.

Cost and Hours: €7.50, don't bother with the combo-ticket that includes the unimpressive Maffei Museum, Tue-Sun 8:30-19:30, Mon 13:30-19:30, closes earlier—likely around 16:00—during mid-June-early Sept opera season, last entry one hour before closing, WC near entry, tel. 045-800-3204.

• *As you exit the arena, look to your right. Where the street splits you'll see a column.*

❸ Devotional Column

In the Middle Ages, this column blessed a marketplace held here. Ten yards in front of it, a bronze plaque in the sidewalk shows the Roman city plan—a town of 20,000 placed strategically in the bend of the river, which provided protection on three sides. A wall enclosed the peninsula. The center of the grid was the forum, today's Piazza Erbe. (Look down Via Mazzini, the busy main pedestrian drag—the bell tower in the distance marks Piazza Erbe.)

• *After viewing the bronze plaque, turn around so your back is to the arena. Head straight down Via Oberdan (bearing left at the fork) and continue a couple of blocks (passing a derelict fascist-era theater, the Astra, set back from the street on the left, at #13) until you see an ancient gate to your right, the Porta Borsari. Walk up to it.*

❹ Porta Borsari and Corso Porta Borsari

You're standing before the main entrance to Roman Verona; back then, this gate functioned as a tollbooth (*borsari* means purse, referring to the collection of tolls that once took place here). Carved into the rock below the spiral, fluted columns (which parents nickname *"tortiglioni"*—a pasta kids can relate to), is a tribute to the emperor who restored this gate. Outside the adjacent Caffè Rialto, the stone on the curb is from a tomb: In Roman times, the roads outside the walls were lined with tombstones, be-

cause burials were not allowed within the town itself. Turn around, look down Corso Cavour, and imagine it in Roman times, leading away from the city gate and lined with tombs. Step into the café. A glass panel in the floor shows the original Roman foundations and pavement stones.

Back outside, cross under the Roman gate and head into the ancient city. Walk down Corso Porta Borsari, the Roman main drag, toward what was the forum. Make it a scavenger hunt. As you walk, discover bits of the town's illustrious past—chips of Roman columns, medieval reliefs, fine old facades, fossils in marble—as well as its elegant present of fancy shops, in a setting that prioritizes pedestrians over cars. On the right, you'll pass the recommended Osteria del Bugiardo, a popular wine bar and a good place to take a break and hang out with Verona's young and trendy.

• *Between Corso Porta Borsari 13 and 15, detour right down Vicolo San Marco in Foro, following the* Pozzo dell'Amore *sign. Twenty yards ahead on your right, you'll find...*

❺ Enoteca Oreste

This funky wine-and-grappa bar is still run by Oreste (with his Chicagoan wife, Beverly) like a 1970s, old-style *enoteca*. Browse and sample and clown around with Oreste. This historic *enoteca* was once the private chapel of the archbishop of Verona. Traces of the past hide between the bottles—ask Beverly to tell you the story (light food, Vicolo San Marco in Foro 7, tel. 045-803-4369).

• *Return to Corso Porta Borsari and continue one block until you hit a big square.*

❻ Piazza Erbe

This bustling market square is a photographer's delight. Its pastel buildings corral the fountains, pigeons, and people who have congregated here since Roman times, when this was a forum. Notice the Venetian lion hovering above the square atop a column, reminding locals of the conquest of 1405. Wander into the market, to the fountain in the middle. A fountain has bubbled here for 2,000 years. The original Roman statue lost its head and arms. After a sculptor added a new head and arms, the statue became Verona's Madonna. She holds a small banner that reads, roughly, *"The city of Verona deserves respect and justice."* During medieval times, the stone canopy in the center of the square (past the fountain) held the scales where merchants measured the weight of goods they bought and sold, such as silk and wool.

If you were standing here in the Middle Ages, you would have been surrounded by proud noble-family towers. Medieval nobles showed off with towers. Renaissance nobles showed off with finely painted facades on their palaces. Find remnants of the 16th-century days when Verona was nicknamed "the painted city."

Locals like to start their evening with an *aperitivo* here. Each bar caters to a different market segment. Survey the scene and, if or when the time is right, choose the terrace that suits you and join in the ritual. It's simple: Grab a spot, adjust your seat for the best view, and order a *spritz* to drink (€4 with a plate of olives and chips).

• *At the far end of Piazza Erbe is a market column featuring St. Zeno, the patron of Verona, who looks at the crazy crowds flushing into the city's silly claim to touristic fame: the House of Juliet (100 yards down Via Cappello to #23, on the left—just follow the crowds). Side-trip there now (but watch your wallet—it's a pickpocket's haven).*

❼ House of Juliet

The tiny, admittedly romantic courtyard is a spectacle: Tourists from all over the world pose on the balcony, while those hoping

for love wait their turn to polish Juliet's bronze breast. Residents marvel that each year, about 1,600 Japanese tour groups break their Venice-Milan ride for an hour-long stop in Verona just to see this courtyard (free, gates open roughly 8:30-19:30 or longer). It's fun to stand in the corner and observe the scene, knowing that all this commotion was started by a clever tour guide in the early 1970s as a way to attract visitors to Verona.

The courtyard walls have long been filled with amorous graffiti. The latest trend is to affix a paper note to the gates or walls with chewing gum. The wall of padlocks is another gimmick, enabling lovers to blow money in an attempt to prove that their hearts are thoroughly locked up. (The shop that sells the locks also sells pens to write on them.) The red mailbox is for love letters to Juliet. There's actually a Juliet Club that reviews these—and all the letters mailed from around the world to "Juliet, Verona, Italy." Each year, the club awards the author of the sweetest letter a free vacation to Verona.

Even those who milk their living out of this sight freely admit,

"While no documentation has been discovered to prove the truth of the legend, no documentation has disproved it either." The "museum," which displays art inspired by the love story, plus costumes and the bed from Franco Zeffirelli's film *Romeo and Juliet*, is certainly not worth the €6 entry fee.

Was there ever a real Juliet Capulet? You just walked down Via Cappello, the street of the cap makers. Above the courtyard entry (looking out) is a coat of arms featuring a hat—representing a family that made hats and which would be named, logically, Capulet.

The public's interest in a fictional Romeo and Juliet—or at least Juliet—is a sign that there's a hunger for a Juliet in our world. Observing the mobs clamoring to polish her breast or blow kisses from her bogus balcony, I try to appreciate what she means to people, and to psychoanalyze what she provides to those who come to Verona specifically for this: the message that love will prevail. In love, you can lose, and still be a winner. Juliet is brave, tragic, honest, outspoken, timeless, and passionate. She's a mover and a shaker, a dreamer and a fighter. In a way, this is a pagan temple where the spirit of Juliet gives people something to believe in...or maybe it's just a bunch of baloney appreciated by a simple-minded crowd.

• *Return to Piazza Erbe. From the middle of the piazza, head right on Via della Costa. Walk down Via della Costa, into the big square.*

❽ Piazza dei Signori

Literally the "Lords' Square," this is Verona's sitting room, quieter and more harmonious than Piazza Erbe. The buildings—which span five centuries—define the square and are all linked by arches. From one arch dangles a whale's rib. It was likely a souvenir brought home by a traveling merchant from a trip to the Orient, reminding the townspeople that there was a big world out there. The long portico on the left is inspired by a building in Florence: Brunelleschi's Hospital of the Innocents, considered the first Renaissance building.

Locals call the square Piazza Dante for the statue of the Italian poet **Dante Alighieri** that dominates it. Dante—always pensive, never smiling—seems to wonder why the tourists choose Juliet over him. Dante was expelled from Florence when that city sided with the pope (who didn't appreciate Dante's writing) and banished its greatest poet. Verona and its ruling Scaligeri family, however, were at odds with the pope (siding instead with the Holy Roman Emperor), and granted Dante asylum.

With the whale's rib behind you, you're facing the brick, crenellated, 14th-century Scaligeri residence. Behind Dante is the yellowish, 15th-century Venetian Renaissance-style Portico of the Counsel. At Dante's two o'clock is the 12th-century Romanesque Palazzo della Ragione.

Looking back the way you came, follow the white *toilette* signs into the courtyard of the **Palazzo della Ragione**. The impressive stairway is the only surviving Renaissance staircase in Verona. Within the palazzo you can visit the Gallery of Modern Art (skippable) and climb the 13th-century **Torre dei Lamberti** for a grand city view. The elevator saves you 243 steps—but you'll still need to walk up 46 more to get to the tower's first viewing platform. It's not worth continuing up 79 more spiral stairs to the second viewing platform (€8 ticket covers tower and Gallery of Modern Art, €4 for just the gallery, no individual tower tickets sold, Mon-Fri 10:00-18:00, Sat-Sun 11:00-19:00, ticket office next to staircase, tel. 045-800-1903, www.palazzodellaragioneverona.it).

• *Exit the courtyard the way you entered and turn right, continuing downhill. Within a block, you'll find the...*

❾ Tombs of the Scaligeri Family

These exotic and very Gothic 14th-century tombs, with their fine, original, wrought-iron protective cages, evoke the age when one family ruled Verona. The Scaligeri were to Verona what the Medici family was to Florence. These were powerful people. They changed the law so that they could be buried within the town. They forbade the presence of any noble family's towers but their own. And, by building tombs atop pillars, they arranged to be looked up to, even in death.

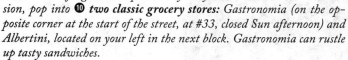

• *Continue 15 yards to the next corner and take the first left on Vicolo Cavalletto. At the first corner, turn right along Corso Sant'Anastasia toward the big, unfinished brick facade of Verona's largest church. For a fragrant and potentially tasty diversion, pop into* ❿ *two classic grocery stores: Gastronomia (on the opposite corner at the start of the street, at #33, closed Sun afternoon) and Albertini, located on your left in the next block. Gastronomia can rustle up tasty sandwiches.*

⓫ Church of Sant'Anastasia

This church was built from the late 13th century through the 15th century. Although the facade was never finished (the builders ran out of steam), the interior was—and still is—brilliant. Step inside to see the delightful way this region's medieval churches were painted. Note the grimacing hunchbacks holding basins of holy water on their backs (near main entrance at base of columns). And don't miss Pisanello's fresco of *St. George and the Princess of Trebizond* (1438; at the tip of the arch, high above chapel to right of altar). Once color-

ful, it has oxidized over time to its current monochrome state. For a closer look at its wonderful detail, check out the images on the computer terminal below the fresco. Ask for the English brochure, which describes the story of the church.

Cost and Hours: €2.50; Mon-Sat 9:00-18:00, Sun 13:00-18:00; Nov-Feb Mon-Sat 10:00-13:00 & 13:30-17:00, Sun 13:00-17:00; www.chieseverona.it.

• *Leaving the church, make two lefts, and walk along the right side of the church to Via Sottoriva. To the right, the Sottoriva arcade was once busy with colorful wine bars and osterie, some of which still exist (see "Eating in Verona," later). But for now, head to the left on Via Sottoriva. In a block, you'll reach a small riverfront area with stone benches that usually have a few modern-day Romeos and Juliets gazing at each other rather than at the view. Belly up to the river view.*

⓬ Ponte Pietra and River View

The white stones of the Ponte Pietra footbridge are from the original Roman bridge that stood here. After the bridge was bombed in World War II, the Veronese fished the marble chunks out of the river to rebuild it. From here, you can see across the river to the Roman Theater, built into the hillside behind the green hedge (see page 369). Way above the theater (behind the cypress trees) is the fortress, Castello San Pietro.

The wide spot in the river here was called the "Millers' Widening," where boats stopped and unloaded grain to be milled. Water wheels once lined the river and powered medieval Verona,

VERONA

employing technology imported from the Holy Land by 10th-century Crusaders.

Continue up the river toward the bridge. Keep an eye out for the recommended **Gelateria Ponte Pietra,** at #13, where Mirko, Mariam, and Stefano dish out fine gelato. Walk to the high point on the bridge and enjoy the view.

• *From the bridge, look back 200 yards at the tall white spire...that's where you're heading. Walk back off the bridge, then turn right, keeping an eye on the left for the steeple of the...*

⓭ Duomo

Started in the 12th century, this church was built over a period of several hundred years. Before entering, note the fine Romanesque carvings on its facade.

Cost and Hours: €2.50; Mon-Sat 10:00-17:00, Sun 13:30-17:00, shorter hours off-season.

Visiting the Church: Step inside, pick up the leaflet that explains the church's highlights, and head to the back-left corner of the church. In the last chapel on the left is Titian's 16th-century *Assumption of the Virgin.* Mary calmly rides a cloud—direction up—to the shock and bewilderment of the crowd below. Notice a handful of tombs embedded in the walls about 15 feet above floor level—an unusual feature. (Generally, tombs are found in the floor of the church or in crypts below.)

Now head up the aisle to the last door on the left (left of high altar), where you'll find the **ruins** of an older church. These are the 10th-century foundations of the Church of St. Elena, turned intriguingly into a modern-day chapel featuring exposed fourth-century mosaic floors from the Roman church that originally stood here.

From there, pass through the little open-air courtyard into the adjacent **baptistery,** with its clean Romanesque lines, hanging 14th-century crucifix, and fine marble font. Try to identify the eight biblical scenes carved on its panels before referring to my answers. (Answers, starting with the panel just to the right of center and working counterclockwise: Annunciation; first Christmas, with animals licking Baby Jesus and giving him a barnyard welcome; announcement to shepherds of Jesus' birth, with their flock stacked on one side; Epiphany, with the Three Kings giving their gifts to Baby Jesus; Herod commanding that all male infants be killed; Slaughter of the Innocents; flight to Egypt; and finally, facing the entry door, John the Baptist baptizing Christ.)

Finally, after leaving the church, circle around its left side (as you face the main facade) to find the peaceful Romanesque **cloister** *(chiostro)*, with mosaics from a fifth-century Christian church exposed below the walk.

Sights in Verona

IN THE TOWN CENTER

▲▲Evening *Passeggiata*

For me, the highlight of Verona is the *passeggiata* (stroll)—especially in the evening. Make a big circle from Piazza Brà through the old town on Via Mazzini (one of Europe's many "first" pedestrian-only streets) to the colorful Piazza Erbe, and then back down Corso Porta Borsari to Piazza Brà. This is a small town, where people know each other, and they're all out on parade. Like peacocks, the young and nubile spread their wings. The classy shop windows are integral to the *passeggiata* as, for many of the ladies, shopping is a sport. Their never-finished wardrobes are considered a work in progress, and this is when they gather ideas. If you're going to complement your stroll with a stop in a café or bar, the best plan is to enjoy a *spritz* drink—not on Piazza Brà, but on Piazza Erbe (the oldest and most elegant bars are on the end farthest from Juliet's balcony).

ArenaMuseOpera (AMO)

This slick museum, which opened in 2013 to celebrate the 100th anniversary of the city's renowned opera festival, fills the old Palazzo Forti in the sleepy streets at the northern edge of downtown. The underwhelming permanent exhibit, swaddled in red velvet, uses a few scant artifacts, sparse descriptions, and a handful of interactive touchscreens to trace the creation of an opera from words *(libretto)* to score *(partitura)* to staging (*rappresentazione,* including designers' sketches, along with actual sets and costumes from some of the performances that have graced the arena's stage). Opera lovers may enjoy this museum—particularly if it's hosting any interesting special exhibits (these can be excellent).

Cost and Hours: €8, more with special exhibits, Tue-Sun 10:30-18:30, closed Mon, closed Nov-March except by request, Via Massalongo 7, tel. 045-803-0461, www.arenamuseopera.com.

WEST OF PIAZZA BRÀ AND THE ARENA

▲Castelvecchio

Verona's powerful Scaligeri family built this castle (1343-1356) as both a residence and a fortress. The castle has two parts: the family palace and the quarters for their private army (separated, for the nervous family's security, by a fortified wall and an internal moat).

Today, it houses the city's art gallery, with an extensive, enjoyable collection of sculpture and paintings.

Cost and Hours: €6, Tue-Sun 8:30-19:30, Mon 13:30-19:30, last entry 45 minutes before closing, Corso Castelvecchio 2, tel. 045-806-2611, see map on page 371 for location. Info sheets are available throughout, but the €4 audioguide (€6/2 people) is still worthwhile.

Visiting the Castle: Religious statues were Verona's medieval forte, while paintings were the city's Renaissance forte. From the entrance, you'll head right toward the **statues,** once brightly painted. Cross to the next wing and head upstairs to walk through two floors that trace the evolution of **painting** from the 13th through the 17th century, including minor works by many major masters (such as Bellini, Mantegna, and Veronese). You'll also pass by a small armory collection.

En route, watch for the chance to roam the **ramparts** with fine views of the city, river, and Ponte Scaligero (described below). Kids (and kids at heart) enjoy scrambling across the delightfully crenellated parapets. Verona was an independent city-state from 1176 to 1387. Then came a long period of subjugation under other powers which, in more modern times, included the Austrians. From the ramparts you can see remnants of Austrian rule: the arsenal across the river and the castle atop the distant hill.

Nearby: Next to Castelvecchio, the picturesque red-brick bridge called **Ponte Scaligero**—fortified and crenellated, as if a continuation of the castle—is free, open to the public, and fun to stroll across. Destroyed by the Germans in World War II, it was rebuilt in the 1950s using many of its original bricks, which were dredged out of the river. Today it's understandably a favorite for wedding-day photos.

▲Basilica of San Zeno Maggiore

This church, outside the old center, is dedicated to the patron saint of Verona, whose remains are buried in the crypt under the main altar. In addition to being a fine example of Italian Romanesque, the basilica features Mantegna's *San Zeno Triptych* (1456-1459) with its marvelous perspective, peaceful double-columned cloisters, and a set of 48 paneled 11th-century bronze doors nicknamed "the poor man's Bible." Pretend you're an illiterate medieval peasant and do some reading. Facing the altar, on the walls of the right-side aisle, you can see frescoes painted on top of other frescoes and graffiti dating from the 1300s. These were done by people who fled into the church in times of war or flooding and scratched prayers into the walls. Druidic-looking runes are actually decorated letters typical of the Gothic period, like those in illuminated manuscripts.

Cost and Hours: €2.50, Mon-Sat 8:30-18:00, Sun 12:00-18:00; Nov-Feb Mon-Sat 10:00-13:00 & 13:30-17:00, Sun 12:00-17:00; located on Piazza San Zeno, a 15-minute walk upriver beyond Castelvecchio, www.chieseverona.it.

ACROSS THE ROMAN BRIDGE, NORTH OF THE CENTER

Roman Theater (Teatro Romano)

Dating from about the time of Christ, this ancient theater was discovered in the 19th century and restored. Admission includes the Roman Museum, located high in the building above the theater (reach it via elevator—start at the stage and walk up the middle set of stairs, then continue straight on the path through the bushes).

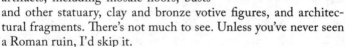

The museum displays a model of the theater, a small chapel, and Roman artifacts, including mosaic floors, busts and other statuary, clay and bronze votive figures, and architectural fragments. There's not much to see. Unless you've never seen a Roman ruin, I'd skip it.

Cost and Hours: €4.50—only €1 if museum is closed for restoration, Tue-Sun 8:30-19:30, Mon 13:30-19:30, last entry one hour before closing, theater located across the river near Ponte Pietra footbridge, tel. 045-800-0360. From mid-June through August, the theater stages Shakespeare plays—only a little more difficult to understand in Italian than in Elizabethan English.

Giusti Garden (Giardino Giusti)

You'll see this picturesque Renaissance garden capping the steep

hilltop just across the Roman Bridge at the northern edge of the city. It's a little oasis with manicured box hedges, towering cypress trees, and a city view from the top of its hill. For most people, however, it's not worth the hike, time, or money.

Cost and Hours: €7, daily 9:30-20:00, Oct-March 9:00-19:00, across the river, beyond Ponte Nuovo.

Sleeping in Verona

Hotel prices soar (at least €20-30 more per night) from mid-June through early September (opera season), in early April (during the Vinitaly wine festival—see "The Wines of Verona" sidebar, later), and during big trade fairs or major holidays. Unless your goal is opera, consider coming before mid-June or after early September. Prices are lowest from November to March.

NEAR PIAZZA ERBE

$$$ Hotel Aurora, at the corner of Piazza Erbe and Via Pelliciai, has friendly, family management, attention to detail, a welcoming terrace with wonderful piazza views, and 18 fresh, modern rooms (family rooms, elevator, air-con, Piazzetta XIV Novembre 2, tel. 045-594-717, www.hotelaurora.biz, info@hotelaurora.biz, Rita). Coming from the train station, you can hop off at Piazza Brà, cross the square, and walk 10 minutes up the main pedestrian street; or, for a slightly shorter walk, stay on the bus two stops longer until the San Fermo stop (from here, walk away from the river, following signs for *Piazza Erbe*).

$ Protezione della Giovane, run by an association that houses poor women, also rents rooms and dorm beds to female tourists (and their children, up to age 12 for boys). Buried deep in the old town and up several flights of stairs, this place offers 20 cheap beds in a clean, institutional, and peaceful setting (women only, dorm bed-€22, private rooms available, no breakfast, 23:00 curfew, reception open 9:00-20:00, Wi-Fi in common areas, self-service coin-op washing machine but no dryer, Via Pigna 7, tel. 045-596-880, www.protezionedellagiovane.it, info@protezionedellagiovane.it).

NEAR PIAZZA BRÀ

You'll find several options in the quiet streets just off Piazza Brà, within 200 yards of the bus stop. From the square, white or yellow signs point you to the hotels. Most of these are big, fairly impersonal business-class places; the Torcolo is more homey and friendly. Albergo Arena is a little farther out, near Castelvecchio (10-minute walk to Piazza Brà).

$$$$ Hotel Giulietta e Romeo is on a quiet side street just 50 yards behind the Roman Arena. It's stylish and well-managed; 10 of its 37 sexy, ultra-modern rooms have balconies (air-con, elevator, free loaner bikes, fitness room, pay parking in garage or ask for free street parking permit, Vicolo Tre Marchetti 3, tel. 045-800-3554, www.hotelgr.it, info@hotelgr.it).

$$$ Hotel Colomba d'Oro is a sprawling, stately, elegant place renting 51 spacious rooms with Baroque flourishes. It has generous public spaces, including a serene garden, and overlooks a

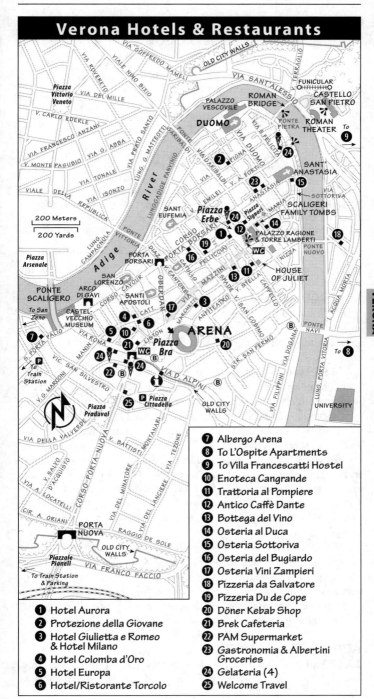

Verona Hotels & Restaurants

VERONA

❼ Albergo Arena
❽ To L'Ospite Apartments
❾ To Villa Francescatti Hostel
❿ Enoteca Cangrande
⓫ Trattoria al Pompiere
⓬ Antico Caffè Dante
⓭ Bottega del Vino
⓮ Osteria al Duca
⓯ Osteria Sottoriva
⓰ Osteria del Bugiardo
⓱ Osteria Vini Zampieri
⓲ Pizzeria da Salvatore
⓳ Pizzeria Du de Cope
⓴ Döner Kebab Shop
㉑ Brek Cafeteria
㉒ PAM Supermarket
㉓ Gastronomia & Albertini Groceries
㉔ Gelateria (4)
㉕ Welcome Travel

❶ Hotel Aurora
❷ Protezione della Giovane
❸ Hotel Giulietta e Romeo & Hotel Milano
❹ Hotel Colomba d'Oro
❺ Hotel Europa
❻ Hotel/Ristorante Torcolo

Sleep Code

Hotels are classified based on the average price of a standard double room with breakfast in high season.

$$$$	**Splurge:** Most rooms over €170
$$$	**Pricier:** €130-170
$$	**Moderate:** €90-130
$	**Budget:** €50-90
¢	**Backpacker:** Under €50
RS%	**Rick Steves discount**

Unless otherwise noted, credit cards are accepted, hotel staff speak basic English, and free Wi-Fi is available. Comparison-shop by checking prices at several hotels (on each hotel's own website, on a booking site, or by email). For the best deal, *book direct with the hotel*. Ask for a discount if paying in cash; if the listing includes **RS%,** request a Rick Steves discount.

quiet and central street (air-con, elevator, Via C. Cattaneo 10, tel. 045-595-300, www.colombahotel.com, info@colombahotel.com).

$$$ Hotel Europa offers 46 slightly dated rooms with spring-time colors and classic comfort. Try to request a balcony overlooking the *piazzetta* below (air-con, elevator, a couple of blocks off Piazza Brà at Via Roma 8, tel. 045-594-744, www.veronahoteleuropa.com, info@veronahoteleuropa.com).

$$$ Hotel Milano is an arty hotel with 57 rooms. The lobby and fancier rooms are tricked out in black and chrome. It has a wonderful terrace and hot tub overlooking the Roman Arena (air-con, elevator, pay parking in garage, Vicolo Tre Marchetti 11, tel. 045-596-011, www.hotelmilano-vr.it, info@hotelmilano-vr.it).

$$ Hotel Torcolo offers 19 comfortable, lovingly maintained rooms with Grandma's furnishings (breakfast extra, air-con, fridge in room, elevator, pay parking in garage; from Piazza Brà promenade, head down the alley to the right of #16 and walk to Vicolo Listone 3; tel. 045-800-7512, www.hoteltorcolo.it, hoteltorcolo@virgilio.it, well-run by Silvia, Diana, Riccardo, and helpful Caterina).

$$ Albergo Arena, a little dreary but with no-frills 1960s charm, is a good value for those on a budget. Located in a peaceful courtyard off a busy street a few blocks from Piazza Brà, it offers 15 very basic, quiet rooms (air-con, elevator, just west of Castelvecchio at Stradone Porta Palio 2, tel. 045-803-2440, www.albergoarena.it, info@albergoarena.it, Francesco and Elena).

ACROSS THE RIVER

$$ L'Ospite, a 10-minute walk across the river from Piazza Erbe, has six cozy, immaculate, fully equipped apartments and lots of stairs. The rooms, warmly managed by English-speaking Federica De Rossi, sleep two to four (family rooms, no reception or daily cleaning, air-con, Via XX Settembre 3, tel. 045-803-6994, mobile 329-426-2524, www.lospite.com, info@lospite.com). Coming from the station by bus (ride same buses as those headed downtown—see page 355), get off three stops past Piazza Brà, just after crossing the bridge, at the XX Settembre stop (across the street from the apartments).

¢ **Villa Francescatti** is a good, church-affiliated hostel in a pretty hillside setting (dorm bed-€18, private rooms available, cash only, includes breakfast, Wi-Fi in common areas, rooms closed from 9:00 to 17:00 but reception open all day, 24:00 curfew; Salita Fontana del Ferro 15, bus #73 or #91 from station to Piazza Isolo plus short steep walk, tel. 045-590-360, www.ostelloverona.it, info@villafrancescatti.it).

Eating in Verona

Every restaurant listed here is within a 10-minute walk of the others. They're mostly small and intimate and found along side streets. It's tempting to grab a table next to the *passeggiata* action along Piazza Brà, but you'll be sacrificing service, value, and quality for your view of the floodlit Roman Arena and Verona on parade (perhaps a fair trade-off). Except for Brek Cafeteria, restaurants on the piazza tend to charge a cover and service fee, making even pizza a pricey choice.

FINE DINING
$$$$ Enoteca Cangrande is enthusiastically run by Giuliano and Corrina, who enjoy turning people on to great, well-matched food and wine. You can sit on a quiet street or in a plush little dining area inside. Their star offering is a €40 set menu, a festival of *antipasti* treats, an imaginative pasta, a meat or fish course, and dessert. They also offer a light à la carte menu at lunch (daily 12:00-22:30, closed Tue off-season; a block off Piazza Brà at Via Dietro Liston 19D—if the equestrian statue jogged slightly right, he'd head straight here; tel. 045-595-022, www.ristorantecangrande.it).

$$$ Trattoria al Pompiere, which has a commitment to regional traditions, is bigger, with formal waiters weaving among its tight tables and walls plastered with photos of big shots from the area. This bustling place is a favorite of local foodies. Marco and his gang serve gourmet meats and cheeses as *antipasti* from their larger-than-life back counter, ideal for a mixed plate to complement the huge selection of fine wines. Reservations are wise (Mon-Sat 12:40-14:00 & 19:40-22:30, closed Sun, chivalry lives—ladies' menus come without prices; halfway between Piazza Erbe and

VERONA

Restaurant Price Code

I've assigned each eatery a price category, based on the average cost of a typical main course (pasta or *secondi*). Drinks, desserts, and splurge items (steak and seafood) can raise the price considerably.

$$$$	**Splurge:**	Most main courses over €20
$$$	**Pricier:**	€15-20
$$	**Moderate:**	€10-15
$	**Budget:**	Under €10

In Italy, pizza by the slice and other takeout food is **$**; a basic trattoria or sit-down pizzeria is **$$**; a casual but more upscale restaurant is **$$$**; and a swanky splurge is **$$$$**.

Juliet's courtyard—head down narrow side street next to Via Cappello 8 to Vicolo Regina d'Ungheria 5; tel. 045-803-0537, www.alpompiere.com).

$$$ Antico Caffè Dante is a high-end place with a 19th-century pedigree and elegant service on the coziest and classiest square in town. You can enjoy a memorable meal of classic Veneto cuisine either at romantic tables on the square or inside. While it's not cheap, if you want to dress up and enjoy a slow, romantic, memorable meal, this can be a good value (Mon-Sat 12:30-14:30 & 19:30-22:30—but closed Mon in summer, Sun 12:00-14:30, Piazza dei Signori 2, tel. 045-800-0083, www.caffedante.it).

$$$ Bottega del Vino is pricey, venerable, and a bit pretentious. Under a high ceiling and walls of wine bottles, brisk, black-vested waiters match traditional dishes (polenta, duck, game) with glasses of fine wine. Choose from 40 open bottles. The waitstaff, ambience, and food have deep roots in local culture. I like their front room best. Reservations are smart for dinner (good daily specials, daily 12:00-23:00—kitchen closed 14:30-19:00, bar open later, off Via Mazzini at Via Scudo di Francia 3, tel. 045-800-4535, www.bottegavini.it).

MODERATE RESTAURANTS

$$ Osteria al Duca is a fun, family-run place with a lively atmosphere and good traditional dishes. Locals line up for its affordable, two-course, €18 fixed-price meal with lots of choices. I much prefer their ground floor (*piano terra*—worth requesting). Reservations are advised (Mon-Sat 12:00-14:30 & 18:30-22:30, closed Sun, half-block east of Scaligeri family tombs at Via Arche Scaligere 2, tel. 045-594-474, www.osteriaalduca.it, Alessandro or Daniela).

$$ Ristorante Torcolo is a family restaurant, with mom (Paola) running the kitchen, and father and son (Roberto and Luca) serving the meals. While it feels a bit dressy, it lacks pretense. They

The Wines of Verona

Wine connoisseurs love the high-quality wines of the Verona area. The hills to the east are covered with grapes to make Soave; to the north is Valpolicella country; and Bardolino comes from vineyards to the west.

Valpolicella grapes, which are used to make the fruity, red Valpolicella table wine (found everywhere), are also the basis for full-bodied red Amarone and the sweet dessert wine Recioto. To produce Amarone, grapes are partially dried (*passito*) before fermentation, then aged for a minimum of four years in oak casks, resulting in a rich, velvety, full-bodied red. Recioto, which in local dialect means "ears," uses only the grapes from the top of the cluster (so they sort of look like the "ears" of the cluster's "head"). Because these grapes get the most sun, they mature the fastest and have the highest concentration of sugar. Before pressing, the grapes are dried for months until all moisture has gone out; the wine is then aged for one to three years.

Bardolino, from the vineyards near Lake Garda, is a light, fruity wine, like a French Beaujolais. It's a perfect picnic wine.

Soave, which might be Italy's best-known white wine, goes well with seafood and risotto dishes. While Soave can vary widely in quality, the best are called "Soave Classico" and come from the heart of the region, near the Soave Castle. Soave is sometimes aged in oak casks, giving it a mellow, rounded flavor.

Sample these and many others at the numerous *enoteche* (wine-tasting bars) or at any restaurant around town. In early April, Verona hosts Vinitaly, the most important international convention of domestic and international wines. Vintners vie for prestigious awards for the past year's vintage. Tourists are welcome to attend at the end of the week and are shuttled to the convention hall from Piazza Brà. Hotels book up months in advance. Check with the TI and www.vinitaly.com for details.

If you're visiting the area in the fall, consider a day trip to nearby Monteforte d'Alpone, east of Verona. The town hosts a fun, raucous wine festival in September—ask at the TI for more information on this and other regional wine festivals.

VERONA

serve all the classics, including a €35 fixed-price meal featuring traditional Verona dishes, and have an accessible menu and extensive wine list. Eat in their dining hall or on the tiny courtyard outside (Tue-Sun 12:30-14:30 & 19:00-22:30, closed Mon, just behind the Piazza Brà scene on a quiet street, Via Carlo Cattaneo 11, tel. 045-803-3730).

EATING IN *OSTERIE* (OLD BARS)

Wandering around the old town, you'll see plenty of Verona's thriving little watering holes. While these traditional old bars focus more on wine than on food, most serve memorable, characteristic, and affordable plates. Menus are simple and rustic—sometimes just bar munchies and the daily pasta. Service is relaxed and the clientele is young and local. For drinks it's mostly wine or water—fine wines are served by the glass, with bottles open and prices listed on blackboards. (I saw one sign suggesting that patrons "don't drive too much to drink.")

I've listed three places below: a classic antique *osteria* with more of a menu; a trendy, more modern place in the old center; and a small one-man show just off Piazza Brà, where you're most likely to make a new friend.

$$ Osteria Sottoriva survives from an era when Verona's river served as the town thoroughfare, and business deals could be made over a glass of wine at rustic riverside eateries. Located in a fine old covered arcade (the portico of Via Sottoriva), Sottoriva offers simple soups and pastas, with both cozy indoor and outdoor seating (daily 11:00-15:00 & 18:00-22:30—but open all day long in summer, closed Wed in winter, behind the Church of Sant'Anastasia at Via Sottoriva 9, tel. 045-801-4323). Don't confuse this with the nearby Ostregheteria Sottoriva23.

$$ Osteria del Bugiardo is jammed with a hip young crowd that spills out into the pedestrian-filled Corso Porta Borsari. They have a buffet of little sandwiches, can whip up a plate of top-quality cheeses, and serve a good pasta-of-the-day. They showcase their own Buglioni wines and are proud to tell you more about them (daily 11:00-24:00, Corso Porta Borsari 17a, tel. 045-591-869).

$$ Osteria Vini Zampieri, with a tiny bar and five tables, keeps a tradition of stoking conviviality with good wine since 1937. Its young and energetic manager, Leo, is passionate about organic wines, slow food, and his own home-brewed beer. As the drinks are their priority, they don't serve much food—just some bar munchies and a nice *antipasti* plate—but at lunchtime, Leo can whip up a simple pasta to complement your wine (Tue-Sun 11:00-14:00 & 17:00-late, Mon 17:00-late, a few steps off Piazza Brà and next to Via Mazzini at Via Alberto Mario 23, tel. 045-597-053). You're welcome to play foosball downstairs on what Italians call the *calcio balilla* ("the little boy soldiers of Mussolini").

PIZZA, CHEAP EATS, AND SWEETS

$ Pizzeria da Salvatore, Verona's first pizzeria, opened in 1963, when pizza was considered a foreign food...from Naples. They serve the best pizza in town, and a visit here offers a nice excuse to stroll across the river into a part of town with no tourists. It's family-friendly, not fancy or romantic, and you'll squeeze into a tight row of tiny tables, rubbing elbows with your neighbors. While it's not quite Naples, it's justifiably popular—come early, or plan to leave

A Mobile Feast Through Verona

Verona is a great town to sample the *aperitivo* ritual. All over town, locals enjoy a refreshing *spritz*, ideally on Piazza Erbe between 18:00 and 20:00. Choose a nice perch, and then, for about €4, you'll get the drink of your choice and a few nibbles (olives and/or potato chips) and a chance to feel very local as you enjoy the *passeggiata* scene.

Consider this for a fun sampling of many dimensions of the Verona eating and socializing scene: Start with an *aperitivo* on **Piazza Erbe** (the most refined bars are the farthest from Juliet's balcony), then walk across Ponte Nuovo to **Pizzeria da Salvatore** and enjoy the town's best pizza. If you have to wait for a table, have another *spritz* at the neighboring bar. Then stroll along the river to **Osteria Sottoriva**, and enjoy a little sampling of bar food with a glass of Amarone (wine to meditate with) under the old arcade. Finish by meandering through the old center back to Piazza Brà for a gelato at **Gelateria Savoia**. *Buon appetito!*

your name on the list and wait awhile (Tue-Sat 12:30-14:30 & 19:00-23:00, Sun 19:00-23:00 only, closed Mon, no reservations, across Ponte Nuovo to Piazza San Tomaso 6, tel. 045-803-0366).

$$ Pizzeria Du de Cope is a colorful, high-energy, informal place (with paper placemats) that buzzes with smartly attired young waiters and locals who keep coming back for the pizza (daily 12:00-14:30 & 19:00-23:00, flamboyant desserts, families welcome, no reservations, at Galleria Pelliciai 10, tel. 045-595-562).

$ *Döner kebab* shops all over town serve hearty, cheap kebabs to munch on from a stool or to take out (most open daily roughly noon-midnight). *Piadine* (pita-bread) kebabs are worth the €4, and the super-sized kebabs can fill a couple on a very tight budget for a total of €7. The best kebabs, according to local assessments, are behind the Roman Arena at Via Leoncino 44. There's another good place on the other side of Piazza Brà, near Hotel Europa, at Via Teatro Filarmonico 6b. The benches in the center of Piazza Brà are handy for a scenic place to munch your cheap meal.

$ Brek Cafeteria, a well-run and modern chain right on Piazza Brà, offers a cheap and easy self-serve option inside. Or, if you want to sit out on the square, you can order off the pricier menu—and enjoy a view that's worth paying a little extra for (daily 11:30-15:00 & 18:30-22:00, longer hours for outdoor seating during summer, facing equestrian statue at Piazza Brà 20).

Groceries: PAM supermarket is just outside the historic gate on Piazza Brà (Mon-Sat 8:00-21:00, Sun 9:00-20:00, exit Piazza Brà through the gate and take the first right to Via dei Mutilati 3).

Near the Church of Sant'Anastasia are two classic grocery stores, **Gastronomia** and **Albertini** (described on page 364).

Gelato: The venerable **Gelateria Savoia** has been in business since 1939. It's in an arcade just off Piazza Brà, marked by a crowd licking their distinctive *semi-freddo*—a specialty of bitter-almond amaretto, cream, and cookie (open long hours daily, just off Piazza Brà at Via Roma 1b). On the other side of town, near Ponte Pietra and the Duomo, is **Gelateria Ponte Pietra** (open late most nights in summer, Via Ponte di Pietra 13). **Gelato Pretto,** a pricey gourmet *gelateria*, has two prime locations—right on Piazza Erbe (at #40) and near Piazza Brà (on Porta Nuova, just past the main arch).

Verona Connections

You have three options for getting train tickets in the Verona station: the standard station ticket office (with slow-moving lines, daily 6:00-21:00), a bank of modern machines (good English descriptions, cash and credit cards accepted), and the Deutsche Bahn ticket office (20 yards from baggage check office in the tunnel, offering tickets at the same cost as the station office but with German efficiency and no lines, Mon-Sat 8:00-18:00, closed Sun).

Every hour, at least two trains connect Verona with Venice, Padua, and Vicenza. Choose one of the cheaper regional trains (R or RV) instead of the faster Frecce express train, which gets you there slightly sooner but costs much more.

From Verona by Train to: Venice (2/hour, 1.5-2.5 hours), **Padua** (2/hour, 40-80 minutes), **Vicenza** (2/hour, 30-60 minutes), **Florence** (*Firenze*, about hourly, 1.5 hours direct or 2.5 hours with transfer in Bologna), **Bologna** (hourly, 1.5 hours), **Milan** (2/hour, 1.5-2 hours), **Rome** (at least hourly, 4-5 hours, often with transfer in Bologna, also 1 direct night train, 6.5 hours), and **Bolzano** (about hourly, 2-2.5 hours, avoid "fast" trains that take the same amount of time but cost much more).

RAVENNA

Ravenna is on the tourist map for one reason: its 1,500-year-old churches, decorated with best-in-the-West Byzantine mosaics. The city's churches and mosaics date from the time (c. A.D. 400-600) when it was the center of Western civilization—a civilization in transition, from Roman to barbarian to Byzantine to medieval. You'll see all these layers in Ravenna.

In 402, barbarian tribes were zeroing in on the city of Rome. The Roman emperor moved his capital to Ravenna, a city well-known as a home port for the imperial navy (today's Classe). Because of its location, Ravenna kept close ties with the other Roman capital at Constantinople (called Byzantium).

Ravenna was conquered by the Goths (via Hungary) in 476, and the 1,000 years of the Roman Empire came to an end. But Ravenna continued on as the Goths' capital. They kept much of the Roman infrastructure and legitimized their rule by building sophisticated palaces and churches in the Roman style.

In 540, the Byzantine emperor Justinian conquered the Goths. This reunited Italy with the still-thriving Empire to the east. Justinian turned Ravenna into a pinnacle of civilization. It remained a flickering light in Europe's Dark Ages for another 200 years, until the Lombard tribes of Germany booted out the Byzantines (in 751). Ravenna then melted into the backwaters of medieval Italy, staying out of historical sight for a thousand years.

In your sightseeing, you'll see art from each of these periods: Roman (Mausoleum of Galla Placidia, Neonian Baptistery), barbarian/Gothic (Arian Baptistery, Basilica di Sant'Apollinare in Nuovo), Byzantine (Basilica di San Vitale, House of Stone Carpets, Church of Sant'Apollinare in Classe), and medieval (Tomb of Dante, Basilica di San Francesco).

Today, Ravenna's economy booms with a big chemical industry, the discovery of offshore gas deposits, and the construction of a new ship canal. More cruise ships than ever are stopping here, six miles from the town center.

From a traveler's perspective, Ravenna has a delightful worka-day quality, providing relief from the touristic intensity of Venice and Florence. The bustling town center is Italy's best for bicyclists. Residents go about their business, while busloads of tourists (mostly cruise-ship passengers and Italian school groups) slip quietly in and out of town for the best look at the glories of Byzantium this side of Istanbul—specifically, the richest collection anywhere of mosaics from the fifth and sixth centuries. Many are pleasantly surprised by the peaceful charm of this low-key town. If it seems less prettied-up than some of the more famous Italian towns, well...that's sort of the point.

PLANNING YOUR TIME

While the highlights of Ravenna can be seen in a four-hour stop-over, the city can provide an entire day of relaxing and enjoyable sightseeing—particularly for mosaic lovers. Its inexpensive lodg-ings and restaurants offer good value for your money. The town is a doable, though long, day trip from Venice or Padua (about three hours by train each way). It's more pleasant to spend the night. You could also stop here on your way from Venice or Padua to Florence. Ravenna is busiest between March and mid-June—prime field-trip season.

Famous but Skippable: Nearly all train travelers to Ravenna change in the regional capital of **Bologna.** While it might be tempting to check your bag at Bologna's station and spend a few hours in town, I'd resist—Ravenna is much more pleasant. Though well-preserved, Bologna is huge (three times the size of Ravenna), congested, and relatively charmless. If you decide to stop off here anyway, head straight to Piazza Maggiore (a 20-minute walk from the station), home to the Town Hall, the TI, and a famous statue of Neptune. The big Gothic building across the square is the un-finished 14th-century Basilica di San Petronio—destined to be one of the biggest churches in Christendom until the Vatican put the brakes on the project. A few blocks west are Bologna's twin sym-bols, a pair of leaning brick towers.

The nearby beach town of **Rimini** is an overrated, crowded mess.

Orientation to Ravenna

Particularly because its sights are concentrated right downtown, Ravenna feels small for a city of 160,000. Central Ravenna is quiet, with a pedestrian-friendly core and more bikes than cars. Subtle white-brick paving down the center of "pedestrian" streets indicates the bike lane: Keep to the sides and listen for the outta-my-way bells (while watching local pedestrians flagrantly stroll right down the middle). To join the two-wheeled crowd, you can rent a bike right next to the station or borrow one from your hotel.

On a quick visit to Ravenna, follow my self-guided walk and visit the Basilica di San Vitale, its adjacent Mausoleum of Galla Placidia, and the Basilica di Sant'Apollinare Nuovo (all covered by one combo-ticket—see "Helpful Hints," below).

TOURIST INFORMATION

The TI is a 15-minute walk (or a 5-minute pedal) from the train station (Mon-Sat 8:30-19:00, Sun 9:30-17:30; Oct-March Mon-Sat 8:30-18:00, Sun 10:00-16:00; Piazza San Francesco 7, tel. 0544-35404, www.turismo.ra.it). Pick up their quarterly *Welcome to Ravenna* publication for a review of events and activities in town.

ARRIVAL IN RAVENNA

By Train: The compact, manageable train station has all the basic services (ticket windows open long hours, ATMs, fast food, newsstand). The ticket machines are just for regional trips. While there's no baggage storage inside the station, if you exit to the left and walk two minutes, you can pay to **check your bag** at the Co-op San Vitale bike-rental shop, listed on the next page.

The station is just a few minutes' walk east of the main pedestrian street: Exit through the front of the station and keep going straight ahead until you hit the main square, Piazza del Popolo (my self-guided walk begins with this same stroll from the station). If you prefer to bike, you can rent wheels at the Co-op San Vitale.

By Car: Don't drive into the center, as you'll be fined. Two inexpensive lots are near the historic core: one accessible from the west side of Via Roma, at Piazzale Torre Umbratica (€1.80/day), and another at Largo Giustiniano just north of the Basilica di San Vitale (€3/day). Or find a free lot south of the station, on Circonvallazione Piazza d'Armi; another is north of the Piazzale Torre Umbratica lot, on Via Monsignore F. Lanzoni. Many lots and places on the street are free overnight (20:00-8:00), and most are free on Sunday.

HELPFUL HINTS

Exchange Rate: €1 = about $1.10

Country Calling Code: 39 (see page 450 for dialing instructions)

Combo-Ticket: Five of Ravenna's best mosaic sights are covered by a single €11.50 combo-ticket that's good for seven days; just buy it at the first sight you visit. Included are the Basilica di San Vitale, Mausoleum of Galla Placidia, Basilica di

Sant'Apollinare Nuovo, Archiepiscopal Museum (with its Chapel of Sant'Andrea), and Neonian Baptistery. All five sights are church-run, distinctly different, and well worth visiting.

Laundry: The self-service **Fastclean Lavanderia** is a five-minute walk from the train station (€3.50 wash, €3.50 dry, daily 7:00-22:00, go left as you exit the station, then take your first left over the rail crossing to Via Candiano 16, mobile 331-130-2072).

Bike Rental: Co-op San Vitale, in front of the train station, rents bikes (€1.50/hour, €12/day, Mon-Fri 7:00-19:00, also June-Aug Sat-Sun 8:00-12:00, photo ID required, tel. 054-437-031). Many hotels have loaner bikes.

Local Guide: Private guide **Claudia Frassineti** is excellent (€100/half-day, mobile 335-613-2996, claudia.frassineti@gmail.com).

Ravenna Walk

A visit to Ravenna can be as short as a four-hour loop from the train station. This 45-minute self-guided walk brings you from the train station to Ravenna's top draw (Basilica di San Vitale), quickly taking in a few other sights on the way. When done, you'll be oriented and can use any remaining time to visit more of Ravenna's sights.

• *Start at the train station, and walk (or pedal) directly into town on the main drag...*

Viale Farini

The station and surrounding neighborhood were bombed in World War II, when Ravenna was right on the so-called Gothic Line—the Nazis' last line of defense against an encroaching Allied surge in 1944. The architectural heritage of the 20th century is a mix of old-fashioned Italian buildings; stern, interwar, fascist structures; and postwar concrete gloom.

After a block, on the left, you'll pass the **St. John the Evangelist** church, with a rebuilt facade. This was the palace church of the fifth-century Empress Galla Placidia (the namesake of one of Ravenna's major sights, a mausoleum we'll see later on this walk). She and her children were caught at sea in a storm, prayed to St. John (the protector of sailors), and survived. In thanks, she had this church built at the site of their first safe step ashore. At least that's the story. It is true that in ancient times, the town harbor came right up to here. Historic churches are so abundant in Ravenna that we'll skip this one.

The next big building is the high school, with students' motorbikes parked in front. After that, the boulevard becomes **Via**

Diaz, an arcaded pedestrian shopping street. Note that the lighter cobbles are for the bikes.

• *At the intersection with Via degli Ariani, side-trip to the right 50 yards to find the...*

Arian Baptistery

Built during the reign of the Goths (c. 526), this small octagonal building marks the center of their Arian-style Christian faith (see sidebar).

Cost and Hours: Free, daily 8:30-19:30, off-season until 16:30, tel. 0544-543-711, www.turismo.ra.it.

Visiting the Baptistery: Theodoric the Great, the Gothic king of Italy (r. 493-526), built the church next door, with this as his baptistery. Imagine the small baptismal pool that once stood beneath this gloriously decorated dome.

The mosaic-covered dome shows Christ standing waist-deep in the River Jordan, being baptized by John the Baptist (in leopard-skin robe), as the dove of the Holy Spirit descends. The body builder on the left is the personified River Jordan, next to a vase from which the river springs. Notice the realism in John's stance. The 12 apostles, dynamic, with feet in motion, proceed around the dome. The empty throne between Paul (with scroll) and Peter (with keys) is a reminder that Judgment Day will come.

The mosaic is Arian, stressing Jesus' human rather than divine nature. Jesus is naked, with his genitals only partly obscured by the water. This emphasizes his mortal body, not his divine spirit. He's a beardless youth, suggesting his recent creation by God. The descending dove spews water to purify Jesus, marking the exact moment when Arians believed Jesus' divine nature emerged. Besides heretical Arian elements, there's also the pagan river god, shown in (pagan) Roman fashion as a bearded old man with a vase and river plant.

To modern eyes, these subtle details mean little. But to Byzantine Emperor Justinian and the Nicenes, these were red flags announcing heresy. While most of Ravenna's Arian art was destroyed when Justinian took control, this ceiling is one of the rare survivors.

The adjacent church is closed to the public. It was the cathedral of the Goths, with a simple main structure surviving from the sixth century and a Renaissance portico.

• *Now, return to the pedestrian boulevard, turn right, and continue to...*

Piazza del Popolo

Marking the town center, this square was created by Ravenna's Venetian rulers in the 15th century. Today's shipping canal was once a river that flowed to about where the two columns stand. But it got mucky and full of mosquitoes. (Dante died here...of malaria.)

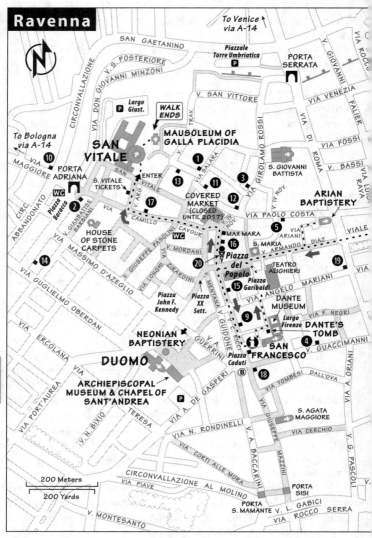

One column was topped by a Venetian lion until 1509 when, with the support of Rome, Ravenna won its independence from Venice. Ravenna's citizens pulled down that symbol of Venetian rule and did the local equivalent of tarring and feathering it. The lion was replaced by St. Vitale (a first-century Christian martyr). The column on the left is topped by Ravenna's first bishop, St. Apollinare. Behind the twin pillars stands City Hall. To the left is a Venetian palace decorated with granite columns and capitals, plundered from a heretical Arian church that was destroyed and then used as

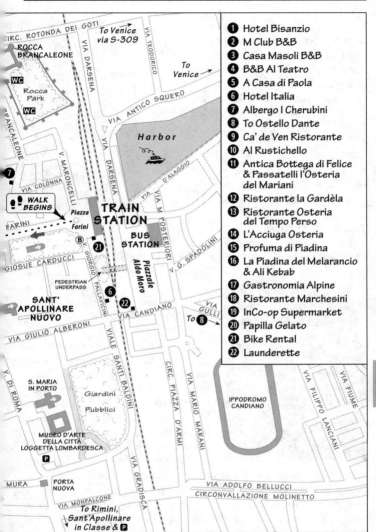

1. Hotel Bisanzio
2. M Club B&B
3. Casa Masoli B&B
4. B&B Al Teatro
5. A Casa di Paola
6. Hotel Italia
7. Albergo I Cherubini
8. To Ostello Dante
9. Ca' de Ven Ristorante
10. Al Rustichello
11. Antica Bottega di Felice & Passatelli l'Osteria del Mariani
12. Ristorante la Gardèla
13. Ristorante Osteria del Tempo Perso
14. L'Acciuga Osteria
15. Profuma di Piadina
16. La Piadina del Melarancio & Ali Kebab
17. Gastronomia Alpine
18. Ristorante Marchesini
19. InCo-op Supermarket
20. Papilla Gelato
21. Bike Rental
22. Launderette

a quarry. This square is a fine place to join the old guys on benches, watching the community parade by.

• *At the end of Piazza del Popolo, turn left down Via Cairoli and walk two blocks—crossing a busy street and passing some heavy-handed fascist architecture—to find the...*

Basilica di San Francesco

Pop into this basilica to see its flooded mosaic-covered crypt below the main altar. Today's water table is about three feet above the Roman crypt's floor level—so there's a pond with goldfish over the fifth-century mosaics (insert a €1 coin to turn on the light). The interior is simple and Franciscan; the altar features a fourth-century Christian sarcophagus with Jesus in the center and the 12 apostles.

Cost and Hours: Free, daily 7:00-12:00 & 15:00-19:00 (but closed during Masses), Piazza San Francesco, tel. 054-433-256.

• *With your back to the church, cut right through the small wooded park. On your right, next to the double archway, a tall, white, domed chapel marks the...*

Tomb of Dante

After he was exiled from Florence for his political beliefs, Dante lived out the rest of his life in Ravenna. The Florentines forgave

Dante posthumously and wanted to bring their famous poet's bones home to rest. To protect Dante's relics from theft by the Florentines, in 1519 Ravenna hid his bones inside the wall of the Monastery of San Francesco. There the bones lay forgotten for three centuries, until they were rediscovered and eventually placed here in 1865. (Florence's Santa Croce Church has a Dante memorial that's often mistaken for a tomb—but it's empty.)

The mausoleum is loaded with symbolism. High above the door, for example, the bronze snake eating its own tail—a symbol of eternity—suggests that Dante's soul (or, at least, his works) will have everlasting life. Capping the structure is an allegorical pinecone: A tasty pine nut hides inside the cone's lifeless exterior—a reminder of how our spirits can transcend the death of our earthly form. (And, not coincidentally, the pine tree is the symbol of Ravenna.)

Just to the right of the tomb, peer through the clever hanging fence with the pine tree city medallions (give it a jiggle) to the garden with the mound *(tumulo)* where Dante's bones were briefly hidden during World War II.

Cost and Hours: Free, daily 10:00-18:00, Nov-Feb until 16:00, Via D. Alighieri 9.

Nearby: The door to the left of the tomb leads into the peaceful twin cloisters of a former Franciscan monastery

The Arian Heresy

Ravenna's art reflects a centuries-long battle of ideas among Europe's Christians that came to a violent head right here. As you wonder at the beauty of Ravenna's mosaics, you're also witnessing an epic clash between two different interpretations of Christianity.

Around A.D. 320 in Alexandria, a devout Christian priest named Arius (c. 256-336) began preaching a seemingly simple idea: Jesus, being the Son of God, was therefore created by God the Father. This idea touched off a firestorm of debate and division unmatched in Christianity until the Protestant Reformation. Arius had raised questions about the very nature of the Christian God: Is God a single entity (as the head of a monotheistic religion should be), three different persons (God the Father, Jesus Christ, and the Holy Spirit), or something in between?

To keep the peace, Roman Emperor Constantine convened a Council at Nicea (in A.D. 325, near modern Istanbul). Arius was accused of doubting the divinity of Christ, by making him separate from and inferior to God the Father. The Council branded Arius a heretic and burned his books. After splitting many theological hairs, they issued the Nicene Creed, which defined God as a Trinity: There was one God, existing in three persons "of the same substance." (Don't make me try to explain it further, or this book may end up getting burned by some sect somewhere.) The three-in-one Trinity became the standard throughout the Empire, and Arian sects were brutally suppressed. (Don't confuse the Arian sect with Nazi Germany's idea of an Aryan race.)

But that didn't settle the matter. Constantine's own son, a fervent Arian, sent missionaries north across the Danube to convert the barbarian Goths to Arian-style Christianity. A century later, as Rome was falling, those same Goths came knocking on Italy's doorstep. They overran Ravenna (476) and made Arian Christianity the official religion of state, though they tolerated the Nicene Christianity of their Italian subjects.

The churches the Goths built—including the Arian Baptistery and Basilica di Sant'Apollinare Nuovo—reflected their Arian faith. Arian mosaics of Jesus emphasized his humanness rather than his divinity.

In 540, the Byzantine Emperor Justinian drove out the Goths. To unite his empire, he demanded both political and theological conformity. Anything with the slightest whiff of Arianism was wiped out. Mosaics were stripped from the walls, statues defaced, and churches were renamed for saints famous for fighting heretics. In their place came art that reflected Byzantine tastes and Trinitarian theology. You'll see evidence of this shift at many of Ravenna's top sights.

Ravenna was Arianism's Waterloo. Sects were snuffed out, Trinitarians triumphed, and the Nicene Creed (in some form) is still said in many Christian churches today.

RAVENNA

(attached to the Basilica di San Francesco, which we saw earlier). Today this complex houses a fascinating-to-Italians **Dante Museum,** which is worth a visit if you're a fan (otherwise, save your sightseeing stamina for what's coming up; museum described on page 396).

• *Turn your back to Dante's tomb and walk straight ahead until you pop out into...*

Piazza Garibaldi

With a statue of Giuseppe Garibaldi (a heroic leader in Italy's unification struggle in the mid-1800s) in the center and the stately, vivid-yellow Alighieri Theater (named for Dante) on the right, this is the humbler of Ravenna's two main squares. On the wall on your left, in a building housing Ravenna's post office, look for the plaques honoring patriots from Ravenna *(patrioti ravennati)* who died in World War II. You'll see both *morti sul patibolo nelle carceri in esilio* (died in prisons in exile) and *caduti sui campo di battaglia* (killed on the field of battle). In the summer and fall of 1944, the Nazis—steadily losing their grip on Italy—dug in near Ravenna and fought determinedly to hang on. The countryside surrounding Ravenna is dotted with several WWII cemeteries, as well as a few remaining "bailey bridges"—temporary bridges erected quickly by Allies on the march.

Next to the plaque listing the war dead is one listing the names of the Nazis' Jewish victims *(ebrei)* from Ravenna and their age at death. Notice how young many of them were.

Continue under the arcade back into Piazza del Popolo, and look at the *Il Comune di Ravenna* plaque on the towered building to your right, dedicated *ai suoi caduti per la liberta* (to those "fallen for freedom"). Those killed included *partigiani caduti in combattimento* (patriots lost in battle) and *per rappresaglia*—killed by the Nazis in retribution for Allied successes. Ravenna was ultimately liberated by mostly Canadian forces.

• *From here, you'll walk six blocks to the* **Basilica di San Vitale:** *With your back to the tower, turn and cross to the far-right corner of the piazza. Turn right and head one block up Via IV Novembre. At the old covered market (and the Max Mara shop), turn left and head down Via Cavour, Ravenna's favored street for evening strolling and shopping.*

About two blocks down Via Cavour, on the right, at #43, peek into the courtyard that holds **Gastronomia Alpine,** *a deli selling top-quality local meats and cheeses—you could pull together a classy picnic here (see shop listing on page 402).*

As you approach the end of the block, the yellow **Porta Adriana** *city gate comes into view (straight ahead). A few steps later, turn right onto Via Argentario. Halfway down this block on the left, at #22, is the ticket office for Ravenna's big sights. Buy your ticket here, then continue down* *the street to Ravenna's crown jewel, the Basilica di San Vitale (through the gateway at the end of this block). Of Ravenna's many impressive and important buildings from this time, the next sights are two of the finest: first the basilica itself, with its dazzling mosaics, and then, across the yard, the small but poignant Mausoleum of Galla Placidia.*

▲▲▲Basilica di San Vitale

Imagine: It's A.D. 540. The city of Rome has been looted, the land is crawling with barbarians, and the infrastructure of Rome's thou-

sand-year empire is crumbling fast. Into this chaotic world comes the emperor of the East (Justinian), bringing order and stability, briefly reassembling the empire, and making Ravenna a beacon of civilization.

Cost and Hours: Covered by €11.50 combo-ticket that includes (and is also sold at) four other worthwhile sights: the Mausoleum of Galla Placidia, Basilica di Sant'Apollinare Nuovo, Archiepiscopal Museum, and Neonian Baptistery. The church is open daily 9:00-19:00, March and Oct 9:00-17:30, Nov-Feb 9:30-17:00 (Galla Placidia has the same hours). Tel. 0544-541-688, www.ravennamosaici.it.

Visiting the Basilica: Step into the church, circle around to the middle of the nave and take it all in.

The basilica—standing as a sanctuary of order in the midst of the madness after the fall of Rome—is covered with lavish **mosaics:** gold and glass chips the size of your fingernail. It's impressive enough to see a 1,400-year-old church, but it's rare to see one decorated in such brilliant mosaics, which still manage to convey their intended message: "This sense of peace and stability was brought to you by your emperor and God." The art is an intricate ensemble of images that, with the help of a medieval priest, would teach volumes.

The centerpiece, high above the altar, is God in heaven, por-

trayed as Christ sitting on a celestial orb, overseeing his glorious creation.

Step up to the **altar.** Position yourself to best see the side walls flanking it. Running the show on earth is Justinian (left side), sporting both a halo and a crown to indicate that he's leader of both the

Church and the State. Here Justinian brings together the military leaders and the church leaders, all united by the straight line of eyes. The bald bishop of Ravenna—the only local guy in this group—is portrayed most realistically (with a name tag above reading *Maximianus*).

On the opposite wall, facing the emperor, is his wife, Theodora, flanked by her entourage. Decked out in jewels and pearls,

the former dancer who became Justinian's mistress (and then empress) carries a chalice with which to consecrate the new church.

The border inside the apse's arch, high above, is decorated with horns of plenty (cornucopia), promising prosperity in return for the people's obedience to the Church and State (Justinian and Theodora).

Back up a bit to let this space work its magic. Get in a medieval frame of mind and study the composition—with floor, walls, and ceiling all integrated into a cohesive meaning. Stand immediately under the **main dome** surrounded by scallop-shell designs, symbolizing St. James, the patron saint of pilgrims. From there the mosaic floor directs your journey to a 16th-century inlaid marble labyrinth which, if you do it right, leads you on to the altar. The lesson: The pilgrimage of faithful life on earth leads to salvation through Christ.

While the decor behind you is Baroque and of no particular artistic importance, the walls and ceilings above and in front sparkle with colorful biblical scenes told with a sixth-century exuberance. (Viennese artist Gustav Klimt sat right here around 1900 and was inspired by the glint of the light on the gold leaf.)

Now take a longitudinal, **ground-up tour** from your spot before the altar: The inlaid floor leads to the sixth-century marble altar (busy with iconography). High on the wall above that is Christ on the globe. Appreciate the symmetry. At the top of the arch, the circle with the monogram of Christ (*I* for Jesus and *X* for Christ) symbolizes perfection and eternity. Floating above the arch, two angels hold rays of sun (Christ is the origin of light). The scene is bookended by two cities: Bethlehem and Jerusalem (each the same but labeled, where Jesus was born and died). Above each city are potted grapevines producing wine, symbols of the blood of Christ.

The **ceiling** above is a festive celebration of God's creation, with 80 different birds from the sixth century—most still flying around Ravenna today. (Bird-watchers—who visit with binoculars, of course—can easily identify these by their exquisitely detailed and accurate feathers.) At the very top, all creation swirls around Christ as the sacrificial lamb, supported by four angels.

Framing the entire apse, arcing high above, is a triumphal **arch.** Its 15 medallions depict 12 apostles, 2 sons of St. Vitale,

and a medieval bearded Christ. Notice the realism...the eyes, the hairstyles.

The mid-sixth century was a time of transition, and many consider Ravenna's mosaics to be both the last ancient Roman and the first medieval European works of art. Standing here, we can witness a culture sud-

denly lurching forward out of antiquity and into the Middle Ages. Notice, for example, that the Christ who hovers above the altar is beardless (per standard ancient-Roman depiction), whereas it's the usual medieval bearded Jesus who's encircled atop the arch—and yet these mosaics were created within the same generation.

The church's **octagonal design**—clearly Eastern in origin—inspired at least two influential churches, including Hagia Sofia, the church-turned-mosque-turned-museum built 10 years later in Constantinople (today's Istanbul). Hagia Sofia, in turn, became the classic architectural model for mosques around the world. In A.D. 787, Emperor Charlemagne traveled to Ravenna and was so impressed with San Vitale that he returned to Aix-la-Chapelle (now Aachen, Germany) and built a new palace—the power base for his vast empire—with a San Vitale-esque chapel at its core. It still stands as part of Aachen Cathedral, making it the oldest great stone building in northern Europe.

The intricate basketlike **capitals** were built to order and shipped from Constantinople to Ravenna. The pilasters surrounding you are brick, covered by sliced marble veneers. Similar marble sheets once covered all the walls. Many were scavenged by Charlemagne to provide flooring for his grand church.

• *When you're ready, exit through the door on the left (as you face the altar) and head across the grounds to the much smaller but even older Mausoleum of Galla Placidia.*

▲▲Mausoleum of Galla Placidia

Just across the courtyard from the Basilica di San Vitale is a tiny, humble-looking mausoleum, with the oldest—and, to many, the most precious—mosaics in Ravenna. Ninety-five percent of the mosaics here are originals, dating from the late Roman period, when Ravenna was the capital of a declining West.

Cost and Hours: Covered by Basilica di San Vitale combo-ticket, same hours.

Visiting the Mausoleum: The Mausoleum of Galla Placidia (plah-CHEE-dee-ah) was designed to be the burial place of this daughter, sister, and mother of emperors, who died around A.D. 450. But Galla Placidia died in Rome and wasn't buried here. The three sarcophagi, built for the imperial family but likely only used by later Christian leaders, stand empty today. The original floor was about four feet lower, explaining the stunted feel of the interior. The art's realistic portrayal of tunics and sandals gives us a peek at the fashions of fifth-century Romans.

The little light that sneaks through the thin alabaster panels brings a glow and a twinkle to the early Christian symbolism that fills the small room. Opposite the door is St. Lawrence being martyred on a fiery grill. He's legendary for mocking his executioners, reportedly saying something like, "I'm done on this side. You can turn me over now." He was famous as an example of the strength of the feisty early Christians. Note the four Gospels clearly labeled on the bookshelf, another inspiration for these first believers as they were persecuted by the Romans.

The dome is filled with stars. Along with Mark's lion, Luke's ox, Matthew's angel, and John's eagle, the golden cross rises from the east, bringing life to all. Doves drink from fountains, symbolic of souls finding nourishment in the Word of God. In both transepts are deer, reminding worshippers of Psalms 42: "Like the thirsty deer longs for spring water, so my soul longs for you, my God."

Look toward the back of the mausoleum. Cover the light from the door with this book (or close the curtain) to see the standard Roman portrayal of Christ—beardless and as the Good Shepherd. Jesus, dressed in gold and purple like a Roman emperor, is the King of Paradise—receiving the faithful (represented by lambs). The Eastern influence (perhaps inspired by the designs on fine Persian carpets or silks) is apparent in the vault's decorative patterns.

• *Our walk is done. Got a train to catch? Head straight back to the station. If you have more time, visit the other sights included on your basilica ticket on your way: the Neonian Baptistery, the Archiepiscopal Museum, and the Basilica di Sant'Apollinare Nuovo.*

More Sights in Ravenna

EAST OF PIAZZA DEL POPOLO
▲▲Basilica di Sant'Apollinare Nuovo

This austere sixth-century church has a typical early Christian-basilica floor plan and two huge and wonderfully preserved side

panels. The only noteworthy sight in this part of town, it's on Via di Roma, just a short detour off the main road back to the train station.

Cost and Hours: Covered by €11.50 combo-ticket, daily 9:00-19:00, March and Oct 9:30-17:30, Nov-Feb 10:00-17:00, tel. 0544-541-688, www.ravennamosaici.it.

Eating: You can have a quick lunch at the air-conditioned, efficient Sant'Apollinare self-serve cafeteria on the church grounds (Mon-Fri 12:00-15:00, closed Sat-Sun).

Visiting the Basilica: Head inside. Ignoring the Baroque altar from a thousand years later, you can clearly see the rectangular Roman hall of justice (basilica) floor plan—which was adopted by Christian churches and used throughout the Middle Ages.

The important art here is the decoration along the sides of the nave, just above the symmetrical arches. The one on the left side is a procession of haloed virgins, each bringing gifts to the Madonna and the Christ Child; the three wise men are at the head of the queue. Opposite, Christ is on his throne with four angels, awaiting a solemn procession of 26 martyrs.

Notice on each side how the processions lead to segments from an earlier Arian design—each about 50 years older. This basilica started (c. 500) as an Arian church—the palace church of King Theodoric of the Goths. Theodoric decorated it with scenes of himself and his royal palace amid Christ and the saints. Look for original, surviving Arian art in the front (on the left, Mary and Baby Jesus; on the right, Jesus and four angels) and in the rear (two cityscapes: *Civi Classis*—Classe; and *Palatium*, for the palace in Ravenna).

When Justinian arrived, he transformed the church in the Byzantine (and Nicene) style. If you study the arcades in the Ravenna cityscape (rear of church, above where you entered), you can see how the palace was kept while the Arian figures were erased, leaving only bits of hands and fingers on the columns and blotted-out haloes behind the curtains. On the opposite side, see three ships in the ancient harbor and a palace where golden bricks were used to cover Arian figures. The brilliant white-robed figures parading on both sides were remade in the mid-500s with a Byzantine rather than an Arian message.

The uppermost panels (hard to see without binoculars) are original Theodoric Arian: prophets (between windows), miracles of Christ (top row on the left), and scenes from the last week of Jesus' life and his Resurrection (top row on the right).

SOUTH OF PIAZZA DEL POPOLO

The first three sights described below cluster near Ravenna's modest Duomo, about a 10-minute walk from Piazza del Popolo. The last sight, the Dante Museum, is a few minutes' walk east of here, right next to the Basilica di San Francesco and Dante's tomb (both described earlier, on my self-guided walk).

▲▲Archiepiscopal Museum

This impressive museum, in Ravenna's Duomo, complements all the relatively empty buildings you've seen and contains the sixth-century Chapel of Sant'Andrea.

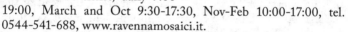

Built as the private prayer chapel for the Catholic bishop during Theodoric's time (c. 500), today it anchors a fine collection of Roman, Byzantine-Christian, and pagan statues, reliefs, and mosaics—all very well-described.

Cost and Hours: Covered by €11.50 combo-ticket, daily 9:00-19:00, March and Oct 9:30-17:30, Nov-Feb 10:00-17:00, tel. 0544-541-688, www.ravennamosaici.it.

Visiting the Museum: From the museum entrance on Piazza Arcivescovado, follow signs to the *Cappella di Sant'Andrea,* in Room IE. Enter the room, turn around, and look above the door to see a sixth-century mosaic showing Christ as a religious warrior, stepping triumphantly on a lion and snake (ancient symbols of evil) and carrying the cross as if it were a weapon. The book he holds reads in Latin, "I am the way, the truth, and the life." This is a strong pro-Trinity statement (Jesus, God, and the Holy Spirit are one) against the Arian heresy. The main chamber of the charming chapel is covered in rich mosaics, with lots of sixth-century symbolism and realistic portrait medallions. Topping the arch just over the door is another clean-shaven Jesus.

Exiting the chapel, turn left into Room IF to see the museum's other highlight, an exquisite sixth-century Byzantine ivory throne, decorated with intricate scenes from the life of Christ. It was carved for Bishop Maximianus, Justinian's Trinitarian appointee, the man who oversaw construction of the Basilica di San Vitale, and whose bald head appears in its mosaics. Nearby, in Room IG, is an interesting circular calendar designed to keep track of the dates for Easter between the years 532 and 626. The upstairs, worth a quick look, offers a chance for a close-up view of mosaics and more Byzantine and Venetian-era church art.

• *Exiting the museum, turn left to find the...*

▲Neonian Baptistery

Also known as the Baptistery of the Orthodox, this octagonal space dates from about the year 400. Imagine pagan adults immersed in the pool under glorious ceiling mosaics as they convert to Christianity. The mosaic portrays the common baptistery theme: John the Baptist baptizing Christ, with the personification of the River Jordan looking on. The scene is ringed by empty chairs, waiting to welcome you into the eternal heavenly banquet. Twelve apostles with dancing feet—their tunics and cloaks alternating between gold and white—give the room a joyful visual sense of rhythm. The acanthus

flowers dividing the apostles were the botanical inspiration for the Corinthian capital, the Roman capital of choice. Decoration on the lower walls features dark purple disks made of precious porphyry stone and a gold leafy arcade creating almond-shaped frames for the prophets.

Over the last 15 centuries, the building (being far heavier than the streets around it) has sunk about 10 feet into the mucky local soil. That's why the floor is higher than the architect planned, which messes up his intended proportion. For that reason also, the baptismal font is not original.

Cost and Hours: Covered by €11.50 combo-ticket, daily 9:00-19:00, March and Oct 9:30-17:30, Nov-Feb 10:00-17:00, tel. 0544-541-688, www.ravennamosaici.it.

• *While you're here, consider at least popping into Ravenna's Duomo for a quick peek. From the Baptistery, walk away from the Archiepiscopal Museum and hook left to reach the front door of the...*

Duomo

Ravenna's main church is a typically big, Baroque house of worship. Like nearly everything else in this town, it's built on much older rubble. In the 18th century, to make way for the current structure, its builders razed the gigantic five-nave Basilica Ursiana—but pragmatically repurposed big chunks of the old church to build the new one. Pay close attention to the inlaid floors, made with cross-sections of columns, capitals, and other decorations from the previous church, all neatly sliced and joined together. Just before the right transept, notice the fine sixth-century marble-carved pulpit, covered with two-dimensional images of animals (typical of the Byzantine style). The Latin inscription, referring to the bishop who reconsecrated the Arian churches, reads, "Agnellus made this pulpit."

Cost and Hours: Free, Mon-Fri 7:00-12:00 & 14:30-18:30 (off-season until 17:00), Sat-Sun until 19:00.

Nearby: The free **botanical garden** (Giardino Rasponi)—with a great view of the cathedral—is a delightful spot to rest after so much sightseeing. Exiting the Duomo, turn right and walk up Via G. Rasponi. After one block, turn right on Via A. Guerrini to find the garden entrance.

Dante Museum (Museo Dantesco)

This small museum celebrates Dante Alighieri, "the Italian Shakespeare," who spent his last three years in Ravenna and now rests next door in the former Monastery of San Francesco. It was here that a 19th-century bricklayer stumbled upon the author's long-lost remains, tucked in a wooden box—now displayed in the museum—simply marked *Dantis ossa* ("Dante's bones"). The exhibit includes good descriptions, but it takes a strong background on Dante and his *Divine Comedy* to make a visit here worthwhile. If you do go in, request an English showing of the seven-minute film (theater on ground floor). Then climb to the first floor where the exhibit circles the courtyard: Be prepared to visit hell, purgatory, and paradise (or at least halls representing each of these). Outside, enjoy the two restful, grassy courtyards, one of them with modern statues of St. Francis and St. Claire.

Cost and Hours: €3, Tue-Sun 10:00-18:00, Nov-Feb until 16:00, closed Mon year-round, Via—what else?—Dante Alighieri 4, tel. 0544-215-676.

NORTHWEST OF PIAZZA DEL POPOLO

House of Stone Carpets (Domus dei Tappeti di Pietra)

Discovered in 1993, the stone mosaic floors of this sixth-century Byzantine house show both pictorial images and abstract designs. Excavations revealed many layers, dating back to the second century B.C. All were peeled away and preserved elsewhere. Only the sixth-century floor (12 rooms on one level) was put back and exhibited here, very close to its original location. Because this was a private home, its art could break from the conservative norms for public art of the age. The highlight is the wonderfully realistic *Dance of the Four Seasons* (displayed on the wall on your right as

RAVENNA

you descend the stairs). Don't miss the fourth-century *Christ as a Shepherd,* which some consider the earliest portrayal of Jesus (it's on the wall facing the *Four Seasons;* part of the face was lost to modern excavations). A visit here is almost meaningless without the €2 audioguide.

Cost and Hours: €4, €7 combo-ticket includes TAMO and Rasponi Crypt; daily 10:00-18:00, shorter hours and closed Mon in off-season; ask for the 10-minute English-language video—the computer-generated images help visitors envision the place in action; entrance through Church of Sant'Eufemia, on Via Barbiani just off Via Cavour near Piazza Baracca, tel. 0544-32512, www.domusdeitappetidipietra.it.

More Mosaics: The same association that runs the House of Stone Carpets also runs two other mosaic sights: **TAMO** has little in the way of historical artifacts but tells the story of mosaic-making (€4, €7 combo-ticket includes House of Stone Carpets and Rasponi Crypt, daily 10:00-18:30, June-Aug until 14:00, Via Rondinelli 2); **Rasponi Crypt** displays a floor of mosaics pieced together from different sites, crazy-quilt style (€2, €7 combo-ticket includes House of Stone Carpets and TAMO, Tue-Sun 10:00-18:30, June-Aug until 14:00, closed Mon, Piazza San Francesco 1).

NEAR RAVENNA
▲▲Church of Sant'Apollinare in Classe
The final major sight for Byzantine mosaic fans is a sixth-century church standing a few miles outside Ravenna in the suburb of Classe. It's impressive, but it comes in fourth place after the Basilica di San Vitale, Mausoleum of Galla Placidia, and Basilica di Sant'Apollinare Nuovo. On a quick day trip, it's certainly skippable.

Cost and Hours: €5, Mon-Sat 8:30-19:30, Sun 13:00-19:30, closed during services, Via Romea Sud, tel. 0544-473-569, www.turismo.ra.it. If trying to see it Sunday morning, you can generally get in for free between Masses until 13:00.

Getting There: The church is three miles out of town—an easy bike ride. To go by bus, buy two local bus tickets (€1.30 each) at any tobacco shop, newsstand, or the TI, then catch bus #4 across the street from the train station (on the corner by the park; 3/hour Mon-Sat, 1/hour on Sun, 15 minutes; save second ticket for return trip). The bus also leaves from Piazza Caduti (near the TI, stop is on the corner). To return to Ravenna from the church, walk back toward town along the main road about 100 yards to find the bus shelter on the right. You could also pay for a taxi (figure around €12 one-way, or €25 round-trip if your visit is quick).

Visiting the Church: The statue of Emperor Augustus, standing in front of the church, is a reminder that Classe was a strategic navy base in Roman times. In early Christian days, Classe was a big pilgrimage destination and home to a large Christian community. Today little remains other than its church, and even that was nearly bombed-out in World War II when the Germans used its medieval tower as a lookout.

The artistic treasure here is the mosaic work in the apse, 90 percent of which is original from the sixth century. The scene is an abstract portrayal of the Transfiguration of Jesus. The cross with a tiny portrait of Christ in its center beams light. God's hand above affirms that "This is the Truth." The three lambs represent James, John, and Peter. The landscape is of pine trees, which once forested the region. And St. Apollinare, the first local bishop, is celebrated because it was he who brought Christianity to the area.

The rest of the church—its mosaics lost to time—is pretty plain. While many churches this old have settled and the bases of their columns are no longer visible, here the floor level remains unchanged, and you can admire the columns' original bases. Near the entrance, a bilingual display panel gives detailed information on the church.

Sleeping in Ravenna

IN THE PEDESTRIAN ZONE, NEAR PIAZZA DEL POPOLO

$$$ Hotel Bisanzio is a business-class hotel with dated public spaces and 38 rooms in the city center (air-con, elevator, usually free on-street parking with hotel permit; Via Salara 30, tel. 054-421-7111, www.bisanziohotel.com, info@bisanziohotel.com).

$$ M Club B&B is a creative, comfortable, and stylish five-room place with an elegant breakfast room, spacious bedrooms, and thoughtful touches. Its website describes each unique room in detail (one family room, loaner bikes, Piazza Baracca 26, mobile 333-955-6466, www.m-club.it, info@m-club.it, Michael). The M Club faces the Porta Adriana gate at the far end of the old town from the train station (a 15-minute walk).

$$ Casa Masoli B&B, in an updated 17th-century building, has six elegantly outfitted rooms with giant bathrooms in a wood-paneled Art Deco style (peaceful garden, air-con, library, Via G. Rossi 22, tel. 0544-217-682, mobile 335-609-9471, www.casamasoli.it, info@casamasoli.it).

$ B&B Al Teatro fills an elegant townhouse with three rooms, one two-level apartment, and shared lounges and a courtyard that invite you to linger (air-con, elevator, loaner bikes, closed Nov-March, Via Guaccimanni 38, tel. 0544-188-1011, mobile 348-708-3867, www.bbalteatroravenna.com, info@bbalteatroravenna.com, Daniella).

$ A Casa di Paola is a converted private home (Paola's mother

Sleep Code

Hotels are classified based on the average price of a standard double room with breakfast in high season.

$$$$	**Splurge:** Most rooms over €170
$$$	**Pricier:** €130-170
$$	**Moderate:** €90-130
$	**Budget:** €50-90
¢	**Backpacker:** Under €50
RS%	**Rick Steves discount**

Unless otherwise noted, credit cards are accepted, hotel staff speak basic English, and free Wi-Fi is available. Comparison-shop by checking prices at several hotels (on each hotel's own website, on a booking site, or by email). For the best deal, *book direct with the hotel.* Ask for a discount if paying in cash; if the listing includes **RS%,** request a Rick Steves discount.

has an apartment on the ground floor) with eight nicely decorated rooms, comfy common spaces, and a treehouse floor plan (family rooms, air-con, free drinks, loaner bikes, Via P. Costa 31, tel. 0544-39425, mobile 347-730-6386, www.acasadipaola.it, info@acasadipaola.it). They also rent three rooms in their art-cluttered home a half-block away, at #26 (same prices).

NEAR THE TRAIN STATION
These places are convenient but have less atmosphere.

$$ Hotel Italia, just 100 yards from the train station, feels like a chain hotel but is actually family-owned. Its 45 rooms lack character but provide comfort and lots of space (family rooms, air-con, elevator, loaner bikes, free parking on first-come, first-served basis, turn left out of station, Viale Pallavicini 4, tel. 0544-212-363, www.hotelitaliaravenna.com, info@hotelitaliaravenna.com).

$ Albergo I Cherubini is a last-resort budget option with 18 basic, no-frills rooms and dark hallways. Ask for a room off the street (fans, cheaper rooms with shared bathrooms, Via R. Brancaleone 42, tel. 0544-39403, www.albergoristoranteicherubini.it, info@albergoristoranteicherubini.it, Donatella).

Hostel: ¢ Ostello Dante, a 15-minute walk from the station, has private and family rooms, loaner bikes, and a game room (12:00-14:30 lockout, 23:30 curfew or magnetic entrance key available with €20 deposit, closed Nov-Feb, Via Nicolodi 12, bus #1 or #70 from train station, tel. 0544-421-164, www.hostelravenna.com, hostelravenna@hotmail.com).

Eating in Ravenna

Located in the cuisine-crazy Emilia-Romagna region—famous for its cheeses and *salumi*—Ravenna has more than its share of great restaurants. Emilia-Romagna, nestled between farm fields and the sea, boasts seafood that's as good as its landfood. A local staple—served at carryout stands as well as fine restaurants—is *piadina* (pee-ah-DEE-nah), unleavened flatbread served plain or with a wide variety of fillings. At the top of every pasta menu is *cappelletti* ("little hats"), small doughy raviolis of cheese in a variety of sauces. Chefs here also make ample use of *squacquerone* ("shapeless"), a soft cream cheese that, by necessity, comes in a bowl. (For more on *salumi* and other Italian treats, see page 439.)

RESTAURANTS

$$ Ca' de Ven ("House of Wine"), the most famous restaurant in town, is surprisingly affordable. It fills a 16th-century warehouse with communal seating and residents enjoying quality wine and traditional regional cuisine. Up front is a bar with tables under ornately decorated Baroque domes, with 15-foot-tall wine cabinets towering above; in back is a huge hall under rough barrel vaults. For a light meal, order one of their *piadine*. Reserve ahead for dinner, and avoid weekend evenings when it's often overwhelmed (€38 fixed-price meal, no cover, Tue-Sun 11:00-14:15 & 18:30-23:00, closed Mon, 2-minute walk from Piazza del Popolo on Via Cairoli, which turns into Via C. Ricci—look for #24, tel. 0544-30163, www.cadeven.it). You can enjoy light meals and/or a glass of fine wine at the bar.

$$ Al Rustichello, a classic trattoria just outside the Porta Adriana city gate, has cozy ambience under heavy timbers. While you can ask for a printed menu, the owner ignores it—he just comes to your table and rattles off the options. Few diners can resist their *cappelletti,* served in the pan it was cooked in. Their €7 *antipasti* plate is a fun, splittable starter, with enticing samples of four local dishes (closed Sat lunch and all day Sun, Via Maggiore 21, tel. 0544-36043).

$$ Antica Bottega di Felice, behind the covered market, has a cheese-and-meat shop in front and an unpretentious sit-down eatery in back, serving up delicious local cuisine. While the space is more functional than atmospheric, the cuisine more than compensates (Mon-Sat 8:00-24:00, closed Sun, Via Ponte Marino 23, tel. 0544-240-170).

$$ Passatelli l'Osteria del Mariani has turned a former cinema into a fun and lively place to dine. The big screen adds to the bright, modern, and spacious atmosphere, as does the open kitchen where *piadina* and pasta are made. They offer modern Italian fare

> # Restaurant Price Code
>
> I've assigned each eatery a price category, based on the aver-
> age cost of a typical main course (pasta or *secondi*). Drinks,
> desserts, and splurge items (steak and seafood) can raise the
> price considerably.
>
> | | |
> |---|---|
> | **$$$$** | **Splurge:** Most main courses over €20 |
> | **$$$** | **Pricier:** €15-20 |
> | **$$** | **Moderate:** €10-15 |
> | **$** | **Budget:** Under €10 |
>
> In Italy, pizza by the slice and other takeaway food is **$**; a basic
> trattoria or sit-down pizzeria is **$$**; a casual but more upscale
> restaurant is **$$$**; and a swanky splurge is **$$$$**.

and a hearty salad bar (daily 12:00-15:00 & 19:00-24:00, Via Ponte
Marino 19, tel. 0544-215-206). For a cheap light meal, drop by
their bar in front, where they offer an inviting *aperitivo* (free appetizers with your drink) from 18:00 to 24:00 each evening.

$$ Ristorante la Gardèla is a local fixture—if Ravenna had
a town dining room, this would be it. The fun-loving waitstaff has
been here for years, and the restaurant has all the nice touches
without the pretense. While there are a few tables outside and up-
stairs, I like the jolly main floor. Their *cappelletti* is served *in brodo*
(soup) or *al ragù* (with meat sauce; €15 and €25 fixed-price meals,
Fri-Wed 12:00-14:30 & 19:00-22:00, closed Thu, tucked behind
the covered market at Via Ponte Marino 3, tel. 0544-217-147).

FISH AND SEAFOOD

$$$ Ristorante Osteria del Tempo Perso is a red-velvet-romantic
choice for seafood, with service as warm as its color scheme, mel-
low jazz on the soundtrack, and a grown-up vibe. I'd ignore the
forgettable outdoor seating (daily 19:30-23:00, also Sat-Sun 12:30-
14:00, Via Gamba 12, tel. 0544-215-393).

$$$ L'Acciuga Osteria ("Anchovy"), hiding at the back of
a little courtyard on a residential street just outside the old town
center, is well-respected for its intentionally short menu of fresh
seafood. Because everything is fresh and priced by the weight, this
can get expensive, but it's worth a trip for seafood lovers. The res-
taurant is done up like the lower holds of a submarine, but—thanks
to the tasteful, dressy decor—seems stylish rather than tacky (€39
fixed-price meal, Tue-Sat 12:00-15:00 & 19:30-23:30, Sun 12:00-
15:00 only, closed Mon, Viale Baracca 74, tel. 0544-212-713).

QUICK SNACK SPOTS

$ *Piadina* Stands: For the best cheap, traditional lunch in Ravenna,
skip the pizza and instead grab a *piadina*. These tasty flatbread

sandwiches are stuffed with a variety of local meats, vegetables, and cheeses (including *squacquerone*), then folded over and grilled. You'll see several takeout windows in the downtown pedestrian zone selling them. Consider the popular-with-students **Profuma di Piadina** (on the way from Piazza del Popolo to the Basilica di San Francesco, at Via Cairoli 24) and **La Piadina del Melarancio** (just off Piazza del Popolo at Via IV Novembre 31). For a break from Italian food, **Ali Kebab**, across from La Piadina del Melarancio at Via IV Novembre 26, is cheap, fast, and inviting.

Local Products: Gastronomia Alpine, a "gastronomic boutique" selling regional cheeses, *salumi*, country bread, and other products, treats in-the-know picnic shoppers to the bounty of Emilia-Romagna. It's conveniently located right along the main pedestrian street (Mon-Wed 8:00-16:00, Thu-Sun 8:00-21:00, Via Cavour 43, tel. 0544-37529). **Antica Bottega di Felice,** recommended earlier as a restaurant, also has a fine cheese and *salumi* shop up front.

Supermarkets: For lunch, assemble a picnic at the **InCo-op** store at the corner of Via di Roma and Via A. Mariani (Mon-Sat 8:00-20:30, Sun 9:00-13:30 & 16:30-20:30). A fine place to enjoy your feast is in the shady gardens of the Rocca Brancaleone fortress (daily until 18:00; 5-minute walk from station, follow Via Maroncelli until you see the walls).

Self-Service Cafeteria: Ristorante Marchesini, near the Basilica di San Francesco, is an upscale self-serve restaurant (over a street-level delicatessen) offering delicious salads and homemade pastas (Mon-Sat 11:00-14:30 & 18:00-22:30, closed Sun, 5-minute walk from Piazza del Popolo, on corner of Piazza Caduti at Via Mazzini 6—ride elevator to first floor, tel. 0544-212-309).

Gelato: Papilla Gelato is bright, mod, and trendy, with free dips from its chocolate fountain if you like (pricey cones, but small is big here, a block off Piazza del Popolo at Via IV Novembre 8).

Ravenna Connections

From Ravenna by Train to: Venice (roughly hourly, 3 hours), **Padua** (roughly hourly, 2.5-3.5 hours), **Florence** (about hourly, 2.5 hours by fast train, no slow train option). All of these trips require a change in either Ferrara or Bologna.

VENETIAN HISTORY

In the Middle Ages, the clever Venetian aristocracy became Europe's middlemen for East-West trade, creating a great merchant empire presided over by a series of elected dukes, called doges. By smuggling in the bones of St. Mark, Venice gained religious importance as well. But after the discovery of America and new trading routes to the Orient, Venetian power ebbed. Yet as Venice fell, her appetite for decadence grew. Throughout the 17th and 18th centuries, Venice partied on the wealth accumulated during its time as a trading power.

That's Venetian history in a seashell. Want more? Read on.

ROME FALLS, VENICE RISES (A.D. 500)

In A.D. 476, the last Roman emperor abdicated, the empire's infrastructure was crumbling, and northern Italy was crawling with

Germanic-speaking "barbarian" invaders. Hoping these Visigoths, Huns, and Lombards didn't like water, Latin-speaking mainlanders took refuge on the marshy, uninhabited islands of the Venetian lagoon.

The refugees squatted on this wet and miserable land. Eventually, they sank pilings in the mud to build on, channeled water into canals, and constructed bridges to lace together the motley collection of more than 100 natural islands that would eventually become Venice.

MEDIEVAL GROWTH (500-1000)

These first Venetians harvested salt and fish for their livelihood, and traded it on the mainland. Though Venice's islands were desolate, the area—known to the Romans as the "Seven Seas"—was strategically important. In about 540 A.D., the Byzantine Emperor Justinian reconquered Italy from the barbarians and briefly reunited the Roman Empire. He established a capital at Ravenna, bringing the Venetian islands under Byzantine influence.

Soon, Venetians began to elect local rulers whom they called "doges"—the first of many who would rule for more than a thousand years. (Though "doge" is linguistically related to our word "duke," Venetian rulers were more like constitutional monarchs, elected by their fellow nobles and expected to govern according to the rule of law.) As early as 810, one doge had his seat in the settlement of Rivo Alto ("High Bank"), near today's Rialto Bridge.

Under Byzantine protection, Venetians became prosperous seagoing merchants. Acting as middlemen, they bought goods from the sophisticated Byzantine and Islamic lands to the East and sold them to consumers in the West.

Venice's merchant economy boomed while the rest of Europe languished under land-based feudalism. Charlemagne, the Holy Roman Emperor who'd conquered much of Italy (c. 800), eyed the region hungrily. But Venetians, wanting to keep their independence, deposed Charlemagne's bishop and chose one who was loyal to (distant) Byzantium.

To legitimize their new bishop, the Venetians managed to smuggle the holy relics of St. Mark from Egypt in 828, thus becoming a religious power overnight. To seal the city's oriental orientation, Venetian leaders had the grand St. Mark's Basilica built in a distinctly Eastern style.

Sights
- Gondolas and the network of canals
- Old crypt under San Zaccaria Church
- Santa Maria Assunta Church on Torcello Island

A SEAFARING POWER (1000-1500)

Venetian sea traders established trading outposts in Byzantine and Muslim territories to the east. They used the same alpine passes that we travel today to ship luxury goods to Western Europe. At home, a stable, constitutional government ran an efficient, state-operated multinational corporation. The shallow lagoon was easily

Venice's Empire

London • Amsterdam
• Bruges
Paris •
Atlantic
Ocean
• Vienna
Verona
Milan • ★ **Venice**
Genoa • DALMATIA
Ravenna • Black
Pisa • Adriatic Sea Sea
Florence • Constantinople •
Rome • •
Amalfi • Corfu • Aegean To China →
Gibraltar Mediterranean Sea
• BATTLE OF Rhodes
LEPANTO
(1571) Nafplio •
Sea Crete Cyprus
Alexandria • HOLY LAND

■ Lands united with or linked to the
  Venetian Empire over the centuries

···· Current National Borders

defended against attack, making fortifications unnecessary. Grand buildings reflected Venice's wealth.

Venetian merchants ran a profitable trading triangle: timber from Venice's mainland to Egypt for gold to Byzantium for luxury goods to Venice. Its merchant fleet was the biggest in the Mediterranean, backed by powerful warships.

By the 12th century, tiny Venice had effectively established itself as an independent, self-ruling country and was running Europe's first industrial complex, the Arsenale (1104). With more than 1,000 workers using an early form of assembly-line production, the Arsenale could produce about one warship a day.

This put the "fear of Venice" into visiting rulers. When France's King Henry III dropped by the Arsenale, Venice entertained him with a shipbuilding spectacle: from ribs to finished product in four hours.

When Europe launched its Crusades to the Holy Land (1095-1272), Venice transported soldiers and defended Byzantine and Crusader ports in return for commercial privileges. This made the eastern Mediterranean a virtual free-trade zone for a very aggressive Venetian trading community to exploit.

Wealthy Venetian nobles built lavish homes. With a natural lagoon as a defense, these were not fortified castles like the rest of Europe but luxurious *palazzi*, complete with loading docks, warehouses, and chandeliered ballrooms. The streets were paved. The government provided oil and required that streets be lit—a first in Europe.

Besides sea trade, Venice established strong local industries. Having mastered the art of making glass, Venice was on the cutting edge of the new science of grinding lenses for eyeglasses and telescopes. Understanding medicine as a chemical rather than an herbal pursuit, Venetians developed Europe's first real pharmaceutical industry. They made Europe's first affordable paper, from rags rather than from sheepskin (parchment). As the city offered the world's first copyright protection, its printing and bookmaking industry boomed. With mountains of capital and a sophisticated trade system of insurance, joint ventures, and money drafts, Venice's merchants eventually became bankers, loaning money at interest—making them early capitalists.

Rather than being ruled by a king—as was standard in feudal Europe—Venice developed a sophisticated government run by voting aristocrats. By the 13th century, Venice was fast becoming a Mediterranean superpower. During the Fourth Crusade (1204), Venetian troops joined other Crusaders in attacking and looting Christian Constantinople. The haul of booty enriched the city, enabling Venice to stand up to its former Byzantine protectors. When Venetian ships routed the fleet of their Genoan rivals at Chioggia (on the south end of the lagoon) in 1381, Venice became the undisputed master of the eastern Mediterranean. Next, they launched attacks on the mainland, conquering much of northern Italy. By 1420, Venice was at the height of its power, with mainland possessions and a powerful overseas trading empire to the east.

HISTORY

Sights
- Doge's Palace
- St. Mark's Basilica
- Frari Church
- Buildings decorated in ornate Venetian Gothic style
- Doge paraphernalia and city history at Correr Museum
- Glass and lace industries (including the Murano glassworks)
- Arsenale shipbuilding complex

Noteworthy Residents
Enrico Dandolo (r. 1192-1205): Doge during the Fourth Crusade, when Venetian crusaders looted Constantinople, helping to enrich Venice.

Marco Polo (1254-1324): Traveler to faraway China whose journal, *The Book of Marvels*, was dismissed by many as fiction.

Paolo Veneziano (1310-1358): Painter who mastered the Byzantine gold-icon style, then added touches of Western realism.

Francesco Foscari (1373-1457): Doge at the peak of Venice's power, whose ill-advised wars against Milan and the Ottoman Turks started the Republic's slow fade.

Jacopo Bellini (c. 1400-1470): Father of painting family. His training in Renaissance Florence brought 3-D realism to Venice.

Gentile Bellini (c. 1429-1507): Elder son of painting family, known for straightforward, historical scenes of Venice.

RENAISSANCE AND SEEDS OF DECLINE (1500-1600)

In 1500, Venice was a commercial powerhouse—among the six biggest cities in Europe. Of its estimated 180,000 citizens, nearly

1,000 were of Rockefeller-esque wealth and power. Europe's richest city-state poured money into the arts. Titian, Tintoretto, Sansovino, the Bellini family, and Palladio called Venice home. St. Mark's Square became the gathering place for merchants and nobles from Venice's vast trading empire. Across Europe, Venice had a reputation as a luxury-loving, exotic, cosmopolitan playground.

But Venice's power had started to wane. The seeds had been sown in the 15th century. In 1492, Columbus sailed the ocean blue, and began to trade with a World that was New. In 1498, Vasco da Gama circled Africa's Cape of Good Hope, finding a new sea route to eastern markets. Venice's monopoly was broken.

On the Italian mainland, Venice became locked in draining wars against its rival Milan. Meanwhile, Ottomans were expanding in the East, encroaching on Venice's former dominions. Venetians and Ottomans became wary trade partners, sometimes dealing peacefully but sometimes battling over strategic ports. In 1453, the Ottomans took Constantinople, and Venice suddenly lost one of its best customers. Venice (and its European allies) scored a temporary victory over the Ottomans at the Battle of Lepanto (1571), but Venice's navy suffered major damage. Spain, England, and Holland, with their oceangoing vessels, emerged as superior traders in a more global economy.

Sights
- St. Mark's Square facades and other work by Sansovino
- Palladio's classical facades (San Giorgio Maggiore and Il Redentore churches)
- Masterpiece paintings by Titian, Giovanni Bellini, Giorgione,

HISTORY

Church Architecture

History comes to life when you visit a centuries-old church. Even if you wouldn't know your apse from a hole in the ground, learning a few simple terms will enrich your experience. Of course, not every church has every feature. It's worth noting that a "cathedral" (*duomo* in Italian) isn't a type of church architecture, but rather a designation for a church that's a governing center for a local bishop.

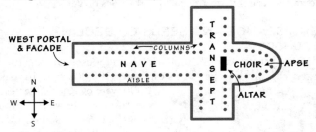

Aisles: The long, generally low-ceilinged arcades that flank the nave.

Altar: The raised area with a ceremonial table (often adorned with candles or a crucifix), where the priest prepares and serves the bread and wine for Communion.

Apse: The space beyond the altar, generally bordered with small chapels.

Barrel Vault: A continuous round-arched ceiling that resembles an upside-down "U."

Choir: A cozy area, often screened off, located within the church nave and near the high altar, where services are sung in a more intimate setting.

Cloister: Covered hallways bordering a square or rectangular open-air courtyard, traditionally where monks and nuns got fresh air.

Facade: The front exterior of the church's main (west) entrance, viewable from outside and generally highly decorated.

Groin Vault: An arched ceiling formed where two equal barrel vaults meet at right angles. Also: a medieval jock strap.

Narthex: The area (portico or foyer) between the main entry and the nave.

Nave: The long, central section of the church (running west to east, from the entrance to the altar) where the congregation sits or stands through the service.

Transept: In a traditional cross-shaped floor plan, the transept is one of the two parts forming the "arms" of the cross. The transepts run north-south, perpendicularly crossing the east-west nave.

West Portal: The main entry to the church (on the west end, opposite the main altar).

and Tintoretto (Accademia, Frari Church, Doge's Palace, San
Zaccaria Church, Correr Museum, Scuola San Rocco)
- Jewish Ghetto and Jewish Museum

Noteworthy Residents
Giovanni Bellini (c. 1430-1516): The most famous son in the
painting family, whose glowing, colorful, 3-D Madonna-and-
Childs started the Venetian Renaissance. Teacher of Titian and
Giorgione.

    Vittore Carpaccio (c. 1460-1525): Painter of realistic, secular
scenes and the impressive Scuola Dalmata di San Giorgio.

    Giorgione (c. 1477-1511): Innovative painter whose moody
realism influenced Bellini (his teacher) and Titian (his friend and
fellow painter).

    Jacopo Sansovino (1486-1570): Renaissance architect who
redid the face of Venice (especially St. Mark's Square), introducing sober, classical columns and arches to a city previously full of
ornate Gothic.

    Titian (Tiziano Vecellio, c. 1490-1576): Premier Venetian Re-
naissance painter. Master of many styles, from teenage Madonnas
to sober state portraits to exuberant mythological scenes to center-
fold nudes.

    Andrea Palladio (1508-1580): Influential architect whose
classical style was much imitated around the world, resulting in villas, government buildings, and banks that look like Greek temples.

    Tintoretto (Jacopo Robusti, c. 1518-1594): Painter of dramatic
religious scenes, using strong 3-D, diagonal compositions, twisting
poses, sharp contrast of light and shadow, and bright, "black velvet"
colors (late Renaissance/Mannerist style).

    Paolo Veronese (1528-1588): Painter of big, colorful canvases,
capturing the exuberance and luxury of Renaissance Venice.

ELEGANT DECLINE (1600-1800)

New trade routes, new European powers, and
belligerent Ottomans drained Venice's economy
and shrank its commercial empire. At home,
however, Venice's reputation for luxury—and
even decadence—still made it a popular tourist
destination for Europe's gentry. In some ways,
this is the period that most defines Venice: the
city of Baroque monuments, masked balls at
Carnevale, velvet-dressed nobles at opera de-
buts, and the roguish debauchery of Casanova.

Venice's empire dwindled economically and politically. In 1669,
its last major outpost, Crete, fell to the Ottomans. Several devastating plagues gutted the population at home. The once-enlightened

government gained a nasty reputation for corruption and for locking away dissidents in the dank prisons of the Doge's Palace. In 1797, Napoleon Bonaparte rolled into Venice and toppled the final doge. A thousand-year era of independent rule was over.

Sights

- Ca' Rezzonico (Museum of 18th-Century Venice)
- La Salute Church
- Masks of the Carnevale tradition
- Old cafés (e.g., the Florian and the Quadri, both on St. Mark's Square)
- La Fenice Opera House
- Baroque interiors in many churches
- Canova sculptures (Correr Museum, Frari Church)
- G. B. Tiepolo paintings (Accademia, Doge's Palace, Ca' Rezzonico)
- Paintings of Canaletto, Guardi, and G. D. Tiepolo (Ca' Rezzonico)

Noteworthy Residents

Claudio Monteverdi (1567-1643): The composer and *maestro di capella* at St. Mark's Basilica who wrote in a budding new medium—opera.

Baldassare Longhena (1598-1682): Architect of the Baroque La Salute Church.

Antonio Vivaldi (1678-1741): Composer of *The Four Seasons* ("Dah dunt-dunt-duh dutta dah-ah-ah").

G. B. Tiepolo (Giovanni Battista, 1696-1770): Painter of mythological subjects in colorful Rococo ceilings.

Giovanni Antonio Canal, a.k.a. Canaletto (1697-1768): Painter of photo-realist Venice views.

Carlo Goldoni (1707-1793): Comic playwright who brought refinement to commedia dell'arte buffoonery.

Francesco Guardi (1712-1793): Painter of proto-Impressionist Venice views.

Giacomo Casanova (1725-1798): Gambler, womanizer, and adventurer whose exaggerated memoirs inspired Romantics.

G. D. Tiepolo (Giovanni Domenico, 1727-1804): Painter son of the famous G. B. Tiepolo.

Lorenzo Da Ponte (1749-1838): Mozart's librettist, who popularized Venice's sophisticated and decadent high society.

Antonio Canova (1757-1822): Neoclassical sculptor whose beautiful polished-white statues were especially popular in Napoleon's France.

HISTORY

MODERN VENICE (1800 TO THE PRESENT)

After Napoleon's defeat at Waterloo, the European allies placed Venice under Austrian rule. Sophisticated Venetians chafed against their Viennese masters. However, Venice was still a key stop on any traveler's Grand Tour, and Europe's young aristocrats visited the city to "complete" their education. Venice and Italy became a political backwater as Austrian and French influence dominated.

In 1866, when Prussia dealt Austria a humiliating military defeat, rebellious Venetians seized the moment to join Italy's independence movement, and annexed themselves to the newly unified, democratic nation of Italy.

Venice joined the Industrial Revolution only reluctantly. A two-mile railroad causeway was built to connect the island city with the mainland during the Austrian period (1846). This was later paralleled by a highway for cars (1932). On the mainland, unbridled industrialization produced pollution (mainly sulfuric acid) that threatened Venice's stone monuments. In 1966, Venice suffered a disastrous flood, which prompted many plans and projects to control future flooding—some have been enacted, while others are still on the drawing board.

Inside Venice proper, however, there has been little new building for centuries. Today, Venice remains a museum piece for

foreigners—one increasingly threatened by mainland pollution, climate change, floods, and hordes of tourists. In the 2000s, Venice—ever an obligatory destination—became a hugely popular stop for cruise ships. Local and UNESCO regulations try to preserve Venice as a cultural landmark. When Venice's venerable La Fenice Opera House burned down in 1996, it was rebuilt right away. Recent repairs to the Rialto Bridge have been largely funded by the Diesel fashion line, whose owner pledged €5 million in response to the city's pleas for sponsorship (but only in return for advertising space on the scaffolding). While keeping up with what's new, Venice remains a historic wonderland. Venice is timeless—a place where visitors can easily blink away elements of the modern world and find themselves transported back in time.

HISTORY

Sights
• Correr Museum's Risorgimento wing

- Statue of Daniele Manin (between St. Mark's Square and Rialto Bridge)
- Motorized *vaporetti* and taxis
- Train station (1954)
- Peggy Guggenheim Collection
- Biennale International Art Exhibition (held in odd years)
- Pollution from the mainland city of Mestre
- Calatrava Bridge (2008)
- Stazione Marittima cruise port
- Burger King

Noteworthy Residents

Daniele Manin (1804-1857): Rebel who led 1848 Venetian revolt against the city's Austrian rulers, eventually allowing Venice to join a united, democratic, modern Italy.

Peggy Guggenheim (1898-1979): American-born art collector, gallery owner, and friend of modern art and artists.

For more on the history of Venice and on Europe throughout the centuries, consider Europe 101: History and Art for the Traveler, *written by Rick Steves and Gene Openshaw (available at www.ricksteves.com).*

PRACTICALITIES

This chapter covers the practical skills of European travel: how to get tourist information, pay for things, sightsee efficiently, find good-value accommodations, eat affordably but well, use technology wisely, and get between destinations smoothly. To study ahead and round out your knowledge and skills, check out "Resources from Rick Steves."

Tourist Information

The Italian national tourist offices **in the US** offer many brochures and a free, general Italy guide. Before your trip, scan their website (www.italia.it) for downloadable materials or contact the nearest branch to request information. If you have a specific problem, they're a good source of sympathy (New York: Tel. 212/245-5618, newyork@enit.it; Chicago: Tel. 312/644-0996, chicago@enit.it; Los Angeles: Tel. 310/820-1898, losangeles@enit.it).

In Venice, TIs are generally understaffed and not very helpful. For more on their services and locations, see page 16.

Travel Tips

Emergency and Medical Help: In Italy, dial 113 for English-speaking police help. To summon an ambulance, call 118. If you get sick, do as the locals do and go to a pharmacist for advice. Or ask at your hotel for help—they'll know the nearest medical and emergency services. For the hospital and first-aid help, see page 19.

Theft or Loss: To replace a passport, you'll need to go in person to an embassy (see page 469). If your credit and debit cards disappear, cancel and replace them (see "Damage Control for Lost Cards" on page 418). File a police report, either on the spot or within a day or two; you'll need it to submit an insurance claim for lost or stolen rail passes or travel gear, and it can help with replacing your passport or credit and debit cards. For more information, see www.ricksteves.com/help.

Time Zones: Italy, like most of continental Europe, is generally six/nine hours ahead of the East/West Coasts of the US. The exceptions are the beginning and end of Daylight Saving Time: Europe "springs forward" the last Sunday in March (two weeks after most of North America), and "falls back" the last Sunday in October (one week before North America). For a handy online time converter, see www.timeanddate.com/worldclock.

Business Hours: Traditionally, Italy has used the siesta plan, with people generally working from about 9:00 to 13:00 and from 15:30 or 16:00 to 19:00 or 19:30, Monday through Saturday (though in tourist areas, larger shops may be open through lunch). In Venice, some stores and restaurants close on Sunday, or at least one other day per week. Banking hours are generally Monday through Friday 8:30 to 13:30 and 15:30 to 16:30, but can vary wildly.

Saturdays are virtually weekdays, with earlier closing hours. Sundays have the same pros and cons as they do for travelers in the US: Sightseeing attractions are generally open, while banks and many shops are closed, public transportation options are fewer (for example, no bus service to or from the smaller towns), and there's no rush hour. Friday and Saturday evenings are lively; Sunday evenings are quiet.

Watt's Up? Europe's electrical system is 220 volts, instead of North America's 110 volts. Most newer electronics (such as laptops, battery chargers, and hair dryers) convert automatically, so you won't need a converter, but you will need an adapter plug with two round prongs, sold inexpensively at travel stores in the US. However, sockets in Italy (and Switzerland) only accept plugs with slimmer prongs, so don't buy an adapter with the thicker ("Schuko" style) prongs—it won't work. Avoid bringing older appliances that don't automatically convert voltage; instead, buy a cheap replacement in Europe.

Discounts: Discounts for sights are generally not listed in this book. Italy's national museums generally offer free admission to children under 18, but some discounts are available only for citizens of the European Union (EU). However, Venice's city museums offer youth and senior discounts to Americans and others who are not citizens of the EU—bring an ID. These museums include the Doge's Palace, Correr Museum, Clock Tower on St. Mark's Square, Ca' Rezzonico, Ca' Pesaro, Palazzo Mocenigo Costume Museum, Murano's Glass Museum, and Burano's Lace Museum.

Online Translation Tips: Google's Chrome browser instantly translates websites. You can also paste text or the URL of a foreign website into the translation window at http://translate.google.com. The Google Translate app converts spoken English into most European languages (and vice versa) and can also translate text it "reads" with your mobile device's camera.

Money

This section offers advice on how to pay for purchases on your trip (including getting cash from ATMs and paying with plastic), dealing with lost or stolen cards, VAT (sales tax) refunds, and tipping.

WHAT TO BRING

Bring both a credit card and a debit card. You'll use the debit card at cash machines (ATMs) to withdraw local cash for most purchases, and the credit card to pay for larger items. Some travelers carry a third card, in case one gets demagnetized or eaten by a temperamental machine.

For an emergency stash, bring $100-200 in hard cash. Although banks in some countries don't exchange dollars, in a pinch you can always find exchange desks at major train stations or airports—convenient but with crummy rates.

CASH

Although credit cards are widely accepted in Europe, day-to-day spending is generally more cash-based. I find cash is the easiest—and sometimes only—way to pay for cheap food, bus fare, taxis, and local guides. Some vendors will charge you extra for using a credit card, some won't accept foreign credit cards, and some won't take credit cards at all. Having cash on hand can help you avoid a stressful predicament if you find yourself in a place that won't accept your card.

Throughout Europe, ATMs are the easiest and smartest way for travelers to get cash. They work just like they do at home. To

Exchange Rate

1 euro (€) = about $1.10

To convert prices in euros to dollars, add about 10 percent: €20=about $22, €50=about $55. (Check www.oanda.com for the latest exchange rates.) Just like the dollar, one euro is broken down into 100 cents. Coins range from €0.01 to €2, and bills from €5 to €200 (bills over €50 are rarely used; €500 bills are being phased out).

withdraw money from an ATM (known as a *bancomat* in Italy), you'll need a debit card (ideally with a Visa or MasterCard logo), plus a PIN code (numeric and four digits). For increased security, shield the keypad when entering your PIN code, and don't use an ATM if anything on the front of the machine looks loose or damaged (a sign that someone may have attached a "skimming" device to capture account information). Try to withdraw large sums of money to reduce the number of per-transaction bank fees you'll pay.

When possible, use ATMs located outside banks—a thief is less likely to target a cash machine near surveillance cameras, and if your card is munched by a machine during banking hours, you can go inside for help. Stay away from "independent" ATMs such as Travelex, Euronet, YourCash, Cardpoint, and Cashzone, which charge huge commissions, have terrible exchange rates, and may try to trick users with "dynamic currency conversion" (described later). Although you can use a credit card to withdraw cash at an ATM, this comes with high bank fees and only makes sense in an emergency.

While traveling, if you want to access your accounts online, be sure to use a secure connection (see page 453).

Pickpockets target tourists. To safeguard your cash, wear a money belt—a pouch with a strap that you buckle around your waist like a belt and tuck under your clothes. Keep your cash, credit cards, and passport secure in your money belt, and carry only a day's spending money in your front pocket or wallet.

CREDIT AND DEBIT CARDS

For purchases, Visa and MasterCard are more commonly accepted than American Express. Just like at home, credit or debit cards work easily at larger hotels, restaurants, and shops. I typically use my debit card to withdraw cash to pay for most purchases. I use my credit card sparingly: to book hotel reservations, to buy advance tickets for events or sights, to cover major expenses (such as car rentals or plane tickets), and to pay for things online or near the end of my trip (to avoid another visit to the ATM). While you could instead use a debit card for these purchases, a credit card offers a greater degree of fraud protection.

Ask Your Credit- or Debit-Card Company: Before your trip, contact the company that issued your debit or credit cards.

Confirm your **card will work overseas,** and alert them that you'll be using it in Europe; otherwise, they may deny transactions if they perceive unusual spending patterns.

Ask for the specifics on transaction **fees.** When you use your credit or debit card—either for purchases or ATM withdrawals—you'll typically be charged additional "international transaction" fees of up to 3 percent (1 percent is normal). If your card's fees seem high, consider getting a card just for your trip: Capital One (www.capitalone.com) and most credit unions have low-to-no international fees.

Verify your daily ATM **withdrawal limit,** and if necessary, ask your bank to adjust it. I prefer a high limit that allows me to take out more cash at each ATM stop and save on bank fees; some travelers prefer to set a lower limit in case their card is stolen. Note that foreign banks also set maximum withdrawal amounts for their ATMs.

Get your bank's **emergency phone number** in the US (but not its 800 number, which isn't accessible from overseas) to call collect if you have a problem.

Ask for your credit card's **PIN** in case you need to make an emergency cash withdrawal or encounter payment machines using the chip-and-PIN system; the bank won't tell you your PIN over the phone, so allow time for it to be mailed to you.

Chip and PIN: While much of Europe is shifting to a chip-and-PIN security system for credit cards, Italy still uses the old magnetic-stripe technology. (European chip-and-PIN cards are embedded with an electronic security chip and require a four-digit PIN to make a purchase.) If you happen to encounter chip and PIN, it will probably be at payment machines, such as those at toll roads or unattended gas pumps. On the outside chance that a machine won't take your card, find a cashier who can make your card work (they can print a receipt for you to sign), or find a machine that takes cash. Most American travelers don't run into problems. Still, it pays to carry euros; remember, you can always use an ATM to withdraw cash with your magnetic-stripe debit card.

If you're concerned, ask if your bank offers a chip-and-PIN card. Andrews Federal Credit Union (www.andrewsfcu.org) and the State Department Federal Credit Union (www.sdfcu.org) offer these cards and are open to all US residents.

Dynamic Currency Conversion: If merchants or hoteliers offer to convert your purchase price into dollars (called dynamic currency conversion, or DCC), refuse this "service." You'll pay extra for the expensive convenience of seeing your charge in dollars. Some ATMs and retailers try to confuse customers by presenting DCC in misleading terms. If an ATM offers to "lock in" or "guarantee" your conversion rate, choose "proceed without conversion." Other prompts might state, "You can be charged in dollars: Press YES for dollars, NO for euros." Always choose the local currency.

Damage Control for Lost Cards

If you lose your credit or debit card, you can stop people from using your card by reporting the loss immediately to the respective global customer-assistance centers. Call these 24-hour US numbers collect: Visa (tel. 303/967-1096), MasterCard (tel. 636/722-7111), and American Express (tel. 336/393-1111). In Italy, to make a collect call to the US, dial 800-172-444. Press zero or stay on the line for an English-speaking operator. European toll-free numbers (listed by country) can also be found at the websites for Visa and Master-Card.

If you are the secondary cardholder, you'll need to provide the primary cardholder's identification-verification details (such as birth date, mother's maiden name, or Social Security number). You can generally receive a temporary card within two or three business days in Europe (see www.ricksteves.com/help for more).

If you report your loss within two days, you typically won't be responsible for any unauthorized transactions on your account, although many banks charge a liability fee of $50.

TIPPING

Tipping in Italy isn't as automatic and generous as it is in the US. For special service, tips are appreciated, but not expected. As in the US, the proper amount depends on your resources, tipping philosophy, and the circumstances, but some general guidelines apply.

Restaurants: In Italy, a service charge *(servizio)* is usually built into your bill, so the total you pay already includes a basic tip. It's up to you whether to tip beyond this. For more details on restaurant tipping, see page 432.

Taxis: To tip the cabbie, round up your fare a bit (for instance, if the fare is €4.50, pay €5). If the cabbie hauls your bags and zips you to the airport to help you catch your flight, you might want to toss in a little more. But if you feel like you're being driven in circles or otherwise ripped off, skip the tip.

Services: In general, if someone in the tourism or service industry does a super job for you, a small tip of a euro or two is appropriate...but not required. If you're not sure whether (or how much) to tip, ask a local for advice.

PRACTICALITIES

GETTING A VAT REFUND

Wrapped into the purchase price of your Italian souvenirs is a Value-Added Tax (VAT) of about 22 percent. You're entitled to get most of that tax back if you purchase more than €155 (about $170) worth of goods at a store that participates in the VAT-refund scheme. Typically, you must ring up the minimum at a single retailer—you can't add up your purchases from various shops to reach the required amount.

Getting your refund is usually straightforward and, if you buy a substantial amount of souvenirs, well worth the hassle. If you're lucky, the merchant will subtract the tax when you make your purchase. (This is more likely to occur if the store ships the goods to your home.) Otherwise, you'll need to:

Get the paperwork. Have the merchant completely fill out the necessary refund document. You'll have to present your passport. Get the paperwork done before you leave the store to ensure you'll have everything you need (including your original sales receipt).

Get your stamp at the border or airport. Process your VAT document at your last stop in the European Union (such as at the airport) with the customs agent who deals with VAT refunds. Arrive an additional hour early before you need to check in for your flight to allow time to find the local customs office—and to stand in line. It's best to keep your purchases in your carry-on. If they're too large or dangerous to carry on (such as knives), pack them in your checked bags and alert the check-in agent. You'll be sent (with your tagged bag) to a customs desk outside security; someone will examine your bag, stamp your paperwork, and put your bag on the belt. You're not supposed to use your purchased goods before you leave. If you show up at customs wearing your new Italian leather shoes, officials might look the other way—or deny you a refund.

Collect your refund. You'll need to return your stamped document to the retailer or its representative. Many merchants work with services—such as Global Blue or Premier Tax Free—that have offices at major airports, ports, or border crossings (either before or after security, probably strategically located near a duty-free shop). These services, which extract a 4 percent fee, can refund your money immediately in cash or credit your card (within two billing cycles). Other refund services may require you to mail the documents from home, or more quickly, from your point of departure (using an envelope you've prepared in advance or one that's been provided by the merchant). You'll then have to wait—it can take months.

CUSTOMS FOR AMERICAN SHOPPERS

You are allowed to take home $800 worth of items per person duty-free, once every 31 days. As for food, you can take home many processed and packaged foods: vacuum-packed cheeses, dried herbs, jams, baked goods, candy, chocolate, oil, vinegar, mustard, and honey. Fresh fruits and vegetables and most meats are not allowed, with exceptions for some canned items. As for alcohol, you can bring in one liter duty-free (it can be packed securely in your checked luggage, along with any other liquid-containing items).

To bring alcohol (or liquid-packed foods) in your carry-on bag on your flight home, buy it at a duty-free shop at the airport. You'll increase your odds of getting it onto a connecting flight if it's packaged in a "STEB"—a secure, tamper-evident bag. But stay away from liquids in opaque, ceramic, or metallic containers, which usually cannot be successfully screened (STEB or no STEB).

For details on allowable goods, customs rules, and duty rates, visit http://help.cbp.gov.

Sightseeing

Sightseeing can be hard work. Use these tips to make your visits to Venice's finest sights meaningful, fun, efficient, and painless.

MAPS AND NAVIGATION TOOLS

A good map is essential for efficient navigation while sightseeing. The black-and-white maps in this book are concise and simple, designed to help you locate recommended destinations, sights, and local TIs, where you can pick up more in-depth maps. Maps with even more detail are sold at newsstands and bookstores.

You can also use a mapping app on your mobile device. Be aware that pulling up maps or looking up turn-by-turn walking directions on the fly requires an Internet connection: To use this feature, it's smart to get an international data plan (see page 449) or only connect using Wi-Fi. With Google Maps or Apple Maps, it's possible to download a map while online, then go offline and navigate without incurring data-roaming charges, though you can't search for an address or get real-time walking directions. A handful of other apps—including City Maps 2Go, OffMaps, and Navfree—also allow you to use maps offline.

PLAN AHEAD

Set up an itinerary that allows you to fit in all your must-see sights. For a one-stop look at opening hours, see "Venice at a Glance" on page 40 (also see the "Daily Reminder" on page 17). Most sights keep stable hours, but you can easily confirm the latest by checking with the TI or visiting museum websites.

If you plan to visit Padua's Scrovegni Chapel, make reservations in advance (see page 330). Also consider reserving an entry slot for St. Mark's Basilica or to tour the Clock Tower on St. Mark's Square in Venice (see page 81).

Don't put off visiting a must-see sight—you never know when a place will close unexpectedly for a holiday, strike, or restoration. Many museums are closed or have reduced hours at least a few days a year, especially on holidays such as Labor Day (May 1), Christmas, and New Year's. A list of holidays is on page 470; check online for possible museum closures during your trip. In summer, some sights may stay open late. Off-season, many museums have shorter hours.

Going at the right time helps avoid crowds. This book offers tips on specific sights. Try visiting popular sights very early or very late. Evening visits are usually peaceful, with fewer crowds.

Study up. To get the most out of the self-guided tours and sight descriptions in this book, read them before you visit.

AT SIGHTS

Here's what you can typically expect:

Entering: Be warned that you may not be allowed to enter if you arrive less than 30 to 60 minutes before closing time. And guards start ushering people out well before the actual closing time, so don't save the best for last.

Some important sights have a security check, where you must open your bag or send it through a metal detector. Some sights require you to check daypacks and coats. (If you'd rather not check your daypack, try carrying it tucked under your arm like a purse as you enter.)

Photography: If the museum's photo policy isn't clearly posted, ask a guard. Generally, taking photos without a flash or tripod is allowed. Some sights ban photos altogether; others ban selfie sticks.

Temporary Exhibits: Museums may show special exhibits in addition to their permanent collection. Some exhibits are included in the entry price, while others come at an extra cost (which you may have to pay even if you don't want to see the exhibit).

Expect Changes: Artwork can be on tour, on loan, out sick, or shifted at the whim of the curator. Pick up a floor plan as you enter, and ask the museum staff if you can't find a particular item. Say the title or artist's name, or point to the photograph in this book and ask, *"Dov'è?"* (doh-VEH, meaning "Where is?").

Audioguides and Apps: Many sights rent audioguides, which generally offer excellent recorded descriptions in English. If you bring your own earbuds, you can enjoy better sound and avoid holding the device to your ear. To save money, bring a Y-jack and share one audioguide with your travel partner. Museums and sights often offer free apps that you can download to your mobile

PRACTICALITIES

device (check their websites). And, I've produced free, download-able audio tours for my Grand Canal Cruise, as well as my tours of Venice's St. Mark's Square, St. Mark's Basilica, and Frari Church; look for the 🎧 in this book. For more on my audio tours, see page 8.

Dates for Artwork: In Italian museums, art is dated with *sec* for *secolo* (century, often indicated with Roman numerals), A.C. (*avanti Cristo,* or B.C.), and D.C. (*dopo Cristo,* or A.D.). OK?

Services: Important sights may have an on-site café or caf-eteria (usually a handy place to rejuvenate during a long visit). The WCs at sights are free and generally clean.

Before Leaving: At the gift shop, scan the postcard rack or thumb through a guidebook to be sure you haven't overlooked something that you'd like to see.

Every sight or museum offers more than what is covered in this book. Use the information in this book as an introduction—not the final word.

FIND RELIGION
Churches offer some amazing art (usually free), a cool respite from heat, and a welcome seat.

A modest dress code—no bare shoulders or shorts for anyone, even kids—is enforced at larger churches, such as St. Mark's Ba-silica and the Frari Church, but is often overlooked elsewhere. If you're caught by surprise, you can improvise, using maps to cover your shoulders and a jacket for your knees. (I wear a super-light-weight pair of long pants rather than shorts for my hot and muggy big-city Italian sightseeing.)

Some churches have coin-operated audioboxes that describe the art and history; just set the dial on English, put in your coins, and listen. Coin boxes near a piece of art illuminate the art (and present a better photo opportunity). I pop in a coin whenever I can. It improves my experience, is a favor to other visitors trying to ap-preciate a great piece of art in the dark, and is a little contribution to that church and its work. Whenever possible, let there be light.

Sleeping

I favor hotels and restaurants that are handy to your sightseeing ac-tivities. Rather than list hotels scattered throughout a city, I choose hotels in my favorite neighborhoods. My recommendations run the gamut, from dorm beds to fancy rooms with all of the comforts.

Extensive and opinionated listings of good-value rooms are a major feature of this book's Sleeping sections. I like places that are clean, central, relatively quiet at night (except for the singing of gondoliers), reasonably priced, friendly, small enough to have a hands-on owner and stable staff, and run with a respect for Ital-

Sleep Code

Hotels are classified based on the average price of a standard double room with breakfast in high season.

$$$$	**Splurge:** Most rooms over €170
$$$	**Pricier:** €130-170
$$	**Moderate:** €90-130
$	**Budget:** €50-90
¢	**Backpacker:** Under €50
RS%	**Rick Steves discount**

Unless otherwise noted, credit cards are accepted, hotel staff speak basic English, and free Wi-Fi is available. Comparison-shop by checking prices at several hotels (on each hotel's own website, on a booking site, or by email). For the best deal, *book direct with the hotel*. Ask for a discount if paying in cash; if the listing includes **RS%**, request a Rick Steves discount.

ian traditions. I'm more impressed by a convenient location and a fun-loving philosophy than flat-screen TVs and a fancy gym. Most places I recommend fall short of perfection. But if I can find a place with most of these features, it's a keeper.

Book your accommodations well in advance, especially if you want to stay at one of my top listings or if you'll be traveling during busy times. See page 470 for a list of major holidays and festivals in Venice; for tips on making reservations, see page 428.

RATES AND DEALS

I've categorized my recommended accommodations based on price, indicated with a dollar-sign rating (see sidebar). The price ranges suggest an estimated cost for a one-night stay in a standard double room with a private toilet and shower in high season, include breakfast, and assume you're booking directly with the hotel (not through a booking site, which extracts a commission and logically closes the door on special deals). Room prices can fluctuate significantly with demand and amenities (size, views, room class, and so on), but these relative price categories remain constant. The city of Venice levies a tax on hotel rooms to generate income for infrastructure and restoration projects. This tax is generally not included in the prices in this book, and must be paid in cash at checkout. It varies from €1 to €4 per person, per night, depending on how many stars the hotel has.

Room rates are especially volatile at larger hotels that use "dynamic pricing" to predict demand. Rates can skyrocket during festivals and conventions, while business hotels can have deep discounts on weekends when demand plummets. For this reason, of

PRACTICALITIES

the many hotels I recommend, it's difficult to say which will be the best value on a given day—until you do your homework.

Once your dates are set, check the specific price for your preferred stay at several hotels. You can do this either by comparing prices online on the hotels' own websites, or by emailing several hotels directly and asking for their best rate. Even if you start your search on a booking site such as TripAdvisor or Booking.com, you'll usually find the lowest rates through a hotel's own website.

Many hotels offer a discount to those who pay cash or stay longer than three nights. To cut costs further, try asking for a cheaper room (for example, with a shared bathroom or no window) or offer to skip breakfast.

Additionally, some accommodations offer a special discount for Rick Steves readers, indicated in this guidebook by the abbreviation "RS%." Discounts vary: Ask for details when you book. Generally, to qualify you must book direct (that is, not through a booking site), mention this book when you reserve, show the book upon arrival, and sometimes pay cash or stay a certain number of nights. In some cases, you may need to enter a discount code (which I've provided in the listing) in the booking form on the hotel's website. Rick Steves discounts apply to readers with ebooks as well as printed books. Understandably, discounts do not apply to promotional rates.

TYPES OF ACCOMMODATIONS
Hotels

The double rooms in Venice listed in this book will range from about €90 (very simple, toilet and shower down the hall) to €400 (plush Grand Canal views and maximum plumbing), with most clustered around €140-180 (with private bathrooms).

Most listed hotels have rooms for any size group, from one to five people. Some hotels can add an extra bed to a double to make a triple for a small charge, and some offer larger rooms for four or more people (I call these "family rooms" in the listings). If there's space for an extra cot, they'll cram it in for you. In general, a triple room is cheaper than the cost of a double and a single. Three or four people can economize by requesting one big room.

Traveling alone can be expensive: A *camera singola* is often only 25 percent less than a *camera doppia*.

Nearly all places offer private bathrooms. You'll save €30/night if you book a room with the shower down the hall. Generally rooms with a bath or shower also have a toilet and a bidet (which Italians use for quick sponge baths). The cord over the tub or shower is not a clothesline. You pull it when you've fallen and can't get up.

Double beds are called *matrimoniale*, even though hotels aren't interested in your marital status. Twins are *due letti singoli*.

The Good and Bad of Online Reviews

User-generated review sites and apps such as Yelp, Booking. com, and TripAdvisor are changing the travel industry. These sites can give you a consensus of opinions about everything from hotels and restaurants to sights and nightlife. If you scan reviews of a hotel and see several complaints about noise or a rotten location, it tells you something important that you'd never learn from the hotel's own website.

But review sites are only as good as the judgment of their reviewers. And while these sites work hard to weed out bogus users, my hunch is that a significant percentage of user reviews are posted by friends or enemies of the business being reviewed.

As a guidebook writer, my sense is that there is a big difference between this uncurated information and a guidebook. A user-generated review is based on the experience of one person, who likely stayed at one hotel and ate at a few restaurants, and doesn't have much of a basis for comparison. A guidebook is the work of a trained researcher who visited many alternatives to assess their relative value. I recently checked out some top-rated user-reviewed hotel and restaurant listings in various towns; when stacked up against their competitors, some were gems, while just as many were duds. Both types of information have their place, and in many ways, they're complementary. If something is well-reviewed in a guidebook, and also gets good ratings on one of these sites, it's likely a winner.

When you check in, the receptionist will normally ask for your passport and keep it for anywhere from a couple of minutes to a couple of hours. Hotels are legally required to register each guest with the police. Relax. Americans are notorious for making this chore more difficult than it needs to be.

Hotels and B&Bs are sometimes located on the higher floors of a multipurpose building with a secured door. In that case, look for your hotel's name on the buttons by the main entrance. When you ring the bell, you'll be buzzed in. Hotel elevators are becoming more common, though some older buildings still lack an elevator, or you may have to climb a flight of stairs to reach it (if so, you can ask the front desk for help carrying your bags up). Also, elevators are often very small—pack light, or you may need to send your bags up one at a time.

Italian hotels typically include breakfast in their room prices. If breakfast is optional, you may want to skip it. While convenient, it's usually pricey for what you get: a simple continental buffet with (at its most generous) bread, ham, cheese, yogurt, and unlimited

PRACTICALITIES

Keep Cool

If you're visiting Italy in the summer, the extra expense of an air-conditioned room can be money well spent, particularly in the south. Most hotel rooms with air-conditioners come with a control stick (like a TV remote; the hotel may require a deposit) that generally has similar symbols and features: fan icon (click to toggle through wind power, from light to gale); louver icon (choose steady airflow or waves); snowflake and sunshine icons (cold air or heat); clock ("O" setting: run X hours before turning off; "I" setting: wait X hours to start); and the temperature control (20 degrees Celsius is comfortable; also see the thermometer diagram on page 476). When you leave your room for the day, turning off the air-conditioning is good form.

---

caffè latte. A picnic in your room followed by a coffee at the corner café can be lots cheaper.

More pillows and blankets are usually in the closet or available on request. Towels and linens aren't always replaced every day. Hang your towel up to dry. Some hotels use lightweight "waffle," or very thin, tablecloth-type towels; these take less water and electricity to launder and are preferred by many Italians.

Most hotel rooms have a TV, telephone, and free Wi-Fi (although in old buildings with thick walls, the Wi-Fi signal doesn't always make it to the rooms; sometimes it's only available in the lobby). Sometimes there's a guest computer with Internet access in the lobby. Simpler places rarely have a room phone, but often have free Wi-Fi. Pricier hotels usually come with a small fridge stocked with beverages called a *frigo bar* (FREE-goh bar; pay for what you use).

If you're arriving in the morning, your room probably won't be ready. Check your bag safely at the hotel and dive right into sightseeing.

Hoteliers can be a great help and source of advice. Most know their city well, and can assist you with everything from public transit and airport connections to finding a good restaurant, the nearest launderette, or a late-night pharmacy. English works in all but the cheapest places.

Some hotels occupy one floor of a building with a finicky vintage elevator or slightly dingy entryway. The hotelier doesn't control the building's common areas, so try not to let the entryway atmosphere color your opinion of the hotel. Even at the best places, mechanical breakdowns occur: Sinks leak, hot water turns cold, toilets may gurgle or smell, the Wi-Fi goes out, or the air-conditioning dies when you need it most. Report your concerns clearly and calmly at the front desk. For more complicated problems, don't expect instant results.

If you suspect night noise will be a problem, ask for a quiet room in the back or on an upper floor. In Venice, a canalside room sounds romantic, but in reality you might be sleeping next to a busy, noisy, boat- and gondola-clogged "street." The quietest Venetian rooms will probably face a courtyard. Once you actually see your room, consider the potential problem of night noise. Don't hesitate to ask for a quieter room.

To guard against theft in your room, keep valuables out of sight. Some rooms come with a safe, and other hotels have safes at the front desk. I've never bothered using one.

While it's customary to pay for your room upon departure, it can be a good idea to settle your bill the day before, when you're not in a hurry and while the manager's in. That way you'll have time to discuss and address any points of contention.

Above all, keep a positive attitude. Remember, you're on vacation. If your hotel is a disappointment, spend more time out enjoying the place you came to see.

Short-Term Rentals

A short-term rental—whether an apartment, house, or room in a local's home—is an increasingly popular alternative to a B&B or hotel, especially if you plan to settle in one location for several nights. For stays longer than a few days, you can usually find a rental that's comparable to—or even cheaper than—a hotel room with similar amenities. Plus, you'll get a behind-the-scenes peek into how locals live.

The rental route isn't for everyone. Many places require a minimum night stay, and compared to hotels, rentals usually have less-flexible cancellation policies. Also, you're generally on your own: There's no hotel reception desk, breakfast, or daily cleaning service.

Finding Accommodations: Websites such as www.airbnb.com, www.roomorama.com, and www.vrbo.com let you browse properties and correspond directly with European property owners or managers. For more guidance, consider using a rental agency such as www.interhomeusa.com or www.rentavilla.com. Agency-represented apartments may cost more, but this route often offers more help and safeguards than booking direct. Or try Steve and Linda of **Cross-Pollinate,** a booking service for private rooms and apartments in the old centers of Rome, Florence, and Venice; rates start at €30 per person (www.cross-pollinate.com).

Before you commit to a rental, be clear on the details, location, and amenities. I like to virtually "explore" the neighborhood using the Street View feature on Google Maps. Also consider the proximity to public transportation, and how well-connected it is

PRACTICALITIES

Making Hotel Reservations

Reserve your rooms several weeks or even months in advance—or as soon as you've pinned down your travel dates. Note that some national holidays merit your making reservations far in advance (see page 470).

Requesting a Reservation: It's easiest to book your room through the hotel's website. (For the best rates, use the hotel's official site and not a booking agency's site.) If there's no reservation form, or for complicated requests, send an email. Most recommended hotels take reservations in English.

The hotelier wants to know:
- the size of your party and type of rooms you need
- your arrival and departure dates, written European-style—day followed by month and year (for example, 18/06/17 or 18 June 2017); include the total number of nights
- special requests (such as en suite bathroom vs. down the hall, cheapest room, twin beds vs. double bed, quiet room)
- applicable discounts (such as a Rick Steves reader discount, cash discount, or promotional rate)

Confirming a Reservation: Most places will request a credit-card number to hold your room. If they don't have a secure online reservation form—look for the *https*—you can email it (I do), but it's safer to share that confidential info via a phone call or fax.

Canceling a Reservation: If you must cancel, it's courteous—and smart—to do so with as much notice as possible, especially for smaller family-run places. Cancellation policies can be strict;

with the rest of the city. Ask about amenities that are important to you (elevator, laundry, coffee maker, Wi-Fi, parking, etc.). Reading reviews from previous guests can help identify trouble spots that are glossed over in the official description.

Apartments: If you're staying somewhere for four nights or longer, it's worth considering an apartment (anything less than that isn't worth the extra effort involved, such as arranging key pickup, buying groceries, etc.). Apartment rentals can be especially cost-effective for groups and families. European apartments, like hotel rooms, tend to be small by US standards. But they often come with laundry machines and small, equipped kitchens *(cucinetta)*, making it easier and cheaper to dine in. If you make good use of the kitchen (and Europe's great produce markets), you'll save on your meal budget.

Private and Shared Rooms: Renting a room in someone's home is a good option for those traveling alone, as you're more likely to find true single rooms—with just one single bed, and a price to match. Beds range from air-mattress-in-living-room basic to plush-B&B-suite posh. Some places allow you to book for a

From:	rick@ricksteves.com
Sent:	Today
To:	info@hotelcentral.com
Subject:	Reservation request for 19-22 July

Dear Hotel Central,
I would like to stay at your hotel. Please let me know if you have a room available and the price for:
• 2 people
• Double bed and en suite bathroom in a quiet room
• Arriving 19 July, departing 22 July (3 nights)

Thank you!
Rick Steves

read the fine print or ask about these before you book. Many discount deals require prepayment, with no cancellation refunds.

Reconfirming a Reservation: Always call or email to reconfirm your room reservation a few days in advance. For B&Bs or very small hotels, I call again on my day of arrival to tell my host what time I expect to get there (especially important if arriving late—after 17:00).

Phoning: For tips on calling hotels overseas, see page 450.

single night; if staying for several nights, you can buy groceries just as you would in a rental house. While you can't expect your host to also be your tour guide—or even to provide you with much info—some may be interested in getting to know the travelers who come through their home.

Local TIs can give you a list of possibilities (or try the free Ciao Italia Bed & Breakfast, which books B&Bs and hostels in Rome, Florence, and Venice; www.ciaoitalia-bb.com). These rooms are usually a good budget option, but since they vary in quality, shop around to find the best value. It's always OK to ask to see the room before you commit.

Other Options: Swapping homes with a local works for people with an appealing place to offer, and who can live with the idea of having strangers in their home (don't assume where you live is not interesting to Europeans). A good place to start is HomeExchange (www.homeexchange.com).

To sleep for free, Couchsurfing.com is a vagabond's alternative to Airbnb. It lists millions of outgoing members, who host fellow "surfers" in their homes.

PRACTICALITIES

Hostels

A hostel provides cheap beds in dorms where you sleep alongside strangers for about €20-30 per night. Travelers of any age are welcome if they don't mind dorm-style accommodations and meeting other travelers. Most hostels offer kitchen facilities, guest computers, Wi-Fi, and a self-service laundry. Hostels almost always provide bedding, but the towel's up to you (though you can usually rent one for a small fee). Family and private rooms are often available.

Independent hostels tend to be easygoing, colorful, and informal (no membership required; www.hostelworld.com). You may pay slightly less by booking direct with the hostel. **Official hostels** are part of Hostelling International (HI) and share a booking site (www.hihostels.com). HI hostels typically require that you be a member or pay extra per night.

Eating

The Italians are masters of the art of fine living. That means eating long and well. Lengthy, multicourse meals and endless hours sitting in outdoor cafés are the norm. Americans eat on their way to an evening event and complain if the check is slow in coming. For Italians, the meal is an end in itself, and only rude waiters rush you.

A highlight of your Italian adventure will be this country's cafés, cuisine, and wines. Trust me: This is sightseeing for your palate. Even if you liked dorm food and are sleeping in cheap hotels, your taste buds will relish an occasional first-class splurge. You can eat well without going broke. But be careful: You're just as likely to blow a small fortune on a disappointing meal as you are to dine wonderfully for €25.

In general, Italians eat meals a bit later than we do. At 7:00 or 8:00, they have a light breakfast (coffee—usually cappuccino or espresso—and a pastry, often standing up at a café). Lunch (between 13:00 and 15:00) is traditionally the largest meal of the day. Then they eat a late, light dinner (around 20:00-21:30, or maybe earlier in winter). To bridge the gap, people drop into a bar in the late afternoon for a *spuntino* (snack) and aperitif.

RESTAURANT PRICING

I've categorized my recommended eateries based on price, indicated with a dollar-sign rating (see sidebar). The price ranges suggest the average price of a typical main course—but not necessarily a complete meal. Sticking to pastas will save you plenty over order-

Restaurant Price Code

I've assigned each eatery a price category, based on the average cost of a typical main course (pasta or *secondi*). Drinks, desserts, and splurge items (steak and seafood) can raise the price considerably.

$$$$	**Splurge:** Most main courses over €20
$$$	**Pricier:** €15-20
$$	**Moderate:** €10-15
$	**Budget:** Under €10

In Italy, pizza by the slice and other takeaway food is **$;** a basic trattoria or sit-down pizzeria is **$$;** a casual but more upscale restaurant is **$$$;** and a swanky splurge is **$$$$.**

ing meat-and-fish *secondi*. Obviously, expensive items (steak, seafood, truffles), fine wine, appetizers, and dessert can significantly increase your final bill.

The dollar-sign categories also indicate the overall personality and "feel" of a place:

$ Budget eateries include street food, takeaway, order-at-the-counter shops, basic cafeterias, and bakeries selling sandwiches.

$$ Moderate eateries are typically nice (but not fancy) sit-down restaurants, ideal for a straightforward, fill-the-tank meal. Most of my listings fall in this category—great for getting a good taste of the local cuisine on a budget.

$$$ Pricier eateries are a notch up, with more attention paid to the setting, service, and cuisine. These are ideal for a memorable meal that's relatively casual and doesn't break the bank. This category often includes affordable "destination" or "foodie" restaurants.

$$$$ Splurge eateries are dress-up-for-a-special-occasion-swanky—Michelin star-type restaurants, typically with an elegant setting, polished service, pricey and intricate cuisine, and an expansive (and expensive) wine list.

To assign price ranges for restaurants in Italy, these price points were my rule of thumb: **$$$$**—most pastas over €13, *secondi* over €20; **$$$**—most pizzas/pastas €11-12, *secondi* €15-20; **$$**—most pizzas/pastas under €11, *secondi* under €15; **$**—meals under €10. I haven't categorized places where you might snack, graze, or assemble a picnic: supermarkets, delis, ice-cream stands, cafés or bars specializing in drinks, chocolate shops, and so on.

BREAKFAST

Italian breakfasts, like Italian bath towels, are small: The basic, traditional version is coffee and a roll with butter and marmalade. These days, most places also have yogurt and juice (the delicious red orange juice—*spremuta d'arancia rossa*—is made from Sicilian blood oranges), and possibly also cereal, cold cuts and sliced cheese, and eggs (typically hard-boiled; scrambled or fried eggs are rare). Small budget hotels may leave a basic breakfast in your room (stale croissant, roll, jam, yogurt, coffee).

If you want to skip your hotel breakfast, consider browsing for a morning picnic at a local open-air market. Or do as the Italians do: Stop into a bar or café to drink a cappuccino and munch a *cornetto* (croissant) while standing at the bar. While the *cornetto* is the most common pastry, you'll find a range of *pasticcini* (pastries, sometimes called *dolci*—sweets). Look for *otto* (an 8-shaped pastry, often filled with custard, jam, or chocolate), *sfoglia* (can be fruit-filled, like a turnover), or *ciambella* (doughnut filled with custard or chocolate)—or ask about local specialties.

ITALIAN RESTAURANTS

While *ristorante* is self-explanatory, you'll also see other types of Italian eateries. A *trattoria* and an *osteria* (which can be more ca-

sual) are both generally family-owned places serving home-cooked meals, often at moderate prices. A *locanda* is an inn, a *cantina* is a wine cellar, and a *birreria* is a brewpub. *Pizzerie, rosticcerie* (delis), *tavola calda* bars (cafeterias), *enoteche* (wine bars), and other alternatives are explained later.

When restaurant-hunting, choose a spot filled with locals, not the place with the big neon signs boasting, "We speak English and accept credit cards." Restaurants parked on famous squares and canals generally serve bad food at high prices to tourists. Venturing even a block or two off the main drag leads to higher-quality food for less than half the price of the tourist-oriented places. Locals eat better at lower-rent locales. Family-run places operate without hired help and can offer cheaper meals.

Most restaurant kitchens close between their lunch and dinner service. Good restaurants don't reopen for dinner before 19:00. Small restaurants with a full slate of reservations for 20:30 or 21:00 often will accommodate walk-in diners willing to eat a quick, early meal, but you aren't expected to linger.

When you want the bill, mime-scribble on your raised palm or request it: *"Il conto, per favore."* You may have to ask for it more than once. If you're in a hurry, request the check when you receive the last item you order.

Cover and Tipping

Before you sit down, look at a menu to see what extra charges a restaurant tacks on. Two different items are routinely factored into your bill: the *coperto* and the *servizio*.

The **coperto** (cover charge), sometimes called *pane e coperto* (bread and cover), is the fee for your table setting (including the typical basket of bread). It's not negotiable, even if you don't eat the bread. Think of it as covering the cost of using the table for as long as you like. (Italians like to linger.) Most restaurants add the *coperto* onto your bill as a flat fee (€1-3 per person; the amount should be clearly noted on the menu).

The **servizio** (service charge) of about 10 percent is similar to the mandatory gratuity that American restaurants often add for groups of six or more. Most legitimate eateries don't have a service charge: The words *servizio incluso* on the menu and/or the receipt indicate that you're not required to pay anything beyond the listed prices (the *servizio* is built in). You can add an additional tip, if you choose, by including €1-2 for each person in your party. While Italians don't think about tips in terms of percentages—and some don't tip at all—this extra amount usually comes out to about 5 percent (10 percent is excessive for all but the very best service).

Some touristy or trendy restaurants don't include the service in the menu prices—instead they tack a *servizio* charge onto your bill. In these cases you'll see something like "*servizio 10%*" on the menu, and the fee will be added onto your bill (so you don't need to calculate it yourself and pay it separately). Rarely, you'll see the words *servizio non incluso* on the menu or bill; here you are expected to add a tip of about 10 percent.

Most Italian restaurants have a cover charge and include service in the menu prices. A few have just a service charge. Places with *both* a cover and a tacked-on service charge are best avoided—that's a clue that a restaurant is counting on a nonlocal clientele who can't gauge value. Self-service restaurants never have a cover or service charge, and in recent years some (especially less formal) cafés and restaurants with table service have stopped charging these fees as well.

Courses: Antipasto, *Primo*, and *Secondo*

For a list of Italian cuisine staples, including some of the most common dishes, see page 439. A full Italian meal consists of several courses:

Antipasto: An appetizer such as bruschetta, grilled veggies, deep-fried tasties, thin-sliced meat (such as prosciutto or carpaccio), or a plate of olives, cold cuts, and cheeses. To get a sampler plate of cold cuts and cheeses in a restaurant, ask for *affettato misto* (mixed cold cuts) or *antipasto misto* (cold cuts, cheeses, and marinated vegetables). This could make a light meal in itself.

Primo piatto: A "first dish" generally consisting of pasta, rice,

PRACTICALITIES

or soup. If you think of pasta when you think of Italy, you can dine well here without ever going beyond the *primo*.

Secondo piatto: A "second dish," equivalent to our main course, of meat or fish/seafood. Italians freely admit the *secondo* is the least interesting part of their cuisine. A vegetable side dish *(contorno)* may come with the *secondo* but more often must be ordered separately.

For most travelers, a meal with all three courses (plus *contorni*, dessert, and wine) is simply too much food—and euros can add up in a hurry. To avoid overeating (and to stretch your budget), share dishes. A good rule of thumb is for each person to order any two courses. For example, a couple can order and share one antipasto, one *primo*, one *secondo*, and one dessert; or two *antipasti* and two *primi*; or whatever combination appeals.

Another good option is sharing an array of *antipasti*—either by ordering several specific dishes or, at restaurants that offer self-serve buffets, by choosing a variety of cold and cooked appetizers from an *antipasti* buffet spread out like a salad bar. At buffets, you pay per plate; a typical serving costs about €8 (generally Italians don't treat buffets as all-you-can-eat, but take a one-time moderate serving; watch others and imitate).

To maximize the experience and flavors, small groups can mix *antipasti* and *primi* family-style (skipping *secondi*). If you do this right, you can eat well in better places for less than the cost of a tourist *menù* in a cheap place.

A few restaurants serve a *piatto unico*, with smaller portions of each course on one dish (for instance, a meat, starch, and vegetable).

Ordering Tips

Seafood and steak may be sold by weight (priced by the kilo—1,000 grams, or just over two pounds; or by the *etto*—100 grams). The abbreviation *s.q. (secondo quantità)* means an item is priced "according to quantity." Unless the menu indicates a fillet *(filetto)*, fish is usually served whole with the head and tail. However, you can always ask your waiter to select a small fish for you. Sometimes, especially for steak, restaurants require a minimum order of four or five *etti* (which diners can share). Make sure you're clear on the price before ordering.

Some special dishes come in larger quantities meant to be shared by two people. The shorthand way of showing this on a menu is "X2" (for two), but the price listed generally indicates the cost per person.

In a traditional restaurant, if you order a pasta dish and a side salad—but no main course—the waiter will bring the salad after the pasta (Italians prefer it this way, believing that it enhances digestion). If you want the salad with your pasta, specify *insieme* (een-see-YEH-meh; together). At eateries more accustomed to tourists, you may be asked when you want the salad.

Because pasta and bread are both starches, Italians consider them redundant. If you order only a pasta dish, bread may not come with it; you can request it, but you may be charged extra. On the other hand, if you order a vegetable antipasto or a meat *secondo,* bread is often provided to balance the ingredients.

At places with counter service—such as at a bar or a freeway rest-stop diner—you'll order and pay at the *cassa* (cashier). Take your receipt over to the counter to claim your food.

Fixed-Price Meals and Ordering à la Carte

You can save by getting a fixed-priced meal, which is frequently exempt from cover and service charges. Avoid the cheapest ones (often called a *menù turistico*), which tend to be bland and heavy, pairing a very basic pasta with reheated schnitzel and roast meats. Look instead for a genuine *menù del giorno* (menu of the day), which offers diners a choice of appetizer, main course, and dessert. It's worth paying a little more for an inventive fixed-price meal that shows off the chef's creativity.

MENU € 19,00
TURISTICO
ANTIPASTO di MARE
PRIMI PIATTI
RISOTTO alla PESCATORA
SPAGHETTI alla MARINARA
SPAGHETTI allo SCOGLIO
TRENETTE al PESTO
SECONDI PIATTI
PESCE ai FERRI
FRITTO MISTO
GRIGLIATA di CARNE
CONTORNI
PATATE FRITTE o INSALATA

While fixed-price meals can be easy and convenient, galloping gourmets prefer to order à la carte with the help of a menu translator (see "Italian Cuisine Staples," later). When going to an especially good restaurant with an approachable staff, I like to find out what they're eager to serve. Sometimes I'll simply say, *"Mi faccia felice"* (Make me happy) and set a price limit.

BUDGET EATING

Italy offers many budget options for hungry travelers, but beware of cheap eateries that sport big color photos of pizza and piles of different pastas. They often have no kitchens and simply microwave disgusting prepackaged food.

Self-service cafeterias offer the basics without add-on charges. Travelers on a hard-core budget equip their room with a pantry stocked at the market (fruits and veggies are remarkably cheap), or pick up a sandwich or *döner kebab,* then dine in at picnic prices. Bars and cafés are also good places to grab a meal on the go.

Pizzerias

Pizza is cheap and readily available. Stop by a pizza shop for stand-up or takeout (*pizza al taglio* means "by the slice"). Supermarkets usually have a pizza counter too. Some shops sell individual slices of round, Naples-style pizza, while others feature *pizza rustica*—thick pizza baked in a large rectangular pan and sold by weight. If you simply ask for a piece, you may wind up with a gigantic slab and be charged top euro. Instead, clearly indicate how much you want: 100

grams, or *un etto*, is a hot and cheap snack; 200 grams, or *due etti*, makes a light meal. Or show the size with your hands—*tanto così* (TAHN-toh koh-ZEE; this much). They'll often helpfully cut it up into smaller pieces. If you want your pizza warm, say *"sì"* when they ask if you want it heated up (*scaldare;* skahl-DAH-ray). For a rundown of common types of pizza, see page 439.

Bars/Cafés

Italian "bars" are not taverns, but inexpensive cafés. These neighborhood hangouts serve coffee, minipizzas, sandwiches, and drinks from the cooler. Many dish up plates of fried cheese and vegetables from under the glass counter, ready to reheat. This budget choice is the Italian equivalent of English pub grub. In Venice, *cicchetti* bars serve a fun assortment of appetizer-sized plates (see the Eating in Venice chapter for recommendations).

Many bars are small—if you can't find a table, you'll need to stand or find a ledge to sit on outside. Most charge extra for table service. To get food to go, say, *"da portar via"* (for the road) or *"da portar canale"* (for the canal). All bars have a WC *(toilette, bagno)* in the back, and customers—and the discreet public—can use it.

Food: For quick meals, bars usually have trays of cheap, pre-made sandwiches (*panini,* on a baguette; *piadini,* on flatbread; or *tramezzini,* on crustless white bread)—some are delightful grilled. (Others have too much mayo.) To save time for sightseeing and room for dinner, stop by a bar for a light lunch, such as a ham-and-cheese sandwich (called *toast*); have it grilled twice if you want it really hot.

Prices and Paying: You'll notice a two- or three-tiered pricing system. Drinking a cup of coffee while standing at the bar is cheaper than drinking it at an indoor table (you'll pay still more at an outdoor table). Many places have a *lista dei prezzi* (price list) with two columns—*al bar* and *al tavolo* (table)—posted somewhere by the bar or cash register. If you're on a budget, don't sit down without first checking out the financial consequences. Ask, "Same price if I sit or stand?" by saying, *"Costa uguale al tavolo o al banco?"* (KOH-stah oo-GWAH-lay ahl TAH-voh-loh oh ahl BAHN-koh). Throughout Italy, you can get cheap coffee at the bar of any establishment, no matter how fancy, and pay the same low, government-regulated price (generally less than a euro if you stand).

If the bar isn't busy, you can probably just order and pay when you leave. Otherwise: 1) Decide what you want; 2) find out the price by checking the price list on the wall, the prices posted near the food, or by asking the barista; 3) pay the cashier; and 4) give the receipt to the barista (whose clean fingers handle no dirty euros) and tell him or her what you want.

For more on drinking, see "Beverages" on page 444.

Ethnic Food

A good bet for a cheap, hot meal is a *döner kebab* (Middle Eastern-style rotisserie meat wrapped in pita bread). Look for little hole-in-the-wall kebab shops, where you can get a hearty takeaway dinner wrapped in pita bread for €3.50. Pay an extra euro to supersize it, and it'll feed two. Asian restaurants, although not as common as in northern Europe, usually serve only Chinese dishes and can also be a good value.

Tavola Calda Bars and Rosticcerie

For a fast and cheap lunch, find an Italian variation on the corner deli: a *rosticceria* (specializing in roasted meats and accompanying *antipasti*) or a *tavola calda* bar (a "hot table" point-and-shoot cafeteria with a buffet spread of meat and vegetables; sometimes called *tavola fredda,* or "cold table," in the north). For a healthy light meal, ask for a mixed plate of vegetables with a hunk of mozzarella (*piatto misto di verdure con mozzarella;* pee-AH-toh MEE-stoh dee vehr-DOO-ray). Don't be limited by what's displayed. If you'd like a salad with a slice of cantaloupe and a hunk of cheese, they'll whip that up for you in a snap. Belly up to the bar; with a pointing finger, you can assemble a fine meal. If something's a mystery, ask for *un assaggio* (oon ah-SAH-joh) to get a little taste. To have your choices warmed up, ask for them to be heated (*scaldare;* skahl-DAH-ray).

Wine Bars

Wine bars (*enoteche;* sometimes called *bacari* in Venice) are a popular, fast, and inexpensive option for lunch. Surrounded by the office crowd, you can get a salad, a plate of meats (cold cuts) and cheeses, and a glass of good wine (see blackboards for the day's selection and price per glass). A good *enoteca* aims to impress visitors with its wine, and will generally feature excellent-quality ingredients for the simple dishes it offers with the wine (though the prices add up—be careful with your ordering to keep this a budget choice). For more on Italian cocktails and wines, see page 445.

Aperitivo Buffets

The Italian term *aperitivo* means a predinner drink, but it's also used to describe their version of what we might call happy hour: a light buffet that many bars serve to customers during the predinner hours (typically around 18:00 or 19:00 until 21:00). The drink itself may not be cheap (typically around €8-12), but bars lay out an enticing array of meats, cheeses, grilled vegetables, and other *antipasti*-type dishes, and you're welcome to nibble to your heart's content while you nurse your drink. While it's intended as an appetizer course before heading out for a full dinner, light eaters could discreetly turn this into a small meal. Drop by a few bars around this time to scope out their buffets before choosing.

Groceries and Delis

Another budget option is to visit a supermarket, *alimentari* (neighborhood grocery), or *salumeria* (delicatessen) to pick up some cold cuts, cheeses, and other supplies for a picnic. Some *salumerie*, and any *paninoteca* or *focacceria* (sandwich shop), can make you a sandwich to order. Just point to what you want, and they'll stuff it into a *panino;* if you want it heated, remember the word *scaldare* (skahl-DAH-ray). If ordering an assortment of cold cuts and cheeses, some unscrupulous shops may try to pad the bill by pushing their most expensive ingredients. Be clear on what you want: *"antipasto misto da __ euro, per favore."* For more on *salumi* and cheeses, see page 442.

Picnics

Picnicking saves lots of euros and is a great way to sample regional specialties. A typical picnic for two might be fresh rolls, 100 grams—or about a quarter pound—of cheese (*un etto,* EH-toh, plural *etti,* EH-tee), and 100 grams of meat, sometimes ordered by the slice *(fetta)* or piece *(pezzi).* For two people, I might get *cinque pezzi* (five pieces) of prosciutto. Add two tomatoes, three carrots, two apples, yogurt, and a liter box of juice. Total cost: about €10.

In the process of assembling your meal, you get to deal with Italians in the market scene. For a colorful experience, gather your ingredients in the morning at a produce market; you'll probably need to hit several market stalls to put together a complete meal (note that many stalls close in the early afternoon).

While it's fun to visit small specialty shops, an *alimentari* is your one-stop corner grocery store (most will slice and stuff your sandwich for you if you buy the ingredients there). A rare *supermercato* (look for the Conad, Despar, and Co-op chains) gives you more efficiency with less color for less cost. At busier supermarkets, you'll need to take a number for deli service. And *rosticcerie* sell cheap food to go—you'll find options such as lasagna, rotisserie chicken, and sides like roasted potatoes and spinach.

Picnics can be an adventure in high cuisine. Be daring. Try the fresh mozzarella, *presto* pesto, shriveled olives, and any regional

specialties the locals are excited about. If ordering *antipasti* (such as grilled or marinated veggies) at a deli counter, you can ask for *una porzione* in a takeaway container *(contenitore)*. Use gestures to show exactly how much you want. The word *basta* (BAH-stah; enough) works as a question or as a statement.

Shopkeepers are happy to sell small quantities of produce, but it's customary to let the merchant choose for you. Say *"per oggi"* (pehr OH-jee; for today) and he or she will grab you something ready to eat. To avoid being overcharged, know the cost per kilo, study the weighing procedure, and do the arithmetic.

ITALIAN CUISINE STAPLES

Much of your Italian eating experience will likely involve the big five: pizza, pasta, *salumi,* cheese, and gelato. For a look at cuisine you'll likely find in Venice, see the sidebar on page 274. For more food help, try a menu translator, such as the *Rick Steves Italian Phrase Book & Dictionary,* which has a menu decoder and plenty of useful phrases for navigating the culinary scene.

Pizza

Here are some of the pizzas you might see at restaurants or at a pizzeria. Note that if you ask for pepperoni on your pizza, you'll get *peperoni* (green or red peppers, not sausage); request *diavola, salsiccia piccante,* or *salame piccante* instead (the closest thing in Italy to American pepperoni).

Bianca: White pizza with no tomatoes (also called *ciaccina*).

Capricciosa: Prosciutto, mushrooms, olives, and artichokes—literally the chef's "caprice."

Eating with the Seasons

Italian cooks love to serve you fresh produce and seafood at

its tastiest. If you must have porcini mushrooms outside of fall, they'll be dried. Each region in Italy has its specialties, which you'll see displayed in open-air markets. To get a plate of the freshest veggies at a fine restaurant, request *"Un piatto di verdure della stagione, per favore"* (A plate of seasonal vegetables, please). Italians take fresh, seasonal ingredients so seriously that a restaurant cooking with frozen ingredients must note it on the menu—look for *congelato*.

Here are a few examples of what's fresh when:

April-May: Calamari, green beans, and artichokes
April-May and Sept-Oct: Black truffles
April-June: Asparagus, zucchini flowers, and zucchini
May-June: Mussels, cantaloupe, loquats, and strawberries
May-Aug: Eggplant, clams
July-Sept: Figs
Oct-Nov: Mushrooms, white truffles, persimmons, and chestnuts
Nov-Feb: Radicchio, cardoon (wild artichoke)
Fresh year-round: Meats and cheese

Funghi: Mushrooms.
Margherita: Tomato sauce, mozzarella, and basil—the red, white, and green of the Italian flag.
Marinara: Tomato sauce, oregano, garlic, no cheese.
Napoletana: Mozzarella, anchovies, and tomato sauce.
Ortolana: "Greengrocer-style," with vegetables (also called *vegetariana*).
Quattro formaggi: Four different cheeses.
Quattro stagioni: Different toppings on each of the four quarters.

Pasta

While we think of pasta as a main dish, in Italy it's considered a *primo piatto*—first course. There are more than 600 varieties of Italian pasta, and each is specifically used to highlight a certain sauce, meat, or regional ingredient. Italian pasta falls into two broad categories: *pasta lunga* (long pasta) and *pasta corta* (short pasta).

Pasta lunga can be round, such as *capellini* (thin "little hairs"), *vermicelli* (slightly thicker "little worms"), and *bucatini* (long and hollow), or it can be flat, such as *linguine* (narrow "little tongues"), *fettuccine* (wider "small ribbons"), *tagliatelle* (even wider), and *pappardelle* (very wide, best with meat sauces).

The most common *pasta corta* are tubes, such as *penne, rigatoni, ziti, manicotti,* and *cannelloni;* they come either *lisce* (smooth) or *rigate* (grooved—better to catch and cling to sauce). Many short pastas are named for their shapes, such as *conchiglie* (shells), *farfalle* (butterflies), *cavatappi* (corkscrews), *ditali* (thimbles), *gomiti* ("elbow" macaroni), *lumache* (snails), *marziani* (spirals resembling "Martian" antennae), and even *strozzapreti* (priest stranglers). Some are filled *(ripieni),* including *tortelli* (C-shaped, stuffed ravioli) and *angolotti* or *mezzelune* (shaped like "priest's hats" or "half-moons").

Most types of pasta come in slightly different variations: If it's a bit thicker, *-one* is added to the end; if it's a bit thinner, *-ine, -ette,* or *-elle* is added. For example, *tortellini* are smaller *tortelli,* while *tortelloni* are bigger. Most pastas in Italy are made fresh.

Here's a list of common pasta toppings and sauces. On a menu, these terms are usually preceded by *alla* (in the style of) or *in* (in):

Aglio e olio: Garlic and olive oil.

Alfredo: Butter, cream, and Parmesan.

Amatriciana: Pork cheek, Pecorino cheese, and tomato.

Arrabbiata: "Angry," spicy tomato sauce with chili peppers.

Bolognese: Meat and tomato sauce.

Boscaiola: Mushrooms and sausage.

Burro e salvia: Butter and sage.

Cacio e pepe: Parmigiano cheese and ground pepper.

Carbonara: Bacon, egg, cheese, and pepper.

Carrettiera: Spicy and garlicky, with olive oil and little tomatoes.

Diavola: "Devil-style," spicy hot.

Frutti di mare: Seafood.

Genovese: Basil ground with Parmigiano cheese, garlic, pine nuts, and olive oil; a.k.a. pesto.

Gricia: Cured pork and Pecorino Romano cheese.

Marinara: Usually tomato, often with garlic and onions, but can also be a seafood sauce ("sailor's style").

Norma: Tomato, eggplant, and ricotta cheese.

Pajata: Calf intestines (also called *pagliata).*

Pescatora: Seafood ("fisherman style").

Pomodoro: Tomato only.

Puttanesca: "Harlot-style" tomato sauce with anchovies, olives, and capers.

Ragù: Meaty tomato sauce.

Scoglio: Mussels, clams, and tomatoes.
Sorrentina: "Sorrento-style," with tomatoes, basil, and mozzarella (usually over gnocchi).
Sugo di lepre: Rich sauce made of wild hare.
Tartufi: Truffles (also called *tartufate*).
Umbria: Sauce of anchovies, garlic, tomatoes, and truffles.
Vongole: Clams and spices.

Salumi

Salumi ("salted" meats), also called *affettati* ("cut" meats), are an Italian staple. While most American cold cuts are cooked, in Italy they're far more commonly cured by air-drying, salting, and smoking. (Don't worry; these so-called "raw" meats are safe to eat, and you can really taste the difference.)

The two most familiar types of *salumi* are *salame* and prosciutto. *Salame* is an air-dried, sometimes spicy sausage that comes in many varieties. When Italians say "prosciutto," they usually mean *prosciutto crudo*—the raw ham that air-cures on the hock and is then thinly sliced. Produced mainly in the north of Italy, prosciutto can be either *dolce* (sweet) or *salato* (salty). Purists say the best is *prosciutto di Parma*.

Other *salumi* may be less familiar:
Bresaola: Air-cured beef.
Capocollo: Peppery pork shoulder (also called *coppa*).
Culatello: Prosciutto made with only the finest cuts of meat.
Finocchiona: *Salame* with fennel seeds.
Lonzino: Cured pork loin.
Mortadella: A finely ground pork loaf, similar to our bologna.
Pancetta: Salt-cured, peppery pork belly meat, similar to bacon; can be eaten raw or added to cooked dishes.
Quanciale: Tender pork cheek.
Salame di Sant'Olcese: What we'd call "Genoa salami."
Salame piccante: Spicy hot, similar to pepperoni.
Speck: Smoked pork shoulder.

If you've got a weak stomach, avoid *testa in cassetta* (head-cheese—organs in aspic) and *lampredotto* (cow stomach that resembles a lamprey—eel).

Cheese

When it comes to cheese *(formaggio),* you're probably already familiar with most of these Italian favorites:
Asiago: Hard cow cheese that comes either *mezzano* (young, firm, and creamy) or *stravecchio* (aged, pungent, and granular).
Burrata: A creamy mozzarella.
Fontina: Semihard, nutty, Gruyère-style mountain cheese.

PRACTICALITIES

Gorgonzola: Pungent, blue-veined cheese, either *dolce* (creamy) or *stagionato* (aged and hard).

Mascarpone: Sweet, buttery, spreadable dessert cheese.

Mozzarella di bufala: Made from the milk of water buffaloes.

Parmigiano-Reggiano: Hard, crumbly, sharp, aged cow cheese with more nuanced flavor than American Parmesan; *grana padano* is a less expensive variation.

Pecorino: Either *fresco* (fresh, soft, and mild) or *stagionato* (aged and sharp, sometimes called *Pecorino Romano*).

Provolone: Rich, firm, aged cow cheese.

Ricotta: Soft, airy cheese made by "recooking" leftover whey.

Scamorza: Similar to mozzarella, but often smoked.

Gelato

While American ice cream is made with cream and has a high butterfat content, Italian gelato is made with milk. It's also churned more slowly, making it denser. Connoisseurs believe that because gelato has less air and less fat (which coats the mouth and blocks the taste buds), it's more flavorful than American-style ice cream.

A key to gelato appreciation is sampling liberally and choosing flavors that go well together. At a *gelateria,* ask, as Italians do, for a taste: *"Un assaggio, per favore?"* (oon ah-SAH-joh pehr fah-VOH-ray). You can also ask what flavors go well together: *"Quali gusti stanno bene insieme?"* (KWAH-lee GOO-stee STAH-noh BEH-nay een-see-EH-may).

Most *gelaterie* clearly display prices and sizes. But in the textbook *gelateria* scam, the tourist orders two or three flavors—and the clerk selects a fancy, expensive chocolate-coated waffle cone, piles it high with huge scoops, and cheerfully charges the tourist €10. To avoid rip-offs, point to the price or say what you want—for instance, a €3 cup: *"Una coppetta da tre euro"* (OO-nah koh-PEH-tah dah tray eh-OO-roh).

The best *gelaterie* display signs reading *artiginale, nostra produzione,* or *produzione propia,* indicating that the gelato is made on the premises. Seasonal flavors are also a good sign, as are mellow hues (avoid colors that don't appear in nature). Gelato stored in covered metal tins (rather than white plastic) is more likely to be homemade. Gourmet gelato shops are popping up all over Italy, selling exotic flavors. Avoid a chain called Grom—it's the Starbucks of gelato in Italy.

Classic gelato flavors include:

After Eight: Chocolate and mint.

Bacio: Chocolate hazelnut, named for Italy's popular "kiss" candies.

Cassata: With dried fruits.

Cioccolato: Chocolate.

Crema: Vanilla.

Croccantino: "Crunchy," with toasted peanut bits.
Fior di latte: Sweet milk.
Fragola: Strawberry.
Macedonia: Mixed fruits.
Malaga: Similar to rum raisin.
Riso: With actual bits of rice mixed in.
Stracciatella: Vanilla with chocolate shreds.
Tartufo: Super chocolate.
Zabaione: Named for the egg yolk and Marsala wine dessert.
Zuppa inglese: Sponge cake, custard, chocolate, and cream.

Gelato variations or alternatives include *sorbetto* (sorbet—made with fruit, but no milk or eggs); *granita* or *grattachecca* (a cup of slushy ice with flavored syrup); and *cremolata* (a gelato-*granita* float).

BEVERAGES

Italian bars serve great drinks—hot, cold, sweet, caffeinated, or alcoholic.

Water, Juice, and Cold Drinks

Italians are notorious water snobs. At restaurants, your server just can't understand why you wouldn't want good water to go with your good food. It's customary and never expensive to order a *litro* or *mezzo litro* (half-liter) of bottled water. *Acqua leggermente effervescente* (lightly carbonated water) is a mealtime favorite. Or simply ask for *con gas* if you want fizzy water and *senza gas* if you prefer still water. You can ask for *acqua del rubinetto* (tap water) in restaurants, but your server may give you a funny look. Chilled bottled water—still *(naturale)* or carbonated *(frizzante)*—is sold cheap in stores. Half-liter mineral-water bottles are available everywhere for about €1. (I refill my water bottle with tap water.)

Juice is *succo*, and *spremuta* means freshly squeezed. Order *una spremuta* (don't confuse it with *spumante*, sparkling wine)—it's usually orange juice *(arancia)*, and from February through April it's almost always made from blood oranges *(arance rosse)*.

In grocery stores, you can get a liter of O.J. for the price of a Coke or coffee. Look for *100% succo* or *senza zucchero* (without sugar) on the label—or be surprised by something diluted and sugary sweet. Hang on to your water bottles. Buy juice in cheap liter boxes, then drink some and store the extra in your water bottle.

Tè freddo (iced tea) is usually from a can—sweetened and flavored with lemon or peach. Lemonade is *limonata*.

Coffee and Other Hot Drinks

The espresso-based style of coffee so popular in the US was born in Italy. If you ask for *"un caffè,"* you'll get a shot of espresso in a little cup—the closest thing to American-style drip coffee is a *caffè americano*. Most Italian coffee drinks begin with espresso, to which they add varying amounts of hot water and/or steamed or foamed milk. Milky drinks, like cappuccino or *caffè latte*, are served to locals before noon and to tourists any time of day (to an Italian, cappuccino is a morning drink; they believe having milk after a big meal or anything with tomato sauce impairs digestion). If they add any milk after lunch, it's just a splash, in a *caffè macchiato*. Italians like their coffee only warm—to get it very hot, request *"Molto caldo, per favore"* (MOHL-toh KAHL-doh pehr fah-VOH-ray). Any coffee drink is available decaffeinated—ask for it *decaffeinato* (deh-kah-feh-NAH-toh). *Cioccolato* is hot chocolate. *Tè* is hot tea.

Experiment with a few of the options:

Cappuccino: Espresso with foamed milk on top (*cappuccino freddo* is iced cappuccino).

Caffè latte: Espresso mixed with hot milk, no foam, in a tall glass (ordering just a "latte" gets you only milk).

Caffè macchiato: Espresso "marked" with a splash of milk, in a small cup.

Latte macchiato: Layers of hot milk and foam, "marked" by an espresso shot, in a tall glass. Note that if you order simply a *"macchiato,"* you'll probably get a *caffè macchiato*.

Caffè corto/lungo: Concentrated espresso diluted with a tiny bit of hot water, in a small cup.

Caffè americano: Espresso diluted with even more hot water, in a larger cup.

Caffè corretto: Espresso "corrected" with a shot of liqueur (normally *grappa, amaro,* or *sambuca*).

Marocchino: "Moroccan" coffee with espresso, foamed milk, and cocoa powder; the similar *mocaccino* has chocolate instead of cocoa.

Caffè freddo: Sweet and iced espresso.

Caffè hag: Instant decaf.

Alcoholic Beverages

Beer: While Italy is traditionally considered wine country, in recent years there's been a huge and passionate growth in the production of craft beer *(birra artigianale)*. Even in small towns, you'll see microbreweries slinging their own brews. You'll also find local brews (Peroni and Moretti), as well as imports such as Heineken. Italians drink mainly lager beers. Beer on tap is *alla spina*. Get it *piccola* (33 cl, 11 oz), *media* (50 cl, about a pint), or *grande* (a liter). A *lattina* (lah-TEE-nah) is a can and a *bottiglia* (boh-TEEL-yah) is a bottle.

Cocktails and Spirits: Italians appreciate both *aperitivi* (palate-stimulating cocktails) and *digestivi* (after-dinner drinks

PRACTICALITIES

designed to aid digestion). Popular *aperitivo* options include Campari (dark-colored bitters with herbs and orange peel), Americano (vermouth with bitters, brandy, and lemon peel), Cynar (bitters flavored with artichoke), and Punt e Mes (sweet red vermouth and red wine). Widely used vermouth brands include Cinzano and Martini.

Digestivo choices are usually either a strong herbal bitters or something sweet. Many restaurants have their own secret recipe for a bittersweet herbal brew called *amaro;* popular commercial brands are Fernet Branca and Montenegro. If your tastes run sweeter, try *amaretto* (almond-flavored liqueur), Frangelico (hazelnut liqueur), *limoncello* (lemon liqueur), *nocino* (dark, sweet walnut liqueur), and *sambuca* (syrupy, anise-flavored liqueur; *con moscha* adds "flies"—three coffee beans). *Grappa* is a brandy distilled from grape skins and stems; *stravecchio* is an aged, mellower variation.

Wine: The ancient Greeks who colonized Italy more than 2,000 years ago called it Oenotria—land of the grape. Centuries later, Galileo wrote, "Wine is light held together by water." Wine *(vino)* is certainly a part of the Italian culinary trinity—grape, olive, and wheat. (I'd add gelato.) Ideal conditions for grapes (warm climate, well-draining soil, and an abundance of hillsides) make the Italian peninsula a paradise for grape growers, winemakers, and wine drinkers. For regional wines produced near Venice, see the sidebar on page 274.

Even if you're clueless about wine, the information on an Italian wine label can help you choose something decent. Terms you may see on the bottle include *classico* (from a defined, select area), *annata* (year of harvest), *vendemmia* (harvest), and *imbottigliato dal produttore all'origine* (bottled by producers). To figure out what you like—and what suits your pocketbook—visit an *enoteca* (wine bar) and sample wines side by side. For tips on ordering wine, see the sidebar.

In general, Italy designates its wines by one of four official categories:

Vino da Tavola (VDT) is table wine, the lowest grade, made from grapes grown anywhere in Italy. It's often inexpensive, but Italy's wines are so good that, for many people, a basic *vino da tavola* is just fine with a meal. Many restaurants, even modest ones, take pride in their house wine *(vino della casa),* bottling their own or working with wineries.

Denominazione di Origine Controllata (DOC) meets national standards for high-quality wine. Made from grapes grown in a

Ordering Wine

To order a glass of red or white wine, say, *"Un bicchiere di vino rosso/bianco."* House wine comes in a carafe; choose from a quarter-liter pitcher (8.5 oz, *un quarto*), half-liter pitcher (17 oz, *un mezzo*), or one-liter pitcher (34 oz, *un litro*). When ordering, have some fun, gesture like a local, and you'll have no problems speaking the language of the *enoteca. Salute!*

English	Italian
wine	*vino* (VEE-noh)
house wine	*vino della casa* (VEE-noh DEH-lah KAH-zah)
glass	*bicchiere* (bee-kee-EH-ree)
bottle	*bottiglia* (boh-TEEL-yah)
carafe	*caraffa* (kah-RAH-fah)
red	*rosso* (ROH-soh)
white	*bianco* (bee-AHN-koh)
rosé	*rosato* (roh-ZAH-toh)
sparkling	*spumante/frizzante* (spoo-MAHN-tay/freed-ZAHN-tay)
dry	*secco* (SEH-koh)
earthy	*terroso* (teh-ROH-zoh)
elegant	*elegante* (eh-leh-GAHN-tay)
fruity	*fruttato* (froo-TAH-toh)
full-bodied	*corposo/pieno* (kor-POH-zoh/pee-EH-noh)
mature	*maturo* (mah-TOO-roh)
sweet	*dolce* (DOHL-chay)
tannic	*tannico* (TAH-nee-koh)
young	*giovane* (JOH-vah-nay)

defined area, it's usually quite affordable and can be surprisingly good. Hundreds of wines have earned the DOC designation. In Tuscany, for example, many such wines come from the Chianti region, located between Florence and Siena.

Denominazione di Origine Controllata e Guarantita (DOCG), the highest grade, meets national standards for the highest-quality wine (made with grapes from a defined area whose quality is "guaranteed"). These wines can be identified by the pink or green label on the neck...and the scary price tag on the shelf. Only a limited number of wines in Italy can be called DOCG. They're generally a good bet if you want a quality wine, but you don't know anything else about the winemaker. (*Riserva* indicates a DOC or DOCG wine matured for a longer, more specific time.)

Indicazione Geographica Tipica (IGT) is a broad group of wines that range from basic to some of Italy's best. These wines don't follow the strict "recipe" required for DOC or DOCG status,

PRACTICALITIES

Hurdling the Language Barrier

Many Italians—especially those in the tourist trade and in big cities—speak English. Still, you'll get better treatment if you learn and use Italian pleasantries. In smaller, non-touristy towns, Italian is the norm. Italians have an endearing habit of talking to you even if they know you don't speak their language—and yet, thanks to gestures and thoughtfully simplified words, it somehow works. Don't stop them to tell them you don't understand every word—just go along for the ride. For a list of survival phrases, see page 479.

Note that Italian is pronounced much like English, with a few exceptions, such as: *c* followed by *e* or *i* is pronounced ch (to ask, *"Per centro?"*—To the center?—you say, pehr CHEHN-troh). In Italian, *ch* is pronounced like the hard c in Chianti (*chiesa*—church—is pronounced kee-AY-zah). Adding a vowel to the English word often gets you close to the Italian one. Give it your best shot. Italians appreciate your efforts.

but give local vintners creative license. This category includes the Super Tuscans—wines made from a mix of international grapes (such as cabernet sauvignon) grown in Tuscany and aged in small oak barrels for only two years. The result is a lively, full-bodied wine that dances all over your head...and is worth the steep price for aficionados.

Staying Connected

One of the most common questions I hear from travelers is, "How can I stay connected in Europe?" The short answer is: more easily and cheaply than you might think.

The simplest solution is to bring your own device—mobile phone, tablet, or laptop—and use it just as you would at home (following the tips below, such as connecting to free Wi-Fi whenever possible). Another option is to buy a European SIM card for your mobile phone—either your US phone or one you buy in Europe. Or you can travel without a mobile device and use European landlines and computers to connect. Each of these options is described below, and you'll find even more details at www.ricksteves.com/phoning. For a very practical one-hour lecture covering tech issues for travelers, see www.ricksteves.com/travel-talks.

USING YOUR OWN MOBILE DEVICE IN EUROPE

Without an international plan, typical rates from major service providers (AT&T, Verizon, etc.) for using your device abroad are about $1.70/minute for voice calls, 50 cents to send text messages, 5 cents to receive them, and $10 to download one megabyte of data.

At these rates, costs can add up quickly. Here are some budget tips and options.

Use free Wi-Fi whenever possible. Unless you have an un-limited-data plan, you're best off saving most of your online tasks for Wi-Fi. You can access the Internet, send texts, and make voice calls over Wi-Fi.

Many cafés (including McDonald's) have free hotspots for customers; look for signs offering it and ask for the Wi-Fi password when you buy something. You'll also often find Wi-Fi at TIs, city squares, major museums, public-transit hubs, airports, highway rest stops (Autogrills), and aboard trains and buses.

Sign up for an international plan. Most providers offer a global calling plan that cuts the per-minute cost of phone calls and texts, and a flat-fee data plan. Your normal plan may already in-clude international coverage (T-Mobile's does).

Before your trip, call your provider or check online to confirm that your phone will work in Europe, and research your provider's international rates. Activate the plan a day or two before you leave, then remember to cancel it when your trip's over.

Minimize the use of your cellular network. When you can't find Wi-Fi, you can use your cellular network to connect to the Internet, text, or make voice calls. When you're done, avoid further charges by manually switching off "data roaming" or "cellular data" (in your device's Settings menu; for help, ask your service provider or Google it). Another way to make sure you're not accidentally using data roaming is to put your device in "airplane" or "flight" mode (which also disables phone calls and texts), and then turn on Wi-Fi as needed.

Don't use your cellular network for bandwidth-gobbling tasks, such as Skyping, downloading apps, and watching YouTube: Save these for when you're on Wi-Fi. Using a navigation app such as Google Maps over a cellular network can take lots of data, so do this sparingly or use it offline.

Limit automatic updates. By default, your device constantly checks for a data connection and updates apps. It's smart to disable these features so your apps will only update when you're on Wi-Fi, and to change your device's email settings from "auto-retrieve" to "manual" (or from "push" to "fetch").

It's also a good idea to keep track of your data usage. On your device's menu, look for "cellular data usage" or "mobile data" and reset the counter at the start of your trip.

Use Skype or other calling/messaging apps for cheaper calls and texts. Certain apps let you make voice or video calls or send texts over the Internet for free or cheap. If you're bringing a tablet or laptop, you can also use it for voice calls and texts. All you have to do is log on to a Wi-Fi network, then contact any of your friends

PRACTICALITIES

How to Dial

International Calls

Whether phoning from a US landline or mobile phone, or from a number in another European country, here's how to make an international call. I've used one of my recommended Florence hotels as an example (tel. 055-213-154).

Initial Zero: Drop the initial zero from international phone numbers—except when calling Italy.

Mobile Tip: If using a mobile phone, the "+" sign can replace the international access code (for a "+" sign, press and hold "0").

US/Canada to Europe

Dial 011 (US/Canada international access code), country code (39 for Italy), and phone number.

▶ To call the Florence hotel from home, dial 011-39-055-213-154.

Country to Country Within Europe

Dial 00 (Europe international access code), country code, and phone number.

▶ To call the Florence hotel from Germany, dial 00-39-055-213-154.

Europe to the US/Canada

Dial 00, country code (1 for US/Canada), and phone number.

▶ To call from Europe to my office in Edmonds, Washington, dial 00-1-425-771-8303.

Domestic Calls

To call within Italy (from one Italian landline or mobile phone to another), simply dial the phone number, including the initial 0 if there is one.

▶ To call the Florence hotel from Rome, dial 055-213-154.

More Dialing Tips

Italian Phone Numbers: Italian phone numbers vary in length; a hotel can have, say, an eight-digit phone number

or family members who are also online and signed into the same service.

You can make voice and video calls using Skype, Viber, FaceTime, and Google+ Hangouts. If the connection is bad, try making an audio-only call. You can also make voice calls from your device to telephones worldwide for just a few cents per minute using Skype, Viber, or Hangouts if you buy credit first.

To text for free over Wi-Fi, try apps like Google+ Hangouts,

and a nine-digit fax number. Italy's landlines start with 0; mobile lines start with 3 and cost substantially more to dial.

Toll and Toll-Free Calls: Italy's toll-free lines, called *numero verde* (green number), begin with 800 or 803. They can be dialed free from Italian phones without using a phone card but don't work from the US. Any Italian phone number that starts with 8 but isn't followed by a 0 is a toll call (generally costing €0.10-0.50/minute). International rates apply to US toll-free numbers dialed from Italy—they're not free.

More Phoning Help: See www.howtocallabroad.com.

European Country Codes			
Austria	43	Italy	39
Belgium	32	Latvia	371
Bosnia-Herzegovina	387	Montenegro	382
Croatia	385	Morocco	212
Czech Republic	420	Netherlands	31
Denmark	45	Norway	47
Estonia	372	Poland	48
Finland	358	Portugal	351
France	33	Russia	7
Germany	49	Slovakia	421
Gibraltar	350	Slovenia	386
Great Britain	44	Spain	34
Greece	30	Sweden	46
Hungary	36	Switzerland	41
Ireland & N. Ireland	353 / 44	Turkey	90

Whats App, Viber, Facebook Messenger, and iMessage. Make sure you're on Wi-Fi to avoid data charges.

USING A EUROPEAN SIM CARD IN A MOBILE PHONE

This option works well for those who want to make a lot of voice calls at cheap local rates, and those who need faster connection speeds than their US carrier provides. Either buy a basic cell phone in Europe (as little as $40 from mobile-phone shops anywhere), or

PRACTICALITIES

bring an "unlocked" US phone (check with your carrier about unlocking it). With an unlocked phone, you can replace the original SIM card (the microchip that stores info about the phone) with one that will work with a European provider.

In Europe, buy a SIM card. Inserted into your phone, this card gives you a European phone number—and European rates. SIM cards are sold at mobile-phone shops, department-store electronics counters, newsstands, and vending machines. Costing about $5-10, they usually include about that much prepaid calling credit, with no contract and no commitment. A SIM card that also includes data costs (including roaming) will cost $20-40 more for one month of data within the country in which it was purchased. This can be faster than data roaming through your home provider. To get the best rates, buy a new SIM card whenever you arrive in a new country.

I like to buy SIM cards at a mobile-phone shop where there's a clerk to help explain the options and brands. In Italy, the major mobile phone providers are Wind, TIM, Vodafone, and 3 ("Tre"). Certain SIM-card brands—including Lebara and Lycamobile, both of which operate in multiple European countries—are reliable and economical. Ask the clerk to help you insert your SIM card, set it up, and show you how to use it. In some countries—including Italy—you'll be required to register the SIM card with your passport as an antiterrorism measure (which may mean you can't use the phone for the first hour or two).

Find out how to check your credit balance. When you run out of credit, you can top it up at newsstands, tobacco shops, mobile-phone stores, or many other businesses (look for your SIM card's logo in the window), or online.

UNTETHERED TRAVEL: PUBLIC PHONES AND COMPUTERS

It's possible to travel in Europe without a mobile device. You can check email or browse websites using public computers and Internet cafés, and make calls from your hotel room and/or public phones.

Phones in your **hotel room** generally have a fee for placing local and "toll-free" calls, as well as long-distance or international calls—ask for the rates before you dial. Since you're never charged for receiving calls, it's better to have someone from the US call you in your room.

If these fees are low, hotel phones can be used inexpensively for calls made with cheap international phone cards (*carta telefonica prepagata internazionale,* KAR-tah teh-leh-FOHN-ee-kah pray-pah-GAH-tah in-ter-naht-zee-oh-NAH-lay—sold at many post offices, newsstands, street kiosks, tobacco shops, and train sta-

Tips on Internet Security

Using the Internet while traveling brings added security risks, whether you're getting online with your own device or at a public terminal using a shared network. Here are some tips for securing your data:

First, make sure that your device is running the latest version of its operating system and security software, and that your apps are up-to-date. Next, ensure that your device is password- or passcode-protected so thieves can't access it if your device is stolen. For extra security, set passwords on apps that access key info (such as email or Facebook).

On the road, use only legitimate Wi-Fi hotspots. Ask the hotel or café staff for the specific name of their Wi-Fi network, and make sure you log on to that exact one. Hackers sometimes create a bogus hotspot with a similar or vague name (such as "Hotel Europa Free Wi-Fi"). The best Wi-Fi networks require a password. If you're not actively using a hotspot, turn off your device's Wi-Fi connection so it's not visible to others.

Be especially cautious when accessing financial information online. Experts say it's best to use a banking app rather than sign in to your bank's website via a browser (the app is less likely to get hacked). Refrain from logging in to any personal finance sites on a public computer. Even if you're using your own mobile device at a password-protected hotspot, there's a remote chance that a hacker who's logged on to the same network could see what you're doing.

Never share your credit-card number (or any other sensitive information) online unless you know that the site is secure. A secure site displays a little padlock icon, and the URL begins with *https* (instead of the usual *http*).

tions). You'll either get a prepaid card with a toll-free number and a scratch-to-reveal PIN code, or a code printed on a receipt.

Although they're becoming rare, you'll see **public pay phones** in a few post offices and train stations. The phones generally come with multilingual instructions, and most work with insertable Telecom Italia phone cards (sold at post offices, newsstands, etc.). With the exception of Great Britain, each European country has its own insertable phone card—so your Spanish card won't work in an Italian phone.

Public computers are easy to find. Many hotels have one in their lobby for guests to use; otherwise you can find them at Internet cafés and public libraries (ask your hotelier or the TI for the nearest location). If typing on a European keyboard, use the "Alt Gr" key to the right of the space bar to insert the extra symbol that appears on some keys. Italian keyboards are a little different from ours; to type an @ symbol, press the "Alt Gr" key and the key that shows the @ symbol. If you can't locate a special character, simply copy it from a Web page and paste it into your email message.

MAIL
You can mail one package per day to yourself worth up to $200 duty-free from Europe to the US (mark it "personal purchases"). If you're sending a gift to someone, mark it "unsolicited gift." For details, visit www.cbp.gov, select "Travel," and search for "Know Before You Go."

The Italian postal service works fine, but for quick transatlantic delivery (in either direction), consider services such as DHL (www.dhl.com).

Transportation

If your trip will cover more of Italy than just Venice, you may need to take a long-distance train or bus, rent a car, or fly. Buses are an alternative to trains (and may be your only option for reaching some small Italian towns), but they are generally slower and less efficient. Renting a car is great for touring the countryside outside of Venice. I give some specifics on trains, buses, and flights here. For more detailed information on transportation throughout Europe, including trains, flying, buses, renting a car, and driving, see www.ricksteves.com/transportation.

TRAINS
To travel by train affordably in Italy, you can simply buy tickets as you go. For travelers ready to lock in dates and times weeks or months in advance, buying nonrefundable tickets online can cut costs in half. Note that the Italy rail pass is generally not a good value; but if your travel extends beyond Italy, there are various multicountry rail passes that might be worth checking into. For advice on figuring out the smartest train-ticket or rail-pass options for your trip, visit the Trains & Rail Passes section of my website at www.ricksteves.com/rail.

Types of Trains
Most trains in Italy are operated by the state-run **Trenitalia** company (www.trenitalia.com, a.k.a. Ferrovie dello Stato Italiane, abbreviated FS or FSI). Since ticket prices depend on the speed of the train, it helps to know the different types of trains: pokey R

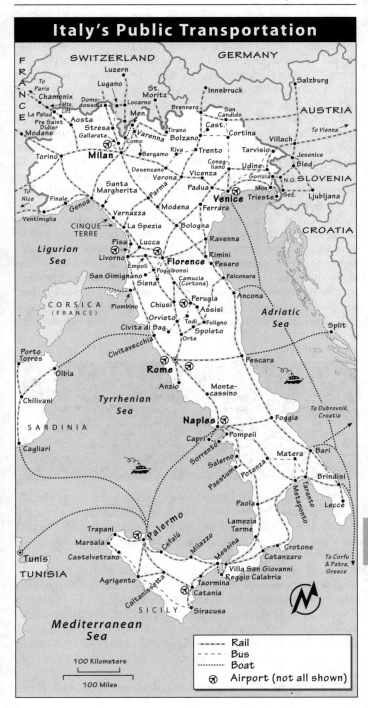

Italy's Public Transportation

Rail

Bus

Boat

✈ Airport (not all shown)

100 Kilometers

100 Miles

or REG *(regionali);* medium-speed RV *(regionali veloce),* IR (InterRegio), D *(diretto),* and E *(espresso);* fast IC (InterCity) and EC (EuroCity); and super-fast Frecce trains: Frecciabianca ("White Arrow"), faster Frecciargento ("Silver Arrow"), Frecciarossa ("Red Arrow"), and the newest Frecciarossa 1000 or Freccemille (up to 225 mph). You may also see the Frecce trains marked on schedules as ES, AV, or EAV. If you're traveling with a rail pass, note that reservations are required for IC, EC, and international trains (€5) and for Frecce trains (€10). You can't make reservations for regional trains, such as many Venice-Padua connections.

A private train company called **Italo** runs fast trains on major routes in Italy. Italo is focused on two corridors: Venice-Padua-Bologna-Florence-Rome and Turin-Milan-Bologna-Florence-Rome-Naples. Their high-speed trains have fewer departures than Trenitalia, but they do offer discounts for tickets booked well in advance. In some cities, such as Milan, their trains use secondary stations—if taking an Italo train, pay attention to which station you need. Italo does not accept rail passes, but they're a worthy alternative for point-to-point tickets. You can book in person (look for Italo ticket offices or their red machines), by phone (tel. 06-0708), or on their user-friendly website (www.italotreno.it).

Schedules

DEPARTS		DEPARTURES			SALIDAS		ABFAHRTEN		
NETTUNO	REG	14.45	14		NAPOLI C. LE	IR	15.15	15
CASSINO	REG	14.55	18		FIUMICINO A.	DIR.	15.15	22
ANCONA	?	14.55	3		NAPOLI C. LE	DIR.	15.20	12
FRASCATI	REG	15.05	19					
MILANO C. LE	X	15.05	8		ANCONA	IR	15.25	5
TARANTO		15.05	13		CASSINO	REG	15.30	17
NAPOLI C. LE		15.10	9		FIUMICINO A.	DIR.	15.35	21
UDINE	I	15.15	6					

At the train station, the easiest way to check schedules is at a handy ticket machine (described later, under "Buying Tickets"). Enter the desired date, time, and destination to see all your options. Printed schedules are also posted at the station (departure—*partenzi*—posters are always yellow).

Newsstands sell up-to-date regional and all-Italy timetables (€5, ask for the *orario ferroviaro*). You can also check www.trenitalia.it and www.italotreno.it (domestic journeys only); for international trips, use www.bahn.com (Germany's excellent all-Europe schedule website). Trenitalia offers a single all-Italy telephone number for train information (24 hours daily, toll tel. 892-021, in Italian only, consider having your hotelier call for you). For Italo trains, call tel. 06-0708.

Be aware that Trenitalia and Italo don't cooperate at all. If you

Deciphering Italian Train Schedules

At the station, look for the big yellow posters labeled *Partenze—Departures* (ignore the white posters, which show arrivals). In stations with Italo service, the posted schedules also include the FS or Italo logos.

Schedules are listed chronologically, hour by hour, showing the trains leaving the station throughout the day. Each schedule has columns:

- The first column *(Ora)* lists the time of departure.
- The next column *(Treno)* shows the type of train.
- The third column *(Classi Servizi)* lists the services available (first- and second-class cars, dining car, *cuccetta* berths, etc.) and, more importantly, whether you need reservations (usually denoted by an R in a box). All Frecce trains, many EuroCity (EC) and InterCity (IC) trains, and most international trains require reservations.
- The next column lists the destination of the train *(Principali Fermate Destinazioni)*, often showing intermediate stops, followed by the final destination, with arrival times listed throughout in parentheses. Note that your final destination may be listed in fine print as an intermediate destination. For example, if you're going from Venice to Verona, scan the schedule and you'll notice that many trains that terminate in Milan stop in Verona en route. Travelers who read the fine print end up with a far greater choice of trains.
- The next column *(Servizi Diretti e Annotazioni)* has pertinent notes about the train, such as "also stops in..." *(ferma anche a...)*, "doesn't stop in..." *(non ferma a...)*, "stops in every station" *(ferma in tutte le stazioni)*, "delayed..." *(ritardo...)*, and so on.
- The last column lists the track *(Binario)* the train departs from. Confirm the *binario* with an additional source: a ticket seller, the electronic board that lists immediate departures, TV monitors on the platform, or the railway officials who are usually standing by the train unless you really need them.

For any odd symbols on the poster, look at the key at the end. Some of the phrasing can be deciphered easily, such as *servizio periodico* (periodic service—doesn't always run). For the trickier ones, ask a local or railway official, try your *Rick Steves Italian Phrase Book & Dictionary*, or simply take a different train.

You can also check schedules—for trains anywhere in Italy, not just from the station you're currently in—at the handy ticket machines. Enter the date and time of your departure (to or from any Italian station), and you can view all your options.

buy a ticket for one train line, it's not valid on the other. Even if you're just looking for schedule information, the company you ask will most likely ignore the other's options.

Point-to-Point Tickets

Train tickets are a good value in Italy. Fares are shown on the map on page 462, though fares can vary for the same journey, mainly depending on the time of day, the speed of the train, and advance discounts. **First-class** tickets cost up to 50 percent more than **second-class.**

Frecce and Italo trains each offer several classes of service where all seats are reserved: Standard, Premium, Business, or Executive on Frecciarossa; Smart, Prima, or Club on Italo; and standard first and second class on other trains. Buying up gives you a little more elbow room, or perhaps a better chance at seating a group together, if you're buying on short notice. Ticket price levels for both companies are Base (full fare, easily changeable or partly refundable before scheduled departure), Economy (one schedule change allowed before departure, for a fee), and Super Economy or Low Cost (sells out quickly, no refund or exchange). Discounted fares typically sell out several days before departure. Fares labeled *servizi abbonati* are available only for locals with monthly passes—not tourists.

Speed vs. Savings: For point-to-point tickets, you'll pay more the faster you go. Spending a modest amount of extra time in transit can save money. On longer, mainline routes, fast trains save more time and provide most of the service. For example, super-fast Rome-Venice trains run hourly, cost €76 in second class, and make the trip in 4 hours, while infrequent InterCity trains (only 1-2/day) cost €50 and take 6 hours. On routes like Verona-Padua-Venice, regional trains cost considerably less than IC and ES express trains, and are only a little slower. For more on regional versus express trains in northern Italy, see page 318.

Discounts: Families with young children can get price breaks—kids ages 3 and under travel free; ages 4-11 at half-price. Ask for the "Offerta Familia" deal when buying tickets at a counter (or, at a ticket machine, choose "Yes" at the "Do you want ticket issue?" prompt, then choose "Familia"). With the discount, families of three to five people with at least one kid (under 12) get 50 percent off the child fare and 20 percent off the adult fare. The deal doesn't apply to all trains at all times, but it's worth checking out.

Discounts for youths and seniors require purchase of a separate card (Carta Verde for ages 12-26 costs €40; Carta Argento for ages 60 and over is €30), but the discount on tickets is so minor (10-15 percent respectively for domestic travel), it's not worth it for most.

Buying Tickets: Avoid train station ticket lines whenever possible by using the ticket machines in station halls. Pay all ticket costs in the station before you board, or you'll pay a penalty on the train. You'll be able to easily purchase tickets for travel within Italy (not international trains), make seat reservations, and even book a *cuccetta* (koo-CHEH-tah; overnight berth). If you do use the ticket windows, be sure you're in the correct line. Key terms: *biglietti* (general tickets), *prenotazioni* (reservations), *nazionali* (domestic), and *internazionali*.

Trenitalia's ticket machines (either green-and-white or red; marked *Trenitalia/Biglietti*) are user-friendly and found in all but the tiniest stations in Italy. You can pay by cash (they give change) or by debit or credit card (even for small amounts, but you may need to enter your PIN). Select English, then your destination. If you don't immediately see the city you're traveling to, keep keying in the spelling until it's listed. You can choose from first- and second-class seats, request tickets for more than one traveler, and (on the high-speed Frecce trains) choose an aisle or window seat. Don't select a discount rate without being sure that you meet the criteria (for example, Americans are not eligible for certain EU or resident discounts). Rail-pass holders can use the machines to make seat reservations. If you need to validate your ticket, you can do it in the same machine if you're boarding your train right away.

For longer-haul runs, it can be cheaper to buy Trenitalia tickets in advance, either at the station or on their website. Because most Italian trains run frequently and there's no deadline to buy tickets, you can keep your travel plans flexible by purchasing tickets as you go. (You can buy tickets for several trips at one station when you are ready to commit.) For busy weekend or holiday travel, however, it can be a good idea to buy tickets in advance, whether online or at a station. Reserved, domestic train tickets purchased online offer a "ticketless" option that means you only need the booking code.

To buy tickets for **Italo** trains, look for a dedicated service counter (in most major rail stations) or a red ticket machine labeled *Italo*. You can also book Italo tickets by phone (tel. 06-0708) or online (www.italotreno.it).

You can't buy most international tickets from machines; for this and anything else that requires a real person, you must go to a ticket window at the station. A good alternative, though, is to drop by a local travel agency. Agencies sell domestic and international tickets and make reservations. They charge a small fee, but the language barrier (and the lines) can be smaller than at the station's ticket windows. For German-run trains in northern Italy, you can also buy tickets at www.bahn.com.

Validating Tickets: If your ticket includes a seat reservation on a specific train *(biglietto con prenotazione)*, you're all set and can just get on board. An open ticket with no seat reservation (generally

PRACTICALITIES

Open or Non-Reserved Ticket—Need to Validate

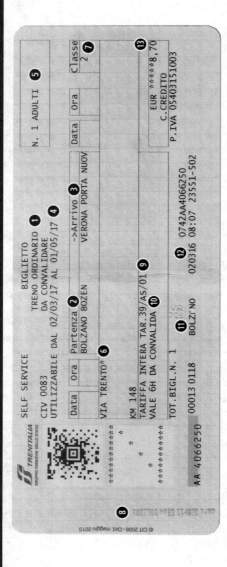

1 Open ticket for non-express train, must be validated
2 Point of departure
3 Destination
4 Period in which ticket is valid
5 Number of passengers
6 Route
7 Class of travel (1st or 2nd)
8 Validation stamp
9 Full fare for non-express train
10 Ticket good for 1 trip within 6 hours after validation
11 Location of ticket sale
12 Date of ticket purchase
13 Ticket cost

Reserved Ticket (Fast Train)—Need Not Validate

TRENITALIA
GRUPPO FERROVIE DELLO STATO

SELF SERVICE   BIGLIETTO CON PRENOTAZIONE **④**
                          FRECCIARGENTO
CIV 0083 **⑧**   BASE
DA ESIBIRE IN CASO DI CAMBIO TRENO
① Con questo viaggio risparmi circa 11kg di co2 (vedi retro**)** **⑮**

| Data | Ora | Partenza **②** | ->Arrivo **③** | Data **⑥** | Ora | Classe |
| 08.03 | 10.33 | FERRARA | VENEZIA S. LUCIA | 08.03 | 11.33 | 2 **⑦** |

                                                        N. 1 ADULTI **⑤**

TRENO 9402 **⑨** CARROZZA 005   POSTI 81 FINESTRINO

TARIFFA BASE AV **⑩**

TOT.BIGL.N.1   830925400112 **⑫**
                              0741AA3903232
                     040316 17:49 23278-501

⑪ PADOVA 00167 0345   EUR ****22,00 **⑭**
                                          C.CREDITO
                          P.IVA 05403151003
                          PNR: BF7WYR CP:254002 **⑬**

AA 3903232

① Departure date & time
② Point of departure
③ Destination
④ "Ticket with reservation"
⑤ Number of passengers
⑥ Arrival date & time
⑦ Class of travel (1st or 2nd)
⑧ "Present to official if changing trains"
⑨ Train, car & seat numbers (finestrino = window seat)
⑩ Fast-train fare
⑪ Location of ticket sale
⑫ Date of ticket purchase
⑬ Booking ID
⑭ Ticket cost
⑮ Amount of CO_2 usage reduced by this train trip

PRACTICALITIES

© CIT 2006 - Ord. maggio 2010

for a *regionali* train) must always be validated. Stamp your ticket (it may say *da convalidare* or *convalida*) before you board in the machine near the platform (usually marked *convalida biglietti* or *vidimazione*). Once you validate a ticket, you must complete your trip within the timeframe shown on the ticket. If you forget to validate your ticket, go right away to the train conductor—before he comes to you—or you'll pay a fine. Note that you don't need to validate a rail pass each time you board (just make sure you've validated it before its first use).

Rail Passes

The **Italy Pass** for the Italian state railway may save you money if you're taking three long train rides or prefer first-class travel, but don't count on it for hop-on convenience on every train. Use the price map on page 463 to add up your ticket costs (prices on the map are for the fastest trains on a given route, many of which have reservation costs built in). Remember that rail passes are not valid on Italo-brand trains.

Rail pass travelers must make separate seat reservations (€5-10 each) for the fastest trains between major Italian cities, but can just hop on regional trains (no reservations possible). Reservations for berths on overnight trains cost extra, aren't covered by rail passes, and aren't reflected on the ticket-cost map.

A **Global Pass** can work well throughout most of Europe, but it's a bad value for travel exclusively in Italy. A cheaper version, the **Select Pass,** allows you to tailor a pass to your trip, provided you're traveling in two to four adjacent countries directly connected by rail or ferry. For instance, with a four-country pass allowing 10

Rail Passes

Prices listed are for 2016 and are subject to change. For the latest prices, details, and train schedules (and easy online ordering), see www.ricksteves.com/rail.

"Saver" prices are per person for two or more people traveling together. "Youth" means under age 26. Up to two kids age 4-11 travel free with each adult on any Eurail-brand pass. Additional kids pay the youth rate. Kids under age 4 travel free.

Map key: Approximate point-to-point one-way second-class rail fares in US dollars. First class costs 50 percent more.

Before purchasing a rail pass, add up the approximate ticket costs for your itinerary. If you'll be making short, inexpensive trips each day, you'll probably find it's cheaper to buy tickets as you go in Italy.

ITALY PASS

	1st Class Adult	1st Class Saver	1st Class Youth	2nd Class Adult	2nd Class Saver	2nd Class Youth
3 days in 1 month	$226	$193	$182	$182	$155	$149
4 days in 1 month	271	231	218	218	186	178
5 days in 1 month	312	266	251	251	214	205
8 days in 1 month	421	359	338	338	288	275

Select Pass prices vary depending on which countries they cover. Two-country pass options allow you to combine Italy with Spain, France, Austria, or Greece, but not Switzerland. Spain-Italy pass does not cover travel through France. Passes do not cover private trains operated by Italo or Thello (which includes the night trains to/from Paris). See website www.ricksteves.com for 4-country option and more details.

EURAIL SELECT PASS–UPPER PRICE RANGE

3 Countries	1st Class Indiv.	1st Class Saver	1st Class Youth	2nd Class Youth
5 days in 2 months	$440	$375	$354	$289
6 days in 2 months	485	413	389	318
8 days in 2 months	567	483	455	372
10 days in 2 months	638	543	512	417

2 Countries	1st Class Indiv.	1st Class Saver	1st Class Youth	2nd Class Indiv.	2nd Class Saver	2nd Class Youth
4 days in 2 months	$362	$308	$291	$291	$248	$238
5 days in 2 months	408	348	328	328	280	268
6 days in 2 months	451	384	362	362	309	296
8 days in 2 months	525	447	421	421	359	344
10 days in 2 months	591	504	474	474	404	387

days of train travel within a two-month period (about $700 for a single adult in 2016), you could choose France-Switzerland-Italy-Greece or Benelux-Germany-Austria-Italy. A two-country version could cover France and Italy or Austria and Italy, but there isn't one for Switzerland and Italy. Note that none of these passes covers overnight trains between Italy and Paris—they require a separate ticket. Before you buy a Select Pass, consider how many travel days you'll really need. Use the pass only for travel days that involve long hauls or several trips. Pay out of pocket for tickets on days you're taking only short, cheap rides.

Train Tips

Seat Reservations: Trains can fill up, even in first class. If you're on a tight schedule, you'll want to reserve a few days ahead for fast trains (see "Types of Trains," earlier). Purchasing tickets or pass-holder reservations onboard a train comes with a nasty penalty. Buying them at the station can be a time waster unless you use the ticket machines.

If you don't need a reservation, and if your train originates at your departure point (e.g., you're catching the Venice-Verona train in Venice), arriving at least 15 minutes before the departure time will help you snare a seat.

On the platforms of some major stations, posters showing the train composition *(composizione principali treni)* indicate where first- and second-class cars will line up when the trains arrive (letters on the poster are supposed to correspond to letters posted over the platform—but they don't always). Other stations may post the order of the cars on video screens along the track shortly before the train arrives. Since most trains now allow you to make reservations up to the time of departure, conductors post a list of the reservable and nonreservable seat rows (sometimes in English) in each train car's vestibule. This means that if you board a crowded train and get one of the last seats, you may be ousted when the reservation holder comes along.

Baggage Storage: Many Italian stations have *deposito bagagli* where you can safely leave your bag for a standardized but rather steep price (€6/5 hours, €12/12 hours, €17/24 hours, payable when you pick up the bag, double-check closing hours; they may ask to photocopy your passport). Because of security concerns, no Italian stations have lockers.

Theft Concerns: In big cities, exercise caution and prudence at train stations to avoid thieves and con artists. Homeless and marginalized people lurk around the station trying to skim tips (or worse) from unsuspecting tourists. If someone helps you to find your train or carry your bags, be aware that they are not an official porter; they are simply hoping for some cash. And if someone other than a uniformed railway employee tries to help you use the ticket machines, politely refuse.

Italian trains are famous for their thieves. Never leave a bag unattended. Police do ride the trains, cutting down on theft. Still, for an overnight trip, I'd feel safe only in a *cuccetta* (a bunk in a special sleeping car with an attendant who keeps track of who comes and goes while you sleep—approximately €20 in a six-bed compartment, €25 in a less-cramped four-bed compartment, €50 in a more private, double compartment).

Strikes: Strikes, which are common, generally last a day (often a Friday). Train employees will simply explain, *"Sciopero"* (strike). But in actuality, a minimum amount of "essential" mainline service is maintained (by law) during strikes. When a strike is pending, travel agencies (and hoteliers) can check to see when the strike goes into effect and which trains will continue to run. Revised schedules may be posted in Italian at stations, and station personnel still working can often tell you what trains are expected to run. If I need to get somewhere and know a strike is imminent, I leave early (before the strike, which often begins at 9:00), or I just go to the station with extra patience in tow and hop on anything rolling in the direction I want to go.

BUSES

You can usually get anywhere you want to in Italy by bus, as long as you're not in a hurry and plan ahead using bus schedules (pick up at local TIs). For reaching small towns, buses are sometimes the only option if you don't have a car.

Long-distance buses are catching on in Italy as an alternative to the train. They are usually cheaper, modern, and often (unlike trains) have free Wi-Fi. They're especially useful on routes poorly served by train. Some of the operators you'll see are Eurolines/Baltour (www.baltour.it), Megabus (www.megabus.com), Flixbus (www.flixbus.com), and Marozzi (www.marozzivt.it). In general, orange buses are local city buses, and blue buses are for long distances.

Larger towns have a (usually chaotic) long-distance bus station *(stazione degli autobus)*, with ticket windows and several stalls (usually labeled *corsia*, *stallo*, or *binario*)—but to save time, buy your ticket at a travel agent or online, and print it out. Smaller towns—where buses are more useful—often have a central bus stop *(fermata)*, likely along the main road or on the main square, and maybe several more scattered around town. In small towns, buy bus tickets at newsstands or tobacco shops (with the big *T* signs). When buying your ticket, confirm the departure point *("Dov'è la fermata?")*.

Before boarding, confirm the destination with the driver. You are expected to stow big backpacks underneath the bus (open the luggage compartment yourself if it's closed). Upon arrival, double-check that the posted schedule lists your next destination and departure time.

Sundays and holidays are problematic; even from large cities, schedules are sparse, departing buses are jam-packed, and ticket offices are often closed. Plan ahead and buy your ticket in advance. Most travel agencies book bus (and train) tickets for a small fee.

FLIGHTS

The best comparison search engine for both international and intra-European flights is www.kayak.com. For inexpensive flights within Europe, try www.skyscanner.com.

Flying to Europe: Start looking for international flights at least four to six months before your trip, especially for peak-season travel. Off-season tickets can usually be purchased a month or so in advance. Depending on your itinerary, it can be efficient to fly into one city and out of another. If your flight requires a connection in Europe, see my hints on navigating Europe's top hub airports at www.ricksteves.com/hub-airports.

Flying Within Europe: If you're considering a train ride that's more than five hours long, a flight may save you both time and money. When comparing your options, factor in the time it takes to get to the airport and how early you'll need to arrive to check in.

Well-known cheapo airlines include easyJet (www.easyjet.com), which serves Venice Marco Polo (airport code: VCE), and Ryanair (www.ryanair.com), which serves Treviso, 12 miles northwest of Venice (airport code: TSF). Airport websites may list small airlines that serve your destination.

Be aware of the potential drawbacks of flying with a discount airline: nonrefundable and nonchangeable tickets, minimal or nonexistent customer service, pricey and time-consuming treks to secondary airports, and stingy baggage allowances with steep overage fees. If you're traveling with lots of luggage, a cheap flight can quickly become a bad deal. To avoid unpleasant surprises, read the small print before you book.

These days you can also fly within Europe on major airlines affordably—and without all the aggressive restrictions—for around $100 a flight.

Flying to the US and Canada: Because security is extra tight for flights to the US, be sure to give yourself plenty of time at the airport. It's also important to charge your electronic devices before you board because security checks may require you to turn them on (see www.tsa.gov for the latest rules).

Resources from Rick Steves

Begin your trip at www.ricksteves.com: My mobile-friendly **website** is *the* place to explore Europe. You'll find thousands of fun articles, videos, photos, and radio interviews organized by country; a wealth of money-saving tips for planning your dream trip; monthly travel news dispatches; a collection of over 30 hours of practical travel talks; my travel blog; my latest guidebook updates (www.ricksteves.com/update); and my free Rick Steves Audio Europe app. You can also find links to follow me on Facebook and Twitter.

Our **Travel Forum** is an immense, yet well-groomed collection of message boards, where our travel-savvy community answers questions and shares their personal travel experiences—and our well-traveled staff chimes in when they can be helpful (www.ricksteves.com/forums).

Our **online Travel Store** offers travel bags and accessories that I've designed specifically to help you travel smarter and lighter. These include my popular bags (rolling carry-on and backpack versions, which I helped design...and live out of four months a year), money belts, totes, toiletries kits, adapters, other accessories, and a wide selection of guidebooks and planning maps.

Choosing the right **rail pass** for your trip—amid hundreds of options—can drive you nutty. Our website will help you find the perfect fit for your itinerary and your budget: We offer easy, one-stop shopping for rail passes, seat reservations, and point-to-point tickets.

Tours: Want to travel with greater efficiency and less stress? We organize **tours** with more than three dozen itineraries and more than 900 departures reaching the best destinations in this book...and beyond. Our Italy tours include "the best of" in 17 days, Village Italy in 14 days, South Italy in 13 days, Sicily in 11 days, Venice-Florence-Rome in 10 days, the Heart of Italy in 9 days, a My Way: Italy "unguided" tour in 13 days, and a week-long Rome tour. You'll enjoy great guides, a fun bunch of travel partners (with small groups of 24 to 28 travelers), and plenty of room to spread out in a big, comfy bus when touring between towns. You'll find European adventures to fit every vacation length. For all the details, and to get our Tour Catalog, visit www.ricksteves.com/tour or call us at 425/608-4217.

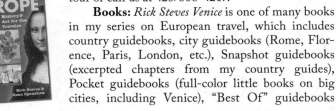

Books: *Rick Steves Venice* is one of many books in my series on European travel, which includes country guidebooks, city guidebooks (Rome, Florence, Paris, London, etc.), Snapshot guidebooks (excerpted chapters from my country guides), Pocket guidebooks (full-color little books on big cities, including Venice), "Best Of" guidebooks (condensed country guides in a full-color, easy-to-scan format), and my budget-travel skills handbook, *Rick Steves Europe Through the Back Door*. Most of my titles are available as ebooks.

My phrase books—for Italian, French, German, Spanish, and Portuguese—are practical and budget-oriented. My other books include *Europe 101* (a crash course on art and history designed for travelers); *Mediterranean Cruise Ports* and *Northern European Cruise Ports* (how to make the most of your time in port); and *Travel as a Political Act* (a travelogue sprinkled with tips for bringing home a global perspective). A more complete list of my titles appears near the end of this book.

TV Shows: My public television series, *Rick Steves' Europe,* covers Europe from top to bottom with over 100 half-hour episodes. To watch full episodes online for free, visit www.ricksteves.com/tv.

Travel Talks on Video: You can raise your travel I.Q. with video versions of our popular classes (including talks on travel skills, packing smart, cruising, tech for travelers, European art for travelers, travel as a political act, and individual talks covering most European countries). See www.ricksteves.com/travel-talks.

Audio: My weekly public radio show, *Travel with Rick Steves,* features interviews with travel experts from around the world. A complete archive of 10 years of programs (over 400 in all) is available at www.ricksteves.com/radio. I've also produced free, self-guided audio tours of the top sights in Rome. Most of this audio content is available for free through my **Rick Steves Audio Europe app,** an extensive online library organized by destination. For more on my app, see page 8.

APPENDIX

Useful Contacts

Emergency Needs
Police, Fire, and Ambulance (Europe-wide): Tel. 112
Police: Tel. 113
Ambulance: Tel. 118
Road Service: Tel. 116

Embassies and Consulates
Nearest US Consulate: Tel. 02-290-351 (Via Principe Amedeo 2/10, Milan, http://milan.usconsulate.gov)
US Embassy: 24-hour emergency line—tel. 06-46741, non-emergency—tel. 06-4674-2420 (Via Vittorio Veneto 121, Rome, http://italy.usembassy.gov)
Canadian Embassy: Tel. 06-854-442-911 (Via Zara 30, Rome, www.italy.gc.ca)

Directory Assistance
Telephone Help: Tel. 170 (in English; free directory assistance)

Holidays and Festivals

This list includes selected festivals in Venice, plus national holidays observed throughout Italy. Many sights and banks close on national holidays—keep this in mind when planning your itinerary. Before planning a trip around a festival, verify its dates by checking the festival's website or TI sites (www.italia.it and www.turismovenezia.it).

In Venice, hotels get booked up on Carnevale, Easter weekend, Liberation Day/St. Mark's Day, Labor Day, Feast of the Ascension Day, the Feast and Regatta of the Redeemer, the Historical Regatta, All Saint's Day, the Feast of our Lady of Good Health, Christmas, and New Year's Eve, and on Fridays and Saturdays year-round. Some hotels require you to book the full three-day weekend around a holiday.

Jan 1	New Year's Day
Jan 6	Epiphany
Jan/Feb	Carnevale: Feb 11-28, 2017; Jan 27-Feb 13, 2018
March/April	Easter weekend (Good Friday-Easter Monday): April 14-17, 2017; March 30-April 2, 2018
April 25	Italian Liberation Day, St. Mark's Day (Venetian patron saint)
May 1	Labor Day
May	Feast of the Ascension Day: May 25, 2017; May 10, 2018
Late May-Early June	Vogalonga Regatta
May/June	Feast of Corpus Christi: June 15, 2017; May 31, 2018
June 2	Anniversary of the Republic
July (third weekend)	Feast and Regatta of the Redeemer (Festa del Redentore)
Aug 15	Assumption of Mary (Ferragosto)
Sept (first weekend)	Historical Regatta
Nov 1	All Saints' Day
Nov 21	Feast of Our Lady of Good Health
Dec 8	Feast of the Immaculate Conception
Dec 25	Christmas
Dec 26	St. Stephen's Day

FESTIVALS IN VENICE

Venice's most famous festival is **Carnevale,** the celebration Americans call Mardi Gras (Feb 11-28 in 2017; Jan 27-Feb 13 in 2018; www.carnevale.venezia.it). It's most festive on weekends, and can be particularly quiet during the first week. Carnevale, which means "farewell to meat," originated centuries ago as a wild, two-month-long party leading up to the austerity of Lent. In Carnevale's heyday—the 1600s and 1700s—you could do pretty much anything with anybody from any social class if you were wearing a mask. These days it's a tamer 18-day celebration, culminating in a huge dance lit with fireworks on St. Mark's Square. Sporting masks and costumes, Venetians from kids to businessmen join in the fun. Drawing the biggest crowds of the year, Carnevale has nearly been a victim of its own success, driving away many Venetians (who skip out on the craziness to go skiing in the Dolomites).

Every year, the city hosts the **Venice Biennale International Art Exhibition,** a world-class contemporary fair, alternating between art in odd years and architecture in even years. The exhibition spreads over the Arsenale and Giardini park. When the Biennale focuses on visual art, representatives from 70 nations offer the latest in contemporary art forms: video, computer art, performance art, and digital photography, along with painting and sculpture (take vaporetto #1 or #2 to Giardini-Biennale; for details and an events calendar, see www.labiennale.org). The actual exhibition usually runs from June through November, but other events loosely connected with the Biennale—film, dance, theater—are held throughout the year (starting as early as February) in various venues on the island.

Other typically Venetian festival days filling the city's hotels with visitors and its canals with decked-out boats are **Feast of the Ascension Day** (May 25 in 2017; May 10 in 2018), **Feast and Regatta of the Redeemer** (Festa del Redentore) on the third weekend in July (with spectacular fireworks show Sat night), and the **Historical Regatta** (old-time boats and pageantry, first Sat and Sun in Sept). **Vogalonga** is a colorful regatta that attracts more than 1,500 human-powered watercraft; teams of often-costumed participants follow a 20-mile course through the canals and lagoon (late May-early June, www.vogalonga.it). Smaller regattas include the **Murano Regatta** (early July) and the **Burano Regatta** (mid-Sept).

Venice's patron saint, **St. Mark,** is commemorated every April 25. Venetian men celebrate the day by presenting roses to the women in their lives (mothers, wives, and lovers).

Every November 21 is the **Feast of Our Lady of Good Health.** On this local "Thanksgiving," a bridge is built over the Grand Canal so that the city can pile into La Salute Church and remember how Venice survived the gruesome plague of 1630. On this day, Venetians eat smoked lamb from Dalmatia (which was the cargo of the first ship admitted when the plague lifted).

Recommended Books and Films

To learn more about Italy past and present, and specifically Venice, check out a few of these books and films. For kids' recommendations, see page 288.

NONFICTION

The City of Falling Angels (John Berendt, 2005). A best-selling author slowly solves the real-life mystery of a 1996 fire that destroyed Venice's La Fenice Opera House.

A History of Venice (John Julius Norwich, 1977). English Lord Norwich's engaging account spans more than a century, from Venice's fifth-century origins to the arrival of Napoleon.

Italian Journey (Johann Wolfgang von Goethe, 1786). In his 18th-century collection of writings, Goethe describes his travels to Rome, Venice, Sicily, and Naples.

A Literary Companion to Venice (Ian Littlewood, 1992). Seven detailed walking tours show Venice's impact on writers such as Byron, Goethe, James, Proust, Lawrence, and Pound.

The Science of Saving Venice (Caroline Fletcher and Jane da Mosto, 2004). This readable introduction to the ecology of Venice's lagoon asks if Venice can survive in the 21st century.

Venice: Lion City (Garry Wills, 2001). One of America's greatest historians tackles the provocative history of Venice in the 15th and 16th centuries.

Venice Observed (Mary McCarthy, 1963). This snappy and engaging memoir details the Venetian ethos through the eyes of a sharply critical writer.

Venice: The Tourist Maze (Robert C. Davis and Garry R. Marvin, 2004). This history of tourism in Venice warns how the city is now being loved to death.

A Venetian Affair (Andrea di Robilant, 2003). Based on letters found in a palazzo, this is a true love story between an aristocrat and an illegitimate girl in 18th-century Venice.

The Venetian Empire: A Sea Voyage (Jan Morris, 1990). Morris brings a maritime empire to life in this book that illustrates the city's place on a larger historical canvas.

FICTION

The Aspern Papers and Other Stories (Henry James, 1894). An American editor travels to Venice in search of letters written to his mistress. Other James works about Italy include *Italian Hours* and *Daisy Miller.*

Death at La Fenice (Donna Leon, 1992). This chilling Venetian mystery and the others in Leon's Commissario Brunetti series reveal more about "real" Italy than many memoirs do.

Death in Venice and Other Tales (Thomas Mann, 1912). The centerpiece of this collection is an eloquent classic that explores obsession, beauty, and death in plague-ridden Venice (also a 1971 film).

The Glassblower of Murano (Marina Fiorato, 2009). A 17th-century glassblower reveals the secrets of his trade to the French, which has repercussions for his descendants in the 21st century.

Invisible Cities (Italo Calvino, 1972). Marco Polo tells of the fantastical cities he's seen...or is he just describing the many facets of his beloved Venice?

The Merchant of Venice (William Shakespeare, 1598). In addition to *Merchant,* other Shakespearean plays set in Italy include *Romeo and Juliet* (Verona), *Much Ado About Nothing* (Sicily), *The Two Gentlemen of Verona,* and *The Taming of the Shrew* (Padua).

The Passion (Jeanette Winterson, 1987). Set in the Napoleonic era, this is both a complex love story and a work of magical realist fiction.

The Rossetti Letter (Christi Phillips, 2007). Shifting between past and present, this novel explores the legacy of a mysterious courtesan in 17th century Venice.

FILM AND TV

Bread and Tulips (2000). A harassed Italian housewife left behind by her family at a roadside café discovers beauty, love, and her true self in Venice.

Casanova (2005). This comic romp, set in 18th-century Venice, stars the late Heath Ledger as the master of *amore.*

Dangerous Beauty (1998). A 16th-century prostitute accused of witchcraft confronts the impossible choices for women in Venetian society.

Don't Look Now (1973). Venice is both threatening and beautiful when a couple (Donald Sutherland and Julie Christie)—grieving the death of their daughter—encounter what may be her ghost.

Letters to Juliet (2010). A would-be writer comes to Verona and discovers a 50-year-old letter left at a statue of Juliet—sparking several unexpected romances.

Summertime (1955). Director David Lean's film follows a melancholy

Ohio schoolteacher (Katharine Hepburn) who travels to Venice looking for romance and finds more than antiques in Rossano Brazzi's shop.

The Wings of the Dove (1997). Based on the Henry James novel, this romantic drama is a tale of desire that takes full advantage of its Venetian locale.

Conversions and Climate

NUMBERS AND STUMBLERS

- Europeans write a few of their numbers differently than we do. 1 = *1*, 4 = *4*, 7 = *7*.
- In Europe, dates appear as day/month/year, so Christmas 2018 is 25/12/18.
- Commas are decimal points and decimals are commas. A dollar and a half is 1,50, one thousand is 1.000, and there are 5.280 feet in a mile.
- When counting with fingers, start with your thumb. If you hold up your first finger to request one item, you'll probably get two.
- What Americans call the second floor of a building is the first floor in Europe.
- On escalators and moving sidewalks, Europeans keep the left "lane" open for passing. Keep to the right.

METRIC CONVERSIONS

A kilogram is 2.2 pounds, and 1 liter is about a quart, or almost four to a gallon. A kilometer is six-tenths of a mile. I figure kilometers to miles by cutting them in half and adding back 10 percent of the original (120 km: 60 + 12 = 72 miles, 300 km: 150 + 30 = 180 miles).

1 foot = 0.3 meter	1 square yard = 0.8 square meter
1 yard = 0.9 meter	1 square mile = 2.6 square kilometers
1 mile = 1.6 kilometers	1 ounce = 28 grams
1 centimeter = 0.4 inch	1 quart = 0.95 liter
1 meter = 39.4 inches	1 kilogram = 2.2 pounds
1 kilometer = 0.62 mile	32°F = 0°C

ROMAN NUMERALS

In the US, you'll see Roman numerals—which originated in ancient Rome—used for copyright dates, clocks, and the Super Bowl. In Italy, you're likely to observe these numbers chiseled on statues and buildings. If you want to do some numeric detective work, here's how: In Roman numerals, as in ours, the highest numbers (thousands, hundreds) come first, followed by smaller numbers. Many numbers are made by combining numerals into sets: V = 5, so

VIII = 8 (5 plus 3). Roman numerals follow a subtraction principle for multiples of fours (4, 40, 400, etc.) and nines (9, 90, 900, etc.); the number four, for example, is written as IV (1 subtracted from 5), rather than IIII. The number nine is IX (1 subtracted from 10).

Big numbers such as dates can look daunting at first. The easiest way to handle them is to read the numbers in discrete chunks. For example, Michelangelo was born in MCDLXXV. Break it down: M (1,000) + CD (100 subtracted from 500, or 400) + LXX (50 + 10 + 10, or 70) + V (5) = 1475. It was a very good year.

M = 1000	XL = 40
CM = 900	X = 10
D = 500	IX = 9
CD = 400	V = 5
C = 100	IV = 4
XC = 90	I = duh
L = 50	

CLOTHING SIZES

When shopping for clothing, use these US-to-European comparisons as general guidelines (but note that no conversion is perfect).

Women: For clothing or shoe sizes, add 30 (US shirt size 10 = European size 40; US shoe size 8 = European size 38-39).

Men: For shirts, multiply by 2 and add about 8 (US size 15 = European size 38). For jackets and suits, add 10. For shoes, add 32-34.

Children: For clothing, subtract 1-2 sizes for small children and subtract 4 for juniors. For shoes up to size 13, add 16-18, and for sizes 1 and up, add 30-32.

Venice's Climate

First line, average daily high; second line, average daily low; third line, average days without rain. For more detailed weather statistics for destinations in this book (as well as the rest of the world), check www.wunderground.com.

J	F	M	A	M	J	J	A	S	O	N	D
42°	46°	53°	62°	70°	76°	81°	80°	75°	65°	53°	46°
33°	35°	41°	49°	56°	63°	66°	65°	61°	53°	44°	37°
25	21	24	21	23	22	24	24	25	24	21	23

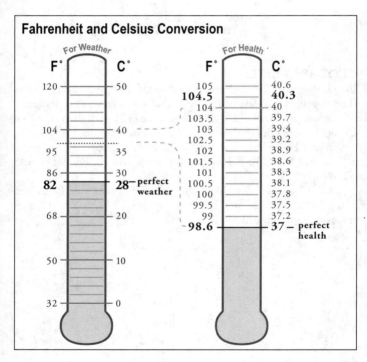

Fahrenheit and Celsius Conversion

Europe takes its temperature using the Celsius scale, while we opt for Fahrenheit. For a rough conversion from Celsius to Fahrenheit, double the number and add 30. For weather, remember that 28°C is 82°F—perfect. For health, 37°C is just right. At a launderette, 30°C is cold, 40°C is warm (usually the default setting), 60°C is hot, and 95°C is boiling. Your air-conditioner should be set at about 20°C.

Packing Checklist

Whether you're traveling for five days or five weeks, you won't need more than this. Pack light to enjoy the sweet freedom of true mobility.

Clothing

- ☐ 5 shirts: long- & short-sleeve
- ☐ 2 pairs pants (or skirts/capris)
- ☐ 1 pair shorts
- ☐ 5 pairs underwear & socks
- ☐ 1 pair walking shoes
- ☐ Sweater or warm layer
- ☐ Rainproof jacket with hood
- ☐ Tie, scarf, belt, and/or hat
- ☐ Swimsuit
- ☐ Sleepwear/loungewear

Money

- ☐ Debit card(s)
- ☐ Credit card(s)
- ☐ Hard cash ($100-200 in US dollars)
- ☐ Money belt

Documents

- ☐ Passport
- ☐ Tickets & confirmations: flights, hotels, trains, rail pass, car rental, sight entries
- ☐ Driver's license
- ☐ Student ID, hostel card, etc.
- ☐ Photocopies of important documents
- ☐ Insurance details
- ☐ Guidebooks & maps
- ☐ Notepad & pen
- ☐ Journal

Toiletries Kit

- ☐ Basics: soap, shampoo, toothbrush, toothpaste, floss, deodorant, sunscreen, brush/comb, etc.
- ☐ Medicines & vitamins
- ☐ First-aid kit
- ☐ Glasses/contacts/sunglasses

- ☐ Sewing kit
- ☐ Packet of tissues (for WC)
- ☐ Earplugs

Electronics

- ☐ Mobile phone
- ☐ Camera & related gear
- ☐ Tablet/ebook reader/media player
- ☐ Laptop & flash drive
- ☐ Headphones
- ☐ Chargers & batteries
- ☐ Smartphone car charger & mount (or GPS device)
- ☐ Plug adapters

Miscellaneous

- ☐ Daypack
- ☐ Sealable plastic baggies
- ☐ Laundry supplies: soap, laundry bag, clothesline, spot remover
- ☐ Small umbrella
- ☐ Travel alarm/watch

Optional Extras

- ☐ Second pair of shoes (flip-flops, sandals, tennis shoes, boots)
- ☐ Travel hairdryer
- ☐ Picnic supplies
- ☐ Water bottle
- ☐ Fold-up tote bag
- ☐ Small flashlight
- ☐ Mini binoculars
- ☐ Small towel or washcloth
- ☐ Inflatable pillow/neck rest
- ☐ Tiny lock
- ☐ Address list (to mail postcards)
- ☐ Extra passport photos

Italian Survival Phrases

English	Italian	Pronunciation
Good day.	Buon giorno.	bwohn **jor**-noh
Do you speak English?	Parla inglese?	**par**-lah een-**gleh**-zay
Yes. / No.	Sì. / No.	see / noh
I (don't) understand.	(Non) capisco.	(nohn) kah-**pees**-koh
Please.	Per favore.	pehr fah-**voh**-ray
Thank you.	Grazie.	**graht**-see-ay
You're welcome.	Prego.	**preh**-go
I'm sorry.	Mi dispiace.	mee dee-spee-**ah**-chay
Excuse me.	Mi scusi.	mee **skoo**-zee
(No) problem.	(Non) c'è un problema.	(nohn) cheh oon proh-**bleh**-mah
Good.	Va bene.	vah **beh**-nay
Goodbye.	Arrivederci.	ah-ree-veh-**dehr**-chee
one / two	uno / due	**oo**-noh / **doo**-ay
three / four	tre / quattro	tray / **kwah**-troh
five / six	cinque / sei	**cheeng**-kway / **seh**-ee
seven / eight	sette / otto	**seh**-tay / **oh**-toh
nine / ten	nove / dieci	**noh**-vay / dee-**ay**-chee
How much is it?	Quanto costa?	**kwahn**-toh **koh**-stah
Write it?	Me lo scrive?	may loh **skree**-vay
Is it free?	È gratis?	eh **grah**-tees
Is it included?	È incluso?	eh een-**kloo**-zoh
Where can I buy / find...?	Dove posso comprare / trovare...?	**doh**-vay **poh**-soh kohm-**prah**-ray / troh-**vah**-ray
I'd like / We'd like...	Vorrei / Vorremmo...	voh-**reh**-ee / voh-**reh**-moh
...a room.	...una camera.	**oo**-nah **kah**-meh-rah
...a ticket to ____.	...un biglietto per ____.	oon beel-**yeh**-toh pehr ____
Is it possible?	È possibile?	eh poh-**see**-bee-lay
Where is...?	Dov'è...?	doh-**veh**
...the train station	...la stazione	lah staht-see-**oh**-nay
...the bus station	...la stazione degli autobus	lah staht-see-**oh**-nay **dehl**-yee **ow**-toh-boos
...tourist information	...informazioni per turisti	een-for-maht-see-**oh**-nee pehr too-**ree**-stee
...the toilet	...la toilette	lah twah-**leh**-tay
men	uomini / signori	**woh**-mee-nee / seen-**yoh**-ree
women	donne / signore	**doh**-nay / seen-**yoh**-ray
left / right	sinistra / destra	see-**nee**-strah / **deh**-strah
straight	sempre dritto	**sehm**-pray **dree**-toh
What time does this open / close?	A che ora apre / chiude?	ah kay **oh**-rah ah-**pray** / kee-**oo**-day
At what time?	A che ora?	ah kay **oh**-rah
Just a moment.	Un momento.	oon moh-**mehn**-toh
now / soon / later	adesso / presto / tardi	ah-**deh**-soh / **preh**-stoh / **tar**-dee
today / tomorrow	oggi / domani	**oh**-jee / doh-**mah**-nee

In an Italian Restaurant

English	Italian	Pronunciation
I'd like...	Vorrei...	voh-**reh**-ee
We'd like...	Vorremmo...	vor-**reh**-moh
...to reserve...	...prenotare...	preh-noh-**tah**-ray
...a table for one / two.	...un tavolo per uno / due.	oon **tah**-voh-loh pehr **oo**-noh / **doo**-ay
Is this seat free?	È libero questo posto?	eh **lee**-beh-roh **kweh**-stoh **poh**-stoh
The menu (in English), please.	Il menù (in inglese), per favore.	eel meh-**noo** (een een-**gleh**-zay) pehr fah-**voh**-ray
service (not) included	servizio (non) incluso	sehr-**veet**-see-oh (nohn) een-**kloo**-zoh
cover charge	pane e coperto	**pah**-nay ay koh-**pehr**-toh
to go	da portar via	dah **por**-tar **vee**-ah
with / without	con / senza	kohn / **sehnt**-sah
and / or	e / o	ay / oh
menu (of the day)	menù (del giorno)	meh-**noo** (dehl **jor**-noh)
specialty of the house	specialità della casa	speh-chah-lee-**tah deh**-lah **kah**-zah
first course (pasta, soup)	primo piatto	**pree**-moh pee-**ah**-toh
main course (meat, fish)	secondo piatto	seh-**kohn**-doh pee-**ah**-toh
side dishes	contorni	kohn-**tor**-nee
bread	pane	**pah**-nay
cheese	formaggio	for-**mah**-joh
sandwich	panino	pah-**nee**-noh
soup	zuppa	**tsoo**-pah
salad	insalata	een-sah-**lah**-tah
meat	carne	**kar**-nay
chicken	pollo	**poh**-loh
fish	pesce	**peh**-shay
seafood	frutti di mare	**froo**-tee dee **mah**-ray
fruit / vegetables	frutta / legumi	**froo**-tah / lay-**goo**-mee
dessert	dolce	**dohl**-chay
tap water	acqua del rubinetto	**ah**-kwah dehl roo-bee-**neh**-toh
mineral water	acqua minerale	**ah**-kwah mee-neh-**rah**-lay
milk	latte	**lah**-tay
(orange) juice	succo (d'arancia)	**soo**-koh (dah-**rahn**-chah)
coffee / tea	caffè / tè	kah-**feh** / teh
wine	vino	**vee**-noh
red / white	rosso / bianco	**roh**-soh / bee-**ahn**-koh
glass / bottle	bicchiere / bottiglia	bee-kee-**eh**-ray / boh-**teel**-yah
beer	birra	**bee**-rah
Cheers!	Cin cin!	cheen cheen
More. / Another.	Di più. / Un altro.	dee pew / oon **ahl**-troh
The same.	Lo stesso.	loh **steh**-soh
The bill, please.	Il conto, per favore.	eel **kohn**-toh pehr fah-**voh**-ray
Do you accept credit cards?	Accettate carte di credito?	ah-cheh-**tah**-tay **kar**-tay dee **kreh**-dee-toh
tip	mancia	**mahn**-chah
Delicious!	Delizioso!	day-leet-see-**oh**-zoh

For more user-friendly Italian phrases, check out *Rick Steves' Italian Phrase Book & Dictionary* or *Rick Steves' French, Italian, & German Phrase Book.*

INDEX

INDEX

MAP INDEX

Start your trip at

Our website enhances this book and turns

Explore Europe

At ricksteves.com you can browse through thousands of articles, videos, photos and radio interviews, plus find a wealth of money-saving travel tips for planning your dream trip. And with our mobile-friendly website, you can easily access all this great travel information anywhere you go.

TV Shows

Preview the places you'll visit by watching entire half-hour episodes of Rick Steves' Europe (choose from all 100 shows) on-demand, for free.

rickstevers.com

your travel dreams into affordable reality

Radio Interviews

Enjoy ready access to Rick's vast library of radio interviews covering travel

tips and cultural insights that relate specifically to your Europe travel plans.

Travel Forums

Learn, ask, share! Our online community of savvy travelers is a great resource for first-time travelers to Europe, as well as seasoned pros. You'll find forums on each country, plus travel tips and restaurant/hotel reviews. You can even ask one of our well-traveled staff to chime in with an opinion.

Travel News

Subscribe to our free Travel News e-newsletter, and get monthly updates from Rick on what's happening in Europe.

Pack Light and Right

Gear up for your next adventure at ricksteves.com

Light Luggage

Pack light and right with Rick Steves' affordable, custom-designed rolling carry-on bags, backpacks, day packs and shoulder bags.

Accessories

From packing cubes to moneybelts and beyond, Rick has personally selected the travel goodies that will help your trip go smoother.

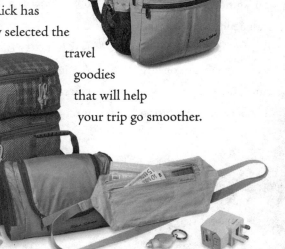

Experience maximum Europe

Save time and energy

This guidebook is your independent-travel toolkit. But for all it delivers, it's still up to you to devote the time and energy it takes to manage the preparation and logistics that are essential for a happy trip. If that's a hassle, there's a solution.

Rick Steves Tours

A Rick Steves tour takes you to Europe's most interesting places with great

great tours, too!

with minimum stress

guides and small groups of 28 or less. We follow Rick's favorite itineraries, ride in comfy buses, stay in family-run hotels, and bring you intimately close to the Europe you've traveled so far to see. Most importantly, we take away the logistical headaches so you can focus on the fun.

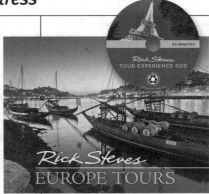

customers—along with us on 40 different itineraries, from Ireland to Italy to Istanbul. Is a Rick Steves tour the right fit for your travel dreams? Find out at ricksteves.com, where you can also get Rick's latest tour catalog and free Tour Experience DVD.

Join the fun

This year we'll take 18,000 free-spirited travelers—nearly half of them repeat

Europe is best experienced with happy travel partners. We hope you can join us.

See our itineraries at ricksteves.com

Rick Steves

BEST OF GUIDES

Best of France
Best of Germany
Best of Ireland
Best of Italy
Best of Spain

EUROPE GUIDES

Best of Europe
Eastern Europe
Europe Through the Back Door
Mediterranean Cruise Ports
Northern European Cruise Ports

COUNTRY GUIDES

Croatia & Slovenia
England
France
Germany
Great Britain
Ireland
Italy
Portugal
Scandinavia
Scotland
Spain
Switzerland

CITY & REGIONAL GUIDES

Amsterdam & the Netherlands
Belgium: Bruges, Brussels, Antwerp & Ghe
Barcelona
Budapest
Florence & Tuscany
Greece: Athens & the Peloponnese
Istanbul
London
Paris
Prague & the Czech Republic
Provence & the French Riviera
Rome
Venice
Vienna, Salzburg & Tirol

SNAPSHOT GUIDES

Basque Country: Spain & France
Berlin
Copenhagen & the Best of Denmark
Dublin
Dubrovnik
Edinburgh
Hill Towns of Central Italy
Italy's Cinque Terre
Krakow, Warsaw & Gdansk
Lisbon

Credits

RESEARCHER

To update this book, Rick and Gene relied on...

Amanda Zurita

Amanda Zurita caught the travel bug early—she's been flying since before she could walk. When she's not hovering over a bowl of *cacio y pepe* in Rome, checking out vintage shops in Florence, or riding bikes around Lucca, she lives in Seattle with her beloved Labrador, Hadrian.

Avalon Travel
An imprint of Perseus Books
A Hachette Book Group company
1700 Fourth Street
Berkeley, CA 94710

Text © 2016 by Rick Steves' Europe, Inc.
Maps © 2016 by Rick Steves' Europe, Inc.
Printed in Canada by Friesens
First printing December 2016

ISBN: 978-1-63121-455-4
ISSN: 1538-1595

For the latest on Rick's lectures, guidebooks, tours, public radio show, and public television series, contact Rick Steves' Europe, 130 Fourth Avenue, Edmonds, WA 98020, 425/771-8303, www.ricksteves.com, rick@ricksteves.com.

Rick Steves' Europe
Managing Editor: Jennifer Madison Davis
Special Publications Manager: Risa Laib
Editors: Glenn Eriksen, Tom Griffin, Katie Gustafson, Mary Keils, Suzanne Kotz, Cathy Lu, John Pierce, Carrie Shepherd
Editorial Production Assistant: Jessica Shaw
Editorial Intern: Megan Simms
Researcher: Amanda Zurita
Graphic Content Director: Sandra Hundacker
Maps & Graphics: David C. Hoerlein, Lauren Mills, Mary Rostad

Avalon Travel
Senior Editor and Series Manager: Madhu Prasher
Editor: Jamie Andrade
Associate Editor: Sierra Machado
Copy Editor: Patrick Collins
Proofreader: Denise Silva
Indexer: Claire Splan
Cover Design: Kimberly Glyder Design
Maps & Graphics: Kat Bennett, Mike Morgenfeld

Photo Credits
Front Cover: © Brian Jannsen / Alamy Stock Photo
Title Page: Gondoliers in St. Mark's Square © Dominic Arizona Bonuccelli
Additional Photography: Dominic Arizona Bonuccelli, Ben Cameron, Simon Griffith, Jennifer Hauseman, Cameron Hewitt, David C. Hoerlein, Gene Openshaw, Michael Potter, Rick Steves, Bruce VanDeventer, Laura VanDeventer, Ian Watson, Wikimedia Commons (PD-Art/PD-US) (photos are used by permission and are the property of the original copyright owners)

More for your trip!
Maximize the experience with Rick Steves as your guide

Guidebooks
Florence, Rome, and Italy guides make side-trips smooth and affordable

Phrase Books
Rely on Rick's Italian Phrase Book & Dictionary

Rick's TV Shows
Preview where you're going with 18 shows on Italy

Free! Rick's Audio Europe™ App
Free audio tours for Venice's top sights

Small Group Tours
Rick offers several great itineraries through Italy

For all the details, visit ricksteves.com